LIBRARY OF ART
PUBLISHER - DIRECTOR: GEORGE RAYAS

THE PARTHENON
AND ITS IMPACT IN MODERN TIMES

THE PARTHENON
AND ITS IMPACT IN MODERN TIMES

General Editor
PANAYOTIS TOURNIKIOTIS

"MELISSA" PUBLISHING HOUSE

Editorial Supervisor:
LAMBRINI VAYENA-PAPAIOANNOU

English translation:
COX and SOLMAN

PHOTOGRAPHERS:
Alinari-Giraudon, Yannis Yannelos,
Giraudon, Bruno Jarret, Kostas Manolis,
Sokratis Mavrommatis, Kostas Megalokonomou,
Spyros Meletzis, Makis Skiadaresis,
E.M. Stresow-Czako, Yannis Tsangaris

Art Editor: SPYROS KARACHRISTOS

Electronic pagination: SET E. ANTONIOU Co.
Reproductions of illustrations: K. ADAM
Printed by EPIKOINONIA SA
Bound by Y. ILIOPOULOS & Y. MOUTSIS Co.

Pp. 368, 30 x 25 cm.
Colour illustrations: 138
Monochrome illustrations: 198
Drawings and diagrams: 105
Paper: Phoenix-imperial mat Scheufelen, 150 gr.

© MELISSA Publishing House, G. Rayas & Co., 1994
10 Navarinou St, 106 80 Athens, Greece
Tel. no. (01) 3611 692, Fax (01) 3600 865

ISBN: 960-204-019-X
Published in Greek and English

CONTENTS

FOREWORD

Today, the Parthenon is recognised as the most important monument of Western civilisation. Its architecture and sculptural decoration are seen as the culmination of ancient Greek art. Yet the contemporary approach to the temple is not confined to the outstanding results of ancient Greek mastery in construction and art. The Parthenon, built by the Athenians of Pericles, is also viewed as the expression par excellence of the spirit of an era which the collective memory of our Western culture has called the 'golden age' and acknowledges as the cornerstone of its lengthy history. This single building – a work of art in its entirety – is a distillation not only of the skills of the specific people who created it, but also of the political and philosophical thought of their society.

Although today this approach to and interpretation of the monument strikes us as self-evident, it has not always been a shared value during the twenty five or so centuries which separate us from the time of Pericles. The Parthenon as a supreme creation is a relatively recent discovery, one which emerged along with the rediscovery of the ancient Greek world in the eighteenth and nineteenth centuries. This is not to say that the building was viewed with indifference by the generations which experienced its creation and its functioning as a place of worship – a role which it held almost continuously, despite radical changes in the religion practised in it, down to modern times – and its recognition as a monument. Quite the reverse; but in those days the Parthenon was recognised and admired only within the narrow confines of Greek society.

The break which radically altered the manner in which the Parthenon was viewed was associated with the re-organisation of Western thought which occurred during the eighteenth century, and in particular with the structuring of historical thought. As soon as the attempt began to make an overall approach to, and interpretation of, the long march of humanity on the criterion of the cultural and social relationship between its successive eras, the Greece of the Classical period laid claim to a distinctive position. It was recognised as the first epoch in which all society's forms of creative expression had flowered at the same time, reaching a climax which subsequently remained unsurpassed and was the model par excellence against which later periods could compare themselves and compete. Since apart from organising the overall achievements of humanity into an upward historical progress, historians also viewed each important creation of society as a faithful expression of the spirit of the age, it was only reasonable that the Parthenon should be recognised as the most faithful expression of the Classical period in Greece. It has survived almost intact down to modern times, allowing our eyes to admire it, our hands to touch it, and the modern mind to measure it with exactness and study it from every angle and in all possible ways so as to discover the secrets of ideal creation. In this new approach to the world, one which placed the new on the foundations of a more complex understanding and interpretation of the old, the Parthenon emerged as an artistic, architectural and ideological model for the nineteenth and twentieth centuries – often, indeed, a pre-eminent model. There can be no doubt that this was a new Parthenon, one which was no longer a place of worship but a monument, a vehicle for the collective memory of our own civilisation.

It is this part of the history of the Parthenon and its impact in recent times which form the subject of this book. It begins, naturally enough, with a broad overview of the long history of the concepts and ideals which its presence has fertilised down the centuries. Next come two important chapters examining the architecture and sculptural decoration of the ancient monument in the light of the most recent research. An extensive account of the modern history of the monument then links us to the events of recent years.

The Parthenon's return to the forefront of attention is examined first through the descriptions and depictions of travellers, architects and archaeologists whose wanderings in difficult times formed part of their search for the ideal works of man. The impact and multi-faceted influence which the architecture and sculptural decoration of the Parthenon have had on the architecture and art of the nineteenth and twentieth centuries is the central theme of three chapters which bring the examination of the subject down to the works of our own times. This general approach is followed by a composite search for the ideological presence of the Parthenon in contemporary Greek society and a theoretical contribution to the successive efforts to restore the monument, culminating in the work of the Committee for the Conservation of the Acropolis Monuments, which is still going ahead. The volume ends with a text on the Parthenon in modern Greek literature.

The extensive and varied illustrative material, brought together from leading institutions and collectors around the world, is not intended simply to provide documentation for the texts: it also constitutes a separate account of the impact of the Parthenon. As a result, the book allows the reader to form a multi-faceted view of the long history of the temple, from the Classical period down to our own day.

To conclude this brief foreword, I would like to take this opportunity of thanking the publisher, the authors and all those – named or unnamed – who have contributed to the best of their ability to the completion of this wide-ranging effort to comprehend what is, perhaps, the most important monument of our civilisation.

Panayotis Tournikiotis

ACKNOWLEDGEMENTS

The publication of this collective work on the Parthenon would not have been possible without the valuable contributions made by the many institutions, collectors, associates and scholars who responded to our invitation. We thank them cordially for their kind assistance.

Our particular thanks to: the Archive of the Committee for the Conservation of the Acropolis Monuments, Ministry of Culture; the Benaki Museum; the Gennadios Library; the German Archaeological Institute; the Museum of the City of Athens; the National Gallery; the National Historical Museum; the Photographic Archive of the Municipal Art Gallery, Athens; the Museum of Tiniot Sculptors, Tinos. The Skulpturenhalle, Basle; the Deutsches Archäologisches Institut, the National Gallery, the Kunstbibliothek and the Technische Universität, Berlin; the City Museum and Art Gallery, Birmingham; the Kunstmuseum, Bonn; the Kongelige Danske Kunstakademiet and the Thorvaldsen Museum, Copenhagen; the National Galleries of Scotland and the Royal Commission of Ancient Monuments of Scotland, Edinburgh; the Deutsches Architektur Museum and the Städelsches Kunstinstitut und Städtlische Galerie, Frankfurt; the British Museum, the British Architectural Library (RIBA) and the Victoria and Albert Museum, London; the Architekturmuseum of the Technische Universität, the Bayerische Staatsbibliothek and the Bayerische Verwaltung der staatlichen Schlösser, Gärten und Seen, Munich; the Avery Architectural and Fine Arts Library, Columbia University, New York; the Bibliothèque Nationale, the Ecole Nationale Supérieure des Beaux Arts, the Institut de France, the Louvre and the Rodin Museum, Paris; the Art Museum, Princeton University, Princeton; the Library of Congress, Washington; the Semperarchiv of the Institut für Geschichte und Theorie der Architektur, Eidgenössische Technische Hochschule, Zurich.

Our thanks also to Stavros and Stella Stavridis, Nikolaos Catsimpoolas, Georgios Despinis, Alexandros Tombazis, Cornilia Hadjiaslani, Dimitris Mantzounis, Pavlos Kalligas, Fani Konstantinou, Fani-Maria Tsigakou, Kostas Paraschos, Nelli Lazaridou, Petros Koufopoulos, and to Dimitris Philippides for his contribution to the English edition.

Endpaper: Edward Dodwell, The Acropolis under Turkish rule. Source: E. Dodwell, Views in Greece, London 1821; Athens, Gennadios Library.

Page 7: View of the Acropolis from the west. Photograph by S. Meletzis.

Pages 8-9: Detail of the west facade of the Parthenon. Photograph by S. Meletzis.

Page 12: The Parthenon from the west. Photograph by S. Meletzis.

Page 15: Detail of the west frieze of the Parthenon. Photograph by S. Meletzis.

Page 17: Section of the Parthenon colonnade. Photograph by S. Mavrommatis.

SAVAS KONDARATOS

The Parthenon as Cultural Ideal

The Chronicle of its Emergence
as a Supreme Monument
of Eternal Glory

An association with legends or important historical events, a charge of religious, political or ideological configurations, an overwhelming presence in space, antiquity, recognised artistic value or, simply, peculiarity of form: these are usually the factors which, individually or in conjunction, cause an architectural work to emerge as a monument or symbol of an idea, a place or an entire culture. Occupying a position somewhere between the Pyramids of Giza and the Eiffel Tower, the Parthenon is undoubtedly such a monument and symbol, one of the best-known of our times. As a creation of Athenian democracy at the height of its powers, as a ruin whose presence on the Acropolis rock continues to impress, and as a building whose worn marbles still reveal the exceptional care taken with their shaping, it is only natural that the Parthenon should recall to the memory the most renowned achievements of ancient Greek civilisation, in which modern Western civilisation boasts of having its roots (fig. 1). Nor is it strange that almost all famous visitors to Athens – heads of state, stars of the stage and screen, eminent authors, scientists, artists and architects – see it as their duty to ascend the sacred rock, to stand, manifestly moved, before the majestic temple, and, as a rule, to be photographed with its Doric columns as a backdrop (figs. 2-5). Such photographs are not just the souvenirs of a visit. They are destined to be published in the daily and periodical Press; they can connote a dedication to the democratic ideal, a sensitivity towards artistic values, or living beauty which has nothing to fear from a comparison with the eternal but cool splendour of the monument. It was also to be expected that the Parthenon should acquire an emblematic function, often appearing as a name or image in the titles or signs of businesses of all kinds (fig. 6), pervading advertisements for 'high quality' goods (fig. 7) and cropping up every so often in the rhetorical figures of Greek politicians.

Other monuments of symbolic importance have, of course, been similarly abused in our days. If, however, as would appear to be the case, the Parthenon outdoes all the others, that is because – apart from its associative connotations – it itself is regarded as a work of unsurpassed perfection and, consequently, of eternal glory. The Parthenon has indeed succeeded not only in overshadowing all the other architectural creations of Classical Greece, but also in establishing itself as a kind of absolute canon for the evaluation of all architectural achievements, even those of an entirely different nature. It is typical that as far back as the 19th century, the French architect and theorist of architecture E.E. Viollet-le-Duc, wishing to praise the beauty of the Gothic cathedral at Amiens, described it as "the Parthenon of France".[1]

It would be a relatively simple task to anthologise the views of archaeologists, theorists and historians of art, and architects to confirm that the Parthenon functions in the minds of experts not only as the outstanding architectural creation of a great civilisation but also as an eternal model of plastic perfection in which the quintessence of architecture as an art is innate. And we would be justified in concluding that the fame of the monument has proved its ability to stand the test of time, which is, perhaps, the surest criterion for judging the value of a work of art.[2] Yet as André Malraux points out, "Every work of art in fact tends to develop into a myth".[3] We might add that this is especially true of great works of art, and the Parthenon could not, of course, be an exception. After the mid-19th century, at the latest, communion with its mythical essence preceded any immediate acquaintance with the monument or enjoyment of its perceptible presence.

1. *The Parthenon and the Propylaea from the Pnyx.* Source: G. Fougères, L'Acropole, Le Parthénon, *Paris 1910; Athens, collection of Stavros and Stella Stavridis.*

Ordinary yet adequately-read visitors, like the experts, approach the Parthenon for the first time prepared to admire it and emotionally charged with the idea that they are about to undergo a unique experience. Allow me to cite two eloquent examples.

In 1904, Siegmund Freud – whose heretical views on psychiatry had already caused a furore in Vienna – visited Athens with his younger brother. Their initial destination had been Corfu, but the prompting of an acquaintance in Trieste had triggered hours of querulous indecision leading to a change of plan. When they found themselves on the Acropolis on the afternoon of their arrival, Freud was struck by a peculiar thought: "So all this really *does* exist, just as we learnt at school!" Much later (1936), in a letter to Romain Rolland which served as his contribution to the *Festschrift* to mark the French author's seventieth birthday, Freud – by now the famous proponent of psychoanalysis – attempted to analyse his experience on the sacred rock. It was as if the remark had been made by one person, he wrote, and addressed to another. "The first behaved as though he were obliged, under the impact of an unequivocal observation, to believe in something the reality of which had hitherto seemed doubtful. [...] The second person, on the other hand, was justifiably astonished, because he had been unaware that the real existence of Athens, the Acropolis, and the landscape around it had ever been objects of doubt. What he had been expecting

was rather some expression of delight or admiration."[4] Freud was ultimately able to interpret the depression at Trieste – self-punishing pessimism over a journey that was "too good to be true" (in English in the original) – and the "feeling of derealisation" (Entfremdungsgefühl) he had on the Acropolis (from which he protected himself with the illusion that he had been in doubt as to its existence) as a "sense of guilt" attached to filial superiority over the father, of having "got further" than the father who was never able to make such a journey. "Our father had been in business, he had had no secondary education, and Athens could not have meant much to him. Thus what interfered with our enjoyment of the journey to Athens was a feeling of *filial piety*. And now you will no longer wonder that the recollection of this incident on the Acropolis should have troubled me so often since I myself have grown old and stand in need of forbearance and can travel no more."[5]

"To see the Acropolis is a dream one treasures without even dreaming to realise it", wrote the young architect Charles Edouard Jeanneret – later the famous Le Corbusier – who arrived in Athens in 1911 on his 'journey to the East' with his friend Auguste Klipstein.[6] Before setting foot in the city, and from his confinement in quarantine on the islet of Ayios Yeorgios off Piraeus, he wrote to his mentor William Ritter, "I have high hopes of the

2. *George Bernard Shaw at the Parthenon; photograph by K. Megaloconomou.*

3. *Dwight Eisenhower at the Parthenon; photograph by K. Megaloconomou.*

Acropolis! I shall preen myself like a vain and fragile lover. I shall wait to land at Piraeus and, in the solitude of the night, I shall go to pay homage [to the Parthenon]".[7] In fact, when he eventually arrived in Athens at eleven in the morning he thought up hundreds of pretexts for not going "up there" at once. However, we should include an extract from Le Corbusier's reminiscences of his visit (fig. 8): "I don't really know why this hill harbours the esssence of artistic thought. I can appreciate the perfection of these temples and realise that nowhere else are they so extraordinary; and a long time ago I accepted the fact that this place should be like a repository of a sacred standard, the basis for all measurement in art. Why this architecture, and no other? For how much have I already been led by an absolute enthusiasm for the works of other peoples, other times, other places? Yet why must I, like so many others, name the Parthenon the undeniable Master, as it looms up from its stone base, and yield, even with anger, to its supremacy?"[8]

In the case both of the Viennese psychiatrist and the young Swiss architect, the mythical proportions assumed in their minds by the triptych of Athens, the Acropolis and the Parthenon are plain to see. The former was haunted even in old age by his guilt over having tasted an experience which his father could not even have conceived of, while the latter never ceased to emphasise the absolute superiority of the Parthenon. Later, as the

acknowledged pioneer of architectural modernism, he visited Greece again, and said "I did what I did with that Acropolis in my bowels."[9] Is it really the case that the myth is so strong that it permeates, superimposes itself on, and even acts as a surrogate for the immediate impression? Or could it be that the impression is so moving as to exceed even the expectations generated by the mythical image? One thing of which we can be sure is that contact with the physical reality of the monument is far from a disappointment for the devotees of its fantasy ideal. Perhaps the mythical representation and direct perception are inextricably entwined, each enhancing the other.

Our purpose in this article is not to 'demystify' the Parthenon or to praise its 'true' value as a work of art. What we shall be trying to do is describe the historical background of our impressions of it in various periods, from the time of its construction to the present day, in the hope of helping readers to identify the ideological elements which, from time to time, have contributed to the renown of the monument and the formation of myths around it. The accounts to which we have access – scanty as far as the distant past is concerned, abundant in more recent times – are not, of course, sufficient by themselves for us to identify and understand the ways in which the Parthenon was dealt with in other times. They must be seen in their contexts – that is, they must be taken in conjunction with what we know about the broader cultural framework, the mentality and the inclinations of each specific age. Naturally enough, our attempt to reconstruct the successive images of the Parthenon and the horizons of experience and expectation from which they emerged cannot make any claim to scholarly completeness. An exhaustive investigation of the sources to identify suitable testimony and a systematic search for, and study of, works connected with the subject would have required time and stamina not at our disposal. However, we hope that the historical sketch which follows will be adequate for the purposes of this book.

The Political and Ideological Framework for the Construction of the Parthenon: the Building's Purpose and its Reception

The battles of Plataea and Mycale (479 BC) marked the end of the Persian Wars. Sparta, which as the strongest Greek power had always been the leader in the fighting on land and at sea – sometimes in actuality, though sometimes only officially – did not seem inclined to continue the struggle against the Persians. Athens, however, which

had made the greatest sacrifices, realised that it still possessed a battleworthy army and, above all, a strong fleet and wished to make the most of the opportunities which had arisen to liberate Asia Minor and extend its power in the Aegean. The dissolution of the Panhellenic alliance, the Delos congress and the formation of the first Athenian League (478/7 BC) laid the foundations for the hegemony which Athens sought. The military operations of the allies, which drove the Persians out of gold-rich Thrace and back from the coast of Asia Minor, the increase in the membership of the League and the willingness of some members to contribute in cash terms rather than by joining the campaigns were not long in bringing Athens unprecedented power and vast wealth.

The democratic reforms of Ephialtes, the ostracising of Cimon, and the assassination of Ephialtes the reformer (462 BC) paved the way for Pericles, the genius and aristocrat who emerged as leader of the democratic party. Democratic support did not prevent Pericles from imposing his personal authority – "a government ruled by its foremost citizen" is how Thucydides describes his regime[10]– and adopting a policy best characterised as imperialist. A series of operations succeeded in achieving three interconnected goals: the complete neutralisation of the Persians, maintenance of the cohesion of the League

4. Jayne Mansfield at the Parthenon, 1957; photograph by K. Megaloconomou.

5. John Wayne at the Parthenon, 1960; photograph by K. Megaloconomou.

6. *An exhibition catalogue bearing the logo of the Scandinavian publishing house Parthenon.*

7. *An advertisement for Philips: "From the splendour of the Parthenon to the mystery of space".*

Όταν ο Περικλής έχτιζε τον Παρθενώνα, διάλεξε το φυσικό φως της Αθήνας για να τονίσει το μεγαλείο της τέχνης και της αρχιτεκτονικής του. Κάτι που κανένα άλλο φως στον κόσμο δεν θα μπορούσε να κάνει τόσο καλά. Γι' αυτό και ίσως υπάρχει μόνο ένας Παρθενώνας. Αυτό το μεγαλειώδες έργο χρόνια τώρα φωτίζει η Philips. Είναι αυτό που ξέρουμε σαν "Ηχος και Φως.

Χάρη στην τεχνολογία και την πείρα της, η Philips προβάλλει τα ανεπανάληπτα στοιχεία του Παρθενώνα σ' όλο το μεγαλείο τους ακόμα και τη νύχτα.

Και φυσικά η τεχνολογία της Philips δεν σταματάει στο φωτισμό του πιο σπουδαίου ίσως – ιστορικού – Μνημείου στον κόσμο, είναι ήδη στο διάστημα.

Η τεχνολογία της Philips ρίχνει φως στο μυστήριο του διαστήματος.

Η SODERN, η υψηλής τεχνολογίας Γαλλική εταιρία ερευνών, θυγατρική της Philips παίρνει μέρος σε ένα από τα πιο φιλόδοξα διαστημικά προγράμματα «την επιστημονική εξερεύνηση του ήλιου» που γίνεται από τη NASA σε συνεργασία με την Ευρωπαϊκή Υπηρεσία Διαστήματος (ESA).

Και πιο συγκεκριμένα τρεις SODERN SED 04 Startrackers έχουν τοποθετηθεί στο Spacelab 2,

Philips.
Από το μεγαλείο του Παρθενώνα στο μυστήριο του διαστήματος.

το διαστημικό εργαστήριο που εξερευνά τον ήλιο.

Οι Startrackers αυτοί – που έχουν τοποθετηθεί στο Σύστημα Κατεύθυνσης Οργάνων που προσδιορίζει τη θέση της πλατφόρμας στο διάστημα – δίνουν τη δυνατότητα στο ισχυρό τηλεσκόπιο του Spacelab 2 που είναι στραμμένο προς τον ήλιο να κάνει ελιγμούς υψίστης ακριβείας με τηλεχειριστήριο χωρίς να επηρεάζεται από τις κινήσεις του Spacelab 2.

Εκτός όμως από την εξερεύνηση του ήλιου, η SODERN έχει πάρει μέρος στα μεγαλύτερα Αμερικανικά και Ευρωπαϊκά διαστημικά προγράμματα μια και είναι πρώτη στον κόσμο σε συστήματα ελέγχου και πλοήγησης διαστημικών σταθμών. Η SODERN έχει στο διάστημα 90 ηλεκτρονικά οπτικά συστήματα με συνολική λειτουργία περισσότερο από 200 χρόνια χωρίς ούτε μία βλάβη.

Ένα μοναδικό ρεκόρ τεχνολογίας!

Philips. The sure sign of expertise worldwide.

 PHILIPS

DOC:ESA/NASA

by means of the exemplary punishment of secession, and confrontation with Sparta from a position of strength. However, his purpose was to establish Athens not only as a military and political power, but also as the provider of "the school of Hellas",[11] which involved, *inter alia*, the construction of monuments which would do the city credit. After the peace arranged by Callias, Pericles attempted to call a Panhellenic congress to deliberate concerning the Hellenic sanctuaries which the barbarians had burned down.[12] We do not know whether such a decision was in any way connected with the oath that the Greeks are said to have taken before the battle of Plataea, not to rebuild the sanctuaries which the Persians had destroyed, but to leave them in ruins "as a reminder to coming generations of the impiety of the barbarians".[13] In any case, the Lacedaemonians were opposed to the idea and the congress never took place, but Pericles was determined to go ahead.

The Athenians had already embarked upon a frenzy of building, mostly in the Agora area, but no attempt had so far been made to reconstruct the sanctuaries of the Acropolis which Xerxes had burned. It was Pericles who inaugurated the reconstruction, in 447 BC, a move of the greatest symbolic significance: its purpose was to emphasise the ancestor-myths of Attica, with which the Sacred Rock was inextricably bound up, to hymn the final victory over the barbarians, to which Athens had contributed so much, and to promote the contemporary grandeur of the city, at the height of its military, economic and intellectual power. As Plutarch points out,[14] Pericles may also have had another purpose: to provide work for the unemployed and distribute the city's wealth more fairly.

The projects on the Acropolis began with the construction of the Parthenon, to use the name later given to the large temple of Athena Polias which was "indissolubly linked to the very essence of Athens" and which to some extent "constituted the apotheosis of the Athenian republic or, more precisely, its divine essence".[15] Shortly after the victory at Marathon – and, most probably, as a result of it – a large temple to Athena, now called the Pre-Parthenon, had begun to be built on the Acropolis. The Persian invasion occurred while this temple was being constructed. Its superstructure had been demolished (some of the drums of its columns were later incorporated into the north Acropolis wall) but its stereobate had survived. It was on more or less the same base, a broad platform towards the south side of the Acropolis, that the new temple rose, using such materials from the old building as had not been ruined beyond repair. Right from the start this was an ambitiously-designed project. Pericles, the architects Ictinus and Callicrates, and the sculptor Pheidias, who undertook the general supervision of the work (Plutarch calls him "the general overseer"[16]) had lofty aims. And, indeed, they achieved a feat which it would be difficult to surpass.

Leaving aside aesthetic judgements, let us examine some more tangible facts. With a stylobate measuring 30.88 metres by 69.50 metres, the Parthenon is the largest Doric temple in the Greek world to reach the stage of completion.[17] It is the only Greek temple to have been built entirely of marble. It is also the temple in which the so-called 'refinements' of the Doric order were most fully employed: these caused the construction costs to soar, since they required the marble to be dressed with the greatest accuracy. However, what made the temple truly unique was the unusual richness of its sculptural decoration. To begin with, the entire temple was designed to house the chryselephantine statue of Athena, 12 metres in height, which Pheidias was to create. This meant that the temple would have to be of large dimensions, and in particular dictated the unusual width of its cella (19 metres). The statue itself, made of the most costly materials, was a kind of treasure: just before the outbreak of the Peloponnesian War, Pericles was able to reassure the Athenians by pointing out that even if their other funds were exhausted, "they might use even the gold plates with which the statue of the goddess herself was overlaid. The statue, as he pointed out to them, contained forty talents' worth of pure gold, and it was all removable."[18] The temple, too, was exceptionally highly-ornamented. The Parthenon is the only Doric temple to have carved scenes on all its metopes (92 in number) and to have its cella surrounded by a continuous Ionian frieze (with a length of 160 metres) – a stylistic innovation which is anything but insignificant. And thanks to the breadth of the temple, the pedimental groups of sculptures were extremely elaborate.

What is of particular importance, however, is the visual symbolism of the sculptural ornamentation, "which was always intended to make the topicality of history emerge through legend".[19] On the eastern and most important pediment was the birth of Athena, shown standing and already fully-armed by the side of the lord of Olympus in a fitting mythological scene of Panhellenic appeal. On the west pediment, the scene of the dispute between Athena and Poseidon for the patronage of Attica was a theme of purely local interest, a reference to the *genius loci* of the Acropolis itself. The motifs for the metopes were partly connected with the Theseus cycle of myths, which told of the Athenian hero and founder but were also well-known outside Attica. The scenes showing the Battle of the Centaurs, the Battle of the Amazons, the Battle of the Giants and the Fall of Troy, however, were all symbolic of the victories of Greeks over barbarians. It is no coincidence that the shield of the Athena statue bore a representation of the Amazons, defeated, on the foothills of

8. Ch. E. Jeanneret photographed at the Parthenon by Auguste Klipstein, 1911. Source: G. Gresleri, Le Corbusier Viaggio in Oriente, Venice - Paris 1985.

the Acropolis. Yet the most delicate symbolism was that of the frieze, which showed the sacred procession of the Panathenaic Festival. This was not simply a depiction of a religious ceremony. As Manolis Andronikos has pointed out,[20] the protagonists in the procession are the people of Athens themselves, "modest and happy, respectful yet simultaneously proud, disciplined but free", in a "poetic" place "where men and gods could freely coexist". In this highly original composition, the ancient myths have been put aside so as to allow the ideal of Athenian democracy itself to be expressed in plastic form and triumphantly praised. "How proud the Athenian people must have been", wrote Henri Lechat,[21] "to see this noble and glorious image of themselves, as if reflected in their eyes by a kind of ideal mirror, and to be justified in recognising themselves as they were, or as they would like to be in the most sublime moments of their existence as a nation".

Even today, one is stunned by the rapidity with which the building was constructed. In 438 BC, only nine years after work had begun, the Parthenon was in a position to be dedicated to its goddess, whose statue was already inside it. Only the ornamentation of the pediments had not been completed, and was to take six more years. Let us not forget that many more public buildings were going up in the Agora and on the foothills of the Acropolis at this time, along with other large temples, such as that of Hephaestus (the 'Theseum') on the knoll of Agoraeus Colonus and of Poseidon at Sounion. And as soon as the Parthenon was finished work began on another ambitious and costly project on the Acropolis: the Propylaea. After the death of Pericles – but in accordance with his plans – the Nike Temple and the Erechtheum were built. These achievements would have been impossible if Athens had not amassed tremendous wealth – more specifically, if Pericles had not drawn on the funds in the allied treasury. However, it also presupposed an unprecedented mobilisation of human resources, involving the work of free artisans as well as slaves.

Unfortunately, we have no accounts by contemporary writers of the planning and construction of the Parthenon and the other works of Pericles, or of the impression they made once completed.[22] According to Vitruvius,[23] Ictinus himself and Carpion composed treatises on the Parthenon, but these have not survived, and neither have any of the other ancient Greek texts on architecture listed by the Roman author. Of course, Thucydides gives us a very clear picture of the grandeur of Athens during the famous fifty years (especially in the Funeral Oration of Pericles), but he refers only in passing to the "Propylaea of the Acropolis and the other buildings".[24] However, it would not be excessively bold to say that the scale, perfection and speed of execution of the works impressed both Athenians and outsiders. Although Plutarch was writing five centuries later, he must certainly be reflecting some degree of historical truth when he says that the construction of the monuments "brought most delightful adornment to Athens, and the greatest amazement to the rest of mankind". The buildings were proud in their size and incomparable in their form and elegance, "yet the most wonderful thing about them was the speed with which they rose".[25] We can be even more certain that the building achievements of Pericles provoked the envy of his opponents: they accused him of spending "Hellas' enforced contributions for the war" on showcase works. As a result, they said, he was bringing disgrace upon the whole of Greece, which watched while the money the other cities had contributed and which was necessary for the war was spent on prettifying and gilding Athens, "which, for all the world like a wanton woman, adds to her wardrobe precious stones and costly statues and temples worth their millions".[26] One of the victims of the outcry was Pheidias, Pericles' closest associate and friend, who according to some sources was imprisoned and according to others was forced to flee Athens before perfecting the ornamentation of the Parthenon.

In 406 BC, when the Erechtheum was finished, the works on the Acropolis were complete. A year later, at Aegospotami, the former might of the Athenian democracy, already economically exhausted by the long Peloponnesian War, collapsed entirely. Even into the first half of the 4th century BC, of course, Athens experienced periods of recovery and continued to be the unchallenged intellectual centre of Greece. But the splendour of the great fifty years now lay in the past. Isocrates, who gave expression to an early stage in the efforts to reconstitute Athenian power, invoked it: "for it is admitted that our city is the oldest and the greatest in the world and in the eyes of all men the most renowned", he wrote in 380 BC.[27] Much later, he paid tribute to Pericles, who "so adorned the city with temples, monuments and other projects of beauty, that even today visitors who come to Athens think her worthy of ruling not only the Hellenes, but all the world; and more than this, he stored away in the Acropolis a sum of not less than ten thousand talents".[28] Plato, on the other hand, saw Pericles, Themistocles and Cimon, who had supposedly "made the city great", as "those who caused the mischief" and as responsible for its decline. This Athenian philosopher would undoubtedly have included the Parthenon among the "trash" with which the great leaders of the previous century had filled the city.[29] Aristotle, too, was indifferent to the work done by Pericles in the cultural sphere, confining himself to the comment that "as long as Pericles was leader of the people, the state was still in a fairly good condition".[30]

The absence of references to the Parthenon and Pericles' other projects in the writings of the Classical period does not necessarily mean that they were not sufficiently discussed or that they were not admired. Most of the texts of this period are lost, and in some of those which survive the omission is easy to explain. However, a later source does tell us that the Cynic philosopher Diogenes, who divided his time between Corinth and Athens, claimed that both were much more beautiful than Ecbatana or Babylon, and that "the Craneion and the Athenian acropolis with the Propylaea were far more beautiful structures than those abodes of royalty, yielding to them only in size".[31]

The glory which surrounded Athens, the Acropolis and the Parthenon – a glory which, as we shall see, continued to glimmer faintly even in the darkest of the subsequent ages – can be seen in a hard historical fact. Although Alexander the Great had no reason to be particularly well-disposed towards the Athenians, nevertheless after the battle of the Granicus (334 BC) he sent them three hundred Persian shields, "to be set up to Athena on the acropolis".[32] Some of those shields were hung up on the architrave of the Parthenon, confirming the significance of the temple as a monument to the victorious struggles of the Greek people against the barbarians of Asia.

The Fate and Memory of the Temple from the Hellenistic Period to the End of the Middle Ages

In the Hellenistic period, the Acropolis continued to be the religious centre and adornment of an Athens which was no longer a great power but which nonetheless still reigned supreme in the arts and letters. The sanctity of the Rock, however, was often defiled – and most seriously only thirty years after Alexander's tribute. When Demetrius Poliorcetes, 'liberator' of Athens, visited the city in 304 BC, the Athenians went far beyond the bounds of flattery in offering him the opisthodomus of the Parthenon as accommodation: "and there he lived, and there it was said that Athena received and entertained him, although he was no very orderly guest and did not occupy his quarters with the decorum due to a virgin".[33] Sure enough, the goddess's eminent guest (who wished to be regarded as her younger brother) defiled the temple by living a dissolute life there with "well-known prostitutes", and, later, on his next visit, by debauching "free-born youths and native Athenian women".[34]

By way of contrast, Athens was honoured and often visited by the rulers of the Seleucid and Attalid dynasties. King Attalus I of Pergamon dedicated some votive offerings of superb art on the Acropolis in 201 BC, to mark his victories over the Gauls, and provided money for the ornamentation of the gymnasia belonging to the Academy and the Lyceum. In 178 BC, Attalus' successor Eumenes II visited Athens with his brothers, in order to take part in the Panathenaic Games. Indeed, one of the brothers, subsequently Attalus II, stayed on in the city (with a friend, subsequently to rule Cappadocia as Ariarathes V) to attend the classes of the philosopher Carneades. Both Eumenes II and Attalus II built famous stoas in Athens, one above the Theatre of Dionysus and the other on the east side of the Agora. The Seleucid monarch Antiochus IV Epiphanes, too, displayed a generous interest in continuing the building work on the temple of Olympian Zeus. A visit to Athens and liberality towards the city were for these rulers, who were striving to Hellenise Asia, the most effective ways of developing their public relations. Furthermore, the buildings of the age of Pericles still stood there in all their glory, reminders of the past splendours of Athens. It was no coincidence that a copy of the Athena Parthenos by Pheidias stood in the library of distant Pergamon.

It was in the Hellenistic period, around 200 BC, that the renowned traveller Polemon, whose descent was from Ilium in the Troad but who had been honoured with the title of citizen of Athens, wrote his *Concerning the Acropolis of Athens*. Unfortunately, this treatise – which could have enlightened us as to the views of that time about the Periclean monuments – has not survived.[35]

Throughout the period when Roman sovereignty was consolidating itself in the Greek peninsula, Athens continued to be a *civitas libera et amica populi Romani* and also attracted large numbers of Romans who admired Greek culture. The Roman consul Aemilius Paullus toured Greece after his victory over Perseus in 168 BC and did not omit a visit to Athens; in fact, he prolonged his stay there in order to admire the city's monuments. Even after the Athenian rebellion which Sulla punished so cruelly in 86 BC, the city was not long in regaining the favour of Rome. Although the army commander Gaius Verres, notorious for his greed, showed no hesitation about plundering the city's sanctuaries in 80 BC, Cicero succeeded in obtaining his conviction ten years later, after he had wrought similar havoc in Sicily.[36] Cicero himself had visited Athens in his youth, in order to round off his Greek education at the Academy, where he spent six months. As an older man, he sent his son Marcus to the Academy, too. In a letter, he urged Marcus to benefit as much as possible from his teacher Cratippus and the authority of the city ("doctoris auctoritatem et urbis"), ending by expressing his regret that other duties prevented him from coming to Athens in person.[37] And in his *De Re Publica* the great Roman orator refers twice to the greatness of Pericles.[38]

Mark Antony spent time in Athens on a number of occasions; he "delighted to be called a Philhellene, and still more to be addressed as Philathenian, and he gave the city very many gifts".[39] For a time, the city was his military headquarters. Shortly after the battle of Actium (31 BC), Octavian passed through Athens, but – perhaps angered by the Athenians, who had been particularly fond of Antony – he cut short his stay. However, he came back as Augustus in 20 BC, and perhaps in 19 BC as well; according to traditional accounts, on the foothills of the Acropolis he met the poet Virgil, who was struggling to complete his *Aeneid*.[40] The small but ponderous temple of Rome and Augustus built on the Acropolis slightly later – 20 metres in front of the Parthenon, but with details inspired by the Erechtheum – was probably a tribute to the Greek monument by the standards of the time, rather than a manifestation of disrespect.

Augustus was the dedicatee of the *De Architectura* of Vitruvius, a unique – and for that reason invaluable – written source of information about the architecture of antiquity. Yet the Parthenon receives only a mention in this work,[41] despite the fact that this was a time of growing interest in the art-works of the Greeks and, as a consequence, of classicist tendencies. The historian Diodorus Siculus, who also flourished during the reign of Augustus, writes with what we could describe as nostalgia of the time of Pericles: "In these years, ... plenty brought increase to the arts, and the greatest artists of whom we have record, including the sculptor Pheidias, flourished at that time".[42] Strabo, another contemporary, did not omit to describe the Acropolis in his *Geography* and to note the presence of the Parthenon: "the city itself is a rock situated in a plain and surrounded by dwellings. On the rock is the sacred precinct of Athena, comprising both the old temple of Athena Polias, in which is the lamp that is never quenched, and the Parthenon built by Ictinus, in which is the work in ivory by Pheidias, the Athena".[43] Of course, his description is frustratingly brief, but the author excuses himself by saying that to dwell any longer on an account of "the multitude of things in this city that are lauded and proclaimed far and wide"[44] would be to lose sight of his purpose.

Although it was artistic interest which motivated Nero to seize treasures from sanctuaries all over Greece – to remove "most of the statues on the Acropolis of Athens"[45] – in order to adorn the *Domus Aurea*, his palace, some of the other Roman emperors were more positive in their Philhellenism and behaved more generously towards the city of Pallas Athena. The position of greatest eminence among these emperors belongs to Hadrian, who not only endowed the city with some superb – and useful – building projects but also made it the seat of the League of United Greeks (131/132 AD), thus restoring it as the capital of the Greek nation. During the two first Imperial centuries, the main representatives of what is often called the 'second Sophistic' stood out for their love of Greece – or, rather, for their nostalgia for the glorious Greek past. Dio Chrysostom, a harsh critic of his own age and a fiery devotee of the Classical heritage, often mentions the "memorials of the good old days" such as the Propylaea and the Parthenon.[46] Aelius Aristides praised Athens as "most fitting for the beauty of temples and statues",[47] and belatedly defended Pericles against the criticism of Plato.[48] Lastly, the "most learned" Herodes Atticus,[49] a friend of Hadrian and teacher of the Emperor Marcus Aurelius (another Philhellene), became one of Athens' greatest benefactors, with donations and building projects.

Bearing in mind that the traveller Pausanias, usually of the greatest value as a source of information about the ancient monuments of Greece (though not always particularly sensitive to their beauty), ignores the Parthenon as a piece of architecture in order to linger over his description of the chryselephantine statue of Athena,[50] the writer of Roman times who is of most importance for our subject is Plutarch. His *Life of Pericles*, to which we have referred frequently so far, provides us not only with important information about Pericles' achievements but also with the first aesthetic evaluation of them. Acknowledging that "deftness and speed" in a project do not necessarily guar-

antee it perfection and the ability to last, Plutarch stresses that the works of Pericles are so much admired because although they were performed with such rapidity they have shown their capacity to withstand time as art-works: "each one of them, in its beauty, was even then and at once antique; but in the freshness of its vigour it is, even to the present day, recent and newly wrought. Such is the bloom of perpetual newness, as it were, upon these works of his, which makes them ever to look untouched by time, as though the unfaltering breath of an ageless spirit had been infused into them".[51] However, it is nonetheless the case that Plutarch makes no special reference to the Parthenon. It seems very likely that in his day, as during the five centuries which had gone before, the work of Pericles which was most impressive and most widely admired was the imposing Propylaea, both imposing and original in its composition. That, at least, is the conclusion to be drawn from the scanty mentions of the works in the authors of antiquity. The Parthenon may have been treated simply as a suitably magnificent housing for the much-famed statue of Athena.

Christianity had already begun to spread in Plutarch's time, and its ultimate triumph marked the end of the ancient world. In Athens, St Paul responded to an invitation from the insatiably curious Athenians to preach to them on the Areopagus, beginning with a rhetorical reference to the existence of an altar dedicated "to the unknown god".[52] We do not know whether the Apostle of the Gentiles took the trouble to climb up to the Acropolis. But centuries later, under Turkish rule, French Ambassador to the Porte Deshayes heard the Athenians saying that the Parthenon had once been a temple of the Unknown God and that Paul had preached in it.[53] His sermon had little effect, however. Even after Constantine the Great established Christianity as the official religion of the Empire, Athens had only a small Christian community and it jealously protected its institutions, its temples and its famous schools of philosophy. In the mid 4th century, Basil the Great, Gregory of Nanzianzus (future Fathers of the Church) studied in Athens, as did Julian, who as Emperor would attempt to reinstate the old religion. When Basil and Gregory were already leading the monastic life in their hermitage in Pontus, Julian, marching against Constantius, would appeal to the Athenians in the hope that they had kept alive "some small spark" of the virtues of their ancestors, reminding them that it was on their Acropolis that he had raised his arms in supplication to Athena, imploring her to protect him from his enemy.[54]

With the death of Theodosius I in 395 AD and the division of the Empire, Greece became part of the Eastern Roman state. In the same year, Athens experienced the invasion of Alaric, who, however, was halted by a flash of light from the raised spear of Athena Promachus, according

9. R. Ceccoli, *View of the Acropolis from the South-West, 1853, oils; Athens, private collection.*

to the traditional account.[55] The city's renown as an intellectual centre lived on through the 5th century, despite the growing attraction of Constantinople – especially after the founding of a university there by Theodosius II. As a result, it was in Athens that Proclus, the last great Neoplatonic philosopher, chose to settle, and it was in the school of Athens that he taught. A pious pagan, he had a dream of Athena (whose chryselephantine statue had already been removed "by those who could move the immovable") prophesying her expulsion and asking him to take her into his humble house.[56]

The death-blow to those like Proclus who hankered for the pagan past was delivered by Justinian in 529, when he issued a decree ordering the closure of the schools of the pagan philosophers, including the famous school of Athens. In building the Church of St Sophia, Justinian's aim was to rival Solomon, not Pericles.

After the 6th century, Athens disappeared into obscurity. Early in the following century, the Parthenon itself was converted into a Christian church dedicated to the Holy Wisdom of God. During the conversion, the sculptures in the centre of the east pediment had to be sacrificed. However, the glory of Athens and of the Parthenon – or 'Our Lady of Athens', as it was now known – flared up again briefly in 1017, when the city was visited by the Emperor Basil II Bulgar-Slayer. After crushing the Bulgars, the Emperor made his way to the ancient temple in order to "make an offering of thanks for his victory" to the Mother of God. Could it be that his visit was of special symbolic value? Was Basil's real intention "to celebrate his triumph on the venerable Acropolis, and to pay respectful homage to the focal point of ancient Hellenism before returning to Byzantium, the capital of modern Hellenism", as G. Schlumberger speculated?[57] Perhaps it may have been so.

Michael Choniates Acominatus, a man of wide classical learning, expected to find at least a little of the former glory of Athens when he arrived, full of enthusiasm, in the city in 1182 in order to take up the post of metropolitan bishop there. But no: "once-golden" Athens, "formerly the mother of wisdom of all kinds and leader in every virtue", was merely an insignificant and poor village. Acominatus' disappointment was boundless:

"Alas for what I suffer and say and write!
I live at Athens, but see no Athens -
rather, doleful dust and hollow happiness.
Where now is your grandeur, saddest of cities?
All the renown of Athens has been lost
and not even a faint trace of it remains."[58]

Despite this disillusionment, Acominatus stayed on in Athens and did his best to help his impoverished flock. But his pastoral tasks were rudely interrupted in 1204, when the Crusaders, after capturing the 'Queen of Cities' (Constantinople), also occupied Athens. The title of Grand Seigneur was given to the Burgundian knight Othon de la Roche, who set himself up in the castle of the Acropolis and was not long in converting the church of Our Lady of Athens into one of Notre Dame. Indeed, in 1206, by a bull of Pope Innocent III, the Latin archbishopric of Athens was placed under the direct protection of the Holy See. This move was not unrelated to the "glorious name and perfect beauty" of the ancient city. The papal bull made it clear that "the grace of God does not permit the ancient glory" of Athens to be lost, especially since the city had succeeded in exchanging "the study of pagan science for the love of divine wisdom", in converting "the bastion of the famous Athena into a humble house of the Mother of God", and in acquiring "a knowledge of the true God, after erecting an altar to the unknown god years ago".[59] Much later, in 1380 – when Athens was in the hands of the Catalans – King Pedro IV of Aragon described the Acropolis as "the most precious jewel which exists in the world" ("la plus richa joya qui al mont sia"), whose like not all the kings of Christendom together could have created.[60]

However, these admiring comments were not the result of knowledge, direct or indirect. Athens and its history had been forgotten by medieval Europe. What they stood for belonged to the realm of myth. Some of the pilgrims to the Holy Land who visited Greek cities and harbours (such as the Englishman Saewulf in 1103 and the German Sudheim in 1350) remembered that there was a place called Athens: of course, they did not go out of their way to visit it, but they did feel the obligation to mention it in their accounts.[61] This state of affairs changed very little when, in the late 14th century, the Duchy of Athens passed to the Florentine Acciaiuoli family and caught a tinge of the brilliance of the early Renaissance.

The 'Discovery' of the Monument by the West in Modern Times

Acciaiuoli hegemony in the Duchy of Athens undoubtedly facilitated contact between the Italians and the city's monuments. Both Nerio I and his successor Antonio (his illegitimate son by Maria Renti, a Greek) received eminent visitors from Italy in the Palazzo d'Acropoli. We do not know whether these visitors included learned men or artists who would have been particularly interested in the monuments on the Rock. It is possible that at this time (around 1425) the painter Francesco Squarcione of Padua,[62] an admirer of things ancient, visited Greece. Indeed, it has been argued that some of the drawings in the famous albums of Jacopo Bellini, foremost representative of Venetian painting in the early Renaissance, are so strongly reminiscent of one of the metopes from the Temple of Hephaestus and a horseman from the Parthenon frieze as to justify the hypothesis that Bellini had seen drawings produced by Squarcione in Athens. However, most students of the period doubt whether Squarcione ever visited Greece at all.[63] As a result, the first proven visit to the Acropolis by a devotee of the ancient world was that of Cyriacus of Ancona, a merchant, man of letters and enthusiastic traveller. He visited Athens on two occasions – in 1436 and 1444, when the Duchy was ruled by the third Acciaiuoli prince, Nerio II – in order to admire the monuments of the city.[64]

The *Commentaria* which Cyriacus wrote about his journeys, which – and this was most important – were accompanied by numerous sketches, were, unfortunately, destroyed when the Sforza library in Pesaro burned down in 1514. However, some extracts from the texts have survived, along with a few drawings which had in the meantime been copied by friends or men of letters of the next generation. As a result, Cyriacus' impressions of his trips to Athens are not entirely unknown to us. "Athenas veni!" he notes triumphantly, and hurries on to record his admiration for the Parthenon, without noting its conversion into a Christian church. "The most spectacular monument stands on the Acropolis. This is the magnificent and admirable marble temple of Pallas Athena, the divine work of Pheidias, with its 58 superb columns. It is everywhere decorated with the most noble reliefs ever carved by the sublime art of a sculptor."[65] However, Cyriacus' sketches of the west side of the temple are far from accurate: they show the temple as hexastyle and the sculptures of the pediment are rendered with a considerable degree of imagination. Yet these drawings (together with the much greater number lost) "were the first authentic notes on Greek art to reach the West since ancient times", and they must certainly have had some influence on the artists of the Renaissance.[66]

10. *Athens as a Flemish city, from the 15th century chronicle of Jean de Courcy. Source: L. de Laborde,* Athènes au XVe, XVIe et XVIIe siècles, *Paris 1854; Athens, Gennadios Library.*

The fall of the Byzantine Empire and the conquest of Greece by the Ottomans did not much sadden the West. The rivalry between the Churches, prejudices towards the Greeks fostered by Latin literature, and the belief that the Turks were descendants of the Trojans (and thus distant relatives of the Italians) created feelings which were anti-Greek rather than otherwise. Only the humanist Aeneas Sylvius Piccolomini, later Pope Pius II, mourned the end of "noble Greece" and the destruction of its glorious cities when he heard of the fall of Constantinople.[67] And when Athens itself was taken by Omar in 1456, Europe shed not a tear for the city of Pallas Athena, as Laborde tells us.[68]

The installation of Turks on the Acropolis (which led to the conversion of the Christian Parthenon into a mosque) inaugurated a long period in which visits from Western travellers were not encouraged. Shifts in Western policy towards the Porte made the Ottoman authorities highly suspicious of foreigners, and often hostile towards them. Thus, despite the constantly growing interest of the West in Greek antiquity, Athens was for long an unknown city. Although the eminent 16th century Hellenist Crusius attempted to gather information about the city's fate by corresponding with Greek priests, early in the next century Johannes Meursius, professor of Greek at Leyden, was forced to describe the Greek antiquities on the basis solely of literary sources.[69] As a rule, Athens was not mentioned in the illustrated albums of the great cities of the known world published at this time. Pictures of Athens, although numerous, are entirely imaginary: these are renderings of German or Flemish medieval cities (figs. 10-12). Even the nautical charts of the period record Athens under the corrupt name 'Settines' (from 'eis tais Athenais', 'at Athens'). Travellers to Greece who passed through Attica or the port of Piraeus were few and far between, and they rarely visited Athens itself. It was still more uncommon for them to take an interest in its monuments. Those who wrote down their impressions of their travels merely referred to the city's glorious past or its current decline.[70] The only exception to this rule in the 16th century is the German apothecary Reinhold Lubenau, a member of the delegation which Rudolph II sent to the Sultan; with the greatest difficulty, he succeeded in visiting Athens and its antiquities in 1589. But his efforts to climb the Sacred Rock were in vain. Hiding his disappointment, he began to draw the monuments on the Acropolis from a concealed position on a nearby hill, but in the end three janissaries arrested him and confiscated his drawings and notes.[71] The French traveller Sieur du Loir – another devotee of things ancient and Greek – who arrived in Athens in 1639 flooded with feelings of "pious veneration", was equally unsuccessful. Before long he was forced to flee Athens in secret, fearful of the Voivod's suspicions.[72]

On the other hand, the renowned Turkish traveller Evliya Çelebi was able to enter the Acropolis castle and admire the Parthenon at his leisure. He began his tour of Greece in 1667, in Thrace, and passed through Athens on his way to Crete. The chapter he devoted to the city in Volume VIII of his ten-volume *Seyahatnamesi* is entitled, characteristically, "Description of the Ancient and Great City of Athens, Abode of the Wise Men of Antiquity".[73] Evliya was no historian. As a rule, he gathered his information from the inhabitants of the places he visited. As a result, his inaccuracies are frequently gross: for example, he attributes the founding of Athens to Solomon, obviously confusing him with Solon. Nonetheless, his descriptions reveal that he was touched with genuine emotion when confronted with the works of ancient art: "In this wondrous city", he wrote, "are assembled the most elaborate and admirable works of art anywhere in the world. There are thousands of sculptures and reliefs, carved on natural marble, showing weird beasts and strange scenes, all worked with incomparable skill... The visitor to the city will find himself face to face with these superb examples of fine art and will be overcome by emotion so great as to provoke a shiver". And he concludes, "no one who wanders the world should regard himself as travelled until he has visited the city of Athens".[74]

In the middle of the Acropolis castle, Evliya came face to face with the Parthenon mosque. He was, of course, aware that this was "an ancient building, which is seen as a model of its kind and is renowned among the travellers and wanderers of the world", and he gives a very vivid description of the monument, telling us that this was where 'Ilahi Eflatun', 'the divine Plato', had once taught. He was struck by the perfection with which the marbles of the columns and walls were assembled, making the joints invisible beneath the gleaming surfaces. But what triggered his unbounded enthusiasm was the sculptural ornamentation of the temple: "The sculptures and the statues are a 'wonder of wonders', and they outstrip in conception and construction the power of the minds of ordinary people... Whatever statue you examine closely, you will discover upon it the seal of creation. And perhaps then you will understand that these creations are not just the product of human skill, but of a divine mandate. Because all the things which the God of the world made on the day of creation, and whatever man has made or will make in the future (from the time of Adam to the end of the centuries), all those things, but all of them, are to be found narrated by the chisels of divine craftsmen on this temple in Athens".[75] In his belief that "the atlas of the world contains no other such mosque, capable of opening up brilliantly-lit pathways in the soul of man", he ends with a wish: "may it stand firm to the end of the centuries, and for ever be a house of prayer".[76]

Evliya Çelebi's unfeigned admiration for the Parthenon and the other antiquities of Athens was not, of course, the result of interests fostered by humanist studies. It reflects his own personal sensitivity, and also the vigour of a long oral tradition which allowed the Athenians of his time to retain "an awareness of the intellectual and spiritual grandeur to which their city had aspired in ancient times".[77] However, by this time conditions had begun to become a little easier for Western antiquarians, thanks largely to the capitulations which the European Powers had imposed on the Ottoman Empire, now in decline.

As early as 1641 France had sent Jesuits to Athens as part of its more active diplomacy towards the Porte; these were followed in 1659 by Capuchin friars who established themselves near the choragic monument of Lysicrates. It

11. H. Schedel, Athens as a German fortress. Source: H. Schedel, Liber Chronicorum, Nuremberg 1493; Athens, Gennadios Library.

is to these Capuchins that we owe a relatively accurate picture of the Acropolis, probably drawn in 1670, showing the Parthenon with a minaret but still intact (fig. 13). However, it was still hard for foreigners to visit the monument, as we can see in a letter from a nameless traveller dated 27 July 1669: "The temple of the Parthenon is still intact in the castle, and by means of a gift we succeeded in having the gate opened, even though the greedy commander was most jealous of the place ... but I was unable to make any drawings of the castle, although I had hoped to be able to measure the temple of Pallas Athena as easily as I had the Theseum. Unfortunately for us, however, the events at Candia had their repercussions in these parts, too, forcing us to leave."[78] In the same year, the Capuchin friar Robert de Dreux (in the retinue of the French Ambassador to the Porte, as his spiritual adviser) managed to bribe the Aga of the castle into letting him approach the Parthenon. "As soon as I entered, I felt great joy to have satisfied my burning dream of seeing the legendary temple, and I realised that my desire had been a justifiable one. Although the Romans, when they were masters of the city, removed the most beautiful works of art, they were unable to detach the admirable sculptures surrounding the temple, since these were firmly attached to the building."[79]

Three highly important visitors during the 1670s expressed their particular admiration for the Parthenon and must receive every credit for the care they took to hand down to us valuable information about the state of the monument before it was so severely damaged by Morosini's mortar bomb. These visitors were Father Jacques Paul Babin, a missionary of the Society of Jesus, the Marquis Olier de Nointel, Louis XIV's Ambassador to the Porte, and Dr Jacob Spon of Lyons. In his report on Athens to the learned Abbé Pécoil, Father Babin describes in some detail the monuments of the city and in particular the Parthenon, expressing the opinion that this temple "surpasses the church of St Sophia which Justinian built in Constantinople" and that "superb in its materials as it is, it is still more admirable for the manner in which it is made and the art which can be observed in it". Above all, however, he was overwhelmed by the sculptures on the west pediment: "The figures and statues of Richelieu's palace, which are the wonder of all France and the masterpiece of the craftsmen of our age, have nothing comparable to these beautiful and massive figures of men, women and horses, of which there are some thirty on this side and as many more on the other, behind the position of the high altar of Christian times".[80] Of

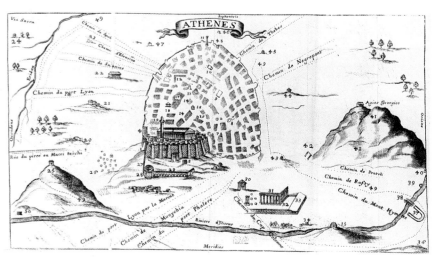

14. J. Spon, Athens in 1676. Source: J. Spon, G. Wheler, Voyage d'Italie, de Dalmatie et de Grèce ..., Lyon 1678; Athens, Gennadios Library.

12. André Thevet, Imaginary View of Athens, 1575, woodcut; Museum of the City of Athens.
13. Athens around 1670 in a drawing by Capuchin monks. Source: H. Omont, Athènes au XVIIe siècle, Paris 1898; Athens, Gennadios Library.

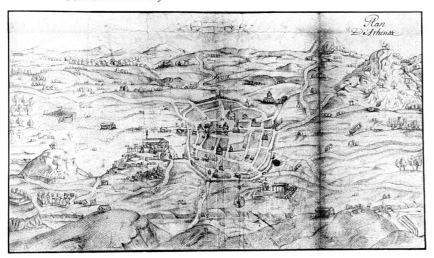

course, these comparisons are sufficient evidence of the superiority which the Parthenon was beginning to gain over other works of architecture, whether ancient or modern.

Nointel visited Athens in 1674, during a pleasure voyage which he made after safeguarding French privileges in the Levant by the renewal of the capitulations. Thanks to his ambassadorial capacity, he ascended the Acropolis with pomp and circumstance and obtained a permit to visit it again and admire the ancient monuments at his leisure. Nointel's knowledge of history was limited, which makes his enthusiasm all the more spontaneous: "If, my Lord" – he wrote to his monarch – "I were able to convey the confusion of mind which this living beauty has caused in me or the host of emotions which are left in my soul I would do so. But I must think again, and concentrate. You will allow me, my Lord, to speak of these things on another occasion."[81] Most important of all, Nointel succeeded in gaining permission for the artist who accompanied him to sketch the Parthenon sculptures, and it is to this initiative that we owe what are called the 'Carrey drawings', kept in the Paris National Library.[82] Although far from perfect – they were sketched from a distance and in something of a hurry – they are valuable evidence for a reconstruction of the sculptural compositions of Pheidias.[83]

Spon made two tours of Greece, most probably on the prompting of the Abbé Pécoil and armed with a letter of introduction from Nointel. He visited Athens on his second trip, in 1676, accompanied by the Englishman George Wheler (fig. 14). Some gifts to the Aga enabled the two men to make the ascent of the Acropolis for which they had longed. A man of literary and historical knowledge, the doctor from Lyons included a relatively responsible and accurate description of the Acropolis monuments in the second of his three volumes of travels, published two years later.[84] Of course, he made some serious errors: he thought that in ancient times, too, the entrance to the Parthenon would have been on the west side, and this led to confusion in the description of the pedimental compositions, with whose themes he was already familiar from Pausanias. In addition, he attributed the temple sculptures to the time of Hadrian.[85] We should remember that when he was writing very little was known about ancient Greek sculpture.

Spon's account of his travels became very popular and made a decisive contribution to stimulating an interest in archaeology.[86] But history has its tragic ironies: it would seem that the book by this French doctor, the last Western European traveller to see the Parthenon intact, was in the possession of officers in Morosini's mercenary army which besieged the Parthenon in 1687 and seriously damaged the temple with its mortar bombs (fig. 15). The commander of the besieging force, the Swedish Count Königsmark, was a man of humanist education and it is certain that "His Excellency was repelled by the idea of destroying the beautiful temple", as we are told in a letter written by one of the Countess's aides. Even Morosini himself did not omit to pay tribute to the city's ancient glory when informing the Venetian Senate of his triumph: "Athens has fallen into our hands, Athens the city of such glory and renown, with its magnificent monuments associated with notable memories of history and learning".[87] In other respects, however, the destruction of the Parthenon does not seem to have set off even a ripple of interest in the rest of Europe at the time.

Even in its ruinous state, the Parthenon continued to call forth the admiration of travellers who were devotees of the ancient world and who grew in number during the 18th century: thanks to the progress made in seamanship and to the relative peace which prevailed in the area, it was much easier now to sail east. "Nothing in all Greece, nor even the whole world, was equal to the magnificence of this temple", wrote the young Earl of Sandwich, who visited the Acropolis in 1738.[88] Even Francisco de Miranda from far-away Venezuela made the following diary entry about the Athenian temple in 1786: "Oh! What a superb monument! Nothing I have seen so far deserves to be compared with it!"[89] However, the Sicilian traveller Xavier Scrofani outdid all the other visitors in sincere emotion. Scrofani, a historian and economist endowed with a romantic sensibility, arrived in Athens in 1795 and, spiritually uplifted, made this entry in his journal: "The sun has just risen, and I am already on the Acropolis. The light from the sky gives the temple of Athena greater majesty ... Oh, my parents, why could you not be with me at this hour?" And a little further on: "I look at the temple, which threatens to bury me beneath its remains, and I think of you, of Athens and of the future. A sweet melancholy

15. The destruction of the Parthenon in 1687. Drawing by the engineer G.M. Verneda. Source: F. Fanelli, Atene, Attica ..., Venice 1707; Athens, Gennadios Library.

envelops my soul. I see nothing before me now, I am dreaming. I am tired of seeing and feeling."[90]

The reports and accounts of travellers increased the interest of Europeans in the Greek antiquities, but did very little to promote archaeological knowledge. The major Classical monuments – including the Parthenon – remained unknown. The image of them conveyed by the travellers' incomplete descriptions and clumsy sketches remained faint and hazy. It was not until the second half of the 18th century that the situation changed, with the publication of two impressive works, *Les Ruines des plus beaux Monuments de la Grèce* of the French architect Julien David Le Roy, published in 1758,[91] and *The Antiquities of Athens* by the English painters and architects James Stuart and Nicholas Revett, published in 1762 (the first volume) and 1787 (the second volume, with drawings of the Parthenon).[92] The Englishmen visited Athens before Le Roy: their journey, sponsored by the antiquarian Society of Dilettanti, began in 1751 and they spent three whole years in the city, measuring and drawing its monuments (fig. 16). Le Roy studied and drew the monuments of Athens in 1754, but he managed to publish before Stuart and Revett and he was undoubtedly the first person to provide Western Europe with a faithful image of the Parthenon (fig. 17). Relatively good representations of the temple and its sculptures, by Richard Dalton, had, however, already been published in Britain (fig. 18).[93]

Apart from the works of Le Roy and Stuart and Revett, which inaugurated the 'scientific' study of the Parthenon and many other Greek monuments, an important contribution to acquainting the European public with the Greek antiquities was made by the most notable of the 18th century travellers' accounts, the *Voyage pittoresque de la Grèce* of Count Choiseul-Gouffier, the first volume of which was published in Paris in 1782.[94] This was a massive illustrated work based on material which the young Count had gathered in 1776, when, accompanied by an entire team of artists, he toured the archaeological sites of Greece. Choiseul-Gouffier revisited Greece and Athens in 1785, on his way to take up the post of ambassador at Constantinople to which Louis XVI had appointed him. In 1780, the necessity of supplementing the material for the second volume of the account caused him to send to Greece the architect and engineer Foucherot, an associate for some years, and the young painter Louis Fauvel. Fauvel was to be sent to Athens again, from Constantinople, with the special mission of making plaster casts of the Parthenon sculptures and collecting as many antiquities as

16. J. Stuart and N. Revett, column capital and pediment from the Parthenon. Source: J. Stuart, N. Revett, The Antiquities of Athens..., vol. 2, London 1787.

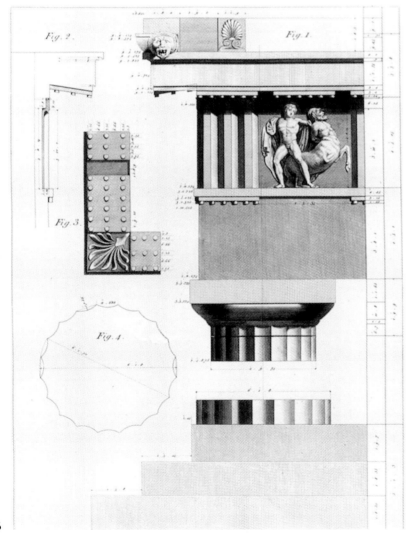

he could. It is worth digressing at this point to note that after the French Revolution (and before he was judged to be a counter-revolutionary and forced to take refuge in Russia), Choiseul-Gouffier recommended Fauvel to the Polish Diet as the artist best qualified to undertake the construction of the Church of Divine Wisdom and Goodness in Warsaw, which was to be an exact replica of the Parthenon.[95] This plan, however, was never proceeded with.

In 1802, Fauvel – who had by now returned to France – was appointed Vice-Consul in Athens and was instructed by Talleyrand to work once more on behalf of Citizen Choiseul-Gouffier. The latter had been restored to his chair in the Académie Française and was preparing the second volume of his *Voyage*. But when the French painter reached Athens, he found his colleague Lusieri dismantling the Parthenon sculptures on behalf of Lord Elgin, who had obtained the permission of the Turkish authorities not only to make plaster casts but also to remove "various pieces of stone with inscriptions and figures". As we know, this operation eventually yielded twelve statues from the pediments, fifteen metopes and fifty six slabs from the frieze.

We are familiar with the storm of protest provoked by this act of vandalism and theft. The only thing that can be said to mitigate Elgin's offence is that he was not the first person to attempt to dismantle and abstract sculptures from the Parthenon: he was merely the first person to succeed. Many European travellers hoped to find and abstract antiquities. Nointel told the Sun King that the sculptures of the temple of Athena "deserve to be placed in His Majesty's libraries and galleries, where they would enjoy the protection which that great monarch affords to the arts and sciences which produced them".[96] Morosini ordered the removal from the facade of the temple "of the statue of a Zeus [in fact, Poseidon] and the reliefs of two majestic horses", which would "add fresh glory to the Republic", but the collapse of the apex of the pediment halted the work.[97] Even Choisel-Gauffier had instructed Fauvel to make the most of every opportunity "to abstract from Athens and its surroundings anything that can be abstracted".[98] Elgin himself acknowledged that the Frenchman was his forerunner: "you opened up the path, along which happier circumstances allowed me to continue".[99] Byron may have castigated Elgin's depredations in a famous phrase –"quod Gothi non fecerunt Scotus fecit!"– but the French archaeologist Quatremère de Quincy praised his "warm and enlightened zeal", which allowed the sculptures to be preserved and appreciated by others.[100]

It is true that the 'Elgin Marbles', which were ultimately bought by the British government for display in the British Museum, made an enormous contribution to acquainting Western Europeans with Classical Greek sculpture (fig.

17. *J.D. Le Roy, elevation and section of the entrance to the Parthenon. Source: J.D. Le Roy,* Les Ruines de plus beaux monuments de la Grèce..., *Paris 1758; Athens, Gennadios Library.*

18. *R. Dalton, frontal view of the Parthenon. Source: R. Dalton,* Antiquities and Views in Greece and Egypt ..., *London 1791; Athens, Gennadios Library.*

A View of the PARTHENION or Temple of Minerva at Athens.　　Vûe du PARTHENION ou Temple de Minerve a Athènes.

19). Above all, however, they were responsible – after the work done by Le Roy and Stuart and Revett – for making the Parthenon more widely known and elevating it to the status of the sublime monument of Greek antiquity.

Reception of the 'Discovery' and the Formation of the Parthenon's Prestige in Modern Times

The growing familiarity of the modern European world with the Parthenon by means of the generally enthusiastic descriptions of travellers, and the sudden rush of publicity which the ruinous temple gained after the illustrated archaeological publications of Le Roy and Stuart and Revett, were necessary – though not sufficient – conditions for it to acquire the status of a sublime work of architecture. It was also necessary that the atmosphere should be suitable for the reception and recognition of this 'discovery'. The fact that precisely such an atmosphere did begin to exist around the mid 18th century – just at the right time, that is – should probably be seen as the outcome of interaction between advancing knowledge of ancient Greek culture and the aesthetic concepts taking shape at the time, rather than as a fortunate coincidence.

A deliberate turn towards Graeco-Roman culture was one of the principal features of the Renaissance, the first period in the modern age. However, the Renaissance knew very little about ancient Greek art and architecture. Such information as it did have came largely from literary sources such as Pausanias or Pliny the Elder, from Roman copies of Greek statues and, later, from a small number of late Hellenistic sculptures such as the Belvedere torso and Laocoon. In architecture, the textbook of Vitruvius was the only source of information. Rome, on the other hand, was from the start a much more advantageous field of research. Men of letters, architects and artists studied and described or drew the topography of the Eternal City and the antiquities which had survived or were discovered there. As a period of creativity *par excellence*, the Renaissance never regarded the ancient model as an absolute: it combined the ancient with the element of nature in order to contrast it with the medieval. Indeed, after the mid 16th century the 'maniera moderna' had begun to be commended, and the works of the great contemporary masters were promoted as models. Giorgio Vasari believed that Michelangelo had surpassed all the ancient sculptors, and that he had perfected the 'composite' architectural order to such a degree as to make comparison between it and the other Classical orders impossible.[101] As for antiquity itself, the author of the *Vite* expresses the view in the foreword to his work that the *disegno* arts started with the Egyptians and the Chaldeans, developed and "flourished in an admirable manner" in Greece, but

19. L. Jewitt, *The Elgin Hall of the British Museum, copper engraving; Athens, collection of Stavros and Stella Stavridis.*

did not reach perfection until they came to Rome.[102] This was to remain the prevailing belief throughout the 17th century, at least in those cases in which some attempt was made to distinguish between Greek and Roman art. We should not forget that the famous 'querelle des Anciens et des Modernes' began when Charles Perrault had the effrontery to compare "the age of Louis with the great age of Augustus" – and not with that of Pericles.[103] However, the reputation of Greece was maintained by the learned tradition and was very far from decline; Athens, "the eye of Greece, Mother of Arts and Eloquence"[104] occasionally served as a stimulus to the literary imagination.

The balance began to turn more decisively in favour of Greece after the mid 18th century, precisely at the time when its ancient monuments started becoming more widely known.[105] Le Roy himself contended that the Etruscans had handed on elements of Greek art to the Romans in contaminated form, thus explaining why Roman art was inferior to Greek in terms of simplicity and nobility. The Comte de Caylus, one of the first French archaeologists, pointed out that the Romans developed their art only after 146 BC, subsequent to their conquest of Greece and their encounter with Greek artistic achievements.[106] Before

Le Roy and Caylus, the superiority of the Greeks over the Romans had been advocated by the Scottish painter Allan Ramsay, who went so far as to claim that it would be impossible to undo the rules of Greek taste "unless Europe should become a conquest of the Chinese".[107] During the period of the Enlightenment, and down to the time of the French Revolution, references to ancient Greece formed an integral part of the polemics of the 'philosophes' against traditional society and the Judaeo-Christian myth on which it was based.[108] Of course, there was frequent mention of Lycurgus' Sparta, but the Athens of Pericles had its supporters, too, with Voltaire at their head. Indeed, in 1770, when Catherine the Great wrote to tell him of the Greek rising in the Morea, the Philhellene patriarch of Ferney composed an ode to what he hoped was the imminent resurrection of Athens: "Come forth, be re-born, beloved Arts, from beneath the wretched ruins whose fragments concealed you; assume once more your ancient brilliance".[109]

The task of defending 'romanità' against the growing cult of Greece was undertaken by the outstanding Italian engraver G.B. Piranesi. In earlier works (*Le Antichità Romane*, 1756, and *Della Magnificenza ed Architettura de' Romani*, 1761) but above all in his *Parere su l'Architettura*, written in dialogue form (1765), Piranesi argued that architecture and the arts reached their highest form in Rome and not in Athens: this was because the Romans had continued the original creative work done by the Etruscans, which had deteriorated in Greek hands.[110] Among the admirers of Roman architecture were Robert Adam, a friend of Piranesi and the originator of the Classical Revival in Britain, and Sir William Chambers, an advocate of the Palladian tradition. Chambers did not hesitate to describe as wholly barbaric the authentic Doric order, which had become known from Stuart and Revett's first volume on the antiquities of Athens and Soufflot's drawings of the temples of Paestum. The cumbersome proportions and absence of a base were unacceptable to followers of the Palladian school. Yet even in England the 'Greek Revival' was not long in coming, growing in parallel with the Gothic Revival that Horace Walpole had inaugurated at Strawberry Hill. In 1758, Stuart – 'Athenian' Stuart, as he was often called – built a replica Doric temple in a garden at Hagley, near Birmingham. Next to it, however, the landowner was careful to erect an edifice in the form of a Gothic ruin.[111]

On the Continent, recognition of Greek architecture was helped by the rationalist theories of the Frenchmen Cordemoy, Laugier and Blondel and of the Italians Lodoli, Algarotti and Milizia. Laugier (*Essai sur l'architecture*, 1753), who had discovered the essence of architecture in the construction of the 'primitive hut', saw in the Doric temple the most inspired interpretation of that archetype in marble, and the purest architectural form in all history. Blondel (in an entry in the *Encyclopédie*, 1751) rejected "imitations of Rome", regarded Greece as the cradle of good architecture, and preferred the authentic Doric order to the 'composite' order invented by the Romans. Milizia, too (*Dizionario delle belle arti del disegno*, 1787) viewed only Greek and Gothic architecture as truly original. And Pierre Jean Mariette, a French antiquarian, hastened to write a letter to the *Gazette litteraire de l'Europe* (1764) rejecting Piranesi's theories as groundless and championing the Greeks.[112]

However, it was the German archaeologist Johann Joachim Winckelmann who finally established the idea of Greek superiority over Piranesi's 'romanità'.[113] In 1755, when Winckelmann was forty four years of age and totally unknown, he gained recognition throughout Europe for his essay entitled *Thoughts on the Imitation of Greek Works in Painting and Sculpture (Gedanken über die Nachahmung der griechischen Werke in der Malerei und Bildhauer-kunst)*, in which he praised the "noble simplicity and sedate grandeur" ("edle Einfalt und stille Grosse") of Greek art.[114] However, Winckelmann's main claim to fame was his *History of Ancient Art (Geschichte der Kunst des Alterthums)*, published in 1764. He was the first scholar to attempt to see Greek culture whole and explain the Greek miracle. In the *Thoughts* he had attributed the creative genius of the Greeks to the climate of their land.[115] In his *History*, he returned to the importance of the climatic factor, but pointed out simultaneously that "Beauty ... was not a general quality, even among the Greeks" and that Athens was able to surpass all the other cities because "after the expulsion of the tyrants, a democratic form of government was adopted, in which the entire people had a share".[116] Winckelmann discerned four periods in the evolution of Greek art, from its genesis to its decline. For him, Greek art in its period of greatest glory was the embodiment of ideal beauty, and for that reason imitation of it was the safest method by which the artists of his own time could achieve a second Renaissance. To some extent, neo-Classicism was the historically concrete response to Winckelmann's challenge.

Winckelmann himself knew very little about ancient Greek art and architecture. He had, of course, studied the principal collections of antiquities of his day, had visited Paestum and knew the treatise of Le Roy. To visit Greece was his dream. In 1768, he set out on a journey through Central Europe to raise money for an excavation at Olympia. But in that same year he was found dead in an inn in Trieste (where he had been waiting for a boat to Venice), stabbed by a young 'friend' who had attempted to rob him. And so this lover of Greek art never saw his ideals at close quarters. No single person in his age made a greater

20. *C.R. Cockerell,* The Athens of Pericles: an imaginary reconstruction. *Source: H.W. Williams,* Select Views in Greece, *London 1829; Athens, Gennadios Library.*

contribution than Winckelmann to establishing the belief that ancient Greece – and, more specifically, Athens in the time of Pericles – created masterpieces which were truly incomparable. As G. Bazin points out, it is paradoxical that Winckelmann also contributed to detaching those masterpieces from the timeless pedestal on which they had been placed by the tradition before him: "He transformed a deathless civilisation into a historical moment; he reduced that civilisation from the absolute to the relative. Believing that he was merging himself with that civilisation, he separated himself from it by the very act in which he objectified it and simultaneously deprived it of its sanctity".[117]

The relativity introduced here took a more integrated form in the philosophy of history advanced by Herder.[118] Although an admirer of Winckelmann,[119] this dissenter from the doctrines of the Enlightenment questioned the extent to which civilisations could be ranked and argued that each period should be treated as a complete world of self-contained value, as one unique step in the creative march of history.

Herder's anti-rationalist philosophy fuelled the famous Sturm und Drang movement which for approximately a decade (1770-1780) set the intellectual life of Germany in turmoil. The young Goethe played a leading part in the movement.[120] It was at this time that he wrote his essay *On German Architecture (Von deutscher Baukunst)*, inspired by his admiration of Strasbourg Cathedral.[121] Later, however, in Weimar – and especially after his first journey to Italy (1786-1788) – Goethe and his younger friend Schiller turned away from Herder towards the classicising ideal of Winckelmann (fig. 21). In the journal he kept of his trip to Italy, Goethe made the following note on the Greek sculptures he saw in Rome: "These great works of art also stand as sublime works of Nature, produced by man in accordance with true and natural laws. All things arbitrary and artificial collapse: here is necessity, here is God."[122]

Goethe was so closely identified with the Classical spirit that Schiller could write to him in 1794, "Since you were born a German and since your Greek spirit found itself cast into this northern Creation, you had no other choices than either to become a northern artist yourself, or, by the power of contemplation, to replace with your imagination

21. J.H.W. Tishbein, Goethe on the Campo at Rome, oils; Frankfurt, Städtisches Kunstinstitut und Städtische Galerie.

what reality could not offer you and, so to speak, to generate a Greece from within ['von innen heraus'] and in a rational manner ['auf einem rationalen Wege']".[123] In his famous *Briefe über die aesthetische Erziehung des Menschen*, written the following year, Schiller notes that, "Artists are, of course, the children of their age, but woe betide them if they are its pupils or, still worse, its pets. A benevolent deity should snatch these infants from their mother's breast in good time, send them to feed on the milk of a better age and allow them to mature under the distant Greek sky ['unter fernem griechischen Himmel zu Mündigkeit reifen']".[124]

Although neither Schiller nor Goethe ever saw the "Greek sky", they strove to create a Greece "from within". Schiller discovered in the ancient Greeks "a representation of our lost childhood ['Darstellung unserer verlorenen Kindheit'] which always remains the most dear thing to us, so that they fill us with a certain nostalgia".[125] Goethe, composing the second part of *Faust* in old age, exalted in the persons of Euphorion, son of his hero, and of Helen, beautiful as ever, the union of the northern soul and the indomitable Greek spirit. In this same work, the poet who never saw the Parthenon puts these lines into the mouth of the Astrologer:

"Der Säulenshaft auch die Triglyphe klingt
Ich glaube gar der ganze Tempel singt".
['The shaft of the column and the triglyph still ring,
And I think the whole temple is singing.'][126]

Towards the end of his life, in *Kalligone* (1800), Herder came out openly against this classicising aesthetics which elevated the Greek monuments to the status of timeless and absolute measures for any judgement in the sphere of art. Furthermore, the late 18th century had seen the first stirrings in Germany of the Romantic movement, of which Herder was an early exponent and Sturm und Drang a forerunner. Goethe's reaction in 1805 (year of the death of his friend Schiller) took the form of the publication of an essay on Winckelmann and constituted a kind of anti-Romantic manifesto, but it was already too late.

Right from the start, the Romantic movement opposed itself to the classicist ideal. This contrast was based on the distinction between the Classical and the Romantic spirit;

22. Richard-Banks Harraden, View of Athens from Philopappus Hill, c. 1820, oils; Athens, Benaki Museum.

23. *L. von Klenze, View of Athens in Antiquity: Imaginary Reconstruction, 1862, oils; Munich, Bayerische Verwaltung der staatlischen Schlössen, Gärten und Seen.*

the distinction was to some extent heralded by Schiller,[127] but it was August Wilhelm Schlegel who expressed it clearly for the first time in lectures he delivered in Berlin and Vienna: "all ancient poetry and art is a rhythmic Law ['ein rhythmischer Nomos'], a harmonious proclamation of the legislation, specified for all time, of a beautifully ordered Cosmos in which the perpetual archetypes of the Beings are reflected. Romantic poetry and art, on the other hand, is an expression of the secret course of Chaos as it ceaselessly strives towards new and wonderful births ['der Ausdruck des geheimen Zuges zu dem immerfort nach neuen und wundervollen Geburten rigenden Chaos'], of the Chaos concealed beneath orderly Crea-

tion, and, indeed, within its ranks... The one [ancient poetry and art] is simpler, clearly, similar to Nature in the self-contained perfection of its individual works; the other [Romantic poetry and art], despite its fragmentary appearance, is closer to the mystery of the Universe."[128] Jean Paul Richter conceived the same difference almost simultaneously. These theorists of German Romanticism had realised that they belonged to a new era and that they were expressing a new, anti-Classical sensibility. And yet they were unable to escape the allure of the Greek spirit. Schlegel, a fine classicist, always had his gaze fixed firmly on ancient Greece. In his *Vorschule der Aesthetik*, Richter praised Classical beauty in tones reminiscent of

Winckelmann and admired the Greeks who knew "how to make their bodies alive and spirited and how to give their spirits a bodily habitation".[129] Friedrich Schlegel, the younger brother of August Wilhelm, not only accepted the absolute superiority of Greek art, but hoped that Romantic poetry itself was opening up "a vista toward a limitless growing classicity" ['Aussicht auf eine gränzenlos wachsende Klassizität'].[130] It is characteristic that at the same time – in the late 18th century – as the classicists Goethe and Schiller were issuing a periodical entitled *Die Propyläen*, the Schlegel brothers were publishing another under the equally 'classical' title *Athenäum*.

The Romantic movement developed in a period of increasingly acute social contradictions and of disappointment of the expectations raised by the optimistic worldview of the Enlightenment. Among the principal features of the movement were a desire for flight and a nostalgia for anything distant in terms of place or time. The Middle Ages, folk legends and exotic cultures provided an abundance of motifs capable of stimulating the Romantic imagination. Yet for the Romantics Greece remained the supreme theme (figs. 20, 22, 23). Most of them were not acquainted with Greece at close quarters. They formed an image of it by reading the texts of ancient authors, works by more recent historians, travellers' descriptions, and occasional fictional accounts of the geographical space of Greece, such as the famous tale by Abbé Jean-Jacques Barthélemy (*Voyage du jeune Anacharsis en Grèce*, 1788).[131] Nor were they emotionally indifferent to the plight of the enslaved Greeks and, later, to their struggle to throw off the Ottoman yoke.[132]

Hölderlin had already written his lyrical novel *Hyperion (Hyperion oder der Eremit in Griechenland*, 1797, 1799), inspired by the 1770 rising in the Morea. In his poem 'The Archipelago', he expressed an aching nostalgia for ancient Greece:

"Tell me, how stands Athens? Over the urns of the teachers
Has your beloved city, here on your sacred banks,
Oh sorrowing god! Has it sunk completely into ash?
Or does some trace of it remain, such that a passing mariner
Might mark and remember?
Did not the columns rise there, and did the figures
Of the celestial ones not shine, once, from high on the roof of the acropolis?"[133]

It was in England, however, that poetic Philhellenism of a Romantic nature took hold at an early date.[134] The subjects for the annual poetry prize competitions at Oxford University were frequently related to ancient Greece. In 1811, the topic was the Parthenon, and the prize was awarded to the otherwise unknown Richard Burton, whose lines stressed the beauty emanating from the monument in the midst of the ruins of forgotten years, and despite the desecration of the site by barbaric mosques. Burton did not, however, mention the abstraction of the sculptures, which at that time were on show in Park Lane, London.[135] Shelley and Keats, the greatest poets of English Romanticism, both adored Greece from afar. When Shelley, who was thoroughly versed in classical literature and a fine translator of it, heard that Ipsilantis had declared the commencement of the War of Independence, he composed his lyrical drama *Hellas* (1821) and dedicated it to his friend, Prince Alexander Mavrokordatos. In the Preface to the work, brimming with pro-Greek sentiments, he wrote: "We are all Greeks. Our laws, our literature, our religion, our arts have their root in Greece".[136] Keats was no scholar, but he admired the poetry of Homer (which he read in Chapman's translation); when he saw the Elgin Marbles, he wrote an excellent sonnet which concluded with these lines:

"So do these wonders [bring] a most dizzy pain,
That mingles Grecian grandeur with the rude
Wasting of old Time – with a billowy main
A sun, a shadow of a magnitude."[137]

And in his wonderful 'Ode on A Grecian Urn' he elevated a probably imaginary piece of Greek pottery to the status of a symbol of the eternal functioning of art.[138]

Other Romantics, however, had the good fortune to travel to Greece and visit Athens and its monuments. The first of them was Chateaubriand, in 1806, who was in search of images for his *Les Martyrs*. Although he was an admirer of Gothic architecture – only naturally, for a true Christian – he left us a lyrical description of his impressions from the Acropolis: "Athens, the Acropolis and the ruins of the Parthenon were coloured the most beautiful shades of peach flower; the sculptures of Pheidias, struck horizontally by a golden ray of sun, came to life and the mobility of the shadows of the relief seemed to make them move on the marble".[139] Nor did Chateaubriand hesitate to denounce Elgin for his "mutilation" of the Parthenon and the Erechtheum. The last Romantic visitor was Lamartine, who came to Athens – now free – in 1832. He described the Parthenon as "a unique and exclusive type of the beautiful in the arts of architecture and sculpture – a kind of divine revelation of ideal beauty received one day by a people *par excellence* of artists and passed on to later generations as pieces of indestructible marble and as sculptures which will live for ever". It was, he said, "the most perfect poem ever written in stone on the surface of the earth".[140]

24. The Parthenon after rain; photograph by F. Boissonas; Athens, collection of Stavros and Stella Stavridis.

In between these two Frenchmen, the most famous Romantic visitor to the Acropolis was undoubtedly Byron. When he ascended the Sacred Rock in 1809, with his close friend John Cam Hobhouse, he did not appear to be particularly impressed; when his companion commented on the majesty of the Parthenon, he replied coldly, "Very like the Mansion House".[141] The Philhellene poet seems to have been moved more by the historical associations set in train by the visit rather than by the beauty of the monument itself. In his *Childe Harold's Pilgrimage* (1812), a poetic work in which memories of the Greek landscape and history are often interwoven with the author's hopes of modern Greek resurrection, Byron expressed his revulsion at "the modern Pict's ignoble boast / To rive what Goth, and Turk, and Time hath spared".[142] And in 1811, back in Athens, he wrote the poem 'The Curse of Minerva'.[143]

As Constantine Tsatsos rightly points out, the Romantics had ceased to see the Classical world "as an eternal example, as indestructible life". They viewed it "as something which had passed, which time had destroyed [and] it is that time which, deep down, generates the sadness and nostalgia which characterise the Romantic approach".[144] If, however, 'nostalgia for Greece' was one basic component in the Romantic (and pre-Romantic) idealistic mentality,[145] this was chiefly because the Greek phenomenon was seen as unique and inimitable, interwoven with the adolescence of a civilisation in which the relationships be-

tween mankind, nature and art were still primary and unaffected, lacking the mediation of later elaboration. For Richter, to take one example, the Greeks were "creatures of the morning-time and the morning-land" ['Geschöpfe einer Morgenzeit und eines Morgenlandes'], and simplicity as a component of the Beautiful "came almost by itself to be taken for granted by them, since they did not have to describe again what had already been described and thus to beautify the Beautiful, as is the case with us, the imitators of the centuries...".[146]

Nostalgia for ancient Greece is also latent in the work of the leading German philosophers of the age, who attempted to construct a systematic philosophy of beauty and art. Schelling, nurtured on the Sturm und Drang movement, a contemporary in his maturity with the growth of Romanticism, and a faithful adherent of Winckelmann, was above all the philosopher who put art in a central position in his system. He raised it to be an activity in which the "eternal and primordial unity" of nature and Ego is revealed – and this, of course, appealed strongly to the Romantics.[147] His historical and critical analyses are rather high-handed, especially where architecture is concerned, but it should be remembered that he ranked Greek architecture far above Gothic architecture. The Gothic style, he contended, "is entirely naturalistic and coarse, and is nothing more than a direct imitation of nature (the plant organism). Nothing in it reminds us of deliberate, free art". Even the earliest Doric columns, on the other hand, which freely imitate the stripped trunks of trees – being, in other words, a mechanical task "raised above utility and necessity, orientated towards the beautiful and already significant" – lead us into the sphere of art.[148] Indeed, with the symmetry of the whole and the perfection of its forms, Greek architecture succeeded in being "an allegory of the higher organic" – that is, animal forms and the human body.[149] According to Schelling, architecture is "frozen music" ['gefrorene Musik'] and the Greeks – who were aware of this, as we can see from the myth of Amphion – succeeded in expressing rhythm, harmony and melody in symbolic form by the Doric, Ionian and Corinthian orders, respectively.[150]

For Hegel, too, Classical art represented a liberation from the direct imitation of the organic forms of nature, but in relation to the symbolic art which preceded it (Egyptian, Asiatic) rather than to later Romantic art, whose roots lie in the Middle Ages and which represents the final and culminating stage in the history of art. Classical architecture, in particular, "rather invents its forms and their configuration, so far as the content is concerned, from ends of spiritual import and in respect to form from human reason without any prototype". However, this undoubted freedom was exercised across a limited area, according to Hegel, and as a result it is somewhat of an abstract and dry character.[151] The Greeks, of course, continued to be the people whose instinct discovered the secret principle of rhythmical order on which beauty was founded. Thus, the ancient Greek temples "present an aspect which both satisfies, and if we may use the expression, sates us to the full".[152]

For both Schelling and Hegel, as for the Romantic poets, the works of Greek antiquity were the remains of a world which had disappeared beyond recall. They can be revived by imbuing them with something of our own spirit, but their original life is over. It is as if the melancholy which emanates from them stems from their own awareness of their imminent end. The Romantics may have knocked the Greek model off its supra-historical pedestal, incorporating it into the specific and irrecoverable past to which it belonged, but they also made it less abstract. They elevated it qualitatively, they endowed it with the power of appeal and, above all, they made it more widely known, thus giving neo-Classicism fresh impetus.

German neo-Classicism in architecture began in Berlin with the Brandenburger Tor, built in 1793 by Gotthard Langhans as the formal entrance to the city on the prototype of the Athenian Propylaea as surveyed by Stuart and Revett. Not long afterwards, the proposal of Friedrich Gilly for the Frederick the Great monument in Leipzigerplaz consisted of a 'Parthenon' raised on an impressive pedestal. The capital of Prussia had the ambition

of becoming a new Athens. Winckelmann called Dresden, the city where the Romantic movement took shape, the 'Athens of the North', but Romanticism found more complete architectural expression in another 'Athens of the North', Munich, thanks to the campaign of public building undertaken by King Ludwig I of Bavaria. The architect Leo van Klenze, protégé of the King (an art-lover and devotee of things Greek), was able there to build his Propyläen and Glyptothek in a flawless neo-Classical idiom. Klenze also had the good fortune to be able to build – on the banks of the Danube near Regensburg – the work which was the most characteristic blend of the Romantic spirit and the models of ancient Greek architecture: the Valhalla monument. Later, he recalled the laying of the foundation stone for this work, in which he was permitted to attempt to imitate "the creator of the Parthenon", as one of the two moments of greatest artistic joy in his life. The other was the beginning of the work of restoring "the most beautiful monument in the world", the Parthenon itself.[153]

However, the neo-Classicism of the first half of the 19th century was only one of the expressions of German Romanticism in the spheres of architecture and the visual arts. The most important building Klenze designed in Munich, the Pinakothek, is in the neo-Renaissance style. And the finest neo-Classical building in Berlin, Karl Friedrich Schinkel's Altesmuseum (opened in 1830), housed a collection of works of medieval and modern Christian art, which Frederick Wilhelm III of Prussia regarded as being more 'ethnic'. He and his successor Frederick Wilhelm IV were primarily supporters of the Nazarene artists, who opposed themselves to the Hellenising tendency and attempted to revive the religious art of the German Middle Ages. It was not long before similar endeavours were undertaken in Bavaria, during the reign of Maximilian II. Of course, it was in England that the Gothic Revival reached its apogee, especially after A.W. Pugin had endowed it with a moralistic tone which was to take it down to the end of the century.[154] In Germany, on the other hand, the Gothic Revival provoked opposition which favoured retention of the glory of the 'Greek' spirit.

Heinrich Heine, a severe critic of Romanticism, was the first writer to denounce as reactionary the pro-medieval artistic trend in Germany.[155] A pupil of Hegel and an advocate of Saint-Simon's view of the artist as pioneer, Heine countered the spirituality of the Nazarenes with the 'Greek' ideal of expressive freedom and aesthetic beauty. The leading Hegelians of the Left adopted a similar stance: Bruno Bauer attempted to correct the image of Hegel as a defender of Romantic art and Prussian totalitarianism, and to portray him as an admirer of the Greeks and a liberal. He condemned the Nazarenes'

Judaic and Christian morality and extolled Hellenism as "a religion of beauty, art, freedom and humanity". Feuerbach inverted the classification of Hegel in order to assert that it was Christian spirituality which had alienated man from his true human essence and that, by way of contrast, the insistence of the Greeks on the perceptible world had a liberating effect.[156] Even in Victorian England, the critic Matthew Arnold –under the influence of Heine– contrasted Judaism and Hellenism as the basic opposing forces by which our world is attracted alternately. He accepted that since the Renaissance progress had been bound up with the Greek values, and expressed his regret that in his own country Puritanism continued to strive against that natural order.[157]

These anti-Romantic outbursts of 'Hellenicity', associated as they were with political Jacobinism, could not but leave their mark on the young Marx. In the Introduction to his *Grundrisse*, Marx attempted to explain why it was that although the art of Greece flourished in unripe conditions of social development, its works "still afford us artistic pleasure and ... in a certain respect they count as a norm and as an unattainable model". "Why", he asked, "should not the historic childhood of humanity, its most beautiful unfolding, as a stage never to return, exercise an eternal charm? There are unruly children and precocious children. Many of the old peoples belong in this category. The Greeks were normal children. The charm of their art

for us is not in contradiction to the undeveloped stage of society on which it grew. [It] is its result, rather, and is inextricably bound up, rather, with the fact that the unripe social conditions under which it arose, and could alone arise, can never return."[158] There was, of course, nothing original about this idea. It had already been expressed by Schiller and most of the Romantics. But once restated by the pen of a philosopher and revolutionary who wished to change the world rather than simply interpreting it, it shows that the appeal of ancient Greece had gone beyond the historical bounds of the Enlightenment and Romanticism. Sure enough, after this time the offshoots of these two opposing traditions would continue to intersect in the interpretation and evaluation of ancient Greek civilisation, and they still do so today. Ernest Renan is a typical example. An heir to both traditions, like Marx, he abandoned his critical lucidity after a visit to the Acropolis in 1865 and found romantic and lyrical tones in which to sing the praises of "the perfect beauty" of its monuments. In his famous 'Prayer' to Athena, he wrote: "Yes, I shall cling to the stylobate of your temple; I shall forget every discipline but yours; I shall become a stylite on your columns; my cell will be on your architrave; and more difficult still! For your sake I shall, if I can, become bigoted, prejudiced. I shall love none other but you."[159]

The Emergence of the Parthenon as a Work of Unique and Matchless Perfection

Romantic and Late Romantic historicism included the publication, after the early 19th century and with ever-greater frequency, of historical works on the Athenian republic and the century of Pericles[160] and of studies of the art of Pheidias.[161] These enhanced the cultural context of the image of the Parthenon, and intensified its reflective power. Above all, however, a more careful study had begun of the monument itself, which the liberation of Greece had made easier of access. As far back as the mid 19th century, the famous 'refinements' of the temple – that is, its deviations from geometrical regularity, which the earliest students of it had not noticed – had been identified and interpreted in a number of ways.[162] The work in this area of F.C. Penrose and J. Pennethorne was as revelatory as that of Le Roy and Stuart and Revett a century earlier. Although some archaeologists were harder to convince, famous historians and theorists of art and architecture vied with one another in their statements of admiration for the wisdom of those who had created the monument, who knew how to give vitality to the simple 'post-and-lintel' building system by means of almost imperceptible gradients and curves. The Parthenon now

25. Auguste Choisy, axonometric drawing of the Parthenon. Source: A. Choisy, Histoire de l'architecture, *Paris 1889.*

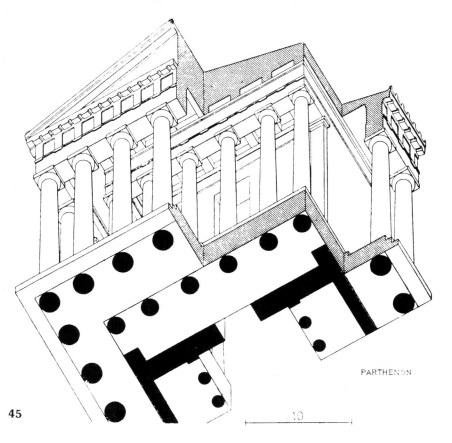

PARTHENON

45

emerged not only as a highly important masterpiece of Greek architecture but also as a sublime model of incomparable perfection, capable of withstanding the changes of the times and any shifts in aesthetic beliefs.[163]

The reception by the great men of the age of the discovery of these 'refinements' was truly enthusiastic. Viollet-le-Duc, a tireless student of the cathedrals of France, an admirer of the rationalism of Gothic construction, and a perceptive theorist of architecture in general, concluded that "the Greeks were capable of anything in the sphere of art; their sense of sight enjoyed pleasures which we are too uncouth ever to be able to appreciate".[164] The great Ruskin, on the other side of the English Channel – another Late Romantic opponent of classicality – was fascinated by the "latent picturesqueness" of this Classical monument *par excellence* and wrote: "Let it not be said, as it was of the late discoveries of subtle curvature in the Parthenon, that what is not to be demonstrated without laborious measurement, cannot have influence on the beauty of the design. The eye is continually influenced by what it cannot detect; nay, it is not going too far to say, that it is most influenced by what it detects least".[165] And at the turn of the century, Jacob Burckhardt, an outstanding historian of the civilisations of the Renaissance and ancient Greece, took the refinements as an occasion to return to the parallel between architecture and music: "We are not interested here in ascertaining the extent to which the refinements which Penrose discovered were deliberate and intentional. If it is indeed for reasons of optics that the columns of the peristyle have a slight inward inclination, that the corner columns are rather thicker and the intercolumnation denser, and that the steps and even the horizontal entablature rise a little in the centre, then we are faced with a phenomenon corresponding to the most delicate contrivances of Greek metric, and we have the words of the Astrologer in the second part of Goethe's *Faust* almost to the letter".[166] Almost at the same time, Auguste Choisy saw the Doric order in his superb *Histoire de l'architecture* as the fullest expression of the high quality of plastic elaboration ("modenature") of Greek construction, and underscored the superiority of the Parthenon: "Its style can only just be distinguished from that of the Theseum; when art its approaching its climax, it can be subjected only to almost imperceptible variations. But on this occasion absolute correctness ['l'absolue justesse'] was achieved, and the predominant impression is one of moderation, serenity and superiority. To the extent, at least, to which a masterpiece can sum up an age, these are the characteristics of architecture in the century of Pericles" (fig. 167).[167] Reared in the French tradition of structural rationalism but also free of the compositional prejudices of the Beaux-Arts, Choisy was able to praise the dynamic balance of landscape and building masses in the free arrangement of the monuments on the Acropolis.[168]

Many interpretations of the refinements on the Doric order were advanced, the initially most convincing being that which treated them as optical corrections in accordance with the writings of Vitruvius. The question took on a new slant before the end of the century with the theory – of Romantic origin – of empathy ('Einfühlung'), which generally attributed the expressiveness of forms to psychological roots. Theodor Lipps, one of the leading representatives of this school, used the Doric column as a characteristic example: there, he said, the aesthetic experience is generated when the observer combines his knowledge of the mechanical forces acting inside the column with his image of the muscle tensions which his body would develop if it were in the position of the column.[169] Slightly later, Wilhelm Worringer attempted to expand the empathy theory by contrasting a liking for the organic with a primordial impulse towards abstraction which, he claimed, was characteristic of primitive peoples. Thus, he saw in the refinements "organic tendencies which heralded the evolution of the future". Such tendencies succeeded in moderating the stereometric austerity of the Doric temple which, by way of contrast with the Ionic temple, "still seems to be the pure product of an artistic will orientated towards the abstract".[170]

These observations, interpretations and evaluations were made at a time at which the Parthenon had ceased to be a design model. The neo-Classicism which had often imitated it for monuments and memorials (in Europe) and for the temples of money (in the United States)[171] had waned, giving place to a rather degraded form of eclect-icism. And the architects who were to play the leading part in detaching design practices from the eclectic use of historical forms had already made their appearance. In a manner which is rather paradoxical (though not too difficult to explain), the Parthenon, now endowed with its refinements, acquired all the greater value as an exemplar as it gradually ceased to be a possible source for morphological borrowings. Henry van de Velde, a creative expon-ent and theoretician of the radical Art Nouveau (and also profoundly influenced by the empathy theory) was particularly struck by the columns of the temple when he visited Greece in 1903. It is as if they do not exist, he observed, and yet "between them gigantic, perfect vases are poised, containing life, space and sun, sea and mountains, night and the stars. The entasis of the columns is so transformed until the resultant space between one and the other has attained a perfect, eternal form".[172] Van de Velde also proclaimed that "we must acquaint ourselves with the meaning, the form and the purpose of all the things in the material world with the same truth by which the Greeks, among so much else, recognised the

46

meaning, the form and the purpose of the column ... As soon as the task of catharsis has been accomplished and the true form of things has reappeared in the light of day, we must search for the perfection of that form with exactly the same patience, spirit and logic as the Greeks possessed."[173]

Apart from the invocations of the Greek spirit which are abundant in the manifestos and theoretical texts written by the avant-garde architects of the period, there are also stylistic references (few in number, but nonetheless characteristic), which led Rayner Banham to write that "in the German-speaking countries of Europe the new architecture of the 20th century was born under the sign of the Doric column".[174] Sure enough, the Doric column – "always a telling sign of a longing for severity", according to Pevsner[175] – is to be seen in works by Behrens (the Mannesman building in Düsseldorf), Mies van der Rohe (the Perls house in Berlin) and Loos (the Villa Karma in Montreux and the Michaelerplatz building in Vienna). Indeed, Loos went so far as to expand the column into a

self-contained architectural form in the proposal he submitted to the famous architectural competition of 1922 for the Chicago Tribune Building.[176]

Also in 1922, Le Corbusier – already one of the pioneers of Modernism – published in the periodical *L'Esprit Nouveau* an article on architecture entitled 'The Pure Creation of the Spirit'. Illustrated with superb photographs of the Acropolis by Fred Boissonas, this article was in effect a hymn to the Parthenon and the "Doric ethos". Le Corbusier enlisted his memories of the reverent pilgrimage he had made to the Sacred Rock in 1911 and what he had assimilated from reading the *Entretiens* of Viollet-le-Duc, the *Histoire* of Choisy and the recently-published *Eupalinos* of Valéry, to write: "Greece, and in Greece the Parthenon, have marked the apogee of this pure creation of the mind: the development of profile and contour".[177] By this term, borrowed from Choisy, Le Corbusier meant the plastic expression of the work, the "skilful, accurate and magnificent play of masses seen in light". For that reason, the caption beneath a photograph

PAESTUM, de 600 à 550 av. J.-C.

Le Parthénon est un produit de sélection appliquée à andart établi. Depuis un siècle déjà, le temple grec était organ ans tous ses éléments.

Lorsqu'un standart est établi, le jeu de la concurrence imn iate et violente s'exerce. C'est le match; pour gagner, il fa

ché Albert Morancé.   PARTHÉNON, de 447 à 434 av. J.

ire mieux que l'adversaire *dans toutes les parties*, dans la lig ensemble et dans tous les détails. C'est alors l'étude poussée d irties. Progrès.

Le standart est une nécessité d'ordre apporté dans le trav: imain.

Le standart s'établit sur des bases certaines, non pas arl

26, 27. Le Corbusier: comparative juxtaposition of a temple at Paestum (600-550 BC) and the Parthenon (447-434 BC) with Humbert (1907) and Delage Grand-Sport (1921) cars. Source: Le Corbusier, Vers une architecture, *Paris 1923.*

juxtapose photographs of the Parthenon with pictures of motor cars, ocean liners, aeroplanes and electric generators (figs. 26, 27). The message was clear enough, but the contiguity was seen as sacrilegious. Even a fellow-Modernist, the Dutch architect J.J.P. Oud, another apostle of "unhistorical Classicism", reacted by saying, "I bow the knee to the wonders of technology, but I do not believe that a liner can be compared to the Parthenon".[181]

28. L. Krier, *Drawing for the Piazza Sedile, Filadelfia, Calabria, 1983. Source:* Architectural Design 7/8, 1984.

29. R. Stern, *drawing for a pavilion at the Forum Design Exhibition, Linz 1980. Source:* Architectural Design 5/6, 1980.

of the curving steps of the temple read as follows: "The Greeks created a plastic system directly and forcibly affecting our senses: columns and their flutings, a complex entablature rich in meaning; steps which set off and link on to the horizon. They employed the most delicate distortions, applying to their contours an impeccable adjustment to the laws of optics".[178]

Yet why, during the most iconoclastic phase of the Modern movement, should the movement's most combative exponent have chosen to praise the Parthenon in such terms? Of course, references to the past are to be found in every revolution, and one might interpret the invocation of the Parthenon as a rhetorical device designed to give prestige to the new ideas. But today, after a more careful and objective overview of the Modern movement,[179] we are in a position to know that Le Corbusier and many of the other pioneers were imbued with Classical ideals, even if they did attempt to express them in an abstract language which, they believed, was in harmony with the demands of the industrial age. In his controversial book *Vers un architecture*[180] (which contained the article we have already referred to), Le Corbusier dared to

Such a reaction should not come as a surprise to us. It was precisely in this period of a heroic quest for a new plastic language founded not on historically established conventions but on primary and universal values that the Parthenon consolidated its position, as a work in which those values had been accomplished with incomparable perfection – a work which, to quote Le Corbusier once more, touches inside us, in a unique manner, the 'axis' of harmony which places us "in perfect accord with nature and probably with the universe".[182]

Does the Parthenon still occupy such a position in our consciousness today? No, we would reply. Its recognition as a supreme work of architecture, which came many years ago, is still in force, but as part, now, of an established cultural convention which undergoes very little renewal. Its image has been irreparably damaged in our eyes. Although the photographs of Boissonas (figs. 24, 30) were still able to convey to his contemporaries some sense of the plastic qualities of the monuments, the countless photographic and other reproductions which have followed have diluted its aura of grandeur. And though full-size replicas of the Parthenon were once attractions

30. *The western peristyle of the Parthenon; photograph by F. Boissonas. Source: G. Fougères,* L'Acropole, Le Parthénon, *Paris 1910.*

for visitors to international exhibitions in distant America,[183] the monument itself is now consumed on the spot each year by the eyes of scores of thousands of tourists, while Classical art as a whole has been delivered into the hands of the greed of advertisers.[184] Even in the theory and practice of architecture, the Parthenon has long lost the position it once enjoyed either as the model *par excellence* for imitation or as a culminating example of plastic truth. The classicising revivals undertaken by totalitarian regimes in the inter-War period have made any reference to Greek antiquity suspect, and the 'Doric ethos' praised by Le Corbusier bears the fresh scars of the Nazi misinterpretation.[185] Lastly, contemporary 'post-Modernism' in architecture has been largely unsuccessful in its attempt to reactivate historical memory. Although for some persistent yearners after Classicality, such as Aldo Rossi or the Krier brothers, the image of the Parthenon has retained the significance of an 'archetype' (fig. 28), for libertarian eclecticists after the manner of Venturi, Moore and Stern it has dissolved into the heterogeneous iconographic fragments of a caleidoscopic view of the architectural past (fig. 29).[186]

However, the monument itself is still there, and nowadays it is the object of care and study by experts whose relationship with it is undoubtedly less disturbed by ideological interference. Their task is to try to save its mutilated body from further damage, and also to study it and carefully to measure its members – continuing a tradition 240 years old – in the hope of revealing more of the mysteries of its construction and original form. Who knows – perhaps the fruit of their toil will suffice to renew yet again our interest in, and admiration of, the Parthenon.

Notes

1. See Ch. Bouras, *Mathimata Istorias tis Architektonikis* ('Lessons on the History of Architecture'), vol. II, Athens 1975, p. 209, where the quotation is given.
2. See in this respect Anthony Savile, *The Test of Time: An Essay in Philosophical Aesthetics*, Oxford 1982.
3. André Malraux, *La Voie Royale*, 1930. See E.H. Gombrich, *Meditations on a Hobby Horse and other Essays*, London/New York 1978, p. 80, where the quotation is given.
4. Sigmund Freud, 'A Disturbance of Memory on the Acropolis', *The Standard Edition of the Complete Psychological Works of Sigmund Freud* (translated from the German under the general editorship of James Strachey in collaboration with Anna Freud, assisted by Alex Strachey and Alan Tyson), vol. XXII, Hogarth Press and the Institute of Psychoanalysis, London 1964, p. 241.
5. *Ibid.*, pp. 247-48.
6. Le Corbusier's impressions of his journey were written three years after it had taken place and published a year after the architect's death (Le Corbusier, *Le Voyage d'Orient*, Paris 1966; *Journey to the East*, Cambridge, Mass. 1987, p. 216). The passages about Greece, together with other relevant texts and drawings, have been superbly compiled by Yorgos Simeoforidis in *Le Corbusier, Keimena yia tin Ellada* ('Texts on Greece'), Athens 1987.
7. *Keimena, op. cit.*, p. 167.
8. Le Corbusier, *Journey, op. cit.*, pp. 216-217.
9. Le Corbusier, *Keimena, op. cit.*, p. 131. The saying was uttered during the lecture which Le Corbusier delivered at the National Technical University of Athens on his second trip to Greece, in 1933, for the IV International Congress of Modern Architecture.
10. Thucydides, II, 65, 9-10. All quotations from ancient authors are taken from the Loeb Classical Library editions, unless otherwise indicated.
11. *Ibid.*, II, 41, 1.
12. Plutarch, *Pericles*, XVII. Plutarch's reference is the only one to this congress.
13. The only reference to the oath is in Diodorus Siculus (XI, 29, 3), and most modern historians doubt whether it was ever taken.
14. *Op. cit.*
15. M. Andronikos, 'I Klassiki Techni' ('Classical Art'), *Istoria tou Ellinikou Ethnous* ('History of the Greek Nation'), Ekdotike Athinon, vol. C2, p. 280.
16. *Op. cit.*, XIII.

17. The only temples which were larger were temple T at Selinus and the temple of Zeus at Acragas, neither of which was completed.

18. Thucydides, II, 13, 5. The 'forty talents' correspond to more than a thousand kilos. The gold was 'removable' so that it could be detached, weighed and put back on the statue.

19. Charles Picard, *L'Acropole d'Athènes*, Paris 1929.

20. *Op. cit.*, pp. 298-302 and 304-305.

21. Henri Lechat, *Phidias et la sculpture grecque au Ve siècle*, Paris 1924, p. 126.

22. However, many of the building inscriptions have survived, and these provide us with valuable information about the way in which the work was done and how much it cost.

23. Vitruvius, *De Architectura*, VII, Foreword, 12.

24. Thucydides, II, 13, 3.

25. Plutarch, *op. cit.*, XII and XIII.

26. *Ibid.*, XII.

27. Isocrates, *Panegyricus*, 23; see also 50.

28. Isocrates, *On the Antidosis*, 234-235; see also 307-308.

29. "For with no regard for temperance and justice they have stuffed the city with harbours and arsenals and walls and tribute and suchlike trash", Plato, *Gorgias*, 518E-519A; see also 515E.

30. Aristotle, *Athenian Constitution*, XXVII, 1.

31. Dio Chrysostom, *Diogenes, or, on Tyranny*, 4.

32. "He sent to Athens three hundred Persian panoplies, to be set up to Athena on the acropolis; he ordered this inscription to be attached: 'Alexander son of Philip and the Greeks, except the Lacedaemonians, set up these spoils from the barbarians dwelling in Asia'"; Arrian, *Anabasis of Alexander*, I, 16, 7, and Plutarch, *Alexander*, XVI, which called them 'shields' rather than panoplies. Note also that according to Dio Chrysostom (*The Second Discourse on Kingship*, 36) Alexander told his father Philip that the spoils of war were a more honourable offering than "the Propylaea of the Acropolis and the Olympeum".

33. Plutarch, *Demetrius*, XXIII, 2-4.

34. *Ibid.*, XXIV, 1.

35. Polemon's work is mentioned by Strabo (*Geography*, IX, 1, 16), but not by Pausanias.

36. In the famous *In Verrem* speeches.

37. Cicero, *De Officiis*, I, 1 and III, 121.

38. Cicero, *De Re Publica*, I, 25 and IV, 11.

39. Plutarch, *Antony*, XXIII, 2-3; see also XXXIII, 4, for Antony playing the role of 'gymnasiarch' in Athens. According to Dio Cassius (*Roman History* XLVII, 39, 2), on one of his visits to Athens, Antony, like a new Dionysus, accepted the Athenians' invitation to wed Athena and received the corresponding dowry.

40. Virgil's visit to Athens is a matter of historical fact. In the same year, he fell ill at Megara and died at Brindisi on his way home. His epic, of course, is anything but pro-Greek.

41. As the subject of the treatises of Ictinus and Carpion.

42. Diodorus Siculus, XII, 1, 4; see also XII, 39, 1 for the statue of Athena.

43. Strabo, *Geography*, IX, 1, 6.

44. *Ibid.*

45. Dio Chrysostom *The Rhodian Oration*, 148. According to Dio Cassius (*Roman History*, LXII, 14, 3), Nero avoided visiting Athens for fear of the Furies.

46. Dio Chrysostom, *Oration Delivered in his Native City on Concord with the Apameians*, 8; see also *The Statesman in the Assembly*, 12.

47. Aelius Aristides, *Panathenaic Oration*, 162D. Later (306D): "Again in the matter of art, what should we judge greatest or speak of first? For the temples are here both the greatest and the fairest of those anywhere, and the statues, apart from those which fell from heaven, hold the highest place in the highest form of art, both the ancient and the modern ones." Elsewhere (309D), on the Athena of Pheidias: "there are admired statues, and that one of yours in the city is the best and first of those".

48. In his *In Defence of Oratory*.

49. Born at Marathon, and not in Asia Minor as were Dio and Aristides. Unfortunately, of all his works only one fragment of a set oration has survived, and the authenticity even of that is disputed.

50. Pausanias, *Attica*, I, 24, 5-7.

51. Plutarch, *Pericles*, XIII.

52. *Acts* 17, 16-34.

53. Jean Baelen, *La chronique du Parthénon*, Paris 1956, p. 70.

54. "Then if this was your conduct of old, and from that day to this there is kept alive some small spark as it were of the virtue of your ancestors..."; "But what floods of tears I shed and what laments I uttered when I was summoned, stretching out my hands to your Acropolis and imploring Athena to save her suppliant and not to abandon me...", Julian, *Letter to the Senate and People of Athens*, 269D and 275A.

55. The tradition is preserved by the 5th century historian Zosimus (*Historia Nova*, E, 6, 1:"Alaric, coming against the city with his whole army, saw Athena Promachus stalking the wall, as she is seen in statues, fully-armed and ready to resist attackers; and on the walls, Achilles, standing forth as Homer showed the hero to the Trojans when he fought in vengeance for the death of Patroclus, in anger. Alaric was unable to bear this spectacle and abstained from any operation against the city, sending ambassadors to sue for peace." (Our translation).

56. We are told this by his pupil and successor in the Academy of Plato, Marinus (*Proclus, or, concerning happiness*, XXX): "As he became beloved of this philosopher-goddess, the choice of a life of philosophy attracted him, this coming to pass as the word had indicated; and the goddess appeared clearly to him, at the time when her statue, which had formerly stood in the Parthenon, was being shifted by those who could move the immovable. The philosopher saw himself visited in a dream by a beautiful woman who told him that he must speedily make ready his house, 'for the lady Athena', she said, 'has chosen to lodge with you.'" (Our translation).

57. *L' epopée byzantine à la fin du dixième siècle*, transl. from the Greek edition (vol. II, Athens 1905, p. 177).

58. M. Acominatos, *Ta Sozomena* ('Remains'), ed. S. Lambros, vol. II, Athens 1880, p. 398.

59. Baelen, *op. cit.*, p. 86.

60. *Ibid.*, pp. 86-87.

61. See Kyriakos Simopoulos, *Xenoi Taxidiotes stin Ellada* ('Foreign Travellers in Greece'), vol. I, *333 BC – 1700*, Athens 1970, pp. 194-195 and 242-243.

62. According to B. Scardeone in his work on Padua published in 1560. See also the next note.

63. Anna Maria Tamassia, 'Jacopo Bellini e Francesco Squarcione: due cultori dell' antichita classica', *Il mondo antico nel Rinascimento, Atti del V Convegno Internazionale di Studi sul Rinascimento (Firenze – Pallazo Strozzi, 2-6 Sett. 1956)*, Florence 1958, pp. 159-166.

64. On Cyriacus, see B. Ashmole, *Cyriac of Ancona*, London 1957, and E. Bodnar, *Cyriacus of Ancona and Athens*, Brussels/Bergen 1960.

65. See Simopoulos, *op. cit.*, pp. 307-308.

66. Carlo Claudio Van Essen, 'I Commentaria di Cyriaco d'Ancona', *Il mondo antico ...*, *op. cit.*, pp. 191-194.

67. "O nobilis Graecia, ecce nunc tuum finem, nunc demum mortua es", he wrote to Pope Nicholas V. In this regard, see Terence Spencer, *Fair Greece, Sad Relic: Literary Philhellenism from Shakespeare to Byron*, London 1954, pp. 6-14.

68. Comte de Laborde, *Athènes aux XVe, XVIe, et XVIIe Siècles*, vol. 1, Paris 1854, p. 4.

69. Crusius (Martin Kraus), a professor at Tübingen, published such information as he was able to gather about the state of the Greek lands and their antiquities in his massive *Turco-Graeciae libri octo ...* (Basle 1854). Meursius' work *Athenae Atticae* (Leyden 1624) was relatively complete and accurate and served as a useful guide for learned visitors to Athens for many years.

70. "The entire country is in such a state of ruin as to make it seem incredible that it was ever glorious", wrote Jean Chesneau in his travels: he came through Attica in 1546 on his way to Constantinople with the French Ambassador, D'Aramon (see Simopoulos, *op. cit.*, pp. 375-376). The Scottish traveller William Lithgow, who visited Athens in 1609, calls the city "the Mother and Well-Spring of all liberal Arts and Sciences, ... but now altogether decayed", and simply mentions the existence of "a Castle which formerly was the Temple of Minerva" (see Spencer, *op. cit.*, pp. 62-63).

71. Simopoulos, *op. cit.*, pp. 158-167.

72. *Ibid.*, pp. 512-518.

73. The first translation of the *Travels* into a European language was the English edition of 1834, which was followed by a number of others. In Turkey, publication was not completed until 1939 (Evliya Çelebi, *Seyahatnamesi*, Istanbul 1898-1938). Extracts from, or summaries of, the chapters referring to Greece have been published in Greek from time to time; the most important work on the chapters dealing with Attica was that of Kostas Biris, *Ta Attika tou Evliya Çelebi* ('Evliya Çelebi on Attica'), Athens 1959. Nikos Cheiladakis relied on earlier attempts at translation for his own literary rendering (Evliya Çelebi, *Taxidi stin Ellada* ['Journey to Greece'], Athens 1991), to which my references and from which the passages translated here.

74. Çelebi, *op. cit.*, pp. 170-171 and 178.

75. *Ibid.*, p. 177.

76. *Ibid.*, p. 178.

77. Biris, *op. cit.*

78. The letter is in the collection of the National Library, Paris. See Baelen, *op. cit.*, pp. 106-107, from which the quotation is taken.

79. Simopoulos, *op. cit.*, p. 632.

80. Baelen, *op. cit.*, p. 112.

81. Simopoulos, *op. cit.*, p. 657.

82. These drawings, which were published by Henri Omont (*Athènes au XVIIe siècle*, Paris 1898), were initially attributed to the French painter Jacques Carrey, but Albert Vandal has argued very persuasively that they were actually the work of a Flemish painter who accompanied Nointel on his tour.

83. See, for example, F. Brommer, *Die Skulpturen der Parthenon-Giebel*, Mainz 1963.

84. Baelen, *op. cit.*, pp. 112-114, and Simopoulos, *op. cit.*, pp. 689-698.

85. Even in the time of Napoleon, some people believed that the Parthenon had been built by Hadrian; that, at least, is the conclusion to be drawn from the first leaf of the album with Carrey's drawings, written by the curator of the National Library, Paris.

86. Spon's companion on his travels, Wheler, attempted to expropriate his work, translating it into English and publishing it over his own name.

87. Baelen, *op. cit.*, pp. 113-121, and Simopoulos, *op. cit.*, pp. 698-706.

88. *A Voyage Performed by the Late Earl of Sandwich Round the Mediterranean in the Years 1738 and 1739*, London 1799, p. 51.

89. Simopoulos, *op. cit.*, p. 480.

90. *Ibid.*, p. 635.

91. Julien David Le Roy, *Les Ruines des plus beaux Monuments de la Grèce considérées du côté de l'histoire et du côté de l'architecture*, Paris 1758, revised edition 1770.

92. *The Antiquities of Athens Measured and Delineated by James Stuart, F.R.S. and F.S.A., and Nicholas Revett, Painters and Architects*, London 1762-1816. This work was frequently reprinted in English and translated into other languages during the 19th century.

93. Dalton's drawings of various Greek monuments were produced during the Grand Tour of the young Earl of Charlemont, which began in 1749, and were engraved by various well-known artists of the time. See Spencer, *op. cit.*, pp. 158-160.

94. The first volume, with a particularly pro-Greek foreword, was published two years later as a self-contained book (*Discours préliminaire du Voyage pittoresque de la Grèce*, Paris 1783). The second volume was published in two parts in 1809.

95. Baelen, *op. cit.*, p. 125.

96. *Ibid.*, p. 112.

97. *Ibid.*, p. 121, and Simopoulos, *op. cit.*, p. 703.

98. Baelen, *op. cit.*, pp. 124-125.

99. Simopoulos, *op. cit.*, p. 459.

100. Baelen, *op. cit.*, pp. 126 and 130. Quatremère de Quincy believed that the antiquities of Rome ought to be left in place but that those of Athens should be moved because they were at risk. In the particular case of the Elgin Marbles, he thought that exhibiting them in a museum would allow them to be seen and enjoyed much more than if they were left on the monument. For these views, which he explained in letters to the sculptor Canova (first published in 1818), see Yannis Tsiomis, 'Apo ti Romi stin Athina' ('From Rome to Athens'), *Athina, Protevousa Poli* ('Athens, Capital City'), Ministry of Culture, Athens 1985, pp. 40-43.

101. See Paola Barochi, 'Il valore dell'antico nella storiographia vasariana', *Il mondo antico ...*, *op. cit.*, pp. 215-236. This also contains extracts from letters from Aretino and Doni to Michelangelo, acknowledging his superiority over the ancients. Doni, in particular, wrote: "I could now glorify you by saying that your statues ... surpass the majesty of the marbles of Pheidias".

102. Giorgio Vasari, *Les vies des meilleurs peintres, sculpteurs et architectes* (édition commentée sous la direction d'André Chastel), 3rd (revised) edition, vol. 1, Paris 1989, pp. 98-100.

103. The comparison is to be found in Perrault's poetic work *Le siècle de Louis le Grand*, read by the poet himself in the Academy in January 1687. The controversy lasted until 1700. Fontenelle and a large part of public opinion sided with Perrault, while among the supporters of the superiority of the ancient were the poets Boileau, Racine and La Fontaine, together with scholars such as Dacier and Menage. Perrault returned to the theme in his *Parallèle* (1688): in the second of the five dialogues of which this consists, he argues that the Louvre, with its famous east facade designed by his brother Claude, was superior to the temple of Ephesus or the Colosseum, since in the meantime there had been a great advance in technical knowledge.

104. John Milton, *Paradise Regained*, IV, 240.

105. Apart from the travellers' accounts and the works of Le Roy and Stuart and Revett, much was done to publicise the Greek monuments by publications such as the *Ruins of Athens and other Valuable Antiquities in Greece*, by Robert Sayer, which appeared in 1759. In parallel, the monuments of Magna Graecia and in particular the temples of Paestum were publicised by the engravings which Q.C. Antonioni began to bring out in 1744, by the drawings of Soufflot in 1764 and by the *Ruins of Paestum* of Thomas Major, published in 1768.

106. In his seven-volume *Récueil d'antiquités, égyptiennes, étrusques, grécques et romaines* (1757-1767).

107. In his text 'A Dialogue on Taste', published anonymously in the London magazine *The Investigator* in 1755. Above all, however, Ramsay was an admirer of Gothic art.

108. See Pierre Vidal-Naquet, 'Parisi - Athina kai Epistrophi' ('Paris -

Athens and Back'), *Athina, Protevousa Poli, op. cit.*, pp. 36-39. For fuller documentation, see N. Loraux and P. Vidal-Naquet, 'La formation de l'Athènes bougeoise. Essai d'historiographie 1750-1850', *Classical Influence on Western Thought 1650-1870*, R.R. Bolgar (ed.), Cambridge University Press 1978.

109. See Spencer, *op. cit.*, pp. 186-187, where the quotation is given.

110. Piranesi was writing at a time when Etruscan archaeology was flourishing. Thomas Coke had already published his *De Etruria Regali* (1723-26) and Gori his *Museum Etruscum* (1737-43), museums of Etruscan art had been founded at Volterra and Montepulciano, and in 1744 the Vatican gallery with the so-called 'Etruscan' vases had opened. Knowledge of Roman architecture, too, had expanded, with the excavations on the Palatine Hill in Rome, the Tivoli and in Pompeii, with the archaeological expeditions to Palmyra and Baalbeck, and with the publication of Robert Adam's drawings of Diocletian's palace at Spalato (*Ruins of Spalato*, 1763).

111. See Nikolaus Pevsner, *An Outline of European Architecture*, 7th ed., Harmondsworth 1963, p. 357.

112. Piranesi replied the following year in his *Osservazioni sulla lettera di M. Mariette*, persisting in his views and emphasising that the Greeks did not allow their artists enough freedom. However, he inadvertently contributed to the reception of 'the Doric', with his engravings of the temples at Paestum, which began to circulate in the year of his death (1778).

113. See also Vasiliki Petridou, 'Piranesi kai Winckelmann: mia Theoritiki Diamachi' (1755-1965)' ('Piranesi and Winckelmann: a Theoretical Dispute'), *Athina, Protevousa Poli, op. cit.*, pp. 44-46.

114. Winckelmann, *Writings on Art*, selected and edited by David Irwin, London 1972, p. 72.

115. *Ibid.*, p. 61.

116. *Ibid.*, p. 107. In the first chapter of the fourth book, entitled 'Grounds and Causes of the Progress and Superiority of Greek Art Beyond That of Other Nations', Winckelmann sums up his explanation as follows: "The superiority which art acquired among the Greeks is to be ascribed partly to the influence of climate, partly to the constitution and government, and to the habit of thinking which originated therefrom, and in an equal degree also, to respect for the artist, and the use and application of art" (*ibid.*, p. 113).

117. Germain Bazin, *Histoire de l'histoire de l'art de Vasari à nos jours*, Paris 1986, pp. 108-109.

118. First in his essay *Auch eine Philosophie zur Geschichte der Bildung der Menschheit* (1774) and later in his fine work *Ideen zur Philosophie der Geschichte der Menschheit* (1784-1791).

119. In 1777, Herder dedicated an essay (*Denkmal Johann Winckelmanns*) to his memory, calling him a "hero" and terming his *Geschichte* "a gigantic work".

120. In his encomium on Shakespeare (*Zum Shakespeares Tag* 1771), in his drama *Götz von Berlichingen* (1773), and, above all, in his novel *Die Leiden des jungen Werthers* (1774).

121. This essay was Goethe's contribution to the volume *Von deutscher Art und Kunst* which Herder was responsible for publishing in 1773.

122. Goethe, *Italienische Reise* (6 Sept. 1787), in *Sämtliche Werke*, Eduard von der Hellen, Stuttgart 1902-1907, vol. 27, p. 108.

123. See Panayiotis Kanellopoulos, *Istoria tou Evropaikou Pnevmatos* ('History of the European Spirit'), vol. VII, Athens 1976, p. 425.

124. Schiller, *Briefe über die aesthetische Erziehung des Menschen*, parallel edition with French translation, Aubier-Montaigne, 1976, p. 134.

125. Schiller, *Über naive und sentimentalische Dichtung*, in *Sämtliche Werke*, Stuttgart/Tubingen 1818, vol. VIII, part 2, p. 46.

126. Goethe, *Faust*, Neue Gesamtausgabe, Leipzig 1941, p. 322.

127. In his essay on naive and sentimental poetry of 1796 (see note 125, above), where he notes the contradiction between ancient naive poetry and modern sentimental poetry.

128. A.W. Schlegel, *Über dramatische Kunst und Literatur*, vol. III, Heidelberg 1817, pp. 14-15.

129. Jean Paul Richter, *Vorschule der Aesthetik* (1804), 17, *Werke* X-VIII, p. 79.

130. *Friedrich Schlegel 1794-1802: seine prosaischen Jugendschriften*, ed. J. Minor, vol. 2, Vienna 1882, p. 220.

131. In the imaginary journey to 4th century Greece of the young Scythian Anacharsis, Barthelemy relied on historical information to provide an authentic and eloquent guide for Europeans wishing to communicate with ancient Hellenism. The book was a tremendous success and was translated into many European languages. Rigas Velestinlis was among its first translators into Greek.

132. Quite a number of travellers discerned in the modern Greeks physical and moral virtues which reminded them of the ancients. One of the main advocates of the belief that the modern Greeks were the descendants of their ancient forefathers was the French traveller and student of folklore Pierre Augustin Guys, in his *Voyage littéraire de la Grèce, ou lettres sur les Grecs, anciens et modernes, avec un parallèle de leurs moeurs* (1783).

133. An excellent Greek translation of the entire poem, by Stella Nikoloudi, was published in the periodical *Logou Harin*, no. 2, spring 1991, pp. 99-106.

134. See Bernard Herbert Stern, *The Rise of Romantic Hellenism in English Literature, 1732-1786*, Menasha 1940, reprinted New York 1969, and Spencer, *op. cit.*

135. Spencer, *op. cit.*, p. 278. The poem was included in the collection *Oxford Prize Poems*, 5th ed., Oxford 1816, p. 173.

136. See George E. Woodberry, *The Complete Poetical Works of Percy Bysshe Shelley*, New York 1901, p. 319.

137. John Keats, sonnet V, 'On seeing the Elgin Marbles for the first time', *Poems*, ed. Selincourt, p. 275.

138. John Keats, 'Ode on A Grecian Urn', *English Poetry in Three Volumes* (The Harvard Classics), vol. II, pp. 878-879.

139. Francois-Réné de Chateaubriand, *Itinéraire de Paris à Jérusalem …*, vol. I, Paris 1831, p. 205.

140. A. de Lamartine, *Voyage en Orient*, vol. I, Paris 1855, offset reprint 1978, p. 95.

141. See André Maurois, *Byron*, English translation by Hamish Miles, New York 1930, p. 133.

142. Byron, *Childe Harold's Pilgrimage*, 2, XII, *The Poetical Works of Lord Byron* (Oxford Edition), London/New York/Toronto/Melbourne 1914, p. 191.

143. Byron, 'The Curse of Minerva', *ibid.*, pp. 138-141.

144. C. Tsatsos, 'O Romantismos, o Satovriandos kai i Hellas' ('Romanticism, Chateaubriand and Greece'), *Nea Estia*, Christmas 1968, no. 885, p. 177.

145. See Jacques Taminiaux, *La nostalgie de la Grèce … l'aube de l'idealisme allemand*, La Haye 1967.

146. See Kanellopoulos, *op. cit.*, where the quotation is given. Cf. Pascal's observation 160 years earlier: "Those whom we call 'ancient' were in reality 'new' in everything … and as we have brought together with our knowledge the experience of all the centuries which followed them, it is in us that the antiquity we honour in others is to be found" (*Fragment d'un traité sur le vide*, 1647).

147. In his work *System des transzendentalen Idealismus* (1800).

148. In his lectures in Jena (1802-1803), which were published much later as *Kunstphilosophie* (1859). See F.W.J. Schelling, *Textes esthétiques* (trans. Alain Pernet and intro. Xavier Tilliette), Paris 1968, p. 120.

149. *Ibid.*, p. 121.

150. *Ibid.*, pp. 123-131.

151. G.W.F. Hegel, *The Philosophy of Fine Art* (trans. F.P.B. Osmaston), vol. III, New York 1975, p. 65.

152. *Ibid.*, pp. 66 and 77-78.

153. See Florian Hufnagl, 'O Klenze kai i archaiotita' ('Klenze and Antiquity'), *Athina, Protevousa Poli, op. cit.*, pp. 58-61.

154. See Kenneth Clark, *The Gothic Revival*, Pelican Books, Harmondsworth, 1964.

155. In his works *Romantische Schule* (1836) and *Ludwig Borne* (1841).

156. See Margaret A. Rose, *Marx's Lost Aesthetic: Karl Marx and the Visual Arts*, Cambridge/New York 1984.

157. In the fourth chapter of his essay on *Culture and Anarchy* (1869), entitled 'Hebraism and Hellenism'; see Matthew Arnold, *Selected Prose*, Penguin Books, Harmondsworth 1970, pp. 273-286.

158. Karl Marx, *Grundrisse* (English trans. Martin Nicolaus), Harmondsworth 1979, pp. 110-111.

159. Ernest Renan, 'Prière sur l'Acropole', *Souvenirs d'enfance et de jeunesse* (1883); see *Oeuvres Complètes*, vol. II, Paris 1948, pp. 752-759.

160. Indicatively: W. Young, *History of Athens* (1804), J. Boot, *Vita Periclis* (1834) and *De Pericle eiusque meritis* (1835), J.A. Kutzen, *Perikles als Staatsmann* (1834), C. Wendt, *Perikles und Kleon* (1836), C. Wordsworth, *Athens and Attica* (1836-1855), H. Sauppe, *De demis urbanis Athenarum* (1846), V. Schneiderhahn, *Die Entwicklung des attischen Demokratie* (1866), E. Filleul, *Histoire du siècle de Périclès* (1872), E. Burnouf, *La légende athénienne* (1872), W. Lloyd, *The Age of Pericles* (1875), A. Schmidt, *Perikles und sein Zeitalter* (1877-79), J. Larocque, *La Grèce au temps du Périclès* (1883), K. Beloch, *Die attische Politik seit Perikles* (1884), E. Abbot, *Pericles and the Golden Age of Athens* (1898).

161. E. Toelken, *De Phidiae Jove Olympico* (1812), K.O. Müller, *De Phidiae vita et operibus* (1827), E. Petersen, *Die Kunst des Pheidias* (1873), C. Walston, *Essay on the Art of Pheidias* (1885).

162. The 'entasis' of the columns had been noted by C.R. Cockerell in 1810, and their slant by T.L. Donaldson in 1829. The curvature of the stylobate was first identified by J. Pennethorne around 1837, and almost simultaneously by J. Hoffer and E. Schaubert. C. Bötticher and J. Durm attributed the curvature to subsidence, while Dörpfeld interpreted it as a means of facilitating the run-off of rain water. For more details and a bibliography, see the first chapter, by M. Korres, of this book.

163. The practice of 'refinement' was known long before the Parthenon was built. However, its systematic and complete application began in Attica around 450 BC, and lasted for some thirty years. Even then, it was not used in all monuments. The columns of the temple of Poseidon at Sounion do not have 'entasis'. The temple of Apollo at Bassae, although the work of Ictinus, has no refinements other than 'entasis'. Refinements are a feature primarily of the temple of Hephaestus (the 'Theseum'), the Parthenon and the Propylaea.

164. E.E. Viollet-le-Duc, *Dictionnaire raisonné de l'architecture française*, Paris 1854-68.

165. J. Ruskin, *Stones of Venice*, vol. II, chapter 5. The expression 'latent picturesqueness' belongs to P.A. Michelis (see note 169, below).

166. J. Burckhardt, *Griechische Kulturgeschichte, op. posth.* 1892-1902, vol. II, p. 134.

167. A. Choisy, *Histoire de l'architecture* (1899), vol. 1, Paris 1954, pp. 232 and 238.

168. *Ibid.*, pp. 327-334.

169. T. Lipps, 'Aesthetische Einfühlung', *Zeitschrift für Psychologie,* 22, 1900, p. 439. See also the same author's *Raumaesthetik und geometrische-optische Tauschungen*, Barth 1897, and his *Aesthetik*, Leipzig 1903 (vol. 1) and 1906 (vol. 2). The Greek architect P.A. Michelis relied on the 'aesthetic mechanics' of Lipps in interpreting the refinements; see his articles 'Ekleptynseis Morphis stin Architektoniki' ('Refinements of Form in Architecture') and 'Lanthanousa Kinisi i Lanthanousa Graphikotita;' ('Latent Motion or Latent Picturesqueness?') in P.A. Michelis, *Aisthitika Theorimata* ('Aesthetic Theorems'), vol. A, 2nd ed., Athens 1971, pp. 301-337 and 110-142, respectively.

170. W. Worringer, *Abstraktion und Einfühlung* (1908), French translation *Abstraction et Einfühlung*, Paris 1978, p. 105.

171. See the chapter by P. Tournikiotis in this book, with comments on the partial and complete imitations of the monument during the neo-Classical period.

172. See K. Frampton, *Modern Architecture: A Critical History*, London 1980, p. 98, where the quotation is given.

173. *Notizen von einer Reise nach Griechenland*, Weimar 1905.

174. R. Banham, 'Neoclassicism', *Encyclopaedia of Modern Architecture* (G. Hatje, general editor), London 1963, p. 203.

175. Pevsner, *op. cit.*, p. 372.

176. For the controversial proposal by this 'enigmatic' Viennese architect, see P. Tournikiotis, *Adolf Loos*, New York 1993.

177. Le Corbusier, *Towards a New Architecture, op. cit.*, p. 202.

178. *Ibid.*, p. 192.

179. By way of contrast with the first historians of the movement, who stressed the innovative elements in the ideas and works of the pioneers, more recent writers have drawn attention to their more profound Classical inclinations. See, in particular, R. Banham, *Theory and Design in the First Machine Age*, London 1960, and Colin Rowe, *The Mathematics of the Ideal Villa and Other Essays*, Cambridge, Mass. and London 1976.

180. Le Corbusier, *Vers une architecture*, Paris 1923.

181. See Banham, *Theory and Design ..., op. cit.*, pp. 157-158.

182. Le Corbusier, *Towards a New Architecture, op. cit.*, p. 192.

183. See once more the chapter by P. Tournikiotis in this book.

184. See C. Bouliotis, 'I Archaiotita stin Diaphimisi' ('Antiquity in Advertising'), *Archaiologia*, no. 27, June 1988, pp. 22-29.

185. See Andreas Ioannidis, 'Klassiki Archaiotita kai Fasismos' ('Classic Antiquity and Fascism'), *ibid.*, pp. 16-21.

186. See Savas Kondaratos, 'I Evropaiki Architektoniki tou Aiona mas kai i Ellada ('European Architecture of Our Century and Greece'), *ibid.*, pp. 70-74.

MANOLIS KORRES

The Architecture
of the Parthenon

I

In the early 5th century, down to the time of its burning by the Persians in 480 BC, the Acropolis retained its ancient Mycenean walls. The terrain, too, was still laid out as it had been in former times, though it was no longer occupied by the palaces of the mythical kings, the heroes who founded the city, but by temples and other sacred buildings of the Archaic period. After the Persian Wars, this complex form which was the result of a millennium of the presence of the state and of lively artistic creation, underwent a radical change. That change took place in a very brief space of time, which, however, encompassed events that even today, twenty five centuries later, stand out as the most important occurrences in Greek history from the point of view of world interest. Those events owe their importance to their unique combination of the appearance of new institutions (or the evolution of earlier ones) and the accomplishment of intellectual and spiritual creative work which was of supreme significance for the development of European civilisation.

The Parthenon is the most striking product of that great historical juncture. Although constructed very rapidly in the middle of the century, it is also – and indeed to a considerable extent – a work and monument of the early 5th century. In other words, it was accomplished by those who established democracy and fought at Marathon.

Systematic excavation of the ground around the monument and expert studies of its stones (those still on the site and those scattered elsewhere) allow us to say with confidence today[1] that the construction of a first marble Parthenon (the Pre-parthenon, or P2, fig. 1) on the site of still earlier sanctuaries began in 490 BC or the following year, and that it was an expression of gratitude and honour for the great victory won on the field of Marathon. Indeed, it is possible that the gigantic base of that first marble Parthenon was originally intended to bear a large poros temple (P1),[2] a project which the founders of democracy were never able to put into effect. This base, the famous stereobate of the Parthenon, of which a section is still visible beneath the Classical temple (or P3), was 78 metres long and is solid throughout its length.[3] It consists of stones from Piraeus weighing two tons and is bedded on large horizontal steps cut into the rock, at depths of up to 11 metres on the south side (fig. 3). Given the size and the solidity of the stereobate, a search for earlier historical phases on the same site would be exceedingly difficult, if

not impossible. However, it seems possible that such phases occurred, for a variety of reasons. It has been contended,[4] with convincing arguments, that the Hekatompedon, the temple of the time of Pisistratus with which we are familiar from the poros sculptures of its entablature, should not be seen as a forerunner of the Old Temple – that is, the Pisistratid temple between the Parthenon and the Erechtheum – but as an Urparthenon, a previous occupant of precisely the same ground now covered by the stereobate of the Parthenon. It seems likely that an even earlier temple, probably dating from the late Geometric period and known only from the fragments of its roof tiles, stood on the site of the Urparthenon.

The other large Archaic temple also had its Geometric forerunner, perhaps the oldest of all as its subsequent name (the 'Old Temple') would suggest, of which the stone bases for two wooden columns have survived.

The original name of the Periclean marble temple is not known. The earliest surviving reference to the name 'Parthenon' dates from the 4th century. Uses of the name 'the temple' ('ho neos') are slightly earlier. A number of other names are also found: 'the great temple', 'the Hekatompedon Parthenon', 'the temple of Athena', 'the great temple of Athena', 'the Hekatompedon temple', 'the Hekatompedon'.[5] The word 'hekatompedon', as adjective or noun, may be a reference to the interior length of the temple itself, or a survival of the name of the hypothetical earlier temple, a hundred ('hekaton') feet ('podes') long.

We do not know exactly how the Parthenon functioned. The fact that an altar has been found to the east of the Old Temple but that a Parthenon altar has never come to light, the absence (or, at any rate, failure to survive) of the names of Parthenon priests or priestesses, the keeping of the most sacred ancient statue of Athena in the Old Temple and then in the Erechtheum, and the ending there of the Panathenaic Procession with the depositing of the newly-woven peplos, are all reasons which have led many to question whether the Parthenon had a religious function at all.[6] Such scholars prefer to believe that it was a huge public votive offering of political and religious importance.[7] Yet the fact that temples formerly occupied the same site, and that long before the foundation of the Delian League and the need for a large treasury the Pre-Parthenon had its own spacious western apartment (fig.

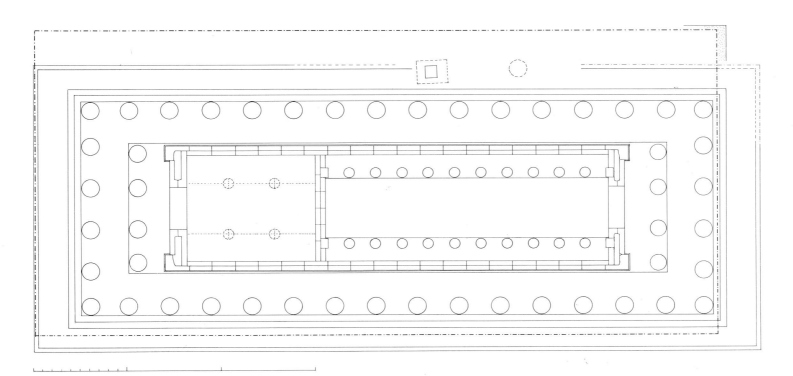

1. The Pre-parthenon; reconstruction of its plan and the building composition of its walls to the level of the upright blocks. The outline of the later Parthenon is shown as dashes and a dotted line. Scale 1:400. Drawing by M. Korres.

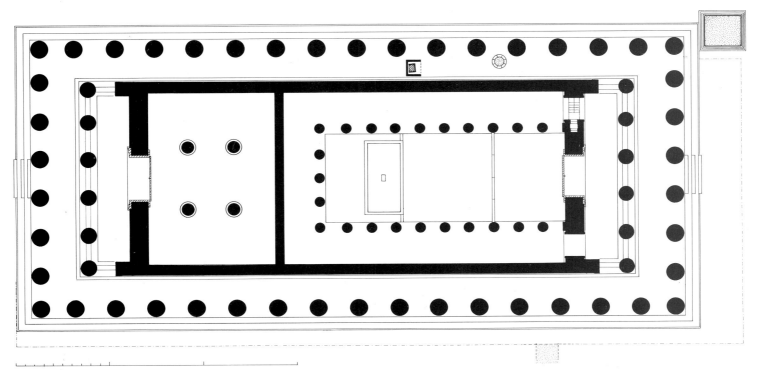

2. The Parthenon: reconstruction of the plan on the basis of recent findings. There are windows in the pronaos and a staircase in the thickness of the east wall, a small temple and a circular altar in the north pteroma, and a tower-like plinth for a statue of a four-horse chariot in the north-east corner. Scale 1:400. Drawing by M. Korres.

3. *The stereobate of the Parthenon visible to its full height (11 metres) during excavations along the south side (1888). Photograph: German Archaeological Institute, Athens.*

4. *Drums and blocks from the Pre-parthenon crepidoma in the north wall (479 BC). The drums are between 1.94 and 1.98 metres in diameter and weigh between seven and nine tons. Photograph by M. Korres.*

1) makes it likely that the Parthenon had at least some religious functions.[8] However the matter may be, the temple should also be seen as a public votive offering, in the period after the city was saved by the victory at the battle of Marathon. Such an approach would be consistent with the information provided by Demosthenes (XXII, 13) that the booty from the battle was used to build the temple. The destruction of the half-built Parthenon by the Persians in 480 BC and its reconstruction, using the same marbles, after the fresh Greek victory redoubled its symbolic power and made it a memorial to a number of battles. The stones, most of them marble drums cracked by the flames the Persians lit, which were deliberately built into the north wall of the Acropolis as sights and exhibits, were in ancient times and still are today unpleasant but useful reminders of the dangers facing the nation (fig. 4).

As a monument to the city as a whole, the Parthenon was ornamented with an Ionic frieze whose theme was not connected with heavenly things, as was the case with the sculptures on the east side, or heroic and mythical, as with the sculptures on the other sides. It was an earthly, Athenian theme (fig. 5). It showed Athenians of various classes grouped so as to correspond to the organisation of the Athenian state: in fact, the groups reflect the successive forms of that organisation, with the earlier system on the north side of the temple and the more recent, the democratic system, on the south.[9] To look at the Parthenon is to feel that this huge temple is, to some extent, a monument to co-existence. It depicts the earlier and more recent gods and citizens from different political periods, and it includes artistic elements from varying systems, with Doric figures and decorations sharing the space with their Ionic counterparts. At the same time, however, the temple is a monument to the idea of the Agon, the struggle. The themes on most of the metopes involve fighting, and this is true of the west pediment, too. Yet what is primarily conveyed is not the victory of one side or the other – of the gods, the Lapiths or the Greeks – and consequently the defeat of the other (the Giants, the Centaurs or the Trojans). As a result, and given that the outcome of the struggle is not emphasised, what emerges in the end is the Agon as a concept, as a perpetual relationship of opposing forces – natural, supernatural, historical, social, individual, ideological and psychological (Centaurs) forces. The Parthenon as a monument of Athenian policy contains a whole host of messages and allusions to the

58

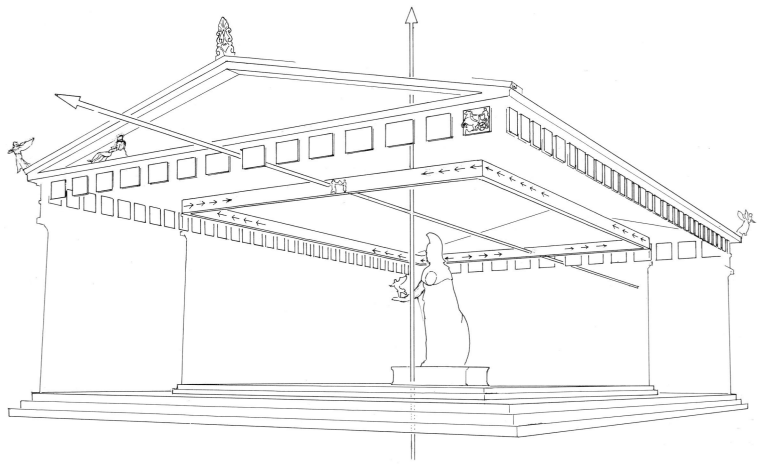

5. Spatial diagram of the general layout of the Parthenon sculptures. The arrows show the ranking of the themes by height and length. Drawing by M. Korres.

values and the aims of the Athenian state. It is clear enough that this major project lends itself to a number of possible readings over and above those which might be confirmed as the intentions of those who built it. However, while a reading of the sculptural compositions can rest on firm foundations, since those are representational works, a reading of the architecture of the temple (a composition of geometric, abstract forms) is a more theoretical and less certain task.

As a building, the Parthenon (fig. 2) employs a temple type unknown in the rest of Greece: it is an octastyle peripteral Doric temple with a hexastyle double-prostyle cella. Apart from the main temple, there is also a hall to the rear, which for the sake of simplicity we shall call the west chamber.

In the Parthenon, as in all the ancient Greek temples, the architectural forms largely coincide with the structural features, as can be seen from the brief description which follows (figs. 6, 9).

The 46 external columns have a diameter of 1.91 metres and a height of 10.43. Each consists of eleven drums[10] weighing between five and ten tons, and a capital with a breadth of 2.00-2.09 metres and a weight of eight to nine tons.

The crepidoma has general dimensions of 72.31 x 33.68 metres, and consists of three steps of a total height of 1.59. The stones of the steps vary in length between 1.30 and 3.84 metres. Those of the upper step – also called the stylobate – are the heaviest: there are 130 ordinary stones, weighing five tons, and four corner stones weighing seven tons. The joints of the crepidoma are not strictly ordered, but – excluding the cornerstones – each third joint of the stylobate and the first step coincides with the axis of a column.

The architrave is one block high (1.35 metres) and three blocks thick (1.80 metres). Thus it consists of 138 (= 3 x 46) blocks[11] measuring 4.30 metres in length for the regular intervals and up to 4.70 metres for the corners. Only the outer side of the architrave was ornamented, and extremely simply at that: above, a continuous protrusion in rectangular section, the fascia, beneath which are the regulae. The regulae correspond exactly in location and size to the triglyphs above them and, beneath them, have their own ornamentation in the form of the 'nails': six cylindrical replicas of real nails, arranged at equal intervals, with a diameter of 6.7 cm. The genera-

60

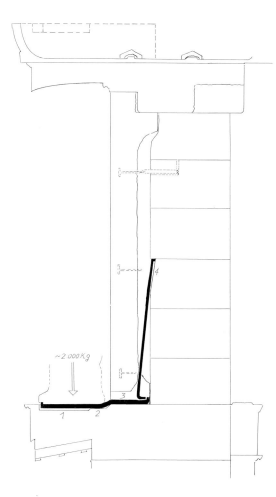

7. *The west pediment of the Parthenon: a section showing the structure of the tympanum, the shape of the upper cornice and the manner in which the lower cornice was relieved of the weight of the larger sculptures using concealed iron brackets. Drawing by M. Korres.*

◁ 6. *The Parthenon: exploded axonometric drawing of part of the east side of the pronaos, by M. Korres.*

tion of this form can be traced back to the corresponding structural and ornamental features of a hypothetical but theoretically necessary stage of evolution of Doric temples in which the entablature was still made of wood[12] (6 x 96 = 576 'nails').

The Doric frieze is the same height as the architrave (1.35 metres) and consists of an alternating series of triglyphs (with a consistent breadth of 84.5 cm.) and metopes. The triglyphs are borne on the joints and centres of the architrave blocks, and so there are two metopes to each block in the architrave, or 14 metopes on each of the short sides and 32 on each of the long sides.

The cornice has a height of 60 cm., projects to an extent of 70 cm., and bears the monumental perimetric termination of the roof tiling, which is approximately as high again and quite plainly projects beyond the cornice. The lower visible surface of the cornice is not horizontal, but slopes outwards at an inclination of 1:6. It consists of a densely-arranged series of plaque-like mutules: they have exactly the same breadth as the triglyphs and there is one above each triglyph and the centre of each metope (92 + 92 + 4 = 188 mutules). The spaces between the mutules, equal in width to half the difference in width between the metopes and the triglyphs, are called guttae. The mutules also have 'nails', like the regulae, but arranged in three rows (3 x 6 x 188 = 3,384 'nails').

The joints of the cornice are so arranged that each ordinary block has one mutule and one gutta (172 blocks, weighing four tons). The corner blocks have four mutules, two guttae and one corner vault (four blocks, weighing 9-10 tons each).

The tympanum of each pediment consists only of upright stones (that is, laid with the long edges vertical, of which the two central blocks, measuring 3.50 x 2.80 x 0.50 m., were the heaviest) set 20 cm. back from the level of the front of the triglyphs so as to increase the depth of the space for statues. The marked projection (90 cm.) of the cornice beneath the pediment stressed the triangular shape of the pediment and its function as part of the roof. However, many of the pedimental sculptures were so large, or, when placed with others in the same position (at different depths within the pediment), would not fit inside the 'covered' area and project quite plainly beyond it, some of them for as much as 30 cm. For additional safety, strong iron brackets concealed in close-fitting recesses relieved the horizontal cornices of some of the weight of the larger sculpture[13] (fig. 7). The corner acroteria, extremely heavy marble sculptures – surely winged Victories[14] whose straining forward movement would have meant that most of their bodies projected beyond the perpendicular surface of the cornice – posed an even greater static problem. In order to solve it, these statues

8. The Parthenon: an axonometric reconstruction of the upper part of the north-east corner, and a detailed cutaway drawing of the base for the acroterium and its system of iron anchors. The shape and dimensions of the base and the anchors tell us that the corner acroteria, which have not survived, must have been large marble Victories in a stance marked by movement forwards and out. The excess mass of the base on the inner side acted as a counterbalance to the statue, and the large iron anchors ensured that the sculpture was safe from toppling off its counterweight (the base). Another anchor at the other end of the base helped prevent a fall of the statue and the base together. Drawing by M. Korres.

9. The Parthenon, an exploded axonometric reconstruction of part of the south side, by M. Korres.

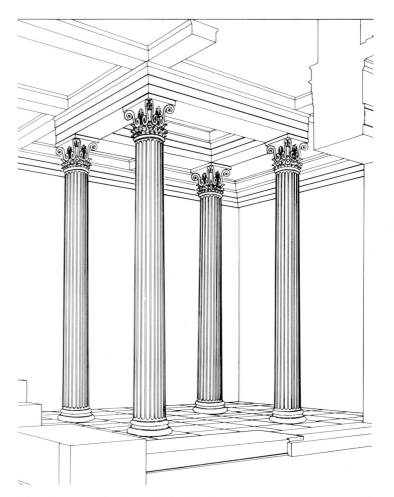

10. The west chamber of the Parthenon; a reconstruction with Ionic columns. Drawing by M. Korres.

11. The west chamber of the Parthenon; a reconstruction with Corinthian columns. Source: P. Pedersen, The Parthenon and the Origin of the Corinthian Capital, Odense University Press 1989.

were placed on plinths consisting of specially elongated marble blocks, weighing some four tons, the greater part of which acted as a counterweight,[15] and strong iron anchors were used to restrain the statues, set off-centre in the outer corners of the plinths (fig. 8). Together with the leaf-form antifixes at the crown of the pediments, almost four metres high,[16] the total height of the facades of the temple reached nearly 24 metres.

The exterior of the cella corresponds to the exterior of the temple: it has its own crepidoma, though with only two steps, tall columns, though only on the two fronts, an entablature and even its own cornice (the thranos or hypodokion) which, however, did not project nearly so far as the exterior cornice. Of course, the particular feature of the cella was its·frieze – in the continuous Ionic, not Doric, form – which was 160 metres long and ran along all four sides of the cella.

The hexastyle porticoes between the antae, although almost the same height as those of the outer portico and spaced at corresponding intervals, are so much lighter in their proportions that the various architectural members of which they consist – drums, capitals and architraves – are anywhere between 1/2 and 2/3 of the weight of

those in the exterior portico.

The walls consist of a series of blocks set upright and slightly projecting (height 1.15-1.17 metres, projection 0.7 cm.) surmounted by courses of stone blocks: 17 of them to the external entablature, and 22 to the architraves of the interior of the cella or main temple and the west chamber (a total of 231 upright blocks weighing 2.7-7 tons and 3,690 blocks of a weight of 1-5 tons).

The walls were topped by the blocks of the architrave (more than 100 of them, weighing 3.5-6 tons) and then by the gigantic lintels of the doors (eight in number, with a total weight of more than 90 tons) and the two windows in the east wall (eight in number, weighing a total of 50 tons).

The columns of the cella were Doric, with 16 flutes, and they formed a two-storey colonnade (that is, one colonnade on top of another) with a height of 13.5 metres around three sides of the cella with 23 columns on each level. The shafts of the upper columns were monolithic. In the west chamber (fig. 10) there were only four columns: they had a height of 12.5 metres and were in the Ionic order or a very early form of the Corinthian order[17] (fig. 11). They, too, had strong architraves in marble (12 of

12. The tiled roof of the Parthenon: we can see the two types of over tile (ordinary and leading, or antifixum), the corner under tile with the lion's head (false gutter) and the base for the acroterium. Source: A. Orlandos, I architektoniki tou Parthenonos, *vol. 1, Athens 1976.*

them, each five metres long and weighing nine tons).

The ceilings of the pteroma and the areas behind the porticoes were marble, consisting of beams (of a length of up to five metres and a weight of seven tons) and coffered panels (36 of which weighed two tons each, 80 weighed 0.6 tons and 106 weighting four tons). The ceiling of the cella was wooden, consisting of very heavy beams (with a section 70 x 70 cm.) and light coffered panels. We do not know whether the ceiling of the west chamber (which had beams seven metres long) was wooden or marble.

Above the ceiling was the roof. Strong marble piers which were square in section (1.23 x 1.23 m.) bore thick beams arranged length-wise along the temple and they, in turn, supported the rafters on which the marble tiles rested. The rafters were wooden, with a section of approximately 0.30 x 0.30 cm., laid in 93 rows at equal distances from each other. The beams were also wooden, but it seems possible that some of them – with a breadth of 90 cm. – were marble.[18] The interior of this gigantic work of construction was reached by a staircase concealed within the thick (2.05 m.) east wall.

The roof consisted of flat undertiles and cover tiles, totalling 8,957 pieces, of which 8,480 (= 2 x 22 x 96) were ordinary tiles (flat under tiles weighing 50 kg. and over tiles weighing 20-30 kg.). The remainder were special forms of tile, such as the 88 verge tiles (sima) above the pediments, each 210 kg. in weight, the 64 eave undertiles, weighing 1.3 tons each, the four corner tiles with the lions' heads, each weighing 1.15, the 130 leaf-shaped leading cover tiles and false over tiles, the tiles covering the spine or ridge of the roof, and some others (fig. 12).

This enumeration – of necessity, in brief – of the principal structural components of the building reveals some of its outstanding features: its size, and the manner in which all its stones are perfectly distinguished from one another and precisely defined in terms of their types. Given these features, each stone has an identity of its own, which allows them to be termed 'architectural members'. The stones in each category are perfectly equal in their shared characteristics, and so each can be taken as an exact representative of all those similar to it. However, each stone also possesses its own informal characteristics (angles which almost imperceptibly differ from a right angle, depending on the position in which the stone was to be placed on the deliberately curved lines of the building, dressing for joints, bolts, etc.), which mean that when it is judged strictly it can be seen to be ultimately unique and not interchangeable with the others in its course. It is the study of precisely these informal features which forms the foundation of the scientific method by which it is possible to identify the original position of stones which have survived detached from the building. However, the scale of these informal features is such as to make precise measurement – to a point on the borderline of practical feasibility – essential if they are to be made use of. Yet the work of the ancient designers and builders of the Parthenon must have required still greater accuracy – indeed, vastly greater accuracy. Recent observations and measurements have added much to our knowledge of the celebrated precision with which the Parthenon was constructed: for instance, the resting and bearing surfaces of the middle drums of all the columns are so perfectly flat that at no point is there a divergence from the mathematical plane of more than 1/20 of a millimetre – and this in more than 1,000 seats of an area of 1.5-3 square metres. These surfaces are so perfectly parallel that along the perimeter of any of the drums its height fluctuates by no more than 15/100 of a millimetre. And – wherever they have survived – the joints in the crepidoma are so hermetically tight that they cannot be examined even when seen under a microscope

with a power of x 60. It is clear, then – at least to those sufficiently familiar with the quality of engineering work – that even the most refined structures built in other countries and in other eras (including our own) often lag far behind the constructional precision of the Parthenon.

In striking contrast to the buildings of other cultures (including those of our own day), the Parthenon resembles many other buildings of its time in not being entirely rectilinear. In elevation, its lines are systematically curved, while the columns, walls and all the other upright features of its surface deviate from the perpendicular. In its floor plan, on the other hand, its form is regular and rectilinear. These deviations and curves are called 'refinements', and they serve the aesthetic functions of the building. The most important of the refinements are as follows (fig. 13): 1. The upward curvature of all the horizontal lines and surfaces: this begins in the foundations, continues in the crepidoma and the entablature, and applies even to the ceilings, the roof and the tiles. 2. The inward inclination of the long sides of the cella and of the columns of the outer portico and their entablature. The corner columns are diagonally inclined (that is, they are angled towards both sides). There is also evidence to suggest that the sides of the two-story colonnades inclined inwards. The pediments, the columns between the antae, the door walls and the partition wall do not deviate from the perpendicular.

Notes

1. The dating of the Pre-parthenon to before the time of the Persian wars was first supported by W.M. Leake (1821) and L. Ross (1835), and has since been the theory favoured by most experts. Dörpfeld (*Mitteilungen des Deutschen Archäologischen Instituts, Athenische Abteilung* [= AM] 10, 1885, pp. 275-277) was the first archaeologist to propose a post-Persian dating, but he himself retracted the theory before long (*AM* 27, 1902, pp. 379-416). However, the second theory has found a number of advocates since that time, although they have lacked sound arguments. Recent work on the restoration of the building has provided new and very powerful proof in favour of the original theory.

2. *AM* 27, 1902, pp. 382, 416. A similar hypothesis had been made earlier by Penrose, *The Principles of Athenian Architecture*, 1st ed., London 1851 (hereinafter Penrose), p. 17.

3. Sample drillings made in 1984 at four different points on the floor down into the depths of the rock passed only through compacted stone. M. Korres, *Perilipseis dialexeon* ('Summaries of Lectures') 1984-85, National Technical University of Athens, History of Architecture Research Centre, p. 13.

4. E. Buschor, *AM* 42, 1922, p. 98. W.B. Dinsmoor, *American Journal of Archaeology* (= AJA) 51, 1947, pp. 108-151.

5. O. Jahn, A. Michaelis, *Arx Athenarum a Pausania descripta*, Bonn 1901, pp. 53ff.

6. A. Michaelis, *Der Parthenon*, Leipzig 1871, pp. 27, 28.

7. F. Preisshofen, *Parthenon-Kongress, Basel, 1982*, E. Berger (ed.), Mainz 1984, pp. 15-18.

8. C.J. Herington, *Athena Parthenos and Athena Polias*, Manchester 1955.

9. L. Beschi, *Il fregio del Partenone, una proposta di lettura*,

Accademia Nazionale dei Lincei, Rendiconti...., Serie VIII, 1984, pp. 3-23. For other interpretations, see J. Boardman, 'The Parthenon Frieze - Another View', *Festschrift für F. Brommer*, 1977, pp. 39-49; A.E. Raubitschek, *Parthenon-Kongress, op. cit.*, p. 19.

10. With the exception of the north-east column and the second on the south side, which consist of 10 and 12 drums, respectively.

11. The middle blocks on the architraves of the north and south sides are lower, as a rule, but other stones above make up the necessary height.

12. N. Weickenmeier, *Theorienbildung dur Genese des Triglyphon*, Darmstadt 1985.

13. A. Orlandos, *I arhitektoniki tou Parthenonos* ('The Architecture of the Partenon'), vol. C., Athens 1978, pp. 525-530, figs. 342-344, 346, 348-354, 356-357.

14. M. Korres, Ch. Bouras, *Meleti Apokatastaseos tou Parthenonos* ('Study of the Reconstruction of the Parthenon'), vol. 1, Athens 1983 (hereinafter *Meleti* 1), p. 41. See also A. Delivorias, *Parthenon-Kongress, op. cit.*

15. *Meleti* 1, pp. 39, 463. See also J. Hoffer, 'Der Parthenon zu Athen in seinem Haupttheilen neu genessen', *Allgemeine Bauzeitung* 3, Vienna 1838, p. 389.

16. P. Danner, *Jahreshefte des Österreichischen archäologischen Instituts in Wien* (= ÖJh), 58, 1988, pp. 41-51.

17. P. Pedersen, *The Parthenon and the Origin of the Corinthian Capital*, Odense 1989.

18. The same hypothesis had been made much earlier by Hoffer (*op. cit.* p. 388) and Penrose (Penrose, pp. 11, 45), and had been accepted by A. Burford ('The Builders of the Parthenon', *Greece and Rome*, vol. 10, Suppl. 1, Oxford 1963, pp. 23-25, plates 3, 4).

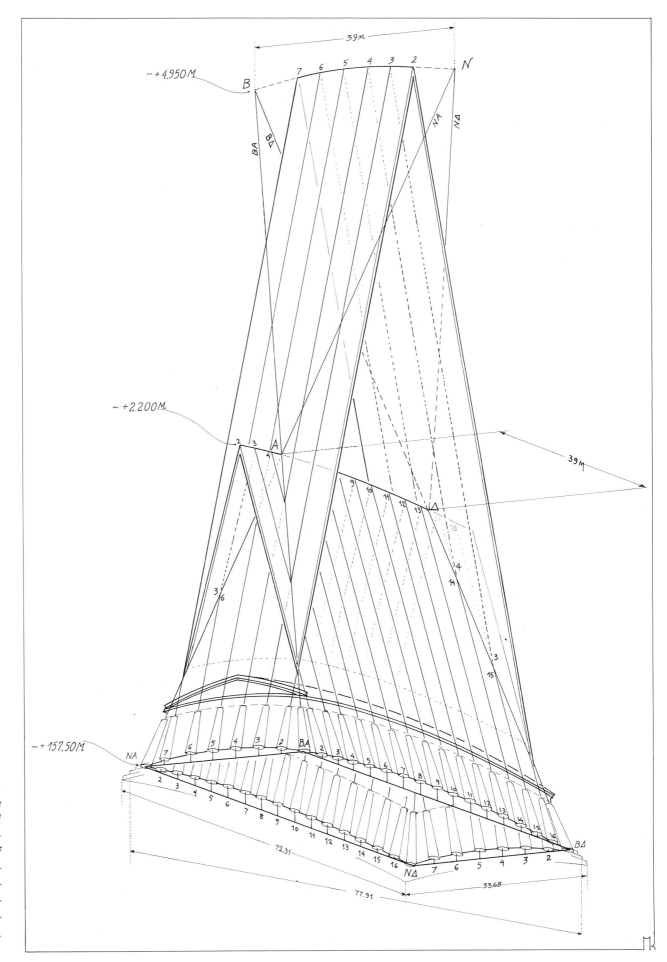

~ +4.950M

39M

~ +2.200M

39M

~ +157.50M

72.31

77.91

33.68

13. The curvature of the horizontal lines and the inward inclination of the external columns of the Parthenon; extrapolated graphic depiction by M. Korres.

14. The Parthenon from the north-west. Photograph by S. Mavrommatis.

15. Part of the north side of the Parthenon. Photograph by S. Mavrommatis.

16. The west facade of the Parthenon. Photograph by S. Mavrommatis.

17. The south pteroma of the Parthenon. Photograph by S. Mavrommatis.

18. Detail of the architrave on the west side of the Parthenon; the last surviving traces of the original painted ornamentation can still be discerned. Photograph by E.M. Stresow-Czako, 1960.

19. Detail of the south-west corner of the Parthenon; the last surviving traces of the original painted ornamentation can still be discerned. Photograph by E.M. Stresow-Czako, 1960.

20. The capital of the third column on the north side. Photograph by S. Mavrommatis.

21. The south side of the Parthenon. Photograph by S. Mavrommatis.

22. Detail of the south-west corner. The metope relief shows a scene from the Battle of the Centaurs. Photograph by S. Mavrommatis.

23. Detail of the west facade. Photograph by S. Mavrommatis.

24. Detail of the Parthenon stereobate. Photograph by S. Mavrommatis.

25. The Parthenon from the Propylaea. Photograph by S. Mavrommatis.

26. Columns on the south side, from within. Photograph by S. Mavrommatis.

27 28

27. *The third column in the north colonnade, from within. Photograph by S. Mavrommatis.*

28. *Columns in the east portico, from within. Photograph by S. Mavrommatis.*

29. *Capital of a column in the peristyle. Photograph by S. Mavrommatis.*

30. *Capital of a column in the pronaos. Photograph by S. Mavrommatis.*

31. *Detail of the entablature on the north side. Photograph by S. Mavrommatis.*

30

31

II

So many studies of the architecture of the Parthenon have been published that they far outnumber the writings about any other building in the world. Unfortunately, however, the most important of those studies – the treatise by Ictinus mentioned by Vitruvius[1] – has not survived. Of course, various other accounts – quite a number of them – are still at our disposal, scattered throughout the works of ancient literature,[2] and others are to be found in pieces of inscriptions,[3] but they are fragmentary, very brief or of a general nature.

Critical classification and archaeological utilisation of this highly valuable information was begun as far back as the 17th century, by amateur antiquarians. It continued through the following century, by the end of which it had acquired a reasonable standard of academic credibility. It then took on monumental proportions in the work of A. Michaelis and the other great philologists and has since proceeded at varying paces in the form of contributions to the examination of various issues of detail. Unfortunately, it seems that the chance of discovering other written testimony is, for the time being, negligible.

Scope for study in terms of the history of art, of architecture and in particular of the history of architecture, however, is very far from exhausted.[4] The field of study consists, on the one hand, of the extant building, of the marbles detached from it, and of the landscaping of its environment in ancient times and, on the other, of an abundance of comparative material composed of other ancient monuments. The breadth of this field of study is constantly expanding. Details which in the past could not have received enough attention are forever 'coming to light', and the various types of analysis are being distinguished with greater and greater clarity: typological analysis (of the floor plans, elevations, forms and ornamentation), analysis of the construction methods, analysis of the order and style (of the forms and ornamentation), geometrical analysis, metrological analysis, and aesthetic analysis. Apart from these areas of study, questions also arise of the historical topography of the Parthenon, of the possible stages or changes of plan during the course of building, of the alterations which may have come about when it was functioning, and of how the building is to be reconstructed.

Needless to say, considerations of the space of this chapter by comparison with the breadth and depth of the issues listed above make it impossible to produce even a general review, no matter how we may try to compress each issue. It seems, therefore, that it might be advisable to deal selectively with only some of them: those concerning the typology of the architectural composition of the Parthenon. Such issues deserve our preference here because they take us back to the most fundamental causes of the architectural uniqueness of this great temple. Nonetheless, they have never been developed as they ought, in contrast to the questions of order, style, measurement, history, etc., with which we are familiar.

1. The basic architectural studies

The earliest studies of the temple as a building were composed by architects and were primarily of a mixed nature. As a rule, they contained analysis of order, geometry and measurement, and dealt with questions of the functioning and reconstruction of the building. The Classicist architects, equipped by their training with a knowledge of architectural order, a positivist spirit and skill as draughtsmen, were important pioneers for the study of the Parthenon.[5]

This first period of purely scientific study of the architecture of the Parthenon was inaugurated by James Stuart and his associate Nicholas Revett in 1751 and 1762.[6] At that time, piles of fallen marble and various leantos covered large parts of the crepidoma of the temple,[7] and its curvature (whose recognition, for the forewarned visitors of the present day, is no more than a fashionable way of gaining acknowledgement of one's powers of observation), still unknown, was anything but easy to see,[8] even for Stuart. However, he did manage to measure the stylobate, with an error of only a few millimetres, and other basic magnitudes. He noted the thickening of the corner columns,[9] hypothesised the existence of an integral metrological relationships of 100:225 between the breadth and width of the stylobate,[10] distinguished the inward inclination of the architrave,[11] and recognised, from their traces, the positions of some of the later interior columns of the cella. Stuart realised that the main facade of the temple was that on the east, and, relying on a familiar reference in Vitruvius (III, 3, 8) introduced for the first time the question of reconstructing the Parthenon as an open-air temple – that is, without a ceiling or roof over the central part of the cella.[12]

For half a century after the publication of the second volume of Stuart and Revett's work in 1787, very little was added to the bibliography on the Parthenon. The detailed studies (1810-1817) of C.H.V. Hallerstein[13] and C.R. Cockerell were unpublished. Their discovery of 'entasis' in the columns was not announced until 1830, when W. Jenkins Jr. published it together with the observation of the inclination of the columns made by T.L. Donaldson in 1820.[14]

In 1838, the results were published of the work (1836-1838) of J. Hoffer.[15] Apart from the major discovery of the curvature in the crepidoma, the walls and the entablature, Hoffer contributed the first systematic descriptions and accurate drawings of the east side of the temple (to produce which he used rope ladders and various kinds of scaffolding) and of many other representative parts of the building. Accurate surveying and measurement of the heights of the drums led for the first time to recognition of the correlations between the unusual geometrical features which Hoffer chose to call subtleties[16] rather than merely corrections. Hoffer accepted the Vitruvian theory about optical illusion and corresponding corrections,[17] but he went beyond it to advance a more profound interpretation.

"The Parthenon, full of majesty, is an outstandingly impressive and fascinating sight to those who view it. Calculations cannot explain precisely what it may be that conquers our senses and captivates us in this ruin, especially since it can provide us with only a scanty idea of what it once was.

"In modern times, colonnades have been built on at least a similar monumental scale, but without achieving such a satisfactory visual result. The reason for this becomes plain only after an exact study of the ancient remains. It is then we discover that the Greeks were not satisfied to use excessively constraining rules, or a single 'rule' in the sense meant by Vitruvius or as the architects of the present day would like to impose. For them, the work was as a whole a question of sensation. They had the conviction – and they were favoured in this by their advanced education and the mild climate – that straight lines create an oppressed, rigid impression; they saw that nature itself abhors everything rectilinear and develops its most alluring forms with beautiful curves. For that reason, they tried to harmonise the constructional aspect of their buildings with nature, transplanting into them the vibrant forms of their natural environment and, in this manner, imbuing the dead measures of art with the life of nature."[18]

Although very many years have passed since those sublime thoughts were expressed for the first time, it would be difficult even today to find a better way of stating the question.

The superb studies of F.C. Penrose on the Parthenon took place in the winter of 1846-47, ten years after those of Hoffer, Schaubert[19] and Hansen[20] and immediately subsequent to the – unfortunately incomplete – work of A. Paccard (1844-46).[21] Penrose made original observations of unique importance and produced the most refined architectural measurements of all time, using instruments of the greatest accuracy manufactured specially for the purpose. The outcome of this work, his *An Investigation of the Principles of Athenian Architecture*, is the best work ever printed on the Parthenon: it is a monument of scientific method, consistency and unparalleled human skill. The main subject of the book is what Penrose now called "optical refinements".[22] But the discussion – in a purely supplementary manner, in appendices, lengthy notes, etc. – of a whole host of other questions is amazingly comprehensive despite its brevity, making the book a still richer original monograph of Classical Athenian architecture from the thematic point of view. Penrose repeated the survey of the east side – from scaffolding attached to the entablature – and both confirmed and considerably expanded the work of Hoffer and Schaubert. The frequent inequality of length in the architrave blocks, the metopes and the cornice blocks (which vary by up to 18,[23] 16[24] and 7 cm., respectively), more marked on the east facade and less on the west and the two long sides; the striking fluctuations in the breadth of the capitals (between 1.999 and 2.058 cm. for the middle columns[25] and between 2.04 and 2.09 for the corner columns); the differences in altitude of the corners of the temple (up to 5 cm.)[26]; the deviation of only 2 cm (to the east) from the apparently and formally central position of the cella with reference to the peristyle[27]; the major difference (16 cm.) of level between the formally equivalent areas of the pronaos (which is deeper) and the opisthodomos, and the reverse difference (6 cm.) in thickness between the columns in the corresponding hexastyle porticoes (which, however, is not echoed in the width of the antae, as a result of which the architrave of the opisthodomos portico is thicker only on the west side of the cella);[28] the greater length to which the antae project on the east side, and the various minor fluctuations in length of the spaces between the columns[29] in the peristyle, are all indubitable geometrical particularities. Measured by Penrose to a highest level of approximation of 3/10 of a millimetre (!),[30] they show the Parthenon to have been the most undogmatic achievement of Classical architecture. One consequence of this outstanding merit is that while in other ancient monuments documentation can be confined to the surveying of certain representative sections alone, in the case of the Parthenon each section is in effect unique and, consequently, cannot be truly understood until it has been exhaustively measured, drawn and explored in all its details and then systematically compared with other similar – and apparently identical – parts of the building.

Another consequence of this quality of the Parthenon is the building's incomparable resistance to the various theoretical attempts to reduce it to perfect numerical systems and harmonious proportions. Such theoretical endeavours have declined to the level of quasi-science or pseudoscience, for the following reasons:

1) They do not respect the true dimensions of the building, as determined by Penrose. Whenever the theoretical definitions proposed clash with reality,[31] the propounders of the theory have the naivity (or impertinence) to allege errors in the bibliographic source or in the building itself.

2) In general, they refuse to be bound by the methodological requirement that the degree to which a theoretical definition (whether metrological, geometrical, or whatever) approximates to the actual building should be no less

than the degree of accuracy with which the building itself was constructed[32] (which in any case such theorists are incapable of conceiving); when, now and then, the theorists pretend to be bound by this requirement, they have no hesitation in falsifying the numerical facts.

3) When the theories try out geometrical proportions, they make use of inaccurate drawings on scales of the order of 1:100 or, at best, 1:50, doing violence to the geometrical constructions or fixing as typical points of intersection, etc., points which are often fortuitous or even, sometimes, located in the air inside or outside the building. Obviously, the application in graphic form of geometrical proportions to such small-scale drawings is incapable of dealing with magnitudes in the real structure of less than five centimetres. Only the conversion of the geometrical shapes into equivalent numerical systems belonging to analytical geometry would allow them to be checked with credibility (and theories of this kind are incapable of standing up to such tests). Apart from the question of their methods, efforts of this kind have dubious motivation, and could often be said to conceal a kind of intellectual totalitarianism, mysticism or some other obsession.

After excluding approaches of this kind, we are left only with simple metrological analysis and strictly numerical analysis[33] of basic proportions as capable of scientific substantiation. It is no coincidence that analysis of these kinds began with the work of Stuart and is still proceeding today. Yet the only widely-accepted product of this analysis is the famous 4:9 ratio (or 100:225, as expressed by Stuart). Thanks to Penrose and Lloyd,[34] this ratio can be identified in the Parthenon as follows:

A. Diameter of column to intercolumniation=4:9 $(=2^2.3^2)$
B. Principal rectangle of floor plan (stylobate) = 4:9
C. Principal rectangle of facade (including the cornice)[35] = 4:9
D. Principal rectangle of the long sides[36] = 16:81 $(=4^2.9^2 = 2.3)$

Of these ratios, only ratio A is generally accepted. Ratio B is only applicable by approximation,[37] and Ratio C is, of course, a product of those which precede it.

Other metrological ratios can be elicited from smaller magnitudes, as Penrose was once more responsible for showing: the taper in the peristyle column to the inclination of the column to the 'entasis' of the column to the height of the curvature in the stylobate on the facade[38] = 24:4:1:4.

Using the Cymagraph, a special automatic device,[39] Penrose surveyed the curving profile of the column flutes, of the echinus of the capitals, of all the volutes, of the cornice below the pediment and even of the flutes of the semi-dressed marble drums from the Pre-parthenon built into the north wall[40] and produced an exact mathematical analysis. He found that all these curves are equivalent to

simple conical sections or consist of a number of different conical sections or the radii of circles.[41]

As for the question of how intentional the refinements were, Penrose generally accepted the arguments put forward by Hoffer, but he placed greater emphasis on the issues of optical illusion and correction.[42] Of the greatest importance is his central idea that the starting-point for the evolutionary development of the horizontal curvature should be sought in the pediment and the initial need to offset the apparent concave curve which would appear in its horizontal cornice because of the visual side-effects of the acutely inclined sides of the pedimental triangle.[43] The theories of Hoffer and Penrose were immediately and generally accepted. Only a few scholars treated them with caution, including the highly influential figure of Karl Bötticher[44] and, strangely enough, J. Durm.[45] However, the unfair comments of Bötticher provided the stimulus for an important piece of field-work and a paper by E. Ziller,[46] the main aim of which was to present in more detail the proof for the intentional nature of the curves and to disprove, once and for all, the contention that they might have been produced by uniform yet differential subsidence or by systematic building errors, etc.

Another publication, by A. Thiersch,[47] demonstrated the authenticity of the refinements, rebutted Durm's arguments to the contrary, analysed the phenomenon of the optical illusions and provided scientific proof of Penrose's views on the questions of the apparent concave curvature and visual correction of the pedimental triangle.

Since then, there have been very many publications,[48] some of them dealing largely or only with the aesthetic aspect and others largely or only with the optical aspect. However, the publications of the former kind have added very little to earlier statements of the issue, and those of the latter kind almost nothing. Many scholars, in their desire to gain the status of basic propounders of theories which have already been quite adequately grounded, have gone so far as to reiterate familiar statements, changing only the wording, or sometimes – in the name of still greater would-be originality – have added explanations of their own. These explanations, usually weak or even erroneous, have probably done more to damage than to advance the original purpose, leaving later scholars with the rather vague and always mistaken impression that the question is still in doubt.

Wilhelm Dörpfeld's first paper on the Parthenon was published in 1881.[49] It inaugurated the most modern period of studies of the architecture of the temple, with a new and more 'archaeological' method beginning to emerge out of the older approach. Such a method did not demand more difficult measurements or better drawings: rather the reverse. Interest now shifted more in the direction of a comparative view and the historical integration of details, and preference was often given to

32. *The Parthenon and the stepped substructure of its base, from the north-west. Source: G.P. Stevens, 'The Setting of the Periclean Parthenon'*, Hesperia, Suppl. 3, 1940.

constructional analysis instead of the morphological approach which had been predominant down to that time.

Dörpfeld, working with simple yet in practical terms infallible data based on the existence of general constructional rules which he himself had observed, was able to add one more method of proof to those which had already been applied. His method was valuable, to begin with, in reconstructing those parts of the monument which have not survived. In order to produce such reconstructions, earlier scholars had searched for what they would have done if they had been in the place of the ancient architect. Dörpfeld, on the other hand, kept a level-headed distance[50] from the problem and looked only for the evidence – or even just the traces of evidence – which would allow the discovery and proof of what had really existed. He never went beyond the bounds of what could be proved.

This method ruled out, *inter alia*, the possibility of there having been staircases and upper chambers in the cella, together with the theory proposed by Bötticher that the statue of Athena Parthenos was placed at the back of the cella in a specially arranged position with pilasters on either side.[51] It proved the correctness of the Penrose reconstruction,[52] although it did not settle the question of whether the ceiling and roof ought to be reconstructed with or without an opening above the centre of the cella.[53]

This problem was solved as follows: in 1883, Penrose's excavations in the Temple of Olympian Zeus revealed that the building was narrower than had formerly been supposed, the scholars having been misled by its great length.[54] For the first time, it was confirmed that the Temple of Olympian Zeus had eight columns, not ten, and this allowed Dörpfeld to revise the view generally held at the time that the Parthenon was an open-air temple.[55] The reference in Vitruvius to an open-air octastyle temple in Athens could now be detached from the Parthenon and attributed to its real subject, the Temple of Olympian Zeus.

Those, then, were the last major revisions, and after them the much-debated theoretical form of the Parthenon was finally settled, at least as far as its basic

33. Perspective reconstruction of a section of the ceiling in the south pteroma. Source: Orlandos, op. cit.

components were concerned. A new period of deeper penetration into the questions of reconstruction, history, historical phases, etc., began with the addition of certain specialised issues on the part of Penrose in the second edition (1888) of his great work. In the case of Penrose, however, it was already too late, while Dörpfeld did no work on the Classical Parthenon after this time. W.B. Dinsmoor, the great continuer of their work, devoted numerous studies to highly important questions of a chiefly historical nature: building inscriptions,[56] historical stages, repairs,[57] construction methods,[58] phases of construction, structural questions relating to the frieze,[59] metrology,[60] the ancient design method,[61] the dating of the foundations,[62] and so on. Yet although Dinsmoor was a good draughtsman, he published no drawings or reconstructions. G.P. Stevens, on the other hand, published such drawings, contributing to reconstruction of the large-scale railings which blocked off the intercolumniation of the porticoes between the antae,[63] reconstruction of the pedestal of the statue of Athena and the wooden ceilings, and reconstruction of the layout of the surrounding ground, the most important votive offerings, subsequent additions to the crepidoma and the architrave, etc.[64] (fig. 32).

The last increase before 1978 in our knowledge of the authentic structural materials was that provided by Orlandos' specialised studies of the panels[65] (p. 33) and the tiled roof,[66] together with his work on the general measuring and design documentation of the building[67] (fig. 40). Unfortunately, however, these measurements are not as precise as they ought to have been, and, consequently, are not suitable for metrological analysis and exact theoretical calculation.[68]

It could be said of the lengthy period which we have been examining that despite the scores of basic studies and the hundreds (if not thousands) of theoretical papers derived from them, and for all the vast number of published and unpublished drawings which we have at our disposal, there has been something of a delay in producing real design documentation for the monument. Without such documentation, it is impossible to penetrate effectively to greater depth in certain areas – primarily of a constructional nature – which although not of the greatest interest in themselves (e.g., which stones, and in what structural order, made up one part or another of one of the walls), are today the sole requirement for very interesting studies of much more important topics. Those topics include: a more exact understanding of the way in which the material was worked and structured,[69] the spatial and chronological development and process of the individual tasks over the incredibly short space of time (447-438 BC) in which the monument was built,[70] the economic and technical organisation of the project, the plan and the changes it underwent before completion of the building,[71] the effects which the sculptural programme had on the architectural design and, perhaps, on the time-scale of the project, metrological analysis and – most important of all – more scientifically accurate reconstructions.

It is only since 1980 that drawings suitable for these purposes have been available in large quantities. Yet since the standards of quality and completeness of work of this type are constantly rising (e.g., the 'Gruben school'), the design documentation of the Parthenon which is now under way still has a long way to go. Although the work of E. Hansen (1987) on the Treasury of the Siphnians[72] could be selected as a model of completeness, we have no idea how long the process of producing new drawings of the Parthenon may take.

2. Some basic issues
a. Corner contraction of the Doric order

As we know, the order of a colonnade demands the equality in size of the columns and the spaces between them. This is also true of the triglyphs, whose axes must coincide with the axes of the columns and the middle of the intercolumniation. As a rule, the architrave is placed with its breadth (B) equally divided (B/2, B/2) on either side of the column axis, so as to bring its weight to bear on the centre of the column.[73] As a result, in the four corners of a Doric temple the architrave comes to an end at a distance of one half of its own breadth (B/2) beyond the axis of the corner column.

Since the breadth of the architrave is usually much greater than the width of the triglyph (in the case of the Parthenon it is more than double, 1.774 as against 0.844[5]), the placing of a corner triglyph involves a serious disturbance of the order: the eccentricity (EK) of the faces of the triglyph to the axis of the column. This eccentricity will equal one half of the difference between the breadth of the architrave and the width of the triglyph (EK=B-T/2).[74] Consequently, the end metopes would have to be made larger (by EK, which would be aesthetically

34. The problem of the corner in the Doric colonnade. Drawing by M. Korres.

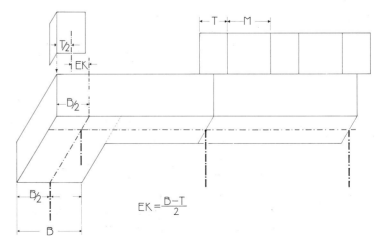

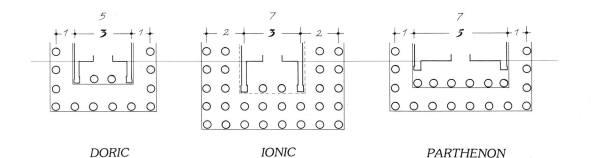

35. A typological juxtaposition of the Parthenon against a regular Doric temple and an Ionic octastyle. Drawing by M. Korres.

36. Perspective reconstruction of the pronaos. Drawing by M. Korres.

unacceptable), or the space between the last columns would have to be smaller (complete single contraction, C1 = EK), or the two methods would have to be combined (partial single contraction, C1 < EK, with a corresponding increase in the metopes)[75] or the immediately adjacent spaces beween columns and triglyphs would have to be modified so as to distribute the discrepancies between a number of features and thus make them difficult to perceive (complete double contraction, C1+C2 = EK, partial double contraction C1+C2 < EK, with a corresponding almost imperceptible increase in a number of metopes).[76] Studies to date of most Doric temples testify to the wide variety of solutions given to the problem of the corners. However, the fact that partial single or double contraction were often chosen is an indication of how irritating the ancient Greeks found the marked evidence of inequality in the spaces between the columns or the triglyphs. It is thus reasonable to conclude that the corners of the Parthenon must – to begin with – have surprised, if not shocked, those involved in the designing and constructing of buildings. In these corners, the contraction is generally single – that is, it applies only to the space between the first and second columns: this is obviously the most brutal form of contraction. Yet it is not even partial, as is often the case in other temples: it is plainly greater than the ordinary full contraction (= EK) and in fact is almost double that measurement, thus saving the end metopes from the 'threat of elongation' not by making them, too, of a regular size but by making them ultimately smaller than the regular metopes! This phenomenon, of which the corners of the Parthenon are the only known examples, is called single overcontraction. The Parthenon itself provides us with a variation on the phenomenon: at the eastern extremities of its north and south sides, the overcontraction is double, not single.[77]

b. The regular Doric temple. The octastyle Doric temple, a breach of the rule. The Ionic and Cycladic factors. The Attic blend

In the case of the orders and columniation of ancient temples, we have to clarify a point which is usually omitted in general-purpose textbooks and of which non-experts are often unaware: the types of columniation – that is, the tetrastyle, hexastyle, octastyle, etc. types[78] – could not be chosen among freely for alternative solutions in conjunction with the order or the size of the temple. Each was in fact closely linked only with specific types of temple and specific orders (fig. 35).

So the regular Doric temple – built in limestone, sandstone or tufa – was customary only on the Greek mainland and especially in its western parts. It was always peripteral and hexastyle, with a cella which was distyle in antis, as a rule, and not prostyle.[79] The octastyle facade and the use of marble as a building material were usually among the features of Ionic temples, which were the custom to the east of the Aegean.[80] The only feature shared by the two contrasting types was their roof, the bearing elements of which were wooden.[81] In the Cyclades – with Naxos and Paros as the centres for development – various types of smaller marble Ionic temples were predominant, but there were also instances of buildings whose floor plans were Ionic and their orders Doric.[82] The use of marble alone for roofs and ceilings was another feature of Cycladic architecture.[83]

These definitions are based on hundreds of examples of monuments, archaeological finds and scattered materials, and new finds constantly confirm them. In the meantime, the exceptions to the definitions have also been identified. They can be summed up as follows: Doric architecture penetrated the Ionic area only very slightly,[84] while the penetration of Ionic forms, and indeed of the order as a whole, into the Doric area was incomparably greater.[85] (There are four or five complete Ionic temples in Doric areas, and many more instances of Ionic ornamentation or full columns in Doric temples.)

In the particular case of the universality of the hexastyle in antis arrangement as the external form of the Doric temple, three divergement cases have long been known, apart from the Parthenon: octastyle temples at Corfu, Selinus and Cyrene.[86] Yet even these cases cannot be described as genuine exceptions, since the increase in the number of columns is superficial in all three, and confined to the outer appearance; the form of the interior (the cella) retains unchanged all the formal features of the corresponding interior of a regular hexastyle temple, and its breadth is equal only (or almost only) to that of the three

84

middle spaces between the columns of the facade (of the seven).[87] The only genuine exception, then, is the Parthenon. Here the increase in the number of columns on the exterior is reflected in a corresponding expansion of the interior form, combined with unprecedented qualitative development of the interior space of the temple. The breadth of the cella corresponds to that of the five middle spaces of the facade (of the seven). (Indeed, since the end spaces are much smaller than those in the centre because of the overcontraction applied to them, the width of the cella, which is correlated precisely with that of the five middle spaces on the facade, is still greater than it would have been if the arrangement of the columns had been regular.) While in the case of the three other octastyle Doric temples – those of Corfu, Selinus and Cyrene – the breadth of the cella amounts to 40%, 41% and 54%, respectively, of the total breadth of the temple, in the Parthenon it amounts to 70%. The interior of the temple in the Parthenon is thus as spacious as that of the gigantic octastyle temple at Selinus or the huge octastyle Ionic temples – despite the fact that those large temples, whose width is between 51 and 55 metres, are 70% broader on the outside than the Parthenon, which measures only 30.88 metres.

However, the Parthenon is not unique only for being the most striking exception to the Doric peripteral temple type, or because its interior is unusually spacious. Under the definitions given above of the Doric, Ionic and Cycladic types of temple in terms of their floor plan, type of stone and roofing, the Parthenon has to be recognised as unique for the early date and importance of its blend of Doric, Ionic and Cycladic features. The manner in which that blend of features is achieved is further proof of the monument's uniqueness.

Before analysing the way in which these heterogeneous elements are combined in the Parthenon, we should note, in general, that the manner in which such elements were used in the architecture of other Doric buildings of the same or earlier date was largely a matter of juxtaposition. Their inclusion had not the slightest effect on the shaping, proportions or character of the Doric or Ionic forms beside which they were set.[88] Unfortunately, however, considerations of space do not permit even a rudimentary exploration of this question, which could be discussed with reference to a whole host of monuments (e.g., the temple of Athena at Paestum, the Doric temple at Locri, the Amycleum, etc.).

The largest non-Doric element in the Parthenon – after the great Ionic frieze, of course – was one of which little or nothing has survived: the columns which bore the roof of the west chamber (fig. 10). The composition of the floor paving and the survival of the faint trace of the seat of a column – first noticed in 1810 or shortly afterwards[89] – are the sole (yet certain) evidence for the reconstruction of four slim columns in the Ionian order[90] or, according to P. Pedersen,[91] of a type which must have been the true (not mythical) archetype of the third order, the Corinthian (fig. 11).

In other respects, the smaller yet emblematically significant Ionian elements are common knowledge: the mouldings of the triglyphs, metopes, capitals and panels, the sculptured Ionic eggs and darts, the Lesbian cymas of the ceiling beams and the cornices beneath the pediment, the sima which is identical with an Ionic moulding, and the leading cover tiles with their Ionic volutes and anthemia in light relief. However, a listing of the features of the Parthenon which are typical of the Ionic order does not exhaust the extent to which the building refers to the Ionic style. We also have an even larger set of features to be found in the Doric forms themselves and, more generally, in the building as an architectural composition.[92] These are the type, character and style of the facades, and of the facades of the cella in particular. They are octastyle rather than hexastyle – thus making them Ionic and not Doric – and with the larger number and slimmer proportions of the columns, together with the overcontraction of the corners, the facades of the temple must have struck observers in ancient times as bearing a marked Ionic imprint. A comparison between the Parthenon and the temple at Olympia or with other contemporary or later Doric temples outside Attica, on the one hand, and with the polystyle Ionic temples, on the other (this second comparison is only possible in practical terms using drawings of reconstructions, of which, fortunately, there is an abundance) will suffice to support this contention. The Ionic influence on the hexastyle facades of the cella (figs. 36, 37) is still stronger. The columns are much lighter in proportion than those of the outer colonnade. The steps of the stylobate and the architrave are still more delicately proportioned; the slabs making up the architrave are approximately the same length as those in the outer architrave, but are only 3/4 of the height. The ratio of their height to their length is exactly 1:4, thus approaching that of the architrave of the Erechtheum,[93] and is clearly entirely alien to the Doric order of the Classical period. The only element which reminds us that these architraves are in the Doric style is the Doric taenia on their upper part, with Doric regulae and guttae (and not a cyma, as is the case on the corresponding architrave of the temple of Hephaestus). Yet the presence immediately above of the large Ionic frieze, in the position where the type of architrave would normally require there to be triglyphs and metopes, justifies the low Ionic proportions of the Doric architrave. It does not, however, do any injustice to the type of the architrave, showing up the Doric regulae as pointless and erroneous. Without precluding the earlier view of Dörpfeld (with their more recent renewed theoretical support from Wesenberg[94]) to the effect that the

37. Doric and Ionic columns drawn as equal in height to make comparison of their proportions easier.
1. From the peristyle of the Temple of Zeus at Olympia.
2. From the east side of the Parthenon.
3. From the pronaos of the Parthenon.
4. From the north portico of the Erechtheum.
5. From the Monument (Sphinx) of the Naxians at Delphi.
The columns of the Parthenon, and of the pronaos in particular, are clearly Ionising in their proportions. The Athenian Ionic columns, on the other hand, are somewhat Doric in proportion. Similar proportions can be observed in the stylobate and the architrave.

initial plan of triglyphs and metopes was cancelled in favour of a continuous frieze, the present form – deliberate and projected from the start – thus poses no difficulties in bringing about a theoretical compromise between the presence of regulae and the absence of triglyphs. Suffice it to mention the architraves of the interior two-storey colonnades of the temples of Aphaea or Paestum, which lack triglyphs, etc., but have both taenias and regulae. This, then, is a more general phenomenon of the acquisition of autonomy on the part of certain forms. In the case of the Parthenon, however, it requires a rather more specialised explanation. The detail which we are discussing forms part of a wider system of arrangements which, along general lines, was intended to serve the process of interpenetration of the two orders: the Doric order for the bearing structure, and the Ionic order for the superstructure. Thus, gradually – as we move up the building – the Doric element becomes ever lighter and the Ionic element is introduced, first as the imposition of Ionic proportions on the Doric forms and then as the introduction of true Ionic forms at a height at which the Doric element has begun to gently ebb away.[95] In this band, Ionic and Doric forms simply alternate in an upward direction: taenia, regulae, guttae, frieze, Lesbian cyma, Doric cyma, Ionic beams, Ionic mouldings and Doric meanders on the ceiling cross-beams, and Ionic decorative motifs on the frames and coffers of the ceiling panels. This is not an isolated phenomenon, but part of a much more general set of components of the inspired artistic composition of the building.[96]

Apart from these Ionic features, a Cycladic influence can also be recognised in the Parthenon, including, as Professor G. Gruben has argued convincingly,[97] its marble ceilings.

We have already accumulated sufficient evidence of the special way in which forms, modes of construction and metrological proportions are blended in the works of the Classical Athenian period. The result of this blend is an architectural idiom generally known as the Attic idiom, or, more specifically, the Attic Doric order (the Parthenon, inter alia) and the Attic Ionic order (temple of Athena Nike, etc.).[98]

As we know, the Athenians believed they were an indigenous population and not Dorians. At the time when they were building the Parthenon, they were the leaders of a major league, most of whose members were Ionians. The architectural works of Athens, built in marble – the 'Ionian' material par excellence – and with their wealth of Ionic features, were an indication of the agreement which Attica and Ionia had reached and also a demonstration of the capacity of the leading power to assimilate foreign models. Although it would appear from this that the Attic architectural idiom was intended to serve the ideal of Attic hegemony, it should certainly not be deduced that the idiom was the outcome of a policy of that kind. Marble had been introduced into Athenian architecture, along with a number of other Ionic elements, some decades before Athens emerged as a leading power and prior to the foundation of the league. The use of marble spread gradually. The earliest Hecatompedon temple had marble tiles round the periphery of its roof;[99] later, the Old Temple was all in marble from the horizontal cornice upwards (pediments, racing cornices, etc.).[100] The new Athenian facade of the temple of Apollo at Delphi was built at about the same time, using marble throughout.[101] The next and final step, the construction in marble of an entire Doric building, was taken with the Treasury of the Athenians at Delphi and the incomplete Pre-parthenon or Older-Parthenon (490-485 BC).[102] At this time, Ionic forms were gaining more and more ground in Athens; suffice it to mention only the famous Archaic Ionic frieze in the Acropolis Museum[103] and the monumental Lesbian cyma of the base of the Pre-parthenon walls.

c. Rules and terms of the architectural arrangement of the transverse sections of the Parthenon

The selection of the questions discussed above and the

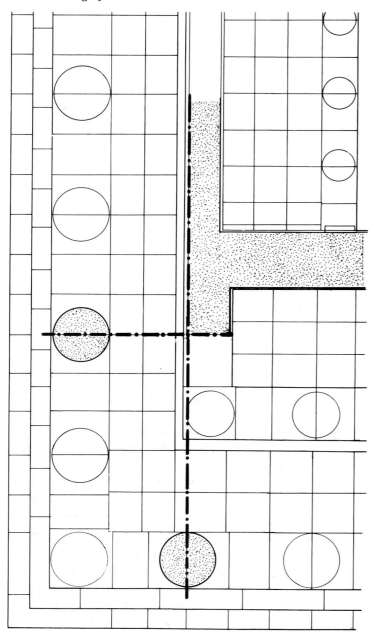

38. The axes of the second and third columns (counting from the corners) as the lines which define the sides and the antae of the cella. Drawing by M. Korres.

order in which they have been explained is the result of a much more wide-ranging exploration of the historical and technical considerations required to reveal the primary terms of the architecture of the temple and to deduce the most likely sequence in which those terms occurred. Thinking about this question dates back a long time and is extensive in the sense that it has sought out answers by means of an exploration of the terms for the architectural composition of other Doric temples.

To begin with, it can be observed that there is a rule for the mutual definition of the external colonnade and the cella: 'A line extrapolating either side of the cella will pass through the axis of the second column from each corner of the two facades' (fig. 38). This principle, which could be called the 'rule of the second column', applies to almost all the temples of Greece proper and to some of those in the western colonies dating from the mid 5th century BC.

One consequence of the application of this simple rule is that the ratio of the breadth of the cella to that of the temple as a whole is always constant. In the majority of cases (hexastyle temples) the ratio is about 57-58%, with rarer instances in which it is as little as 56% or as much as 60%.

By way of contrast, the earlier temples (Archaic and early Classical periods) of the western colonies entirely lack this rule,[104] and the width of the cella is smaller than the interval between the three middle columns on the facade of the external colonnade, sometimes being as little as 1/3 of the total width. In these temples, it has been argued, the composition of the external colonnade and of the cella were two quite separate acts.[105]

In the cases to which the rule of the second column was applied, there are two possible sequences of stages in the process of design: first the outlining of the cella and from that the definition of the colonnade, or vice versa. As for the composition of the colonnade itself, two methods have been proposed: 1. Selection of the general dimensions and proportions of the stylobate, followed by definition of the positions and sizes of the columns, by division of the general outline. As a rule, this sequence leads to, or is combined with, disparity among the columns and the intercolumniation on the facades and the long sides. 2. Selection of the diameter of the columns and of the intercolumniation intervals as the fundamental magnitudes, and production of the overall dimensions by multiplication of the intercolumniation and addition of the two end intervals from the axis of the column to the edge of the stylobate. As a rule, this sequence leads to general dimensions related in a way which does not contain any notable numerical ratio. Good arguments have been advanced for making this the method most probably used for the temples of the Classical period.[106] However, Gruben's view is also worthy of note: he believes that in the case of the Parthenon a particularly difficult feat was accomplished and that both methods were employed simultaneously,[107] with equal intervals between the columns and, this notwithstanding, a simple metrological ratio (4:9) in the rectangle of the stylobate and between the diameter of the columns and the space between them. This, of course, would not be possible if the corners of the temple were not overcontracted.

As for the columns, we know with certainty what was the factor which determined their diameter: the hundreds[108] of drums which, dislodged, were lying around the Pre-parthenon, incomplete and burned by the Persians (fig. 4). Another important factor which acted as a constraint on the scale of the temple was first hypothesised by Penrose, with reference to the length of the architrave blocks: the geological capacity of the quarries.[109]

At this point, and without having completed our review of the basic factors in the architectural composition of the Parthenon, it would, perhaps, be fitting to interpolate the most fundamental question in critical thought, given that the discussion so far suffices to show that a number of different factors – heterogeneous factors, to some extent – are concealed in each of a number of the steps in the process of composition. Thus, the following factors have a part to play in the condensation of the columns: one term of an aesthetic nature, one structural consideration, one typological element and one idealistic factor (the numerical relations in the ground plan). The three first factors are organic terms and, to some extent, are flexible within a given direction. The fourth is absolute – that is, inflexible – and lacks any manifest aesthetic, functional or constructional purpose, though it does, perhaps, have a philosophical object. It was required that the building be highly satisfactory not only in practical terms, as a visual image and for the ideological programme (which will not be discussed here), but also for thought – and, furthermore, not just the kind of thought which deals with material questions, perceiving the physical, functional, economic, ideological, artistic and other elements in the architectural achievement, but also the type of thought which inclines towards incorporeal and thus absolute magnitudes, such as numbers and the perfect formations of theoretical geometry.

The architectural achievement itself and such ancient accounts as have survived demonstrate that the intention of the great artists who created the Parthenon was to satisfy a large number of different requirements, including those of a physical, functional, technical, economic and ideological nature.

We are left, consequently, with the need to conduct a rational investigation of the possibility or impossibility of a process of composition in which each individual act has more than one different and self-contained causes.

This question could be framed in approximately the following terms: why was the Parthenon – and the Parthe-non alone, indeed – designed in a manner so different from that of the large number belonging to the sole regular type, the hexastyle Doric temple?

Was the chryselephantine statue of Athena Parthenos and the demand for more space around it the primary consideration?[110] In other words, was the external octastyle pattern the inevitable consequence of an increase in the size of the building from within? Or, conversely, was the new interior space, with its unprecedented capacity, chiefly the inevitable consequence of another primary cause which involved the whole of the building – that is, the creation of a truly enormous temple, of a temple larger not only than its incomplete predecessor, but even than that of Olympia?

Until the time of the Parthenon, the Doric temple could be made larger only by proportionally increasing the size of all its parts (and not by numerical increase). But a proportional increase in the width of the Pre-parthenon to an extent capable of meeting the demand for a genuinely larger temple (whether solely to increase the overall size or solely to provide a more spacious interior for the statue of Athena, or for both reasons) would have approximately doubled the mass and weight of the columns, the architraves, etc.[111] Even if the builders had not been obliged to use the existing half-finished drums (that is, if the question of selecting the size of the columns, etc., were still unsettled), would the construction of a hexastyle temple equivalent in size to the actual octastyle building have been possible if it had to consist of architectural members of double the mass?

The geological capacity of even the best strata on Mt Pentelikon precluded this, of course.[112] Yet even had such pieces of marble – hundreds of them, with lengths of up to six metres and a weight of 20 tons – been less uncommon, how much more would it have cost to extract them, transport them, haul them up on to the rock and put them in place in the building? By using limestone instead of marble the cost of a large hexastyle temple would not have been so excessive, but it would still not have been less than that of a marble octastyle temple for which the materials were already to hand.

But if, ultimately, the choice of an octastyle form and construction in marble was dictated by economic considerations, what remains of the position that the marble and the eight columns were the result of Ionic influence? The answer to this is rather complex. The use of marble for the Parthenon was more economical because a large part of the necessary quantity was already available. Yet the original use of this material in the Pre-parthenon had been anything but economically preferable. It follows that the initial choice of the material had been dictated by its suitability for more delicate forms and proportions – that is, for an architectural idiom whose principal presumption was an Ionic influence.

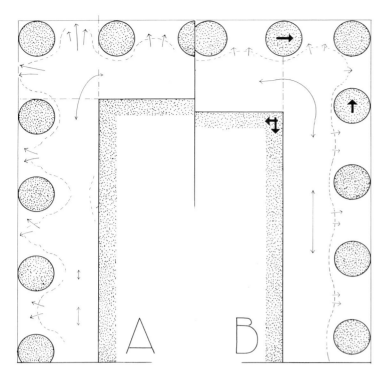

39. Differing proportional relations between the thickness of the columns and their distance from the wall define and hold in to differing extents the space between the wall and the columns. Drawing by M. Korres.

The choice of the octastyle form was indeed dictated by the serious economic considerations explained above. But how easily would such a solution have gained acceptance, given that it obviously ruined beyond repair the ideal proportions of the regular Doric type, the only one applied up to that time? Although the various economic factors are generally sufficient to explain compromises of this kind, there ought nonetheless, among all the peripteral Doric temples with which we are familiar, to be some whose shape is not regular. If such a step could not be taken in, for instance, Olympia, but could – for very important economic reasons – be taken in Athens, it is a result of the fact that Athenian architecture had already acquired an inclination towards the Ionic (marble, lighter proportions, etc.), as can be seen in the Athenian treasury at Delphi. Consequently, it was possible for the various difficulties which loomed in the anticanonical octastyle form to be overcome.

This, then, was the background against which Ictinus prepared his plans. To begin with, the project would have to be an architectural design capable of satisfying the demand for a building of large volume with a spacious interior – and also the requirement that the drums and other marbles which had been prepared forty years earlier for quite a different temple should be used in the most economical manner.

Without altering the diameter of the columns, the architect reduced the original intercolumnation by 12 centime-

tres for the middle columns and 36 centimetres for the end columns. At the same time, he increased the original height of the columns by one drum and reduced the width of the capitals from 2.21 metres to between 2 and approximately 2.06 metres. This eliminated some of the elongation of the facade, while the new proportions of the columns conveyed a sense of perpendicularity which was of use in moderating the remaining degree to which the height of the temple really was less than it ought to have been by comparison with the breadth. The denser arrangement of the columns corresponded better to the weight of the pediment, which, proportionally, was larger in the octastyle building than it would have been in a hexastyle temple.[113] This denser arrangement was also essential on the long sides of the temple, so as to 'hold in' the space of the pteroma; it is generally true of colonnades that if the distance between the columns is not sufficiently smaller than the distance between the columns and the wall, the intervening semi-open air space loses its coherence and becomes confused with the space outside (fig. 39). This, indeed, was the reason for the formation of the 'rule of the second column' which we have already encountered. Needless to say, given the overcontraction of the intercolumniation at the corners, application of the rule to the Parthenon would not have been enough to 'hold in' the space of the lateral pteromas unless the colonnade was as densely constructed as it is. In fact, it is the densest colonnade of any known Doric temple in Greece proper. There are thus two opposing forces at work between the cella and the colonnade. One, pushing the pteroma space outwards, originates in the marginal increase in the size of the cella and the fact that its surfaces approach the colonnade.[114] The other, which circumscribes and holds in the pteroma, is the result of the markedly greater density of the columns.

The even greater density of the columns at the corners was also particularly useful in holding in the interior (of the pteroma) at just those points where it was subject to a centrifugal tendency because of the compulsory change in its direction. Thanks to application of the rule of the second column, an observer standing in the pteroma and looking down its length does not see only the open space beside the corner column but also the greater part of the second column on the next side, thus showing him that he is not standing in a simple rectilinear colonnade but in a space which flows around the cella[115] (figs. 39, 40).

d. Terms of the architectural arrangement of the lengthwise parts of the Parthenon

While the architectural arrangement of the transverse parts of the temple was a piece of originality and boldness on the part of those who designed the building, the arrangement of the lengthwise parts seems simply to apply a pre-existing type. The large west chamber, known in the

40. A perspective reconstruction of the west pteroma. Source: Orlandos, op. cit.

41. A perspective reconstruction of the interior of the temple, with the statue of Athena Parthenos. The columns had 16 flutes. The lower columns consisted of drums, and the upper one were monolithic. Drawing by M. Korres.

bibliography as the opisthodomos or the Parthenon proper, is certainly the feature by which the Parthenon can be distinguished from the vast majority of other temples. The prevailing view, of course, is that this was a treasury, necessary for the safekeeping of the alliance's money and other property.[116] Yet ten years prior to the founding of the alliance, the Pre-parthenon had already been given an equally long west chamber.[117] More importantly, the double interior division was a feature not only of the two successive marble Parthenons but also, ultimately, of all the other temples on the Acropolis: of the Erechtheum, and of the Old Temple of Pisistratid times. We do not know exactly what form was taken by the floor plan of the other large Archaic temple, that known as the Hecatompedon,[118] but it seems very likely that it, too, had a similar double division. In general, the double interior division is not uncommon in the temples of other Greek cities, but as a rule it is a division between the temple proper and the adyton, entered from the main temple,[119] and not a division into two self-contained

chambers with separate entrances from the front and rear porticoes, as in the case of the Parthenon and the other temples on the Acropolis.

As a result, it is more correct to class the Parthenon in a separate temple type, that of the 'double temple', the other known examples of which are confined, for the time being, to the Acropolis. That, in turn, allows the phenomenon to be recognised as a tradition belonging only to the temple-building of Athens and connected with the housing of the cult of Athena with other much older yet still flourishing cults.[120]

Another feature of the Parthenon which is not encountered in the temples of other Greek cities is the extreme shallowness of the pronaos and the opisthonaos.[121] This feature is connected with two others, which without being unique are nonetheless rare: a) the pronaos and the opisthonaos are to all intents and purposes equal in size, whereas in other temples the pronaos is obviously deeper, and b) the colonnades of the pronaos and the opisthonaos are prostyle, and not in antis as is the rule in other temples. While the combination of these three elements is so rare as never to be encountered anywhere else, it is the rule on the Acropolis, as we can see from the floor plans of the Pre-parthenon and the Old Temple. As we can see, it is clear that the extremely rare nature of the front and rear porticoes of the Parthenon (pronaos and opisthonaos) was not the creation of the geniuses who designed the Great Temple, but part of the temple-building tradition of the Acropolis.

Thanks to the marked growth in studies of Ionic architecture over the last twenty years, it is now possible to identify the Ionic (or rather, Cycladic) typological origins of the porticoes of the Parthenon and of the other temples on the Acropolis – and not only of the Doric temples we have already described, but also of the Ionic temples (the porticoes of the temple of Athena Nike and of the east side of the Erechtheum; not that of the north side, whose floor plan would be better described as an original Athenian creation).

All that is left now is to state the basic typological features of the large interior of the temple. There are three main features: first, the unusual breadth of the chamber, resulting from the bold composition of the cross-section of the temple; second, the arrangement of the internal two-storey colonnade around its centre, an unprecedented phenomenon for the time,[122] and, third, the placing of the ceiling at the greatest height allowed by the construction of the roof.[123] In the particular case of the arrangement of the two-storey colonnade, it should be noted that as a rule, in other temples, there were two such colonnades, which divided the interior of the temple into three aisles. Of these, the two lateral aisles were very narrow – in effect, they were detached sections of the central aisle – and their only purpose was to create an impression of depth behind the columns.

In the Parthenon, the internal columns formed a three-sided colonnade which was far enough from the side walls and the back wall to divide the interior into two areas of comparable size (fig. 41): a broader central area and a more elongated perimetric area. Those lucky enough to be able to visit the interior of the temple could move in either of the spaces, while in both cases a wide range of angles of vision was available for discovering the simple grandeur of the vast floor and wall surfaces, the richness of the coffered ceilings, the infinite prospects of variations in the rhythmical repetition of columns and chiaroscuro, and the measurements of the space enclosed within these features, with all its stimuli – light, shadow, brilliance, dazzle, echoes, the coolness of the marble and the caress of the gently stirring air. Yet above all, the arrangement of the chamber permitted the unique observation, from all sides, of the greatest masterpiece of all, the chryselephantine statue of Athena Parthenos, standing just a little way behind the middle of this magnificent chamber.

Notes

1. Vitruvius, VII introduction, 12. See also P.M. Mylonas, 'Vitrouviou ta deka prooimia' ('The ten proems of Vitruvius'), *Filia Epi* ('In Token of Friendship'), Archaeological Association, vol. B, Athens 1987, p.63.
2. The ancient accounts are to be found collected in O. Jahn, A. Michaelis, *Arx Athenarum a Pausania descripta*, Bonn 1901, pp. 53-61, 94-98. See also A. Michaelis, *Der Parthenon*, Leipzig 1871, pp. 288-333.
3. For the building inscriptions, see. *IGI²*, pp. 339-354 (*IG = Inscriptiones Graecae*); see *American Journal of Archaeology (AJA)* 17, 1913; 25, 1921. See also *Arx Athenarum*, pp. 94ff. For the treasury inscriptions, see *IGI²*, pp. 232ff, *IGII²*, pp. 1370ff. For the most recent accounts, see D. Lewis, *Comptes et Inventaires dans la cité Grecque*, Neuchatel 1988, pp. 297-308. A monograph on the subject is being prepared by D. Harris (Princeton University). For other inscriptions, see *IGII²*, p. 212, *IGI²*, pp. 339-353. For the Hecatompedon, see *IGII²*, p. 92 (the 'Callias resolution' which refers to completion of the Parthenon pediment).
4. See the bibliography assembled by Ch. Bouras in M. Korres, Ch. Bouras, *Meleti Apokatastaseos tou Parthenonos* ('Study for the Restoration of the Parthenon'), vol. 1, Athens 1983 (hereinafter *Meleti* 1), pp. 169ff. See also *Parthenon-Kongress, Basel, 1982*, E. Berger (ed.), vol. II, Mainz 1984, pp. 461ff (1170 titles, ed. H. van der Meijden).
5. In my opinion, the judgements which underestimate the academic value of the work of the Classicists are superficial and thus unfair; they rely on a critique of only one part of that work, the general reconstructions, where the freedom of their artistic approach is quite plain to see. But those reconstructions were only a part of their work. This is easily demonstrated by the numerous academically original notes they made, by their sketches and their painstaking and usually extremely accurate measurements, by their drawings of the current situation (which often required very great physical effort, involving scrambling among the piles of rocks or up the flimsiest of scaffolding, rope ladders, etc.), by their archaeologically strict reconstructions of details and construction methods, by their inspired interpretations and, in some cases, by a notable knowledge of the ancient world.
6. J. Stuart, N. Revett, *The Antiquities of Athens*, vol. II, London 1787.
7. See the various early depictions of the monument, and especially those of Dalton (1749): R. Dalton, *Antiquities and Views in Greece and Egypt*, London 1791, plates 43-44 and 42 (however, the lean-tos and the medieval staircase were omitted for the purposes of these drawings).
8. F. Penrose, *The Principles of Athenian Architecture*, 1st ed., London 1851 (hereinafter Penrose¹), p. 20.
9. Stuart and Revett, *op. cit.*, plate 2. The thickening is slightly more than four centimetres or 1/44 of the diameter of the column. According to Vitruvius (III, 3, 11) it ought to have been 1/50.
10. Stuart and Revett, *op. cit.*, p. 8.
11. *Ibid.*, plate 6.
12. *Ibid.*, pp. 5-8.
13. *Carl Haller von Hallerstein in Griechenland*, ed. H.G. Bankel, Berlin 1986, pp. 102-106 and esp. p. 104.
14. C.R. Cockerell, *Descriptions of the Ancient Marbles of the British Museum*, vol. 6, London 1830, 'Pediments and Metopes of the Parthenon', and W. Jenkins Jr. in C. Cockerell et al, *Antiquities of Athens and other Places in Greece, Sicily, etc., supplementary to*

the Antiquities of Athens by James Stuart and Nicholas Revett, London 1830, pp. 4ff, plate 4.

15. Josef Hoffer, 'Das Parthenon zu Athen in seinen Haupttheilen neu gemessen', Wiener Allgemeine Bauzeitung 3, Vienna 1838, nos. 27, 41, 42, 43, pp. 249-250, 371-375, 379-383, 387-391, plates 237, 238, 239. The very well-known architect Ed. Schaubert worked with Hoffer on this research.

16. Ibid., p. 372 ("Subtilitäten").

17. Ibid., p. 375; cf. Vitruvius (III, 3, 13; III, 4, 5; V, 9, 4).

18. Ibid., p. 371.

19. Tübinger Kunstblatt, 1843, p. 52. See also F. Koepp, Archäologischer Anzeiger (= AA) 5, 1890, pp. 129-148.

20. Ida Haugsted, 'The architect Christian Hansen, drawings, letters and articles', Analecta Romana Instituti Danici, X, 1982, and A. Papanikolaou-Christensen, Athens 1818-1853, Views of Athens by Danish Artists, Athens 1985, passim.

21. Paris – Rome – Athènes, Ecole Nationale Supérieure des Beaux-Arts, Paris 1982, pp. 162-171, 349-368. See also Michaelis, Der Parthenon, p. 89.

22. The book was subtitled, The results of a recent survey conducted chiefly with reference to the optical refinements exhibited in the construction of the ancient buildings at Athens, London 1851.

23. For example, between the second (-4.15) and fourth (-4.33) architrave blocks on the east facade. See note 29, below.

24. For example, between the first west metope (1.17) and the eighth east metope (1.33); see note 29, below.

25. The eight column capitals on the east side are all larger by ~5.5 cm. than those on the other sides (Penrose[1], plate 5, p. 10). Penrose attributed this to aesthetic considerations (pp. 14, 15, notes). Dinsmoor (The Architecture of Ancient Greece[3], London 1950, p. 162) agrees, and hypothesises that it was a belated improvement carried out during the course of construction. However, recent observations by this author demonstrate that the east side was constructed at the same time as the others, not later – and, indeed, that work on it was constantly in advance of that on the others. The east side was the side finished first. As a result, the broader capitals were among the first decisions taken by the architect. J.J. Coulton (Parthenon-Kongress, p. 43, note 22) judges from the point of view of proportions that the larger, not the smaller, capitals are probably older. For general reasons, Karl Schefold ('Kleisthenes. Der Anteil der Kunst an der Gestaltung des Jungen attischen Freestaates', Museum Helveticum 3, 1946, p. 91) advances the view that construction must have begun on the east side. This view is shared, for all temples, by E. Buschor (Mitteilungen des Deutschen Archäologischen Instituts, Athenische Abteilung [= AM], 51, 1926, pp. 163ff) and G. Walter (Alt Ägina, Berlin 1938, p. 78). However, apart from the aesthetic considerations it seems that the broadening also met the need for the entablature to be located off-centre, in an outward direction, accompanying (or following) the shift in the location of the cella conceived in the same manner (Meleti 1, p. 128, and see note 29, below).

26. Penrose[1], plates 11 and 12, pp. 31-32; Penrose could find no satisfactory explanation for this. His failure to explain it is quite understandable: excavations had not yet revealed the truncated staircase on the west of the Parthenon. It was not until its discovery (1858) that it became possible to make some important observations: the staircase runs parallel to the temple and that it, too, is curved in the same manner as the crepidoma (A. Choisy, 'Note sur la courbure dissumétrique, des degrés qui limitent au couchant la plate-forme du Parthénon', Comptes Rendus de l'Académie des Inscriptions et des Belles Lettres, Paris 1865; N.S.[1] pp. 413-416; by the same author, Histoire de l'architecture, vol. 1, Paris 1899, pp. 331-332).

The necessity of viewing diagonally the Parthenon and the large staircase (original width ~40 metres and height 3.80 metres) eight

metres from it would have produced an irritating clash in perspective of the curvature if the south extremity of the staircase were not lowered (as Choisy mistakenly assumed, though correctly identifying the principle) or if the south-east corner of the temple were not raised, as was eventually done. In the chronological sense, this was the first geometrical deviation in the building: "a refinement for a refinement", as R.E. Wycherley has aptly termed it (The Stones of Athens, Princeton, N.J., 1978, p. 111). See also Meleti 1, p. 17.

27. Penrose[1], p. 8, notes 5, 7. Dinsmoor (op. cit., p. 162) allows another – yet smaller – eccentricity in a northerly direction, and indeed attributes it to an engineering error. B.H. Hill (AJA, 16, 1912, p.551) sees this eccentricity as deliberate: the first step of the cella, he says, has a breadth of one old Athenian foot (of the Pre-parthenon) on its north side and of a new Athenian foot on the south. Was this a practical need to re-use existing earlier materials? Could aesthetic considerations – different lighting – have been responsible? Was it a case of compromising older and more modern units of measurement (and thus institutions), as was also the case with the numerical symbolism of the earlier and later types on the north and south side of the frieze, respectively (L. Beschi, Il fregio del Parthenone, una proposta di lettura, Accademia Nazionale dei Lincei, 39, 1984, pp. 1ff) – or was it a combination of all these factors?

28. The differing widths of the columns in the porticoes on the east and west sides has concerned all the scholars since Penrose and has given rise to various interpretations and theories: columns which were originally equal, with the thinning of those on the east or the thickening of those on the west coming at a later date; columns which were unequal right from the start. As for the causes, the following have been proposed: thicker columns in the opisthonaos would better suggest the idea of the safety of the Treasury; thinner columns in the pronaos were more suitable for making the entrance to the main temple more spacious, with better lighting; thicker columns were more appropriate for re-using the corresponding columns from the portico of the Pre-parthenon. See Penrose[1], p. 8, and W.B. Dinsmoor, The Architecture of Ancient Greece, op. cit., p. 162, and 'How the Parthenon was Planned, Modern Theory and Ancient Practice', Architecture, vol. 47, 1923, no. 6, pp. 177-180, and vol. 48, 1923, no. 1, pp. 241-244 (here no. 47, 1923, p. 243); G.P. Stevens, Hesperia suppl. 3, 1940, p. 67; A. Orlandos, I architektoniki tou Parthenonos ('The Architecture of the Parthenon'), vol. A., 1976 (plates), vol. B, 1977 (text), vol. C (text continued; hereinafter Orlandos, Parthenon), p. 437.

Strangely enough, the difference in depth between these two areas (the pronaos and the opisthonaos) has not so far attracted the interest of scholars. In fact, however, that difference is the most important phenomenon, and the much-debated difference in the columns is only one of its many consequences. Thanks to more recent studies of the question, it has become possible to conclude that in the original plan the pronaos and the opisthonaos had exactly the same architectural design. But in an early stage of construction of the pronaos – immediately after the laying of the blocks to support the columns and walls – the plan was modified so as to increase the depth of the chamber by some 15 centimetres without disturbing the external dimensions of the cella. This increase was dictated by the decision to install an Ionic frieze directly below the ceiling of the pronaos. Since the frieze and the top course of masonry corresponding to it would project, the dimensions of the ceiling would have to be reduced and the proportions of the coffered panels would be disturbed. This could be avoided only by slightly increasing the space beneath this new frieze. The increase was accomplished by reducing the diameter of the columns by 6 cm and by moving the wall in which the door was set back (i.e., in a westerly direction) by ~8 cm. See Meleti 1, pp. 124, 126; Meleti Apokatastaseos tou Parthenonos ('Study for the Restoration of the Parthenon'), vol. 2a, Athens 1989, by M. Korres, in association with N. Toganidis, K. Zambas and Th. Skoulikidis, at the head of a team of restorers (hereinafter *Meleti* 2a), p. 13; M. Korres, *Study for the Restoration of the Parthenon*, vol. 2b, Athens 1989 (hereinafter *Study* 2b), plate 1, column PK3, where the earlier base circle can be seen. The frieze in the pronaos was unknown to scholars and continues to be so today, since it was completely destroyed many centuries ago. Among other recent conclusions about the pronaos and the opisthonaos are those listed below. The west door was one Attic foot narrower than the east door, and one and a half feet lower. There were two large windows on either side, lighting the lateral isles of the main temple and contributing to the creation of indirect side-lighting and consequently to emphasis of the plasticity of the great statue. The marble panels in the ceiling of the pronaos were equal in number to those of the opisthonaos, were in a particular style and more richly decorated: they were thrice-recessed rather than twice, and the coffering was much deeper. (Today we are in a position to say that the large and richly-ornamented panels of the north portico in the Erechtheum were merely copies of those in the pronaos of the Parthenon.) The columns of the pronaos had a greater   entasis than those of the rest of the temple (.02,4 as opposed to .01,7). The top course of masonry in the pronaos was not simply Doric, but also contained a Lesbian cyma which was carved and not simply painted as was the case with the top course of masonry in the peristyle. Inside the thickness of the east wall, to the north of the door, was a gap containing a staircase for access to the space between the ceiling and the roof. See M. Korres, 'Der Pronaos und die Fenster des Parthenon', *Parthenon-Kongress*, pp. 47ff, *Meleti* 1, pp. 122ff and in particular pp. 128 and 129; *Meleti* 2a, p. 13, diagrams 4, 6, figs. 16-19, pp. 43, 47.

29. Penrose[1], plate 4, p. 16, plates 6-8, Orlandos, *Parthenon*, plates 26-29, 31, 32. The fluctuations in the intercolumniation are normally attributed to minor errors of the order of millimetres. The fluctuations in the lengths of the architrave blocks are attributed by Penrose to questions of the rarity of such long pieces of marble and of economy of materials. Once it had been accepted that the lengths could fluctuate, slabs slightly shorter than the proper length could be used if combined with slightly longer slabs. However, Penrose did not omit to hypothesise that the fluctuations in the lengths of the sides of the architrave slabs might be connected with those in the lengths of the metopes, but he was less insistent on this than on the rarity of such marbles and the question of economy. However, it can be stated today, thanks to fresh research, that all the fluctuations of the lengths of the architraves and metopes were planned in advance. Yet the most amazing feature of all is that the advance planning of these lengths was done at a very early stage in the project, before the stylobate for the peristyle had been laid. There must have been an extremely constructive discussion between architect and sculptors at that time. They must have been skilled enough to be able to perceive, with the imagination, optical phenomena which would only become visible once the facades of the temple had been finished, and so broadminded that they could work out solutions and accept major amendments to the regular proportions in the name of improved results. As architectural forms, the metopes ought under the Doric order to have been absolutely equal. But as pieces of sculpture they could not be seen as equal. The number (two to four), type (human beings, horses and other animals, Centaurs, chariots, altars, statues) and arrangement of the figures and objects, and the nature and direction of the movements depicted were terms which had to be – and were – taken seriously into consideration. A part of the length was removed from some of the metopes, and added to others. Then it was decided to make the corresponding alterations to the lengths of the architrave blocks. This shows that the exact order in which the metopes would be placed had also been agreed. The architects had reconciled themselves to the idea that the joints of the architrave slabs and the axes of the triglyphs above most of the columns would be off-centre to an incredible extent: as much as half an Attic foot.

Needless to say, they could not count only on the impressions of visitors whose artistic eye was as untrained as – with very few exceptions – that of most of our contemporaries. In at least two cases, however, they judged that in order to moderate this off-centredness an equivalent number of columns would have to be shifted. The second column on the north side was moved 4 centimetres west. Its original position was defined by the joint in the first step of the crepidoma, and its present one by the corresponding joint in the stylobate – while, as a rule, the joints in question ought almost to coincide, as we can see in the four sides of the crepidoma. The change in the spacing of the crepidoma joints beneath the second north column is a statement of one of Ictinus' acts of composition – couched not in the language of his famous treatise, but in the code of deterministic architecture and of the art of building a large project. The cause of the act itself – and the reason for discovering it – is the theme of the first two metopes, rich in size and motion, and the correspondingly marked off-centredness of the third triglyph. Here we should add that part of the difference (an additional ~4 cm.) was offset in an easterly direction, by placing the entablature of the east side off-centre towards the columns to an equivalent extent (see note 73, below). Furthermore, the particularly large increase in the breadth of the column capital (by ~4 cm.) and in the capital of the column to the east (the corner column) by ~5.5 cm has also been proposed as the reason for the movement of the column westwards (see *Meleti* 1, p. 129).

30. Penrose[1], p. 7 and notes, also pp. 50 and 64, note 2. Precision instruments, etc.

31. For a critique of these theories, see W.B. Dinsmoor (*Architecture*, vol. 47, 1923, pp. 177-180). See also Orlandos, *Parthenon*, pp. 669-735.

32. D. Mertens, 'Zum Entwurf des Parthenon', *Parthenon-Kongress*, pp. 55-58. See also *Meleti* 1, pp. 119-120, 202, and H.G. Bankel, *AA* 1984, pp. 420ff.

33. Penrose[1], pp. 9, 10, 14, 16.; Dörpfeld, *AM* 7, 1882, p. 296, and 15, 1890, p. 170; Dinsmoor, *Architecture*, vol. 48, 1923, p. 242; the same author, *Hesperia*, 9, 1940, p. 22; the same author, *The Architecture of Ancient Greece*[3], pp. 161-163; H.G. Bankel, 'Das Fussmass des Parthenon', *Parthenon-Kongress*, pp. 33ff. See also *AM* 98, 1983. There are a large number of metrological analyses of the Parthenon, and they have produced varying results. See, for example, *Parthenon-Kongress*, pp. 33, 55, 68, 75, 80, 99, 119 (Bankel, Merthens, Mezös, Seki, Stucchi, De Waele, Berger); Büssing, *Jahrbuch des Deutschen Archäologischen Instituts* (= *JdI*) 97, 1982; Wesenberg, *AM* 97, 1982, pp. 111ff, and *AA* 1984, p. 547.

34. Stuart and Revett, vol. II, p. 8; Penrose[1], pp. 8, 10, 78; Penrose[2] (2nd ed., 1888), pp. 111-116 (appendix by W.W. LLoyd).

35. W.B. Dinsmoor, 'The Basis of Greek Temple Design', *Atti del settimo Congresso Internazionale di Archeologia Classica*, vol. 1, Rome 1961, p. 364. The measurements approximate to this figure to within two or three centimetres.

36. Dinsmoor, 'Temple Design', *op. cit.*; G. Gruben, *Die Tempel der Griechen*[1], Munich 1966, p. 167.

37. Penrose attributes this difference to what he saw as a subsequent modification: the thickening of the columns in the west portico. This, however, cannot be the case; see note 28 above. Earlier scholars held the view that the 4:9 proportion on the floor plan was not intentional. See Dörpfeld, *op. cit.*, Dismoor, *Architecture*, vol. 47, 1923, p. 177; H. Riemann, *Zum Griechischen Peripteraltempel*, Düren 1935, p. 99, and see also note 107 below.

38. Penrose[1], p. 36.

39. Penrose[1], p. 50, note 2.

40. A. Tshira, 'Die unfertigen Säulentrommeln auf der Akropolis zu Athen', *JdI* 55, 1940, pp. 242-261.

41. Penrose[1], plates 19-21 and 40, 1, 2.

42. Penrose[1], pp. 77ff.

43. Penrose[1], pp. 78, 79, note 1.

44. K. Bötticher, *Bericht über die Untersuchungen auf der Akropolis von Athen in Frühjahre 1862*, Berlin 1863, pp. 115-141.

45. J. Durm, 'Reisebericht aus Attika', *Zeitschrift für Bauwesen* 21, 1871, pp. 470ff.

46. E. Ziller, 'Über die ursprüngliche Existenz der Curvaturen des Parthenon', *Zeitschrift für Bauwesen* 15, 1865, pp. 35ff.

47. A. Thiersch, 'Optische Täuschungen auf den Gebiete der Architektur', *Zeitschrift für Bauwesen* 23, 1873, pp. 9ff (especially p. 33, with a reference to the treatise *Physiologische Optik* by the famous physicist Helmholz) and plate B.

48. See above, note 31.

49. *AM* 6, 1881, pp. 283-302, plate 12.

50. See A. Mallwitz, 'O Wilhelm Dörpfeld kai i klassiki architektoniki stin Ellada' ('Wilhelm Dörpfeld and Classical Architecture in Greece'), *Epetiris tis Etaireias Lefkadikon Meleton*, E, 1978-1980, p. 44.

51. Bötticher, *op. cit.*

52. Penrose[1], plate 12 (with piers in the corners of the internal colonnade), and also plate 4 (with columns in same position), and p. 6, note 4, which comes out in favour of the second solution.

53. *AM* 6, 1881, p. 298.

54. *Journal of Hellenic Studies* (= *JHS*) 8, 1887, pp. 272-273.

55. See above, note 12, and Penrose[1], p. 11; Vitruvius III 2, 8. See also C. Bötticher, *Der Hypaethral-Tempel auf Grund der vitruvischen Zeugnisses*, 1874, and J. Jeile in *Licht und Architektur*, W.D. Heilmeyer, W. Hoepfner (eds.), Tübingen 1990, p. 31, with technical calculations of the lighting of the interior.

56. *AJA* 17, 1913, pp. 17, 53-80; 25, 1923, pp. 233-245.

57. *AJA* 38, 1934b, pp. 93-106.

58. *The Architecture of Ancient Greece*[3], pp. 167-176.

59. *AJA* 58, 1954, pp. 144ff.

60. See above, note 33.

61. *Op. cit.* and 'The Basis of Greek Temple Design', *Atti del settimo Congresso Internazionale di Archeologia Classica*, *op. cit.*, p. 363.

62. *AJA* 38, 1934a, pp. 408-448.

63. *Hesperia*, Suppl. 3, 1940, pp. 67ff; see also *Hesperia* 11, 1942, pp. 354-364.

64. *Hesperia* 24, 1955, pp. 240-276; *AJA* 38, 1934, pp. 533-542; *Hesperia* 5, 1936, pp. 471ff and Suppl. 3, 1940, pp. 24ff, 41ff, 57ff; 12, 1943, pp. 135-143; 15, 1946, pp. 1-26; *AJA* 66, 1962, p. 337, plate 89.

65. *Praktika tis Akadimias Athinon* (= *PAA*), 21, 1946, p. 224; Orlandos, *Parthenon*, pp. 471-511.

66. *Hesperia*, Suppl. 8, 1949, pp. 259-267, and Orlandos, *Parthenon*, pp. 600-631, and also pp. 547-580.

67. Orlandos, *Parthenon*, plates (1943-1975).

68. For comments on these inaccuracies, see *Parthenon-Kongress*, vol. 2, pp. 367 and 371.

69. *Meleti* 1, pp. 44-53, 90-121.

70. A. Burford, 'The Builders of the Parthenon', *Greece and Rome*, vol. 10, Suppl. 1, Oxford 1963, p. 23.

71. See above, notes 25-28, *JdI* 98, 1983 (Wesenberg on a possible previous plan with triglyphs and metopes in the place of the Ionic frieze), and below, note 94.

72. G. Daux, E. Hansen, *Le trésor de Siphnos*, Paris 1987.

73. The seating of the architrave slabs on the north and south sides is constantly off-centre towards the column capitals by almost one centimetre in a southerly direction; that of the architrave slabs on the east side is off-centre by a factor of almost four (~3.5 cm) in an easterly direction (see above, note 29).

74. F. Krauss, *Paestum*, Berlin 1941, pp. 25-26, fig. 5; G. Gruben, *Die Tempel der Griechen*[1], p. 40; J.J. Coulton, *Greek Architects at Work*, London 1977, pp. 61ff, figs. 18, 20; W. Müller-Wiener, *Griechische Bauwese in der Antike*, 1988, p. 116.

75. As, for example, in temples A and E (of Hera) at Selinus; Gruben, *op. cit.*, p. 227, and D. Mertens, *Die Tempel von Segesta und die dorische Tempelbaukunst des griechischen Westes in klassischer Zeit*, Mainz 1984, pp. 84, 152ff.

76. As, for example, in temple A (facade) at Selinus, the temple of Poseidon (or Zeus or Hera) at Paestum, the temple of Athena at Syracuse and that of 'Concord' at Acragas; Krauss, *op. cit.*, p. 48, Gruben, *op. cit.*, pp. 41, 253, 264, 305, and Mertens, *op. cit.*, pp. 61ff, 73 fig. 27, 112 fig. 60, 152ff.

77. The second gap has a width of ~4.26,0 as opposed to the normal value of almost 4.30 (for an explanation of the phenomenon, see note 29, above). For the overcontraction of the corners of the Parthenon, see also J.J. Coulton, *Annual of the British School at Athens* (= *BSA*) 69, 1974, p. 66; J. Bundgaard, *Parthenon*, Copenhagen 1976, p. 64; *AM* 97, 1982, pp. 114ff (Wesenberg). Of particular interest is the fact that the overcontraction in the corners is also present in the hexastyle east and west porticoes; see M. Korres, *Parthenon-Kongress*, p. 52, and *Meleti* 1, pp. 26-27.

78. Vitruvius, III, 2, 3; Ch. Bouras, *Mathimata istorias tis architektonikis* ('Introduction to the History of Architecture'), Athens 1980, pp. 152ff; see also A. Orlandos, *Elefsiniaka* 1, 1932, pp. 209-223.

79. C. Weickert, *Typen der archaischen Architektur*, Augsburg 1929, pp. 92ff, 105ff, 116ff, 142ff, 182ff and especially p. 185.

80. Weickert, *op. cit.*, pp. 188ff; Gruben, *Die Tempel der Griechen*[3], Munich 1980, pp. 318ff; Bouras, *op. cit.*, pp. 167ff.

81. T. Hodge, *The Woodwork of Greek Roofs*, 1960; Paton, Stevens et al, *The Erechtheum*, Cambridge Mass. 1927, figs. 187, 193, plate 24.

82. For the first category, see Gruben, *op. cit.*, pp. 340-348. See also *Münchner Jahrb. für Bild. Kunst* 1972, pp. 7ff; *PAE* 1976, pp. 299ff (Gruben, Korres); *AA* 1968, p. 693 (Gruben, Könings); 1970, p. 135; 1972, p. 319; 1982, pp. 159-229, 623-689; 1987, pp. 569-621 (Lambrinoudakis, Gruben et al). For the second category, see R. Vallois, *L'architecture hellénique et hellénistique à Délos*, I, 1966; II, 1978; by the same author, 'Topographie délienne I,II', *Bulletin de correspondance hellénique* (= *BCH*) 48, 1924, pp. 411-445; 53, 1929, pp. 185-315; *AA* 1972, pp. 421-430 (H. Fastje); *AA* 1982, pp. 231-264 (M. Schuller); pp. 265-270 (K. Schnieringer); pp. 271-290 (A. Ohnesorg); *AA* 1985, pp. 319-398 (M. Schuller).

83. Gruben, Korres, *PAE*, 1976, pp. 302ff; 1977, pp. 383ff; 1981, pp. 295ff; Gruben, *Architectura,* 1985, pp. 105-116.

84. J.T. Clarke, *Investigations at Assos*, I, 1882; II, 1898; U. Fister-Hotz, *Der Bauschmuck des Athenatempels von Assos*, Rome 1984; B. Wescoat, 'The Temple of Athena at Assos', *AJA* 91, 1987, pp. 553-568.

85. Krauss, *op. cit.* and *AM* 1, 1948, pp. 11-20; Mertens, *op. cit.* and *Mitteilungen des Deutschen Archäologischen Instituts. Römische Abteilung* (= *RM*) 86, 1979, pp. 103-139 ('Der ionische Tempel von Metaport'); D. Theodorescu, *Le Chapiteau Ionique grec*, Geneva 1980; by the same author, 'Chapiteaux Ioniques de la Sicile meridionale', *Cahiers du centre Jean Bérard* I, Naples 1974; B. Barletta, *Ionic Influence in Archaic Sicily*, Gothenburg 1983; F. Benoit, 'Le Chapiteau ionique de Marseille', *Revue archéologique* (= *RA*) 43, 1954, pp. 17-43; E. Petersen, *RM* 5, 1890 ('Tempel in Locri').

86. We could also add the temple of Hera at Selares, Foce del Sele (P. Zancani Montuoro, U. Zanotti Bianco, *Heraion alla Foce del Sele* I, II, 1951-54), the Hellenistic phase in the building of the temple of Apollo at Crimissus (D. Mertens, F. Seiler, 'Crotone', *Atti del 23, convegno ... 1983*, Naples 1984, pp. 223ff) and the temple of Artemis Tauropolos at Loutsa (J. Travlos, *Bildlexikon zur Topographie des antiken Attika*, 1988, pp. 211ff). Of these temples, only the first is of importance for the issue discussed here.

87. See above, note 75, and Gruben[3], p. 238.

88. See above, note 75, and Gruben[3], pp. 239, 253.

89. See *Meleti* 1, pp. 16, 20, 347. The traces were first observed by Cockerell and Woods; Penrose[1], p. 6, and P. Pedersen, *The Parthenon and the Origin of the Corinthian Capital*, Odense University

Press 1989, note 5.

90. Penrose, Paccard, Dörpfeld, Dinsmoor, Orlandos, Gruben and others; Loviot makes a different reconstruction, with successive columns and a tile with a hole for smoke to escape (*Paris – Rome – Athènes, op. cit.*, p. 234).

91. P. Pedersen, *op. cit.*; see also G. Lavas, 'Tholos Bauten', *Epistimoniki Epetiris Panepistimiou Thessalonikis* ('Academic Yearbook of the University of Thessaloniki') F2, 1974, p. 44, and G. Roux, 'Pourquoi le Parthénon?', *Académie des Inscriptions et belles lettres*, Comptes rendus, 1984, p. 302.

92. Gruben[3], p. 178; G. Fougères, 'Les origines du Parthénon et l'influence de l'ionisme sur l'architecture dorique a Athènes', *Hommage a Louis Olivier*, Paris 1911, p. 195, and I.K. Raubitschek, *Ionicizing – Doric Architecture*, Columbia University, Ann Arbor 1982.

93. Ratio of height of architrave slabs to length 1:3.4 on the east side, 1:4.3 on the north portico.

94. *AM* 9, 1884, p. 336 (Dörpfeld). B.R. Demangel (*La frise ionique*, 1933, p. 316) holds a different view, and see also B. Schweitzer, *JdI* 53, 1938, p. 30; Orlandos, *Parthenon*, p. 449, note 5; *JdI* 98, 1983, pp. 57ff (Wesenberg, with note 36 on the opinion of Orlandos).

95. Orlandos, *Parthenon*, p. 449.

96. The type and ornamentation of the pilasters, the type and ornamentation of the ceiling, the type and ornamentation of the pediment, the type and ornamentation of the roof, etc. Unfortunately, nothing is known with exactness about the forms and ornamentation of the interior rooms.

97. Gruben[3], pp. 344, 348, and *Architectura*, 1985, p. 111.

98. See note 92, above.

99. *AM* 60, 1935 (Schuchhardt).

100. Recent research has shown that apart from the parts of the temple which were already known to be marble, the tympanums of the pediment were marble, too.

101. M. Courby, *Fouilles de Delphes*, 1927.

102. *AJA* 16, 1912, pp. 535-558 (D. Hill).

103. Acropolis Museum 1340, 1342, 1343; H. Schrader et al, *Die archaischen Marmobildwerke der Akropolis*, 1939, pp. 387-390, plates 198-200; H. Payne and G.M. Young, *Archaic Marble Sculpture from the Acropolis*, 1936, pp. 47, 50, plates 127, 128; M. Brouskari, *Mouseion Akropoleos* ('The Acropolis Museum'), Athens 1974, pp. 54, 63, fig. 107.

104. Mertens, *Der Tempel von Segesta, op. cit.*, p. 49. For the Parthenon, see Dinsmoor, *Architecture*, vol. 48, 1923, p. 243; and J.J. Coulton, *Greek Architects at Work, op. cit.*, p. 64.

105. Gruben[1], pp. 230, 274.

106. See above, note 33.

107. Gruben[1], p. 167. There are, however, doubts as to the applicability of this view as far as the 4:9 ratio of the general dimensions of the stylobate are concerned, since there is a difference of a few centimetres which is not without significance. See above, note 37.

108. Dinsmoor (*op. cit.*, p. 242) hypothesises that apart from the lower drums (two per columns) which had been part of the Pre-parthenon, all the other drums were also already in situ. Indeed, he gives a figure of 96 drums for those of the first category and 336 for the others. Recent research has revealed that a large number of semi-dressed column capitals were also on the site already, for the same purpose (each weighing 11 tons).

109. See note 29, above, and *Meleti* 1, pp. 44ff. See also M. Korres, 'The Geological Factor in Ancient Greek Architecture', *The Engineering Geology of Ancient Works, Monuments and Historical Sites*, (P.G. Marinos, G.C. Koukis, eds.), vol. 3, Rotterdam 1988, pp. 1779-1793.

110. C. Weickert, *Studien zur Kunstgeschichte des 5 Jh. V. Chr.* II, Abhandlungen der Deutschen Akademie des Wissenshaften zu Berlin, Phil. hist. klasse, 1950, pp. 6ff; Bundgaard, *op. cit.*, pp. 63ff; R. Carpenter, *The Architects of the Parthenon*, Harmondsworth 1970, p. 111; G. Lavas, *Altgriechisches Temenos, Baukörper und Raumbildung*, Basle 1974, p. 108; H. Knell, *Perikleische Baukunst*, Darmstadt 1979, p. 14. According to B. Wesenberg (*AM* 97, 1982, pp. 116ff), the starting point for the composition of the temple was not the cella or the Parthenon proper, but the peristyle. According to the same author (*op. cit.*, p. 112), the theory that Pheidias had a global influence on the temple – and even on its sculpture – is groundless.

111. According to rough estimates made by this author, this hypothetical larger hexastyle temple would have had columns 25% thicker than those of the octastyle actually built; they would also have been 15% taller, making them 80% more massive. The architrave slabs would have been 35-40% longer, thus more than doubling their mass, and so on.

112. Penrose[1], p. 16, and note 109, above.

113. See J.F. Bommelaer, 'Les colonnes du Parthénon, motifs de leur anomalie', *Le dessin d'Architecture dans les Sociétés Antiques*, Strasbourg 1985, pp. 123-134 and in particular fig. 6. For an opposite view, see Bundgaard, *Parthenon, op. cit.*, figs. 38, 39, and Dinsmoor, *Architecture of Ancient Greece, op. cit.*, p. 161, and the same author, *Architecture*, vol. 48, 1923, p. 243, where the fullest account of the phenomenon is given. See also note 77, above. In the case of the pediment, it could be said that the increase in its height as a result of an increase in the number of columns and not of their height would cause the ratio of its surface to the total area of the facade (that is, its visual weight) to increase by the number of columns, as by the numbers 3, 5, 7 and 9, respectively, for a tetrastyle, hexastyle, octastyle and decastyle facade if the intercolumniation and the height of the columns was constant in each case. However, in order partly to moderate the increase in the pediment, the increase in the number of columns was usually combined with contraction of the intercolumniation and an increase in the height of the columns. In the temple of Hephaestus the proportion of the facade occupied by the pediment (without the sime) is 11%. With columns of a similar order, the figure for the Parthenon would have been 15.4%; in reality, however, it is only 13%, a reduction which is primarily due to the denser arrangement and greater height of the columns and, secondarily, to the slightly more acute angle of the sides of the pediment.

114. G. Lavas, *Altgriechisches Temenos, op. cit.*, p. 110; the same author, 'Tholos Bauten', *op. cit.*, p. 39.

115. The entablature should also certainly be counted among the features which help to 'hold' the pteroma; as a rule, its inner surface was the same size as the outer surface.

116. This classic theory was advanced primarily by Michaelis (*Der Parthenon*, pp. 25-27), and has been followed by most scholars down to the present day. See also G. Roux, *op. cit.*, p. 306, and note 3 above. Furtwängler (*Meisterwerke der griechischen Plastik*, 1893, pp. 172ff) held a different view, believing that the west chamber must have had a religious function.

117. *AJA* 16, 1912, plate 9.

118. *JdI* 43, 1928, p.89, plates 34 and 35; *AJA* 51, 1947, pp. 109-151; *JHS* 80, 1960, pp. 127-157.

119. See above, notes 75, 79, 80, 81.

120. M. Nilsson, *Geschichte der Griechischen Religion*[3], 1967-74; W. Burkert, *Homo Necans*, University of California Press 1983.

121. Usually, the width of the interior of the pronaos is manifestly greater than the distance between the columns of the portico.

122. Weickert, *op. cit.*, p. 6; Gruben[3], p. 171; Lavas, *Altgriechische Temenos, op. cit.*, p. 108; Korres, *Parthenon-Kongress*, p. 53.

123. *Meleti* 1, pp. 13, 28.

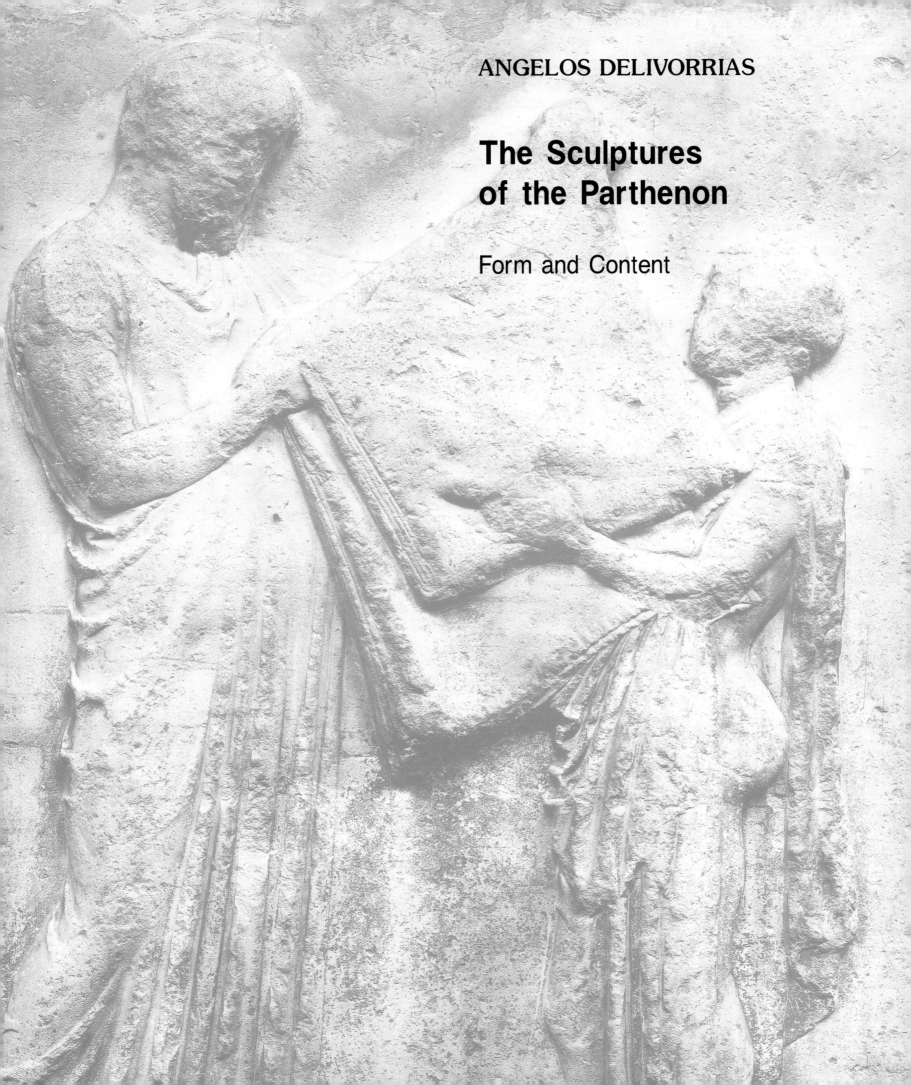

ANGELOS DELIVORRIAS

The Sculptures of the Parthenon

Form and Content

In order to appreciate the cohesion of the ornamental forms of the Parthenon (or rather, their sequentiality) – that is, in order to experience the aesthetic uniqueness and functional role of the sculptures in the organic constitution of the monument – we must first examine the internal relationship between the Parthenon as an act of architectural creation and the rock of the Acropolis. This relationship it is which, apart from giving us a reassuring sense of security as to the static solidity of the building, also provides a more inward certainty: that no matter how the building's axis of meaning may appear to aim high at heavenly co-ordinates, its foundations do in fact lose themselves in the depths of the primordial and unadulterated roots of earthly reality – whence, indeed, it draws the stamina that has allowed it to withstand the ages.

The Acropolis rock is not only the basic geophysical component of the Athens basin. It is also the predominant symbolic form taken by the historicity of the surrounding area; something of a crystallisation of Athenian self-awareness of the indissoluble bond that linked the indigenous nature of their origins with the blessed land of Attica and the mandates of their historical existence. Even today, the rock exudes perceptible sanctity; forged in the consciousness of time, that sanctity recalls to mind the duty of freedom interwoven with the necessity of law, the optimistic message that man is the measure of all things, and the lesson of tragic destiny which determines the sphere of hubris and the permissible. The harmonisation of sensation with knowledge, of ethos with boldness and virtue, of the practical and theoretical approaches to things, of aethetics and poetics; revolutionary inquiries; the power of the imagination to create form and the validity of traditional commitments; the equity of spirit and matter – those are the ideas and values which, in their interrelation, were tried and tested on the Acropolis in order to compose mankind's most valuable experience.

There can be no doubt that the Acropolis itself was taken into consideration as a crucial element during the designing of the architectural work which crowns it, so as to endow that building with the eternal value of solid foundations and also with continuous, vitalising communication with the inexhaustible forces of the Attic soil. We can be sure, too, that it represents one of the two axes around which the allusive references in the ornamental figures of the Parthenon evolve dialectically – and this applies equally to those figures which the current receptiveness of learned thought can easily comprehend, and to those which wide-ranging intellectual sensitivity will continue through the future to track down in the endless circles of interpretative elaboration. Inexhaustible, too, is the content of the messages which the centuries have recorded in its layers, dating from as far back as the dark years of the Bronze Age when the patron goddess of the Athenians first began to haunt the rock as the protectress par excellence of every acropolis and Mycenean palace. And it was from her ill-fated union with Hephaestus that the first mythical king of Athens was born here, shortly before the dawn of Athenian history, as we can trace out in the poetic memory of Homer and the stratigraphy of the Greek past.

On the rock of the Acropolis, Myth and Reality together wove some of their finest incidents, from the stormy confrontation between Athena and Poseidon over which of them was to rule Attica to Theseus' victorious counter-attack on the Amazons and the dramatic self-sacrifice of Codrus when the designs of the Dorian invaders were thwarted. The period of the Pisistratid tyranny, with the stigma it left on the Greek consciousness, and the

100

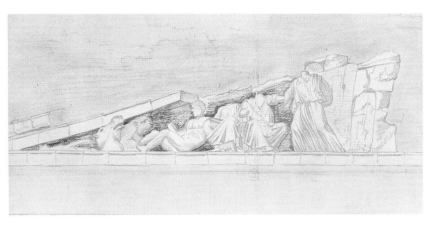

1. J. Carrey, drawing of the left side of the east pediment, 1674. Source: The Carrey Drawings of the Parthenon Sculptures, T. Bowie, D. Thimme (eds.), London 1971.

2. J. Carrey, drawing of the right side of the east pediment, 1674. Source: The Carrey Drawings of the Parthenon Sculptures, op. cit.

triumphant victory of democracy, the purification of the site and its fresh desecration during the ruinous attacks of the Persians are, of course, connected with the self-awareness of the Athenians of the 5th century BC but also interpret the more general recognition of the significance of the Acropolis – in other words, the manner in which its renown has echoed down subsequent ages. For that reason, the emotional charge still emitted by the core of the rock is not capable of reception only by those in tune with the mentality of antiquity, as we can see at other great moments in Greek history; suffice it, for example, to remember the significance of the ripping down of the German flag during the difficult years of the Occupation.

Yet if the rock of the Acropolis constitutes one directly perceptible point of reference for an understanding of the mythological scenes that ornament the Parthenon, projecting their content on to the human level, there is also another rock – imagined, this time – which serves as a second axis to raise associative connotations to a much higher level. This is the rock of Mt Olympus, the ideal location of the divine world, which contains, *inter alia*, the conditions for the miraculous birth of the goddess who

would protect the city of the Athenians. The composition on the east pediment, depicting the birth of Athena on the summit of Olympus, must reflect the significance of a similar miracle which took place around the Acropolis and proved to be equally eternal: the birth of an ideal form of government by means of the co-existence of the components of a community and the fruitful rivalry involved in their equality as elements. That is why the concepts of Athens, Athena and Democracy were more or less identical in content, as we can deduce from the entire intellectual and artistic production of the 5th century BC and as Evelyn B. Harrison has emphasised with epigrammatic clarity.

The dimension of the eternal which surrounds the birth of Athena on the east pediment of the Parthenon takes perceptible form in the 'epiphany' of the entire Greek Pantheon – the assembly, that is, of the gods of Olympus, who as a body look on as the event depicted unfolds, honouring it with their presence and integrating it into the sphere of the sublime. In a manner corresponding to the uniqueness of the theme, the dimension of the eternal is

3. The Madrid relief; a drawing developing the scene. Source: F. Brommer, Die Skulpturen der Parthenon-Giebel, *Mainz 1963.*

4. *The east pediment: Helios and his chariot (A-C); London, British Museum.*

refracted and made perceptible thanks to the genius of the concept and the mastery of the rendering of the theme at a moment in time that forms part of the cosmological rhythm of a universal harmony marked eloquently by the rising of the Sun on one side and the setting of the Moon on the other. This exquisite thematic device, repeated on the north metopes of the temple and in the ornamentation of the cult statue, but above all flanking the birth of Aphrodite on the pedestal of the chryselephantine statue of Zeus at Olympia, has rightly been seen as bearing the personal stamp of the genius called Pheidias.

Of the sculptures on the east pediment, only a small part had escaped the ravages of time when Jacques Carrey drew them in 1674 (figs. 1, 2). Without the invaluable testimony of Pausanias (I, 24, 5) it would thus be im-

5. *The east pediment: head of a horse from the chariot of Selene (O); London, British Museum.*

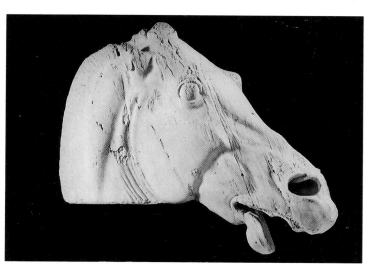

possible to make even the most tenuous hypotheses about the original content of the composition. Equally, any attempt to reconstruct its particular nature would be doomed to failure without the scanty examples provided by the earlier iconographic tradition of the myth. Here it should be noted that the painstaking efforts of archaeologists to discover a few fragments, even, of the lost central figures enhance our hopes that the large gap between the two surviving extremities of the scene may one day be filled. It seems certain that with the constant increase in the amount of surviving material the current wide range of views – expressed almost every day, with ever-fresher design proposals – about how the continuity of the broken composition might be restored, and the infinite variety of theoretical correlations which support those views will, over time, condense into more and more solid and final conclusions.

The scene on the east pediment of the Parthenon develops – and is to be read – from left to right, in accordance with certain unshakeable laws and with a dialectical correspondence in the organisation of the units made up of the individual figures, just as the concepts flow across the canvas of a philosophical text. In this manner, as the sun-god Helios (A) and his four-horse chariot (B-C) emerge from the waves of the Ocean (fig. 4), they correspond in compositional and logical terms to the setting of the Moon (Selene, N), which rounds off the pageant when her own four-horse chariot sinks at the ultimate edge of the earth (figs. 5, 6). The first and last figures in the pedimental composition, with their celestial nature and their symbolic implications, define not only a point in universal time but also the dimensions of the imaginary space in which the action is unfolding. They are followed by Dionysus (D, fig. 7), on the left, and Aphrodite (M, fig. 8), on the right – the two deities bound up more than any of the others with earthly things, with the world of men. They watch the events with differing degrees of attention.

Recognition of the other figures and reconstruction of those which have disappeared from the centre of the pediment are matters of personal belief. These questions seem likely to be the subject of continued debate, and with no hope of unanimity among researchers as long as we lack the basic co-ordinates of the organisational programme on which the design of the scene and the articulation of its ideological objectives were based. As for the difficulties of the problem of interpretation, we should devote more detailed attention to the meaning of the two female figures shown directly next to Dionysus (E-F), brought to life by the moving warmth of the intimacy easy to discern between them (fig. 9). These figures could, of course, be identified as the divine pair of Demeter and Persephone were it not for the fact that the chests on which they are sitting, seen as Eleusinian baskets (kistai) with clear allusions to the specific locality, would be misplaced on Mt Olympus at the time of the birth of Athena. Still more intractable are the problems caused in any case by the presence of Persephone for the consistency of the chronology of the scene, since it would involve a unique deviation from the relevant iconographic tradition. On the other hand, the emotional relationship between both

6. The east pediment: Selene (N); Acropolis Museum. Photograph: German Archaeological Institute, Athens.

7. The east pediment: Dionysus (D); London, British Museum.

103

8. The east pediment: figures K, L and M; London, British Museum.

9. The east pediment: figures E, F and G; London, British Museum.

10. I. Beyer: reconstruction of the east pediment. Source: I. Beyer, Athenische Mitteilungen *89, 1974.*

11. K. Jeppesen: reconstruction of the east pediment. Source: K. Jeppesen, Parthenon-Kongress Basel, E. Berger (ed.), *vol. 1, Mainz 1984.*

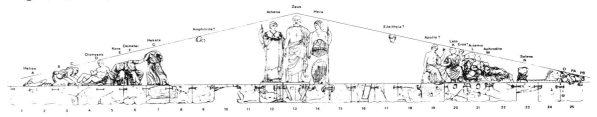

12. O. Palagia: reconstruction of the east pediment (drawing by K. Iliakis). Source: O. Palagia, The Pediments of the Parthenon, *Leiden 1993 (= Monumenta Graeca et Romana VII).*

13. E. Berger: reconstruction of the east pediment. Source: E. Berger, Antike Kunst *20, 1977.*

14. E.B. Harrison: reconstruction of the east pediment. Source: E.B. Harrison, American Journal of Archaeology *71, 1967.*

15. *The east pediment: male torso (H); Acropolis Museum. Photograph: German Archaeological Institute, Athens.*

figures and the female figure which immediately follows them (G), which is hastening to give them the news of the divine birth (fig. 9), conveys to us the impression that the trio of figures is compositionally unified and demands that our search turn in a different interpretative direction.

Divine trios such as the Graces, the Hours, the Nymphs and the Fates are often shown as the guarantors of blessings bestowed upon the order of the world in scenes showing the birth of gods. The Fates, in particular, are depicted in the neo-Attic reliefs which repeat a 4th century scene of the birth of Athena, perhaps from the pedestal of an important cult statue and certainly not from the lost central part of the east pediment of the Parthenon, as used to be thought (fig. 3). According to this line of thinking, however, the corresponding female figures on the other side of the pedimental triangle (K-L) could be a rendering of another trio rather than a depiction of Hestia and Dione or Leto and Artemis. This would involve the addition of a figure moving in a contrary direction, or even the organic incorporation of Aphrodite (M) into the same unit of meaning (fig. 8). Such an arrangement would not be precluded *a priori* by the Athenian cult of the goddess of love, nor is it ruled out by the testimony of Pausanias (I, 19, 2) to her very close connection with the goddesses of destiny, of whom, it must have been widely believed, she was the 'most senior'. These reservations are applicable, of course, only if the composition of the east pediment and its fundamental meaning were predicated on spatial as well as chronological unity; I myself believe that such spatial unity is a characteristic of all the individual the-

matic cycles of which the ornamental programme of the monument is composed.

As we have already noted, all the attempts made so far to reconstruct the lost figures of the east pediment have relied on the large-scale development of subjective judgements as to the system behind the layout of the composition and the internal rationale of the mythological interaction of the figures. They also rely on the equally ambitious development of views as to the decoding of the traces which the figures have left on the horizontal cornice – a matter of some complexity with controversial interpretative approaches whose presentation, even in simplified form, would disorientate rather than help the readers of this text. Nevertheless, the central figure of Zeus was most probably not standing, as Immo Beyer hypothesised using arguments drawn from the example of the east pediment at Olympia (fig. 10) and as Kristian Jeppesen (fig. 11) and more recently Olga Palagia (fig. 12) continue to believe. This is not only because none of the known depictions of the scene shows Zeus standing, but also because the mechanism of meaning at work in the scene could never permit it. It strikes me that to move the thematic core of the scene into the open air, with its protagonist seated on a rock as proposed by Ernst Berger (fig. 13), and not on his throne in the palace of the gods as argued by Evelyn B. Harrison (fig. 14) and more recently advocated by George Despinis (fig. 16), causes still greater problems. Indeed, I believe that before long it will be proved once and for all that the Zeus of the eastern pediment was depicted turning in the direction of the rising sun, where the inviolable 'law of hierarchy' dictates that we reconstruct the fully-armed, new-born Athena. However, the fact that the central items in the theme must have been arranged in such a manner will only be confirmed when other fragments of the enthroned divine figure – apart from the colossal left hand with the thunderbolt discovered by Despinis – come to light.

If Athena was actually shown on the left side of the pedimental triangle and not in the position hypothesised

16. *G. Despinis: reconstruction of the central figures on the east pediment (drawing by Y. Kayas). Source: G. Despinis,* Partheno-neia, *Athens 1982.*

by Harrison, Berger and Despinis (figs. 13, 14, 16) among other researchers, then Hephaestus, the second most important personage in the theme must have occupied a corresponding place to the right, as Erika Simon initially suspected (though her ultimate version of the design differs). However this may be, the much-discussed male torso which has repeatedly been connected with the figure of Hephaestus (fig. 15) must belong to some deity located towards the right-hand extremity of the pediment: to Poseidon, perhaps, and certainly not to Ares, whose physique would have demanded a much more obviously youthful appearance. The reconstruction of the figure proposed by Despinis, in a position at some distance from the centre of the composition (fig. 16), once more fails to correspond to the small size of the torso, strengthening the arguments put forward by Olga Palagia for dismissing the figure from the east pediment altogether. I myself would prefer to continue to regard the figure as a candidate for inclusion in the pediment, at least as long as its movement cannot be interpreted and, as a consequence, the decoding of its content is difficult. Despite the arguments of Jeppesen (fig. 11), it would be hard for the religious context of the myth and its ideological distillation to support the attribution of this torso to a kneeling Atlas; this quite apart from the more general imbalance which it would introduce into the system of proportions of the composition, a disadvantage shared by all the other reconstructions proposed to date.

In the case of the gaps which remain empty between the central and outermost figures of the east pediment, future research will have to choose between two solutions which have been offered – although the magnitude of the genius which conceived and designed the composition is far from precluding the existence of a third, unthinkable for our level of knowledge today and our scope for hypothetical speculation. In order to achieve in visual terms the harmonious agreement of proportions in the balanced blend of figures portrayed – an agreement which, despite the spectacular variety of the poses and the large scale of the movement, is hindered by the compulsory constraint of incorporation of the scene into the triangular ground of the pediment – the areas on either side of the centre must have been occupied either by enthroned figures, as earlier scholars assumed and as some still argue today, or by chariots, as Werner Fuchs proposed, following the example of the composition on the west pediment (fig. 18). Regardless of these alternatives, according to the critique of George Despinis, the bodies of horses used by Immo Beyer for his reconstruction (fig. 10) – which had a direct effect on the reconstructions of Berger, Jeppesen and Simon (figs. 11, 13) – cannot have come from the pedimental decoration of the monument. In both cases, the scene would, however, have been rounded off with

17. The east pediment: fragments of a robed figure; Acropolis Museum. Photograph: German Archaeological Institute, Athens.

18. J. Carrey: drawing of the left side of the west pediment, 1674. Source: The Carrey Drawings of the Parthenon Sculptures, op. cit.

the figures necessary to complete the meaning of the theme. For Despinis, the essential presence of Eileithyia, goddess of childbirth, is confirmed by a fragment of a female hand with a torch, long known to archaeologists. Despinis is also to be credited with the correct interpretation of a part of the lyre of Apollo, another figure present. It is hard to recognise Hera in the monumental robed figure restored to us by Max Wegner's conjunction of two large fragments (fig. 17). Identification of the figure depends on the controversial restoration of its original height and on the ascertaining of its position in the pediment, which according to Despinis was quite a long way from the central unit in the scene (fig. 16).

This brief review of only some of the proposals made for reconstruction of the east pediment will, I am sure, have helped readers to realise that the problems relating to the pediment go far beyond the interpretation of individual figures or questions relating to the reconstruction of the enigmatic composition. They touch upon a whole series of associated issues, of a technical nature. For

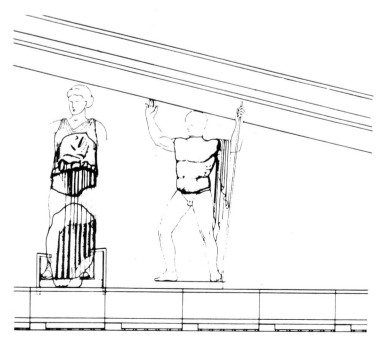

19. G. Despinis: reconstruction of the Wegner robed figure and male torso H (drawing by Y. Kayas). Source: Despinis, op. cit.

20. The east pediment: section of a head with veil; Acropolis Museum. Photograph: German Archaeological Institute, Athens.

N O P Q R S T U V W

21. J. Carrey: drawing of the right side of the west pediment, 1674. Source: The Carrey Drawings of the Parthenon Sculptures, op. cit.

22. The east pediment: section of a female figure; Acropolis Museum. Photograph: German Archaeological Institute, Athens.

example, the grooves which according to Despinis were used to secure the pedestal of Wegner's robed figure on the horizontal cornice by means of large iron hooks (fig. 19) are notable for the unusual roughness of their execution. This is in sharp contrast with the particularly careful workmanship of similar details on some of the sculptures of the west pediment and in many other carvings of the 5th century BC. We cannot fail, for instance, to be impressed by the care which was devoted to dressing the tympanum side of the horses pulling the chariots of Athena and Poseidon, or by the surface of the joint on a marble which Brian F. Cook has attributed to the Cecrops group (fig. 25). The suspicion that the grooves of the robed figure may have been the result of subsequent repairs is reinforced not only by the fact that the hooks project beyond the front of the statue (fig. 19) in a manner impermissible in the aesthetics of the Classical period, but also by the identification of specific repairs to the structural elements of the pediment. One of the horizontal cornice blocks was certainly replaced at a later (though as yet undetermined) time, and apart from the fact that this would inevitably have meant the moving of the sculptures above, it also allows us to hypothesise extensive repairs to other parts of the composition.

The grooves on the neck of the first of the seated figures on the right of the pediment (K, fig. 8) and on the much-debated colossal veiled head which, as is more or less universally accepted, ought to be associated with Wegner's robed figure (fig. 17) and to which Alexandros Mantis recently added new parts (fig. 20), are similarly rough-and-ready. Attribution of the head to the pedimental composition is not disputed, regardless of whether it originally belonged to a seated or a standing figure or, consequently, of the correctness of an idea once advanced by this author that it might be ascribed to the figure of Zeus. To be absolutely honest, however, I have to say that I do not regard as final the arguments on which rejection of the association of the head with Zeus relied, not so much because they fail to answer a series of interlinked questions as because they lead almost inevitably to a compositionally impossible reconstruction of the central figure in the pediment flanked – without organisational flow or the necessary respect for the principles of the smooth development of proportions – by two confused groups of seated and enthroned deities.

In relation to the problem of the repairs which, it seems, were done to the east pediment, we should note here the large section of the legs of a female figure in a peculiar stance, which Max Wegner ascribed to the west pediment (fig. 22). This is because the presence of grooves similar to those on the pieces described above probably mean that it should be connected with the east pediment (as Ernst Berger and Evelyn B. Harrison correctly suspected), although reconstruction of the figure to which it belonged would be difficult to undertake without fresh and additional information. Furthermore, there are a number of other unidentified fragments which are unmistakably of the quality devoted to the Parthenon but which for the time being, at least, cannot be ascribed with certainty to one pedimental composition or the other. These include the famous Laborde head (fig. 24), many of the worn sculptures identified at various times by Ernst Berger and Maria Brouskari, and all the pieces which are constantly being added to an ever-growing repository of fragments from the sculptural decoration of the building.

The quality of the stylistic value of the composition and its content is much more eloquent than its original appearance, despite the fact that the various attempts to link individual pieces of sculpture with the great names of 5th century Athenian art do not stand up to close examination. There is no doubt that the combination of an unparalleled concept with great refinement in elaboration, the admirable organisation of the masses and the inspired design of the structure all transcend by far the aesthetic experience which research can gain of the great creations of the Classical period, known to us only from the frigid copies of the Romans. The strength and grace of the physique of Dionysus (D, fig. 7), and the self-evident air of ease in the development of its movement would be hard to parallel in similar works not only of the same period, but of any other. This applies also to the vigorous shaping of the two female figures of the next group (E-F, fig. 9), to the metal-like sharpness of the folds in their garments, and to the moving tenderness which emerges from the immortalisation of their fleeting inner communication. Equally invigorating is the flow of the cloth in the symphony in movement which is the next figure, with the mantle blowing back from its shoulders (G, fig. 9). But the art of the Parthenon touches the limits of the potential available to expression in the group of three female figures in the right corner of the east pediment (K-M, fig. 8). Here the grandeur, predominance and inspired projection of a physical ideal are blended with the fan-shaped development of the morphology of the attitudes and the contrapuntal composition of the relief found in movement, with the melodious warmth of an incredibly human intimacy, and with a rhythmic reduction of the working of folds in the garments which is not to be found in the past of the visual experiences of earlier times or in the future of the expressive experimentation of later periods. The severity of Selene's garment (N, fig. 6) prepares the viewer for a thrilling experience: the blinding flash of humanity triggered when we catch sight of her horse (O, fig. 5), which exerts the same overpowering force on the human mental world today as it did in the time of Goethe.

23. E. Simon: reconstruction of the central figures in the west pediment (drawing by M. Balestrazzi). Source: E. Simon, Tainia, Festschrift für R. Hampe, Mainz am Rhein 1980.

The west pediment of the Parthenon had survived in much better condition than the east pediment when it was drawn by Jacques Carrey (figs. 18, 21). That was before the destruction wrought by Morosini, which was responsible for the mutilation of such pedimental figures as have not vanished beyond recall. Thanks to Carrey's drawings, it would be possible even without the account of Pausanias (I, 24, 5) to recognise the theme depicted: the contest between Athena and Poseidon over the land of Attica, with the local heroes looking on as judges of the divine gifts offered, the olive tree and the well-spring. In contrast, it would have been much more difficult to ascertain the resolution of the dramatic clash between the two divinities – that is, the termination of their confrontation with the thunderbolt hurled by Zeus – without the

24. *The Laborde head; Paris, the Louvre. Photograph: Giraudon.*

logical proof offered by Erika Simon, based on the details of the myth, the scene on a hydria from Pella and a rare combination of academic skill and mental sensitivity (fig. 23).

The composition of the west pediment corresponds in many ways to that of the east pediment and is a clear dialectical response to it, in that the miracle of divine birth portrayed on the east pediment reaches its semantic completion here with a wonder of equal power. The 'birth' of the olive tree – that is, the burgeoning of Athena's symbol par excellence – is depicted as the invaluable divine gift which endowed the Athenians with the blessings of food and light. The scene is invested with the prestige of the presence of their forefathers, just as the birth of the patron goddess is honoured with the consent of the Greek pantheon. Indeed, it would not be too bold to hypothesise that, apart from revealing a profound awareness of the religious roots of Athens, lost in the distant past of tree-worship, the honour done to Athena was intended as a stimulus to the historic memory, a deliberate invocation of the stamina of the sacred tree, so sorely tried at the time of the Persian invasion, and of the new miracle of its rebirth.

From the dizzying heights of the cliffs of Olympus, these burdens of allusion and codified messages in the use of myth as parable thus bring us to earth on the rock of the Acropolis – a human space. The emotion is a thrilling one, and it derives not only from a direct reading of the topography of the two thematic nuclei but also from the lateral vistas of the context of the entire narrative plot. In other words, the absolutely divine, closed and inaccessible sphere determined by the east pediment contrasts with its praise, in effect, of the world of the heroes, the mythical forefathers of mankind – and not as spectators only, but as judges of the divine discourse in the centre of gravity of the theme. This heroic world, perceived as the connecting tissue in the interlayering of the human and divine elements, brings to mind once again – involuntarily – the famous axiom about man as the measure of all things. It is a unique moment in the history of civilisation; not without some degree of self-importance, it reflects the level of self-knowledge (or rather, self-awareness) which the Classical period in Athens had reached, and which was not, of course, capable of lasting for more than thirty years.

Among the best-preserved figures on the west pediment is Cephissus (A), recumbent in the extreme left corner. He is depicted with his muscular body expressively raised and turning as his attention is momentarily attracted by the happenings in the centre of the composition (fig. 26). The less well-preserved Callirhoe (W) in the right corner (fig. 28) would certainly have had a garment flowing restlessly from her shoulder, in a manner suited to the liquid mobility of the pose of her body. Of the two kneeling figures which came next to Cephissus and Callirhoe, only Ilissus (V) survived down to the time of Carrey, on the right-hand side of the pedimental triangle (fig. 27). Despite the damage which the statue has suffered since then, and the relentless corrosion of its marble skin, we still feel a stir of excitement at its plastic strength and polyphonic articulation of its condensed structure. Most of the figures which come between these statues and the chariots and charioteers of the two gods have been lost or have survived in varying degrees of completeness, and so the tracking down of new fragments and their ultimate reconstruction is possible only with the help of Carrey's drawings (figs. 18, 21). Here extremely valuable assistance is provided by the repetition of the composition, in miniature, on a Roman pediment from Eleusis showing the rape of Persephone, recently restored by Ruth Lindner (fig. 29). The Cecrops group (B-C) is repeated in this later work; until recently, it remained in its original position on the left side of the pediment, suffering the irreversible consequences of pollution by the murky atmosphere of Athens (fig. 25). A scattering of fragments and a severely damaged child's torso have been ascribed to the next group of two female figures and a youth (D-F). On the other side, Oreithyia and one of her twin son – Zetes or Calais – have survived in much better condition (P-R, fig. 32). This is a charming work, where the boundaries of inspiration have coincided with those of skill in the dressing of the marble. The vigorous female figure is

25. The west pediment: the Cecrops group (B-C); Acropolis Museum. Photograph: German Archaeological Institute, Athens.

26. The west pediment: Cephissus (A); London, British Museum.

shown as revelling in the cool breeze rustling the folds of her garment – a reminder in aesthetic terms of the invisible presence of Boreas, 'son-in-law' of the Athenians, and the decisive contribution which his support had made to the outcome of the Persian Wars. Next comes a group consisting of another female figure with a child on her lap (S-T), of which a large section has survived, and one more female figure (U) whose lower parts were recognised by Rhys Carpenter (fig. 31) despite the objections of Ernst Berger and, more recently, Olga Palagia. Frank Brommer attributes a piece to the lower section of another seated figure, also with a child, thus filling in the corresponding gap (U*) in Carrey's drawing (fig. 21).

Various puzzling fragments have from time to time been ascribed to the figure of Nike (Victory) driving the chariot of Athena (G), but it is difficult to see in them the mobility, expressiveness and grace of dress that so struck Carrey. The figure of Hermes (H), on the other hand, has survived in much better condition, especially since the discovery by George Despinis of the right thigh and its attachment to the torso of the statue (fig. 33). The reins of Poseidon's chariot were held by Amphitrite (O), one of the most powerful statues on the Parthenon (fig. 34). The winged female figure accompanying her (N) is of the same outstanding artistic standard, and – by analogy with the Hermes figure – must be identified as Iris, messenger of the gods (fig. 35). Of the horses which drew the chariots, we possess some heads and a considerable number of fragments of bodies, many of them recognised and reassembled by Jean Marcadé. We also have the torso of the 'native' with the serpentine body who, as Kristian

27. The west pediment: Ilissus (V); Acropolis Museum. Photograph: German Archaeological Institute, Athens.

28. The west pediment: Callirhoe (W); London, British Museum.

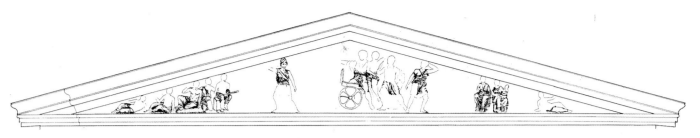

29. *R. Lindner: reconstruction of the Eleusinian pediment.* Source: *R. Lindner,* Jahrbuch des Deutschen Archäologischen Instituts *97, 1982.*

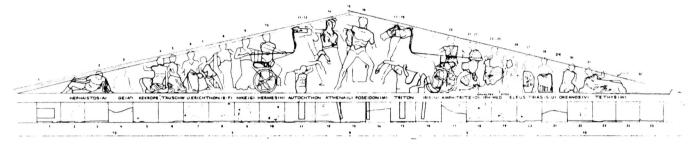

30. *K. Jeppesen: reconstruction of the west pediment.* Source: *K. Jeppesen,* Acta Archaeologica *34, 1963.*

Jeppesen has proved, served to support the horses of Athena, while those of Poseidon were held up by a Triton (figs. 30, 36). There is no doubt that this ingenious solution to a problem of pure static engineering – as dictated by the necessity for compositional and aesthetic justification within the content of the scene – can only be interpreted as the concept of the greatest sculptor of all time. Here, of course, I am referring once again to Pheidias, the prime exponent of the ideals of the Athenian state in the time of Pericles, whose inspiration can be detected even in the less elaborate sculptures on the monument.

The two central figures, in their explosive dimension, leave deep imprints on the composition of the west pediment. Thanks to the painstaking research of Maria Brouskari and an important discovery by Judith Binder, the figure of Athena (L) is drawing ever nearer to completion (fig. 37). Yet despite the optimism of the promises that one day the statue will be restored, as guaranteed by the continuing detective work to identify fresh pieces, I cannot resist the temptation to take this opportunity to emphasise how disgraceful, from every point of view, it is that the sculptures of the Parthenon should be so brutally parcelled out between the British Museum and the Acropolis Museum. I should also make it clear that the force in my tone is not at all the result of influence from the controversial Greek 'campaign' to regain a lost national symbol, but rather of unshakeable logic dictated more generally, I believe, by an ethical position towards the integrity of works of art. Indeed, the figure of Athena is direct evidence of the difficulty involved in reconstructing a statue when its torso is in London and its head, extremities and the other surviving parts of its original form continue to be in Athens. We can see, too, how much delay there will be in the recognition of new fragments when all the rest of the material to which they belong is not as-

sembled in the same place. I pass over, as self-evident, the crucial requirement for the unity of all the component parts of the same artistic creation – that is, of a living organism. No legal or other pretexts can justify the hacking up of that creation, in accordance with principles which were embedded in the human consciousness as far back as the time of Solomon. This also applies, of course, to

31. *The west pediment: section of a female figure (U); Acropolis Museum. Photograph: German Archaeological Institute, Athens.*

32. The west pediment: Oreithyia (P); London, British Museum.

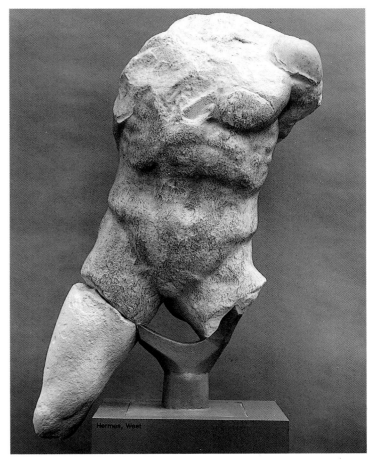

33. The west pediment: Hermes (H) with the thigh restored to its position; London, British Museum. Photograph by G. Despinis.

34. The west pediment: Amphitrite (O); London, British Museum. A plaster cast with the thigh restored to its position. Photograph: German Archaeological Institute, Athens.

35. The west pediment: Iris (N); London, British Museum.

the rugged figure of Poseidon (M), whose torso is shared out between the Acropolis Museum and the British Museum (fig. 38). Scholars are not unanimous about the other pieces ascribed to this statue, and especially about those on which Werner Fuchs based his reconstruction of the legs. However, it does seem certain that the god of the sea had one foot on the rocky projection from which welled his spring of water, leaving the axis of the scene dominated by the olive tree, Athena's gift to the Athenians, which was probably worked in metal rather than marble.

The pedimental scenes on the Parthenon would not have been complete, for the aesthetics of the Classical period, without the two acroterial compositions which crown the pedimental triangles. In earlier times, scholars divided a limited number of fragments of floral motifs among these two compositions. Today, they are ascribed only to the two central floral acroteria, outsized tracery constructions of superb elegance and stone-mason's skill. The side acroteria can be assumed to have been female figures in motion, which were most probably in harmony with the meaning both of the pedimental scene on the east side and with that of the west. No trace of these figures has, however, come to light so far. Our picture of the central acroteria is a much clearer one, thanks to the continuing researches of Ernst Berger, although his recon-

37. The west pediment: Athena (L); British Museum and Acropolis Museum. Plaster cast. Photograph: German Archaeological Institute, Athens.

struction is considerably hampered by the constraint of height, which under no circumstances can have been less than the maximum height of the pediments (fig. 13).

A similar internal correspondence – that is, the conception of the design for the two pedimental compositions and the acroteria above them – is to be found in the intersecting pairs of axes of meaning which penetrate the nuclei of the thematic cycles of the rest of the sculptural ornamentation. Although scholars disagree as to the interpretation of individual details, this similarity can be seen, to begin with, in the four large-scale mythological units depicted on the metopes of all four sides of the building and in their contrapuntal interaction. On the east or 'divine' side of the Parthenon, 14 metopes develop the narrative of the battle of the gods against the Giants, a conflict in which Athena played a major part in ensuring victory for the gods (fig. 39). Of course, the reliefs of the Battle of the Giants were chiselled off in the Early Christ-

36. The west pediment: torso of an 'indigenous Athenian' from beneath the chariot of Athena; Acropolis Museum. Photograph: German Archaeological Institute, Athens.

116

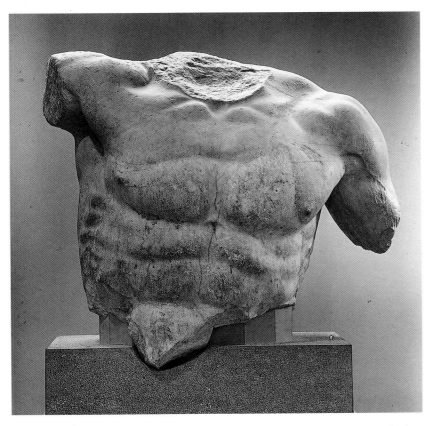

38. The west pediment: Poseidon (M); Acropolis Museum. A plaster cast of the section in the British Museum has been added to the sculpture. Photograph: German Archaeological Institute, Athens.

(Victory) and Zeus in metopes 1, 2, 4 and 8, respectively. Nonetheless, if the male head discovered by George Despinis in the basement of the National Archaeological Museum does in fact belong to these metopes, then it is not at all impossible that other fragments have survived. In such a case, it seems almost certain that our picture of the components of the composition will gradually become clearer in the future. Even in their mutilated form, the east metopes of the Parthenon clearly convey the significance of the myth they depict – a myth whose implications go far beyond the sphere of the divine, as is also the case with the theme of the east pediment. That is because the consolidation of world order symbolised by the defeat of the Giants is derived from the more general co-ordinates of the harmony of the universe. Indeed, the frequent use of the theme for the purposes of propaganda, with its allegorical reference to the results of the barbaric Persian invasion, is much more eloquent as a parable in magnifying the role of Athena, Athens and the democratic form of government than any other encomium would have been. However, while the skilful appropriation by Athenian policy of what was a panhellenic myth is also to be seen in the choice of it to adorn the Panathenaic robe, the presence of Heracles as Athenian hero marks out the limits of this approach, if not a secret wish to subjugate the world of the Peloponnese to that of Athens.

ian era, when the temple of the patron goddess of Athens was converted into a church of Our Lady, and so were the metopes on all the other sides except the south. Consequently, it would have been impossible to 'read' the fragments of these carvings and reconstruct the sequence of episodes without the exhaustive labour of tracing the surviving outlines undertaken by Camillo Praschniker and all the others who at different times have worked to decode the metopes. However, since we are still a long way from a generally accepted interpretation, it is with considerable hesitation that I mention the recognition of Heracles in metope 13 and the relative unanimity which applies to the identification of Hermes, Dionysus, Athena with Nike

The 14 metopes of the west or 'earthly' side of the building – a side which is more closely linked to the human world and with the historical destiny of Athens in particular – portray the battle of the Athenians against the Amazons (fig. 40) in order to counterbalance the battle of the gods against the Giants. Here the leading role of Theseus is singled out not only by its narrative correspondence to that of Athena, but also by the clear contrast between it and the significance latent in the presence

39. M. Cox: drawings of the metopes on the east side. Source: J. Boardman and D. Finn, The Parthenon and its Sculptures, London 1985.

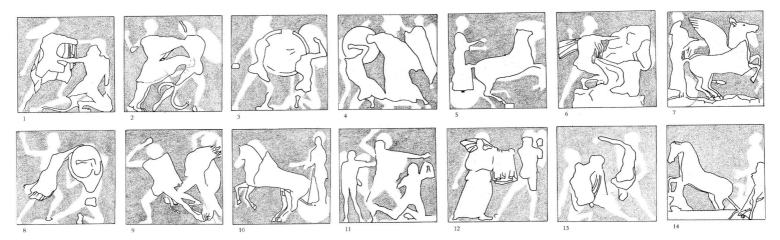

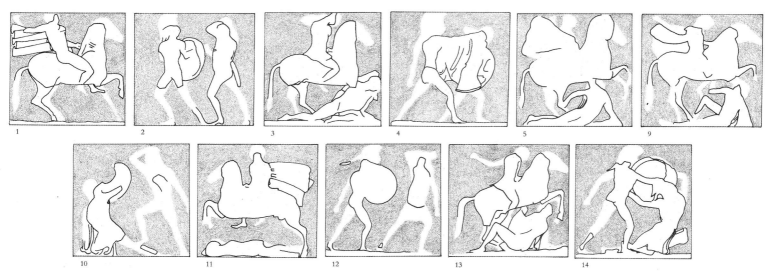

40. M. Cox: drawings of the metopes on the west side. Source: Boardman and Finn, op. cit.

of Heracles. The mythical founder of the Athenian form of government is hard to recognise among the mutilated figures on the chiselled-down metopes, the best preserved of which probably portrays Antiope, queen of the Amazons, on horseback (no. 1). However, such details of the garments as can be distinguished leave no room for doubt as to the identity of the theme, ruling out the hypothesis that the metopes might show some scene from the wars between the Greeks and the Persians. In any case, such direct references to historical events would be incompatible with the spirit of indirect statement which is more generally characteristic of the subjects chosen for the ornamentation of the Parthenon. In contrast, the symbolism contained in the scene showing the battle of the Amazons allows the emergence, projected on to the prestige of the mythical model, of the decisive importance of Athenian democracy for victory over the Persian invaders – that is, of its superiority over the forms of government of the other Greek cities.

Symbolism of a similar kind also emanates from the metopes of the north side. Only 13 of the 32 original metopes have survived, in such a state as to raise serious questions about the unity of the space and time in which they were articulated (fig. 42). Although it is difficult to deny that the main theme of the composition is the Fall of Troy, Erika Simon and José Dörig discern interpolated scenes from earlier episodes in the Trojan myth. I number myself among those who believe that metopes 1 and 29, showing Helios and Selene respectively, are in accordance with the theoretical principles which dictated the presence of those two figures on the east pediment of the temple and mark the beginning and end of a single narrative, outside the unfolding of which are only the gods of metopes 30-32, the instigators and, simultaneously, the

spectators of the Trojan drama. Consequently, metope 2 should be read as a scene of the Greeks preparing for their departure. During this period, Menelaus – probably accompanied by Odysseus (no. 24) – attempts to take revenge on Helen, who appeals to the cult statue of Athena and is eventually saved by the divine intervention of Aphrodite and Eros (no. 25). At the same time, Aeneas and his family manage to escape from the ruin of the city (no. 28). The link between the panhellenic myth and the Athenian past is achieved with the presence of Damophon and Acamas, the two sons of Theseus, who bring Aethra back to Athens. Although the composition has survived in too ruinous a state to permit final conclusions, it has been hypothesised that this incident, which would certainly be present in any Athenian version of the tale, is shown either on metope D (no. 23?) or metope 27. The last metope, no. 32, is undamaged and still in place, thanks to its misinterpretation by the Christians (fig. 41); it serves as a reminder of what the loss of those sculptures which are gone beyond recall means for the history of ancient Greek art.

For some unknown reason – perhaps because they were not directly visible, or because once again their subject was misunderstood by the early Christians – the 32 metopes of the south side of the Parthenon survived in perfect condition down to the time of Morosini. The explosion in the Turkish arsenal caused by the mortaring of the building in 1687 destroyed the central slabs, but these had already been drawn by Carrey (figs. 43, 49-56). Combined study of these drawings and the metopes which have since survived in relatively good condition – no. 1 in its original position (fig. 44), nos. 2-9 and 26-32 in London, no. 10 in Paris and no. 12 in the Acropolis Museum – or have been reassembled from their constituent fragments has led modern scholars, in particular, to a series of conflicting interpretations. It has been argued that, by way of contrast with the other sides of the temple, the south metopes consisted of two independent mythological cycles, with themes taken from the battle of the Lapiths and the Centaurs at either end and an unrelated narrative in the centre. According to Frank Brommer, this is an unknown local myth of Attica; Erika Simon and Martin Robertson believe it to have been the story of Ixion or Daedalus, respectively; Karl Schefold and José Dörig claim it as an episode in the genealogical myths of the Athenians; and Burkhardt Fehr sees in it the myth of Phaedra and Alceste. However, there seems little doubt that the work still being done by Alexandros Mantis, and the new fragments which he is constantly recognising – restoring many of the ruined slabs in a frequently spectacular manner – will eventually prove the unity of meaning of the south metopes. In the centre is the event which provoked the Battle of the Centaurs in Thessaly: the wedding of Perithoüs, among the guests at which was Theseus, who was to play an important part in the fight which followed. The rationale which governs the thematic unity of the scene was advanced by Evelyn B. Harrison and, very recently, by Ursula Höckmann, who, with great perspicacity, has shed much light on the enigmatic content of many individual episodes from these metopes and on their sequence of meaning. The decodification of the messages emanating from the metopes has proved as troublesome as the identification of their content. Although in the established view the depictions of the battle of the Lapiths and Centaurs frequent after the Persian wars reflect, in paradigmatic form, the punishment of the barbarians for their hubris, Ernst Berger discerns here a desire to project Athenian superiority in rivalry amongst the Greeks, for domestic consumption and for the purposes of political propaganda. I would like to point out that the confrontation which ends in the victory of human values over the bestial violence of powers without reason,

41. North metope no. 32: Athena and Hera. Photograph: German Archaeological Institute, Athens.

as the myth is principally expressed in this version on the Parthenon, is imbued with allusiveness on a number of levels which is intensified by the specific reference of the theme to the sanctity of the act of marriage.

Interpretative ambiguity is not the only factor which arrests our attention about the metopes of the south side. We are also fascinated by the fluctuations in the quality of their workmanship, which covers the entire range of skill and fluency from absolutely inspired art to the conventional, flat expression of the stylistic discourse. In this interesting phenomenon of expressive pluralism we can detect the extent to which all the artistic forces of Athens had to be rallied in order to construct this gigantic project in an exceptionally short space of time. Important

42. M. Cox: drawings of the metopes on the north side. Source: Boardman and Finn, op. cit.

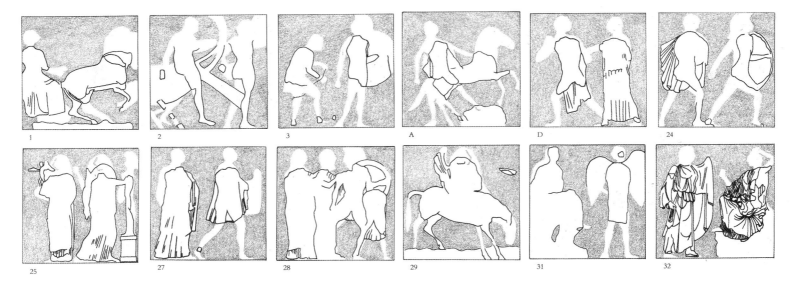

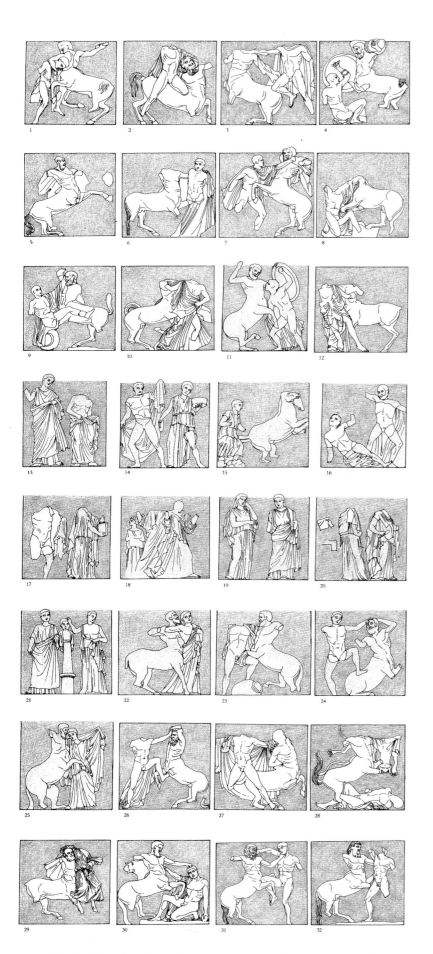

43. M. Cox: drawings of the metopes on the south side. Source: Boardman and Finn, op. cit.

44. South metope no. 1. Photograph: German Archaeological Institute, Athens.

sculptors (though their names have not come down to us) of varying ages and stylistic tendencies must have worked side by side on the completion of the monument with craftsmen of more moderate skills and accomplishments and a whole horde of assistants and associates, gradually forging interpersonal uniformity and with it the unity of Classical art. Stylistic research has relied on the fluctuations in quality of the embellishment of the Parthenon sculptures in its efforts to unseal the secrets of the personal contributions made by each artist, seeking out the expressive features of the pioneers of artistic creation prior to the Parthenon and the distinction between them and the new forces of post-Parthenon art, then being tried out. This is a far from simple undertaking. It is still further complicated by the difficulty of assessing what was the result of uniform planning of the composition and what might fall within the bounds of the freedom of those who executed the composition. Sensitive viewers, unaffected by the questions which torment the experts, automatically perceive the events depicted as tumultuous, as indicative of the inner struggle for expression of the Classical period. This is the impression conveyed by the anguished endeavour of the Lapith in metope 1 to escape from the deadly embrace of his opponent (fig. 44), or by the sense of elevation to a higher ethical plane by means of the nobility of the facial features of the combatants, despite the ferocity of the scene depicted in metope 4 (fig. 45). The same applies to the unparalleled balancing of

120

45. *South metope no. 4; London, British Museum, and Copenhagen, Royal Museum. Plaster cast. Basle, Skulpturenhalle. Photograph by D. Widmer.*

46. *South metope no. 29; London, British Museum.*

47. *South metope no. 28; London, British Museum.*

48. *South metope no. 27; London, British Museum.*

49. J. Carrey: drawings of metopes 1-4 on the south side, 1674. Source: The Carrey Drawings of the Parthenon Sculptures, op. cit.

50. J: Carrey: drawings of metopes nos. 5-8 on the south side, 1674. Source: The Carrey Drawings of the Parthenon Sculptures, op. cit.

51. J. Carrey: drawings of metopes nos. 9-12 on the south side, 1674. Source: The Carrey Drawings of the Parthenon Sculptures, op. cit.

52. J. Carrey: drawings of metopes nos. 13-16 on the south side, 1674. Source: The Carrey Drawings of the Parthenon Sculptures, op. cit.

53. J. Carrey: drawings of metopes nos. 17-20 on the south side, 1674. Source: The Carrey Drawings of the Parthenon Sculptures, op. cit.

54. J. Carrey: drawings of metopes nos. 21-24 on the south side, 1674. Source: The Carrey Drawings of the Parthenon Sculptures, op. cit.

55. J. Carrey: drawings of metopes nos. 25-28 on the south side, 1674. Source: The Carrey Drawings of the Parthenon Sculptures, op. cit.

56. J. Carrey: drawings of metopes nos. 29-32 on the south side, 1674. Source: The Carrey Drawings of the Parthenon Sculptures, op. cit.

forces – or, rather, the wonderful transcription of embattled resistance into the harmonious rhythm of the dance – of metope 27 (fig. 48), or the thrilling composition of metope 28, with its Centaur galloping in triumph over the body of the dead Lapith (fig. 47).

One could spend hours discussing the Battle of the Centaurs metopes of the Parthenon, discovering as one did so more and more planes of interest. Considerations of space urge self-restraint, but a profound need for release compels me to return briefly to one of the problems of the content of the scene. I shall, however, not explain in detail, once more, a suspicion which has been troubling me for some time: that the marital theme, which dialectically weaves together the contradictions in many of the symbolic points and allegorical allusions, can also be traced out beneath other sections of the sculptural ornamentation – such as, for instance, the myth of Pandora, which for reasons that are not entirely clear was given a prominent position on the pedestal of the cult statue of Athena Parthenos. Unless I am very wrong, the more profound reasons for this choice should be sought in Classical antiquity's belief in the antithetical nature of harmony, as expressed – to take an extreme case – in the conjunction of the two sexes in the formation and reproduction of the human community. Thus it is not without significance that in the scene on the east pediment – to look behind the mythological happenings and their religious implications, whatever they were – the female element is projected on an almost equal footing with the male, which while predominant is credited with the capacity of reproduction, the female characteristic par excellence. Nor is it coincidental that, although the conflict is ultimately resolved, the female element is triumphant in the competitive confrontation between the two protagonists on the west pediment. This relationship is only superficially reversed in the metopes of the west side, where it is not difficult to imagine the familiar amatory incident between Theseus and the queen of the Amazons. It is balanced, furthermore, by the symmetrical placing of male and female deities in the Battle of the Giants on the east side. Even clearer hints are inherent in the scene depicted by the metopes of the north side. The violation of marital harmony, though not expressly portrayed, is nonetheless counted as the principal cause of the Trojan drama which is depicted, obviously in a direct correspondence to the meaning of the metopes on the south side.

I hope that the progress so far of these thoughts will have clarified the pressure of meaning which leads me to see in the Parthenon frieze – the greatest composition not only of Greek antiquity but also, if I am not mistaken, of all time (figs. 57-60) – a joyous celebration of an event of 'marital' significance: an equation and union of the human, heroic and divine worlds unique in the history of civilisation. The conjunction of the three planes is extolled and emphasised, and through them the meaning of existence is refracted and becomes perceptible; their conjunction is projected on to the democratic structures of the Athenian form of government, just as those structures themselves are refracted through the religious and cult-derived starting-point for the theme depicted.

With the recent exceptions of Joan B. Connelly and Jerome J. Pollitt, most scholars agree that the Parthenon frieze depicts the Procession of the Panathenaea. However, as can be seen from the unrelenting attempts of researchers to decode the more profound meaning of the scene and the equally continuous stimulation which it exerts on learned curiosity (as evidenced primarily by the interpretative approaches of Evelyn B. Harrison, Erika Simon and Luigi Beschi), the composition on a first level of reading 'marries' the earlier religious tradition and the cult ceremonies carried out in the old temple of Athena with the Hecatomb sacrifice on the great altar which had crystallised by the time of Pericles. The large-scale unity of the individual sections of the scene, starting in the south-west corner of the building, in fact portrays two independent but converging processions, of which the south (fig. 57), offering up ten cows, is proceeding towards the earlier temple, while the west (fig. 58), which continues all along the north side (fig. 59), has a double offering of four cows and four sheep and is heading for the great altar on the Acropolis. On the south side, the regular procession, in order of representation of the ten tribes with the groups of knights, four-horse chariots and sacrificial animals, reflects the democratic organisation of the state in the age of Pericles. On the west and north sides, the formations are in multiples of the number four, which is connected with the earlier tribes of Attica and the social structure of Athens down to the time of Cleisthenes. These four Ionian tribes, subdivided into twelve phratries, could be traced back to the mythical period of the kings, and although they lost their political importance after the reforms of Cleisthenes, they were still prestigious in terms of religious legality. Indeed, it was into the phratries that boys were first inducted, at the festival of the Apaturia, before later being introduced – as ephebes – into the ten tribes by their demes. Thus, when I refer in a manner which is perhaps unorthodox to the 'marrying' of the allusive references in the scene, what I mean is the dialectical transcendence of the contradictions between the traditional customs and the new organisation of the state, between the ancient religious convictions and more recent expressions of faith, between old values and new.

Despite the individual 'breaks' which occur between

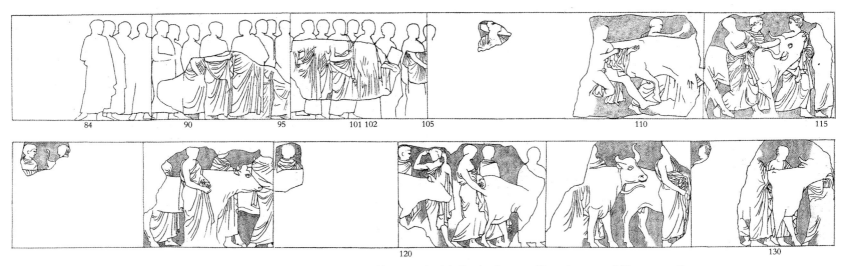

57. *Sections of the south frieze as reproduced by J. Carrey (drawing by M. Cox). Source: Boardman and Finn,* op. cit.

58. *The west frieze as reproduced by J. Carrey (drawing by M. Cox). Source: Boardman and Finn,* op. cit.

the various sections of the procession, stressing the incomparable rhythmic movement of the composition, the interpolation of the ten stewards at the four corners and along the sides unifies the entire processional crowd, just as it unifies the melodious musicality of the hymn being sent up to the patron and the city of Athens. As the development of the theme takes its rising course, and on another level of reading, the contradictions between social classes and ages are 'married', and the differences between the sexes and the varying functions of the system of government are merged in a harmonious conjugation of the past with the present and of space with time. This is easiest to see in the apotheosis which occurs when the

two parts of the procession join, along the axis of the east frieze (fig. 60), where the gods of Olympus and the Eponymous Heroes – also, indicatively, divided into two groups – look on as the ceremony reaches its most sacred moment: the delivery of the robe of Athena (figs. 61-69). As the theme reaches its climax, the honouring and exaltation of the female element becomes obvious (figs. 62, 63, 66), since all the allusive directions of the composition are now clearly projected on to what is, once more, a model of marital consummation crystallised in the *sacra conversatio* between Zeus and Hera, the supreme divine couple (fig. 61). That is why I cannot avoid the temptation of advancing the argument that the nine-month process

125

59. Sections of the north frieze as reproduced by J. Carrey (drawing by M. Cox). Source: Boardman and Finn, op. cit.

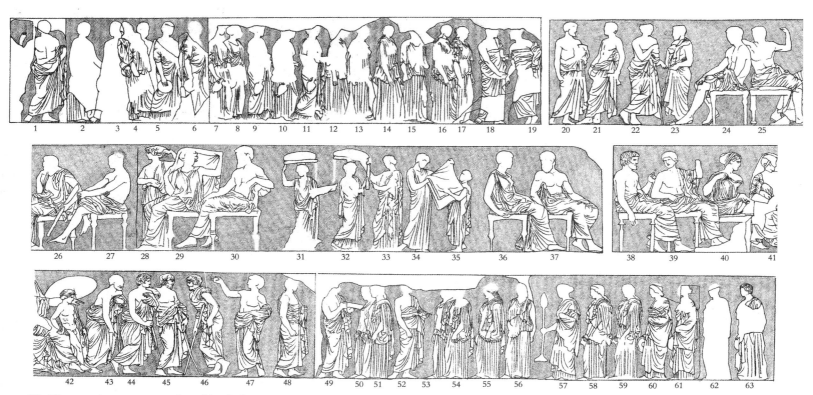

60. The east frieze as reproduced by J. Carrey (drawing by M. Cox). Source: Boardman and Finn, op. cit.

of weaving the robe is an allusion to the 'renewal' of Athena's divinity. Indeed, I would even go so far as to add that the distinct suggestion of a bridal/royal ceremony of the east frieze and the mystical inclination that emanates from it may conceal marital content of some kind. The virgin goddess, shown accompanying Hephaestus in a clearly intimate manner and with an obvious compositional desire to correspond to the supreme divine couple of Olympus, could – somewhat unorthodoxly – be seen as the 'bride' of Athens (fig. 67). We cannot be certain whether this dimension, lost in the most distant past of the cult, was consciously present in the ceremony of the Panathenaea. But it would be difficult to doubt the wish of the period in which the Parthenon frieze was cre-

ated that Athena might unite with the god of the arts par excellence – a union from which the first indigenous king of Athens had already been born.

Since I believe profoundly in the width of the scope for approaches which the sculptures of the Parthenon impose upon us with their deliberate polysemy, I would never regard any interpretation which I might advance as infallible, or rather as absolutely satisfactory by the current standard of thinking. That, of course, is not to say that I am not completely convinced of the correctness of my interpretation. The apparent contradiction is only superficial, and such an accusation involves forgetting that the concept of the frieze coincides with the apogee of the great Sophists; the validity of the various readings finds its philosophical vindication in the theories of phenomenalism and relativism. The obvious timelessness which permeates the composition as a whole, erasing all points of reference to the specific and generalising the theme depicted, thus does not conflict with the mythological interpretation advanced by Chrysoula Kardara and its reduction to the first celebration of the Panathenaic procession, except insofar as this interpretation restrains the frieze within the suffocating confines of the specific. Indeed, for 5th century Athenians, who must have realised the revolutionary transfer of the theme from the mythical to the human world, a shift from one level to the other would have been as automatic as the reflection of one world on the other which can be distinguished in the sculptural ornamentation of the monument as a whole. From this point of view, it is equally valid to relate the scene with the battle of Marathon, not so much because of the numerical co-ordinates of the figures depicted (detected by John Boardman) as for the general level of historicity which permeates the iconographic programme in relation to the

61. The east frieze: Zeus and Hera; London, British Museum.

62. The east frieze: delivery of the robe; London, British Museum.

63. The east frieze: procession of women; Paris, the Louvre.

Persian wars. The same applies to the multiplicity of interpretations to which the location of the scene is open. For example, Werner Gauer's persistent campaign to identify evidence that the scene is taking place in the Agora does not clash with the established view that the location is a single one, stretching from the Kerameikos to the Acropolis, linking in the viewer's mind the memory of his forefathers and those who fell defending the city with public and private life under the canopy of a series of sublime religious mandates.

The multi-level stratification of programmatic wisdom and the multiple systems of indirect reference, interwoven and reflected in the parables of myth and religion, make up a uniform corpus of ideology in the sculptural ornamentation of the Parthenon. It is a proclamation of faith, whose intellectual and spiritual weightiness could be compared only with that of Pericles' Funeral Oration. In the polysemy of its semantics, manifestations of reverence and gratitude are elided with the demands of historical memory and objectives for the future to produce an incomparable paean of praise for the city of Athens and the values of the democratic form of government, a work of greater importance than any other achievement of the aesthetics of the Golden Age, no matter how brilliant. In other words, we are dealing with a codified synopsis of a didactic nature which covers the entire range of processes of the consciousness from the recording of an observation to the reduction of self-knowledge, from self-confirmation to propaganda, from quantitative magnitudes to qualitative values and from ethical principles to aesthetic models.

There can, of course, be no doubt that the execution of this colossal project, the imprinting of all the shades of the system of ideological messages contained in it in the sense of their transference from thought and sensation on to the marble, varies from instance to instance, in line with the particular features of the personality, age and talent of the scores of artists who put the plan into effect. This is most clearly visible in the frieze, despite the fact that there are reliefs of thrilling power and sensitivity on the west (fig. 72), north (fig. 70) and south sides (fig. 71) to add to the rare quality of those on the east side (figs. 61-69). Yet over and above the varying degrees of success in conveying the message, and despite the differences in quality which can be discerned in many parts of the ornamentation, the overall concept and design, with its stunning unity of form and content, cannot but be ascribed to one, and only one, artist of outstanding inspiration – an artist whose experience of the problems of his time was a direct one, stemming from a first-hand view of the vicissitudes of Pericles' visions.

The established view – and this is one of the firmest stepping-stones in the history of 5th century art – is that all the sculptural ornamentation of the Parthenon was designed by Pheidias. Indeed, there has been no shortage of eminent archaeologists (especially of an earlier generation) who discerned the artist's personal seal even in the dressing of some of the most masterly sculptures on the building: in the horse of Selene in the east pediment, for instance (fig. 5), in the first metope on the south side (fig. 44), or in the magnificent central figure of the west frieze (fig. 72). Of course, the written tradition makes no mention of the name of Pheidias, apart from mentioning his supervision of the Acropolis project in general and the

128

construction of the chryselephantine cult statue of Athena Parthenos in particular. The mere fact that the cella of the temple was widened inordinately precisely so as to accommodate this gigantic creation is proof – if not of Pheidias' ability to intervene directly in the architectural planning – at least of the close co-operation between him and the architects of the building. Despite the recent objections of Nikolaus Himmelmann, the similarly multi-level complexity of the programmatic semantics in the statue of Athena Parthenos, with ornamental elements imbued with the same unique creative inspiration, suffices to consolidate our confidence that the sculptures of the Parthenon, too, sprang from the mind of Pheidias.

Thanks to the abundance of information provided by the written tradition and a series of small-scale Roman copies, and thanks above all to the unceasing involvement of research with problems of form or content, we now have a relatively clear idea of what the chryselephantine statue of Athena Parthenos originally looked like. The frigid Varvakeion Athena (fig. 73) is believed to give the closest idea of the complete composition, while the Copenhagen head preserves more, though distant, reflections of the character of the original. The goddess was depicted wearing the simple 'Attic' robe, with a large goatskin (the aegis) across her breast. On her head she wore the Attic helmet, with heads of animals on the visor, griffins in relief on the raised cheek-pieces, and plumes resting on a sphinx flanked by two winged horses. There were precious jewels on the ears, throat and upper arms of the statue, which wore on its feet thick-soled sandals

64. The east frieze: section of a head from the procession of women; Acropolis Museum. Photograph: German Archaeological Institute, Athens.

65. The east frieze: eponymous heroes; London, British Museum.

66. The east frieze: procession of women; London, British Museum.

bearing scenes in relief of the battle of the Centaurs (perhaps that of Heracles). With her right hand resting on a column, the goddess was offering Victory to the assembly of the Athenians, while her left hand rested on, and held, the shield by her side, whose outer side was ornamented with a monumental scene from Theseus' battle against the Amazons. The efforts of archaeologists to reconstruct this scene, using as evidence the numerous neo-Attic copies of individual episodes from it, cannot yet be regarded as having reached completion. There seems still less chance of reconstructing anything of the painting of the battle of the Giants which adorned the inside of the shield, with only a few faint echoes in red-figure vase-painting as assistance. We can, however, detect the presence of the theme of Helios and Selene, one of Pheidias' favourites. Thanks to the Varvakeion copy, however (fig. 73), we do have a much clearer picture of the inner space formed by the concave surface of the shield and the coiled, upward-rearing body of the sacred snake, a reminder of Erichthonius, first indigenous king of the Athenians. The pedestal of the statue narrated the moment when the gods of Olympus, all gathered in assembly, bestowed their gifts on Pandora, Hephaestus' most renowned creation and the first woman of the myths; the sun was shown rising and the moon setting, underlining for one more time the special importance of this theme.

67. The east frieze: Athena and Hephaestus; London, British Museum. Source: J. Boardman et al, Die Griechische Kunst, Munich 1976.

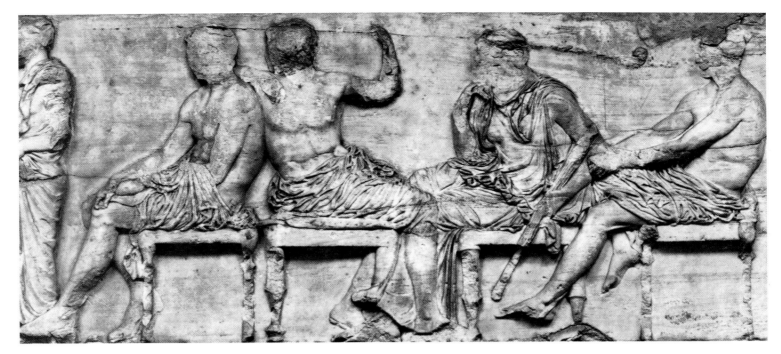

All that has survived of this enigmatic composition is a few fragmentary references in a Hellenistic copy from Pergamon, an incomplete reproduction in miniature from the Pnyx and a section of relief from Rhodes.

Much has been written about the meaning and the semantics of Athena Parthenos. In the most complete – and most recent – review of the ornamental components of Pheidias' work, Burkhardt Fehr notes a sequence of conscious references around the central ideological axis of the Athenian League of Delos. He also detects numerous more indirect hints concerning the rival city of Corinth, whose commercial interests in the western Mediterranean and their clash with Athenian aspirations westward were

68. The east frieze: Hermes, Dionysus, Demeter and Ares; London, British Museum. Source: Boardman et al, op. cit.

69. The east frieze: Poseidon, Apollo, Artemis, Aphrodite and Eros; Acropolis Museum, National Museum of Palermo, and impression of a lost section. Plaster cast. Basle, Skulpturenhalle. Photograph: British Museum.

70. *The north frieze: water-bearers; Acropolis Museum. Photograph: German Archaeological Institute, Athens.*

71. *The south frieze: the sacrificial animals; London, British Museum*

72. *West frieze: central figure; Acropolis Museum. Photograph: German Archaeological Institute, Athens.*

among the most serious causes of the Peloponnesian War. In the scene on the shield, and in the metopes of the west side of the temple, the role of Theseus as the symbolic mouthpiece of Athenian democracy during the attack by the exotic race of the Amazons is a piece of propaganda appropriating for the Athenians the Greek victory over the Persians. And with this indirect attribution of the outcome of the conflict between Greeks and Persians to the decisive intervention of the goddess, the theme takes on a clear function as a deterrent or warning, leaving no doubt in the mind of the viewer that any similar endeavour in the future will once more fall foul of the invincible defensive weapons made by Hephaestus.

For the consciousness of the Classical period, it was self-evident that Athenian superiority in every confrontation with the barbarians, relying on their more advanced know-how and technological equipment, left them in debt to the goddess and her exceptionally close bond with the god of metal-working. This bond, to which the Athenian democracy dedicated the beautiful marble temple which, still intact, dominates the flat field of ruins which is the Agora, would hardly have gone unnoticed by the general spirit of propaganda that permeates the mythological themes of the Parthenon, as we can deduce from the weaponry of the opposing sides in the battle of the Centaurs. The relationship between Hephaestus and Athena is even more clearly recorded in the east pediment of the temple, where the birth of the patron goddess of Athens would have been inconceivable without the decisive intervention of the divine craftsman. Still more eloquent is the east frieze, where the two gods, seated side by side watch with the self-evident courtesy of an established couple the Panathenaic procession. On the pedestal of the cult statue, with the 'birth' of Pandora, with Hephaestus just having completed the moulding of his finest creation, with Athena (first and foremost) and all the other gods of Olympus arriving to offer their divine gifts to the 'newborn', and with the rising sun and the setting moon once more signifying the cosmological dimensions of the theme, the intimacy of the relationship finally transcends both its religious and its historical roots. May I be forgiven by the frigid assessors of data and the strict pragmatists of positivist science, but I believe very deeply – however unable I may be to support my belief with unshakeable arguments – that in the supremely significant ceremonial of the act of human creation depicted the mind of the ancient viewer would be looking (more than in the case of the shield of Athena) for the figure of the greatest creator of all time in the facial features of the divine craftsman. And in the knowledge that the thematic nucleus of the scene contains a latent marriage (that of Pandora and Epimetheus, with its consequences), I be-

lieve the ancient viewer would, quite reasonably, wonder how balance was achieved between the contradictions in the weaving of the human fate, and how the optimism of hope could emerge as the transcendence of accumulated sorrows.

In order to understand the reasons which led to the choice of the myth of Pandora, and in order to cast light on its internal connections with the entire system of references of the statue of Athena, we must first remember that the myth was an Athenian one. Then we must note that similar miraculous 'births' – though of divine figures – were a more general feature of the thematic repertoire of the pedestals on which stood the cult statues of post-Parthenon times. Consequently, we cannot adopt a one-track approach, whether as religion or as propaganda, to the significance of the birth of Athena on the east pediment of the temple, with which the 'narrative' of the history of the Parthenon begins, in relation to the birth of Pandora with which it ends. It is tempting to see in this theme a desire to define and contrast the two poles be-

73. The Varvakeion Athena; Athens, National Archaeological Museum. Photograph: German Archaeological Institute, Athens.

tween which life lies – that is, the creation of man as a counterpoise to the creation of a god. This is particularly true since the continuation of the myth, with punishment not as a threat but as a marking out of the boundaries of destiny expanding to promise hope, also expands the humanitarian measures on which rests the ideological substructure of the values of the Parthenon.

However the matter may be, we can see here, once more, the vista of a sense of marriage in which the value of the divine gifts is perceived in its relativity and where man, not god, will decide as to the inevitability of the outcome of the drama.

Bibliographical note

The bibliography concerning the ornamentation of the Parthenon and its problems is vast. Taking the references in the text as a criterion, we should note the following fundamental works: A. Michaelis, *Der Parthenon*, Leipzig 1870-71; A.H. Smith, *The Sculptures of the Parthenon*, London 1910; E. Thomas, *Mythos und Geschichte, Untersuchungen zum historischen Gehalt griechischer Mythendarstellungen*, Cologne 1976, pp. 47ff, 53, 58ff; H. Knell, *Perikleische Baukunst*, Darmstadt 1979, pp. 30ff; E. Berger (ed.), *Parthenon-Kongress Basel, Referate und Berichte 4. bis 8. April 1982*, Mainz 1984 (with all the bibliography down to that time). See also, since then, G. Despinis, *Parthenoneia* ('On the Parthenon'), Athens 1982, and most recently, J. Boardman and D. Finn, *The Parthenon and its Sculpture*, London 1985; H. Knell, *Mythos und Polis, Bildprogramme griechischer Bauskultur*, Darmstadt 1990, pp. 95ff; D. Castriota, *Myth, Ethos and Actuality. Official Art in Fifth-Century BC Athens*, Madison, Wisconsin 1992, pp. 134ff.

On the more particular topic of the pediments, see M. Wegner, 'Peplosstatue aus dem Ostgiebel des Parthenon', *AM* 57, 1932, pp. 92ff, plates I-II, *Beil*. 17-18; R. Carpenter, 'New Material for the West Pediment of the Parthenon', *Hesperia* 1, 1932, pp. 1ff, plates 1-3; M. Wegner, 'Ein Torso aus dem Westgiebel des Parthenon', *Neue Beiträge zur klassischen Altertumswissenschaft. Festschrift zum 60. Geburtstag von Bernhard Schweitzer*, Stuttgart 1954, pp. 185ff, plates 40-43; F. Brommer, *Die Skulpturen der Parthenon-Giebel*, Mainz 1963; K. Jeppesen, 'Bild und Mythus an dem Parthenon', *ActaArch* 34, 1963, pp. 1ff; 'Evidence for the Restoration of the East Pediment Reconsidered in the Light of Recent Achievements', *Parthenon-Kongress Basel, op. cit.*, pp. 267ff; J. Marcadé, 'Zu den Skulpturen der Parthenon-Giebel', *BCH* 88, 1964, pp. 623ff; E.B. Harrison, 'Athena and Athens in the East Pediment of the Parthenon', *AJA* 71, 1967, pp. 27ff; 'U and her Neighbours in the West Pediment of the Parthenon', *Essays in the History of Art Presented to R. Wittkower*, London 1969², pp. 1ff; M.S. Brouskari, 'Ek tou Dytikou Aetomatos tou Parthenonos' ('From the West Pediment of the Parthenon'), *AD* 24A, 1969, pp. 8ff; E. Simon, *Die Götter der Griechen*, Munich 1969, pp. 211ff, fig. 199; E. Berger, *Die Geburt der Athena im Ostgiebel des Parthenon*, Basle-Mainz 1974; I. Beyer, 'Die Zweigespanne und Mittelgruppen der Parthenongiebel', *AM* 92, 1977, pp. 101ff; E.B. Harrison, 'The Shoulder-Cord of Themis', *Festschrift für F. Brommer*, Mainz 1977, pp. 155ff; R.M. Gais, 'Some Problems of River-God Iconography', *AJA* 82, 1978, pp. 355ff. and esp. p. 362; J. Binder, 'Akropolis 7222', *Stele, Tomos eis Mnimin N. Kontoleontos* ('Stele; a Volume in Memory of N. Kontoleon'), Athens 1980, pp. 487ff; E. Simon, 'Die Mittelgruppe im Westgiebel des Parthenon', *Tainia, Festschrift für R. Hampe*, Mainz 1980, pp. 239ff; A. Delivorrias, 'Zum Problem des Zeus im Ostgiebel des Parthenon', *Praestant Interna, Festschrift für U. Hausmann*, Tübingen 1982, pp. 41ff; R. Lindner, 'Die Giebelgruppe von Eleusis mit dem Raub der Persephone', *JdI* 97, 1982, pp. 303ff and esp. pp. 321ff and 393ff; W. Fuchs, 'Zur Rekonstruktion des Poseidon im Parthenon-Westgiebel', *Boreas* 6, 1983, pp. 79ff; J. Binder, 'The West Pediment of the Parthenon: Poseidon', *Studies Presented to S. Dow on his Eightieth Birthday*, Durham 1984, pp. 15ff; A. Mantis, 'Akropolis 2381', *BCH* 110, 1986, pp. 231ff; E. Simon, 'El Nacimiento de Atenea en el Frontón Oriental del Parthenón', *Coloquio Sobre et Puteal de la Moncloa*, Madrid 1986, pp. 65ff; B. Cook, 'Parthenon West Pediment B/C, the Serpent Fragment', *Kanon, Festschrift E. Berger, AntK* 15, Bh 1988, pp. 4ff, plate 13; M. Oppermann, *Von Medusabild zur Athenageburt, Bildprogramme griechischer Tempelgiebel archaischer und klassischer Zeit*, Leipzig 1990, pp. 155ff; B.S. Spaeth, 'Athenians and Eleusinians in the West Pediment of the Parthenon', *Hesperia* 60, 1991, pp. 331ff; B.B. Shefton, 'The Baksy Krater Once More and Some Observations on the East Pediment of the Parthenon', *Kotinos, Festschrift für E. Simon*, Mainz am Rhein 1992, pp. 241 ff; Olga Palagia, *The Pediments of the Parthenon*, Leiden 1993 (= *Monumenta Graeca et Romana* VII).

For the acroteria, see J. Binder, 'Acropolis Acroterion Fragment', *Festschrift für F. Brommer*, Mainz 1977, pp. 29ff; I.S. Mark, 'New Fragments of the Parthenon Acroteria', *Hesperia* 46, 1977, pp. 241ff; A. Delivorrias, 'Zur Akroterkomposition des Parthenon', *Parthenon-Kongress Basel, op. cit.*, pp. 289ff.

For the metopes, see C. Praschniker, *Parthenonstudien*, Augsburg/Wien 1928; 'Neue Parthenon-Studien', *ÖJH* 41, 1954, pp. 5ff; F. Brommer, *Die Metopen des Parthenon*, Mainz 1967; E. Simon, 'Versuch einer Deutung der Südmetopen des Parthenon', *JdI* 90, 1975, pp. 100ff; J. Dörig, 'Traces de Thraces sur le Parthénon', *MusHelv* 35, 1978, pp. 221ff; E.B. Harrison, 'Apollo's Cloak', *Studies in Classical Art and Archaeology. A Tribute to P.H. von Blanckenhagen*, Locust Valley, New York 1979, pp. 91ff; J. Dörig, 'To Programma tis Glyptis Diakosmisis tou Parthenona' ('The Programme of Sculpted Ornamentation on the Parthenon'), *AE* 1982, pp. 187ff; 'Les metopes Nord du Parthénon', *Parthenon-Kongress Basel, op. cit.*, pp. 202ff; B. Fehr, 'Die 'gute' und die 'schlechte' Ehefrau; Alkestis und Phaidra auf den Südmetopen des Parthenon', *Hephaistos* 4, 1982, pp. 37ff; M.A. Tiverios, 'Observations on the East Metopes of the Parthenon', *AJA* 86, 1982, pp. 227ff; B. Wesenberg, 'Perser oder Amazonen? Zu den Westmetopen des Parthenon', *AA* 1983, pp. 203ff; 'Parthenongebälk und Südmetopenproblem', *JdI* 98, 1983, pp. 57ff; M. Robertson, 'The South Metopes: Theseus and Daidalos', *Parthenon-Kongress Basel, op. cit.*, pp. 206ff; E. Berger (ed.), *Der Parthenon in Basel, Dokumentation zu den Metopen*, Basle-Mainz 1986; K.A. Schwab, 'The Gods of the Parthenon North Metopes N31 and N32', *AJA* 90, 1986, p. 207; A. Mantis, 'Neue Fragmente von Parthenon-Metopen', *JdI* 102, 1987, pp. 163ff; 'I Apokatastasi mias Voreias Metopis tou Parthenona' ('Reconstruction of One of the North Metopes of the Parthenon'), *Ametos, Timitikos Tomos M. Andronikos* ('Ametos, A Volume in Honour of Manolis Andronikos'), I, Thessaloniki 1987, pp. 473ff; K. Schefold, F. Jung, *Die Urkönige, Perseus, Bellerephon, Herakles und Theseus in der klassischen und hellenistischen Kunst*, Munich 1988, pp. 70ff; K.A. Schwab, *The Parthenon Metopes and Greek Vase Painting: A Study of Comparison and Influences*, New York University 1988; A. Mantis, 'Beiträge zur Wiederherstellung der mittleren Südmetopen des Parthenon', *Festschrift für N. Himmelmann*, Mainz 1989, pp. 109ff; U. Höckmann, 'Die Südmetope 21 und das Thema der Parthenon-Südmetopen', paper presented at the conference entitled 'Klassik als exemplarische Bewältigung der Geschichte-Neue Aspekte zu Kunst und Literatur im Jahrhundert der Griechieschen Tragödie', Blaubeuren, 24-27 October 1991.

For the frieze, see C. Kardara, 'Glavkopis - O Archaios Naos kai to Thema tis Zoophorou tou Parthenonos' ('Glaucopis: the Ancient Temple and the Theme of the Parthenon Frieze'), *AE* 1961, pp. 61ff, plates 4-7; E.G. Pemberton, 'The Gods of the East Frieze of the Parthenon', *AJA* 80, 1976, pp. 112ff; J. Boardman, 'The Parthenon-Frieze - Another View', *Festschrift für F. Brommer*, Mainz 1977, pp. 39ff; F. Brommer, *Der Parthenonfries*, Mainz 1977; J.H. Kroll, 'The Parthenon Frieze as a Votive Relief', *AJA* 83, 1979, pp. 349ff; E. Simon, 'Die Mittelszene im Ostfries des Parthenon', *AM* 97, 1982, pp. 127ff; *Festivals of Attica*, Madison 1983, pp. 55ff; W. Gauer, 'Was geschieht mit dem Peplos?', *Parthenon-Kongress Basel, op. cit.*, pp. 220ff; E.B. Harrison, 'Time in the Parthenon Frieze', *Parthenon-Kongress Basel, op. cit.*, pp. 230ff; U. Kron, 'Die zehn attischen Phylenheroen am Parthenonfries', *Parthenon-Kongress Basel, op. cit.*, pp. 235ff; I.S. Mark, 'The Gods on the East Frieze of the Parthenon', *Hesperia* 53, 1984, pp. 289ff; L. Beschi, 'Il fregio del Parthenone: una proposta di lettura', *Atti dell'Accademia Nationale dei Lincei, Rendiconti* 39, 1985, pp. 173ff; M. Cool Root, 'The Parthenon Frieze and the Apadana Reliefs at Persepolis: Reassessing a Programmatic Relationship', *AJA* 89, 1985, pp. 103ff; I.D. Jenkins, 'The Composition of the So-Called Eponymous Heroes on the East Frieze of the Parthenon', *AJA* 89, 1985, pp. 121ff; J. Mansfield, *The Robe of Athena and the Panathenaic 'Peplos'*, Berkeley 1985; E. Berger (ed.), *Der Parthenon in Basel, II, Dokumentation des Nord- und Ostfrieses*, Mainz 1986; R. Osborne, 'The Viewing and Obscuring of the Parthenon Frieze', *JHS* 107, 1987, pp. 98ff; T. Schäfer, 'Diphroi und Peplos auf dem Ostfries des Parthenon: zur Kulturpraxis bei den Panathenäen in klassischer Zeit', *AM* 102, 1987, pp. 185ff; C. W. Clairmont, 'Girl or Boy? Parthenon East Frieze 35', *AA* 1989, pp. 495ff; B. Nagy, 'Athenian Officials on the Parthenon Frieze', *AJA* 96, 1992, pp. 55ff; J.B. Connelly, 'The Parthenon Frieze and the Sacrifice of the Erechtheids: Reinterpreting the Peplos Scene', *Abstracts Arch. Inst. of America* 16, 1992, pp. 25; J.J. Pollitt, 'The Meaning of the Parthenon Frieze', Proceedings of the Symposium on 'The Interpretation of Architectural Sculpture in Greece and Rome',

National Gallery of Art, Washington DC, 22-23 January 1993 (in press).

For the stylistic questions, see N. Himmelmann, 'Phidias und die Parthenon-Skulpturen', *Bonner Festgabe J. Straub*, Bh.BJb 39, 1977, pp. 67ff; 'Ta Glypta tou Parthenonos kai o Pheidias' ('The Parthenon Sculptures and Pheidias'), *EpistEpetAth* 27, 1979, pp. 9ff; 'Zur Entlohnung künstlericher Tätigkeit in klassischen Bauinschriften', *JdI* 94, 1979, pp. 127ff; 'Die zeitliche Stellung der Südmetopen am Parthenon', *Stele, Tomos..., op. cit.*, pp. 161ff; 'Planung und Verdingung der Parthenon-Skulpturen', *Bathron, Beiträge zur Architektur und verwandten Künsten für H. Drerup*, Saarbrücken 1988, pp. 213ff; A.H. Borbein, 'Phidias-Fragen', *Beiträge zur Ikonographie und Hermeneutik, Festschrift für N. Himmelmann*, Mainz 1989, pp. 99ff.

For the statue of Athena Parthenos, see W.H. Schuchhardt, 'Athena Parthenos', *AntPl* 2, 1963, pp. 31ff; N. Leipen, *Athena Parthenos, A Reconstruction*, Toronto 1971; G. Hafner, 'Die Sphinx auf den Helm der Athena Parthenos der Phidias', *StädJb*, N.F. 5,1975, pp. 7ff; W. Schuchhardt, 'Zur Basis der Athena Parthenos', *Wandlungen, Festschrift für E. Homann-Wedeking*, Waldsassen 1975, pp. 120ff; B. Fehr, 'Zur religionspolitischen Funktion der Athena Parthenos im Rahmen des delisch-attischen Seebundes I, 1', *Hephaistos* 1, 1979, pp. 71ff; II, *Hephaistos* 2, 1980, pp. 113ff; III, *Hephaistos* 3, 1981, pp. 55ff; E.B. Harrison, 'Two Pheidian Heads: Nike and Amazon', *The Eye of Greece, Studies in the Art of Athens for M. Robertson*, Cambridge 1982, pp. 53ff; A. Delivorrias, 'To Vathro tis Athenas Parthenou kai o Glyptikos tou Diakosmos' ('The Pedestal of Athena Parthenos and its Sculptural Ornamentation'), *Proceedings of the XII International Conference of Classical Archaeology*, 1983, III, Athens 1988, pp. 53ff; B.S. Ridgway, 'Images of Athena on the Acropolis' in J. Neils (ed.), *Goddess and Polis: The Panathenaic Festival in Ancient Athens* (exhibition catalogue), Princeton 1992, pp. 131ff.

For the shield, see T. Hölscher, E. Simon, 'Die Amazonenschlacht auf dem Schild der Athena Parthenos', *AM* 91, 1976, pp. 115ff; E.B. Harrison, 'Motifs of the City-Siege on the Shield of Athena-Parthenos', *AJA* 85, 1981, pp. 281ff; V.M. Strocka, 'Das Schildrelief zum Stand der Forschung', *Parthenon-Kongress Basel, op. cit.*, pp. 188ff; D. Mauruschat, 'Ein neuer Vorschlag zur Rekonstruktion der Schildamazonomachie der Athena Parthenos', *Boreas* 10, 1987, pp. 32ff; H. Meyer, 'Ein neues Piräusrelief. Zur Überlieferung der Amazonomachie am Schild der Athena Parthenos', *AM* 102, 1987, pp. 295ff; T. Stefanidou-Tiveriou, 'I Synthesi tis Pheidiakis Amazonomachias kai oi Iroes Thiseas kai Kepropas' ('The Composition of Pheidias' Battle of the Amazons and the Heroes Theseus and Cecrops'), *Ametos..., op. cit.*, II, Thessaloniki 1987, pp. 839ff; W. Gauer, 'Parthenonische Amazonomachie und Perserkrieg', *Kanon, Festschrift E. Berger, AntK* 15, Bh. 1988, pp. 28ff.

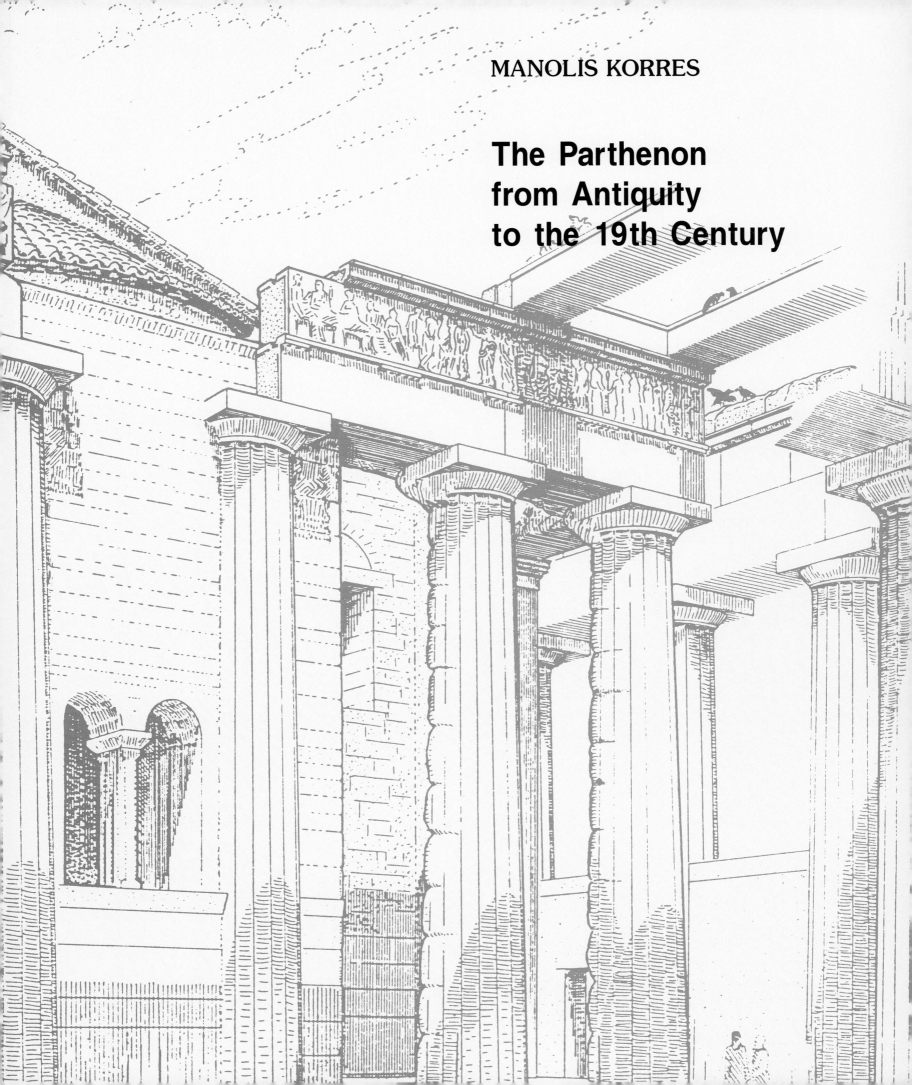

MANOLIS KORRES

The Parthenon
from Antiquity
to the 19th Century

Very few of the works of man could have survived in such good condition as the Parthenon: in its position, to such an age and through such misadventures. Yet although comparisons of this kind may show the Parthenon to be much tougher than the best of other buildings, its state today[1] could hardly be described as worthy of it, especially if we bear in mind the incredible solidity of its compact foundations, the incomparable perfection of its construction, the natural advantages of using marble as the basic building material, and the relatively mild climate of Greece. The natural rate of wear and tear to the Parthenon was always slow, especially during the first seven centuries down to the time when it was severely damaged by fire. More than five centuries after its completion, the temple still looked new enough to have been freshly-built, as Plutarch clearly tells us.[2] A careful examination of the wear to the building reveals that if such extensive exogenous damage had not been done to it, our impression today of its state of preservation would not differ much from Plutarch's. Man alone is undoubtedly responsible for the current state of this ancient masterpiece, and has wrought more damage than all the forces of nature together. It has often, and reasonably, been argued that the preservation of the Parthenon was largely due to the fact that the building did not fall into disuse after the suppression of the ancient religion, but became a Christian church. Then, after its ecclesiastical function came to an end, it was re-used once more, as a Muslim mosque, and thus it was preserved down to modern times at the cost of conversions and a degree of damage. In the case of other structures, though, preservation by use is achieved by means of maintenance – that is, active protection against the elements of nature – while the preservation of the Parthenon by continuous use consisted merely in its protection against other and even more destructive uses, such as demolition to yield stone for rebuilding. It did not involve action to deal with natural wear and tear, to which, in any case, the building seems to have been almost totally resistant. In the case of the Parthenon, it could thus be said that – theoretically – the best way of ensuring optimum preservation would have been a complete lack of any interest in it for use or intervention, from the best to the worst, and consequently absolute abandonment to the elements of nature, which

would have been far from damaging. In this hypothetical case, the monument would still have those wonderful but lost features which only the imagination of a tiny number of experts can reconstruct with any accuracy. Its history alone – an almost uninterrupted sequence of vicissitudes – would be different.

As recent observations have shown, the first external event to have a serious impact on the building was the very powerful earthquake of 426 BC – which can probably be taken to have been among the three or four worst to hit Greece. Our evidence for this comes from the account of Thucydides,[3] almost scientific in its accuracy, and from a detailed study of the damage caused to the Parthenon at this time: a large part of both facades shifted 2 cm. north.[4]

The fourth century was a time of relative peace for the monument. Of course, intervention had begun to take place, principally in the form of the erection of votive and commemorative statues around the temple and on the steps of the crepidoma, but this did not damage the fabric of the building. It may, perhaps, have spoiled its initial appearance and disturbed its complete simplicity in places, but the monuments added at this time were of the greatest importance in their own right, and some of them were the work of the most famous sculptors and makers of statues in bronze. The erection on the architrave of ornate shields – votive offerings out of the booty of war – was, however, less discreet. Those on the east side were the oldest and the largest. With a diameter of 1.25 m., they were exactly the same size as the space remaining on the architrave beneath the taenia, and so they only fitted directly beneath the metopes, occupying the entire space there. There were thus fourteen of them, as many as the metopes. On the other three sides, the shields were somewhat smaller and were mounted only above the columns, numbering a total of 42 (17+8+17).[5]

Real abuse of the Parthenon, one of the symptoms of a growing decline in individual and collective values, began in 304-3 BC, when the Athenians accommodated Demetrius Poliorcetes, conqueror of the city,[6] in the west chamber of the temple. Shortly afterwards (301 BC), the rise to power of the tyrant Lachares proved disastrous not only for the city but for the Parthenon, too. In 295, bankruptcy led Lachares to remove – in the most brutal

1. The large commemorative monument on the north-east corner of the Parthenon (c. 180 BC). The life-size bronze statue of a four-horse chariot concealed part of the epistyle of the temple. Drawing by M. Korres.

manner – the precious metals from many of the votive statues in and around the temple, including the priceless robe of Athena herself and many of the shields.[7] This treasure did not save the tyrant, but the temple lost its original opulence once and for all. The statue of Athena must have been restored not with gold plate, but with sheets of gilded copper.

The third century BC was violent, creative and highly damaging to the entire Greek world; in terms of local history, it was rather an unfortunate time. In the Parthenon and its immediate surroundings, however, new votive and commemorative offerings were set up next to those already in place, twelve new and rather smaller shields replaced the fourteen which had been removed from the east side, and others were added or replaced on the north and south sides.[8] Most important of all, however, and a superb example of an art still flourishing and evolving, must have been the long group of sculptures dedicated to Athena in commemoration of the Galatian wars (241 BC *et seq.*) by Attalus I in around 220 BC. It stood to the south of the temple, near the wall.[9] Of the numerous bronze sculptures, only some Roman copies in marble of dying Gauls have survived; they are considerably larger

than life-size, and are in themselves outstanding examples of anatomical perfection, profound expression of the soul and serious contemplation of the mind.

Another Attalid monument, commemorating Eumenes II or (more possibly) Attalus II, was erected before the middle of the second century on the east side of the temple, directly in front of the column in the north-east corner (fig. 1).[10] This was a towering and massive pier, similar in articulation and dimensions to the pedestal of Agrippa,[11] which, like it, must have borne a large bronze four-horse chariot flanked by standing charioteers or boys. Since this monument was very tall and touched the building, it partially concealed the corner of the temple up to the level of the metopes. This was certainly incompatible with the original meaning of the Parthenon and the spiritual ethos of its creators, and it was a consequence of the subsequent economic and moral decline of the Athenian state. Among the symptoms of that decline was the shameless flattery of the powerful of the day, which often went to extremes such as this instance of the devotion of an entire corner of the Parthenon to the honour of an ordinary mortal. The ascription of titles of divinity to men who may have been extremely powerful but were no less mortal than their fellow humans (in fact, their lives were a good deal more dangerous) was a phenomenon which was beginning to spread at this time. It had much less to do with the actual growth of an absurd faith among some people in the allegedly divine properties of those so elevated as with the linguistic phenomenon of the way in which some words became alienated from much of their original significance and weight. Such questions of politics, however, lay far outside the realm of the artists, who worked to the best of their ability in the service not only of

2. Traces of the votive shields and the bolt holes for the metal letters of the Roman inscription on the east side of the Parthenon epistyle. Photograph by M. Korres.

3. Reconstruction of the fire which burned down the Parthenon, seen from the hill to the west of Lycabettus (now called Strefi). To the left, Lycabettus; in the distance, the heights of Piraeus, the Saronic Gulf and Aegina. Drawing by M. Korres.

the external but also of the internal purposes of their art.

In 31 BC, the huge votive and commemorative monument was rededicated to the emperor Augustus. The original inscription was deleted,[12] a new inscription[13] was added, and it may have been that fresh sculptural work was necessary. Not long afterwards (27 BC), the nine-column circular Ionian temple of Rome and Augustus was built[14] at a distance of only 25 metres from the east facade of the Parthenon and precisely on its axis. However, the new temple, only 10 metres in height as opposed to the 23 metres of the Parthenon, was low enough not to prevent the rays of the sun from penetrating to the back of the chamber where the statue of Athena stood, or even of impeding the horizontal rays of dawn. The great doorway of the cella was almost two metres higher than the top of the roof of the circular temple.

The worst insult to the spirit of the Classical temple was committed in 61 AD when a monumental inscription some 25 metres long was placed on the east architrave in honour of Nero, "dei filius".[15] The inscription cannot have lasted much longer than the reign of the corrupt emperor himself, but its traces will be there for ever: scores of holes in the marble, made for the pins which held up its gilt metal lettering (fig. 2). The general arrangement of these traces makes it clear that the inscription did not dis-

place the twelve more recent shields on the architrave: it was discontinuous, and the letters were fitted into the spaces in between the shields. According to some scholars, the inscription accompanied a large statue of Nero erected nearby, inside or outside the temple. Others, however, believe that the inscription recorded the dedication of the temple itself to Nero.[16] A century later, the traveller Pausanias tells us that a statue of Hadrian stood next to that of Athena.[17]

It does seem, though, that the Roman era produced at least one useful intervention in the Parthenon: the east pediment was repaired to make good earthquake damage. Unfortunately, the state of preservation of the east pediment makes it impossible to ascertain the exact extent of these repairs. Only one repaired section can still be seen on the building: a replacement cornice slab above column 3 from the north. This block, weighing almost four tons, was set in its horizontal position after its predecessor had been removed, but we cannot be sure whether the sculpture it bore was the original or a new work. Strong scaffolding, a crane and two pulleys would have been needed for this arduous yet delicate task.[18]

Although we have no mention of it in the sources, it is clear – and generally accepted today – that long before the historic devastation of 1687 the building had been badly damaged by fire. This was followed by extensive repair work, the most familiar example of which is the reconstruction of the inner colonnade.[19] Many of the marbles from this reconstruction have survived on the Acropolis, and can be dated – on criteria of their order

140

4. *Reconstruction of the interior of the Parthenon immediately after the fire. Drawing by M. Korres.*

and style – to the second century BC.[20] However, as B.H. Hill was the first scholar to observe, the repair work actually took place during the late Roman period: it simply made use of earlier materials produced by the systematic demolition of a Doric colonnade of the Hellenistic period.[21] Unfortunately, no testimony to the details of the damage and the repair work have survived, and so opinions are divided as to the causes and date of either event. There is also a relatively well-known earlier view that the new colonnade must have formed part of the temple's conversion into a Christian church.[22] However, a recent discovery has ruled this out completely: apart from the inner colonnade and the west doorway, the major reconstruction operation also extended to the complete repair of the east door,[23] which would only have been functionally useful if the building was still operating as an ancient temple.[24]

We do not, of course, know exactly when the Parthenon's ancient function ceased, but it is reasonable to assume that this cannot have happened before the official prohibition of the 'old religion' in 397, by decree of the emperor Theodosius I, or – even more likely – before the special decrees on ancient temples issued by Theodosius II in 438. The Athenians, heirs to the sublimest of ancient civilisations, held on for as long as they could to what in Roman times had been the only asset of their once all-powerful city: their traditions, their political institutions, their numerous intellectual foundations, and their ancient religion (we must disregard the familiar 'tradition' – actually constructed at a later date – that Paul's preaching of Christianity had a widespread appeal). Nonetheless, the decrees of Theodosius II must have spelt the end for the ancient function of the temple. Marinus tells us that the neo-Platonist Proclus (412-485) was not allowed to enter the Parthenon.[25]

How long before the building ceased to function as a temple had it been burned down and repaired? First of all, it could be argued that the repairs cannot have taken place before the third century, since one of the marbles used in them bears a third or fourth century inscription from its previous use.[26] According to one theory (1979),[27] the fact that fragments of the original inner columns were

5. Sample reconstruction of the architectural members of a colonnade from which were taken the later internal columns of the Parthenon. Photograph by M. Korres.

6. Heat cracking on the columns of the opisthonaos. Photograph by M. Korres.

7. Reconstruction of the later (4th century AD) internal columns of the Parthenon (cross-section of the interior from the central axis to the south wall). The central column was removed in the 6th century to make way for the arch. Drawing by M. Korres.

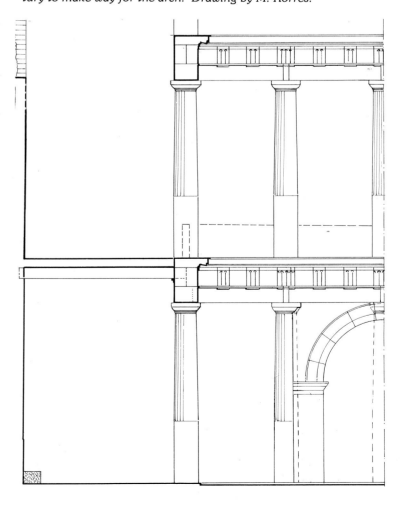

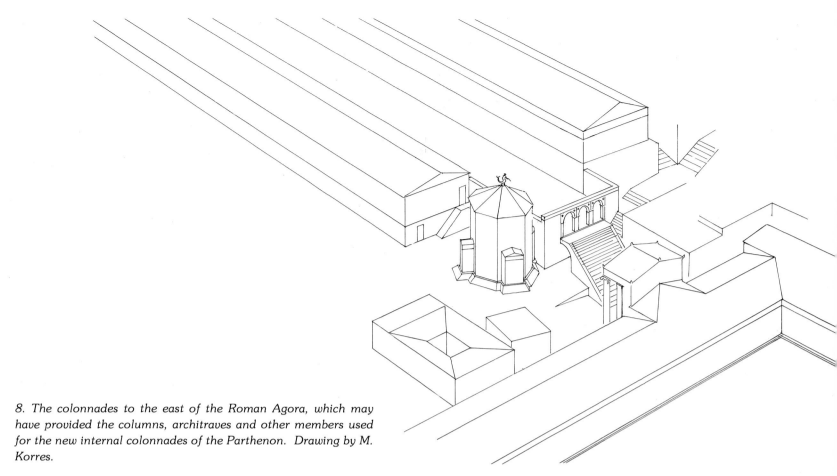

8. *The colonnades to the east of the Roman Agora, which may have provided the columns, architraves and other members used for the new internal colonnades of the Parthenon. Drawing by M. Korres.*

found to have been built into the walls of the ancient Agora, which date from the fifth century,[28] would dictate a dating of the repairs to the early years of that century. This would make it the work of Herculius, proconsul of the province of Illyricum from 402 to 410. Yet various instances of damage and repair to the pivots of the new east door, which left deep scratches on the (equally new) threshold and on the ancient floor, imply such a duration of use[29] that a dating of the repair to the fifth century is quite out of the question. A more likely solution – at least than this theory – is provided by J. Travlos (1970):[30] in his view, the repairs must have been done during the brief period when the Empire was ruled by Julian (362-365). By the same token, the fire (accidental or deliberate) must be attributed to the Heruli.[31] The theory is conjectural. It stems from a overall conclusion to be drawn from the excavations in the ancient Agora as to the destructiveness of the raid of the Heruli (267): in general, it seems that in the 3rd century almost everything in the Agora and throughout the city was laid waste, principally by arson.[32] The fact that the repairs were made using stones taken exclusively from other buildings – buildings which were both numerous and heterogeneous and which were systematically demolished as useless or simply less useful – is important evidence that they followed general destruction of the city and not just isolated damage to the Parthenon. However, the consideration that almost a hundred years elapsed be-

tween the fire and the repairing of the Parthenon may cause some doubt as to the dating of the one event or the other.

The damage caused to the building by the fire was very serious (figs. 3, 4).[33] The gigantic roof beams and rafters (timber with a volume of 480 cubic metres) were consumed by fire, and must have burned for many days. Almost all the marble roof, weighing about 350 tons, crashed to the ground in fragments. The abrupt and extreme rise in the temperature caused severe heat cracking[34] on all the marble surfaces in the areas where there was burning wood: the upper surface of all the panels, the revetments of the pediments, the inner faces of the walls, all the inner columns, many of the outer columns (fig. 6) and the antae, much of the face of the door wall, the entablature and the beams of the opisthonaos and, even more so, of the pronaos. The two colossal doors, masterpieces of many different arts weighing a total of 30 tons, vanished altogether, and the marble lintels above them – with a total weight of 90 tons – were so deeply cracked by the heat that they were ready to fall.

Although the repairing of the temple was done in as economical a manner as possible, it was nonetheless a major undertaking. We have, unfortunately, no accounts of it, but continuing study of the material traces it left – primarily of successively used blocks of stone – is gradually expanding our knowledge. From the numerical point

9. The west doorway after repair, 4th century AD. The brick arch was added in 1872. Scale 1:100, drawing by M. Korres.

of view, the most important source of material for the repairs was the systematic demolition or one – or possibly two – identical Doric colonnades. These produced columns, architraves, friezes and a cornice (fig. 5) with which a new double colonnade was built in the interior of the cella. Traces on the floor indicate the positions and the diameters of these more recent columns and, of course, the length of their architraves. According to Travlos, the columns and other features must have come from the ground-level facade of a two-storey colonnade of the Pergamon type. These must have been used on both levels of the double colonnade,[35] each of whose storeys would have had its own complete entablature and cornice (fig. 7), in violation of the ancient rule according to which the columns on the lower level ought always to be larger and to have an entablature consisting only of an architrave (see p. 92, fig. 41). The unorthodox nature of this composition was presumably a result of the need to give the colonnade the maximum possible height using the only columns available, which were too short.

However, a more detailed examination of certain morphological variations makes it likely that the material did not all come from a single portico or colonnade, but from two different porticoes or, at the least, two different colonnades. Furthermore, the surviving constructional details indicate that the sections of the portico or porticoes from which the cornices were taken had only one storey,[36] not two. These observations, in conjunction with the variety of scattered materials located primarily in the Roman Agora and originating in the upper level of at least two different porticoes of the so-called 'Pergamon type', lead to the conclusion that apart from the Stoa of Eumenes and the Stoa of Attalus the city must have had at least two more porticoes of the same type; if it was not the case that one of these had a single-storey section (since that was its design, or because the upper storey was never finished), then there must have been still another portico, with one storey, perhaps in the vicinity. Unfortunately, the positions of all these porticoes cannot be identified until research into the ground of the ancient city continues.[37] However, evidence has emerged recently of the existence of two formerly unknown porticoes, one or both of which may have some connection with those referred to above. These porticoes flanked an elongated, though not narrow, straight unroofed space which began at the grand staircase directly opposite the east Propylum of the Roman Agora (fig. 8).[38] The arcade – a familiar structure – which still stands in position just behind the Horologion of Cyrrhestus is not part of a building but was simply a kind of ornamental entrance to the unroofed space behind it and between the two porticoes. It seems likely, then, that the materials for the new colonnades inside the cella of the Parthenon were taken in part from at least one of these two porticoes.

The colonnades from which the marble blocks for the repairs were taken seem to have been very long, since they provided not only the 46 new columns for the cella but also at least 13 more which were used, at about the same time, to repair the east portico of the Asclepeum,[39] and the materials to repair the threshold of the east door (with the use of eight surplus architrave slabs) and reconstruct some other parts of the temple. Most importantly, the reconstruction work involved the posts of the east door, which were also repaired using surplus architrave blocks, of which 11 have survived. This brings the total number of intercolumnal spaces to 77 and thus the total length to 193 metres.

In order to construct a strong new west doorway in the ruined opening of its predecessor, 90 different pieces of marble of various sizes weighing a total of 80 tons were used. These came from the demolition of ten large and a greater number of small votive, commemorative and funerary monuments dating from Classical times down to the Roman period (fig. 9).[40]

The fire-damaged surfaces were clad in places with

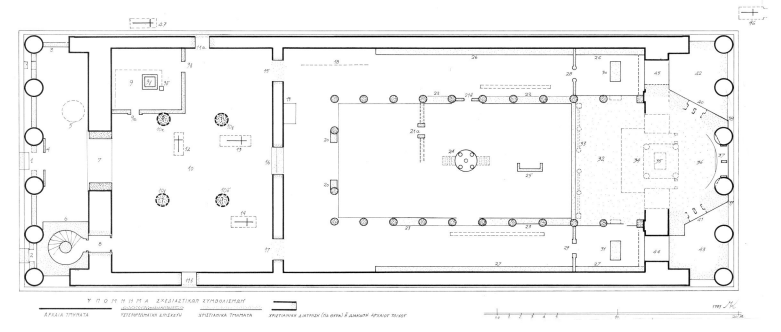

10. *Floor plan of the Parthenon as a Christian church. The most important parts are as follows: 1. Main entrance to the pronarthex. 2. Second main entrance (until the 13th century). 5. Marble receptacle. 6. Staircase (13th century). 7. Main entrance. 8. Second main entrance (until the 13th century). 9. Baptistery. 10. Narthex. 11. Side entrances. 12-14. Vaulted tombs under the floor of the narthex. 16, 15, 17. Central and side entrances to the main church. 18. Staircase to the gallery. 20. Piers of the arch. 21-23. Screens around the nave. 24. Later ambo. 26-27. Gallery support walls. 28-29. Side screens with short piers and rails. 30-31. Marble altars on four short columns. 32. Solea. 33. Hexastyle presbytery screen. 34. Ciborium. 35. High altar. 36. Synthronon. 37, 40, 41. Double apse windows. 38, 39. External corners of the apse. 42. Open water tank. 43. Vaulted tank. 44. Ancient window. 45. Modern window. 46-47. Vaulted tombs beneath the floor of the north pteroma. Drawing by M. Korres.*

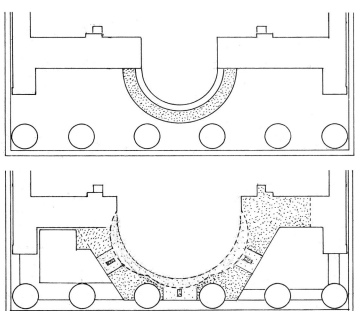

11. *The apse of the Christian Parthenon. Above: from the 6th to the 12th centuries. Below: from the 12th to the 17th-19th centuries. Drawing by M. Korres.*

marble slabs of various sizes, after they had been suitably scraped (walls, floors), or were plastered and remodelled in mortar (walls, columns between the antae). In some cases, the mortar was reinforced with iron pins wedged into holes in the marble (column capitals and architraves between the antae).[41]

The long marble beams in rectangular section which were needed for the roof were obtained by re-dressing and squaring the shafts of monolithic Ionic columns probably taken from the interior of the dismantled portico. Such beams were used in the roof of the pronaos, and in the cella to link the new colonnade and the walls at the height of the ceiling. At least one was used as a lintel for the west door,[42] and others may have been incorporated into the lintel of the east door.

The new roof covered only the cella. The area between it and the peristyle was left completely roofless: the greater part of its marble ceiling had already been removed[43] since the severe thermal damage done to it when the roof caught fire had made it unsafe in many places. Conversion of the pteromas into open spaces made it necessary to hew grooves in the floor to collect and lead off rain-water – most of which came from the roof. There were two more points of difference between the old roof and the new one: it was more steeply-pitched, and its tiles were of baked clay rather than marble. However, there may also have been some marble tiles: those which had been located above the marble entablature of the peristyle could well have escaped destruction by fire or fall.

The materials used for the great statue of Athena would have meant that it was completely destroyed in the fire. It, too, was replaced by a later work. In the floor are the bolt joints of the original pedestal and also of the pedestal belonging to the later statue, which was slightly smaller

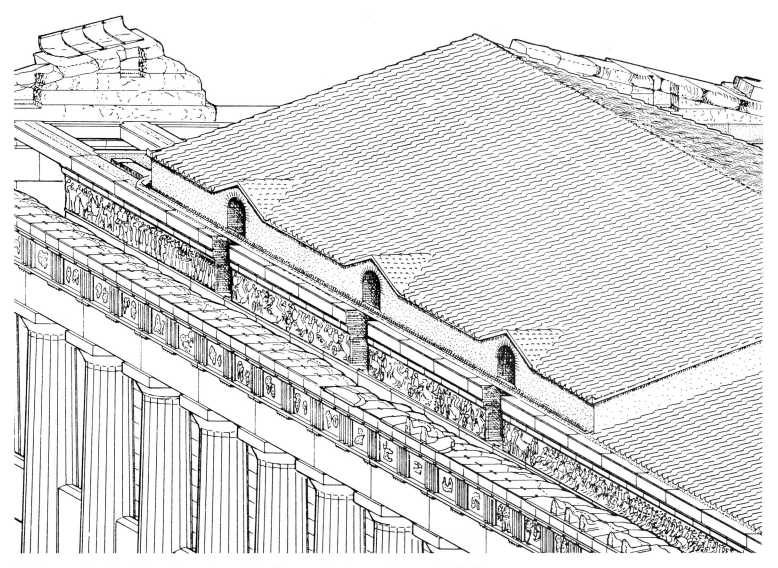

12. The raised roof and the side windows of the Christian Parthenon. Drawing by M. Korres.

(7.45 x 3.50 metres as opposed to 7.85 x 3.90 metres).[44]

After the fourth century, the collapse of the ancient world began to pick up speed as Christianity spread more and more widely. The decree on religious toleration (the Edict of Milan, 312-313), the recognition of Christianity as the official religion of the Roman state, the decrees of Theodosius I forbidding the practising of pagan worship (397), the decrees of Theodosius II (Codex Theodosianus XVI, 10, 25) concerning pagan temples, their purification and the conversion of many of them into Christian churches, and, lastly, the closing of the schools of philosophy under Justinian (529) were all historical landmarks for the fortunes of the Parthenon.

It would seem that the old religion ceased to be practised in the Parthenon some time during the fifth century. Later, possibly under Justinian, the temple was used for Christian rites, although our first firm evidence of this dates from a century afterwards.[45] Given that the plan of the temple resembled that of the basilica type of church, it proved possible to convert it with relatively little interven-

tion (fig. 10). Three doors were made in the wall between the chambers, and the west chamber was connected to the cella and served as a narthex, with its entrance not only through the west door but also through two others made in the side walls. The east door was walled up: its doorway, somewhat widened, became the arch across the front of a large apse built in the centre of the pronaos. This apse was initially semicircular (fig. 11) and was built using stones from ancient monuments, at least one of which was itself semicircular in shape: the monument to commemorate general Cephisodotus,[46] which originally stood inside the Propylaea, in front of the temenos of Artemis Brauronia.

The baptistery had a rectangular floor plan and occupied the north-west part of the narthex, from which it was separated by delicate screens (partitions).[47] It had two doors and a rectangular font in the centre, made out of four slabs of marble set upright along the sides of a gap created by removing an entire slab of the ancient floor.

In the temple itself, the two levels of the colonnades

13. The second stage of the apse of the Christian Parthenon. Drawing by M. Korres.

were used to create galleries simply by installing wooden floors in the side aisles.[48] For architectural reasons, the central column in the transverse colonnade was removed, and to provide better lighting three windows were made high up in each of the side walls. Each of these windows involved the removal of an entire slab of the frieze and the cutting out of part of the top course of masonry and the beam along the wall (fig. 12).

The opisthonaos was converted into a pre-narthex, with stone-built screens[49] and occasional doors in between the columns.[50] Stronger and higher walls were built to block off the spaces between the columns of the peristyle,[51] thus turning the unroofed pteroma into a kind of ambulatory which went some way to making up for the absence of the atreum usual in a basilica.[52] Three large doors and a greater number of small ones allowed access to the pteroma from all four sides of the building. In these places, the steps necessary to mount the crepidoma were added or hewn out, but only on the level of the second step and the stylobate: by that time, the first step had dis-

appeared beneath later deposits of soil. Porches were attached to at least two of these doors round the perimeter, but we do not know at what date (fig. 15).

The conversion from temple into church was generally beneficial to the further conservation of the monument. On the other hand, it was not without certain grave consequences. The raised reliefs of the sculptures of the metopes on the two short sides and the north long side were extensively defaced[53] and the central (and largest) pedimental sculptures on the east pediment were detached, along with the greater part of the cornice beneath the pediment and the tympanum.

While the Parthenon was functioning as a Christian church, there were numerous burials in tombs hewn out of the foundations immediately beneath the floor, in the narthex[54] and in the north pteroma.[55] During the same period, hundreds of inscriptions were carved on the walls and especially on the columns of the peristyle,[56] along with various symbols. These carvings make the Parthenon a still more valuable monument: it constitutes the major part of the city's 'museum in stone', in other words the largest archive of information about the medieval history of Athens.

To date, 232 of these graffiti have been read; 60 of them are precisely dated, and they are spread uniformly over the entire period during which the building functioned as a Christian church, after the mid fifth century. They usually consist of invocations to Christ or the Virgin, or commemorate the deaths of various persons and, more rarely, events of other kinds. Scores of names of bishops, archbishops, other members of the clergy, officers and other persons have been preserved for us thanks to the extremely important 'chronicle in stone' of the medieval Parthenon. The Christian Parthenon was dedicated to the Virgin Mary, and its commonest name for many centuries was Our Lady of Athens.[57] From the 'stone chronicle' we learn that the bishopric of Athens was raised to an archbishopric before 841, and then to a metropolitan bishopric before 981. Some of the archbishops of Athens had notably successful careers: in the time of Archbishop Nikolaos Ayiotheodoritis (1166-1175), for example, the extensive conversion of the Parthenon into a Christian church – the most drastic repair project since Roman times – seems to have taken place.

Most of the east wall, still authentically ancient, and the semicircular Early Christian apse were demolished. Only the section with the south (ancient) window was left.[58] A new wall was built in the same position, but the apse was much larger, with thicker walls and a semihexagonal outer surface (figs. 11, 13).[59]

The middle two columns of the ancient pronaos, which had been free-standing till that time, were engaged into the east wall of the apse. Their architrave was removed, together with the frieze slab above it,[60] all the superior courses of masonry and three of the seven roof beams in the east pteroma. In any case, these had long lost their coffered panels.

A double arched window was built into each of the three sides of the apse.[61] The outer slab from the dismantled architrave was redressed and used as the sill for the middle window.[62]

At this time, or more likely early in the following century, marbles taken from the systematic demolition of the Philopappus monument (specifically, from its rear) were used to build a rectangular tower – that of which part, up to the height of the architrave, has survived.[63] Originally, the tower was higher than the roof.[64] Inside was a spiral staircase leading to the top of the tower. We know none of the details of a rectangular structure which for centuries stood on the entablature of the opisthonaos and the roof beams behind the west pediment.[65] A brick wall containing a blind arch built in the ruinous centre of the west pediment may be connected with this structure.[66] Part of

the purpose of the wall was to hold in place the parts of the sculptures which were ready to fall, and in particular the figure of Poseidon.

The interior layout of the church and its liturgical fittings, the outcome of a long process of addition, was as follows. On the left side of the pronarthex was a phiale, that is, a large tank of water.[67] The sanctuary and the side recesses had marble altars,[68] of which that in the sanctuary was surmounted with a four-pillared ciborium.[69] These areas ended at a screen placed approximately six metres from the east wall and consisting of low piers, a rail and short columns. The floor of the sanctuary was raised only in the nave,[70] and the floor of the apse was elevated still higher above this level.[71] Indeed, it is said that there was a tank of water beneath the floor of the apse.[72] The seats of the bishops and presbyters (the synthronon) consisted of a number of steps, with a throne at the axis and the highest point.[73] Behind this was the large double window; the stone tracery of the two panes in each part of the window was superb.[74]

On the synthronon, on either side of the throne, were box-shaped stone repositories for sacred vessels which opened only from the top and were covered with marble slabs that gave the whole group the appearance of a stone-built altar.[75] Similar structures were attached to both sides of the wall between what had been the cella and the west chamber.

On the left of the nave, not far from the presbytery screen, was the circular marble ambo, standing on what was – initially, at least – a solid pedestal (fig. 14).[76] This ambo, or one like it supported on short columns,[77] is mentioned by the last visitors (before the Parthenon was blown up by Morosini) as standing on the left (north) of the nave, close to the pulpit (on its column) from which the Koran was read.

In the 12th century, when Nikolaos Ayiotheodoritis or possibly Michail Choniatis was archbishop,[78] the walls of the church were extensively painted,[79] and it may well be that the outside was whitewashed at this time.[80]

In 1204, the Greek lands were conquered by the armies of the Fourth Crusade and then distributed among the various leaders. Otto de la Roche occupied Attica and Boeotia, and took the title of Duke of Athens and Thebes.

The Parthenon now became an archepiscopal cathedral of Our Lady – with official approval, by the Papal Bull of 27 November 1206, by virtue of which the newly-installed Archbishop Bérard was given the same jurisdiction as his Orthodox predecessor had had over churches and clergy throughout the province of Athens.[81]

At about this time, the first bell-towers made their appearance outside Athenian churches.[82] The Parthenon may have had one too, possibly as an addition to the watchtower which stood on the south side of the

14. The original form of the ambo in the Christian Parthenon. Scale 1:20. Stone δ1911 was taken from the monument of Conon and Timotheus (4th century BC), stone α1439 from the pedestal of a colossal bronze statue, and stone ν558 from the pedestal of a gigantic bronze tripod. Drawing by M. Korres.

pronarthex[83] or to the structure above the west pediment (fig. 16). In 1261, the Byzantines drove the Westerners from Constantinople and liberated part of the former empire, but Attica and Boeotia remained in the hands of the De La Roche family. In 1311, after the murderous battle of Lake Copais, the lands of the De La Roche passed into the hands of the Catalan Company, who installed their own garrison and command on the Acropolis.[84] In 1378-81, some of the Catalan conquests were held by the company of soldiers of Navarra.

At a special meeting held in the Parthenon on 20 May 1380, the Catalans drew up a report known as *Els Capitols d'Atenes*, addressed to Pedro IV of Arragon and requesting his protection. The king assented. His order appointing a 12-man garrison for the "Acrópolis de Atenas" contains laudatory remarks which, after a thousand years of silence, indifference or ignorance, were the first recognition from the West of the great aesthetic value of the Acropolis.

In general, Pedro was opposed to the damaging of church property in order to facilitate Catalan military works.

In 1388, possession of the Acropolis passed to Neri Acciaiuoli of Florence. The Propylaea was converted into a palace, and strengthened with various fortifications.[85]

Neri Acciaiuoli died in 1394. In his will, he gave instructions that he was to be buried in the Parthenon, and he bequeathed the entire city of Athens to 'Santa Maria de Atene', appointing Venice as the executor of his testament. Three years later, Venice took advantage of the role that Neri had assigned it to occupy the Acropolis. However, before long they had to deal with the claim laid to the Rock by Antonio Acciaiuoli, the Greek-Florentine son of Neri. Reinforcements were requested from the Serene Republic, and the strong but time-worn walls of the Acropolis were repaired (1401).

In 1403, after a siege lasting fifteen months, the Acropolis was back in Acciaiuoli hands.[86] The palace (that is, the Propylaea) was further extended[87] and life returned to peaceful normality. Henceforth, the official language of the Duchy of Athens was Greek, in which even the nobles of Florence spoke and wrote amongst themselves. Antonio also restored the Greek Orthodox bishopric of Athens (which, however, was soon locked in combat with the Latins).

Neri's will (1394) and the account of the Italian visitor

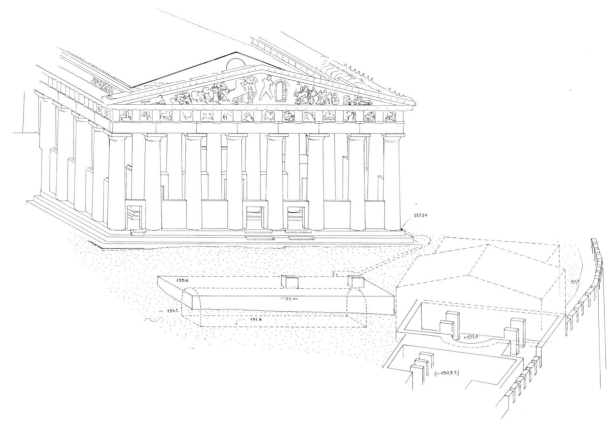

Nicolo da Martoni (1395) provide us with valuable information about the Parthenon. They mention precious highly-ornamented vessels, books, etc., valuable silver ornamentation on the doors, a mosaic of Our Lady with the Holy Infant in the apse of the sanctuary, the famous perpetual light (probably a votive offering of the Byzantine Emperor Basil II) which stood in a recess into which the relics of a saint were probably built, and the ciborium over the altar with its four pillars.

We have no information from this period about the smaller buildings on the Acropolis. We cannot be sure whether the Erechtheum was still functioning as a Christian church, in the form which it had taken in the Early Christian period. Graffiti on the walls and fragments of inscriptions in Greek and Latin are the only archaeological material on which we can base our hypotheses about the Erechtheum under the Franks.[88] We do know, however, that apart from the Parthenon there was another church on the Acropolis, that of San Bartolomeo in the Propylaea.

The famous traveller Ciriaco de Pizzicolli di Ancona[89], the first visitor with a knowledge of antiquity and a systematic interest in archaeology, came to Athens twice, in 1436 and 1444. His descriptions and sketches (on which the familiar depictions of the Parthenon by Guiliano and Francesco da Sangallo were based) are archaeological data of the greatest value.[90] After the death of Antonio Acciaiuoli in 1435, Athens was ruled by his nephews Ranieri (Neri II, 1435-1439, 1441-1451) and Antonio (1439-1441) and by Chiara Zorzi of Venice, widow of Neri II, who in 1453 married – in the Parthenon – Bartolomeo

Contarini, also of Venice. At just this time, pressure from Byzantium and also from the new conquerors of Greece, the Turks, had built up to such an extent that Neri II was forced to pay tribute to the Turks. That state of affairs was only a provisional one, however. In 1456 the Turks took the city and besieged – or rather, blockaded – the Acropolis. Two years later, the last Duke of Athens, Franco Acciaiuoli (son of Antonio), departed with his family from the castle, leaving behind only Nicolo Protimo, the archbishop.[91] An age had come to an end – an age whose only traces in the Parthenon today are a few graffiti and inscriptions (fig. 18).

The governor sent to the city by the Sultan established his headquarters in the west side of Hadrian's Library,[92] while the former administrative building (the Propylaea) now became the offices and living quarters of the garrison commander (the disdar-aga). The harem, however, was installed in the Erechtheum, not the Propylaea.[93]

In the meantime, the Latin clergy departed and the Orthodox Church was restored. For a short while, the Parthenon was officially returned to the Church,[94] but we do not know – given that the Acropolis was a military camp – whether the Turks allowed it to function.

In 1458, Mehmet II, the conqueror of Constantinople, visited Athens and admired the monuments[95] – including, presumably, the Parthenon. On his way back from the Peloponnese in 1460, he stayed in Athens again, and it must have been at this time that the Parthenon was converted into a mosque (figs. 17, 19).[96]

Some information about the monuments is to be gained from two other visitors of this period: a Greek (the

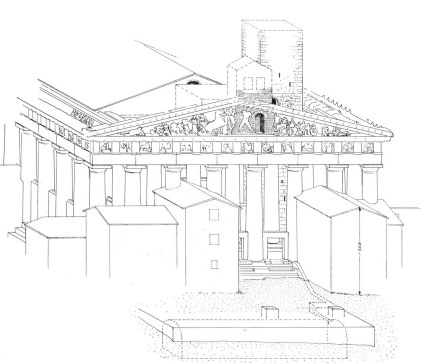

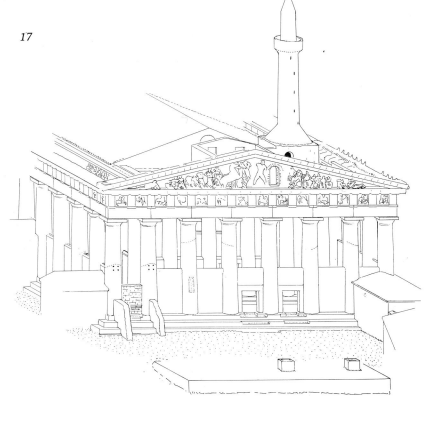

15. The west side of the Parthenon in the 12th century. Drawing by M. Korres.

16. The west side of the Parthenon in the 13th century. Drawing by M. Korres.

17. The west side of the Parthenon in the 17th century. Drawing by M. Korres.

18. Remnants of a monumental Frankish inscription on the west wall of the Parthenon. Photograph by M. Korres.

18

'Vienna Anonymous' of shortly before 1460)[97] and a Venetian who mentions the conversion of the Parthenon into a mosque.[98] The Turkish occupation, however, led to the almost complete disruption of communication between Athens and Western Europe for a long period of time.

References to the forgotten city of Athens were rare, and usually inaccurate. The first pictures of the city – nder the name Settines or Setiné (corruptions of 'Athens') – circulated in the West, but were totally imaginary. They were simply compositions with features of the landscape, architectural forms and human figures borrowed from corresponding pictures of places and cities in Western Europe.[99] In the rare written references, Athens and Piraeus (Porto Leone) were described as almost deserted places full of ruins. Unfortunately, this period also saw the intensification of what had for long been a bad habit among Westerners: the removal of marbles from ruined or complete ancient buildings and their shipping abroad. These vessels were usually bound for Genoa or Venice,[100] although there were other destinations, and the Greek marbles were re-dressed into the architectural and sculptural members of the new and splendid buildings being erected there.

These seaborne undertakings did most damage to the monuments closest to the coast, but even those further inland were affected to some extent. On the other hand, the looting of the same monuments by the local populace, and especially by the Turks for their new building projects, was just as destructive. The Temple of Olympian Zeus in Athens was one of the many monuments to be severely plundered for its material. In the fifteenth century it still had 21 columns, but by the end of the next century only 17 were left. The fragments of columns from the Temple of Olympian Zeus of which many are still to be found on the Acropolis, remnants of the demolition of Turkish structures, are testimony to the way in which the value of historical monuments was perceived at this time. The Parthenon, however, continued to be of functional use as a building and this, fortunately, protected it from the fate of the Temple of Olympian Zeus.

In the 16th century only Turks lived on the Acropolis, while the rest of the city[101] was inhabited primarily by Christians. The Turks allowed Christian Orthodoxy to survive in all the lands they conquered. This was not only a matter of ensuring a quiet life for themselves. The Turks were also able to turn to their own account the schism between Catholics and Orthodox, which, thanks to the boundless fanaticism it released, tended to make the enslaved peoples suspicious of the West and unwilling to receive any support from that source in the direction of their liberation, purely and simply out of the fear that such assistance was aimed at subjugating the weakened Orthodox populations to the papal throne.

Two centuries after the rapid expansion of the Ottoman Empire, however, things were very different. Some of the Western powers had emerged, successively, as economic and military powers on an international scale, while the vigour of Turkey had begun to decline and there was intense interest in the Turkish-occupied areas among diplomatic, business, scientific and artistic circles in the West. At this time, too, Greeks began to distinguish themselves for their social position and learning, and often maintained connections with the West. The teaching of science began again in Athens with Theophilos Korydallefs (1563-1646).

The seventeenth century saw the beginnings of intense interest in French and English high society in acquiring antiquities from Italy, Greece and Asia Minor.

The Acropolis of Athens was, from the start, a suitable source of such acquisitions, but it was far from easy – especially for Christians – to obtain permission to ascend the Rock. Military considerations, and in particular the fear of espionage, outweighed any inclination the garrison commander might have had to be of service to his eminent visitors.

In 1645 a Jesuit mission arrived in Athens. They were followed in 1658 by Capuchin friars, who in 1669 settled in a house they had bought to the east of the Acropolis, on the site now occupied by the square which surrounds the choragic monument of Lysicrates. They went to the trouble of making a topographical plan of the city (1679). The French consul, Jean Giraud, who had arrived at the same time as the Jesuits, was for many years the principal foreign scholar in Athens and served as a guide to visitors.

The cruel Turkish-Venetian war came to an end in 1669, making a visit to Athens easier for those interested. Among the visitors of the period 1671-1679 was the English traveller Bernard Randolph. His book of impressions includes some of the basic dimensions of the Parthenon, which he describes as one of the most glorious buildings of Europe, noting its excellent state of preservation. He also reported the poor lighting of the mosque (light entered only from the east) and that the Turks had whitewashed the interior (presumably partly in order to obliterate the Christian wall-paintings).[102] Francis Vernon gives precisely the same partial measurements in a letter of 1676.[103]

Among the surviving descriptions of the Parthenon[104] prior to 1687, the richest in information are those of the Turkish traveller Evliya Çelebi,[105] who was in Athens shortly after 1634, and of Jacob Spon and George Wheler, who visited Athens in 1675-1676. Of less importance are the accounts of the Jesuit J.P. Babin (1672), of G. de la Guilletière (1674) and of C. Magni (1674). The drawings produced by the painter (believed, with reason, to have been J. Carrey) who accompany C.F. Olier, Marquis de Nointel (French ambassador in Constantinople) on his visit to Athens in 1674 are of the greatest value as documentation of the sculptures of the Parthenon.

These descriptions are notable for their extreme inaccuracy and are rife with misunderstandings. However, they do make clear that the internal layout of the Parthenon as a mosque retained many of the functional features which it had had as a church: the phiale,[106] the ciborium,[107] the synthronon,[108] the episcopal throne,[109] and the old box-shaped repositories for sacred vessels,[110] among others. Strangely enough, the mosaic depiction of Our Lady was also still visible.[111] Indeed, these visitors report that the Turks believed in a legend according to which a divine power had punished with mutilation the first Turk who attempted to damage the mosaic in the apse. They also believed that an epidemic would overwhelm the population if the Christian repositories for sacred vessels were broken open.[112]

We can be certain that when the church was converted into a mosque the bell-tower, the presbytery screen,[113] the high altar,[114] and the altars in the side apses[115] were all removed. There is some uncertainty about the fate of the ambo, about the successive positions of the episcopal throne, about the location of the minber,[116] about the exact position of the mihrab, about whether or not there was a Turkish (?) water-tank beneath the floor of the apse and as to the exact form taken by the internal supports of the side walls so as to hold up the galleries. Was the upper part a series of piers, as Michaelis hypothesised,[117] or was it simply a continuous structure identical to the lower sec-

19. The Parthenon before 1670 (detail of a drawing in the Bonn Kunstmuseum). Source: H. Omont, Athènes au XVII siècle, *Paris 1898; Athens, Gennadios Library.*

tion, of whose form numerous traces have survived in the ancient floor?[118]

There is also uncertainty as to the windows. Most visitors make mention – with considerable vagueness, usually – only of the double window in the centre of the apse. Magni reports small openings for lighting in the roof, while Vernon speaks of windows in the upper part of the side walls.[119] These windows correspond to the breaks in the continuity of the frieze marked with the word "venter" on Carrey's drawings. A recent stone-by-stone study of the material surviving on the ground has shown that these windows broke not only the frieze but also the upper course of masonry and the beam on the top of the wall. They were thus higher than the wall, which allows us to conclude that the apertures shown along the roof of the Parthenon in the drawings of the Acropolis from the south-west[120] of 1670 (fig. 19) are none other than the upper part of these windows, which would be the only section of them visible from a distance.[121] This systematic study of the surviving marbles proved beyond doubt that there were also double windows on the two sides of the apse.[122] Consequently, all that we can assume from the accounts of the seventeenth century is that by that time most of the ancient windows had been blocked up. The phenomenon of a gradual reduction, during the Middle Ages and especially in Turkish times, of the number and size of church windows is in any case far from a rare one.[123]

The nature of the internal colonnades, the ceilings and the roof is another question over which different views have been advanced at different times. Also in dispute are the issues of whether there were internal arcades dating from Christian times with capitals not in the Doric order, of whether there was a barrel vault (at least over the nave) and of whether the roof was covered with marble tiles whose joints were filled with insulating plaster. The reason for the variety of views expressed on these issues is the lack of clarity in the descriptions of the various parts of the building.

Recent research into all the material dating from later phases in the building's history has shown that down to the end (1687) the internal colonnades consisted of the semi-fluted Doric columns[124] which had replaced the originals in late Roman times. Also until the end in 1687, these columns supported the same straight architraves. When the temple, after its repairs, was converted into a Christian church, only one column had been removed: that which stood exactly on the axis of the temple, and only after a broad arch had been constructed in the same position to bear the weight of the entablature. The corresponding column in the upper colonnade remained in position – that is, "above empty space" (the arch), a feature which impressed Evliya Çelebi with the boldness of its construction.[125] As a result, the number of columns in the lower colonnade was 22 (23 minus 1), while above, as Spon and Wheler quite correctly report, it was 23.

Although it is easy enough to discover the truth about the columns, it is much more difficult to reach a final conclusion about the way in which the interior was roofed. Since the building had not been designed for vaults, its

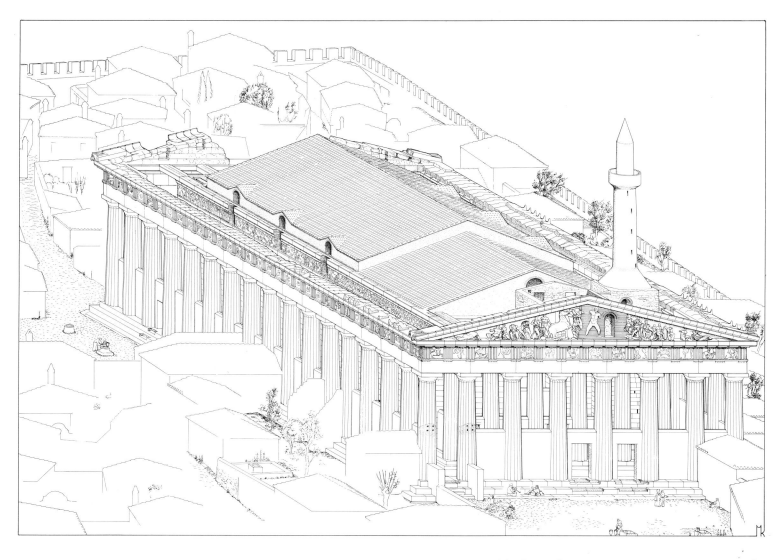

20. *The Parthenon in the 17th century, isometric reconstruction. The peristyle, roofless since the 4th century and with its gaps walled in to a height halfway up the columns, formed a most unusual kind of perimetric courtyard. Drawing by M. Korres.*

walls were unsuitable for such weights. That consideration, however, is not sufficient to reject the possibility of there having been such vaults. The Temple of Hephaestus (often known as the 'Theseum') is statically similar to the Parthenon and yet it was later given a barrel-vault whose thrust the building is still withstanding.[126] It could, of course, be argued that the magnitudes of the Temple of Hephaestus are smaller than those of the nave of the Parthenon (width 6.25 m., maximum height approx. 9 m., as against 10 m. and about 18 m., respectively), but the Parthenon has thicker walls and its peristyle is much heavier. Static calculations have shown that various forms of light vault would have been feasible. The limited number of small windows is an argument in favour of the vault theory, as is the consideration that when the new roof was constructed there would have been every reason to choose materials which would prevent a fresh fire and the renewed destruction of the building. In archaeology, how-

ever, reasonable hypotheses are one thing and proof is quite another.

The wooden roof version is just as possible, if not indeed more so. The appearance of the roof in the drawings of 1670 (fig. 19), for example, is more consistent with a wooden structure. It is also clear from these drawings that the new structure was more steeply raked than its predecessor, that it did not extend as far as the pediments and that it was lower above the west chamber of the sekos (the narthex of the church) and higher above the cella. If the roof actually was wooden and Babin was not using the word "voûte" carelessly,[127] then we could hypothesise that below the roof there was a wooden ceiling which imitated a barrel vault.[128] It is equally difficult to reconstruct the west chamber, whose original columns must also have been destroyed when the temple burned down for the first time. What kind of new ceiling did it have, and how was it supported? How many supports were there – four or six? The travellers' descriptions make it seem likely that the west chamber had marble columns, to which the Turks had added a stone-built pier to make good a fault in one of the columns or in part of the ceiling itself.[129] Our hypotheses about the nature and material of

21. The blowing up of the Parthenon on 26 September 1687. Isometric reconstruction. Drawing by M. Korres.

the roof are connected with another consideration: how safe was the temple as a store for the gunpowder kept there in 1687?

That year, 1687, was unfortunately the unhappiest in the troubled history of the monument. The second Turkish-Venetian war was in full flood, and the Peloponnese had already passed from the hands of the Turks into those of the Venetians, where it was to remain for thirty years. Yet conditions now were no longer so favourable for the establishment of a Venetian presence in Attica. Indeed, the extremely able Venetian commander in chief, Francesco Morosini, had foretold as much. Nonetheless, at a council on 14 September 1687 it was decided to move on the castle of Athens, and before long troops and powerful batteries of cannon and mortars were in battle positions round the Acropolis. The bombardment was merciless and hundreds of shells struck the Parthenon, where the Turks – trusting to the great solidity of the building – had stored enormous quantities of gunpowder. In the end, fate struck. On the evening of 26 September

1687, after four days of bombardment, a shell went through the roof – perhaps entering by an opening which was already there – and ignited the gunpowder, causing an explosion which demolished the central part of the building (fig. 21).[130] After that time, the Parthenon was a roofless ruin. Although the Venetians had won a sweeping victory, they soon decided that it was against their interests to remain in Attica and that they would have to evacuate the castle. The Turks became its masters once more, but it took them a long time to recover from the damage and repair their stronghold. The houses rose once more in the castle, around the proud Classical monuments, but less densely that prior to 1687. Unfortunately, we do not know exactly when the new mosque was built inside the devastated Parthenon. We do, however, have a very clear picture of what it looked like thanks to the many depictions of it: nearly all of them are drawings, but there is one unique photograph, taken by Joly de Lotbinière in 1839.

The general impression that the ruinous state of the Parthenon before the first reconstruction work of 1842 was the outcome of the explosion of 1687 is mistaken. As far as the side walls are concerned, only 2/3 of the damage can be ascribed to the disaster of 1687 (fig. 22).

In 1802, a team of labourers working for Lord Elgin took some two metres[131] off the height of the standing sections in order to remove a total of some 27 metres of frieze.

Twenty years later (1822), the Turks besieged on the Acropolis almost completely demolished the rest of these sections, which still stood to a height of 11 metres, in order to get at the lead in the ancient joints,[132] which they melted down to make bullets. Some 520 ancient stones were moved out of position at this time, 200 of them being cut up for use in makeshift building operations.

The state of the walls before this demolition (fig. 20) was almost exactly that shown in some of the drawings of Dalton (the preservation of the Parthenon down to 1749, where the ruined monument is depicted – strangely enough – without the small mosque in its centre), Stuart and Revett (1751),[133] J.D. Le Roy (1755), Gell (1800) and others.

It would seem from a recent study of the pronaos[134] that a certain amount of demolition had occurred even before 1750. It also seems likely that two or three columns on the south side and in the pronaos had not been felled by the explosion, at least completely, but continued to totter in a precarious state. They must have been brought down soon afterwards, either by the forces of nature or by the inhabitants of the castle so as to remove the risk of an accident.[135] The same may be true of the minaret,[136] which was located in the part of the building that withstood the explosion.

The marbles brought down by the explosion lay in huge tumbled heaps around the building and also inside its ruins. From the start, and down to the middle of the eighteenth century, these stones were used as a source of lime to rebuilt and repair the parts of the walls that had collapsed.[137] This, indeed, was how enough space was made to built the little mosque. The rendering down of the marble continued until almost none was left inside the temple, at which point the surviving part of the south-east anta was demolished[138] and much of the ancient paving was removed from the floor in various positions around the new mosque.[139]

Inside the peristyle, in the pronaos and around the temple, the piles of stones lasted much longer. Until the liberation of the castle in 1833, they were subjected to constant diminution and sifting at the hands of demolition workers, stone-masons and collectors of antiquities.

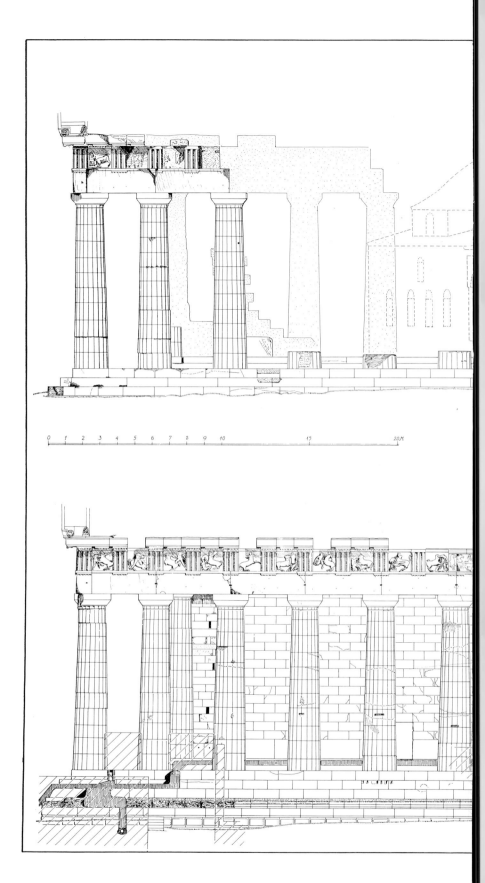

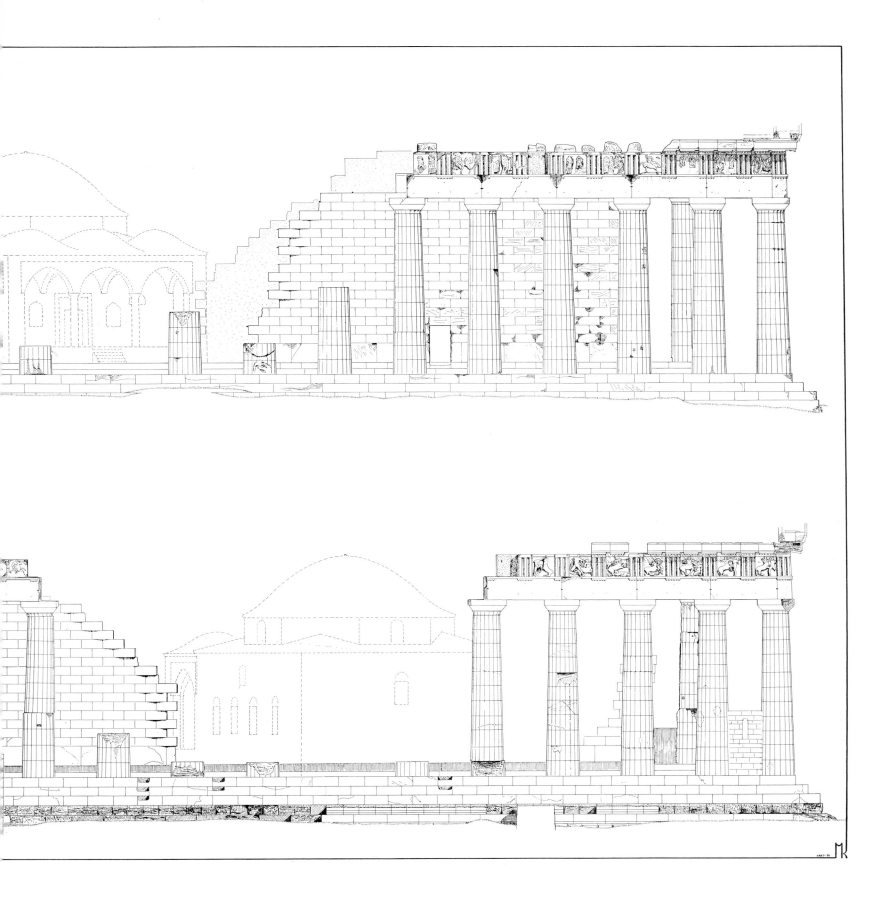

22. The Parthenon in the year 1800. Above: the north side. Below: the south side. The drain along the first step of the crepidoma led rain-water from the tanks on the east side to the much larger tank to the west. The small mosque inside the temple survived until 1843. Drawing by M. Korres.

Notes

1. For the conditions for preservation of the monument, see M. Korres, Ch. Bouras, *Meleti Apokatastaseos tou Parthenonos* ('Study for the Restoration of the Parthenon', hereinafter *Meleti*) vol. 1, Athens 1983, pp. 201-378.

2. *Pericles*, 13, 1.

3. *Peloponnesian War*, C, 89.

4. *Meleti* 1, pp. 328-330.

5. G.P. Stevens, *Hesperia*, Suppl. 3, 1940, pp. 64-66. In general, it would appear that the shields were put up in a number of phases, though not those hypothesised by Stevens. However, Stevens was correct in supposing that the shields on the long sides were put up at a later date. The whole question is still being studied.

6. Plutarch, *Demetrius*, 23, 3.

7. Plutarch, *Isis and Osiris* 379D, *Athenaeus* IX, 405, *Pausanias* I, 25, 7; 29, 16.

8. According to A. Orlandos, *I Architektoniki tou Parthenonos*, vol. I, 1976 (plates), vol. II, 1977 (text), vol. III, 1978 (text), hereinafter Orlandos, *Parthenon*, p. 214, the objects erected on the long sides in this second phase may have been gold wreaths and not shields.

9. R. Wenning, *Pergamenische Forschungen* 4, 1978.

10. *Bulletin de correspondence hellénique* (= *BCH*) 110, 1985, p. 675.

11. R. Bohn, *Die Propyläen der Akropolis zu Athen*, Berlin 1882, pp. 39-40; W.B. Dinsmoor, *American Journal of Archaeology* (= *AJA*) 24, 1920, p. 82.

12. Although traces of the last word can still be discerned.

13. *Inscriptiones Graecae* (= *IG*) II2, p. 3272.

14. *IG*II2, p. 3173; W. Binder, *Der Roma Augustus Monopteros auf der Akropolis in Athen*, Stuttgart 1969.

15. *IG*II2, p. 3277; E. Andrews, *Journal of Hellenic Studies* (= *JHS*) 16, 1896, p. 339; *Class. Rev.* 10, 1896, p. 222.

16. Orlandos, *Parthenon*, p. 215; Kevin K. Carrol, 'The Parthenon Inscription', *Greek, Roman and Byzantine Monographs* no. 9, 1982. The fact that the inscription is off-centre from the axis of the temple is not a coincidence (Carrol, *op. cit.*, p. 20), but was dictated by the fact that the high monument obscured the north-east corner of the temple.

17. I, 24, 7.

18. Initially (*Meleti* 1, p. 330), this author assumed that the new cornice also belonged to the repairs carried out immediately after the earthquake of 426 BC. However, more recent observations allow us to conclude that the new cornice is actually of a much later date. The high quality of the dressing and laying of the cornice probably advocates a date in the 1st century AD. For the repairs to the pediment, see also H. Carpenter, *Hesperia* 2, 1933 and W.B. Dinsmoor, *AJA* 38, 1934, p. 98.

19. F. Penrose, *The Principles of Athenian Architecture*, 2nd. ed., London 1888, p. 20, plate 9A.

20. W.B. Dinsmoor, *AJA* 38, 1934, p. 102; J.J. Coulton, *The Architectural Development of the Greek Stoa*, 1976, p. 225.

21. *AJA* 45, 1941, pp. 399-427, note 89,5 (on p. 426).

22. A. Michaelis, *Der Parthenon*, Leipzig 1871, p. 48.

23. *Meleti* I, pp. 136, 138a; *Meleti Apokatastaseos tou Parthenonos* vol. 2a, Athens 1989, by M. Korres in association with N. Toganidis, K. Zambas and T. Skoulikidis at the head of a team of restorers (hereinafter, *Meleti* 2a), pp. 46-48.

24. When the building was converted into a Christian church, the east door was demolished and the sanctuary apse built in its place.

25. Marinus, *Proclus*, 30.

26. See note 44, below.

27. A. Franz, *AJA* 83, 1979.

28. *Ibid.*, p. 397.

29. According to the programme of restoration currently in progress, the more recent theshold of the east door will be restored to its position. This will show and prove the damage done by the pivots of the leaves of the door and their replacement or repair.

30. G. Travlos, *Bildlexikon zur Topographie des Antiken Athen*, Tübingen 1971 (hereinafter, *Bildlexikon*), p. 444; *Archaeologiki Ephimeris* ('Journal of Archaeology', = *AE*) 1973, pp. 218-236.

31. The Heruli, a Germanic tribe who had been displaced from Scandinavia by the Danes in around 250 AD, invaded Greece in 267 and got as far as the Peloponnese, destroying more or less everything in their path. In the end, they were defeated at the river Nestus by Gallienus. The Athenians, under Dexippus, had previously managed to drive them away, but not before they had ransacked the countryside.

32. Dexippus, fragment 21; H. Thompson, 'Athenian Twilight, AD 267 - 600', *Journal of Roman Studies* (= *JRS*) 49, 1959, pp. 61-72; J. Travlos, *Poleodomiki Exelixis ton Athinon* ('The Urban Planning Development of Athens', hereinafter *Poleodomiki*), Athens 1960, p. 125.

33. *Meleti* 1, pp. 344-354.

34. *Meleti* 1, pp. 288-294.

35. *AE* 1973, p. 288. Dinsmoor (*AJA* 38, 1934, p. 101), under the influence of the well-known account of Magni, hypothesises that the upper columns were probably of another type (possible Aeolic).

36. The upper surface of the cornices is rough rather than flat, as it ought to have been if it once bore the facade of an upper floor.

37. Travlos, *Bildlexikon*, p. 577; Ch. Bouras, 'Hellenistic Athens', *XIII Internat. Kongress für klass. Archäologie*, Berlin 1988, p. 269.

38. Travlos, *Bildlexikon*, pp. 28-31, 36-41.

39. As first demonstrated by B.H. Hill, *AJA* 45, 1941, pp. 399-427, note 89,5; I.T. Hill, *The Ancient City of Athens* 1953, p. 127, and note 7 to chapter XV.

40. N. Kyparissis, *Archaiologikon Deltion* ('Archaeological Bulletin', hereinafter *AD*) 11, 1927-28; G.P. Stevens, *Hesperia* 15, 1946, pp. 17ff. Of the inscriptions removed from the later doorway, the most recent, an epitaph in the neo-Platonic spirit (*IG*II2, p. 3816), provides a lower limit for dating the repairs to the temple. Unfortunately, however, its dating to the third century is not entirely safe.

41. These have been commented on by most students of the monument: Penrose, Bötticher, Durm, Dinsmoor, Orlandos and others. The capitals of the Temple of Apollo at Delphi were repaired in a similar manner after a fire; see P. Amandry, Académie Royale de Belgique, *Bulletin de la classe des lettres...* LXXV, 1989, pp. 32ff.

42. This marble remained in place (see photographs by E. Piot, J. Robertson, W. Stillman, F. Boissonas and others) until being lowered to the ground in 1926 (N. Balanos, *I Anastylosis ton mnimeion tis Akropoleos* ['The Restoration of the Acropolis Monuments'], Athens 1940, p. 123, plates 138, 142, 143). Unfortunately, only a small piece of it has survived.

43. Michaelis, *Der Parthenon*, p. 49. Confirmation was provided by the excavations in the ancient Agora. Fragments of the panels and of the internal columns were found in fifth century walls; W. Dinsmoor Jr., *Hesperia* 40, 1971, pp. 275, 277; *Archaiologika Analekta ex Athinon* ('Archaeological Miscellancy from Athens', = *AAA*) 4, 1971, pp. 264-268; *Hesperia* 43, 1974, pp. 132-135; *AJA* 77, 1973, pp. 211.

44. *AJA* 38, 1934, p. 95, fig. 2; see also *Hesperia* 24, 1955, p. 244.

45. *Jahrbuch des Deutschen Archäologischen Instituts* (= *JdI*) 54, 1939, p. 138; Travlos, *Bildlexikon*, p. 445.

46. *AD* 1889, p. 210; *IGII2*, p. 3828; *Meleti* 2a, p. 53.

47. M. Korres, *5on Symposion Vyzantinis Archaiologias* ('Fifth Symposium on Byzantine Archaeology'), Association of Christian Archaeology, Athens 1985, pp. 36-38. It used to be assumed that the font was in the pronarthex (Michaelis, *Der Parthenon*, p. 46, note 167; *AE* 1960, pp. 4, 12) or outside, to the north of the apse (*JdI* 54, 1937, p. 133).

48. Michaelis, *Der Parthenon*, p. 46; Travlos, *Bildlexikon*. fig. 576. However, the staircases to the galleries were not in the narthex, but in the church itself.

49. Michaelis, *Der Parthenon*, pp. 46, 50.

50. There were three doorways (in the space between the central columns and the spaces between those at each end, as correctly supposed by E. Breton, *Athènes*, Paris 1868, p. 132, floor plan I, G, H) and not two, as later scholars hypothesised. In addition, a single hewn step can still be discerned between the first and second columns, despite the severe damage which the stylobate has sustained at this point (cf. Orlandos, *Parthenon*, plate 1, and see also A. Orlandos, L. Vranousis, *Ta Haragmata tou Parthenonos* ['The Graffiti of the Parthenon'], Athens 1973, p. 13).

51. J.P. Babin (Michaelis, *Der Parthenon*, p. 336). Deichmann believes that these screens date from the Late Byzantine or Turkish period (*JdI* 54, 1939, p. 134). However, it seems that the system of screens was not uniform and they did not all date from the same period. The earlier screens date back to the building's first years as a church. Later, however, they were replaced, some of them being removed entirely and others being substituted by the walls of buildings abutting on the peristyle, erected principally during the period of Frankish rule. The Turks later demolished many of these buildings, leaving the spaces between the columns almost empty.

52. Michaelis, *Der Parthenon*, p. 51.

53. C. Praschniker, *Parthenonstudien*, 1928, pp. 48ff. For the survival of the metopes on the south side and of one on the north side as capable of receiving an 'interpretatio Christiana', see *Archäologischer Anzeiger* (= *AA*) 1933, pp. 401-405 (Rodenwaldt).

54. P. Kavvadias, G. Kawerau, *I anaskafi tis Akropoleos ton Athinon* ('The Excavation of the Acropolis of Athens'), Athens 1907, pp. 103-104, plate 7, nos. 69, 70, 71; J.J. Bundgaard, *The Excavation of the Athenian Acropolis*, Copehagen 1974, vol. I, p. 43, vol. II, plate 111 (sketch by Kawerau).

55. See also A. Norre-Dinsmoor, *Studies in the History of the Parthenon*, University Microfilms Inc., Ann Arbor, Michigan 1966 (hereinafter, A.N. Dinsmoor, *Studies*), p. 34; *AJA* 16, 1912, p. 541, fig. 14. Another tomb, beneath the floor towards the west extremity of the north pteroma, remains unexplored. The square depression midway along this pteroma was a receptacle for bones (see Orlandos, *Parthenon*, plate 1, and *BCH* 112, 1988, p. 612). One of these tombs beneath the floor must have been that of Neri Acciauioli, if, of course, the wish he expressed in his will (1394) was respected.

56. Orlandos and Vranousis, *op. cit.*

57. J. Strzygowski, *Mitteilungen des Deutschen Archäologischen Instituts*, Athenische Abteilung (= *AM*) 14, 1889, p. 276. Earlier visitors mistakenly believed that the church honoured 'the Unknown God' (the Vienna Anonymous) or the Holy Wisdom of God (Guilletière). K. Pittakis' theory, too, about a church of the Holy Wisdom is probably unfounded.

58. *Parthenon-Kongress*, pp. 47-54.

59. *Meleti* 2a, pp. 48-53.

60. See the previous note; F. Brommer, *Der Parthenonfries*, Mainz 1977, pp. 115-116.

61. See above, note 47 (M. Korres).

62. See the previous note and *Meleti* 2a, p. 108.

63. It is shown on almost all the published ground plans. For a section drawing (by Ch. Bouras) and other details, see *AE* 1960, pp. 1-16.

64. *Meleti* 1, p. 151 and notes 7, 8, 9.

65. Remnants and traces of Byzantine plaster at various points behind the pediment and above the beams show the extent of the building. Part of it was still standing in the eighteenth and early nineteenth centuries, and it can be distinguished in various drawings, such as those of J. Stuart and N. Revett, *The Antiquities of Athens*, vol. I, 1762; vol. II, 1787; vol. III, 1794; vol. IV, 1816 (hereinafter, Stuart and Revett; specifically, in vol. II, chapter I, plate I), where it can be seen in the background through the space between the third and fourth columns from the north, of Gell (*Meleti* 2a, p. 143), and of C. Hansen (A. Papanikolaou-Christensen, *Athina, 1818-1853, Erga Danon Kallitechnon* ['Athens, 1818-1853, Works by Danish Artists'], Athens 1985, plate 13). This remnant was demolished before 1842.

66. See the drawings of Carrey and derivatives of them in H. Omont, *Athènes au XVIIe siècle. Dessins de sculptures du Parthénon attribués à J. Carrey et conservés à la Bibliothèque Nationale, accompagnés de vues et plans d'Athènes et de l'Acropole*, Paris 1898 (hereinafter, Omont).

67. This stood to the left of the entrance according to Evliya Çelebi, who thought it was a kind of gigantic wine-cup "belonging to the men who built the Parthenon" (from the Greek edition of Çelebi on Attica, edited by K. Biris, Athens 1959, p. 33). Babin also mentions the *phiale* and interprets it as a font. Spon and Wheler do likewise. For the *phiale* see also *Praktika tis Christianikis Archaiologikis Etaireias* ('Proceedings of the Association of Christian Archaeology', = *XAE*), 1932, pp. 19-32.

68. See above, note 47 (M. Korres). For the high (middle) altar, see A. Orlandos, *I xylostegos palaiochristianiki vasiliki* ('The Wooden-Roofed Early Christian Basilica'), Athens 1954, p. 408.

69. See above, note 47 (M. Korres). The bases of the pillars of the ciborium have recently come to light.

70. This difference in height, marked by steps, is mentioned by early visitors. In both aisles, however, the traces and pin joints of the screens can be seen in the floor itself.

71. This can be deduced from the mentions of a tank beneath the floor of the apse (see the following note) and from the fact that while the first apse was much broader than the original doorway, the posts were left in place – that is, they did not obstruct the space. Of course, this could be the result only of the existence of the *synthronon* and the consequent reduction in the width of the space beneath it. But there are other reasons, too, for believing that the floor was raised. According to travellers, there were two or three steps inside the apse (the fact that we are talking about a *synthronon* and not simply a staircase can be seen in Magni's use of the word "scaglioni"), while the episcopal throne which stood on them was *in front* of the window (see below, notes 73, 74). However, we must retain our reservations about the height of the floor in the apse, since the information we possess to date could also be consistent with a floor lower than that initially advocated – if, for example, the tank (if it existed: see the following note) was very low and if the *synthronon* stood on a pedestal or if its upper part was not a step but a kind of pedestal. The question is still under investigation.

72. There are reservations as to the accuracy of Spon's information: Michaelis, *Der Parthenon*, p. 55, note 216. Was the small stone-built hollow which K. Bötticher (*Bericht Über die Untersuchungen auf der Akropolis von Athen in Frühjahre 1862*, Berlin 1863, p. 160) discovered beneath the floor of the apse the tank in question? Was it in fact the space for the box of relics often placed beneath the altar when a church was founded? Or was it merely a sacrarium, a system for draining off the water left after the washing of the altar and the priests' hands? Whatever it was, this hollow must have been contained within the Byzantine structure, for once it was removed the ancient floor was revealed in its entirety, as it remains today over the area of interest to us here.

73. The throne is mentioned by most visitors. When the first archaeological work was being done on the Parthenon (1835 *et seq.*) there were three or four marble thrones in the building. Of them, the one identified by Ludwig Ross (*Archäologische Aufsätze* I, p. 113) is now in the Acropolis Museum (S. Casson, *Catalogue of the Acropolis Museum*, vol. 2, Cambridge 1921, p. 278, no. 1366; for the inscription see *IG* II 1524, and G. Richter, *Ancient Furniture*, Oxford 1926, p. 13; *AM* 63-64, 1938-39, p. 134, note 7, and *AJA* 58, 1954, pp. 271-276; see also Dinsmoor, *Studies*, p. 22).

74. The tracery is mentioned by all the visitors, but without the requisite clarity. Wheler names the window and gives the exact position of the screens below the opening on either side of the throne (see Michaelis, *Der Parthenon*, p. 48, note 176). Recent research and identification of the surviving marbles of the apse have confirmed his description.

75. The vagueness of the travellers' descriptions has caused the formulation of various misleading hypotheses about the positions of these repositories. However, systematic correlation of all the data leads only to the conclusion that there were four of them, arranged symmetrically on the *synthronon* (for more details, see note 110).

76. Spon wrote that "au milieu du Temple sur le coté gauche est une tribune élevée sur de petites colonnes de marbre, et qui étoit sans doute la chaire du Predicateur". Deichmann hypothesises that it was a platform on six small columns, traces of which have survived in the north aisle (*AM* 63-64, 1938-39, p. 136). Traces of a structure such as that described by Spon are to be seen on the ancient floor (recesses and bolt joints for the columns), but they are exactly in the centre of the nave and not on the left. These allow the reconstruction of an ambo on short columns (K. Biris, *Evliya*, plate 1, with the comment "minper = the ambo of a Christian church"; Dinsmoor, *Studies*, pp. 29-30; Korres, *op. cit.*, note 47). A.N. Dinsmoor (*Studies*, p. 31) hypothesises that the ambo was later moved towards the north-east of the nave. Recent research has led to the reconstruction of an ambo with a solid pedestal which probably predated the structure described by Spon (M. Korres, *7on Symposion Vyzantinis kai Metavyzantinis Archaiologias* ['7th Symposium on Byzantine and Post-Byzantine Archaeology'], Association of Christian Archaeology, Athens 1987, pp. 38-39). The paved floor of this ambo was later used again in the mosque and ultimately remained in the building until the end of the nineteenth century.

77. See the previous note. It seems rather unlikely that the ambos coexisted; the second probably replaced the first. However, if they actually did co-exist, then it seems very likely that the first ambo was re-used not only for the minber but also for the mihrab. If not, then the second ambo may have made use of the upper part of the first.

78. Michael Acominatus, *Sozomena* ('Remains'), ed. S. Lambros, I, II, Athens 1979-80. See also *Armonia* 3, 1902, p. 284; F. Gregorovius,

Geschichte der Stadt Athen im Mittelalter, von der Zeit Justinians bis der türkischen Eroberung, vols. I-II, Stuttgart 1889 (hereinafter, Gregorovius), here vol. I, pp. 204ff; *Proceedings of the XAE* 1932, p. 31; *AE* 1953-54, p. 295; M. Pavan, *L'avventura del Partenone, un monumento nella Storia ...*, Florence 1983 (hereinafter, Pavan, *Partenone*), pp. 46-47.

79. See the previous note. See also *Archaeologia* 51, 1888, p. 175; M. Bruskari, *Les monuments de l'Acropole*, 1978, plates 50, 51; M. Collignon, *Le Parthénon*, (photographs by Boisonnas), plate 135, 1, 2.

80. According to the first observations and conclusions (still under review) of the chemical engineer N. Beloyannis and the restorer D. Dogani.

81. Pavan, *Partenone*, p. 59.

82. *Ibid.*, p. 67; C. Barla, *Morphi kai Exelixis ton Vyzantinon Kodonostasion* ('Form and Development of Byzantine Bell-Towers'), Athens 1959, and esp. p. 42.

83. See above, note 73. See also *JdI* 102, 1987, fig. 28.

84. K.M. Setton, *Catalan Domination of Athens*, London 1975.

85. *JdI* 102, 1987, p. 416 (T. Tanoulas); Travlos, *Poleodomiki*, pp. 163ff, fig. 106; Ministry of Culture, *Catalogue of the Exhibition 'The Acropolis at Athens, Conservation, etc.'*, Athens 1986, p. 106 (T. Tanoulas).

86. Gregorovius, vol. II, pp. 265-267.

87. Pavan, *Partenone*, p. 92.

88. J.M. Paton, *The Erechtheum*, Cambridge, Mass. 1927, pp 512-519.

89. E.W. Bodnar, *Cyriacus of Ancona and Athens*, Brussels 1960.

90. Omont, plate XXIV.

91. Gregorovius, vol. II, pp. 372, 388.

92. I. Knithakis, F. Mallouchou, I. Tinginaga, 'To Voevodaliki tis Athinas' ('The Voevodate of Athens'), *Eponyma Archontika ton Chronon tis Tourkokratias* ('Mansions Belonging to Eminent Families in Turkish Times'), Ch. Bouras (ed.), National Technical University, Athens 1986, pp. 105-124.

93. Paton, *op. cit.*, pp. 523ff.

94. L. Ross, *Archäologische Aufsätz, op. cit.*, pp. 245ff; C. Wachsmuth, *Die Stadt Athen* I, Leipzig 1874, p. 13; Michaelis, *Der Parthenon*, p. 54. Gregorovius (vol. II, p. 390) finds it highly unlikely that the Parthenon functioned as a Christian church after the Turkish conquest (1458). See also Pavan, *Partenone*, p. 108.

95. C.O. Müller, *Fragmenta Historicorum Graecorum*, vol. V, Paris 1870, p. 125, and L. Chalcocondiles, *De Origine ac Rebus Gestis Turcorum*, Bonn 1843, pp. 453-455.

96. See above, note 94.

97. Michaelis, *Der Parthenon*, p. 335 (page erroneously numbered 353).

98. *AM* 24, 1899, p. 72.

99. L. de Laborde, *Athènes aux XVe, XVIe et XVIIe siècles*, vol. I, Paris 1854, p. 39.

100. Pavan, *Partenone*, p. 121.

101. *Ibid.*, p. 104; see also the letter from S. Kavasilas to M. Kraus (1578); Laborde, I, p. 58; Ross, *op. cit.*

102. Michaelis, *Der Parthenon*, p. 336.

103. *Ibid.*, p. 339.

104. Collected by Laborde, Michaelis and others. The fullest collection is that of A.M. Dinsmoor, *Studies*, pp. 216-309 (list of testimonia).

105. Biris, *Evliya*.

106. Evliya, Babin, Spon, Wheler. For a special study, see D. Pallas, *Proceedings of the XAE*, 1932, pp. 12-32. See also Dinsmoor, *Studies*, p. 34.

107. Evliya (who tells us that the canopy of the ciborium was made of ebony) and Spon (who reports that the columns were made of porphyrite with white marble Corinthian capitals). See also note 47 (M. Korres).

108. Babin, Spon, Wheler (who describes the *synthronon* as semicircular with two or three steps), Magni.

109. De la Guilletière, Spon, Wheler; see also note 43.

110. Babin, De la Guilletière, Spon, Wheler. These are described as numbering two or four (on either side of the throne, in the wall) and as being shut (all of them or only half of them). This partially conflicting and partially complementary evidence allows us to conclude that the repositories were either on the upper part of the *synthronon* or, more probably, directly above what was left of the side windows (see notes 47 and 59), the outer side of which must already have been blocked off (thus preventing them from being seen as windows and explaining why the visitors do not mention them).

111. Babin, De la Guilletière, Spon, Wheler; Michaelis, *Der Parthenon*, note 176.

112. See the previous note.

113. Michaelis, *Der Parthenon*, p. 55.

114. Babin, Spon, Wheler.

115. Babin.

116. Dinsmoor, *Studies*, p. 31; Michaelis, *Der Parthenon*, note 216; *AM* 63-64, 1938, pp. 39, 136 (with the minber in the north aisle).

117. Michaelis, *Der Parthenon*, pp. 46, 49.

118. See above, note 47 (Korres). See also *Hesperia* 43, 1974, p. 141 (stalls along the walls), and Travlos, *Bildlexikon*, fig. 576.

119. *AJA* 58, 1954, p. 145.

120. Omont, plates 29, 29´; another copy of the original plan is preserved at Bassano: Pavan, *Partenone*, p. 134, fig. 20.

121. The placing of windows in the upper part of the walls was not in accordance with the rules of Early Christian and Byzantine architecture, but it did provide much better lighting. If the windows had been lower down, they would have been in the shadow of the peristyle. Stones from the courses above the frieze have roughly dressed surfaces which until 1687 were the sides of the windows. A study of these stones has contributed to identifying the position of the windows in terms of the length of the walls. The rainwater gutters around the roof were on top of the walls (that is, along a line interrupted by the windows), but their continuity was ensured by beams which crossed the gaps in front of each window. One such beam, with the gutter dressed and plastered, has still survived, on the ground.

122. *Meleti* 2a, pp. 48ff, figs. 24 and 25.

123. The walling in of windows was done primarily for static reasons. In the case of the Parthenon, however, these reasons cannot have been very strong.

124. Michaelis (*Der Parthenon*, p. 48) believes that when the Parthenon was converted into a Christian church the internal columns were replaced. Deichmann (*AM* 63-64, 1938-39, pp. 129ff) held the earlier view that the older columns were replaced by others which supported arches. In about 1460, 'Anonymous of Vienna' (Michaelis, *Der Parthenon*, p. 335) saw straight white marble beams not only from column to column but also from the columns to the wall. The columns described by Evliya must have been those of the late Roman repairs. Wilkins (1802) observed the traces of Roman columns on the floor of the temple and, inside the temple, semi-fluted columns of a thickness corresponding to that of the traces (*Atheniensia, or, Remarks on the Topography and Buildings of Athens*, London 1816, p. 100). Later (1837-38), J. Hoffer observed the traces and the column sections corresponding to them (*Allgemeine Bauzeitung* 1838, p. 390). This, in conjunction with earlier accounts and some of the first photographs of the sekos, showing it full of ancient marbles (including recognisable sections of the internal columns), make it certain that the columns which replaced the originals at some point were still in place in 1687.

125. Biris, *Evliya*, p. 35.

126. Travlos, *Poleodomiki*, p. 91; John M. Camp, *The Athenian Agora*, London 1986, fig. 187. For the static problem of the vault, see F.C. Penrose, *The Principles of Athenian Architecture*, 1st ed., London 1851, p. 68, note 2.

127. De la Guilletière uses the same word. Babin himself calls one of the flat roofs of the temple a "voûte plate".

128. Evliya describes a closely-fitting wooden ceiling (Biris, *Evliya*, pp. 36-37). Biris himself hypothesises (*ibid.*, p. 41) that there were simple trussed beams above the ceiling.

129. Spon, Wheler; Michaelis, *Der Parthenon*, note 192.

130. For the explosion, see *Meleti* 1, pp. 365-70, and *Die Explosion des Parthenon*, catalogue of an exhibition at the Antikenmuseum, Berlin 1990.

131. To be exact, 1.93 metres (wall beam + top course of masonry + frieze = .56 + .35 + 1.02 = 1.93). The fact that the top course of masonry and the beam still survived above the frieze is clear from the drawing of Gell (F. Brommer, *Die Parthenon-Skulpturen*, Mainz 1979, fig. 17).

132. E. Blaquire, *Narrative of a Second Visit to Greece*, vol. 1, London 1825, p. 157.

133. Stuart and Revett, vol. II, plate 2 (the Erechtheum, with the Parthenon on the left). There are no differences between this drawing and those of Dalton and Gell as far as the break in the north wall is concerned.

134. *Meleti* 2a, pp. 48-54.

135. *Meleti* 1, pp. 365-367.

136. Michaelis, *Der Parthenon*, p. 66.

137. Stuart and Revett, vol. IV, p. 40.

138. As above, notes 134 and 135.

139. This can been seen from the fact that the floor has only survived complete where it was covered by the small mosque.

FANI MALLOUCHOU-TUFANO

The Parthenon from Cyriacus of Ancona to Frédéric Boissonas: Description, Research and Depiction

An Approach to Concepts and Media over Time

First Approaches

Ciriaco de' Pizzicoli of Ancona in Italy (more familiar as Cyriacus) visited Athens in April 1436,[1] ascending the Acropolis and admiring the Parthenon. A man of the Renaissance – but at the same time an eminent personality in his own right – Cyriacus did not gaze upon the church of Our Lady,[2] as all previous visitors had done, but upon "the great marble temple of Pallas Athena, the masterpiece of Pheidias".[3]

Cyriacus of Ancona was an energetic merchant, a self-taught antiquarian, a man of inquiring and highly restless mind. He lived in an era when relations between the West being 'reborn' and the declining Byzantine Empire were becoming closer, in the face of the Ottoman threat. A traveller since extreme youth throughout what had once been the united Graeco-Roman world, Cyriacus was conscious of that world's shared cultural identity. He dissented from the philological approach to antiquity then prevalent in humanist circles and turned towards its other remnants, especially those of Greece. Cyriacus sent manuscripts, coins, seal-stones and sculptures back to Italy to enhance the first collections then being set up in Florence and Venice, was a systematic copier of inscriptions and viewed the architectural monuments.[4] Once more adopting an opinion unusual for his age, he saw those monuments as historical documentation – "historiarum sigilla" – more reliable than that of texts, and as possessing an image which ought by all means to be preserved for the future, in the form of descriptions and drawings.[5]

On his first visit to the Acropolis, Cyriacus was struck by the Parthenon, by the number of columns which surrounded it and by their size, and above all by the sculptures which adorned the temple. On his second visit, in 1444, he was impressed by the same features. This time he kept more notes about the columns, the peristyle, the superb walls and, principally, the plastic ornamentation of the building. He recognised the Centaurs and the Lapiths on the metopes and the Athenian victories during the Periclean period of the frieze, and he admired the colossal statues of humans and horses on the pediments. Standing before the Parthenon, Cyriacus remembered what he had read about the monument in the ancient authors – Aristotle and Pliny – and, for the first time in modern history, connected the ancient sources with the reality of the monument. Thus he proved himself to possess the seeds of original thought and method, a factor which distinguished him from the humanists of his age. On one of his visits, he drew the monument.

Various copies of Cyriacus' drawings have survived, the most important of them being those of the Hamilton Codex in Berlin and those which the architect Giuliano da Sangallo copied into his personal book of drawings (taccuino). The most striking feature about the drawings is how far they lie from architectural reality, which is refracted on the basis of subjective ideas and concepts already in Cyriacus' mind.

This was to be a characteristic of all the subsequent depictions – and even descriptions – of the Parthenon down to the nineteenth century. The architecture and sculpture of the monument were always rendered in accordance with the aesthetic and stylistic concepts prevailing at the time, and in line with the degree of knowledge – or rather, ignorance – of the original draughtsman, the copyist or, later, the engraver as far as the architecture of Classical times and the plastic art of Pheidias were concerned. We should not forget that until the monuments of Paestum and Athens were 'discovered' in the mid-eighteenth century, Western Europe knew of Doric architecture only through Vitruvius, a valuable but sometimes misleading source, and all those who had undertaken to interpret him.[6] Nurtured at best on Hellenistic copies of Classical sculpture, and usually on the Roman imitations which were constantly coming to light in Rome, Western Europe first saw authentic Classical works in the early nineteenth century, when the marbles of the Parthenon and the frieze from the temple of Apollo at Phigaleia arrived in London.

In the Hamilton drawing (fig. 1), the Parthenon acquires a tall, narrow facade with a high pediment filled by the figure of Athena, in the centre, dressed in Renaissance

164

1. Cyriacus of Ancona: the west facade of the Parthenon. Drawing from the Hamilton Codex. Source: H. Omont, Athènes au XVIIe siècle, *Paris 1898; Athens, Gennadios Library.*

robes, by the lively horses of her chariot to the left and a whole host of putti, the winged cherubs of which Italian painters of the fifteenth century were so fond. The Doric order is suggested by the fluted columns without bases, but there are no triglyphs or metopes above the architrave. There is also a sketch, below the building, of scenes from the north and east sides of the frieze, whose figures are pure Renaissance in the moulding of their bodies and in their garments. The drawing itself is rigid and rather childish, presumably because the copyist was trying to be as faithful as possible to the original by the amateur Cyriacus.

In the second drawing (fig. 2) we have clear indications of artistic intervention. Sangallo 'copied creatively', using elements which he liked and which would be familiar to him from the monuments of Rome and from his studies of, or visits to, other places. The Parthenon is transformed into a grand building with better, though rather heavy, proportions, whose general picture – though not its details – is strongly reminiscent of the Pantheon in Rome. It is revealing of the knowledge and spirit of the

age that the south metopes of the monument, with their scenes from the Battle of the Centaurs, have been transferred to the facade, on to a kind of attic above and behind the pediment. Cyriacus must have made two separate drawings, one of the building and one of the metopes (as he had done with the frieze). Sangallo, not knowing where to put the metopes – Alberti, the source of such knowledge as he had, makes no mention of narrative scenes on the metopes of the Doric temple – retrieved from his memory and reproduced the attic, with its reliefs, from a Roman triumphal arch, a form with which he would have been familiar.[7]

These descriptions and drawings of the Parthenon remained in manuscript form and circulated only in the circle of friends and pupils of Cyriacus and Sangallo. They thus had a negligible effect on the aesthetic inquiries of the day. The Renaissance continued to devote its attention to manuscripts and Roman monuments. In effect, its relationship with the Parthenon began and ended with Cyriacus of Ancona.

After Athens was taken by the Ottoman Turks, the city and its monuments slipped out of the sight and minds of Europeans. Tiny, insignificant Athens lay far from the routes to Constantinople or the Holy Land, while the wars which raged across the Aegean throughout the greater part of the fifteenth and sixteenth centuries necessitated the further fortification of the Acropolis and made it difficult for foreigners to visit. Athens and the Parthenon lived on in the memory of Europe only through classical studies, which after the sixteenth

2. Cyriacus of Ancona: the west facade of the Parthenon. Copy by Giuliano da Sangallo. Source: Omont, op. cit.

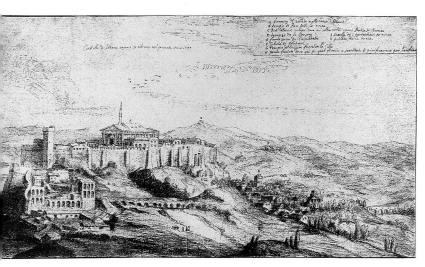

3. The Acropolis and the Parthenon from the south-west, c. 1670; Bonn, Kunstmuseum.

century began to spread beyond the bounds of Italy.

In Athens itself, memories of the glorious past survived, and were linked with Christian traditions in the manuscript, dating from about 1460, known as the 'Anonymous of Vienna'. The Parthenon has become a church to the Mother of God once more, built not by Pheidias but "by Apollos and Eulogius in the name of an Unknown God". The Vienna Anonymous enhances his narrative with on-the-spot observations of the temple, some of them confused and imaginary and others valuable and unexpected – such as the comment on the 'drystone' construction of the temple: "And its walls are made of white marble; and they sit squarely in position, without mortar and lime; each wall is raised with iron and lead".[8] Most of the descriptions of the Parthenon during the first two centuries of Ottoman rule contain a similar mixture of traditions and legends. Although generally vague and full of misunderstandings, they are valuable for modern researchers.

The conversion of the Parthenon into a church dedicated to the Unknown God belongs to the realm of tradition. Indeed, some visitors read an inscription to this effect on the monument.[9] The misfortunes which would befall anyone who dared to damage the interior ornamentation of the building or its functional equipment were legendary.[10]

Comments and observations on the architecture and sculpture of the monument always depend on the level of the viewer or listener, and on the special atmosphere of the environment and period in which he lived. In 1575, Theodosios Zygomalas was unaware of the ancient name of the Parthenon and did not know who had built it. He called it the Pantheon, "a building superior to all other buildings", and attributed its sculpture to Praxiteles – thus incidentally demonstrating how low the standard of learning had fallen in Constantinople at the time.[11] The early travellers, often passing through Athens quite by chance, were not notable for their knowledge of antiquity.[12] They

were impressed most of all by the material aspects of the monument and its quantitative measurements – the brilliance of the marble, the number of columns, the spaciousness of the building and its excellent state of preservation. They did not comprehend the arrangement of the chambers, the architectural order, or the iconography of the plastic ornamentation. They touched spontaneously on topics such as the naturalness and vigour of the sculptures, over which there was to be much controversy in the future.[13] They all expressed profound admiration for something which they did not really understand. The repute of the Parthenon among scholars was already very high, and had been since antiquity.[14] Yet without doubt the most heartfelt account of the Parthenon at this time is that of a man without a classical education: Evliya Çelebi, the much-travelled Turk who, on seeing the building in 1667, exclaimed, "I have seen many mosques in the world, but never one to equal this".[15]

Antiquarians on the Acropolis

By the end of the seventeenth century Western Europe had made a more decisive turn east. The volume of news from such parts increased constantly, as the publication of works of travel grew after the beginning of the century. At the same time, there was more and more demand for antiquities from the Greek world. Interest focused largely on small portable finds, which, together with others from Rome and Italy, adorned and enriched the palaces and collections of monarchs and nobles. The accumulation of archaeological finds contributed to the development of an antiquarian interest which was to come to a head in the eighteenth century. For the time being, attention focused on the external features of the objects as a source of visual pleasure and of information about the ancient world to supplement the texts, and not on the spirit and principles of their art. No attempt was made to classify them by period or style. Similarly, there was no interest in Greek architecture. Rome was the centre of culture: it was the place where artists from all over Europe met, and it was one of the major stops on the continental Grand Tour of stripling members of the English aristocracy. The monuments of Rome continued to be the sole, unquestioned standards in which the rules of formal architecture were sought. At this time, however, the studying and surveying of them became more systematic and, above all, more objective: a contribution to this was made by the foundation, in the seventeenth century, of the first Academies and learned societies. Among the various missions which they organised, that of Antoine Desgodetz, who in 1676/77 surveyed the monuments of Rome with unprecedented accuracy, introducing new methods and a new ethos into the drawing of ancient architecture, was of particular importance for its influence on the way in which the Parthenon and the other Athenian monuments would be approached in the future.[16]

4. J. Carrey: The Acropolis and the city of Athens from the north-east, 1674, oil-painting, detail; Athens, National Gallery.

During this period, European lovers of antiquity – most of them French – turned their attention to Athens and its monuments. On the first map of Athens – a general 'bird's eye view' of the type common at the time, drawn by the French Capuchins who had settled in the city – the Parthenon and the other monuments are shown schematically and conventionally, as map markings. The first depictions of the monument which clearly belong to the visual arts also date from this period. One, dated 1670, is a view from the Hill of the Muses in ink, an example of the Venetian landscape-painting tradition of the time copied in the well-known Bonn drawing (fig. 3).[17] Another, showing the Acropolis from Lycabettus, is the first colour painting (in oils) of the Parthenon, and it was the work of a professional painter, Jacques Carrey. In the painting,[18] all the town of Athens and the Acropolis, on which the Parthenon is the chief feature, serve as the background to the main theme of the scene: the ceremonious entry into the city, in November 1674, of Olier, Marquis de Nointel, Louis XIV's ambassador, and his numerous retinue, of which the painter was part (fig. 4).

Nointel may ultimately have failed in his inspired,

though premature, ambition[19] of introducing Europe to the real Greece, but he left behind a heritage of the greatest value. Carrey's drawings[20] of almost all the plastic ornamentation of the Parthenon are today a unique record of many sculptures which were utterly destroyed just a few years later, in 1687 (see the chapter by A. Delivorrias in this volume). The drawings, in black and red pencil, are generally accurate as far as externals are concerned – that is, in rendering the narrative scenes and the state of preservation of the pieces. Carrey refrained from filling in the figures, and he often recorded the damage which they had suffered (see p. 123, figs. 54, 55). His drawings are also incontrovertible testimony to the beliefs of seventeenth century painters unacquainted with Classical art. Deeply rooted in Carrey were the artistic principles and convictions he owed to his teacher, Charles Le Brun, the painter of Versailles,[21] and when he came to make his copies he transformed the self-controlled Classical gods and heroes into restless figures with strongly emphasised anatomical details and great plasticity which embodied rules for the proportions of the human body of undoubtedly baroque taste.[22]

5. J. Spon: the Parthenon, 1676. Source: J. Spon, G. Wheler, Voyage d'Italie, de Dalmatie et de Grèce..., Lyon 1678; Athens, Gennadios Library.

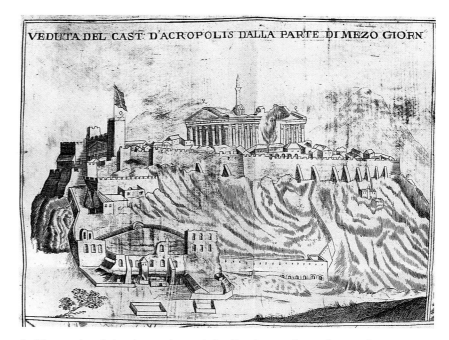

6. The castle of the Acropolis and the Parthenon from the south-west, after the explosion of 1687. Source: F. Fanelli, Atene Attica descritta da suoi principii sino all'acquisto fatto dall'Armi Venete nel 1687, *Venice 1707; Athens, Gennadios Library.*

Nointel was little more knowledgeable. Writing back to France, he boasted of the drawings produced by his artist, copies of sculptures "of which we can say that they surpass the finest reliefs and statues of Rome".[23] Nointel could perceive the quality of the sculptures, but not the difference of style. The same was true of his spiritual father, the Jesuit priest Jacques Paul Babin, who found the west pedimental sculptures of the monument far superior to the statues adorning the palace of Cardinal Richelieu, for him, at least, the "wonder of wonders".[24] Neither Nointel nor Babin – or those who were to follow them – understood the architectural dimension of the monument's plastic ornamentation. They saw the sculptures in the spirit of the seventeenth century, as mere ornamental elements "which deserve to form part of His Majesty's collection", as Nointel wrote[25] – prophetically, as it turned out.

The most important travellers of the period, Jacob Spon and George Wheler, visited the Parthenon in 1676. Their observations and drawings are of the greatest significance because of the tremendous popularity and wide circulation of their work in Western Europe throughout the following century.

In their examination of the monument, Spon and Wheler[26] dismissed the traditions and legends (censuring earlier travellers for having accepted them) and described in detail the various parts of the temple and the arrangement of its sections (the interior). Their description is the last before the explosion. Spon, an early scientific spirit, touched on questions such as the roof of the temple which still concern researchers today. Like all the travellers of their age, Spon and Wheler devoted their attention

to the sculptures, which they described at length. Taking the west facade of the monument to have been its entrance – an understandable error[27] – they thought that the pedimental composition showed the birth of Athena, as in the account of Pausanias. Spon 'Romanised' the monument: the Parthenon, as a symbol of artistic superiority and perfection even in ancient times, had to be made to fit in with the prevailing aesthetic values. Thus the west pedimental sculptures were not by Pheidias, but dated from the time of Hadrian, who was actually depicted, with his

7. G.M. Verneda, ground plan of the Acropolis castle, 1687. Source: Fanelli, op. cit.

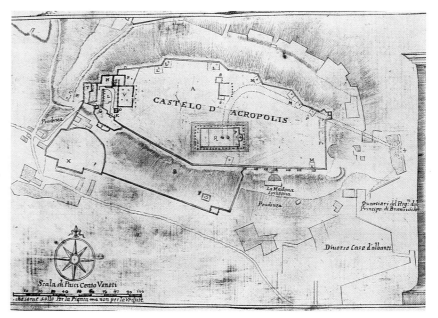

8. R. Pococke, *floor plan and elevation of the Parthenon, 1741. Source: R. Pococke,* A Description of the East and some Other Countries, *vol. II, part II, London 1745; Athens, Gennadios Library.*

consort Sabina, in the group of embracing figures[28] in the north corner of the triangle. This assumption later proved fatal for the reception of the sculptures in England.

Spon and Wheler's drawings (fig. 5), the first drawings of the monument to be printed, reflect their idea (or rather, their rejection) of ancient Greek architecture: the Parthenon is shown outside its actual setting, schematically restored to its hypothetical original form (rendered with mistakes[29]), and as an example of a strange architectural order which was completely alien to the aesthetic ideals of the age.[30] The wide circulation of this image established it as a symbol of the Doric Greek temple before its discovery in the middle of the next century.[31]

The English mathematician Francis Vernon was the last visitor of importance during the seventeenth century. In the most adverse conditions, he attempted to measure the monument with accuracy. In observing the Parthenon, he was the first visitor to suspect that behind Rome lay

Greece: "a procession of people going to sacrifice of very curious sculpture",[32] he wrote of the frieze in 1676.

The Parthenon had survived almost intact for many centuries thanks to its reputation, to the respect which it inspired and, above all, to the fact that it was in constant use, but it was destroyed on the evening of 26 September 1687 (fig. 6). The blast of the mortar fired by Morosini's mercenaries set off another explosion – of publicity. The Serene Republic brought out a whole series of propaganda texts spreading the news of the tragic event and the monument throughout Europe, while the successive editions of Spon and Wheler's travellers' texts in the main European languages made their valuable information – and their misunderstandings – common knowledge. Their drawings were equally widely published, together with other depictions of Athens, notably in the illustrated albums of Marco Vincenzo Coronelli.[33] The culmination of these publishing activities was the *Atene Attica* of F. Fanelli, which appeared in 1707. Together with the depiction of the exploding Parthenon (see p. 34, fig. 15), Fanelli published the first real maps of Athens and the Acropolis, drawn by Venetian army engineers using surveying instruments (fig. 7). *Atene Attica* also included the history of the city from its foundation to Morosini's 'redemption' of it by conquest, and descriptions of its monuments which summarised the archaeological knowledge of the age. All this was enveloped in an ideology which called upon the West to recover Athens in the historical cultural and archaeological sense.[34] At the same time, the pieces of the monument which found their way back to Venice and other cities along with the returning soldiers were an invitation to Europeans to demolish and loot it.

Back to the Fountain-Head of Art: Le Roy, Stuart and Revett

In the eighteenth century, the period of the Enlightenment and a time of an anguished search for new values of life and artistic standards, Europe discovered ancient Greece as an Idea and a Vision of high moral stature and liberty, of democracy, of equality and of justice. Along with the ancient land, the modern Greek world came to light, too, with its monuments, now elevated to the status of incomparable models of beauty and perfection, its landscape, which combined unusual beauty of nature and atmosphere with unique historical and mythological references, and its inhabitants, worthy successors – in their struggle for freedom – of their glorious ancestors. This period of encounter between Greece and Europe lasted some eighty years, from 1750 to the end of the third decade of the nineteenth century, and it proved to be exceptionally beneficial to both sides: Europe discovered its roots and underwent intellectual and architectural renewal, while Greece was helped to regain its independence.

9. R. Dalton: the south-east corner of the Parthenon, 1749. Source: R. Dalton, Antiquities and Views in Greece and Egypt with the Manners and Customs of the Inhabitants, from Drawings Made on the Spot, A.D. 1749, *London 1791; Athens, Gennadios Library.*

The first eighteenth century visitors, most of them British, continued to see the Parthenon through the eyes of Spon and Vitruvius. In 1741, Richard Pococke concluded that the architecture of the temple had not reached a high stage of development when it was constructed, unlike the sculpture, which had attained perfection.[35] His drawing (fig. 8) is confirmation of his opinion: the Parthenon is a Romanised Doric temple, with occasional sprigs of greenery to connect it with a surreal reality.[36] This period also saw the first visits by aristocratic grand tourists, a tendency which was to become much more general by the end of the century. The Earl of Sandwich, an important figure and one of the founder members of the Society of Dilettanti, was in Athens in 1738/39, and Lord Charlemont came with his own painter, Richard Dalton; both men were possessed of a new spirit, an open-minded and unprejudiced one which led them to make penetrating observations about the structure and arrangement of the monument.[37] To Dalton, a poor draughtsman with a limited talent who was imbued with the rococo ornamental trends of his day, we owe weak, anaemic depictions of the Parthenon (fig. 9) set in an environment lacking character and serenity, which were printed in an album in 1751. They were, however, the first attempt to show the monument in its true condition and not in some hypothetical restored form. Dalton's ornamental inclinations, typical of his age, are more manifest in his drawings of the west frieze, where the vigorous figures of Pheidias' horses were transformed into a number of miniatures strongly reminiscent of those of the Roman ring-stones (cammei) so popular among collectors of the period.

These drawings by Dalton were the first depictions of the Parthenon sculptures to be printed.[38]

After the middle of the century, the Parthenon and the other Athenian monuments took an active part in the process of rediscovery and reassessment of ancient Greek architecture. Now the monument began to be approached on the basis of the trends which had become prevalent: on the one hand, the neo-Classical search – addressed to the Greek monuments – for the basic rules of true architecture, and on the other the belief of empiricists that the monuments were a source from which emotional charges could be drawn and a starting-point for associative thought. Now, for the first time, the Parthenon – the monument per se, and not a literary echo of it – became decisively involved in European thinking. Its perfect response to the requirements of intellectuals progressively elevated it to the status of a symbol of Classical perfection – and also of the Romantic ruin, a process

10. J.D. Le Roy: elevation and ground plan of the Parthenon; reconstruction, 1755. Source: J.D. Le Roy, Les ruines des plus beaux monuments de la Grèce, *2nd ed. Paris 1770; Athens, Gennadios Library.*

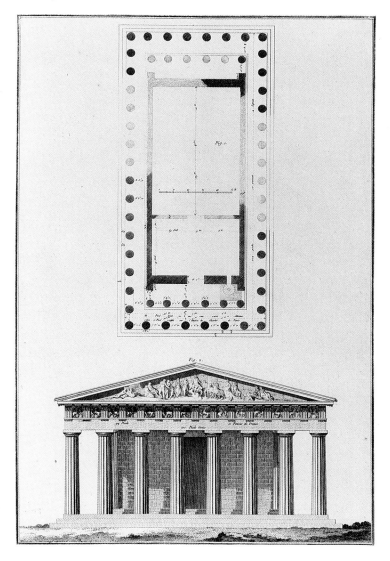

which was to reach its climax in the century to come.

As part of the neo-Classical approach, the monument was systematically explored for the first time by travellers who were also 'scientists', such as the architects Stuart, Revett and Le Roy, by professional painters such as Pars, and by classicists and archaeologists such as Chandler.

Everything began in Rome. In an atmosphere made favourable by the first find of the excavations at Herculaneum and Pompeii, which had brought to light many objects closely connected with Greece, and by the promptings of the first Grand Tourists to the east, Stuart and Revett printed a pioneering text, their Proposals (1748) in which they proclaimed their faith in the superiority of the monuments of Athens. These were monuments of "good sense" and "elevated genius", and the two authors intended to make them known, with drawings produced on the spot, to European artists in search of perfection.[39] This historic declaration, the manifesto of neo-Classicism, set off a chain of highly important events. On the one hand, it inspired Julien-David Le Roy, a scholar of the French Academy at Rome, to set off on his own mis-

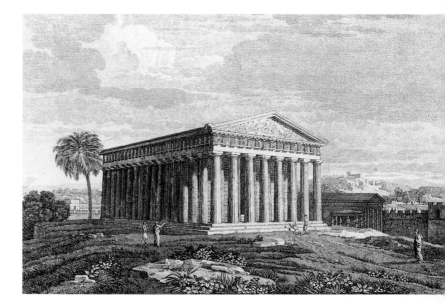

12. 'The Parthenon from Afar'. Source: Atlas of the Travels of the Young Anacharses compiled after J.D. Barbié du Bocage, Vienna, 1820.

sion to Athens, in February 1755. The fruit of his researches was the *Ruines des plus beaux monuments de la Grèce*, published in 1758, one of the earliest works about Greek architecture to be published in Europe and the first to cover the monuments of Greece itself. On the other, it marked the commencement of a series of English expeditions, supported morally and financially by the Society of Dilettanti, which thus ceased to be a social club for aristocrats with vaguely artistic leanings and became the principal lever, for a whole century, in promoting the scientific exploration of the Greek east.[40] These expeditions led to the publication of outstanding archaeological treatises, examples of a first scientific approach to the monuments and of a high aesthetic level, which were to leave their stamp upon the age.

In his treatise, Le Roy examined the monuments in their historical and architectural aspects, providing comments and lengthy references to ancient sources and more recent travellers – in the particular case of the Parthenon, to Spon[41] – ultimately producing more of a synopsis of the knowledge of his age than of an original analysis and contribution. The principal objective of his work, however, was theoretical. In line with the thinking that had become predominant in France as far back as the seventeenth century with regard to the need to revive architecture by means of a return to rationalism and the truth of primordial forms,[42] Le Roy supplemented his treatment of the monuments with a theoretical study of the historical evolution of architecture and the principles which govern it. In those principles, Le Roy demonstrated the advance of Greek architecture towards perfection, while at the same time underscoring its clear superiority over all other architectures, earlier of later.[43]

Le Roy illustrated the architectural part of his study with

11. J.D. Le Roy: details of the column capitals and the entablature; artist's reconstruction, 1755. Source: J.D. Le Roy, op. cit.

13. J.D. Le Roy: the Parthenon from the south-east, 1755. Source: J.D. Le Roy, op. cit.

geometrical drawings, a ground plan, and artist's reconstructions of the west facade and details of the entablature (figs. 10, 11) in which the architecture of the Parthenon was conveyed with unprecedented completeness. The historical part of the treatise was illustrated with vedute of the monuments (fig. 13), after the manner of Le Roy's contemporary Gianbattista Piranesi, who had illustrated the monuments of Rome.[44] What was of prime importance in these views was not exactness in the rendering of architectural and plastic details, but the accentuation of the innate character of the monuments, which caused those who viewed them to experience differing emotions: admiration of the quality of the Greek ruins, awe at the power and majesty of the Roman remains. However, Le Roy's work is permeated by the ornamentalism of the period, which only serves to weaken the final result. This trend came to a head with the *Ruins of Athens with Remains and Other Valuable Antiquities in Greece*, published in London by R. Sayer in 1759, a pirated edition with drawings by Le Roy and texts by Wheler: in it, the Parthenon was reduced to a mere ornamental motif, part – with the remains of Hadrian's aqueduct and the temple of Olympian Zeus – of a more general composition of ruins similar to the souvenir paintings of Rome produced at the same time.[45]

Le Roy's *Ruines* met the demand of the day for pictures of, and information about, the Greek world. It sold large numbers of copies and was an immediate commercial success. It was also the direct cause of the outbreak, in 1761, of a controversy which had been latent for some time over the superiority or otherwise of the Greek ruins over those of Rome. The protagonists in the controversy were Piranesi and the theoretician Pierre Jean Mariette, and it was to lead to the definitive release of architecture from the doctrines and rules of Vitruvius.[46] It also contributed to the short-lived "goût grec" style (c. 1760) in French ornamentation, furniture and miniature works of art.[47] Of decisive importance was Le Roy's encounter with the abbé Barthélemy, author of the idyllic panorama of ancient Greece which for a half-century or so after 1788 was to dominate Europe: it could truly be said that when young Anacharsis looks at the Acropolis, he sees it through the eyes of J.D. Le Roy (fig. 12).[48]

Stuart and Revett turned to the "Fountain-Head of Art",[49] as they called ancient Athens, after experiencing an atmosphere full of philosophical references to the superiority of ancient Greece and as the continuers of a movement for the revival of architecture by means of a return to classicism (even indirect classicism) which had appeared in England early in the eighteenth century.[50] Believers in the purity and clarity of Greek architecture, and

14. *J. Stuart, N. Revett: elevation of the Parthenon peristyle; reconstruction, 1751-1753. Source: J. Stuart, N. Revett,* The Antiquities of Athens, *vol. II, London 1787; Athens, Gennadios Library.*

15. *J. Stuart, N. Revett: section of the Parthenon peristyle; reconstruction, 1751-1753. Source: J. Stuart, N. Revett,* op. cit.

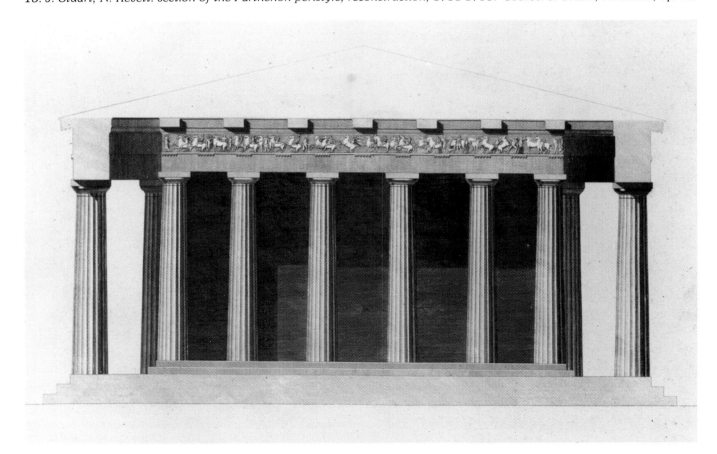

convinced of the need to approach it in a similar spirit, they set hitherto unprecedented standards of accuracy and care in surveying and drawing it,[51] following the example of Desgodetz. These ambitious objectives – together with elements innate in their characters – prevented them from completing their work during the two years they stayed in Athens (from March 1751 to September 1753), and caused an unusually long delay in publication. The fact that almost fifty years – from 1762 to 1816[52] – elapsed before publication was complete was partly responsible for ensuring that this work of the greatest importance for its concept, its quality and volume, and its influence in years to come – *The Antiquities of Athens Delineated by J. Stuart and N. Revett, Painters and Architects* – did not play the part it deserved in the first phase of the discovery of Greek architecture by Western Europe.[53]

Before the publication (which did not take place until 1789) of the second volume of *The Antiquities*, which contained the greatest examples of the Acropolis architecture, Robert Wood and the Society of Dilettanti had published *The Ruins of Palmyra* and *The Ruins of Baalbek* (1753 and 1757, respectively), which established the form for archaeological publications of the time. These were large, de luxe folio volumes, containing historical information about the sites, brief descriptions of the monuments, and a wealth of illustrations: views of the monuments in their current state, and artist's reconstructions of their architecture, both in general and as to their details. In 1764, the Society itself organised its first archaeological expedition, to Ionia. It was led by R. Chandler, an outstanding classicist, and its members were Revett (for the architectural drawings) and the painter William Pars (for the artist's reconstructions). On its way home, the expedition stopped in Athens, staying from September 1765 to June 1766, allowing Revett to add to the work he had done in the past, while Pars spent more than two months high up on the architrave of the Parthenon copying the sculptures "with diligence, fidelity and courage".[54] In 1776, Chandler himself published a work of travel about Greece, containing a history of the Parthenon going back to the time of the Persian Wars, providing and criticising the source material and that of more recent travellers, and describing the sculptures on the basis primarily of Wheler.[55] By 1789, Europe had made the acquaintance of Greek architecture in Le Roy, in the first volume of *Antiquities* (1762), and in *Antiquities of Ionia* (1764), while the publications of English and French scholars about the temples of Paestum dealt more specifically with the Doric order. Nonetheless, the way in which the Parthenon was handled and depicted in *The Antiquities of Athens* constituted a landmark in the discovery of the monument.

Stuart and Revett discredited Spon and Wheler.[56] They definitively clarified the orientation of the temple, and the general arrangement and original function of its various parts.[57] Strangely enough, they made no mention of the

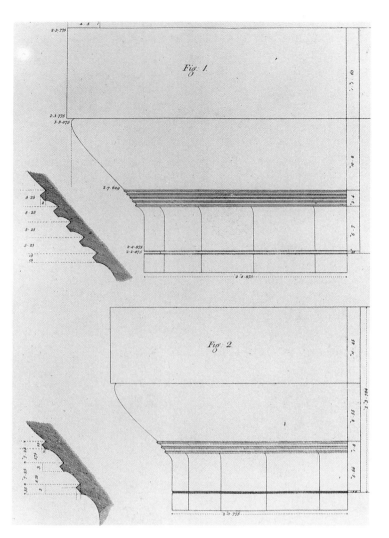

16. *J. Stuart, N. Revett: 1. The cymas of the peristyle column capitals. 2. The cymas of the pronaos column capitals; artist's reconstruction, 1751-1753. Source: J. Stuart, N. Revett, op. cit.*

erroneous identification of the pedimental compositions, though they did question the Roman dating of the sculptures. They touched upon the question of the Hecatompedon and the original roofing of the temple. Here they returned to Vitruvius, and identified the roofless octastyle mentioned there with the Parthenon, an ascription which soon extended to other Doric temples and survived until late in the 19th century, especially in publications of a generally encyclopaedic nature. Stuart and Revett took no interest in constructional questions, nor did they arrive at any more general theoretical conclusions about architecture, as had Le Roy. Their purpose was much more direct and practical: to enrich the range of decorative motifs available to their own time with fresh features of morphology and order.[58]

The architectural drawings of Stuart and Revett are extremely interesting. Their general reconstructions are marked by a painterly texture and plasticity, achieved by the extensive use of chiaroscuro (figs. 14, 15). Like the drawings of Le Roy, those of Stuart and Revett are faithful to the manner of Desgodetz and, more generally, to the seventeenth century style. At the same time, however, some true line drawings began to make a rather timid appearance (fig. 16), in the special depictions of details of the architectural order. They were reminiscent of the manuals of drawing of the time, and they represented the beginning of a trend which was to become more general early in the nineteenth century, when surveying and drawing the monuments was raised to the status of a basic tool in what was a new science: the history of architecture.[59] The drawings are extremely accurate in the rendering of order and morphology, but less so in the general proportions, where Le Roy is superior. In their idealisation of Greek architecture – in accordance with the prevailing beliefs of the time – and in their unshakeable faith in its absolute symmetry, regularity and use of a single colour, Stuart and Revett failed to grasp the irregularity, refinement and polychromy (of which some traces were still visible) that are, in fact, its characteristics.[60]

The Antiquities of Athens was equally important for its renderings of the Parthenon sculptures. For the first time, Europe could gain – in the drawings of Stuart and Pars – an overview of the plastic architectural ornamentation of the Parthenon: the west pediment, the south metopes, the Panathenaic frieze. Both artists were inspired by an idealising trend stemming from neo-Classical aesthetics. Yet there were differences between them. Stuart drew the frieze (fig. 17), which in any case, with its variety and richness, corresponded more closely to the demand of his fellow-countrymen for ornamental scenes. His classicism can be seen in his firm, clear outlines, in the elimination of individual characteristics in the rendering of the figures, and in the smoothing over of irregularities in the surface.[61] Yet his drawings suggest more successfully than any of their predecessors the vigour and movement

of Pheidias' originals. In the drawings of Pars, this idealisation is taken much further. His figures are notable for their purity, nobility and refinement, qualities which give them an unyielding superficial brilliance and overall stylistic uniformity.[62] It is clear that Pars was following the dictate of Reynolds, his contemporary, in searching for "a general and comprehensible beauty" and was striving to convey "an idea which exists only in the temple".[63] This is even more evident in the general view of the monument from the east by the same artist (fig. 18): the Parthenon rises in all its ruined majesty, serene and indifferent towards its surroundings, a symbol of transcendental beauty and eternity.

Drawings of the sculptures by Pars are also to be found in the sumptuous *Museum Worsleyanum...* of 1794, though with considerable stylistic differences from his originals which can be attributed to the copyists and engravers who had intervened.[64] This volume contained a reconstruction of the temple which is indicative of the ignorance of the Greek orders still prevalent despite the progress made,[65] and a general picturesque view of the Acropolis with the Parthenon (fig. 19), enlivened with anecdotal details (also by Pars) which foreshadowed future developments. As the century drew to its end, of the drawings of Carrey, which had just been discovered,[66] were printed for the first time in Barbié du Bocage's atlas of 1799. Europe's discovery of the Parthenon was now complete. The next stage was its looting – accompanied by more profound knowledge of the monument, and an experiential approach to it.

The Upsurge in Travelling: Redefining Relations with the Monument

The looting of the Parthenon, which grew more inten-

17. J. Stuart: detail of the east frieze of the Parthenon, 1751-1753. Source: J. Stuart, N. Revett, op. cit.

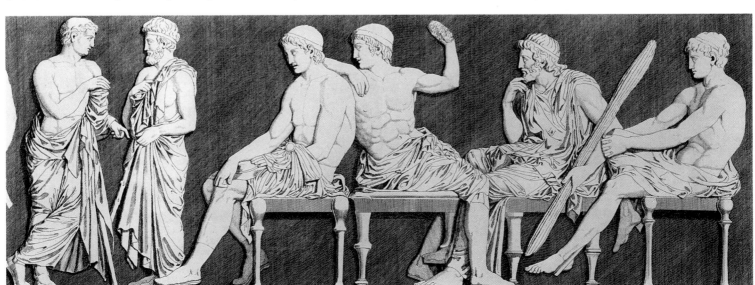

18. W. Pars: the Parthenon from the east, 1765. Source: J. Stuart, N. Revett, op. cit.

19. W. Pars: the Parthenon from the south-east, 1765-1766. Source: Museum Worsleyanum ..., London 1794; Athens, Gennadios Library.

20. Lady Mary Ruthven (copy of a drawing by G.B. Lusieri): the east extremity of the south side of the Parthenon while Lord Elgin's labourers were working on the monument (1819?); Edinburgh, National Galleries of Scotland.

21. G.B. Lusieri: the Parthenon from the north-west, 1802; Athens, Benaki Museum, no. 23979.

sive as time passed and the number of visitors increased, eventually involved the monument in early nineteenth century rivalry between Britain and France for political, economic and cultural sovereignty in Europe. It ended with the systematic ransacking of the ornamental sculpture by Lord Elgin and his agents (figs. 20, 21). When the sculptures arrived in London, a major controversy broke out as to whether they dated from Greek or Roman times. Simultaneously, however, their naturalness, vigour and restrained realism were perceived for the first time – features which demolished the prevailing theoretical superstructure erected by Johann Joachim Winckelmann about the idealised beauty and grace, the "noble simplicity and sedate grandeur" of Greek plastic art.[67] The debate, whose participants included personalities of international standing such as the archaeologists and students of aesthetics Ennio Quirino Visconti and Antoine Chrysostome Quatremère de Quincy and the sculptor Antonio Canova, ended with a definition of the character of Classical art and did much to promote involvement with it.[68]

It would not be an exaggeration to say that Greece flooded Europe in the first three decades of the nineteenth century. In Germany, where the ancient Greek ideal (Griechentum) had been elevated by men of letters into a primary parameter in national rebirth and where classical studies were flourishing, the foundations were laid for a systematic scholarly search for, and identification of, the Greek works of art. With the foundation in 1799 of the Prussian Technical Academy, the scientific exploration of ancient architecture was born, and was to produce the most valuable of results in the second half of the nineteenth century, especially where the Acropolis and the Parthenon were concerned. In Italy, ascription of their true identity to the vases which had come to light in Campagna and Tuscany – and which had at first been thought to be Etruscan – led to the discovery of ancient Greek pottery, following that of architecture and the plastic arts. In France, Coraes, Boissonade and Villemain revived the study of ancient Greek literature, while Quatremère de Quincy and Désiré Raoul Rochette consolidated and popularised Classical archaeology with publications in mass circulation periodicals and public seminars. In parallel, Réné Chateaubriand's Itinéraire de Paris à Jérusalem, a work often imitated by travellers of the period, transformed the travel narrative into a work of pure literature, capable of conveying emotion and images to confirm the vision of Barthélémy. However, it was in Britain that the most striking upsurge of Hellenism took place at this time.

The literature of travel, which was extremely popular in Britain throughout the nineteenth century, emerged as an important source of information about the Greek world – ancient and modern – side by side with the first archaeological expeditions and the cultivation of Classical studies by Richard Porson and his disciples. The growing number

22. R. Smirke: the Parthenon from the west, 1802; London, British Museum.

of works of travel about the Near East and Greece was directly connected with the rapid rise in the volume of travellers to those areas and the increase in interest in them which began in the last quarter of the eighteenth century and became more general during the Napoleonic Wars and the continental blockade. This was, furthermore, a period of much greater British influence over the Ottoman Empire.

In the first twenty years of the nineteenth century, travellers of every social class flocked to Greece and Athens. They represented a cross-section of trends and occupations: aristocrats (and even royalty), prosperous middle-class citizens, scholars and artists, soldiers and diplomats, merchants and scientists. In their traveller's tales – texts in various forms (prose, verse, real or fictitious letters) and of varying quality, which circulated very widely and were much reviewed and reprinted – they described the country and its inhabitants, the monuments and their natural setting, and thus introduced a Greek note into popular taste. One direct result of this (in combination with the upsurge of public interest caused by the Parthenon marbles, and the frieze of Phigaleia and the controversy over it) was an outbreak of Hellenomania in everyday life, affecting hairdressing, clothing, and the faithful copying and transferring, as they stood, of elements of the Greek orders and morphology into furniture, decoration and architecture. The volumes of The Antiquities of Athens proved to be a valuable tool in this respect; they were supplemented, reprinted and translated into the main European languages, while their drawings circulated throughout Europe and were included in manuals of model drawings and the textbooks of technical academies.[69]

The study of the Parthenon was promoted by architects of the time, such as W. Reveley, Joseph Woods, C.R. Cockerell, W. Kinnaird, Thomas Leverton Donaldson,

William Wilkins, J. Scoles, and J. Wolfe, some of whom (Thomas Hope, Robert Smirke – fig. 22 – and others) also figured largely in the Greek Revival and regarded a visit to Athens as an essential part of their professional training. On questions of identification of the parts of the monument or its ground plan, they revised the work of Stuart and Revett and corrected their errors. They were also successful in identifying the subjects of the pedimental compositions – in relation to the orientation of the temple – and, for the first time, turned to questions of construction: Wilkins, Kinnaird, Woods, Reveley and Scoles worked on the assembly, the 'drystone' building method, and the manner in which the blocks of the walls, the entablature and the tympanums of the pediments had been put in place. The nature of the original roof of the Parthenon was always an interesting issue: most scholars accepted the open-air solution suggested by Le Roy and Stuart and Revett, while Kinnaird went so far as to extend it to the Doric temples of Paestum, Aegina, Phigaleia and Olympia. Wilkins was doubtful, while Lucas wrote of a transparent roof and Cockerell of systems involving a raised lightshaft or apertures (fig. 24). An equally wide range of opinions was voiced about the order of the two-storey interior colonnade. There were supporters of all the orders: Ionian (Woods, Wolfe), Corinthian (Donaldson), or a combination of more than one order (Cockerell, Paul Lucas). A deeper

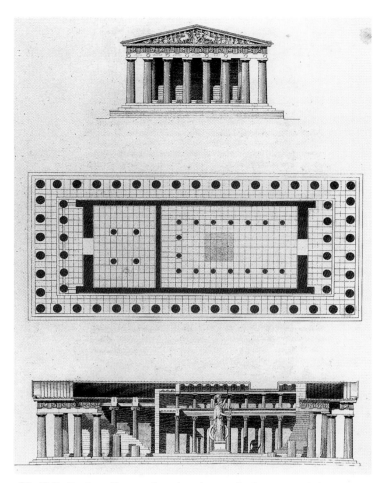

23. C.R. Cockerell: the Parthenon from the east; reconstruction. Source: H.W. Williams, Select Views in Greece with Classical Illustrations, *vol. II, London 1829; Athens, Gennadios Library.*

24. C.R. Cockerell: west facade, plan and elevation of the Parthenon; reconstruction. Source: Description of the Ancient Marbles in the British Museum, *London 1830, part VI; Athens, Gennadios Library.*

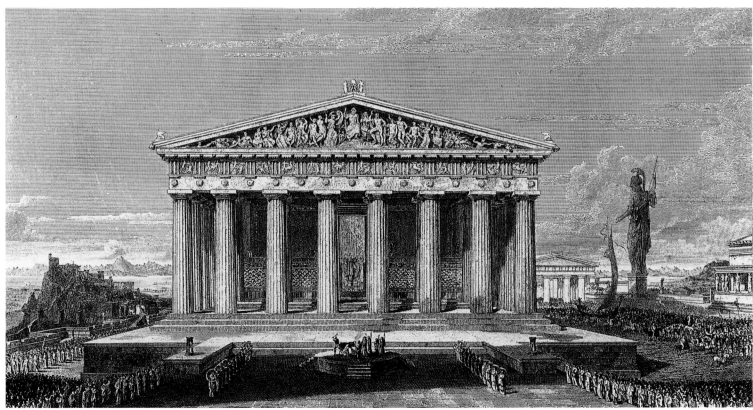

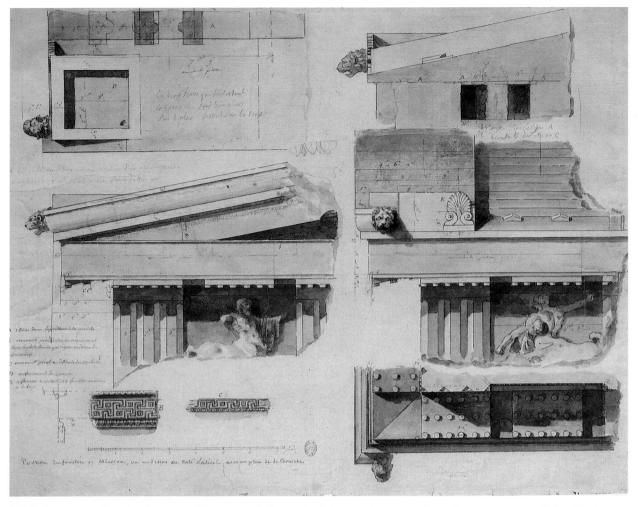

25. L.S. Fauvel: details of the entablature and the roof of the north-west and south-west corners of the Parthenon; reconstruction; Paris, Bibliothèque Nationale, Estampes Gb 15,7.

26. J.M. Karnejefl: the Parthenon from the north-east, 1804. Source: Das Griechenland Album des Grafen K. von Rechberg 1804-1805, Zürich 1974; Berlin, Deutsches Archäologisches Institut.

27. L. Dupré: the Parthenon from the west, 1819. Source: L. Dupré, Voyage à Athènes et à Constantinople, Paris 1825; Athens, Gennadios Library.

study of the questions of order led, eventually, to the discovery of the irregularities and the refinement. Allason and Cockerell discovered the 'entasis' of the columns, while Donaldson and Scoles observed the inward inclination of the columns in the peristyle and of the superstructure of the building. Others, such as Wilkins and Woods, sought the system of proportions governing the monument, while at the same time noticing – and commenting on – the traces of its original polychromy.[70]

These observations were not usually published in self-contained form. A number of them were included in the volumes of *The Antiquities* edited by some of the architects whose names are given above.[71] But the majority circulated by word of mouth, in the circle of foreigners who were residents of Athens or visited the city in those years. The same applied to drawings, many of which were exhibited at the Royal Academy in London or were included in publications of the time: travellers' reminiscences, souvenir albums, and the first catalogues of the British Museum.[72]

This process of publicising and simplifying the most

characteristic learned discoveries of the day was helped considerably by Giovanni Battista Lusieri and Louis François Sébastien Fauvel, permanent residents of Athens who usually guided visitors to the Acropolis and the Parthenon. In the particular case of Fauvel, a personality emblematic of the city and the era, with one foot in the antiquity-hunting camp of the eighteenth century and the other in the scientific approach of the nineteenth, recent publication[73] of his unpublished 'remains' (fig. 25) has revealed the extent of his knowledge. Fauvel was the first to note the existence of traces of polychromy (when the first casts were being made of the Parthenon sculptures), and he went deeply into the way in which the superstructure had been constructed and its parts installed; he also knew much about the refinements, had dated figures on the basis of comparative methods, and had explored the pre-Classical stage of the monument and its fate in later periods.

As a result, we find in the travellers' accounts of this period[74] references to the traces of the painted ornamentation of the monument and to the evidence that its reliefs were gilded (Edward Dodwell, Simone Pomardi, E.D. Clarke, P.O. Bröndsted, William Haygarth), praise or criticism for Stuart and Revett for the image they had conveyed of the Parthenon or even their drawings of it

(Dodwell, Clarke, William Gell), and comments on the constructional details of the Parthenon, such as the spaces behind the metopes and the triglyphs and the fluting of the columns (Clarke, Chateaubriand). Sometimes the Parthenon is taken as a starting-point for more general thoughts about the nature of the Doric order (H.W. Williams), or the character of ancient Greek architecture is compared with that of the Gothic (P.E. Laurent) or even modern architecture: Gell writes of the unfortunate transposition of ancient Greek forms into modern architecture, while Chateaubriand comments on its blind imitation of an architecture whose basic principles and features it distorts.

Above all, however, the visitors to the Parthenon during this period took an active part in the sensationalist and psychological approach to works of art which had grown up during the eighteenth century, particularly in Britain. Their texts are full of references to the emotions which the sight of the Parthenon inspired in them: usually a diffuse mixture of admiration, respect and amazement, dizziness, melancholy nostalgia, sadness and indignation over the imminent total destruction of the monument.[75] All these emotions were directly bound up with the new aesthetic categories of the Sublime and the Picturesque, into which the monuments could now be fitted in parallel with that of the Beautiful. These writers also tried to analyse the causes of their emotion: von Riedesel, John Bramsen, Chateaubriand and the abbé Martin connected it with the masculine simplicity and sense of solidity and durability of the Doric order, Haygarth and T.S. Hughes with the noble simplicity of the structure, Martin, F.C.H.L. Pouqueville and Williams with the beauty and poetry of the reliefs, Alessandro Bisani, Dodwell, J.C. Hobhouse and Laurent with the whiteness and impressive mass of the marble, and most visitors with the harmony and perfect beauty of the monument and the soundness of its proportions (fig. 28). Some visitors sought the causes of their emotion in the unity and austerity of the architectural design (Hughes, Bramsen, Gell, John Fuller); others, such as Dodwell, in the majestic dimensions, the brilliance (Hughes), or the successful combination of severity, strength and grace of the ornamentation (Chateaubriand). Quite a number (Dodwell, Gell, Chateaubriand, William Turner and Laurent) turned to the skill and care of the final elaboration of simple surfaces, sculptures and morphological features – even in places not normally open to view – or in the perfect assembly, the ancient 'harmony', of stones and column drums.

Various opinions were expressed as to the reasons for which the monument was built. The Parthenon was the supreme product of Athenian democracy (von Riedesel), the highest point reached by the political life of the Greeks, and it reflected their nobility of spirit and the sense of truth and beauty innate in them (Bröndsted). According to Hughes, patriotism was the prime motive for creative activity in ancient Athens, while Laurent linked the monu-

28. F. Préaux: the Parthenon from the north-west, 1799; Athens, Benaki Museum, no. 26502.

ment to the intellectual genius of the Athenians, the development of which depends on the climate and on nature.

Now, as never before, the picturesque qualities of the Parthenon and of the general landscape of the Acropolis were emphasised and depicted. They stressed the placing of the Parthenon in perspective, off-centre with reference to the lengthwise axis of the rock; this was a feature noted principally by architects – especially Woods, Cockerell and Carl Haller von Hallerstein – and which was pointed out for the benefit of the visitors they guided round the site (Hughes, fig. 30). Among other features were the majesty with which the Parthenon rises "amongst the heaps of surrounding ruins – itself having severely suffered from the shock of earthquake and the still more desolating hand of man!" (H.W. Williams, fig. 29); and the picture of complete devastation on the Acropolis: "the heaps of ruins of wretched houses and various buildings, constructed part with clay and marble;" (Williams), "scatter'd wide ... shapeless fragments ... the coil'd snake hisses amidst the knotted grass ...:Age's hand" (Haygarth, fig. 32); "the Parthenon in its present corroded state, impresses the mind with the idea of its thousands of years;" (Williams, fig. 31). "if the progress of decay should continue to be as rapid as it has been for something more than a century past, there will, in a few years, be not one marble standing upon another on the site of the Parthenon" (Hobhouse, fig. 26). The effect of time – the most important factor in the acquisition by a monument of the property of picturesqueness, according to the theorists of the period – was plain in the reddish-gold shade which the marbles had taken on and which almost all the travellers commented on.[76] This mature, mellow colour increased the impressiveness and charm of the monument, enhancing and at the same time softening the blinding whiteness of the Pentelic marble (Pomardi, F.S.N. Douglas, Laurent).

The lyrical tone of the pages from these travellers' accounts reaches still greater heights when the monument is described at dawn or sunset: "The ruins are dressed in the first rays, which envelope them. The drops of dew, glistening everywhere like pearls, the contrast between these shadowy masses and the light ... everything floods me with intoxicating fascination", wrote Saverio Scrofani of Sicily in 1795.[77] At the same time of the day, "the ruins of the Parthenon are surrounded in marvellous shades the colour of peach blossom, while the reliefs of Pheidias, lit from the side by a golden ray of sunlight, come to life and seem to move on the marble in the tremor of the light" (Chateaubriand). "At sunset, the temple stands beneath a silver-grey cloud in a brilliant, clear and ethereal atmosphere, surrounded by gentle, transparent light with tints of pink" (Williams, De Marcellus, fig. 27); "night closes silently ... all ... fades in gloom" (Haygarth, fig. 35).

The golden colour of the Parthenon was not the result only of time, but also of the clear sky and bright sunlight of Athens; it was precisely the Attic light which brought out the delicacy of the lines and colours. That, according to Chateaubriand, was why the detached sculptures lost so much of their beauty beneath an English sky. The close

29. H.W. Williams: general view of the Parthenon and the Acropolis from the Propylaea, 1817. Source: H.W. Williams, op. cit.

30. C.R. Cockerell: general view of the Parthenon and the Acropolis from the Propylaea. Source: Descriptions of the Ancient...., op. cit.

31. W. Haygarth: the Parthenon from the west, 1810-1811; Athens, Gennadios Library.

32. W. Haygarth: the east extremity of the south side of the Parthenon, 1810-1811; Athens, Gennadios Library.

connection between the monument and the place where it was built was now emphasised by many travellers. Henry Holland, indeed, discovered a superb blend of nature and art which made the site unique and, more generally, identified a particular *genius loci* that haunted the modern town and linked it to its glorious predecessor with unbreakable bonds.

These travellers were obliged by the dictates of the age to combine aesthetic delight with the setting in motion of a sequence of associative ideas and emotions; on seeing the Parthenon, they were raised to heights of ecstasy and sunk into vivid reveries. Scrofani, for example, when wandering through the interior of the temple, came upon Pericles, Aspasia and Ictinus watching the progress of work and urging on the craftsmen, and Haygarth con-

versed with Athena herself. In 1806, Chateaubriand inaugurated a practice which came to be a rule for later visitors, in climbing to the top of the spiral staircase in the Parthenon and admiring, from there, the panorama of the Attic landscape, reviving in his imagination the glories of the ancient city, and drawing unfavourable comparisons with the sad reality of their own day.

Now some travellers began to comment – though only in passing, and in isolated instances – on the most obvious and direct aspects of that prosaic reality. The Compte de Marcellus and Turner criticised visitors for their habit of carving their names on the marbles of the ruins, and Clarke, Chateaubriand and Woods all deplored the looting of the monuments – regardless of whether or not they indulged in it themselves. Most of the travellers took up a po-

33. L.S. Fauvel: the Parthenon from the west, 1790; Paris, Bibliothèque Nationale, Estampes Gb 15,71.

34. L. von Klenze: the Parthenon from the west, 1834; Princeton University, The Art Museum (C.G. Mather Fund).

sition towards the looting of the Parthenon by Elgin, which occurred in their own times. Opinions differed: Hobhouse, Bramsen, T.R. Jolliffe and Fuller understood and justified Elgin, while others, including Clarke, Dodwell, Chateaubriand and Williams, had only words of scorn for him.

This stirring period of extreme Romanticism – of visions, reveries, outpourings of emotion and of visual delights – came to an end on the outbreak of the Greek War of Independence. During the War, the Acropolis was successively besieged and occupied by Greeks and Turks (June 1822 - July 1827, July 1827 - April 1833), and the Parthenon and the other monuments were isolated, and severely damaged, once again. In 1833, when the Acropolis passed into the hands of the newly-founded Greek state, the monument entered a new phase in its history.

Towards a more Objective Approach: the First Scholarly Studies

The main feature of the new era was that for the first time an objective approach to the Parthenon was adopted. Now it became part of processes of purely scientific investigation, and measures in the form of conservation and restoration were taken to protect and enhance it. Now, too, travel ceased to be a matter of a personal quest through adventure of an identity and a vision, and the monument was accessible to the masses; that, in turn, meant that knowledge about it had to be available in popular form and its image had to circulate widely. In the early years of the century, the image continued to express a subjective view; it was not until after 1840 that a new invention, photography, made it possible to convey a more objective view of reality.

The Parthenon, as the symbol of the revived Greek nation and also as an area in which the new Bavarian dynasty could cover itself with glory, was the focus of state interest and attention from the very start. Leo von Klenze, an influential figure whose opinion weighed heavily in the kingdom of Bavaria, determined in the summer of 1834 (fig. 34) precisely what the policy of intervention on the Acropolis was to be – a policy that lasted throughout the nineteenth century: clearing of the Rock of the medieval and later buildings that covered it, restoration of the monuments, the construction of a museum.[78] Intervention of this kind deepened and promoted still further scientific study of the monument.

During the first twenty years after Liberation, the archaeologists who worked on the Acropolis were German (Ludwig Ross, Joseph Hoffer, Eduard Schaubert, who were responsible for the work in the early years), French (such as Alexis Paccard, who made notable achievements in the 1840s) or British (James Pennethorne, George Knowles, and F.C. Penrose: the continuers of a lengthy tradition). Now the prime source of interest for scholars were the optical refinements and the traces of polychromy. Hoffer, Schaubert and Pennethorne discovered the curvature of the stylobate, and Schaubert – once again – and Paccard recorded such traces of paint as had survived. Their researches came to the attention of the public in papers published in periodicals or presented as lectures, or in publications by third parties in scientific articles or books.[79] Although the important work done in 1845/6 by Paccard, one of the first scholars of the French Academy at Rome to work in Greece, consisting of an exact survey which had claims to being a work of art (pp. 261-263, figs. 1-5), and a detailed examination of the monument from the point of view of its structure, functions and ornamentation, produced important conclusions, it, like the projects of the other scholars who followed, remains unpublished in the archives of the École des Beaux Artes, Paris.[80]

The research of Penrose, on the other hand – carried out simultaneously – was published in 1851 as *The Principles of Athenian Architecture*, most of which deals with the Parthenon. This was a study of unprecedented accuracy and clarity, which finally settled the questions of curvature and inclination in the members of the temple, and of its constructional techniques; it dealt convincingly with the question of the painting of the temple (figs. 37, 38) and provided the most reliable ground plans (both for the current state of the monument and for its reconstruction).[81] *The Principles*, the last publication of the Society of Dilettanti, set a brilliant seal on a century of archaeological exploration. After that time, British researchers dealt with more specialised questions such as the roofing of the temple – leading James Fergusson, in 1883, to wild solutions and fantastic drawings influenced by the aesthetics of the metal architecture of his time (fig. 36).[82]

After the second half of the nineteenth century, the task of investigating the Acropolis passed into the hands of the solidly structured German school of archaeology. The research of Carl Bötticher into the later phases of parts of the building and the original arrangement of its chambers, together with details of their construction, stood out for their positive spirit which was unable to accept instances of deliberate irregularity, such as the curvature of the stylobate and of the entablature above it, which were ascribed to subsidence in the stereobate of the monument.[83] By the early 1870s, when all Europe's attention was fixed on its own medieval and more recent past, A. Michaelis published his study *Der Parthenon*, relating the history of the monument from antiquity to the present day, and collecting and examining sources of all kinds in a critical and scholarly spirit. Michaelis' study is unsurpassed, and will remain for ever a basic tool in the hands of all those involved with the history of the monument.[84] The last scholar in this line was Wilhelm Dörpfeld, who for forty years after the last decade of the nineteenth century dominated archaeological research on the Acropolis. His stream of publications[85] concerning the pre-Classical phases in the building of the Parthenon and the monuments of the Acropolis more generally was directly bound up with the great excavations of the period 1885-1890, which overturned the views then prevalent as to the history of the Rock.

Visitors to the Acropolis: Popularisation and Dissemination of Knowledge and the Image

After 1830, the improved external conditions for travel and the introduction of regular steamship sailings to Greece made the country and its monuments accessible to the masses for the first time. Travellers now became visitors – and visitors not to an ideal land of dreams, but to a newly-formed European state, one which could show them conditions of Levantine charm and picturesqueness, but also much to disconcert and upset them. The Parthenon, however, was never a disappointment, even to the most hostile or indifferent visitors (Joseph d'Estourmel, Alphonse de Lamartine, Edmond About).[86] Now it had risen in the European consciousness to the status of an ar-

36. J. Fergusson: the interior of the Parthenon from the east; artist's reconstruction. Source: J. Fergusson, The Parthenon, London 1833; Athens, Gennadios Library.

chetypal Classical monument thanks to the harmony, grace and severity of its lines and figures, the correctness of its proportions, and the symmetry of its parts, which create a whole marked by perfect equilibrium (Antoine M. Chenavard, Eugène Yemeniz, A Baird, M. Hirstin, Charles de Moüy, M. Bernard). The texts of the time brim over with absolute and dithyrhambic descriptions expressed in almost stereotyped terms: "It would, therefore, be a very erroneous idea to regard this Temple merely as the best school of Architecture in the world. It is also the noblest Museum of Sculpture and the richest Gallery of Painting" (Christopher Wordsworth); "the finest edifice on the finest site in the world" (Walter Colton, Francis Bedford); "the sole perfect work that the hand of Man has ever accomplished" (Jean Alexandre Buchon, S. Hill, Hermann Hettner); "the most perfect poem on earth ever written in stone" (Lamartine); "the finest of all the pagan temples, on which the Attic genius was lavished" (Théophile Gautier); "the ideal crystallised into Pentelic marble" (Ernest Renan).[87]

The ceremony of a visit to the Acropolis was equally stereotyped: contemplation of the monument and the reconstruction of it, in its original form, in the viewer's mind; observation at different times of the day and night, and in various climatic conditions, so as to allow an appreciation of the alternating shades of colour (von Klenze, Buchon, Henry Cook, Hirstin, Yemeniz, Edward Lear, de Moüy); thoughts about the process of decay and an emphasis on the picturesque qualities of the monument (Richard Monckton Milnes, William Hamilton, Lear; figs. 39, 40); and appreciation of the surroundings of the temple from its top (von Klenze, Edgar Garston, Yemeniz, de Moüy). The same applies to the listing of the monument's characteristics as a sublime ruin: colossal magnificence, transcendental beauty, serenity, clarity, purity and power (Colton, Théodore Achille Louis du Moncel, Chenavard, Edmund Spencer, Cook, Hettner). All the familiar emotions were expressed, now with the addition of respectful enthusiasm and an intellectual delight suggested by the Parthenon.[88]

In parallel with this attitude, which continued – though in an exaggerated and standardised form – a long tradition, references to more prosaic issues now became more frequent and more extensive. Such matters included the scourge of the looting of the monuments and of the scattered antiquities lying about, done by visitors and above all by the crews of ships lying at Piraeus, and which the "picturesque" Kyriakos Pittakis, Inspector of Antiquities of Greece, strove to combat. Some visitors dealt exclusively with the current situation and adopted attitudes towards the excavations and the work of removing the traces of subsequent phases of the history of the Acropolis and the Parthenon which was going ahead at this time, or towards the restoration of the monument. Most visitors expressed the wish that the Parthenon marbles could return home, if suitable conditions for their preservation could be guaranteed.

At this time, improvements in typographical methods and the discovery of new techniques for printing drawings and colour pictures[89] led to a renewed upsurge in the printing of lavishly illustrated travel books and souvenir publications. De luxe albums and travel books in formats so large as to approximate to albums were particularly popular, and included those by William Cole, du Moncel, Chenavard, M. Rey and Cook. So, too, were popular publications of a general nature, such as Wordsworth's *Greece: Pictorial, Descriptive and Historical*; their texts, packed with information, were illustrated with small and romantic woodcuts (vignettes) emphasising the picturesque aspect of the monument and reflecting the associative thoughts of readers. Alternatively, the books were illustrated with full-page copper engravings providing dream-like images of the Parthenon in accordance with the idea of the general reading public of Greece as a country of the exotic East (fig. 45).[90] In the publications of this period, science and the work of travel were completely

37. F.C. Penrose: view of the north-west corner of the Parthenon; artist's reconstruction of reliefs, cymas and traces of colour, 1847. *Source:* The Principles of Athenian Architecture, *London 1851.*

38. F.C. Penrose: capital of a doorpost in the opisthodomos and cyma above the Parthenon frieze; artist's reconstruction, 1847. *Source:* The Principles ..., op. cit.

39. J. Skene: the opisthodomos portico from the north-west, 1838-1845; Athens, National Historical Museum.

40. J. Skene: the opisthodomos portico from the north-east, 1838-1845; Athens, National Historical Museum.

41. S. Claudius: the Parthenon from the north-east; Museum of the City of Athens, no. 531.

42. V. Lanza: the Parthenon from the north-east; Museum of the City of Athens, no. 102.

distinct. Of course, the authors referred frequently to the latest scientific discoveries, information about which they obtained from *The Topography of Athens* of W.M. Leake (in its second edition of 1841) and the *L'Acropole d'Athènes* of Ernest Beulé (of 1853),[91]: these were very familiar works which functioned as tourist guides for learned travellers. They also referred to the art periodicals which circulated widely at the time, but unlike their predecessors, they no longer took any part in the procedure of producing the knowledge.

Of all these depictions – not only those which were printed, but many others produced by visitors: pencil drawings, water-colours, full-scale paintings, more and more of them being brought to light by modern research – some, such as those of S. Claudius, Cole, Rey, Freeman and Vicenzo Lanza (figs. 41-43), were in the mode of the pre-Liberation period. The Parthenon is shown in an abstract, romantic setting so as to suggest various emotions or confirm preconceived visions. Others, such as those of du Moncel, Ippolito Caffi, Andrea Gasparini and Cook

43. *E. Rey: the Parthenon from the east, 1843; Athens, Benaki Museum, no. 26438.*

44. *H. Cook: the Parthenon from the north-east, 1851; Athens, Benaki Museum, no. 26446.*

45. Irton: the Parthenon from the east. Source: C. Wordsworth, Greece: Pictorial, Descriptive and Historical, London 1840; Athens, Gennadios Library.

46. Th. du Moncel: the Parthenon from the north-west, 1842. Source: Vues pittoresques des Monuments d'Athènes, Paris 1845; Athens, Gennadios Library.

(figs. 44, 46, 49), were intended more to emphasise the existing picturesque contrasts by means of the introduction of figures and details from contemporary everyday life.[92] A third category lay closer to objective reality: the Parthenon rises as imperious as ever out of a landscape which changes according to the progress of the work being done on the Acropolis (F. Arundale, Christian Hansen, Martinus Gottlieb Rørbye, Giovanni Renica, Harald Conrad Stilling, F. Church, figs. 47, 48). After the fourth decade of the nineteenth century, this category also included photographs.

Photography – a New Means of Depiction

The Parthenon immediately became a subject for this new and truly revolutionary technique: it formed part of the first expedition to photograph Classical sites and monuments which set out in October 1839, only two months after the official announcement of the new invention (fig. 52).[93] The first photographs were of a purely documentary nature, and lacked much of the aesthetic quality of the paintings produced at the same time, by which they were clearly influenced.[94] The new method of making pictures soon entered widespread use, as equipment and techniques improved and the product was marketed. The Parthenon and the other monuments on the Acropolis became a popular subject for the various photographers who passed through Athens (usually on their way to the Near East) or spent longer periods there; it was included in the early albums of photographs[95] and was a common subject for the first Greek photographers who took part in international exhibitions.[96] Before long, photographers began to have artistic ambitions, which did not, of course, spoil the impression of reality but emphasised various aspects of it: the Parthenon was approached

from differing angles, its off-centre position on its site was stressed, and efforts were made to convey the unsettled nature of its setting – caused by the large numbers of scattered ancient marbles and the upheaval created by the excavations (figs. 50, 55). Photographs of this kind are found side by side with others of a more formal and academic nature – frontal shots accentuating the harmony and imposing presence of the building – and were, indeed, often taken by the same photographer (fig. 51).[97]

Among all those who photographed the Parthenon at this time, the most notable cases were those of Alfred Normand (1851, fig. 53),[98] the first architect to attempt to form a systematic archive of shots of Classical monuments, with the assistance of architectural compositions, and William J. Stillman.[99] A roving, independent spirit, Stillman produced incomparable photographs of the Parthenon in 1869: he took pictures from original angles, and succeeded superbly in rendering the atmosphere and allusive nature of the monument, sometimes by using experimental methods (fig. 58).[100]

After 1890 – under the influence of the major works of intervention being carried out on the Acropolis at the time[101] – photographers tended to emphasise still more the Classical nature of the monument. As photographed by the brothers Aristotelis and Konstantinos Rhomaidis from the roof of the Museum (fig. 54), whose top approximates to ground level in ancient times, the Parthenon undoubtedly conveyed an impression closer to that of antiquity.[102] In the photographs taken by Albrecht Meydenbauer[103] during an expedition in 1910, the temple towers imposingly above the newly-discovered Mycenean wall, a monument to the triumph of Reason over the mythical, primordial origins of the mind (figs. 56, 57). This trend culminated in the photographs of Frédéric Boissonas,[104] the

47. C. Hansen: the Parthenon from the north-east, 1835; Photographic Archive of the Athens Municipal Art Gallery.

48. H.C. Stilling: the Parthenon from the north-west, 1853; Photographic Archive of the Athens Municipal Art Gallery.

49. A. Gasparini: the Parthenon from the west, 1843, tinted copper engraving; Museum of the City of Athens, no. 53.

50. *General view of the Parthenon and the Acropolis from the north-west, 1861. Photograph by F. Frith; Boston, collection of N. Catsimpoolas.*

51. *The Parthenon from the east, c. 1865. Photograph by D. Konstantinou; Boston, collection of N. Catsimpoolas.*

52. *P.G. Joly de Lotbinière: the Parthenon from the north-west, 1839, daguerreotype; Athens, Benaki Museum, Yeroyannis-Petmezas collection.*

53. *The Parthenon from the west, 1851. Photograph by A. Normand; Archive of the Committee for the Conservation of the Acropolis Monuments, no. 001438.*

54. *The Parthenon from the south-east, c. 1905. Photograph by A. and K. Romaidis. Source:* Pinacothèque Hellénique: collection A. Rhomaidès: Athènes antiques, *s.a.; Athens, collection of Stavros and Stella Stavridis.*

55. *General view of the Parthenon and the Acropolis from the Propylaea, 1872-1874. Photograph by P. Sebah; Athens, collection of Stavros and Stella Stavridis.*

57. *The Parthenon from the east, 1910. Photograph by A. Meydenbauer; Athens, collection of Stavros and Stella Stavridis.*

56. *The east extremity of the south side of the Parthenon, 1910. Photograph by A. Meydenbauer; Athens, collection of Stavros and Stella Stavridis.*

58. *General view of the Parthenon from the east, c. 1869. Photograph by W.J. Stillman. Source: W.J. Stillman,* The Acropolis at Athens, *1870; Athens, Gennadios Library.*

59. The east extremity of the north side of the Parthenon, c. 1913. Photograph by F. Boissonas. Source: Le Parthénon, l'histoire, l'architecture et la sculpture, Paris 1914; Athens, collection of Stavros and Stella Stavridis.

landscape photographer of Greece *par excellence*, published in attractive folios and encyclopaedic editions.[105] They revealed, as the new century dawned, the unparalleled beauty of the monument, the sense of eternity emanating from Classical art (fig. 59) – and, lastly, the Idea of the Parthenon, which, as Scrofani puts it, has been preserved and handed down over the centuries by the nations and the peoples as some consolation in their tragic fate.

Notes

1. At this time, when Athens was under the sovereignty of the Acciaiuoli Dukes of Florence, the conditions were more suitable for contact with the West. See M. Pavan, *L'avventura del Partenone, un monumento nella storia*, Florence 1983 (hereinafter: Pavan), pp. 77-105.

2. See the article by M. Korres, 'The Parthenon from Antiquity to the Nineteenth Century', in this volume.

3. A. Michaelis, *Der Parthenon*, Leipzig 1871 (hereinafter: Michaelis, *Der Parthenon*), p. 334.

4. For Cyriacus and his age, see J. Colin, *Cyriaque d'Ancone, le voyageur, le marchand, l'humaniste*, Paris 1980, and L. Beschi, 'La scoperta dell'arte greca', *Memoria dell'antico nell'arte Italiana*, S. Settis (ed.), I, II, III, Torino 1986 (hereinafter Memoria); here III (hereinafter Scoperta), pp. 314-338. On Cyriacus' visits to Athens, see E. Bodnar, *Cyriacus of Ancona and Athens*, Brussels 1960.

5. C.R. Chiarlo, 'Gli fragmenti della sancta antiquitate', *Memoria* I, p. 274.

6. P. Mylonas, 'Vitrouviou ta deka proimia' ('The Ten Proems of Vitruvius'), *Philia Epi eis G.E. Mylona* ('G.E. Mylonas: In Token of Friendship'), vol. IV, Athens 1990, pp. 1-29; E. Forssman, 'La teoria vitruviana dell'architettura', *La Fortuna di Paestum e la memoria del dorico 1750-1830*, J. Raspi Serra (ed.), I, II, Florence 1986 (hereinafter, *Fortuna*), here I, pp. 152-158.

7. For the surviving copies of Cyriacus' drawings, see B.L. Brown, D.E. Kleiner, 'Guiliano da Sangallo's Drawings after Ciriaco d'Ancona: Transformations of Greek and Roman Antiquities in Athens', *Journal of the Society of Architectural Historians* XLII, 4, 1983, pp. 321-328, with all the previous specialised bibliography.

8. Michaelis, *Der Parthenon*, p. 335.

9. The dedication of the Parthenon as a Christian church to the Unknown God was repeated, after the Anonymous of Vienna, by S. Kavasilas (1578), F. Arnaud (1602), L. des Hayes Baron de Courmenin (1578) and R. de Dreux (1669). The fact that there was an inscription to this effect on the church is mentioned by Sieur du Loir (1641) and La Guilletière (1674). For their accounts, see Michaelis, *Der Parthenon*, pp. 335, 337-338, and M. Paton, *Medieval and Renaissance Visitors to* *the Greek Lands*, Princeton, NJ, 1951, pp. 52, 62, 17. The inscription on the monument is also mentioned by the legend to the Capuchin map of Athens of c.1670; L. de Laborde, *Documents inédits ou peu connus sur l'histoire et les antiquités d'Athènes*, Paris 1854, p. 15.

10. Anyone who damaged the mosaic of Our Lady in what had been the sanctuary apse of the Christian church would be paralysed, while there was a danger of an epidemic of cholera in the town if the stone receptacles in the santuary were opened; accounts by J. Babin (1672), La Guilletière (1674, Michaelis, *Der Parthenon*, pp. 336-339), and Père Alexis (1672), Laborde, *op. cit.*, p. 18.

11. T. Zygomalas and S. Kavasilas (Michaelis, *Der Parthenon*, p. 335) answer the question of Martin Crusius as to whether Athens still existed: sufficient evidence of the ignorance of sixteenth century Europe as to the contemporary city. For the contribution which Zygomalas' answer made to the confusion which later prevailed concerning the dating of the Parthenon sculptures, see J. Rothenberg, 'Descensus ad Terram', *The Acquisition and Reception of the Elgin Marbles*, New York and London 1977 (hereinafter, Rothenberg, 'Descensus'), pp. 112-113.

12. They were usually sailors, such as the sea-captain F. Arnaud (1602), diplomats (L. des Hayes, 1621), priests (Sieur du Loir, 1641, R. de Dreux, 1669) or merchants (J.B. Tavernier, 1663).

13. "Two prancing horses which to the human eye seem to be alive", wrote Zygomalas of the horses on the west pediment of the temple, while J.B. Tavernier mentioned armed warriors who appeared ready to fight.

14. O. Jahn, A. Michaelis, *Arx Athenarum a Pausania descripta* (reprinted), Chicago 1976, pp. 53-56.

15. For the Parthenon as a mosque, see M. Korres, *op. cit.* See also K. Biris, *Ta Attika tou Evliya Çelebi* ('Evliya Çelebi on Attica'), Athens 1959, p. 42, and G. Seferis, *Dokimes B´* ('Essays II'), Athens 1984, pp. 340-341.

16. W. Herrmann, 'Antoine Desgodetz and the Académie Royale d'Architecture', *The Art Bulletin* 40, 1958, pp. 23-53, and D. Mertens, 'I templi di Paestum nella prima storiografia dell'Architettura antica', *Fortuna* I (hereinafter, Mertens, 'Templi'), p. 160.

17. For the original drawing, see L. Beschi, 'Un disegno veneto dell'Acropoli Ateniese nel 1670', *Arte Veneta* X, 1956, pp. 136-141. This drawing is kept in the Museo Civico of Bassano del Grappa. For the copies of the drawing in the Bonn Kunstmuseum and by the artist A. Perin, see H. Omont, *Athènes au XVIIe siècle. Dessins des sculptures du Parthénon attribués à J. Carrey et conservés à la Bibliothèque Nationale, accompagnés des vues et plans d'Athènes et de l'Acropole*, Paris 1898, plate XXIX.

18. The painting belongs to the Museum of Chartres, but is on permanent loan to the National Gallery and Alexandros Soutzos Museum, Athens.

19. Beschi, 'Scoperta', p. 341.

20. T. Bowie, D. Thimme, *The Carrey Drawings of the Parthenon Sculptures*, London 1971.

21. He was the principal representative of the trend to impose strict rules of composition and expression on seventeenth century painting by means of the Academies.

22. Rothenberg, 'Descensus', pp. 79-84.

23. H. Omont, *Missions archéologiques françaises en Orient au XVIIe et XVIIIe s.*, Paris 1902, pp. 193-194.

24. J. Babin, *Relation de l'état présent de la ville d'Athènes*, Lyon 1674, pp. 25-35.

25. Omont, *Missions....*, *op. cit.*

26. J. Spon, *Voyage d'Italie, de Dalmatie, de Grèce et du Levant fait aux années 1675 et 1676*, Lyon 1678, pp. 142-159, and G. Wheler, *A Journey into Greece, by G. Wheler, Esq., in Company of Dr Spon of Lyon*, London 1682, pp. 360-364.

27. This was the side by which the Christian church, and, later, the Ottoman mosque of the Parthenon were entered. At this time it would have been very difficult to get anywhere near the east side of the temple, because of the houses which covered the entire top of the Acropolis rock.

28. Figures B and C of the west pediment. Spon's attribution survived down to the early nineteenth century, first being rejected by W. Wilkins ('On the Sculptures of the Parthenon', *Walpole's Memoir*, London 1818, pp. 409-420).

29. There were errors in the number of columns on the long sides of the temple, in the number of steps in the crepidoma, in the rendering of the order, and in the triglyphs, which are omitted from both drawings. Furthermore, the capitals are of the Tuscan type. In the Spon drawing the metopes are ornamented with wreaths in relief, after the Roman fashion, while on the facade of the temple the middle space between the columns is shown as excessively wide. This error was corrected in Wheler's drawing, which, however, continues not to show the columns between the antae in the opisthodomos.

30. D. Mertens, 'Jacob Spons Parthenonbild', *Kanon*, Basle 1989, pp. 46-53.

31. The Spon drawing was reproduced by V. Coronelli in numerous editions (see below, note 33), and was copied by C. Magni – another member of Nointel's entourage – in his *Relazione della città di Atene*, Parma 1688. It was also included – though as a representative example of a Greek temple, not as a depiction of the Parthenon – in a plate of examples of ancient architecture (vol. II, 1722, no. 14) from B. de Montfaucon's *L'antiquité expliquée et représentée en figures*, Paris 1719 et seq., which constituted a synopsis of archaeological knowledge of the age.

32. Michaelis, *Der Parthenon*, p. 339.

33. V. Coronelli, *Morea, Negroponte e Adiacenze*, Venice 1708 et seq., plates 75, 82.

34. Pavan, pp. 192-197.

35. R. Pococke, *A Description of the East and some Other Countries*, vol. II, part II, London 1745, p. 162.

36. Pococke's drawing comes closer than any other to the Doric temple according to Vitruvius: a tall, unadorned pediment, and an entablature on the external peristyle which ends with a section of a metope. Some quite arbitrary features, such as the high step along the internal colonnade of the opisthodomos, have been added.

37. Earl of Sandwich, *A Voyage Round the Mediterranean in the Years 1738-1739*, London 1799, p. 62. Lord Charlemont (*The Travels of Lord Charlemont in Greece and Turkey in 1749*, London 1984, p. 130) made original observations about the assembly of the blocks of stone in the temple and was the first visitor to note the irregularity of the intercolumniation, which he regarded as accidental. However, Sandwich and Charlemont were important not so much for their observations (which were not published in their own lifetimes) as for the way in which their attitude and encouragement opened up the way for Stuart and Revett to visit Athens. See D. Wiebenson, *Sources of Greek Revival Architecture*, London 1969 (hereinafter, Wiebenson, *Sources*), p. 23.

38. Drawings by Dalton of the Parthenon were printed for the first time – along with others, of Sicily, Asia Minor and Egypt – in *A Collection of 52 Engraved Plates from Drawings by R. Dalton of Antiquities in Sicily, Greece, Asia Minor and Egypt*, London 1751-2, plates III-VI. See also Rothenberg, 'Descensus', pp. 85, 88-91.

39. J. Stuart, N. Revett, *The Antiquities of Athens*, vol. I (1762), p. V.

40. Wiebenson, *Sources*, p. 28.

41. J.D. Le Roy, *Les Ruines des plus beaux monuments de la Grèce*, Paris 1758, p. 9.

42. R. Middleton, D. Watkin, *Architettura dell'Ottocento*, Milan 1980, pp. 5-24.

43. Le Roy, *op. cit.*, pp. IX-XIV.

44. M. Docci, D. Maestri, *Il rilevamento architettonico, storia, metodi e disegno*, Rome and Bari 1989, pp. 119-125.

45. And especially those of G.P. Pannini; G.C. Argan, *Storia dell' arte Italiana*, vol. 3, Florence 1968, p. 411.

46. R. Wittkower, 'Piranesi's "Parere su architettura"', *Journal of the*

Warburg Institute 2, 1938-1939, pp. 147-158.

47. A contribution to this was also made by the writings of the Belgian architect J.F. Neufforge, who engraved most of the plates in Le Roy's book (Middleton and Watkin, *op. cit.*, pp. 65-71).

48. The album by J.D. Barbié du Bocage, *Recueil des cartes géographiques, plans, vues et medailles de l'ancienne Grèce relatives au voyage du jeune Anacharsis*, Paris, accompanying J.J. Barthélemy's *Voyage du jeune Anacharsis en Grèce, dans le milieu du quartrième siècle avant l'ère vulgaire*, Paris 1788, contained drawings of the Parthenon (a reconstruction of the west facade and a perspective view of the monument) which copy, or are based upon, Le Roy. The tremendous publishing success and wide circulation of the book in the years to come (it went through some forty editions in the most important European languages – even Greek) gave Europe a reasonably accurate image of the monument which was far better than its predecessors in depicting the order of the Parthenon.

49. *The Antiquities of Athens*, vol. I, p. V.

50. Pavan, pp. 208-209 and J. Summerson, *Architecture in Britain 1530-1830*, Harmondsworth 1979, pp. 317-319.

51. *The Antiquities of Athens*, vol. I, p. VII.

52. *The Antiquities of Athens*, vol. I (1762), vol. II (1787, though actually published in 1789, after the death of Stuart), vol. III (1794), and vol. IV (1816).

53. L. Lawrence, 'Stuart and Revett: their Literary and Architectural Careers', *Journal of the Warburg Institute* 2, 1938-1939, pp. 128-146.

54. R. Chandler, *Travels in Greece*, Dublin 1776, p. 54.

55. *Ibid.*, pp. 46-54.

56. *The Antiquities of Athens*, vol. II, pp. 1-9.

57. Of course, they also made certain mistakes with regard to the arrangement of the inner columns in the cella and the number of columns in the west chamber. They also believed there to have been an opening in the partition between the cella and the west chamber (*ibid.*, plate III).

58. J. Landy, 'Stuart and Revett: Pioneer Archaeologists', *Archaeology*, vol. 9, no. 4, 1956, pp. 253-254.

59. Docci and Maestri, *op. cit.*, pp. 110-113, 135; Mertens, 'Templi', pp. 179-181, 190; E.A. Rankin, *Englishmen on the Acropolis. An Historiography of the Architecture of the Parthenon ca. 1750-1850* (typewritten doctoral thesis), Johannesburg 1978 (hereinafter, Rankin, *Englishmen*), pp. 118-119.

60. Landy, *op. cit.*, p. 258.

61. D. Watkin, *Athenian Stuart. Pioneer of the Greek Revival*, London 1982, p. 21.

62. Rothenberg, 'Descensus', pp. 95-100.

63. Sir J. Reynolds, 'Lectures on Art', in M.C. Beardsley, *Istoria ton Aisthitikon Theorion*, ('History of Aesthetic Theories'), Athens 1989, p. 140.

64. *Museum Worsleyanum, or a collection of antique basso relievos, bustos, statues and gems with views of places in the Levant taken on the spot in the years 1785, 1786 and 1787*, II, London 1794, Class V, 'Sculpture of the temple of Minerva in alto e basso relievo'. This contains superb drawings by Pars of the south frieze, drawings of the west frieze by an Italian engraver called Dolcibene, who produced awkward imitations of Pars, and poor – almost distorted – drawings of seven metopes on the south side of the temple.

65. The reconstruction was the work of an artist called Reveley who accompanied Sir R. Worsley on his trip to Athens in 1785. It is typical of his ignorance even of the order with which he was dealing that the drawing depicts, in parallel, both methods of solving the problem of the corner of the Doric entablature familiar from Vitruvius.

66. Of Carrey's drawings, which originally numbered more than four hundred, only those of Athens have survived. They were bought by Louis XV and ended up in the Cabinet des Estampes of the National (formerly Royal) Library of France, where they were rediscovered by accident in 1797. Before their publication in Bocage's album (*op. cit.*), drawings of

two south metopes and slabs from the south frieze by Carrey had been included in Montfaucon's treatise (*op. cit.*) as representative examples of ancient Greek dress as shown in the reliefs on the blocks. In the 1799 album, Bocage's draughtsman added reconstructions of the pedimental sculptures inspired by Carrey to the familiar west facade of Le Roy and to the perspective drawing of the temple.

67. R. Bianchi Bandinelli, *Introduzione all'archeologia classica come storia dell'arte antica*, Rome and Bari 1976, pp. 11-27.

68. Pavan, pp. 289-314, and in particular the special study of this question in Rothenberg, 'Descensus'.

69. The Antiquities was reissued in 1825-1830, edited by W. Kinnaird. In the meantime, it had been translated into French in 1808-1822 and into German in 1828-1833, with a supplementary article by K.O. Müller on the Parthenon metopes and frieze. The textbooks of H. Gentz, A. Hirt and K.F. Schinkel for the Technical Academy of Prussia included drawings by Stuart and Revett (W. Höpfner, E.L. Schwandner, *Archäologische Bauforschung, Berlin und die Antike*, exhibition catalogue, Berlin 1979, pp. 343, 346-347).

70. For the research work done by British architects during the early years of the nineteenth century, see the special study by Rankin, *Englishmen*, which contains material from unpublished archive sources (diaries, etc.).

71. Volume III of *The Antiquities* was edited by W. Reveley, and vol. IV by J. Woods, while 1830 saw the publication of *The Antiquities of Athens and Other Places in Greece, Sicily, etc. Supplement to the Antiquities of Athens, delineated and illustrated by C.R. Cockerell, W. Kinnaird, T.L. Donaldson, W. Jenkins, W. Railton, architects.*

72. The case of Cockerell is typical: he wrote little, but his influence was great. His drawings of the Parthenon were included in the 'learned' traveller's text by P.O. Bröndsted, *Voyage dans la Grèce....*, Paris 1826, plate XXXVIII (reconstructed plan), who dedicated it to him; in the album by H.W. Williams entitled *Select Views in Greece...*, vol. I, London 1829 (reconstructions of the west and east facades, fig. 23); and in the *Description of the Ancient Marbles in the British Museum*, part VI, London 1830, plates XXI-XXIV (reconstructions of the entablature and pediments of the east and west facades, ground plan, lengthwise section, fig. 24, general picturesque view of the Acropolis, fig. 30). Smaller romantic and picturesque sketches by Cockerell were included in Wordsworth's popular *Greece Pictorial...* (see below, note 90).

73. L. Beschi, 'L.S. Fauvel e il Partenone', *Parthenon-Kongress*, 4 bis 8 April 1982, Basle and Mainz 1984, pp. 319-323, plates 56-61.

74. For the full titles and dates of publication of the travellers' texts, see S.H. Weber, *Voyages and Travels in the Near East during the Nineteenth Century*, Princeton, NJ, 1952.

75. The quotations are from texts by von Riedesel (1768), Scrofani (1794-1795), Clarke (1801), Hobhouse (1809-1810), Haygarth (1810-1811), Queen Caroline (1814), Williams (1817?), Laurent (1818) and L. Dupré (1819).

76. At this time, the highly distinctive colour of the surface of the Parthenon marbles was attributed solely to natural causes. The question of the plastering of the monument by human hand had not yet arisen. See I.D. Jenkins, A.P. Middleton, 'Paint on the Parthenon Sculptures', *Annual of the British School at Athens* 83, 1988, pp. 183ff.

77. Cited (in Greek translation) in Kyriakos Simopoulos, *Xeni Taxidiotes stin Ellada* ('Foreign Travellers in Greece'), vol. 1, Athens 1981, p. 635.

78. M. Casanaki, F. Mallouchou, 'Interventions on the Acropolis: 1833-1975', *The Acropolis at Athens, Conservation, Restoration and Research 1975-1983*, Athens 1985, pp. 12-20.

79. Ross excavated around the perimeter of the Parthenon, laying bare the foundations of the pre-Periclean temple, over the period from the autumn of 1834 to the summer of 1836 (see *Archäologische Aufsätze*, vol. 1, Leipzig 1855, pp. 72-142). Hoffer was the first (in 1836) to discover the horizontal curve in the stylobate of the Parthenon. He published his observations in the *Wiener Allgemeine Bauzeitung*, 1838, pp. 294ff (see J. Sisa, 'Joseph Hoffer and the Study of Ancient Architecture', *Journal of the Society of Architectural Historians* XLIX, 4, December 1990, pp. 430-439). The similar observations made by J. Pennethorne in 1837 were published by M.W. Leake, *The Topography of Athens*, London 1841 (2nd ed.), and they thus became immediately widely known. Schaubert published his observations on the curvature of the Parthenon in construction industry newspapers and art periodicals in 1838, 1842 and 1843. A pupil of K.F. Schinkel, Schaubert is the link between Athens and Berlin, where in 1833 he presented a paper to the local association of architects on the question of the polychromy of the Parthenon (Höpfner and Schwandner, *op. cit.*, p. 351).

80. The most important work done by the French on the Parthenon in the fifth decade of the nineteenth century was that of Laborde and Paccard in 1844. Laborde planned to publish a full and final study of the Parthenon in two volumes. In the end, one volume of drawings was published (*Le Parthénon, documents pour servir à une restauration*, Paris 1848), including some drawings by Paccard of the details of the monument. Paccard's study was known to scholars from an article on it by E. Burnouf in *Revue des Deux Mondes*, 1 December 1847, and from the book by E. Beulé, *L'Acropole d'Athènes*, Paris 1853, which included an artist's reconstruction of the ground plan of the temple by Paccard. However, it was not until recently, in *Paris – Rome – Athènes, Le voyage en Grèce des architectes français aux XIXe et XXe*, Paris 1982, pp. 162-171, 351-368, that his drawings and the written commentary on his study were published. This book also contained drawings made by the expeditions of B. Loviot in 1879-1881 (pp. 230-237), which are a riot of outrageous colour, and M. Lambert in 1877 (pp. 252-257), where the Parthenon is shown as part of the group of monuments on the sacred rock.

81. The ground plan of the monument in its current state (plate 3) was by G. Knowles, and the artist's reconstruction (plate 4) by Penrose. Penrose's study stood out for the accuracy of its measurements, achieved by the use of special methods; see M. Korres, Ch. Bouras, *Meleti Apokatastaseos tou Parthenonos* ('Study for the Restoration of the Parthenon'), vol. 1, Athens 1983 (hereinafter, *Meleti* 1), p. 203.

82. J. Fergusson, *The Parthenon*, London 1883, plate IV.

83. C. Bötticher, *Bericht über die Untersuchungen auf der Akropolis zu Athen (im Frühjahre 1862)*, Berlin 1863.

84. Before Michaelis, much information about the history of the Parthenon was brought together in the classic treatise by L. de Laborde, *Athènes aux XVe, XVIe et XVIIe siècles*, vols. I, II, Paris 1854.

85. After 1881, Dörpfeld produced a stream of publications in the *Mitteilungen des Deutschen Archäologischen Instituts, Athenische Abteilung* concerning the Parthenon and the other monuments of the Acropolis. For a full list of his articles on the Parthenon, see *Meleti* 1, bibliographical bulletin on pp. 178-179.

86. See above, note 74.

87. From Renan's 'Prière sur l'Acropole', which, of course, is not a travel text. It was written in 1876, eleven years after Renan visited the Acropolis, and it stemmed from his general philosophical thinking about the relationship between Hellenism and Christianity; see H. Psichari, *La 'Prière sur l'Acropole' et ses mystères*, Paris 1956. Similar thinking about the Parthenon had manifested itself in France as far back as the 1840s, when the values of medieval Christianity were being discovered. A.N. Didron compared the Parthenon to Rouen Cathedral and underlined the contribution which Hellenism had made to consolidating Christian culture, using the conversion of the temples of the Acropolis into Christian churches as an example. E.A. Thouvenal believed the Parthenon was the equal of Reims Cathedral (R. Canat, *L'éveil du Parnasse 1840-1852*, Paris 1955, pp. 14-15, 38).

88. Admiration (Hamilton 1835, Garston 1840, Hinstin 1864); grief (Milnes 1832/3), melancholy nostalgia, intellectual joy (de Beauregard 1899).

89. The steam-powered roller printing press entered use in 1814, with the techniques of lithography and colour lithography being developed in the same year, in parallel with a fresh upsurge in the use of wood-cuts (G. Fioravanti, *Grafica e Stampa*, Bologna 1988, pp. 17, 64-66).

90. Wordsworth's book was published in London in 1840, with 350 wood-cuts to illustrate the text and 28 full-page copper engravings consisting of artist's views (mostly to sketches by Cockerell) and reconstructions of monuments and archaeological groups to drawings by Sargent, Irton and Purser. The book was a great success, and in 1841 was published in French.

91. Leake used the views of Brönsted on the sculptures of the Parthenon, the observations of Pennethorne and a general ground plan of the Parthenon by Penrose. Beulé relied chiefly on Leake, Paccard, Burnouf and Penrose.

92. F.M. Tsigakou, *Anakalyptontas tin Ellada* ('Discovering Greece'), Athens 1981, pp. 25-30, 68-70.

93. The expedition was organised by the Frenchman N.P. Lerebours, a publisher and manufacturer of optical instruments. The Daguerreotypes taken by the Swiss-Canadian P.G.G. Joly de Lotbinière were published in an album by Lerebours, *Excursions Dagueriennes, Vues et Monuments le plus Remarquables du Globe*, Paris 1841-2; see G. Hübner, 'Bild as Botschaft. Das antike Erbe Athens fotographischen Zeugnisser des 19. und 20. Jahrhunderts', *Fotogeschichte*, vol. 8, no. 29, 1988, pp. 3-5.

94. A. Xanthakis, *History of Greek Photography 1839-1960*, Athens 1988, p. 44.

95. Such as E. Piot, *L'Acropole d'Athènes*, 1853; A. Lorent, *Ruinen Athen*, 1875; H. Beck, *Vues d'Athènes et des monuments photographiés d'après nature,* Berlin and London 1868.

96. F. Margaritis exhibited at the Paris World Fair of 1855 and D. Konstantinou at the Paris World Fair of 1867, see Xanthakis, *op. cit.*, p. 68. For photographs of the Parthenon by Greek photographers, see *Athina 1839-1900 Photographikes Martyries* ('Athens 1839-1900, The Evidence of Photographs'), exhibition catalogue, Athens 1985, nos. 76, 297.

97. As was the case with J. Robertson (Hübner, op. cit., p. 10).

98. G. Daux, 'L'Athènes antique en 1851. Photographies d'Alfred Normand', *Bulletin de Correspondance Hellénique* 18, 1956, pp. 619-624, plates XI-XXIV.

99. W.J. Stillman, *The Acropolis of Athens Illustrated Picturesquely and Architecturally in Photography*, London 1870.

100. This dramatic photograph of the Parthenon and, more generally, of the Acropolis from the east was produced by combining two negatives (Xanthakis, *op. cit.*, p. 90).

101. The great excavations of 1885-1890 under P. Kavvadias reached down to the natural rock and removed the last later remains from the Acropolis. The extensive restoration work on the monuments under N. Balanos, which began in 1898 and lasted some forty years, returned a considerable part of the appearance of the temple to its original condition. These interventions gave the Acropolis its appearance today.

102. *Pinacothèque Hellénique: Collection A. Rhomaïdes; Athènes antiques* (s.a.), plate 9. The photographs of the Parthenon date from after 1902.

103. H. Büttner, 'Zur Geschichte der ehemaligen Messbildanstalt und des Messbildarchivs des Instituts für Denkmalpflege', *Materialen und Berichte zur Denkmalpflege in der Deutschen Demokratischen Republik*, Jena 1973, p. 31.

104. Hübner, op. cit., p. 22.

105. *L'Acropole: Le Parthénon*, 2 vols., Paris 1913, with an introduction by G. Fougères, and *Le Parthénon, l'histoire, l'architecture et la sculpture*, Paris 1914, with an introduction by M. Collignon. Both publications contained architectural drawings (water-colours) of the Parthenon by the architects L. and M. Magne dating from 1894 and first published in L. Magne's, *Le Parthénon*, Paris 1895.

PANAYOTIS TOURNIKIOTIS

The Place
of the Parthenon in
the History and Theory
of Modern Architecture

The belief that the Parthenon is the most important building in the world, the most perfect structure ever to have been erected, is deeply rooted in the architectural thought of our times. Almost no one would question it. Very few theoretical statements in relation to architecture over the last two centuries have avoided referring to this Greek monument – in their opening pages – as a climactic moment in history. However, if we look more closely at such statements we will see that apart from their expressions of admiration and interpretations of genius, the Parthenon is often invoked in order to provide a foundation for significant changes in the direction of architectural progress, from mere repetitions of its forms to the most highly subjective compositions in concrete or steel.

As a standard for architecture, the Parthenon is nonetheless a recent discovery. It was effectively unknown until the publication in 1758 of J.D. Le Roy's drawings of it. Descriptions and views of the Parthenon had, of course, been circulating in Europe since the time of Cyriacus of Ancona. Yet despite the fact that Athens was in Florentine hands and that in Florence the Renaissance was at its height, we know of no original depiction of the antiquities of Athens other than that of Cyriacus himself, who visited the city in 1436 and 1444 after four decades of travels in the Mediterranean.[1] Cyriacus' drawings, 'copied' in 1465 by Giuliano da Sangallo (see p. 165, figs. 1, 2)[2], were, consequently, all that quattrocento Italy needed of the monuments of ancient Greece. That image was a vague and timeless one, one which skipped from order to order with only the inscription 'the temple of Minerva in Athens' as a common feature.[3] Similarity to the actual building was not a matter of importance. The rendering of the temple did not go beyond the most rudimentary type of ancient propylum. Furthermore, the Parthenon was completely detached from any kind of environment: there was an entire absence of locus. The temple was, of course, located in Athens; yet in these pictures what is important is the building in isolation, the propylum, the temple in general, whether it was located in Athens or anywhere else. In any case, Athens as represented in the medieval chronicles was not a real place. Its existence was purely imaginary, and closer to the location of the draughtsman – whether that was Nuremberg, Flanders or some other place – than

to the city which he drew but had never seen (see pp. 31-33, figs. 10-12).[4]

Athens and the Parthenon did not 'meet' until the second half of the seventeenth century. Travellers and emissaries marked the antiquities on a diagram of a contemporary city which was in line with the relative geometry of the monuments (see p. 33, figs. 13-14).[5] They also produced views of Athens which showed the Parthenon on top of the Acropolis, but these were merely reproductions of the phenomena. In the report of the Jesuit Father Babin, the Parthenon is described as a "grand mosque" and is shown as such at the highest point of a Turkish city.[6]

The publication in 1678 of Dr Jacob Spon's book of travels was the first time that the Parthenon made its presence felt in the history of modern architecture. Now, as never before, the usual representation of reality was supplemented by depictions of monuments detached from their surroundings and restored to their supposed original form.[7] In fact, Spon travelled the East in search of coins and antiquities of values to collectors, an undertaking in which he was financed by Colbert – who had also sent Antoine Desgodetz to survey the buildings of Rome so that French architects would have proper models, and had commissioned a translation of Vitruvius from Claude Perrault. European architects were not yet interested in Greek ruins. Spon, however, took with him and published the first depiction of the Parthenon detached from its true environment (see p. 168, fig. 5). Despite its obvious inaccuracies, his archetypal representation of the temple made the round of the Western world and was popular for many decades. However, the starting-point of this process was not the real Parthenon but a conventional image which lay outside time and place: an abstract temple type. Visitors did not judge the actual building: they projected on to it the descriptions and judgements of ancient writers. Furthermore, the Parthenon and the other monuments of Athens – which were regarded as being of equal value – were not part of a system of interpretation of the past, not were they in any way involved in a definition of the terms of the architectural process. The image of a Parthenon in isolation was of greater interest to numismatists and collectors of the picturesque antiquities which were

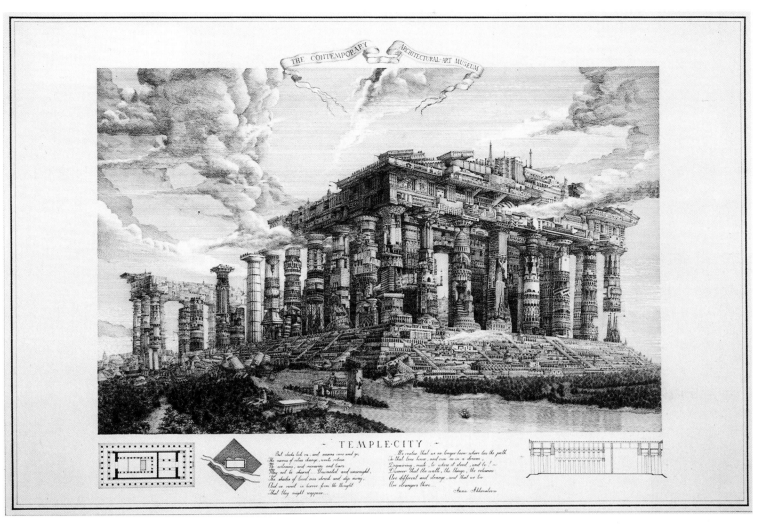

1. I. Galimov: design for a contemporary museum of architecture and art, the Temple-City, 1988; Frankfurt, Deutsches Architekturmuseum.

'worth seeing' in the territories of the Ottoman Empire.[8]

The true dividing line in the Western approach to Athens and the Parthenon ought to be associated with the events of 1687 and the accurate ground plans drawn by the engineer G.M. Verneda under the guidance of the Conte di San Felice.[9] The first depictions of Athens, the Acropolis and the Parthenon drawn on a horizontal projection were purely of a military nature. Their task was to contribute to the reconstruction of the fortifications and to swell the archive of the Serene Republic's fortified sites. When first published, however (by Francesco Fanelli, in 1707;[10] see p. 168, fig. 7), these drawings were a foundation stone in the new approach to the ancient monuments. They were republished many times down to the beginning of the nineteenth century, sliding more and more each time towards the fields of architecture and archaeology.[11]

After that time, the Parthenon ceased to be a physical reference in an ancient text. It was no longer an abstract type detached from an unimportant environment. Now it was subjected to the rationalism of empirical reality: it ex-

isted as it was, it occupied a specific position, and it had an entirely real form. In Spon's drawing, the Parthenon was spatially placed in a qualitative relationship to the monuments of the city as described by Pausanias. In Verneda's ground plan, the Parthenon is above all a rectangle which exactly defines a system of geographical co-ordinates. This new departure led, inevitably, to the strict accuracy of the architectural survey, to an 'anatomy' of the true situation which – alone – can help us know and reconstruct the structure of the original building: the anatomy of a dead organism, of ruins. I am referring here to a very broad set of realignments in the realm of the arts and sciences and, above all, to a method of approaching and interpreting reality which is inevitably associated with anatomy, ballistics, cartography and architecture.[12] The empirical rationalism of anatomy as a method of understanding and reconstructing the natural world was used in precisely the same way, by precisely the same people, for understanding and reconstructing architecture.[13] The Parthenon had to blow up, strange though it may seem, before its ruins could be 'anatomised'. These two successive stages belong to the same rational train of thought. In order to hit the Parthenon with a shell, you have to know its specific position, you have to define its location, and you have to be able to measure with accuracy the distance between it and the observer. Accuracy of that kind is deductive knowledge; it is empirical rationalism. On it was based the expedition to Rome by Antoine Desgodetz, in 1674, to survey the only possible reality of the ancient buildings.[14] On its foundations – which owed much to the analytical spirit of the doctor C. Perrault and the architect F. Blondel – the Englishmen Stuart and Revett were to conduct, a few decades later, the task of surveying the Parthenon and producing artist's reconstructions of it. For the engineer San Felice, who left Paris and abandoned his studies of ballistics in 1685,[15] for the architect François Blondel, who published his *Art of Bombardment*[16] and *New Manner of Fortifying Cities*[17] almost simultaneously, and for Claude Perrault, who made drawings of ballistae after Vitruvius and even constructed them – for Blondel to experiment with[18] – the art of building and the art of demolishing were two sides of the same analytical thinking. The knowledge necessary to knock something down was equally essential in order to put it up again.

The English painters James Stuart and Nicholas Revett and the French architect Julien David Le Roy travelled to Athens, measured the Parthenon, depicted it in its contemporary setting – and then isolated it, reconstructed its ground plan and elevations and analysed it into details (see the articles by S. Kondaratos and F. Mallouchou-Tufano elsewhere in this volume) in the mid-eighteenth century, when the idea of returning to the original sources of Greek architecture had ripened in France and Britain.[19] Although there are differences between the two books, *The Antiquities of Athens measured and delineated*[20] and *Les Ruines des plus beaux Monuments de la Grèce considérées du côté de l'histoire et du côté de l'architecture*[21] both provide direct links between the history and theory of architecture, and put forward the Parthenon – among other important Athenian buildings – as a model ready for use by their authors' contemporaries.

Stuart and Revett treated the monuments which comprised their work in the same manner. To begin with, they provided "first a View of it (...) faithfully exhibiting the present Appearance of that particular Building and of the circumjacent Country".[22] Then they moved on to "Geometrical Plans and Elevations after the manner of Desgodetz, in which will be given, with the greatest accuracy, the measure and proportion of each particular member, as well as the general disposition and ordonnance of the whole Building, restored to its original form".[23] Yet their approach was dominated by the absence of time. Monuments dating from different periods were juxtaposed

purely and simply because they all belonged to the great family of Athenian antiquities. The Parthenon of Pericles' time both precedes and succeeds buildings of the Roman era.[24] The concept of evolution in form and construction is entirely absent. The character of the site is of no interest. The beauties of ancient Greece, absolute and timeless, hold their value everywhere and for ever.

Stuart and Revett had nothing to say about the theory and history of architecture. All they did was to demonstrate images and models, to copy which – as they themselves did in their architecture – was sufficient. In effect, they worked in Athens (as Desgodetz did in Rome) without transcending the thinking of the seventeenth century. Nonetheless, they succeeded in 'establishing' images of the Greek antiquities; neutral, absolute and timeless images, detached from language. It was Stuart and Revett who shaped the modern image of the Parthenon, even if the building could still be said to lie outside the history and theory of architecture.

By way of contrast, Le Roy attempted to base a theory of contemporary architecture on an interpretation of its past. In his *Les Ruines...* he touched on the main issues which concerned architects in his day. He introduced a method of analysing Greek architecture as a part of the sum of all the architecture so far effected which was in line with the emergence of history in the limelight. Le Roy aspired to a 'French' architecture of the second half of the eighteenth century which would simultaneously make the most of the arrangement of Christian churches, the achievements of Gothic architecture and "the beauty" of the Greek orders.[25] His contemporaries would have to comprehend the architecture of Greek temples if it was their ambition to construct masterpieces equivalent to the Parthenon. Yet elevation to the level of Greek architecture did not mean copying Greek forms: it meant acting in the manner of the ancient Greeks, it meant applying the same principles.

Le Roy was not interested in bringing out timeless and universal standards. Instead, he examined the fundamental principles of architecture in relation to the concepts of place, time and society. In his eyes, buildings constructed in a specific period by a given society enclosed within their forms the material, cultural and social essence of the environment which had produced them. Consequently, the forms of architecture evolve along with societies and reflect its inevitable mutations. The Parthenon is a climactic moment in architecture precisely because it expresses the sublimest moments of Athenian democracy. The task of the historiographer is not just to anthologise the best buildings of each place, but also to study them so as to reconstruct "the chain of ideas along which human beings have passed" (fig. 2).[26] This position allowed Le Roy to introduce comparative morphology into the field of

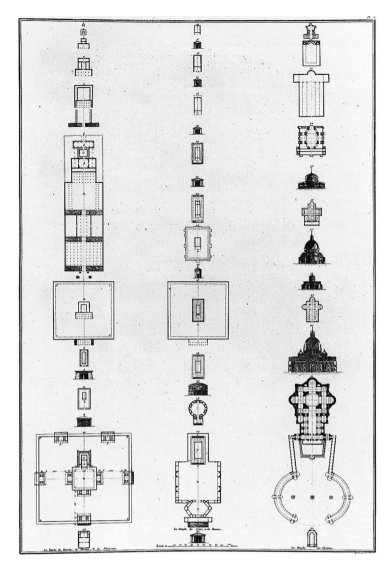

2. Julien David Le Roy: comparative table of architectural history. On the left, Egyptian temples, in the centre, Greek temples, and on the right, Roman temples, on the same scale and in chronological order. Source: J.D. Le Roy, Les Ruines des plus beaux monuments de la Grèce, Paris, 2nd ed. 1970; Athens, Gennadios Library.

architectural theory, marking the emergence of a new way of representing the order of things and thus laying the foundations for the history of architecture in the sense of rational practice which was then to develop during the nineteenth and twentieth centuries.

Le Roy's discourse is structured in a manner quite different from that of Stuart and Revett. For Stuart, the forms of the monuments were not transparent; they did not constitute testimony to the conditions of the past, and existed only as a phenomenon in time present. Perhaps they were even less than that, since the two Englishmen did not succeed – despite the accuracy of their observations and measurements – in 'seeing' the traces of colour on certain members of the temple. For Le Roy, on the other hand, the visible forms bore witness to invisible rela-

tionships which concerned the time at which the monuments were built. The forms were transparent: they tell us about things which cannot be seen in the time present of observation.

This manner of seeing phenomena was what established, for Le Roy, the principle of difference. The Greek buildings belong to the time, the place and the society which produced them. They are to be analysed as part of a past which is completely finished, and they have nothing beyond their fundamental principles to offer the architecture of the present. Stuart, by way of contrast, placed the 'finest' monuments from all periods of history side by side. This was the principle of identity: paradigmatic monuments – that is, models – are equally 'classical' whether they are located in Athens, in Rome or in London, and regardless of the differences in time, place and society. All forms are equally present and valid in the eyes of the observer, who is their sole judge. Stuart and Revett surveyed models; Le Roy sought for fundamental principles and archetypes. If for Stuart and Revett the Parthenon was, par excellence, a model for copying, for Le Roy it was the foundation of an architecture which had not as yet appeared but would be orientated towards the future. In founding his theory of the architectural process on an interpretation of architecture as already effected, Le Roy was proposing a history with an active structure, one which has henceforth been the principal characteristic of 'contemporary' architecture. At the same time, the Parthenon was introduced into the historical and theoretical discourse about architecture as the first moment of culmination in the past and as the starting-point for competition in the direction of the future.

The years which followed the publication of the seminal works of Stuart, Revett and Le Roy coincided with the consolidation of the ideals of neo-Classicism as an intermediate space marked out by their widely differing yet complementary approaches. The prevailing spirit was one of a return to the sources; it brought the inquiring young architects of the first two decades of the nineteenth century to Greece, and to Athens in particular, to see at close quarters, draw and interpret the most important monuments of history. Among them were many architects who became important representatives of neo-Classicism, including the Englishmen Robert Smirke, Charles Robert Cockerell and William Wilkins, and the Germans Carl Haller von Hallerstein and Karl von Fischer. Nonetheless, despite the acute observations made by some of these visitors – such as Cockerell's discovery of the 'entasis' of the Parthenon – and the numerous enlightening comments they made on matters of detail (with the question of paint as the most important), the general level of knowledge did not really improve on Le Roy's seminal studies on the

3. *Friedrich Gilly: final design for a monument to Frederick the Great, 1797, copy of the lost original; Berlin, Technische Universität.*

theoretical and historical level or on the work of Stuart and Revett in drawing the originals. At this time, the drawings of the two English artists circulated very widely.[27] Athenian architecture emerged as a true model for contemporary architectural practice, especially in Germany and England, and in a different manner in the United States of America. Yet the Parthenon always occupied a place of its own; it was not seen simply as an example of the 'Greek order', but as its culmination, a building obviously invested with signifiers originating outside architecture. Starting from its specific and individual features, the Parthenon reappeared in the European and American architecture of the first half of the nineteenth century, where it served as an ideal shell for the introduction of new ideas and new functions. Yet the impact of the Parthenon was only the influence of the original model up to a certain point. After that point, secondary models came into being; they were, of course, indirect vehicles for the original message, but they had a new and additional message, too, which depended on the simultaneous ideological function of the secondary model. It is this reappearance, and the variations on it, which we shall be examining in the rest of this article, from the point of view of a typological approach to the references. We shall deal first with important monuments and then with important public buildings before moving on to the use of individual architectural features from the Parthenon in buildings of the time and concluding with two informal but highly characteristic relationships between the ancient temple and contemporary architectural practice.

A. Important monuments: these are national monuments which express an entire nation or lofty ideas, and monuments to eminent men who embodied the sublimest patriotic or artistic ideals. In this category, we can discern two trends: a) buildings which repeat the entire structural type of the Parthenon, usually standing in a raised site – either a monumental man-made platform or a natural hill – in an allusion to the Acropolis of Athens, and b) buildings which combine the constructional type and the consequent ideological content of the Parthenon (as a propylum) with that of the Roman Pantheon (as the main body of the monument).

It is characteristic that the important buildings which we shall be discussing here are above all 'monuments' in the sense which that word acquired when, in the late eighteenth and early nineteenth century, it was associated with the ideological function of 'preserving in the memory',[28] a function expressed with the arrangement of the monumental mausoleum around a centre and still more clearly in the Roman Pantheon. As a result, the reference to the Pantheon was more or less inevitable. Yet while the Pantheon alludes to the Roman dimension of antiquity, the Parthenon expresses not only its Greek equivalent but also the context of the age of Pericles, in terms of political, social and cultural ideas and the association of the monument with victory over the Persians.

The Parthenon symbolises Greece and all those other things, but it is neither a 'monument' nor a 'Pantheon' (in the ancient sense). The Pantheon of Rome is first and foremost a 'Pantheon' in terms of function; its status as a primary architectural symbol of the Roman Empire is secondary, though equally important. The condensation of both types into a single modern building – which at the same time created a new type – was done so as to embody, by osmosis or mere addition, the values expressed by each.[29] In parallel, it was a statement that the Greek and Roman periods of antiquity were being invoked on an equal footing. Exclusive reference to the Parthenon, on the other hand – especially when combined with the placing of the monument in a raised position – was a statement that Greek antiquity of the Classical period was seen as clearly superior to that of the Roman Empire. We shall refer to the most notable examples of such buildings, taking the important monuments in chronological order.

Friedrich Gilly's drawing for the monument to Frederick the Great (1797, fig. 3)[30] was the archetypal model for a contemporary octastyle Doric temple on a man-made platform. Of course, the reference to the Parthenon has to be deduced rather than being a clear statement, given that Gilly merely noted on a preliminary sketch that "Athens is the model, the Acropolis". Yet the invocation of the Acropolis rock and the Parthenon is quite obvious even if the ideological context of Classical Athens is flanked by those of Egyptian and Roman architecture. Here we also have to note the 'national' importance of

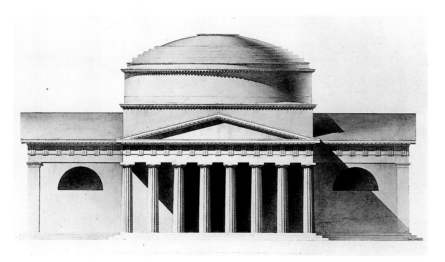

4. Karl von Fischer: first design for the German national monument - Valhalla, 1809; main elevation; Munich, Architekturmuseum, Technische Universität.

5. Karl von Fischer: first design for the German national monument - Valhalla, 1809; section; Munich, Architekturmuseum, Technische Universität.

the Prussian monarch, in doubling the territory of his kingdom, in playing a leading role in European developments, in bringing about fundamental cultural and social reforms, and in cultivating intellectual affairs, all of which elevated him to the status of an exemplary enlightened despot.

The German Valhalla in Bavaria, the largest Doric temple to have been built since antiquity and clearly modelled on the Parthenon, could well be seen as the culmination of neo-Classicism. The idea of building a large national monument symbolising pan-German unity was conceived by Prince Ludwig of Bavaria in 1807, when the power of Napoleon was at its height, for the purpose of boosting German national morale.[31] Ludwig's vision was of a 'German Pantheon' modelled on those of Rome and Paris;[32] it was to contain a collection of busts of the most eminent Germans in history, from Alaric and Theodoric to Mozart, Schiller and Goethe.[33] On the advice of the Swiss historian Johannes von Müller, however, he ultimately decided to 'make reality' the Valhalla of the old Scandinavian myths – the place where virgin female warriors, the Valkyries, received dead heroes before they entered the service of the god Odin. The long story of the design of the monument now began. First of all, Ludwig sought the help of the architect Karl von Fischer, who had just returned from Athens. Fischer proposed two solutions. In that of 1809, a synthesis of the Roman Pantheon and the Parthenon appeared for the first time, in a cruciform building (figs. 4, 5). In the second, of 1810, the Parthenon alone predominates, in conjunction with elements taken from the corresponding temple at Paestum so as to emphasise the nature of the Greek Doric order in its supreme expression, transcending time and place (figs. 6, 7). However, a decisive role in the course of events was played by the Battle of the Nations (or Battle of Leipzig, 1813), which marked Napoleon's retreat from Germany. In February 1814, Ludwig proclaimed an architectural competition for the German Valhalla, which was now to be a Greek temple. The obvious comparisons with the victory over the Persians put the Parthenon in the first rank of possible models. Fischer once more proposed a pure octastyle Greek Doric temple which clearly referred to the Parthenon. The plan submitted by Haller von Hallerstein displayed a similar spirit: his 'Parthenon' could be situated on one of two alternative imaginary sites, obviously referring to the natural height of the Acropolis and culminating in a man-made pedestal (figs. 8, 9). In order to round off the meaning of his composition, Haller von Hallerstein turned to Egyptian features as Gilly had done in 1797. Despite the participation in the competition of many eminent architects,[34] Ludwig was in no hurry to announce the results, and in 1819 he commissioned the project from Leo von Klenze. Von Klenze was torn between modelling himself on the Pantheon, the mausoleum of Hadrian and

6. Karl von Fischer: second design for the German national monument - Valhalla, 1810; main elevation; Munich, Architekturmuseum, Technische Universität.

7. Karl von Fischer: second design for the German national monument - Valhalla, 1809; side elevation and section; Munich, Architekturmuseum, Technische Universität.

Bramante's design for St Peter's before arriving, in his turn (1821), at a 'German Parthenon/Valhalla' which demonstrated and documented the 'common roots' of the ancient Greeks and the modern Germans. The monument was constructed at Regensburg, on a man-made platform on top of a natural hill, and it was completed in 1842 (figs. 10, 11).[35] Despite its striking external similarity with the Parthenon, the building is in fact clearly German and entirely modern, as can be seen from the general arrangement and layout of its interior, the selection and

use of materials, the Valkyries holding up its iron roof, its fifty busts, the narrative of the German epic in its sculptures and the impressive flight of steps by which it is approached.

In Britain, the possibility of building a national memorial was discussed after the victory at Waterloo and, although it would be difficult to underestimate the impact of the drawings for the German Valhalla, already familiar, there were corresponding ideological references to the Parthenon. Indeed, the debate about the construction of a na-

8. Carl Haller von Hallerstein: entry to the architectural competition for Valhalla, 1814; general view; Munich, Bayerische Staatsbibliothek.

9. *Carl Haller von Hallerstein: entry to the architectural competition for Valhalla 1814; perspective drawing; Munich, Bayerische Staatsbibliothek.*

tional monument or Valhalla took place along the lines of that in Germany. The drawing by Thomas Harrison (c. 1815, fig. 12)[36] repeated the blend of the Pantheon and the Parthenon and was strongly reminiscent of Karl von Fischer's original plan (fig. 4). Although Parliament approved the project, it never took specific form.[37] In Scotland, however, where there was a similar ambition, the foundations were laid in 1822 on the natural rise of Carlton Hill in Edinburgh of a 'Parthenon' to adorn the 'Athens of the North', to plans by Cockerell and Playfair.[38] Externally, the building clearly referred to the Parthenon, and even the general lie of the land bore some resemblance to the Acropolis. At the same time, however, the interior of the building – which rivalled von Klenze's Valhalla – was to function as a Christian church. In 1829, when twelve columns had been erected (fig. 13), work came to a halt, largely for financial reasons. Despite the later proposals for its completion by G.M. Kemp (1843, fig. 14), J. Dick Peddie (1886) and G. Washington Brown (1918), the National Monument of Scotland remains as it

was abandoned in 1829, a definitive reminder of the wane of neo-Classicism.

The mausoleum of Antonio Canova, planned and completed at Possagno, near Genoa, between 1819 and 1833 – and ascribed to the architect Giovanni Antonio Selva (figs. 15, 16)[39] – had a completely different starting-point. This, too, was a blend of the Pantheon and the Parthenon, designed to bring out the ideological and artistic connection between the famous sculptor and the worlds of Greece and Rome. Although retaining their proportions, the building is markedly smaller than its models. Yet it is not a copy to scale, which does not seem to have interested the architect. The reliefs of scenes from the Old and New Testaments, the bare drum, the host of functional, constructional and morphological features and, above all, the blend of the Pantheon and the Parthenon show that the neo-Classical architects were not concerned to copy the real models so much as to create new types enhanced with the signifiers of the rich code which a conquest of history could offer them.

10. *Leo von Klenze: the Valhalla at Regensburg, near Munich,*
1821-1842. Source: Claude Mignot, L'architecture au XIXe siècle,
Fribourg 1983.
11. *Leo von Klenze, the Valhalla at Regensburg; interior. Source:*
Oswald Hederer, Leo von Klenze, Persönlichkeit und Werk, *Munich*
1964.

B. Important public buildings: the modern function
of such structures is incorporated into the Parthenon as a
building type and a set of significances, so as to state the
relationship between that function and the values it represents in society and those represented (in the eyes of the
society in question) by the Parthenon for ancient Athens.
Buildings of this type are found only in the United States,
where they house financial and political functions: banks,
a customs house, a capitol.[40] Naturally enough, the complex requirements of the modern function made it necessary to radically rearrange the interior of the 'Parthenon',
since it had to contain a large number of offices set out on
different floors and also a spacious hall for transactions
with the public. The new 'Parthenon' was thus confined to
the general external appearance. For the first time, too, it
entered a densely-built urban environment. The completely different relation in which the American 'Parthenon' stood towards the ancient temple, history in general
and modern society also made it permissible to intervene
in the general building type, which now incorporated
imposing domes with references quite alien to Greek
antiquity.

The first use of the autonomous Parthenon type for a
modern function in the USA was for the Second Bank of
the United States, in Philadelphia. This structure emerged
from an architectural competition held in 1818, whose
terms stated that the building was to be a double-portico
edifice in the simplest and cheapest form of "the Greek
order", with marble facades.[41] The first prize was awarded

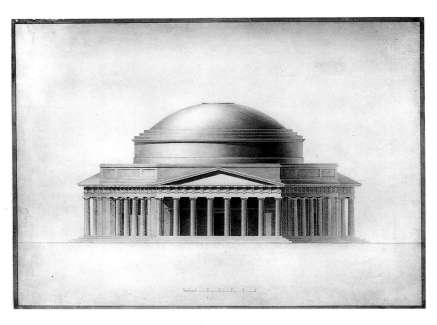

12. Thomas Harrison: design for a British national monument - Valhalla, c. 1815; London, The British Architectural Library, RIBA.

13. C.R. Cockerell, W.H. Playfair: the National Monument of Scotland on Calton Hill, Edinburgh, 1822-1829; Edinburgh, Royal Commission of Ancient Monuments of Scotland.

14. G.M. Kemp: proposal for completion of the National Monument of Scotland on Calton Hill, Edinburgh, 1843; Edinburgh, Royal Commission of Ancient Monuments of Scotland.

15. Giovanni Antonio Selva: the mausoleum of Antonio Canova, Possagno, 1819-1833. Photograph: Alinari-Giraudon.

16. Giovanni Antonio Selva: the mausoleum of Antonio Canova, Possagno, 1819-1833; plan. Source: Allgemeine Bauzeitung 22, 1836.

to William Strickland,[42] a pupil of Benjamin Latrobe, and the building – completed in 1824 (figs. 17-19) – was immediately hailed as a "strikingly beautiful" ornament to the urban landscape of Philadelphia.[43] The two porches were exact copies of those of the Parthenon, reduced to three-fifths of their original size, but as a whole the building – in coloured marble – left no doubt that this was a use of the most characteristic feature of its appearance in order to bestow significance, rather an a replica of the temple. We can see an indication of the climate of the age in Latrobe's own entry (fig. 20), which retained the portico of the Parthenon but changed the entire type of the temple by adding a higher section to make room for the public business hall.[44]

The same rationale was used by the architects Ithiel Town and Alexander Jackson Davis, first in their plans for the Indiana Capitol in Indianapolis (1831-1835, fig. 21), where an imposing dome was added to a double-porticoed building in the general shape of a temple with porches similar to those of the Parthenon, and above all in the New York Customs House, which was designed in 1833 and completed in 1845 (figs. 22-25)[45] – that is, the same year as the German Valhalla. The Parthenon of Wall

17. William Strickland: the Second Bank of the United States, Philadelphia, 1818-1824, water-colour by A.J. Davis; New York, Avery Architectural and Fine Arts Library, Columbia University.

18. William Strickland: the Second Bank of the United States, Philadelphia, 1818-1824. Photograph by Cervin Robinson, 1959; Washington, Library of Congress.

19. William Strickland: the Second Bank of the United States, Philadelphia, 1818-1824; plan. Source: C. Mignot, op. cit.

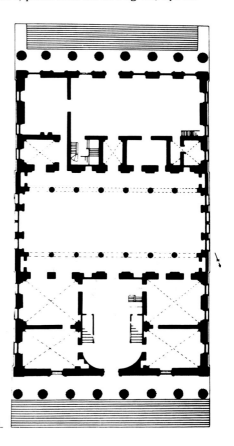

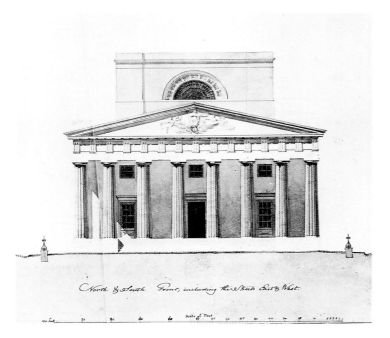

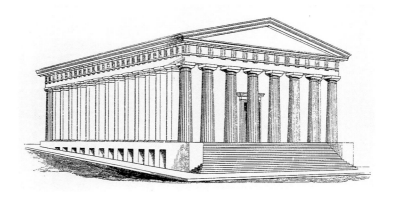

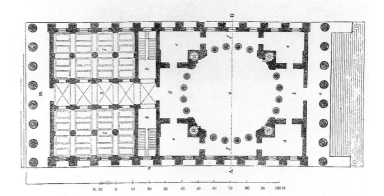

20. *Benjamin Latrobe: entry to the competition for the Second Bank of the United States, Philadelphia, 1818, water-colour; Washington, Library of Congress.*

21. *Ithiel Town and Alexander Jackson Davis: the Indiana Capitol, Indianapolis, 1831-1835; general view, floor plan; New York, Avery Architectural and Fine Arts Library, Columbia University.*

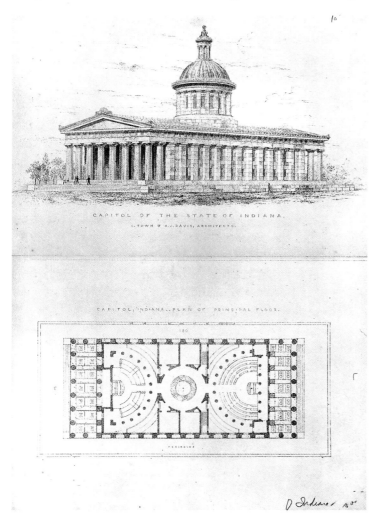

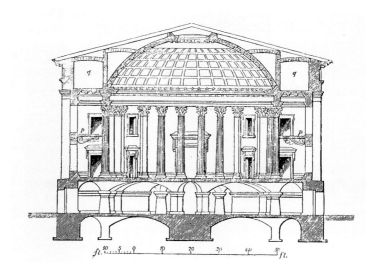

Longitudinal Section.

22. *Ithiel Down and Alexander Jackson Davis: Custom House, Wall St, New York, 1833-1842; revised plan. Perspective drawing, plan, lateral section (source: The Architectural Magazine II, December 1835) and lengthwise section (source: Journal of the Society of Architectural Historians 3, October 1964).*

VIEWS IN NEW-YORK.   BY ROBERT KERR, ARCHITECT

Nº 1

THE CUSTOM HOUSE, WALL STREET

VIEWED FROM BROAD STREET.

23. Ithiel Town and Alexander Jackson Davis: the Custom House, Wall St, New York, 1833-1842, lithograph by Robert Kerr, 1845; Washington, Library of Congress.

Street is a marble double-porticoed building in the shape of a temple adapted to modern functions which demanded that there should be a large number of offices on four storeys and a magnificent cross-in-square rotonda as a hall for the public. A further variation on the same theme can be seen in yet another finance Parthenon, the Boston Customs House, the work of Amni Young (1837-1847). It rounds off a cycle of works which displayed the particular features of American neo-Classicism in the best possible manner.[46]

C. The use of individual architectural features taken from the Parthenon in nineteenth century buildings can be divided into two categories: a) the use of an entire portico which gives the entrance of a building otherwise adapted to modern functions and other typologies a char-

acter so full of significance as to bestow on the entire structure a symbolic and ideological relationship with the Parthenon and the ideals and values of the society which it represented, and b) the use of even more detailed features which in some cases operate as mere references to the values of Classical antiquity, in others constitute statements of identity, and in a third set of instances are charged with specific meanings associated with the sublimest ideals of the ancient world. In the last case, the references are still less overt and retain their allusive nature against a wider background of the symbolic functioning of numerous detailed architectural features.

The following are characteristic examples of the first category of building: 1. The Parthenon-like porch of Haller von Hallerstein's original plan for the Munich Glyptothek, c. 1813 (figs. 26, 27), which has an unusually complex floor plan and contains a reference to the Propylaea of the Acropolis in its entrance.[47] 2. The porch in the plans for the Duke of Wellington's palace, 1816 (fig. 29), which was C.R. Cockerell's first involvement with

24. Ithiel Town and Alexander Jackson Davis: Custom House, Wall St, New York, 1833-1842; original design, section; New York, Avery Architectural and Fine Arts Library, Columbia University.

25. Ithiel Town and Alexander Jackson Davis: Custom House, Wall St, New York, 1833-1842. Photograph by Manolis Korres.

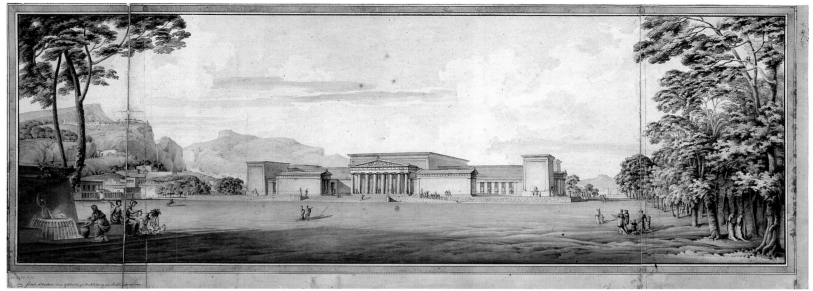

26

26. Carl Haller von Hallerstein: the Munich Glyptothek, proposal I, c. 1813; perspective drawing; Munich, Bayerische Staatsbibliothek.

27. Carl Haller von Hallerstein: the Munich Glyptothek, proposal I, c. 1813; plan; Munich, Bayerische Staatsbibliothek.

28. Théodore Labrouste: the Court of Cassation, entry to the Grand Prix of 1824; elevation. Source: The Beaux-Arts and Nineteenth-Century French Architecture, *R. Middleton (ed.), London 1982.*

29. Charles Robert Cockerell: the palace of the Duke of Wellington, 1816; elevation. Source: D. Watkin, The Life and Work of C.R. Cockerell, *London 1974.*

27

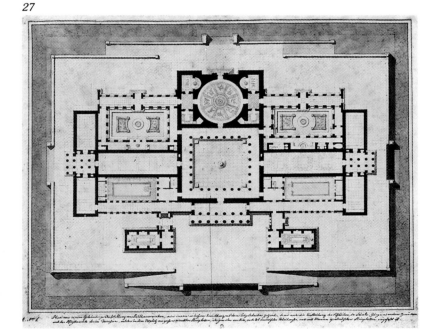

28

29

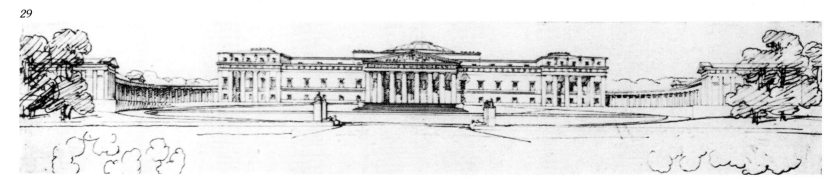

30. Robert Mills: the Patent Office, Washington, 1835-1840, daguerreotype by John Plumbe, c. 1846; Washington, Library of Congress.

design practice.[48] 3. The porch in the design for the Cour de Cassation which was Théodore Labrouste's entry for the Grand Prix of 1824 (fig. 28); it was based on a model Courthouse by Durand, which gave it a clear reference to Greek antiquity as the ideological foundation for the function the building was to house.[49] 4. The porch for the Patent Office in Washington, by Robert Mills, 1835-1840 (fig. 30), which led into the 'temple' of the innovative spirit that supported the 'American miracle'.[50] 5. The porch of the house at Berry Hill, near Halifax, Virginia, c. 1842-1844 (fig. 32); this is a unique yet characteristic example of a residential building with a Parthenon-like porch despite the generally Palladian nature of the layout.[51]

Among good examples of buildings in the second category are the following: 1. The Parthenon-like main entrance – beneath a hexastyle porch – to the Court of Session in Glasgow, by William Stark, c. 1807-1814.[52] 2. The Parthenon-like Doric columns of the tetrastyle porch of the Covent Garden Theatre in London, by Robert Smirke,

1808-1809.[53] 3. The ornamental friezes from the Parthenon inside the Fitzwilliam Museum, Cambridge, by George Basevi, 1834-1835.[54] 4. The copy of the Parthenon frieze which adorns the morning-room of the Reform Club in London, by Charles Barry, 1837-1841.[55]

The proposal produced by Schinkel for a palace on the Acropolis in Athens, as a residence for King Othon (figs. 33, 34)[56], belongs in a category of its own. The most important ruined monuments of Classical Athens made the Acropolis the most suitable place to build a palace for the Bavarian monarch of modern Greece, while at the same time they were to play their part in the architecture of the new building, since the ruins would remain as they were next to the up-to-date and anything but Greek structures proposed by the notable Prussian architect. The attraction of the Parthenon, greater than that of the Erechtheum or the Propylaea, was so strong that it pulled young kings and ambitious architects towards it – to such an extent as to menace their own existence, since in their moment of crowning glory they would also encounter their own self-abnegation.

Although it does not constitute a true category of the influence of the Parthenon on the architecture of the first half of the nineteenth century, the business card of the architect James Dakin (c. 1833), giving his name and profession beneath a perspective view of the temple (fig. 31), makes plain the broader ideological function of the Parthenon – in American society, at least. Dakin,[57] who began his career in the Town and Davis practice, never designed any projects based on the Parthenon but was very 'Greek' in employing a selectivity which adapted all modern buildings to the symbolic charge stemming from the various periods in architectural history. His business card simply promises 'Parthenons' in the sense of the best possible architecture which prospective clients could expect. In that sense, the card conveys the measure and boundaries of the presence of the Parthenon in the Western architecture of the first half of the nineteenth century.

31. J.H. Dakin: the architect's professional card, c. 1833. Source: Arthur Scully Jr., James Dakin, Architect, *Baton Rouge 1973.*

The radical change in this situation followed the liberation of Athens and the first clearing operations on the Acropolis. Of course, it was not only the result of the fact that architects and archaeologists were now able to conduct their studies of the ruins without impediment. Above all, it was a natural consequence of general shifts in the European view of architecture, which moved its approach to things from the level of phenomena and models to be imitated to one of the invisible laws and principles that determine the phenomena of architecture. A decisive role in determining this new direction was played by the detailed

studies and publications of architects who had ascertained the complex web of architectural refinements and structural achievements embodied in the Parthenon, had discovered the widespread use of paint in the monument and had picked up the threads of its history. The Athenian temple had now been awarded the incontrovertible status of the crowning glory not only of Classical architecture but of architecture in general. The works I am referring to here are those of the Englishmen Francis C. Penrose[58] (see p. 188, figs. 37, 38) and James Pennethorne,[59] the

32. Residence at Berry Hill, near Halifax, Virginia, 1842-1844; Washington, Library of Congress.

Frenchmen Alexis Paccard[60] (see pp. 261-263, figs. 1-5) and Benoit Loviot[61] (see pp. 273-275, figs. 18-22), and the Germans Carl Bötticher[62] and Adolf Michaelis.[63]

The recognition of the Parthenon as 'perfect' – that is, as transcending aesthetic preferences and disputes – was followed by a period lasting many decades (at least as far as the mid-twentieth century) in which the architecture of the temple constituted the most important part of the foundations for any theoretical statement about architecture whose ambition was to create new forms in close connection with the social, political and cultural conditions, the climate, the materials and the construction methods of a particular country. The founding of history in the close bond between human creative activities and the place and time of their occurrence ruled out the possibility of repeating in the present the visible models of the past, while at the same time making the Parthenon a paradigm and fulcrum in the search for an architecture – in the immediate future – which would be entirely new and just as much of an achievement. In this line of advance, inaugurated by the pioneering work of Julien David Le Roy, the Parthenon emerged as a timeless and placeless measure of comparison, as a culminating teaching which, *ipso facto*, was incapable of repetition and which could serve only as an exhibit and an example for the information of contemporary architects.

The most important role in mapping out this path was played by the Frenchman Viollet-le-Duc, who studied Gothic architecture by comparison with the present of the nineteenth century and the past of Greek architecture at its zenith, taking the Parthenon as his example *par excellence*.[64] In Viollet-le-Duc's rationalist interpretation, there are basic principles which underlie the architecture of many different periods, producing different results because they are applied in different conditions. He believed that forms ought both to be and to appear to be the natural consequence of the materials available, of the construction methods of the time, of the climate, of social conditions and of the requirements of the specific project. The Parthenon is thus the ultimate Doric temple and the zenith of Greek architecture only when it is located in Athens, in the local conditions which dictated to the architect's 'sense of reason' the specific formal options he took. It would be ludicrous to place the building amidst the mist and cloud of Edinburgh. Its perfection stems not from the forms of which it is composed – that is, from its phenomena – but from the principles which governed its construction – that is, from the logical method. It would be equally unthinkable to build a Parthenon in nineteenth century Paris. Viollet-le-Duc would permit such a thing to be done only by way of exception; for example, the Parthenon might be reconstructed on Monmartre so as to preserve the type of eternal beauty, given that the original

had been so severely damaged, just as a rare natural species is preserved in the controlled conditions of a garden. On the other hand, no part of a building is acceptable when detached from the whole to which it belongs.[65] Viollet-de-Duc denounced in the most scathing terms the use of individual details from the Parthenon (or other buildings of the past) in structures of his own time: this ran counter to the basic principles of architecture, that is, to the rational and organic relationship of the part to the whole and of the whole to the place and time of its creation.

The theoretical structure of Viollet-de-Duc sought to question the 'fraudulent' architecture of his own time and to lay the foundations for a 'true' architecture in the near future. Under the Cartesian method, systematic analysis and classification of the experiences of the past – that is, history – was essential if this aim were to be achieved. Such analysis and classification would make comprehensible the immutable principles of architecture which had always been the source of progress; their application would reveal the 'true' architecture of the near future. In this theoretical framework, the study of Greek or Gothic architecture was not connected with a revival of the masterpieces of the past on the level of phenomena. It was confined to the confirmation of principles – that is, of theory. The rationalism which Viollet-le-Duc recognised in the work of the architects of Classical Greece and the French Middle Ages thus belonged neither to the fifth century BC or to the thirteenth century AD. It was purely a product of the nineteenth century, which was projected on to the past to as to prove a point: that since all true architecture of the past relied on 'reason', then if true architecture were to exist in the near future, it, too, would have to rely once more on 'reason'. Starting from this position, Viollet-le-Duc searched for the true expression of the constructional function of iron, the new building material, and proposed a series of applications that showed the way forward into the third period of architectural sublimity after those of the Parthenon and the cathedrals.

The materialistic interpretation of architecture, whose chief representative was the German Gottfried Semper, headed in a different direction, though one which was complementary as far as the spirit of the age was concerned, giving priority to the principle of 'facing' structural components. Semper devoted much of his research to the colouring of ancient monuments, and in particular of the Athenian monuments, which he visited and studied in 1831-1832[66] (see pp. 264-265, figs. 7-8). According to his 'theory of facing' (Bekleidungstheorie), optimal compliance with functional and constructional requirements is an invisible condition for each modern building. The ultimate surface of the building, however, is a 'skin' of forms and colours which safeguard the cultural function of

33. *Carl Friedrich Schinkel: proposal for a palace for King Othon on the Acropolis, 1834; general view from the west. Source: C.F. Schinkel,* Entwurf zu einem Königspalast auf der Akropolis bei Athen, *Berlin 1878; Athens, Gennadios Library.*

34. *Carl Friedrich Schinkel: proposal for a palace for King Othon on the Acropolis, 1834; general view of the audience hall. Source: C.F. Schinkel,* op. cit.

architecture, and the necessary materials are to be faced with ornamentation, symbols and other elements so as to constitute the 'language of forms'. Semper based his theory on the facing with colour (Farbenbekleidung)[67] of the ancient temples, including the Parthenon with its elegant marbles. Thus he gave the concept of style a new meaning.[68] Simultaneously, he adapted his architecture to the cultural elements in the programme for the project (which depend on location and social conditions), seeking thus to make it absolutely contemporary and familiar in its environment. This justified him in treating Klenze's Valhalla as a prime example of what not to do,[69] and in arguing – with Owen Jones – that the iron of the innovative Crystal Palace in London (1851) ought to be symbolically faced with the eternal colours of the Parthenon.[70]

The purely eclectic approach to architecture cultivated in the second half of the nineteenth century in the unifying light of the 'Classical tradition'[71] also saw the Parthenon as the zenith of Greek architecture and as a model of perfection – one, however, which could not be imitated as a whole in the modern age. Julien Guadet, who crystallised the theoretical approach of the Ecole des Beaux Arts,[72] taught that "the classic is not the privilege of any period, any country or any school".[73] He put the Parthenon, the Baths, the Amphitheatres, St Sophia, Notre Dame, Saint-Ouen, St Peter's, the Villa Farnese and the Louvre on the same pedestal, and gave his pupils the following warning: "Admire these wonderful buildings as they have come down to your hands, but learn to respect them, and never let the thought of rebuilding them cross your minds".[74] The model building of another age was not at the architect's disposal. It belonged inescapably to its age, and to no other. However, it consisted of architectural features which made up the architect's basic vocabulary. In Guadet's *Eléments* the Parthenon is never shown as a single buiding; that would not have been of interest to his students. Only segments of the structure are shown, in their reconstructed original form as part of the comparative presentation of features such as the Doric order, the portico or the pediment.

The lengthy process which began around the middle of the nineteenth century, with the rise of structural rationalism and the materialistic interpretation of phenomena, with documented acknowledgement of the majesty of the Parthenon, and with the questioning of any attempt to repeat its phenomena, culminated during the third and fourth decades of the twentieth century in the theory and practice of the modern movement. Here, too, the Parthenon was constantly present: in the movement's texts, to begin with, but also in a more covert manner in the buildings which were seen as radical models for anti-historical modernism. A typical example is the presence of the Parthenon in the writings of Le Corbusier, and especially in *Towards a New Architecture*,[75] which laid the foundations of his personal concept of architecture as pure spiritual creation – a concept which had a significant impact on subsequent generations. On two famous pages (see p. 47, figs. 26-27), Le Corbusier juxtaposed the temple of Poseidon at Paestum and the Parthenon, above, against the 'Humbert 1907' and 'Delage Grand Sport 1921' motor cars, below.[76]

Starting from his definition of architecture as "the masterly, correct and magnificent play of masses brought together in light",[77] Le Corbusier divided human constructional activity into that which was 'building' and that which was 'architecture'. 'Building' goes no further than practical capacity and produces standardised structures which satisfy functional needs and provide maximum efficiency for a minimum requirement in funds, work and materials, forms, colours, words and sounds. Architecture is an almost imperceptible intervention in a constructional type which is complete in every sense – an invisible intervention in a standard – for the purpose of introducing harmony into the assembly of formal elements and of making a graceful section through the visible details in such a way as to trigger feelings of emotion and spiritual uplift in the viewer.[78] In the same way, the Parthenon is distinct from the standard Doric temple as exemplified by the temple of Poseidon at Paestum. The process by which the type – that is, the Doric temple of Paestum – is produced belongs to the sphere of building. Rational organisation of its forms – geometry, order and measure – is an rule innate in human creation and a characteristic of all buildings, even when we are talking only of a primitive hut. Architec-

ture adds to the innate orderliness of the builder a deliberate pursuit of harmony, of 'the beautiful', in the visible grace of the masses which is perceived by the organ of sight and, on reaching the brain, causes satisfaction of the spirit and the soul.

The comparison between a typical Doric temple and the inspired creation which is the Parthenon thus acquires didactic significance. Le Corbusier's aim was to demonstrate the distance which separates mere fulfilment of needs within the bounds of reason – that is, building – from its creative perfection with the addition of architecture. His age, he explains to his readers, is one of the rational fulfilment of needs: it is the age of the motor car and the aeroplane. In the hands of a Pheidias, however, architecture is something more than that. To use Le Corbusier's own words: "In this period of science, of strife and drama in which the individual is violently tossed about at every moment, the Parthenon appears to us as a living work, full of grand harmonies. The sum of its inevitable elements gives the measure of the degree of perfection to which man can attain when he is absorbed in a problem definitely stated. The perfection in this case is so much outside the normal, that our apprehension of the Parthenon can only correspond nowadays with a very limited range of sensation, and, unexpectedly enough, with sensations of a mechanical kind; its correspondence is rather with those huge impressive machines [automobiles] with which we are familiar and which may be considered the most perfect results of our present-day activities, the only products of our civilisation which have really 'got there'. Pheidias would have loved to have lived in this standardised age. He would have admitted the possibility, nay the certainty, of success (...) Before long he would have repeated the experience of the Parthenon."[79] A reading of those two pages does not, then, place the Parthenon on the same pedestal as the Delage Grand Sport motor car of 1921. It shows that however refined a motorcar may have become between 1907 and 1921, it remains a standard, a creation of reason alone, and it lags far behind the Parthenon, which is a pure creation of the spirit. In other words, Le Corbusier was calling on the architects of his age not to confine their work to fulfilling needs and achieving transparency – that is, truth – in their constructions, but to intervene creatively in noble competition with the model of the Parthenon.

By the late eighteenth century (and certainly by the early nineteenth century), the Parthenon was a fundamental feature on the cognitive horizon of all students of architecture. When the teaching of history and theory was introduced into the schools of architecture, the Parthenon established itself in the collective consciousness of architects as the ultimate moment in Classical Greek

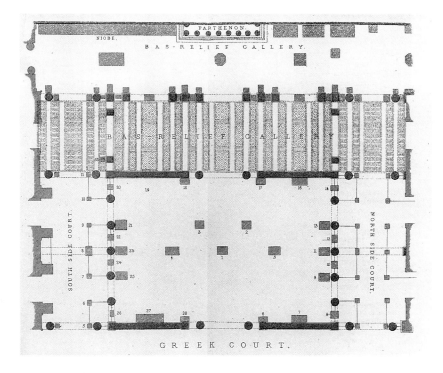

35. Plan of the Greek Court at the Crystal Palace Exhibition, London, 1851. The position of the Acropolis can be discerned at the top. Source: Owen Jones, The Greek Court Erected in the Crystal Palace, *London 1854; Athens, Gennadios Library.*

Even more important, however, was the model of a corner of the Parthenon and copy of its plastic ornamentation erected in the Ecole des Beaux-Arts in Paris (fig. 36).[81] Those who were to become the leading exponents of eclecticism learned their art and architecture (in the most eminent school of the nineteenth century) right next to accurate details of the Parthenon. This was only natural, since the Parthenon was for the most important textbooks – from Choisy's[82] *Histoire* to Guadet's *Eléments* (which left their stamp on the turn of the twentieth century) – the ultimate masterpiece of a Classical tradition which spread down so many centuries and across so many different lands.

The reconstruction of the Parthenon – full-size – for the Tennessee centennial exposition in Nashville (1897)[83] was different in nature but equally didactic. Here the replica of the Parthenon was at the same time the main attraction of the state fair (fig. 37). The rebuilding of the structure in 1931, using concrete (fig. 38) and without the rest of the fair – a process to which the renowned archaeologist W.B.

36. Félix-Jacques Duban and Ernest-Georges Coquart: the Ecole des Beaux-Arts, Paris, 1863-1874; the central covered atrium with a detail of the Parthenon and copies of art-works used in teaching. Photograph: Giraudon, 1929.

architecture and as one of the greatest achievements of the Classical tradition in architecture, equivalent to the Pantheon in Rome, St Sophia and Notre Dame. After the early nineteenth century, more and more books were published and they became much more accessible to a wider expert reading public. The ideogram of the temple, its historical relationship with the golden age of Pericles, its architecture and the vicissitudes of its subsequent fate came down to most scholars in the form of 'history of architecture' (which emerged as a new genre at this time and rapidly multiplied in number) or through the handbooks or catalogues of pictures from different countries and different periods. Later, when the first thorough studies of the temple were carried out, and when detailed drawings and accurate figures were published (exceeding in their volume those relating to any other monument in the history of architecture) – that is, when the 'sublimity' of the architecture of the Parthenon was proved beyond any doubt in all its refinements and in the advanced approach of its aethetics – exact large-scale replicas of the monument were produced so as to inculcate its perfection into trainee architects.

A characteristic example of this trend is the model of the west facade of the Parthenon, on a scale of 2:9, which was shown by Penrose in 1851 at the Exhibition in the Crystal Palace. Penrose constructed his model in accordance with the exact measurements he had made and all the refinements he had observed in Athens (fig. 35).[80]

37. General view of the Tennessee Centennial Exposition, Nashville, 1897, lithograph; Washington, Library of Congress.

38. The Parthenon from the Tennessee Centennial Exposition, c. 1931. Source: Christopher Hitchens, The Elgin Marbles, *London 1987.*

Dinsmoor was a consultant – somewhat improved the impression made by the first approach. Yet the fact that another 'Parthenon' had in the meantime dominated the interest of visitors to the San Francisco Exposition of 1915[84] is sufficient evidence that this was not a random manifestation of the American spirit but rather an ideological syndrome, one which now involved broader masses of the people and demonstrated the appeal which lay in a combination of the Classical temple and the society which had created it.

Our search for the presence of the Parthenon in twentieth century architecture must be conducted on different terms. The theoretical and aesthetic dictates of modernism precluded any obvious invocation of its phenomena. During this period there were no Parthenon-like porticoes, columns or other details, far less any repetitions of the basic building type, even though it is often referred to in the texts of the most important architects, such as Le Corbusier and Walter Gropius.[85] Thus it is very difficult to identify any actual – that is, manifest – presence of the Parthenon in the architecture of modernism. Even were we to suppose that allusive references could be found, it could not be argued with certainty – when indeed it is not

224

39. Le Corbusier: the Villa Savoye at Poissy, near Paris, 1929-1931. Photograph by Alexandros Tombazis.

a fundamental alteration in the means of construction. Stone and brick gave way to reinforced concrete, and the overt morphological expressive form of the octastyle portico – in the static sense – ceased to have any meaning. Delicate columns were arranged at clearly greater intervals in order to bear the same weight, thus restricting the possible similarities with the columns of the past. Despite the inherent doubts, we could risk two references precisely because they appear most likely to conceal a 'Parthenon' and because they also sum up the most successful moments in the putative relationship between the architecture of the Classical temple and the architecture of modernism.

Le Corbusier's Villa Savoye at Poissy (1929-1931, fig. 39) is seen as the culmination of the architect's theoretical and aesthetic quest during the Twenties, a quest which was dominated by the idea of the Parthenon. The austere horizontal arrangement, the purely rectangular outline of the floor plan, and the regular colonnade of which the *pilotis* consists (and which bears horizontal 'taenias' in concrete and glass – that is, empty and filled spaces) are all evidence of references to the Parthenon which may have existed unwittingly in the architect's mind. The connection is further strengthened by the free-standing location of the building in the countryside, which would in effect have been impossible in an urban house such as the Villa La Roche. All these features point to the Villa

expressly stated – that what is behind the colonnade is the Parthenon and not the Doric spirit in general. To put it more simply, it might even be structural rationalism, which dictated a similar approach to architecture by the ancient Greeks and contemporary Europeans. Furthermore, the shift from overt references to the Parthenon in the direction of covert allusions which marked the transition from the nineteenth to the twentieth century was not simply a change in ideology. It was largely the outcome of

40. Walter Gropius: the US Embassy in Athens, 1956-61. Photograph by K. Megaloconomou.

41. Vittorio Mazzucconi: an Academy complex, Athens, 1989; perspective drawing. Source: Vittorio Mazzucconi, L'idea della città, *Florence 1989.*

Savoye as a reference – with a greater or lesser degree of awareness – by Le Corbusier to the Parthenon. This is the 'Parthenon' of his architecture.[86]

The United States Embassy in Athens, by Walter Gropius (1956-1961, fig. 40), has to be seen against the background of US foreign policy in the Fifties, a policy which demanded that 'Americanness' and the most advanced construction techniques be blended with the architectural language of each country.[87] An enumeration of the references to the architecture of the Parthenon in the numerous publications which described the Embassy for the public would be sufficient to demonstrate the close relationship between Gropius' building and the Parthenon in the international collective consciousness of architects.[88] Furthermore, its structure – the peripteral colonnade, the horizontal bands edging the roof, etc. – and the materials used (in particular, the facing of the columns in Pentelic marble) contribute to linking contemporary architecture with the prevailing local model. This, however, was not confined in importance to the extent of Le Corbusier's project, since the nature of the Embassy building – in conjunction with the specifications laid down by the owner – allowed the implication of a relationship between the contemporary and the Classical which was rightly termed 'the Greek Revival' in the international Press.[89]

The developments of recent years will not concern us in the same manner. It is true that since the mid-Sixties the questioning of modernism has gone hand-in-hand with a 'return of the past' – that is, of history – in contemporary architectural practice.[90] Yet the Parthenon is rarely encountered among the host of buildings of all periods depicted in the seminal texts of the period.[91] Furthermore, references to it function on terms different from those which we have seen so far. In the iconographic use of forms from the past and in the linguistic approach to architecture there is room only for the ideogram of the Parthenon as an ornamental element, as the vehicle for messages or as a statement of one's place of origin. Contemporary architects are very little interested in the true significance of the ancient temple or in an understanding of its architecture (fig. 41). The levelling of the image of the Parthenon down to all the other images and all the other types encountered in the history of architecture is a characteristic manifestation of the contemporary mode of thought and of the entire network of prevailing social and cultural values and construction methods. Yet it is far from paradoxical that this same period has seen a revival of interest in studying the Parthenon and the other important monuments of the past from the perspective of the best possible understanding, to date, of their architecture and of detailed maintenance and even restoration.[92] The gradual attenuation of the ideological function of the Parthenon over the period from the late eighteenth to the late twentieth century has contributed to demystifying the symbol and opening up the way for thorough and largely objective study of it from the architect's point of view. The Parthenon thus seems to be acquiring the status of a highly significant heritage which will become more familiar and accessible to us the more that architects can succeed in driving from their minds any thought of working with analogies or images of this, the earliest of the ultimate monuments.

Notes

1. Cyriacus, who visited Athens with the texts of Greek and Latin writers as his guides, described and depicted for us a small number of monuments - those which we find in most of the travellers' accounts down to the eighteenth century: the Parthenon, the Tower of the Winds, the monuments of Lysicrates, Philopappus and Thrasyllus, and the aqueduct of Hadrian. His text focuses on the descriptions and judgements of ancient writers, at the expense of the reality of his own time. In his eyes, the Parthenon was a renowned, exceptional and admirable temple in terms which he had borrowed from Aristotle and Pliny. Cyriacus' drawings were burned in 1514. But the surviving copies - by an unknown hand - served as the starting-point for a whole series of depictions of the Parthenon which marked out its place in the iconographic vocabulary of architecture (cf. Edward Bodnar, *Cyriacus of Ancona and Athens*, Brussels 1960, and 'Athens in April 1436', *Archaeology* 23, 2, 1970, pp. 96-105 and 23, 3, 1970, pp. 188-199; see also Adolf Michaelis, 'Eine Originalzeichnung des Parthenon von Cyriacus von Ancona', *Archäologische Zeitung* XL, 1882, pp. 367-384).

2. The Parthenon was among the collection of architectural monuments produced by Sangallo c. 1465. It forms part of folio 28, containing the antiquities of Athens, a work which many Europeans (including Jacob Spon and Julien David Le Roy) consulted in Rome before travelling on to Athens. Sangallo retained the general form of the original drawing, but converted the order from Doric to Ionic and put the portico (still octastyle) on the facade of the building. Cf. Henri Omont, *Athènes au XVIIe siècle*, Paris 1898, p. 7, and Stefano Borsi, *Guiliano da Sangallo. I disegni di architettura e dell'antico*, Rome 1985.

3. The Parthenon is also shown in a third drawing, by an unknown hand, in Paris. Here a hexastyle portico in the Corinthian order has been added to the temple, and the monument would not be recognisable without the inscription "Temple de Minerve à Athènes" to identify it. See Omont, *op. cit.*, p. 7.

4. Cf. Hartmann Schedel, *Chronicarum Liber*, Nuremberg 1493, and Sebastian Münster, *Cosmographia*, Basle 1541.

5. Visitors to Athens sought out the antiquities with Pausanias in hand and the Capuchin friars as guides. As an aid in their task, the Capuchins made the first plan of Athens, the archetype for a significant number of topographic drawings showing the ancient monuments against the neutral background of the contemporary city. The Capuchin plan was published for the first time in Guillet de St. George, *Athènes ancienne et moderne et l'etat présent de l'empire des Turcs*, Paris 1675. It was the founding father of the family of tourist plans still in use today, and shows the network of monuments which, to use Pausanias' phrase, were "worth seeing". The monuments are realistically depicted, in three dimensions. The contemporary city, on the other hand, exists only in the form of the geometry of the relative positions, topology essential to the visitor looking for the sights.

6. Cf. P. Babin, *Relation de l'etat présent de la ville d'Athènes*, Lyon 1674.

7. Cf. Jacob Spon, *Voyage d'Italie, de Dalmatie, de Grèce et du Levant fait aux Années 1675 et 1676*, vol. II, Lyon 1678, pp. 131ff.

8. Cf. Bernard de Montfaucon, *L'Antiquité Expliquée et Représentée en Figures*, Paris 1719-1724, vol. II, plate XIV.

9. The blame for the bombardment must be placed on the engineer Antonio Mutoni, Conte di San Felice, commander of Morosini's artillery, who had studied mathematics and ballistics in Paris and was a well-known figure. As soon as he had won the day, Morosini demanded exact plans of the city and the Acropolis, which were drawn using mathematical instruments by the engineer Giacomo Milhan Verneda under the supervision of San Felice. Cf. James Morton Paton, *The Venetians in Athens 1687-1688*, Cambridge, Mass. 1940, pp. 72-73.

10. *Atene, Attica. Descritta da suoi Principii sino all'acquisto fatto dall'Anni Venete nel 1687*, Venice 1707, pp. 309 and 317.

11. Cf. the plans published by Richard Pococke (*A Description of the East and Some Other Countries*, vol. II, II, London 1745, plate LXVII; see p. 169, fig. 8) and Richard Chandler (*Travels in Greece*, Oxford 1776, p. 25), and the plan of the Acropolis next to that of the Parthenon as drawn by Stuart in Antoine Chrysostome Quatremère de Quincy (*Restitution des deux frontons du Temple de Minerve à Athènes*, Paris 1825, plate I).

12. The activities of the Royal Academy of Sciences during the second half of the seventeenth century are characteristic of this spirit. The Academy, which was the world of Claude Perrault and François Blondel – that is, the 'anciens' and the 'modernes' – appeared on the frontispieces of both the *Histoire Naturelle des Animaux* of Perrault (Paris 1671) and the *Recueil de plusiers traitez de mathematiques de l'Academie Royale des sciences* (Paris 1676), by F. Blondel, M. Mariotte, M. Picard and others, which covered questions of trigonometric ground surveying, ballistics and descriptive geometry applied to architectural order. On this frontispiece, the Academy is being visited by Colbert with the Sun King, who appears to be pointing to a fortified city in horizontal projection, exactly behind which is a horizontal projection of the innards of a gazelle. In the background, outside the window, is the Observatory, an important project by Perrault which, however, actually stood on a different site.

13. One characteristic example is that of Claude Perrault, who used precisely the same technique of drawing to depict a chameleon, a beaver and other animals in his *Description anatomique des divers animaux dissequez dans l'Academie Royale des sciences* (Paris

1682) and the ancient temples in his translation of Vitruvius (Paris 1673). For Perrault, see Antoine Picon, *Claude Perrault ou la curiosité d'un classique*, Paris 1988, and Wolfgang Herrmann, *La théorie de Claude Perrault*, Brussels 1980.

14. Antoine Desgodetz, *Les édifices antiques de Rome dessinés et mesurés très exactement*, Paris 1682.

15. Cf. Paton, *op. cit.*

16. François Blondel, *L'art de jetter les bombes*, Paris 1683.

17. François Blondel, *Nouvelle Manière de Fortifier les Places*, Paris 1683.

18. *L'art de jetter les bombes*, *op. cit.*, pp. 492ff, 523ff.

19. For the beginning of this return to the roots, see Dora Wiebenson, *Sources of Greek Revival Architecture*, London 1969, and Joseph Rykwert, *The First Moderns. The Architects of the Eighteenth Century*, Cambridge, Mass. 1980.

20. James Stuart, Nicholas Revett, *The Antiquities of Athens Measured and Delineated*, London 1762-1816. The second volume, which concerns the monuments of the Acropolis, was published in 1789 (date printed as 1787).

21. Julien David Le Roy, *Les Ruines des plus beaux Monuments de la Grèce considérées du côté de l'histoire et du côté de l'architecture*, Paris 1758, second (revised) edition, to which my references, Paris 1770.

22. Stuart and Revett, *op. cit.*, I, p. V.

23. Wiebenson, *Sources...*, *op. cit.*, p. 78 (from the Venice Proposals of 1751).

24. The Parthenon follows the Doric portico of the Agora, the Ionic temple on the banks of the Ilissus, the Tower of the Winds and Hadrian's Library, all of which fascinated the experts of the time.

25. Cf. Julien David Le Roy, *Histoire de la disposition et des Formes différentes que les Chrétiens ont donné à leurs Temples, depuis le Régne de Constantin de Grand jusqu'à nous*, Paris 1764.

26. J.D. Le Roy, *Les Ruines...*, *op. cit.*, I, p. XX.

27. In the early nineteenth century *The Antiquities of Athens* was reprinted in English and translated into French (1808-1822), Italian (1832-1844) and German (1829-1833). It later came out in pocket editions such as *Les Antiquités d'Athènes et autres monuments grecs d'après les mesures de Stuart et Revett*, édition portative (Nolau), Paris 1835, reprinted Athens 1850, and *The Antiquities of Athens and Other Monuments of Greece*, London 1905.

28. Cf. Alfred Neumeyer, 'Monuments to "Genius" in German Classicism', *Journal of the Warburg Institute* II, 1938, pp. 159-163.

29. Cf. Carol L.V. Meeks, 'Pantheon Paradigm', *Journal of the Society of Architectural Historians* XIX, 4, 1960, pp. 135-144.

30. Cf. Alste Oncken, *Friedrich Gilly*, Berlin 1935.

31. For particulars of the German Valhalla, see *Die Walhalla. Idee, Architektur, Landschaft*, Jörg Traeger (ed.), Regensburg 1979, and Jörg Traeger, *Der Weg nach Walhalla*, Regensburg 1978. See also Sokratis Yeorgiadis, 'Enas Parthenonas stis ochthes tou Dounavi' ('A Parthenon on the Banks of the Danube'), *Tefchos* 5, 1991, pp. 40-44.

32. Soufflot's church of Sainte-Génévière, which was converted into a Pantheon at the time of the Revolution.

33. Cf. König Ludwig der Ersten von Bayern, *Walhalla's Genossen*, Munich 1842.

34. Including Klenze, Schinkel and Hübsch, but unfortunately very few drawings have survived.

35. Cf. Traeger, *op. cit.*, Leo von Klenze, *Walhalla in artistischer und technischer Beziehung*, Munich 1842, and Oswald Hederer, *Leo von Klenze, Persönlichkeit und Werk*, Munich 1964, pp. 300-314.

36. Cf. J. Mordaunt Crook, *The Greek Revival*, London 1968, pp. 24-26.

37. Cf. Andrew Robertson, *The Parthenon, Adapted to the Purpose of a National Monument to Commemorate the Victories of the Late War; Proposed to be Erected in Trafalgar Square or Hyde Park*, London 1838, and G. Cleghorn, *Remarks on the Intended Restoration of the Parthenon of Athens as the National Monument of Scotland*, Edinburgh 1824, pp. 3-4.

38. For the National Monument of Scotland and the debate around it, see 'Restoration of the Parthenon', *Edinburgh Review*, February 1823, pp. 126-144; G. Cleghorn, *op. cit.*, and J. Mordaunt Crook, *The Greek Revival, Neoclassical Attitudes in British Architecture 1760-1870*, London 1972, pp. 104-105.

39. Cf. 'Über den Bau der Kirche von Possagno, nach dem Plane Canova's', *Allgemeine Bauzeitung*, 1836, no. 21, pp. 162-163 and no. 22, p. 170; Carol L.V. Meeks, *op. cit.*, and the same author, *Italian Architecture 1750-1914*, New Haven and London 1966, pp. 186-188.

40. Cf. Lois Craig, *The Federal Presence. Architecture, Politics and Symbols in United States Government Building*, Cambridge, Mass. 1978.

41. Cf. Marcus Whiffen, *American Architecture 1607-1860*, Cambridge, Mass. 1981, p. 153.

42. Cf. Agnes Addison Gilchrist, *William Strickland: Architect and Engineer, 1788-1854*, Philadelphia 1950, and 'Latrobe vs. Strickland', *Journal of the Society of Architectural Historians* II, 3, 1942, pp. 26-29.

43. Cf. David P. Handlin, *American Architecture*, 1985, pp. 52-54.

44. Cf. Craig, *op. cit.*, p. 54.

45. The building of the New York Custom House was fraught with incident: Samuel Thomson and John Frazee intervened to bring about considerable changes in the interior of the initial award-winning design of Town and Davis. Cf. Louis Torres, 'Samuel Thomson and the Old Custom House', *Journal of the Society of Architectural Historians* XX, 4, 1961, pp. 185-190, and the same author, 'John Frazee and the New York Custom House', *Journal of the Society of Architectural Historians* XXIII, 3, 1964, pp. 143-150.

46. For the special character of American neo-Classicism, see Talbot Hamlin, *Greek Revival Architecture in America*, New York 1944.

47. Cf. *Klassizismus in Bayern, Schwaben und Franken. Architektur-Zeichnungen 1775-1825*, Munich 1980, pp. 230-231.

48. Cf. David Watkin, *The Life and Work of C.R. Cockerell*, London 1974, pp. 26-31.

49. Cf. Neil Levine, 'The competition for the Grand Prix in 1824: a case study in architectural education at the Ecole des Beaux-Arts', *The Beaux-Arts and Nineteenth-Century French Architecture*, Robin Middleton (ed.), London 1982, pp. 66-123, and J.N.L. Durand, *Précis des leçons d'architecture*, Paris 1805, vol.2, 1817² pp. 48-49 and plate 6.

50. Cf. Louise Hall, 'The Design of the Old Patent House', *Journal of the Society of Architectural Historians* XV, 1, 1956, pp. 27-30; Jane B. Davies, 'A.J. Davis' Projects for a Patent Office Building, 1832-1834', *Journal of the Society of Architectural Historians* XXIV, 3, 1965, pp. 229-251.

51. Cf. Mills Lane, *Architecture of the Old South, Virginia*, New York 1987, p. 188; T. Hamlin, *op. cit.*, p. 191, plate L, and William J. Murtagh, *The National Register of Historic Places 1976*, Washington 1976.

52. Cf. J. Mordaunt Crook, *The Greek Revival ..*, *op. cit.*, 1972, p. 147, fig. 182.

53. *Ibid.*, pp. 98, 118, fig. 180.

54. Cf. Robin Middleton, David Watkin, *Architecture Moderne 1750-1870. Du néoclassicisme au néo-gothique*, Paris 1983, p. 261.

55. *Ibid.*, p. 270.

56. Cf. Carl Friedrich Schinkel, *Entwurf zu einem Königspalast auf der Akropolis bei Athen*, Berlin 1878⁴; Paul Ortwin Rave, 'Schinkels Traum von einem Königspalast auf der Akropolis zu Athen', *Atlantis* VI, 3, March 1934, pp. 129-141; Rand Carter, 'Karl Friedrich Schinkel's Project for a Royal Palace on the Acropolis', *Journal of the Society of Architectural Historians* XXXVIII, I, 1979, pp. 34-46.

57. Cf. Arthur Scully Jr., *James Dakin, Architect. His Career in New York and the South*, Baton Rouge 1973.

58. *An Investigation into the Principles of Athenian Architecture*, London 1851.

59. *Elements and Mathematical Principles of the Greek Architects and Artists*, London 1844, and *The Geometry and Optics of Ancient Architecture*, London and Edinburgh 1878.

60. Léon de Laborde, Alexis Paccard, *Le Parthénon, documents inédits pour servir à la restauration de ce monument*, Paris 1848, and *Paris-Rome-Athènes. Le voyage en Grèce des architectes français aux XIXe et XXe siècles*, Paris 1982, pp. 162-171 and 350-368.

61. 'Mémoire sur la restauration du Parthénon', *Revue Archéologique* 39, 1880, pp. 322-331, and *Paris-Rome-Athénes, op. cit.*, pp. 230-237.

62. *Die Tektonik der Hellenen*, Potsdam 1852, and *Die Akropolis von Athen*, Berlin 1888.

63. *Der Parthenon*, Leipzig 1870 and 1871.

64. Eugène-Emmanuel Viollet-le-Duc, *Dictionnaire raisonné de l'architecture française du XIe au XVIe siècle*, Paris 1854-1868, and *Entretiens sur l'architecture*, Paris 1863-1872.

65. Cf. Viollet-le-Duc, *Entretiens..., op. cit.*, I, pp. 55 and 474.

66. Cf. Harry Francis Mallgrave, introduction of Gottfried Semper, *The Four Elements of Architecture and Other Writings*, Cambridge 1989, p. 14, and G. Semper, *Vorläufige Bemerkungen über bemalte Architektur und Plastik bei den Alten*, Altona 1834 (translated in *The Four Elements...* as 'Preliminary Remarks on Polychrome Architecture', pp. 45-73).

67. Cf. G. Semper, 'Preliminary Remarks...', *op. cit.*

68. Cf. G. Semper, *Die vier Elemente der Baukunst*, Braunschweig 1851, and *Der Stil in den technischen und tektonischen Künsten, oder praktische Aesthetik*, Frankfurt and Munich 1860-1863.

69. Cf. G. Semper, 'Preliminary Remarks...', *op. cit.*, pp. 46-47, and Wolfgang Hermann, *Gottfried Semper in Search of Architecture*, Cambridge, Mass. 1984, pp. 158-159.

70. Cf. G. Semper, 'A Fragment on the Origin of Polychromy' in Owen Jones, *An Apology for the Colouring of the Greek Court in the Crystal Palace*, London 1854, pp. 47-56, and 'On the Study of Polychromy and its Revival', *The Museum of Classical Antiquity,* 1, 1851, pp. 228ff.

71. The significance of the term 'the Classical tradition' is analysed by Joseph Rykwert, 'The Ecole des Beaux-Arts and the Classical Tradition', *The Beaux-Arts..., op. cit.*, pp. 9-17.

72. Cf. Julien Guadet, *Eléments et théorie de l'architecture*, Paris 1902.

73. *Ibid.*, vol. 1, p. 83.

74. *Ibid.*, p. 364.

75. Le Corbusier, *Towards a New Architecture*, London 1946.

76. *Ibid.*, pp. 106-107. For the meaning of certain basic terms in Le Corbusier's *Towards a New Architecture*, see my paper 'Orthologismos kai Idealismos. I Antilipsi tis Architektonikis tou Le Corbusier' ('Rationalism and Idealism. The Concept of Le Corbusier's Architecture'), *Deltio Syllogou Architektonon* 16, 1988, pp. 43-47.

77. Le Corbusier, *op. cit.*, p. 31.

78. "ARCHITECTURE is a thing of art, a phenomenon of the emotions, lying outside questions of construction and beyond them. The purpose of construction is to MAKE THINGS HOLD TOGETHER; of architecture TO MOVE US", *ibid.*, p. 23.

79. *Ibid.*, pp. 134-135.

80. Cf. Owen Jones, *The Greek Court Erected in the Crystal Palace*, London 1854, p. 1.

81. Cf. Richard Chafee, 'The Teaching of Architecture at the Ecole des Beaux-Arts', *The Architecture of the Ecole des Beaux-Arts*, Arthur Drexler (ed.), London 1977, pp. 61-109.

82. Auguste Choisy, *Histoire de l'architecture*, Paris 1899.

83. Cf. W.F. Creighton, *The Parthenon in Nashville*, Nashville 1968.

84. Cf. L. Craig, *op. cit.*, p. 222.

85. Cf. Walter Gropius, *Apollon dans la démocratie. La nouvelle architecture et le Bauhaus*, Brussels 1969, pp. 49-50 and 100.

86. Cf. William J.R. Curtis, *Le Corbusier: Ideas and Forms*, New York 1986.

87. Cf. Jane C. Loeffler, 'The Architecture of Diplomacy: Heyday of the United States Embassy-Building Program, 1954-1960', *Journal of the Society of Architectural Historians* XLIX, 3, 1990, pp. 251-278.

88. Cf. 'American Architecture Designed for Export', *The Architectural Review*, October 1957, pp. 237ff; *Architectural Record*, December 1957, pp. 159-164; *Bauen und Wohnen*, December 1959, pp. 412ff; 'The US Builds in Greece', *The Architectural Forum*, December 1961, pp. 118-123; *Edilizia Moderna*, April 1962, pp. 1-6.

89. Cf. 'Greek Revival', *The Architects' Journal*, 22 December 1960, p. 885.

90. Cf. *The Presence of the Past: First International Exhibition of Architecture - Venice Biennale*, Venice and London 1980.

91. Cf. Aldo Rossi, *L'architettura della città*, Padua 1966 (translated into Greek as *I Architectoniki tis Polis*, Thessaloniki 1987), pp. 190-200 and 337, with a photograph of the author among the columns of the Parthenon.

92. Cf. Manolis Korres, Charalambos Bouras, *Meleti Apokatastaseos tou Parthenos* ('Study for the Restoration of the Parthenon'), Athens 1983; M. Korres et al, *Meleti Apokatastaseos tou Parthenonos* ('Study for the Restoration of the Parthenon'), Athens 1989, and the articles by Manolis Korres and Charalambos Bouras in this volume.

STELIOS LYDAKIS

The Impact of the Parthenon Sculptures on 19th and 20th Century Sculpture and Painting

Ideological Conflicts

Heinz Ladendorf

When Lord Elgin was preparing to put his plans into effect, he was unaware – like many of his contemporaries – of the enormous significance which his undertaking was to have for spiritual culture. Yet in the area to which this undertaking was addressed, it bore no fruit. The visual arts gained no direct impetus from the Parthenon sculptures. Artists were able to appreciate the power and majesty of the sculptures, but their form proved to be indissoluble, inaccessible, impossible to use...

Heinz Ladendorf

As soon as artists saw the Parthenon sculptures in the makeshift Park Lane exhibition (fig. 1),[1] they reacted with enthusiasm. The most enthusiastic of all of them was the painter Benjamin Robert Haydon, who studied and painted (fig. 2) the sculptures even at night, and expressed his awe and admiration for them in the most ecstatic terms:[2] "My heart thumped! Here were the first beginnings of art, which the Greeks created at the time of their sublimest achievements... It seemed to me that some divine truth was shining its light on my mind and I realised that these sculptures would awaken the art of Europe...". Haydon also tells us that when his teacher, Johann Heinrich Füssli, saw and examined the pedimental sculptures he exclaimed (in a blend of English and German), "De Greeks were Godes! De Greeks were Godes!"

What Haydon stated in his personal reminiscences – that the sculptures of the Parthenon "would awaken the art of Europe" – was also the pretext and justification used by Elgin, who added that viewpoint to his arguments.[3] Yet the question of the extent to which European art was actually awakened via the Parthenon sculptures and of how far it was influenced by them appears to have little grounding in reality. Although the Elgin Marbles had an immense effect on the intellectual world in general, they had no 'revitalising' impact on the specific sector of art. Artists were able to appreciate the power and majesty of the Parthenon sculptures, yet their form proved unsurpassable, enclosed within itself and unsuitable for variation and development. The Classicist reworking of them seemed hubristic, and even to restore them to completeness struck many as sacrilege.[4]

Nonetheless, there was no shortage of notable conjunctures, which have an importance of their own no matter how peripheral they may have been, and which bring out an inner wish on the part of artists to draw closer to the great models, if only from their own point of view and in line with their own potential.

Goethe was among the first to recognise the superb quality of the Parthenon sculptures.[5] His judgement relied, of course, on the plaster casts which he had seen, and above all on the drawings of the sculptures published by various travellers and artists. Indeed, two drawings from Haydon's set occupied a place of honour in his house.[6] But in London, where the originals could be seen, the circle of admirers and artists who studied and copied them grew steadily wider. Now they flocked to Burlington House, to which the sculptures had been moved, and they included the sculptor John Flaxman ("the Pheidias of our time"), the sculptor John Henning (fig. 3), and the painters Thomas Lawrence and Benjamin West – the latter of whom made use of the Parthenon sculptures as motifs for post-Baroque Classicist compositions on themes from Greek history, an approach which Haydon rejected.[7]

In the meantime, realisation of the unique artistic value of the Parthenon sculptures took on momentum with the views of Ennio Quirino Visconti, director of the Vatican Museum and *conservateur* of the ancient works of art which Napoleon had seized from Rome and borne off to Paris.[8] As the guest of Elgin (and in his role as the elder statesman of the art criticism world as far as Classical sculptures were concerned), Visconti studied the sculptures in London and then wrote from Paris to W.R.

1. A. Archer: The Elgin Room, 1819, oils on canvas; London, the British Museum. Archer himself can be seen on the right; seated, Sir Benjamin West and Joseph Planta (Chief Librarian); extreme left, Benjamin Robert Haydon.

Hamilton expressing his admiration for the collection, especially as a means "for promoting the arts and sciences."[9]

The importance of Visconti's views were overshadowed by the opinions neither of the Earl of Aberdeen nor of R. Payne Knight, Deputy President of the Society of Antiquaries and famous numismatist – who never in fact visited the collection.[10] On the other hand, there were the particularly weighty impressions of Antonio Canova, the renowned sculptor, whom the Pope sent to London to argue the cause of returning to Rome the art-works which Napoleon had seized. Canova visited the collection in the company of Hamilton, with whom he was acquainted and who wrote to Elgin that when Canova entered the hall of sculptures he appeared initially to have been robbed of speech by their beauty and magnificence. Then he said he would have worked differently in his own field if he had been taught on the basis of those models at an early age.[11]

Yet as a typical Classicist, he does not seem to have reconciled himself, inwardly, to the Classical model, which went far beyond his personal aesthetic concept. Evidence of, or references to, the Classical model are rarely found in Canova's later work.

However, an examination of the reactions of the artists then working in England who were invited by the eighteen-member committee on the purchase of the sculptures to express their opinions of them reveals wide differences.[12] Despite these differences, the committee came out in favour of Elgin, agreeing that if the collection were to be bought by the state it would provide "models and examples to those, who by knowing how to revere them and appreciate them, may learn first to imitate and subsequently to rival them". Here again, as in the beginning, we see the leitmotif of the promotion and regeneration of the arts by means of the Parthenon sculptures, a position explained by the 'historical' spirit of Classicism and of the nineteenth century in general, which related the present to the past and, following the example of the Renaissance, sought for great models. At that time, no one was capable of perceiving the difference between the variation and the model, or the completely different influence that

2. Benjamin Robert Haydon: two of the three Fates from the east pediment of the Parthenon, 1809; London, British Museum, Haydon 3(6).

the latter has on artistic creation. Variations are vulnerable and suitable for further elaboration, while the great models, as we have already seen, are inaccessible because they are unsurpassable. Any variation on them will be inferior to them. In this particular case, "the hand is paralysed by our awareness that this is a uniquely great creation, by consciousness of the fact that they are inimitable".[13]

The belief that the ancient sculptures from Greece which ended up in the countries of Western Europe would promote the arts seems to have been used widely as a central justification by those who seized the sculptures. The Bavarian architect Leo von Klenze, delivering a lecture on

31 March 1821 in the Bavarian Academy of Sciences[14] on the "removing of plastic works of art from modern Greece" and attempting to justify the purchase by Prince Ludwig (as he then was) of the sculptures from the temple of Aphaia, brought out all the familiar arguments. The removal and conservation of the Greek monuments, he said, was a work of salvage and possessed enormous educational power while also contributing to the search for artistic perfection. Von Klenze referred to the work of Choiseul-Gouffier and the pieces he had taken to Paris, and to the case of the Parthenon sculptures, whose removal he regarded as a colossal achievement "which has inaugurated a new period in the history of art". For the first time, von Klenze continued, cultured Europe had come in contact with true Greek art, contact of a kind which could not have been created by the travellers in

3. John Henning: section of the procession from the north frieze of the Parthenon, in miniature and with many of the details restored; London, British Museum, GR 1938. 11-18 27.

4. *Decimus Burton: propylum at Hyde Park Corner (London), 1825.*

5. *Decimus Burton: propylum at Hyde Park Corner, detail of the frieze. Source: J. Mordaunt Crook,* The Greek Revival, *London 1972.*

their descriptions or the scholars in their copies. Von Klenze himself was greatly influenced, as an architect, by the architecture of the Parthenon, although its sculpture remained a closed book to him. It is also interesting that in his voluminous design work and painting he returned again and again to architectural and sculptural models such as the Atlases from the temple of Zeus at Acragas or the Caryatids, while he does not seem to have been interested in either the section of the frieze or the group of Cecrops and his daughter which were still on the monument and which he knew at close quarters.[15] On the other hand, the sculptor Ludwig Michael Schwanthaler – who created the statues that adorn von Klenze's Propylaea in the Königsplatz, Munich – had more in common with the general object of ancient sculpture and of the frieze in particular. He was especially attracted by markedly energetic compositions and probably drew on the sculpture of sarcophagi, bearing direct relation to the Parthenon sculptures only in isolated cases. Here we can see the 'echoes' which are more frequent in the minor sculptors of the period than in the work of the great Classicists such as Canova or Thorvaldsen.[16] And although the architects pressed on with Classical architecture, using the Classical orders and rules and even in some cases making direct replicas of the Parthenon,[17] there was great hesitation among the sculptors. It was with relief that they evaded

the great models provided, in particular, by the Parthenon sculptures. The Romantic spirit seemed to be capable of gaining access to the architectural forms of the past, and even those of the Classical age, where it appeared to discover a sense of proportion and a rule capable of use in new structures, in complete contrast to the sense of pro-

6. *Decimus Burton: the Atheneum Club (London), 1827-1830.*

7. *H.W. and W. Inwood: St Pancras' Church (London), 1819-1822. Photograph by Laskarina Boura, Photographic Archive of the Benaki Museum.*

8. *L. Alma Tadema: Pheidias and the Parthenon Frieze, oils; Birmingham City Museum and Art Gallery.*

portion and rule of purely plastic form. Then again, the concept of 'perfection' or 'completion' in the plastic arts ran contrary to Romanticism, which ultimately sought for the incomplete, the 'non finito', an aspect inherent in, for example, the torso. That is why it is not without importance that the torso occupied a special position and was particularly appreciated in the sculpture of the nineteenth century. The case of Asmus Jacob Carstens[18] is a typical one. His search was not for the complete but for the fragmented, once more using antiquity as his pretext. However, the very fluidity of the Romantics prevented them from being able to approach not so much the completeness of the form as the absolute balance of its contents. Latent in Romanticism is an inner existential anxiety which is absent from the Olympian serenity of Classicism. As a result, although we encounter in Romanticism phenomena of acute nostalgia for the complete, in which form and content are in harmony, that nostalgia exists because the complete is impossible.

With these conditions as a basis, the Parthenon sculptures could have no effect on the European sculpture of the nineteenth century. On the other hand, their presence in a field in which antiquity was being exploited for decorative purposes at precisely that time, such as that in

9. Karl Friedrich Schinkel: A Glance at the Golden Age of Greece, oils. The original was destroyed in 1945, and the work is known to us in a copy by Wilhelm Ahlborn; Berlin, National Gallery.
10. Detail of fig. 9.

which John Flaxman worked,[19] allowed some scope for copying, especially of the frieze. The Hennings family (John Henning the Elder and John Henning the Younger, fig. 3) developed a minor industry in reproductions of the frieze in miniature, while Decimus Burton made slight alterations to it and installed it high up on the exterior of the Athenaeum (fig. 4) and on the monumental entrance to Hyde Park in London (figs. 5, 6).[20]

It may have been the frieze which served as the inspiration for decoration of all kinds, but it was the single Caryatid that arrived in London along with the rest of the Parthenon sculptures which served as a model for development. Of course, one cannot ignore the significance of the pioneering work done by Stuart and Revett[21] or all the travellers' accounts which, in their own way, had prepared the ground. The depiction in Volume II of *Antiquities of Athens*, in particular, was the model for the 'replica' of the entire Porch of the Caryatids attached to St Pancras Church in London in 1819-1822, the work of William Inwood (fig. 7).[22] The original, of course, was only a starting-point. Inwood did not succeed in producing an exact copy of it – even assuming that was his intention – yet although his variations were relatively free, the composition is close enough to the general motif of the original to make it impossible to overlook. The atmosphere generated in London by the presence of the Parthenon sculptures also stimulated a number of paintings on connected themes. Sir Lawrence Alma-Tadema, for instance, painted Pheidias up on the scaffolding inspecting the frieze *in situ*[23] at close quarters (fig. 8). Of the same nature, though in a different spirit and style, is Karl Friedrich Schinkel's famous dream-fantasy, which allows our eye to wander across the landscape of the 'Golden Age of Greece'. Indeed, that was the title of the picture: *Blick in Griechenlands Blüte*. The original – unfortunately destroyed in 1945 and known to us only from the copy by Wilhelm Ahlborn[24] in the National Gallery, Berlin – was painted in 1825 and was the city of Berlin's gift to Princess Louise of Prussia on her marriage to Prince Frederick of Orange (figs. 9, 10).[25]

This picture by the architect and painter Schinkel made a profound impression as soon as it was completed. Rarely had such verisimilitude and poetry been seen in a view of ancient Greece, and these features appear to be predominant here in the artist's thoughts and feelings. This was not an echo of a more 'literary' Classicism in the spirit of Stefan George, but a historical and aesthetic approach to Classical Greece assisted by the removal of the Parthenon sculptures to London and their aesthetic assessment. Yet here, too, the ground had been prepared by the famous work of Stuart and Revett, which Schinkel knew and on whose illustrations he drew.

The picture heightens the concept of Classicism with a

11. *Section of the east pediment of the Parthenon (depositing of the robe). Source: J. Stuart, N. Revett,* The Antiquities of Athens, *vol. I, London 1762.*

text, on the left, in Greek, stemming from a hymn by Aristotle to the goddess Arete.[26] The hymn praises the self-sacrifice of warriors, and although Schinkel's immediate reference is to the Persian Wars, he undoubtedly connected them with the struggle of the Greeks for liberation. He also parallels the Athens of Pericles with the Berlin of Frederick William III, urging the age to regenerate itself culturally. When Bettina von Arnim wrote to Goethe in 1826 that anyone looking at the painting would want to live in the place it depicted, she was expressing a Romantic nostalgia for Greece by which Schinkel was also possessed. "Here", he wrote, "one could live with that people and watch all the human conditions in which it subsisted". In other words, there was a desire to revive an ideal world, one identified with Classical Greece and Athens, and the inner wish of the Bavarians to reconstruct Pericles' Athens *in situ* was not unrelated to that desire. The plans which Schinkel himself proposed for King Othon's palace on the Acropolis[27] were one further step in this direction.

Yet to understand the idealistic inclination and interest in Classical Greece of Germany in the first half of the nineteenth century we shall have to add to the factors with which we are already acquainted that which was cultivated by the presence of the Parthenon sculptures in London and the discussions to which they gave rise. The whole question awakened consciences and nurtured a form of aesthetics which sought for constant, integrated models. At the same time, anything relevant to Classical Greece was studied and the accounts of travellers were seen in a new light – as, more importantly, were the depictions in monumental works such as those of Le Roy and Stuart and Revett. Schinkel was an outstanding example of all these trends. He circumvented the model of Italy, which had been the Mecca of German intellectuals since the late eighteenth century, with Goethe as the principal figure. Schinkel's links with Italy were deep. In the spirit of the Grand Tour, he visited Italy in 1803, when he was 22 years of age, and then again in 1824, while he never went to Greece at all. Indeed it is interesting, as Walter Rehm notes,[28] that although there was much nostalgia for

Greece in Germany, the great Germans differed from the French and English in that none of them ever visited the country: "I have heard of Elis and Olympia" (Hölderlin, 'Der Einzige').

All the Germans had heard of the country they admired, and perhaps only Ludwig I of Bavaria (King Othon's father) and the painter Carl Rottmann were exceptions to the rule about visiting the country. Yet Schinkel found himself forced to deal with the real Greece when he received a commission from the Prussian royal family to prepare the plans for a palace on the Acropolis ten years after he had produced his painting – that is, in 1832. He took his topographical particulars from Stuart and Revett, who had been a prerequisite for the picture, too. In the foreground of the picture, which impresses with its size (94 x 235 cm.), we see a temple being built. To the right, a canopy keeps the sun off the workmen assembling a frieze. In the background, the landscape is in line with the type familiar from similar compositions by Poussin, Joseph Anton Koch and Claude Lorrain. The temple itself is most unusual and is employed as an architectural subject rather than in any other way. The city which can be seen in the background has fine buildings: a gymnasium, a mausoleum, an Agora with temples, theatres and colonnades. The temple frieze is of particular interest for its connection with the Parthenon frieze. Although Schinkel never saw the originals, which had already been bought by the British Museum when he was painting his picture, he was stimulated by the debate over them into tracking down the depictions of their outlines in Stuart and Revett and accurately transferred plates XII to XIV of vol. II of *Antiquities of Athens* (fig. 11). He selected a section from the handing over of the robe and the

12. Adolf Menzel: vignette for the letters of Frederick II of Prussia to the Baron de la Motte Fouqué (Berlin, 18 Jan. 1750). Woodcut by Adolf Vogel. Source: Oeuvres de Frédéric le Grand, Imprimerie Royale XI, 1849; Berlin, Kunstbibliothek, SMPK, NB 605.

group of women, into which he interpolated a fragment from the parapet of the temple of Nike Apteros. This is followed immediately by men with objects of sacrifice and a chariot. Schinkel chose from the scene of the handing over of the robe to the goddess Athena, as depicted by Stuart and Revett, the left-hand section with Zeus and Hera seated on thrones. Here, as in the original, Hera is lifting the veil to shade her face. In the originals, the faces of Zeus and Hera are damaged, while Stuart and Revett show them complete. The face of Iris is missing from the slab in the British Museum and is kept in the Acropolis. And although one would have expected Schinkel to take the original as it stood, he reverses it in order to adapt it to the flow of the composition.[29]

Schinkel's painting was undoubtedly a major contribution to the art of the nineteenth century, and it is also important evidence of nostalgia for an ideal world (Arcadia) which is none other than Greece at its most sublime moment. This was proclaimed by Walter Rehm,[30] who in 1836 wrote in his famous book *Griechenland und Goethezeit* of a Greece which was a refuge for all intellectuals, a kind of 'Paradise lost' to which one could return to obtain strength and faith. This, as we have seen, is what Schinkel wrote of his picture: "Here one could live with that people ...".

The Parthenon sculptures gradually acquired in the minds of Europeans the nature of 'absolute sculpture', while it was recognised that the art of sculpture had limits which it itself created and which could not be transgressed. Thus, inwardly, began a process of juxtaposing and comparing Classical sculptures with those of other periods. Although, strictly speaking, this was impermissible – given that conditions differ from age to age and that the comparison leads nowhere – it was also inevitable.

One very interesting example of such a juxtaposition, with ironic undertones, is the vignette by Adolf Menzel for the correspondence of Frederick II of Prussia with the Baron De la Motte Fouqué (Berlin, 18 January 1750), which Otto Vogel transferred to wood (fig. 12).[31]

In the vignette, a nobleman of the time of Frederick the Great is comparing, juxtaposed in a museum, a plaster cast of Cephissus from the west pediment of the Parthenon with the Cleopatra group by the French sculptor François Gaspar Adam, produced in 1750, which Frederick installed on the top terrace of the palace of Sanssouci. In the spirit of Winckelmann, Menzel contrasted the 'noble simplicity' ("elde Einfalt") and 'sedate grandeur' ("stille Grösse") of the Greek sculpture with the 'vulgar taste' ("gemeinsten Geschmack") of modern artists – that is, those of the eighteenth century. Menzel had studied the figure of Ilissus with great care, as many of his drawings show.[32] In his vignette, he presumably also wished to contrast his own age with that of Frederick II, which did not appreciate antiquity. As we know, in his correspondence Frederick lavished praise upon Voltaire and rejected Homer.[33]

The Philhellenic spirit from which all these inclinations and trends stemmed was at its height in the first half of the nineteenth century. In parallel, there was an awareness of the uniqueness and inimitability of Classical Greek art. Apart from England, where the sculptures of the Parthenon stimulated discussion and served to enlighten, the position of Goethe in this respect is of importance because of the effect it had in Germany and, as we have seen, Schinkel was among the most extreme advocates of the Philhellenic spirit.

As early as 1787, when he was in Rome, Goethe had seen drawings of the Parthenon sculptures. "Yesterday I saw a number of drawings by the nobleman Worthley, who has travelled to Greece and Egypt. What interested me in particular were the drawings of the frieze of the temple of Athena, the work of Pheidias. It is impossible to imagine anything more beautiful...".[34] In August 1787 Goethe returned to the same subject: "The sculptures from the facade of the Parthenon, in Worthley's drawings, made a decisive and unforgettable impression on me".[35] Years later, in a letter to Wilhelm von Humboldt of 16 September 1799, he asked for a cast of a rider or a clothed form: "so würden Sie mich äusserst glücklich machen" ('which will make me very happy'). "Even the smallest piece would give me special pleasure."[36]

Goethe ultimately saw plaster casts of the Parthenon frieze in a little museum set up by a man called Schleyermacher in the palace at Darmstadt,[37] and he wrote that he "experienced great joy".

In the meantime, he kept close watch on every step in what was happening to the sculptures themselves, which had reached London and had been offered to the state for purchase. On 23 April 1816 he had in hand Böttiger's translation of the *Memorandum on the Subject of the Earl of Elgin's Pursuits in Greece* by William Hamilton,[38] and on 20 July 1817 he expressed a wish to visit London and see at close quarters the sculptures which were "a law and a bible" to him.[39] In the end, he did not go, contenting himself with 'beneficial indications' ("wohlthätige Andeutungen"): copper engravings and drawings.

Just as Goethe acknowledged the aesthetic level of the Parthenon sculptures, he also recognised the Greeks as great masters,[40] and saw in the works of Pheidias the supreme example.[41] In his 'Advice to a Contemporary Sculptor',[42] Goethe refers to the ease with which the Greeks hit on the correct way of presenting various subjects, such as the battle between two opponents. Setting out from the metopes of the Parthenon, he noted the mastery with which the fortunes of battle change, inclining first one way and then the other.

In the end, he came face to face with plaster casts of the Parthenon sculptures: "Some very precious things have come to us from England. One does not know how to arrange them. The Elgin marbles and all the rest, depicted so many times, are as familiar to us as if we had the originals before us..." And he ended with an ironic comment, half in English, on the commercial exploitation of the casts: "Two of the Fates zehn Guineen. One of the Fates fünf Guineen..."

Goethe seems to have been among those who believed that the Parthenon sculptures would have a significant impact on sculpture in Europe: "This has been a good year for the visual arts. From the Elgin marbles one can learn more and more things."[43] In 1818, he added:[44] "This year was for Great Art the beginning of a new age...". He records his acquaintance with the sculptures of the temple of Aphaia (on Aegina) and Phigaleia, concluding that he had found the "sublime" in the sculptures of the Parthenon. And in a letter to S. Boisserée (7 August 1819), he wrote: "If people did not have such a strong tendency to regress, they would now (with their knowledge of the Parthenon sculptures) have a fresh opportunity to advance".[45] "With our knowledge of the architecture and sculpture of the Greeks, we were encouraged towards the sublime view of art. We were led to the Parthenon by the Elgin marbles. As a result, we came to realise the ultimate limits of man's artistic ability ... and we deemed outselves happy for that reason, too."[46]

The account given by Eckermann in his famous *Conversations with Goethe*[47] is also characteristic of the latter's faith in the regeneration of the arts. Goethe told Eckermann that he had been watching the progress of German painting, with undiminished interest, for fifty whole years without identifying any true values. He believed that a major talent was needed to make the most of whatever the conditions of the times could offer: "The means exist, the ways forward have been indicated and opened up. And now we have Pheidias before our eyes, which was unthinkable in our youth."

Ultimately, Goethe found in the horse's head from the chariot of Selene (east pediment) all the components of "sublime sculpture".[48]

What is of interest in an examination of Goethe's attitude to the Parthenon sculptures is that this great thinker was among the first to recognise their unique artistic value, and this had far-ranging consequences for the more general approach to them. In Europe at this time, certain models came to be seen as classics of absolute value, and an awareness grew of the uniqueness of what was to be called 'classic' in art. Indeed, it could be argued that at this moment Greek Classical art was comprehended and, as a supreme artistic value, entered the consciousness of intellectuals. That art, as revealed by the sculptures of the Par-

13. Auguste Rodin: Two Marshals and Girls (from the east frieze), 1856, ink and water-colours; Paris, Rodin Museum, D.62. Photograph by Bruno Jarret.

14. Auguste Rodin: section from the north frieze, 1856, ink and water-colours; Paris, Rodin Museum, D.61. Photograph by Bruno Jarret.

thenon, was not known to the Renaissance, which did not possess the concept of the 'Classical'. Yet although there was great enthusiasm for Classical art, and the noblest minds of the period – with Goethe outstanding among them – had high hopes that knowledge and understanding of the Classical models would lead to the creation, once more, of classical art, it also had to be admitted that there were boundaries which could not be transcended. Classical art was the exclusive product of a 'classic' age, and it could not be transferred as an intellectual conquest to another epoch – especially to one which did not fulfil any of the conditions that had nurtured the 'classicism' of the earlier period. But this was a time of excessive enthusiasm, and enthusiasm does not usually allow scope for rational evaluation. It should also be remembered that the nineteenth century had a completely different concept of the 'copy' from that of the twentieth century. Copying was an admissible activity, a creative act, and when the English copied the Parthenon frieze this was not seen as sterile repetition. However, when architects copied ancient architectural models it was seen as sterility, although if any variation was included, that sufficed to justify efforts of all kinds.

Even as far back as the time of Frederick II of Prussia, a distinction had been made between 'imitation' and 'copying',[49] with the former being taken to be the creation initiated by a model. The 'copy', on the other hand, was seen as an attempt to repeat or reproduce the original, as Winckelmann wrote in his *Gedanken über die Nachahmung der griechischen Werke* ('Thoughts on the Imitation of the Greek Works'), or as Goethe's friend Karl Philipp Moritz put it later in his *Über die bildende Nachahmung des Schönen* ('Concerning the Visual Imitation of the Beautiful').

The twentieth century was deliberately anti-Classical. In order to find itself, it attempted not only to circumvent the great models of the past but, in some cases, to mock them. Thus Salvador Dali turned the Venus di Milo into a piece of furniture, while the Mona Lisa was subjected both to variation and to despoliation. The views on Greek antiquity of Gaugin and Marinetti are familiar: although we shall be examining them in more detail a little later in this chapter, let it be noted that they viewed Greek antiquity as a disaster for the free visual expression of Europeans. Futurism, in particular, was opposed to historicism of any kind, and its positions contributed to distancing art from the visual solutions of the past. Yet there were moments at which antiquity played an important part in the work of artists representative of the twentieth century, such as Picasso or Moore, and in recent decades there appears once more to have been a return to the models, which have been seen in a new light against the background of post-Modernism.

15. *Théodore Gericault: Rider, wax; Paris, private collection.*

Picasso, in particular, produced hundreds of drawings, engravings, sculptures and pieces of pottery which were inspired by themes from Greek mythology. The works of 1905/6 and the period after 1917, when he visited Italy, could be described as Classical or neo-Classical, and he returned to antiquity again and again when illustrating texts by ancient authors (Ovid, Aristophanes) or when, as between 1933 and 1938,[50] he dealt with themes such as the Minotaur. Picasso's acquaintance with the sculptures of the Parthenon dated back to his boyhood (between the ages of ten and fifteen), when he made drawings in the Le Coruña Academy and in Barcelona from casts of ancient sculptures as was the custom at the time. A marvellous drawing by him, showing the Ilissus or Dionysus figure from the east pediment of the Parthenon (fig. 16),[51] has survived from this period (1893/94). The young Picasso rendered this great sculpture, a favourite with English painters and draughtsmen, with the greatest of accuracy and purity. He had a masterly grasp of its proportions and expression, and emphasised both its highlights and its shadows. Yet although he produced a vast number of variations on sculptural compositions and vase paintings, he never returned to the Parthenon sculptures: their absolute nature was incapable of stimulating his imagination. The classic, completed work can act as a constraint on the creative inclination, which feels unable to add to or subtract from it while mere copying does not satisfy. The inhibition can be suppressed only by restricting oneself to the more general shape, which can be utilised in personal creations. This was the approach adopted by Henry Moore, in whose seated and semi-recumbent forms the influence of the pedimental sculptures of the Parthenon can be detected. The artistic physiognomy of Moore, whose

16. *Pablo Picasso: Ilissus or Dionysus (from the east pediment of the Parthenon), 1893-1894. Source: Picasso und die Antike, Badisches Landesmuseum Karlsruhe, 1974 (catalogue).*

career was set in a country almost entirely lacking in sculptural tradition, is typical of Britain, which while it produced no major artistic trends or notable schools, nonetheless gave birth to individual artists of the highest level. The fact that Moore came from a family of miners and that he was born in the bare landscape of Yorkshire – which also produced sculptors such as Barbara Hepworth and Kenneth Armitage – is of particular importance. At a very early age he became acquainted with 'matter' – stone – and he learned to appreciate the 'general structure' of things as expressed in the simple, pure landscape, Archaic art and the art of primitive peoples. The immediate starting-points for his preferences may be located in the work of Gill, Epstein and Dobson, but Massaccio and Michelangelo also helped to shape him, and side by side with Archipenko, Brancusi and Picasso one must number among the influences on Moore the sculptor of the Parthenon pediments, which he had seen at close quarters in the British Museum. In the case of Moore, it is clear that what is of interest to the artist is not the style of the original but its spiritual strength. That, after all, is what acts on his own spirit and makes it productive. This is not to say that there were no important sculptors in the past, such as Canova, who were closely acquainted with the Parthenon sculptures; what is of importance is the extent to which one is capable of elaborating on the messages one receives. Everything depends on the point of view from which one approaches things, on one's personal theory of the world and on the intellectual 'frequency' on which one operates. Canova worked on the 'frequency' of elegance and harmony, while Moore's was that of the enigmatic and potential, the alienated. The elegance which is a fea-

ture of some of the pedimental sculpture of the Parthenon, such as the figures of Dione and Aphrodite on the east pediment, may have had more of an effect on Canova's spirit than others. For Moore, however, the figure of decisive importance was the seated form known as Hestia, also from the east pediment, whose shape he was to use on many occasions (fig. 17).[52]

The semi-recumbent form (figs. 18, 19) which is so important throughout Moore's work puts one in mind of the so-called Ilissus or Dionysus figure from the east pediment, and the figure called Cephissus from the west pediment (figs. 16, 17). Both sculptures, which are numbered among the most perfect of sculptural solutions, had entered into Moore's plastic thought, which revolved around their basic model. Moore may have transformed the Classical model into a mannerist, primitive shape, but that was because this was the only way of truly making use of them: the further the work lies from its model, the more impor-

17. *Henry Moore: Mother and Child (The Virgin and Child), 1943-1944, stone; St Matthew's Church, Northampton.*

18. Henry Moore: Recumbent Figure 1939, bronze; Victoria and Albert Museum, London.

tant its own presence is. If Canova and Thorvaldsen had based themselves on these models, they would have produced works which were far their inferiors, for the very simple reason that the Classicists tried to stick as close as possible to the Classical model. Moore, the anti-Classicist, overcame this obstacle through mannerism, and the work that resulted is truly interesting from the plastic point of view. What interested Moore was dynamic shape, which bestowed rhythm and intensity on his masses. And just as Cézanne perceived in objects the solid shape that was latent within them, so Moore, when he looked at Dionysus or Cephisus, discovered the solid correlations of their masses; like Brancusi, he attempted to eliminate all the realistic elements so as to reach down to the "skeleton of the primordial masses and shapes". He himself believed that "from these everybody can go on to appreciate more complex forms of combinations of several forms".[53] And since for the sculptor shape, mass, is what colour is to the painter, Moore wanted to train his own eye to see structures and forms: "Do you know that many more people are 'form-blind' than 'colour-blind'?"

What Moore was attempting to do was the outcome of a series of processes which took place in Europe in the early decades of the twentieth century and which, *inter alia*, advocated a return to the primordial or the primitive, thus transcending the cultural saturation which some

thinkers – such Gaugin and the Futurists – believed to stem from an undue attachment to the great models of the past. Those models, which, as we have seen, Moore transmuted into 'purged' creations in the spirit of Brancusi, were seen by the Futurists and Dadaists as the causes of the 'arteriosclerosis' of Western culture. They taught not just that such models should be avoided, but that they should be destroyed. "One should abandon", said Gaugin, "this Europe of the *Graeculi* and search for the best of the savages". He went so far as to argue that "the greatest deception is the Greek model, however beautiful it may be", and he believed that there was more profound content in a child's wooden rocking-horse than in the horses of the Parthenon.[54] These views were an antidote to the saturated Classicising trends of the nineteenth century, while at the same time proposing a "radical return to nature" – though quite a different one to that which Rousseau had had in mind. It would be more accurate to talk of a 'return to the springs of civilisation', 'to Paradise before the Fall'. Now the Classical was treated as constituting that Fall. For that reason, the first Futurist manifesto, that of 20 February 1909, pointed to the need to "destroy the museums and libraries",[55] that is, the vehicles for the Classical models, while proclaiming that "a racing car with its bonnet decorated with thick pipes like snakes [...], a car which roars and flies like a bullet,

19. Henry Moore: Recumbent Figure, 1945-1946, stone; Devon.

is more beautiful than the Nike of Samothrace".[56]

In 'Death to Moonlight' ('Ucciadiamo il chiaro di Luna'), published in April 1909, the Futurists called for the destruction of the Parthenon.[57] Marinetti himself may have been careful to avoid confirming this position when he came to Athens in 1933, stating diplomatically that "Futurism ... has no memory",[58] but in the so-called 'Manifesto to the Young People of Greece', which he wrote "specially for the *Eleftheron Vima*",[59] there are many references to the subject. The reaction of Parthenis, which we discuss below, was directly connected with the negative attitude which Marinetti adopted to the Parthenon as a Classical model.

The 'Manifesto to the Young People of Greece' deserves a little attention, since it clearly reveals the Futurists' attempt to impose their views in the cradle of the Classical itself. Marinetti begins his text with a personification of the Parthenon, and urges young people to distance themselves from tradition: "One night of storm and great artistic inspiration, a night electrified with new stars, the Parthenon, like a harmonium infested with millions of cicadas and bees, pronounced sonorously: Greek students .... leave my columns rapidly, because I am the prison of futile wisdom... Admit that the Parthenon is to you the decayed, grand stove of Greece ... a valuable yet useless stove. It is undoubtedly a rare piece; in its time, there can

have been nothing better. But how is it to be used today, when wisdom is immediate and automatic? The Parthenon may make a good impression as it stands upright on the Acropolis, but would it retain its majesty in the eyes of a Greek aerial poet flying at a height of ten thousand feet? My beloved Greek students, turn your backs on the Acropolis... assassinate melancholy and nostalgia by means of original discoveries."[60]

Konstantinos Parthenis, a broad mind by the standards of the time, commented on this view in his own distinctive way: "There is no need to demolish the Acropolis, our Mother; we shall take it as an example, not as a model to be imitated."[61]

In Greece itself, the Futurist views of the first decades of the century clashed with diametrically opposed concepts of the past and the Great Tradition. Periklis Yannopoulos supported Hellenocentrism, Angelos Sikelianos attempted to revive the Delphic Festival, and Fotis Kontoglou called for devotion to Greek Orthodoxy and the cultivation of a revitalised version of the Byzantine style in painting. Yet for all this the Parthenon was no more than a 'great memory' even for the 'pro-traditionalists' of Greece.

It is as a memory, as nostalgia, as a reference to models of timeless value, that we find the impact of the Parthenon sculptures in the work of contemporary Greek painters

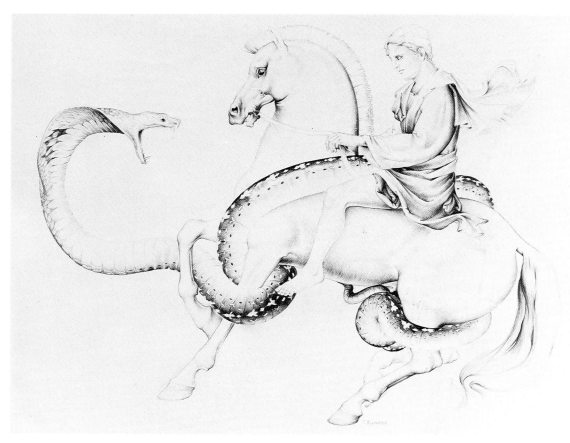

20. Yorgos Derpapas: variation on a theme from the Parthenon frieze, drawing.

and sculptors. By way of contrast with their predecessors, who painted the Acropolis and its monuments but not the sculptures, these artists do not deal with the architectural remains but solely with the sculptures of the Parthenon and, in particular, with those in London. They are acquainted with those sculptures from trips to the British capital – though primarily from photographs and books – and they would seem to be more interested in some than others. The head of the horse from the chariot of Selene (east pediment), Ilissus (west pediment), Cephissus (west pediment) and the frieze (especially the riders) are particular favourites.

In a series of works involving horses and riders (e.g., *Victors and Vanquished*) Paris Prekas took his inspiration directly from the Parthenon frieze (figs. 22, 26). Wherever he uses the rider motif, there is an outline of pulsing, dynamic motion, and the details are circumvented for the sake of a fleeting impression conveyed with Expressionist and abstract media. Where, however, he studies the sculpture in order to assimilate it, the figure is rendered more specifically – not so say scrupulously, and with great accuracy. Prekas is fascinated by the superb craftsmanship of the original, which compels him to observe its details and penetrate into its unique magic. He does not differ greatly from this approach when he deals with the rearing horse from the central section of the west frieze, which is still *in*

situ (fig. 26). The famous relief is rendered in broad terms but with clarity, while the Expressionist atmosphere heightens the explosiveness of the expressive approach.

The horse's head from the chariot of Selene which aroused such enthusiasm in Goethe fascinates Paris Prekas, too, as it has other contemporary artists. In a series of studies (figs. 23-25) made into engravings, Prekas elicited various expressive possibilities from this head using only differences in the rendering of line and in the colour scale; this is a kind of *ars multiplicata*, at least when all the pieces are seen juxtaposed.

Meropi Preka is also inspired by the Parthenon sculptures, but in a different way. While Paris Prekas attempts by reproduction in drawings and paintings to draw closer to and comprehend the original, she assimilates it and incorporates it into her own personal style of expression (figs. 27, 28). With undisguised freedom, she varies the shapes of the originals, which are almost always accompanied by doves, one of the artist's favourite motifs. Meropi Preka has done fine work in coloured glass, and she brings to her sketches the features of that technical dimension. Some of the sketches are in the nature of tracings and preliminary drawings for compositions in coloured glass.

Yorgos Derpapas (figs. 20, 21) incorporates figures

21. Yorgos Derpapas: Untitled, tempera.

22. Paris Prekas: Riders, oils on canvas.

from the Parthenon sculptures – as they stand or in variation – into his imaginary world, which consists of collages of paintings. The figures are transferred with thorough elaboration of the details, and the attempt to produce a naturalistic rendering heightens the Surrealistic character of precisely those naturalistically recorded forms. When an enormous snake wraps itself around the horse of one of the riders from the frieze, the Classical serenity of the composition takes on the atmosphere of a nightmare. The reference to the riders in the frieze is also of interest as an indication, as a mark which has left its stamp on historical thought and consciousness.

Paschalis Angelidis, a member of the younger generation of painters, also makes use of Surrealist juxtapositions to alienate the famous originals. Once again, the horse from Selene's chariot has pride of place: Angelidis hangs it from belts in an indefinable location, or surrounds it with iron bars (fig. 30). Cephissus, too, is hung in the void from belts, but his figure is empty and riddled with holes, as if he were a bronze statue rather than a marble one (fig. 29).

In an admirable and effortless juxtaposition, Kostis Voloudakis incorporates Cephissus into a photographic collage (fig. 31).

Kleio Natsi is another artist who has used the head of the horse from Selene's chariot and sections of the frieze in her paintings. Here we have the emergence of memories into a system consisting of multiple references to the past and the present (figs. 32, 33).

The impact of the Parthenon sculptures on modern Greek sculpture is limited to a very few purely indicative

23-25. Paris Prekas: three variations on the head of the horse from Selene's chariot from the east pediment of the Acropolis, pencil drawings.

248

26. Paris Prekas: the horse from the west frieze of the Parthenon, oils on canvas.

cases. In one of them, the theme, rather than the plastic features themselves, was exploited: this is the central pediment of the Academy of Athens, the work of the sculptor Leonidas Drosis, who took his theme of the Birth of Athena from the east pediment of the Parthenon (figs. 34-36). Against the background of a broader programme symbolising the rebirth of Greece, the birth of Athena, goddess of wisdom and the arts, corresponds to the view that the arts and sciences were now returning to the land where they were born:

> "Sacred Science! A friend of the Muses
> And citizen of Greece is building your Temple;
> He has a will
> That the ancient glories be revived."[62]

Drosis follows the original in placing Zeus on his throne, and Athena and Hephaestus at the centre of the pediment, while the left corner is occupied by the rising Sun (Helios) and the right by the setting Moon (Selene). In between are a number of figures, some of which correspond to those of the original arranged in a manner necessitated by the placing of the composition in the triangle formed by the relatively small pediment. The Classicising formulation of the composition attempts to promote the idea of the Classical, yet Drosis' figures fail to go beyond the formalism typical of such cases. The programme for the composition can no doubt be connected with the scholars of the age, from Alexandros Rizos-Rangavis to Friedrich Thiersch and Eduard Schaubert – the latter of whom had urged Theophil von Hansen, the architect of the Academy building, to design the Athena on the left-hand column as "not a theatening figure, with her spear in hand, but a bringer of peace".[63]

Yeorgios Vitalis took his inspiration from the horses of the Parthenon frieze for a fine composition on the theme

249

27, 28. Meropi Preka: drawings inspired by the sculptures of the Parthenon.

of *Hector's Farewell* to his family (fig. 37) – a sculpture which got no further than the cast and can be seen in the Museum of Tiniot Sculpture on the island of Tinos. Vitalis' originals are the chariot-drivers of the south section of the frieze (and especially nos. XXVII and XXXII).[64]

The head of the horse from Selene's chariot can be seen once again, radically altered and cast in bronze, in a work with a personal Expressionist style by Yannis Parmakelis (fig. 38).

It is interesting, then, to note that when contemporary Greek artists deal with the Parthenon sculptures they tend to revolve around some of the figures, attempting either to render the original faithfully or vary it. The Parthenon sculptures in the Acropolis Museum do not inspire them, with a very few exceptions. For them, the sculptures of the Parthenon are the Elgin Marbles, the pieces which have established themselves in the human mind as types of timeless value. The head of the horse from Selene's chariot is the most common motif and is treated as the quintessence of 'the Classical'. Its careful transcription reveals both respect and interest, while the marked variations on it – to the point of despoliation – are connected with a wish to transcend the Classical when not stemming from Dadaist and Futurist associations similar to those responsible for the transformation of the Venus di Milo (Salvador Dali) or the Mona Lisa.

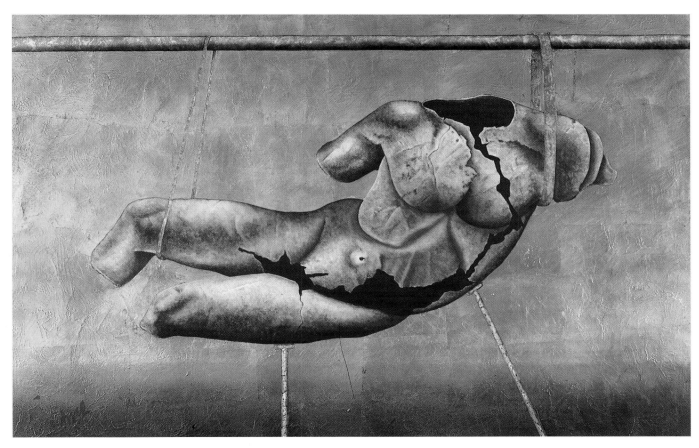

29, 30. *Paschalis Angelidis: paintings inspired by the pedimental sculptures of the Parthenon.*

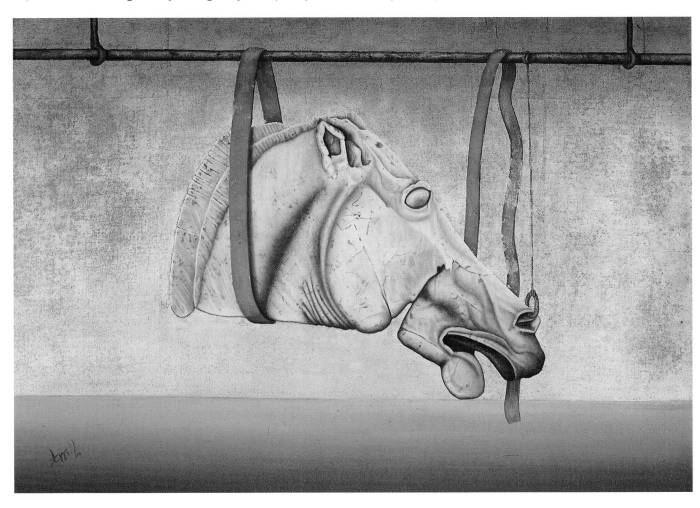

31. Kostis Voloudakis: photographic collage with the figure of Cephissus from the east pediment of the Parthenon.

32, 33. Kleio Natsi: Compositions, oils on canvas.

34. Leonidas Drosis: model for the central pediment of the Academy of Athens, 1870; Athens, National Gallery.

35. Leonidas Drosis: the sculptures from the central pediment of the facade of the Academy of Athens.

36. Leonidas Drosis: the sculptures from the central pediment of the facade of the Academy of Athens. Photograph by P. Tournikiotis.

37. Yeorgios Vitalis: Hector's Farewell to his Family, plaster; Tinos, Museum of Tiniot Sculptors.

38. Yannis Parmakelis: Victor No. 2, 1969, bronze.

Notes

1. The house was bought by Elgin after his release by the French in 1806. In 1807, he erected a makeshift shelter in the courtyard of Gloucester House, as the building was called, and exhibited the sculptures there. See Ioannis Gennadios, *O Lordos Elgin kai oi pro avtou ana tin Ellada idios archaiologisantes epidromeis* ('Lord Elgin and Previous Incursors Throughout Greece, Mostly in the Guise of Archaeologists'), Athens 1930, pp. 45, 46.

2. See T. Taylor, A. Huxley, *The Autobiography and Memoirs of Benjamin Robert Haydon 1786-1846*, 2 vols., London 1926 (new edition).

3. See William St. Clair, *Lord Elgin and the Marbles*, London 1967, pp. 166ff; Heinz Ladendorf, *Antikenstudium und Antikenkopie*, Berlin 1958, p. 49. See also Elgin's letter of 1801 to Lusieri, in which he asks for good casts of details of the sculptures as models for his craftsmen to work from. A.H. Smith, 'Lord Elgin and his Collection', *Journal of Hellenic Studies,* vol. 36, 1916, pp. 163-372; Jacob Rothenberg, 'Descensus ad Terram', *The Acquisition and Reception of the Elgin Marbles*, New York and London 1977.

4. Canova was to refuse to work in Rome on the completion of the Parthenon sculptures, as Lusieri proposed to him in 1801 (see A.H. Smith, *op. cit.*, p. 203). In 1807, Flaxman first hesitated and ultimately declined to complete them, agreeing with Canova's description of completion as sacrilege (see A. Michaelis, *Der Parthenon*, Leipzig 1871, p. 83; W. Rehm, *Griechentum und Goethezeit. Geschichte eines Glaubens*, Leipzig 1936, 3rd ed. Munich 1952, pp. 2, 26).

5. See Enst Grumach, *Goethe und die Antike*, vol. B, Potsdam 1949, pp. 494ff.

6. Ladendorf, *op. cit.*, p. 49. See also Taylor and Huxley, *op. cit.*, and J. Wagner, *Das literarische Werk des Malers Benjamin Robert Haydon*, Göttingen 1934.

7. See Ladendorf, *op. cit.*, chapter VIII, note 23. In the particular case of Flaxman, it should be noted that in 1784 he had applied to the Society of Dilettanti for permission to copy Stuart and Revett's drawings of the Parthenon frieze (see the Hamburger Kunsthalle catalogue, *John Flaxman, Mythologie und Industrie*, Hamburg 1979, p. 7). When faced with the Parthenon sculptures – on which he made a positive report to the Committee considering their purchase – he declared them to be "a tasteless and barbarous forerunner of the age of Pheidias, in which sculpture matured", *ibid.*, p. 155.

8. For Visconti, see C.B. Stark, *Systematik und Geschichte der Archäologie der Kunst*, Leipzig 1880, pp. 167, 243-244 (= Handbuch der Archäologie der Kunst); Andreas Rumpf, *Archäologie*, vol. A: *Einleitung, Historischer Überblick*, Berlin 1953, pp. 62-63, 83, 89, 90; *Der Archäologe. Graphische Bildnisse aus dem Porträtarchiv Diepenbroik*, Kestner-Museum, Hanover 1984, p. 244 (catalogue).

9. This was followed by the memorandum 'Lettre de E.Q. Visconti à un Anglais' (1815), for use in the negotiations for the purchase of the sculptures by the state, and in 1818 by the book *Mémoires sur les ouvrages de sculpture du Parthénon et de quelques édifices de l'Acropole à Athènes.*

10. See Gennadios, *op. cit.*, pp. 51ff.

11. Cf. Canova's letter to Elgin, dated 10 November 1815, in which the famous sculptor congratulated Elgin and stated that he deserved "grace and gratitude". See also Quatremère de Quincy, *Canova et ses ouvrages, mémoires historiques sur la vie et les travaux du célébre artiste*, Paris 1834.

Quatremère de Quincy notes that in his work 'Theseus Overcoming a Centaur' (*Teseo in lotta con il Centauro*), now in the Kunsthistorisches Museum of Vienna (see Mario Praz, *L'opera completa del Canova*, Milan 1976, pp. 174, 175, 176, 177; models in the Museum of Sculpture at Possagno), Canova was directly inspired by the metopes of the Parthenon, which he knew first from Stuart and Revett and later from seeing the originals in London. The work was commissioned from Canova by the Italian state and completed in 1819. Francis I of Austria, who eventually purchased it, put it in a copy of the Temple of Hephaestus (the 'Theseum') which P. Nobile built in the gardens of Hofburg.

The metope which seems to be closest to Canova's composition is no. 2 on the south side, see Frank Brommer, *The Sculptures of the Parthenon*, London 1979, plate 13.

A variation on the same theme was the subject of a work by the famous animalier Louis-Antoine Barye (1796-1875), see *The Art Journal*, vol. 1, 1888, p. 20.

As for Canova's pronouncement on the Parthenon sculptures, "la verità della natura congiunta alla scelta delle forme belle", see Marilena Kasimati, 'Istorismos i to zontanema tou paramithiou. Eikones apo to telos to 19ou ai. ston evropaiko choro' ('Historicism or Bringing the Story Alive. Late Nineteenth Century Pictures from Europe'), *To soma kai to pneuma* ('Body and Soul'), National Gallery, Athens 1989, p. 27 (catalogue).

12. See the Society of Dilettanti, *Specimens of Ancient Sculpture*, XXXIX.

13. Ladendorf, *op. cit.*, p. 49.

14. *Über das Hinwegführen plastischer Kunstwerke aus dem jetzigen Griechenland und die neuesten Unternehmungen dieser Art*, Munich 1821, p. 24.

15. See Norbert Lieb and Florian Hufnagl, *Leo von Klenze. Gemälde und Zeichnungen*, Munich 1979.

16. See the semi-recumbent male figure on the east pediment of the Propylaea, with Ilissus or Dionysus from the east pediment of the Parthenon; Frank Otten, *Ludwig Michael Schwanthaler 1802-1848*, Munich 1970.

A connection between Bertel Thorvaldsen and the Parthenon frieze can be seen in the frieze he created for the Quirinal Palace in Rome between 1810 and 1814, on the occasion of Napoleon's visit to the Eternal City. Drawing a parallel with this visit, Thorvaldsen's frieze showed the 'Entry of Alexander the Great into Babylon'. See Christiane Grunwald, 'Zu den Aegineten-Ergänzungen', *Bertel Thorvaldsen. Ein dänischer Bildhauer in Rom*, Cologne 1977, p. 307 (catalogue of the Museen von Stadt Köln).

17. See J. Mordaunt Crook, *The Greek Revival. Neoclassical Attitudes in British Architecture 1760-1870*, London 1972; Dora Wiebenson, *Sources of Greek Revival Architecture*, London 1969.

18. See Peter Bloch, 'Die Berliner Bildhauerei des 19. Jahrhunderts und die Antike', *Berlin und die Antike*, Deutsches Archäologisches Institut, Berlin 1979, pp. 177ff (catalogue).

19. John Flaxman, *Mythologie und Industrie, Kunst um 1800*, Hamburger Kunsthalle 1979 (catalogue).

20. See John Boardman, *The Parthenon and its Sculptures*, London 1985, p. 252. Boardman is misled – presumably by R. Jenkins (*The Victorians and Ancient Greece*, Oxford 1980) – into attributing to John Henning the work on the Athenaeum Club (1827-1830) and at Hyde Park Corner, when in fact these projects were by Decimus Burton (1800-1881); see Crook, *op. cit.*, pp. 61, 122-4, 128, 135, 136, and figs. 178 and 211).

21. J. Stuart, N. Revett, *The Antiquities of Athens*, 4 vols., London 1762-1816. The Caryatid portico is shown in vol. 2. For a full bibliography on the subject, see Crook, *op. cit.*, pp. 165ff.

22. The Caryatids were very often used in the architecture of Classicism in Germany. See *Berlin und die Antike*, Berlin 1979, pp. 581ff., with numerous illustrations (catalogue).

23. The picture is reproduced in Boardman, *op. cit.*, p. 252.

24. National Gallery, Berlin, SMPK, NG2/54; oils on canvas, 94 x 235 cm., Ahlborn nach Schinkel 1936.

25. Schinkel does not seem to have painted the picture for this purpose, to judge from the letter which Bettina von Arnim wrote to Achim von Arnim on 10 May 1825: "Schinkel has finished his landscape, which he began about a year ago" – that is, before setting out on his second trip to Italy, on 29 June 1824.

26. In the *Anthologia Lyrica Graeca*, E. Diehl (ed.)., fasc. 1, p. 177, it is described as a hymn to Hermes.

27. In this respect, see Schinkel, *Werke der höheren Baukunst, für die Ausführung entworfen*, Potsdam 1840-42, 1. Abteilung, 'Entwurf zu einem Königspalast auf der Akropolis'; F. v. Quast, 'Neubau der Stadt Athen und des Kgl. Schlosses auf seiner Burg', *Museum*, year 2, 1834, pp. 187-190, 227,231; the same author, *Mitteilungen über Alt- und Neu-Athen*, Berlin 1934; P.O. Rave, 'Schinkels Traum von einem Königspalast auf der Akropolis zu Athen', *Atlantis*, year 6, 1934, pp. 129-141.

28. *Op. cit.*, p. 1.

29. Adolf Max Vogt, *Karl Friedrich Schinkel, Blick in Griechenlands Blüte. Ein Hoffnungsbild für "Spree-Athen"*, Frankfurt/M, 1985, p. 57; see also *Berlin und die Antike*, Berlin 1979, pp. 95ff, no. 195 (catalogue).

30. *Op. cit.*

31. Cf. *Oeuvres de Frédéric Le Grand*, Imprimerie Royale, XI (1849), p. 22, Berlin, Kunstbibliothek, SMPK, NB 605; *Berlin und die Antike, op. cit.*, p. 135.

32. Cf. Berlin, Kupferstichkabinett und Sammlung der Zeichnungen, N.899.

33. See *Berlin und die Antike, op. cit.*, p. 201.

34. *Italienische Reise*, Rome, 23 March 1787.

35. *Ibid.*, August 1787.

36. For all the references to the subject, see Ernst Grumach, *op. cit.*, pp. 494ff.

37. Goethe to Christine von Goethe, 22 October 1814.

38. London 1811; 2nd ed., 1815. It was published in German under the title *Denkschrift über Lord Elgins Erwerbungen. Nach der zweiten englischen Auflage bearbeitet*, Leipzig-Altenburg 1817.

39. Grumach, *op. cit.* p. 498; letter to Sartorius, 20 July 1817.

40. J. Wolfgang von Goethe, *Anforderungen an den modernen Bildhauer*, 1817.

41. Goethe, *Verein der deutschen Bildhauer*, 27 July 1817.

42. Grumach, *op. cit.*, p. 499.

43. *Tag- und Jahres-Hefte*, 1817; Grumach, *op. cit.*, p. 501.

44. *Tag- und Jahres-Hefte*, 1818; Grumach, *op. cit.*, p. 502.

45. In 1819, Goethe read the *Lettre du chev. Antonio Canova et deux Mémoires sur les ouvrages de sculpture dans la collection de Mylord comte Elgin par Ennio Quirino Visconti*, London 1816. Over the same days, he also borrowed *The Elgin Marbles from the Temple of Minerva at Athens on 61 Plates*, London 1816, and E.J. Burrows, *The Elgin Marbles, with an abridged historical and topographical account of Athens*, vol. A, London 1817, a work he had known for some years.

46. *Tag- und Jahres-Hefte*, 1820.

47. 13 December 1826, p. 302.

48. Grumach, *op. cit.*, p. 505; Pferdekopf von Gespann der Selene.

49. See Gerhardt Rodenwaldt, *Griechisches und Römisches in Berliner Bauten des Klassizismus*, Berlin 1956, p. 9. The connection between Rodin and the Parthenon sculptures can be seen chiefly in the sketches of two slabs from the frieze (figs. 13 and 14); he knew one of these from the original, since it is in the Louvre (east section of the frieze, pl. VII 49-56, Choiseul-Gouffier), and the other from a cast of the original, which is in London (north section of the frieze, pl. XLII 130-134). The sketches were drawn in 1856, are in ink and watercolour and are kept in the Rodin Museum in Paris. The sketches are accurate, though they do not go into detail and shading is applied only very occasionally. In 1905, when the periodical *Le Musée* (2 March - April 1905, pp. 68ff) sought the views of French artists and intellectuals on the restoration of the Parthenon, Rodin called "dynamically and actively" for the temple to be left as it was and not completed. See Marina Lambraki-Plaka, *O Rodin kai i archaia elliniki techni* ('Rodin and Ancient Greek Art'), Athens 1985, pp. 50ff. In his book on the cathedrals of France (*Les cathédrales de France*, Paris 1914, p. 8) Rodin describes the Parthenon as summing up all of Greece: "The Parthenon has done more to defend Greece than the wisest of her statesmen".

Théodore Géricault made a wax copy, with very few variations, of the rider from the west section of the Parthenon frieze (pl. VI 11.12). The copy is now in a private collection in Paris (see Maurice Rheims, *19th Century Sculpture*, London 1972, p. 298, fig. 3, and see also fig. 15 in this article).

As for Bourdelle, Marina Lambraki-Plaka *(Bourdelle et la Gréce, Les sources antiques de l'oeuvre de Bourdelle*, Athens 1985, figs. 100, 101) draws a connection between a section of the Monument Mickiewicz (specifically, Les Trois Polognes) and the slab from the Parthenon frieze in the Louvre (pl. VII 49-56, Choiseul-Gouffier, see above). The connection, however, is very general and hardly self-evident.

50. *Badisches Landesmuseum Karlsruhe, Picasso und die Antike*, 1974, p. 1 (catalogue).

51. F. Ph. Ingold, *Picasso in Russland*, 1973, pp. 39ff, and especially p. 41.

52. See *Seated Woman*, mixed technique, 71 x 58.5 cm., collection of Irina Moore, London. *Henry Moore, Rijks-museum Kröller-Müller*, Otterlo 1968, fig. 67 (catalogue).

53. From an article by Kaisu-Mirjami Rydberg, written in Helsinki in May 1938.

54. See Werner Haftmann, *Malerei im 20. Jahrhundert*, Munich 1954, p. 34.

55. See G. Lista, *Futurisme – Manifestes, documents, proclamations*, Lausanne 1973.

56. F. Marinetti, 'Futurisme', *Le Figaro*, 20 February 1909, p. 1; Faidon Bouboulidis, 'Apichiseis tou foutourismou sti Neoelliniki Grammateia' ('Echoes of Futurism in Modern Greek Literature'), *Epetiris Idrymatos Neoellinikon Spoudon* ('Yearbook of the Foundation for Modern Greek Studies'), vol. A, 1979-80, p. 10.

57. Lista, *op. cit.*, p. 107.

58. See the newspaper *Eleftheros Anthropos*, 31 January 1933.

59. 10 February 1933, p. 1; the full title of the article was 'Raise your Flag: a Manifesto to the Young People of Greece'.

60. The newspaper *Ellinikon Mellon* (31 January 1933) carried an article signed with the pseudonym 'Diavatis' ('Passer-by') including the following comment: "Stop, oh men of England (travellers)! – What's going on up here? – The moonlight has been executed! – What? – There's no moonlight any more, and the Parthenon's been demolished! – And who killed the moonlight and demolished the Parthenon? – Marinetti! Greece no longer has a Parthenon! – It doesn't have a Parthenon? Then what does it have? – Trams, engine-sheds …".

61. See Ilias Fertis, 'K. Parthenis. O Daskalos' ('K. Parthenis. The Master'), *Zygos*, October 1956, nos. 11-12, p. 26; Stelios Lydakis, *Istoria tis Neoellinikis Zografikis* ('History of Modern Greek Painting'), Melissa, Athens 1976 (= *Oi Ellines Zografoi*, 'Greek Painters', 3).

62. From the 'Ode' which Yeorgios Tertsetis composed for the laying of the foundation stone of the Academy in 1859; see G. Laios, *Simon Sinas*, Athens 1972, p. 186.

63. Königliche Bibliothek, Copenhagen: Hansen-Nachlas; Schaubert to Hansen, 29 November 1856.

64. Stuart and Revett, *op. cit.*, vol. B, 1787, pl. XVIII.

DAVID VAN ZANTEN

The Parthenon
Imagined Painted

Central Athens, with its broad streets and square blocks, is in large part a nineteenth century city, laid out by German architects in 1830s after the establishment of the independent Greek state. The Acropolis rises from its centre cleared, restored and (in the case of the temple of Athena Nike) actually re-assembled from scattered parts during the years after 1830 to assume the iconic shape recorded in later nineteenth century photographs and paintings. The neat city around on the bent spine of University Street was peopled with public buildings in what was imagined to be the style of the Periclean Acropolis: von Gärtner's Old Palace (1835-1841), Christian Hansen's University (1837-1842), Theophile von Hansen's Academy (1859-1887). Yet these exercices in Periclean design differ in many respects from the Parthenon and its entourage visible on the citadel a mile away, most particularly in being touched up with gilding and paint. Their mouldings and capitals are exotically enlivened with gold palmettes and touches of red, blue and green. Their columns are set off against walls frescoed in deep, flat colours, especially red. Their architects believed that this was just the reconstruction of the painted decoration that had originally existed on the Periclean monuments and indeed this treatment seems conservative when compared with the polychromy imagined on the Parthenon by their contemporary scholar-architects Alexis Paccard (figs. 1-5), Gottfried Semper (figs. 7-8) and Benoit Loviot (figs. 18-22).[1]

This polychromatic decoration transformed the appearance of the Parthenon and seemed as outrageous as it was fascinating. Its reconstruction was based on dim traces scattered here and there on the Parthenon, the Propylaea and especially the Theseum, mostly on the frieze and cornice mouldings or the ceiling caissons.[2] These traces had been given substance by the discovery of painted architectural members in the excavations at Aegina in 1811 and later in Sicily. Terracotta cornices from several sites showed brilliant painted patterns. Ancient literary sources supported these indications: Vitruvius says that triglyphs were painted blue, numerous authors speak of paintings on temple walls which might be imagined as murals setting off the peristyle columns.

The mid-nineteenth century discovered Periclean architecture after the Greek War of Independence and imagined it very vividly coloured. There was an engagement and passion in this work that is missing in more recent work, like the 1950s monochrome reconstruction of the Stoa of Attalus. Strangely enough, we still do not know just how – to what degree and in how high a key – the monuments of the Acropolis had originally been painted. All we have, for the moment, is the fascinating imaginings of the scholar-architects of a hundred and fifty years ago.

1. In February 1845, the Académie des Beaux-Arts in Paris established the practice of the architect pensionnaires at the French Academy in Rome spending a year in Athens to produce archaeological studies. In 1846 the French School in Athens was founded and, in 1847, the architects were attached to it (until the change of regulations in 1863).[3] For more than a decade a series of Grand Prix winning architects and students from the Ecole Normale Supérieure worked in Athens to explore Greek culture at its source. Eleven students were initially dispatched, among them the architects Théodore Ballu and Alexis Paccard and the normaliens Emile Burnouf and Charles Levêque. Among those that followed during the years immediately afterward were the architect Charles Garnier (later the designer of the Paris Opera) and the normalien Charles-Ernest Beulé (later permanent secretary of the Académie des Beaux-Arts). Between them this group produced a corpus of drawings and written analyses of the Periclean monuments that embodied a new and vivid conception.

One of the first monuments the French student

1. *Alexis Paccard: reconstruction of the east facade of the Parthenon, 1845-1846, ink wash drawing; Paris, Ecole Nationale Supérieure des Beaux-Arts.*

architects addressed was the Parthenon. Paccard measured and drew it with extraordinary precision in 1845-1846 and proposed a polychromatic reconstruction (figs. 1-5).[4] His friend Emile Burnouf (a future Sankrit scholar) published an essay on the significance of Paccard's findings in the *Revue des Deux Mondes* on 1 December 1847. Paccard projected external painting only above the taenia below the frieze, but here it is complete: blue on the triglyphs, red on the metope grounds, red and blue key patterns on the taenia and the cornice fascia. The sculpture is painted. Bronze shields are shown attached to the architrave. The cella wall is indicated a flat red. Paccard also represented the subtle curves and inclinations in the building's members, documented by a minute measurement and levelling of the remains.

Traces of painted decoration on the cruder stucco coatings of Greek and Republican Roman monuments in Italy and Sicily had alerted the first nineteenth century visitors to Athens to examine the Periclean monuments closely. They found evidence that even the fine Pentelic marble surfaces of the Parthenon had been painted to some degree but also that none of the heavy architectural elements were even, level or square. The English architect C.R. Cockerell during his stay in Athens in 1810-1815 had noted the column's entasis, a sutble bulge at its greatest about a third of the way up the shaft, as well as certain evidence of painted decoration. Twenty years later another English architect, T.L. Donaldson, had observed that the building's columns were not set vertically, but rather leaned slightly inward, the angle increasing in roughly equal increments towards the corner. In 1837 another English architect, James Pennethorne, proved that the Parthenon's stylobate curved upward towards the centre of each facade, following suspicions aroused when he examined the monument for traces of painted decoration in 1832-1835. This evidence had become clearer as the debris cluttering the temple had been cleared away during the 1830s and the German architects established in

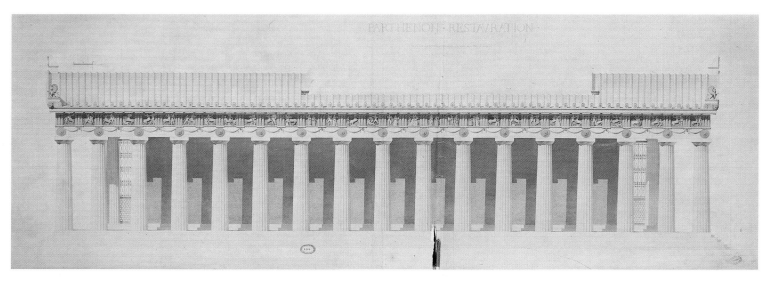

2. Alexis Paccard: reconstruction of the west facade of the Parthenon, 1845-1846, ink wash drawing; Paris, Ecole Nationale Supérieure des Beaux-Arts.

3. Alexis Paccard: reconstruction of the Parthenon, 1845-1846, longitudinal section, ink wash drawing; Paris, Ecole Nationale Supérieure des Beaux-Arts.

Athens, especially Eduard Schaubert and Ludwig Ross, published the discovery in the Vienna *Allgemeine Bauzeitung*.[5] In 1845-1847 Paccard as well as the English scholar Francis Crammer Penrose painstakingly surveyed the Parthenon to reveal a consistent avoidance of regularity as well as scattered traces of painted decoration.

In 1835 the German scholar Franz Kugler offered a very considered, conservative reconstruction of how the Parthenon's painted decoration might have appeared (fig. 6), rationalising that it was mere touches to bring out the translucence of the marble.[6] He was responding to a far more imaginative reconstruction being proposed by another German, the achitect Gottfried Semper (figs. 7, 8).[7] Semper insisted that the Parthenon was completely painted red, marble being used simply as a finer base for colour than the stucco of earlier buildings. His reconstruction drawing shows this red set off by blue and yellow triglyphs, purple, white and gold patterns on the abacus,

and green, red and blue egg-and-dart patterns across the Doric echinus.

Kugler and Semper do not integrate the refinements of form into their hypotheses, nor do they base their idea upon an exhaustive study of the site. This was Paccard and Burnouf's accomplishment. Burnouf, in his 1847 essay, recognised that the painting destroyed the purity of the architectural masses and that the refinements contradicted the modular proportional systems previously assumed to control Greek architectural aesthetics. He accepted the explanation offered by several observers that the refinements were to counteract visual effects of instability, for example, the corner columns compressed and inclined backward to correct a tendency to seem to topple outward. He extended this into the idea that the whole Parthenon was really a work of sculpture, not just made to appear stable, but to seem living and majestic like the colossal statue of Athena once within. Furthermore, in thus

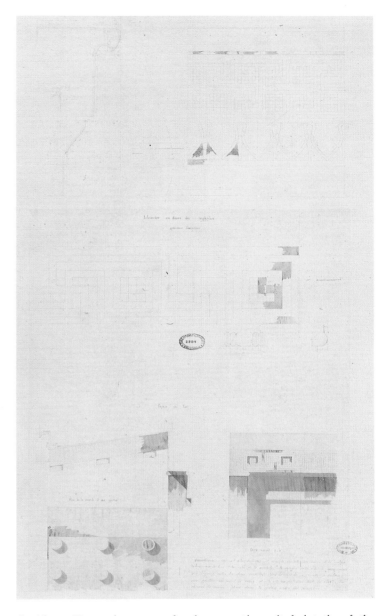

4. Alexis Paccard: reconstruction of the entablature of the Parthenon, 1845-1846, ink wash drawing; Paris, Ecole Nationale Supérieure des Beaux-Arts.

5. Alexis Paccard: traces of colour on the relief details of the Parthenon, 1845-1846; Paris, Ecole Nationale Supérieure des Beaux-Arts.

transcribing the responding curves of sculpture into building, Burnouf continued, the Parthenon simultaneously picked up the geometry and colouring of the sharply-defined Attic landscape around it. The temple became a middle term, a mediating element, between the human body and nature, and its mantle of painted decoration was necessary to echo the colours of the landscape and moderate the brilliance of its Pentelic marble.

"Under the Athenian sun the powerful environment of Greece strikes us immediately, absorbs us in a sense and makes us vibrate with its own life... The colour of ruins is almost always that of their surroundings, of nature itself, into which we seem to be re-absorbed; but nature is not enough for man, he senses in him the urge to make and to vivify, concentrated in a single object, the beauty that he finds scattered around him. [The Greeks] obeyed nature and since in Greece everything is painted, brilliant, they make their temples on that model... Greek art, entirely born of nature and inspired by it fundamentally, curves the steps and pavements of the temples, the architraves, friezes and bases of the pediments, just as nature curves the sea, the horizon and the rounded back of the mountains."

This was a beautiful and riveting evocation. The intellectual construction within which Greek architecture had previously been grasped was that of the great theoretician (and permanent secretary of the Académie) A.-C. Quatremère de Quincy.[8] His relentlessly abstract,

6. *Franz Kugler: reconstruction of the order of the Parthenon, frontispiece, 1835, chromolithograph. Source:* Über die Polychromie der griechischen Architektur und Skulptur und ihre Grenzen, *Berlin 1835; Athens, Gennadios Library.*

doctrinaire three-volume *Architecture* (1788-1825) for the *Encyclopédie méthodique* presented the Greek temple form as absolutely fixed, communicating its specific dedication only by the selection of its order, the orders constituting three fixed sub-systems. The vocabulary of elements and mouldings was unchanging. There were two kinds of architecture: 'regular' and 'irregular': the Greeks created the former as an extension of their philosophical brilliance; weaker cultures fell into the mindless enjoyment of the latter. Extravagant shapes, overt conceits (like caryatids), and painting were irregular and to be avoided.

Quatremère had never been to Greece. Indeed, most early nineteenth century visitors to Greek monuments, whether those of Magna Graecia, Sicily, or of Greece proper, had not spent long time at the sites, only drawing mouldings and details with any care, otherwise sketching overall plans and speculating little on topography or vistas. Most monuments were partially buried or encum-

bered by late building, as at the Acropolis before the 1830s. The first case of systematic excavation and study only came with the German expeditions of the 1870s. The students at the French School at Athens, however, lived in Athens and studied the emerging Acropolis stone by stone. They realised that its monuments could not be explained by Quatremère's idealist typologies but instead were a unique and a very complex whole – an architectural composition, a religious temenos, and a part of the topography of the Attic plain.[9]

In 1851 Burnouf's fellow *normalien* Charles Levêque tried to raise these ideas to a general conception of Greek aesthetics, again in the *Revue des Deux Mondes* (15 August). For him the key was the remarkable Greek landscape, so clearly defined in valleys, unified by the omnipresent blue sea, constantly swelling and folding,

7. *Gottfried Semper: reconstruction of the order of the Parthenon, c. 1834, water-colour; Zurich, Semperarchiv, Institut für Geschichte und Theorie der Architektur, Eidgenössische Technische Hochschule.*

everywhere filled with historical and magical meaning.

"The mountain, the plain, the sea, the islands balance each other and unite in Greece by continual mutual response; leave the shores, seek the highest summits or the most secluded valleys, you believe the sea far off; but look: it is at your feet. Arriving one day at the furthest end of the gorges where Phyle, the fortress of Thrasybulus, is hidden, we thought ourselves emprisoned in the walls of mountains. Suddenly a double ray of sunlight cut between two clouds to show us, to the east, the plain of Athens stretching to Hymettus and, to the south, in a fold of the Aigaleo, a corner of the blue gulf of Eleusis, caught between the rocks like a fragment fallen from the vault of heaven."

Ancient Greek art and architecture was the abstraction and reflection of this.

"Greek art found its model not in the actual appearance of the countryside, but in its physiognomy; if it examined the body, it was only to read the thought within it which it grasped, made its own and put in a new body; beautiful like the first although of a less perfect beauty and of an-

other countenance. This is the action of genius: it shapes and vivifies like Prometheus; but what it steals from heaven is not the clay, it is the fire; and when, inspired by divine creation, without copying it raises sculpture to spirituality, it happens that nature and monuments of art appear like two copies of the same eternal model, one from the hand of God, the other from that of man."

Ten years later in his *Science du Beau* (1861) Levêque expanded this into a general theory of art and especially architecture based on the psychological linkage of emotions to expressively distorted, seemingly animated forms.

The French student architects studied the monuments of the Acropolis one by one, Ballu and Jacques Tetaz the Erechtheum (1844-1845 and 1847-1848), Paccard the Parthenon (1845-1846), Philippe Titeux, Louis Chaudet and Prosper Debuisson the Propylaea (1846 and 1848). They extended their work to the Theseum (Louis André, 1851), to Sounion (Victor Louvet, 1855), Aegina (Charles Garnier, 1852-1853) and even to Bassae (Denis Lebouteux, 1853). The problem was to synthesise this mass of material documenting the complexity and specificity of Greek monuments. This was the accomplishment of the normalien Beulé after his arrival in Athens in 1851.

The Propylea had always been a puzzle. It had a temple's colonnades and pediments yet it seemed some sort of gate. After clearing and after the studies of Titeux, Chaudet and Desbuisson, Burnouf published a study explaining how it could have functioned militarily.[10] This did not satisfy Beulé. He excavated the steps leading down the Acropolis from the building and to his delight discovered the remains of a fortified gateway at the bottom, since named the Beulé Gate. The Propylaea, in Pentelic marble and displaying all the refinements and polychromy of the Parthenon, had seemed too delicate to be a military structure and here was proof that it was not. In his two-volume *Acropole d'Athènes* of 1853-1854 Beulé depicts it as a purely decorative construction. Furthermore, having discovered the point from which it would have first been seen, Beulé explains its proportions and irregular composition as carefully scenographic.

"It is a decorative monument and nothing more, but magnificently decorative, where the artist, without other interference than the shape of the site, could give himself over entirely to his inspirations. Time, millions, the choicest materials, the most skilful craftsmen, he had all at his discretion. Such good fortune is so helpful to talent that it might seem to give birth to it."

In a word, Beulé presented the Propylaea, the Parthenon and the whole architectural ensemble on the Acropolis not as exercises in typology, but as a highly inflected and specific work of composition emerging (in the case of the Propylaea) into pure constructed decoration.

Beulé found refinements of form easier to accept than polychromy. While he could not deny its existence and its brilliance, he imagined that it had become subtler and less obtrusive as Greek architecture evolved, until the Parthenon was only tinted and that in its upper parts, as Paccard showed.[11] Among the French student architects, one was not so hesitant: Charles Garnier, working at Aegina in 1852-1853 (fig. 9). In his memoire accompanying his study[12] he cites Hittorff (whose *Architecture polychrome chez les grecs* had appeared in 1851) and declares that all Greek temples were completely painted. His reconstruction drawings show the column shafts painted yellow, the architrave bright red, the Doric capitals covered with egg-and-dart patterns above gilded necking and below blue abaci. Rhythmic rinceaux are shown on the external and the internal architraves. Here the polychromy did not just bring out the architectural forms but played against them and threatened (to academic eyes) to overwhelm them. But Aegina was a special case. Firstly, the temple's remains had been largely buried and when exhumed in 1811 the members had shown clear traces of bright paint which had faded upon exposure to the air, although only after being recorded. The evidence of polychromy was the strongest here of all Attic monuments. Secondly, the temple was not built of marble, but of stuccoed limestone, and was of pre-Periclean date, like the temples of Magna Graecia and Sicily, so that the question remained whether its treatment could be extrapolated and extended to the monuments of the Acropolis.

2. To the French students in Athens around 1850, ancient Greek polychromy was part of the discovery of the general complexity and subtlety of ancient Greek architecture. It engendered a new vision of classical art. One remarkable German artist, the scholar-architect Gottfried Semper, had preceded them in this, although he created an even more general system, and at the beginning had the benefit of only a few months in Athens.[13] Throughout his distinguished (if also tumultuous) career Semper periodically returned to the formulation of an embracing but obscure system of architectural theory inspired by the problem of Greek polychromy. He sketched it in his *Vorläufige Bemerkungen über bemalte Architektur und Plastik bei den Alten* of 1834. He extended it in his *Vier Elemente der Baukunst* of 1851 (also entitled *Über Polychromie*). He tried to state it definitively in his massive *Stil in den technischen und tektonischen Künsten* of 1860-1863, but could not finish the third and final volume applying his principles to modern design. He summarised it in his *Über Baustil* of 1869.

Semper started from the rejection of the 1820s methods of design which he categorised as either fitting together parts (in the manner of J.-N.-L. Durand) or painting pictures. For him architecture was essentially living and thus unified: painting, sculpture and building interwoven in it, responding to the changing demands of the social community. This ideal was achieved in ancient Greece. "The architect is the chorus leader, he leads the work..." ("Der Architekt war Chorage, er führt sie an...").

Polychromy to Semper was the key to exploring Greek architecture because, narrowly, it showed the painted medium insinuating itself into sculpture and architecture, and broadly, it might preserve memories of vestigial conventions otherwise invisible in remains weathered to whiteness. In two passages in the *Bemerkungen* he hypothesises how motifs and moulding evolved. First came real objects – garlands of flowers; braids of sacrificial victims' hair – looped over the building's members. Then their representation was painted on the surfaces as they became traditional attributes. Then they were carved into the building's mass to achieve permanence. These carvings were also painted to make them resemble the original objects they had come to replace. And so on. To Semper every Greek moulding was the descendant of some meaningful object and thus was carved and painted in the same

266

9. *Charles Garnier: reconstruction of the facade of the temple of Aegina, 1852-1853, ink wash; Paris, Ecole Nationale Supérieure des Beaux-Arts.*

conventional pattern. The echinus of the Doric capital, for example, must always have borne a painted and etched egg-and-dart pattern (fig. 7). Also, while carrying on this symbolism in the conventional patterns, Greek polychromy simultaneously was inflected to articulate the form and relief of the building so that it outlined antae or set off metope sculpture.

In the *Vier Elemente der Baukunst* of seventeen years later Semper expands the memorial aspect of polychromy. Having studied primitive architectural decoration in Paris and London, while in exile from the Dresden rising of 1849, he formulated the theory that such ornament reflected an origin in four primitive crafts which had united to produce the first habitations: stereotomy for plinths and floors, carpentry for ceilings, weaving for walls (once made of tapestries), and clay modelling for the domestic furniture given rise to by the central hearth. Greek and later ornament continued, in conventional patterns, the memory of these different technologies on the appropriate architectural members.

In his *Stil* Semper explored the implications of this: that the decorative vocabulary evolves within subtle limits, that it is not an immediate functional expression of construction, but instead a mantle (Bekleidung) laid over structural forms which retains its conventional patterns despite translation into different materials (Stoffwechsel). It is the task of the modern designer to overcome simple functionalism and to start the huge archaeological task of reconstructing the history and meaning of the building's ornamental garment.

The great example of that ornamental garment was the painted decoration of the Parthenon that Semper had reconstructed in the coloured plates of his *Anwendung der Farben* of 1834-1836 (fig. 7). He tried to balance the traces of the lost vocabulary of Greek mouldings – the purple and green egg-and-dart of Ictinus' echinus – with securely documented traces of patterns. He proceeds with a tremendous sense of colour harmony. And it is this last quality, perhaps, that is the most impressive: the French students of 1850 never made their polychrome reconstructions sing in such an intricate, symphonic manner – even Garnier, who remains flat and self-consciously archaicising.

If Beulé could evoke the Acropolis as a continuously responding composition of curves, angles, truncations, inflections and vistas, Semper could project the lost Periclean polychromatic garment just as richly in the microcosm of the Parthenon's elevation. Semper emphasised that force and clarity were essential in Greek polychromy. In 1851 he published in London one of the most powerful characterisations of what he imagined to have been the effect of this decoration:

"The prevailing colour of the temple burned with all the glowing beauty of the setting sun. The colour may be defined as of a yellow red, very vapoury, resembling that of the finest terracotta. In fact the general appearance of the temple would precisely resemble the appearance of a fine day in an eastern climate".[14]

What they felt they discovered in the painting and refinements of the Acropolis was the tightest unity of effect. Semper became the great architect of relieved surfaces and mouldings in his Dresden Opera House (1838-1841) and museum (1847-1854) as well as later of the Vienna Hofburg (1871-1882). Beulé supported a similar highly

10. Théodore Labrouste: reconstruction of the temple of Heracles at Cori, 1831-1832, ink wash; Paris, Ecole Nationale Supérieure des Beaux-Arts.

modulated, inflected architecture in his capacity as permanent secretary of the Académie in Paris. Garnier, of course, personified it in his great Paris Opera (1861-1875).

3. We have noted that by the time of these explorations of Periclean aesthetics in the 1830s and the 1840s polychromy had already been established as an issue in the context of the Etruscan, Republican Roman and Greek remains of Italy and Sicily. This initial discovery was involved

11. Marie-Antoine Delannoy: reconstruction of the Tiber island, Rome, 1832-1833, ink wash; Paris , Ecole Nationale Supérieure des Beaux-Arts.

with an earlier, 'romantic' re-evaluation of the classical past and produced a series of striking, imaginative reconstructions that would influence the visualisation of the Parthenon (figs.9 to 17).

Traces of painting had been noted by travellers on Greek monuments during the decades around 1800 but little had been made of them.[15] In December 1823 – January 1824 the Cologne-born Parisian architect Jacques-Ignace Hittorff studied the Greek remains in Sicily, specifically seeking traces of painted decoration on their stucco surfaces.[16] In 1824 he displayed reconstructions of this colouring in Rome and Paris and in 1827-1830 began publication of his *Architecture antique de la Sicile* with three chromolithographed plates (fig. 13). This presented, among other things, a complete reconstruction of a little temple at Selinus, hypothesised by Hittorff as dedicated to Empedocles (fig. 14). Contemporaneously, in 1827, the German archaeologists Otto Magnus von Stackelberg and August Kestner together with the architect Joseph Thürmer made the first careful study of the archaic Etruscan tomb paintings at Corneto (Tarquinia) which showed how brilliant Greek colouring might have been and how flat and rhythmical its patterning.[17] Again contemporaneously a brilliant group of French student architects at the French Academy at Rome explored these discoveries, producing a controversial series of reconstructions sent back for display in Paris.[18] These began with Herni Labrouste's Paestum reconstructions of 1828-1829, his brother Théodore's of the Temple of Vesta at Tivoli of 1829-1830 and of the temples at Cori of 1831-1832 (fig. 10), Marie-Antoine Delannoy's of the Tiber island in Rome of 1832-1833 (fig. 11) and finally Simon-Claude Constant-Dufeux's reconstruction of the Republican Capitoline of 1833-1834. A number of personal architectural fantasies water-coloured by Henri Labrouste and Felix Duban at the same time were even more extraordinary. By 1830 these discoveries and reconstructions had attracted such attention that a fierce international controversy broke out, some, like the scholar Raoul-Rochette (Quatremère's successor and Beulé's predecessor as

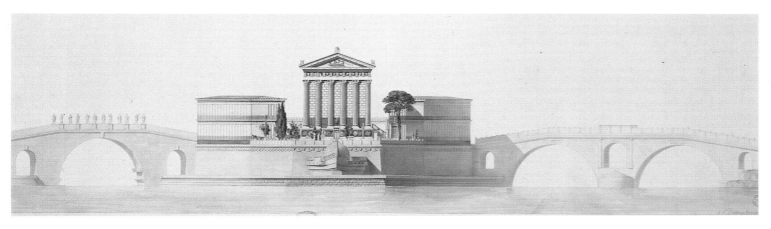

12. Claude-Simon Constant-Dufeux: tomb of Admiral Dumont d'Urville, 1842-1844; Paris, Cimetière Montparnasse. Photograph by D. van Zanten.

13. Jacques-Ignace Hittorff: reconstruction of the entablature of the 'temple of Empedocles', Selinus, c. 1827, water-colour; Paris, Institut de France.

14. Jacques-Ignace Hittorff: reconstruction of the facade of the 'temple of Empedocles', Selinus, chromolithograph. Source: L'architecture polychrome chez les Grecs, Paris 1851.

15. *Gottlieb Bindesbøll: facade of an ideal museum for Thorvaldsen's sculpture, 1836-1837, water-colour; Copenhagen, Det Kongelige Danske Kunstakademiet.*

permanent secretary of the Académie), denying that painted decoration was used at all.[19]

Younger architects studying in Rome during these years worked variations upon this fascinating revelation. The brilliant Dane, Gottlieb Bindesbøll, projected an ideal museum for Thorvaldsen's sculpture in 1836-1837 in the Ionic style with extravagant polychromy, shown applied even to the great sculptor's neo-classical works (figs. 15, 16).[20] In 1839-1844 Bindesbøll got the chance to execute the Thorvaldsen Museum in Copenhagen, the architecture vividly painted with figural friezes in the Etruscan style (fig. 17). Earlier, in 1830, Semper had set out to study the evidence for polychromy in Italy, Greece and Asia Minor with a French friend, Jules Goury, who was gathering material for a compendious study of the subject. When Semper returned to Germany in 1832 Goury continued on with the Englishman Owen Jones. They eventually reached the Alhambra in Granada in Spain where they made an exhaustive study of what they felt to be the most central and sophisticated demonstration of Mediterranean coloured decoration. Goury died there in 1834 but Jones published their work in his pioneering chromolithographic *Plans, Elevations, Sections and Details of the Alhambra* of 1836-1845.[21]

This generation of the pioneers of the polychrome question did not focus on the Parthenon (with the exception of Semper) but used much more scattered evidence to more personal artistic ends. Henri Labrouste and his

16. *Gottlieb Bindesbøll: facade of an ideal museum for Thorvaldsen's sculpture, 1836-1837, water-colour, detail; Copenhagen, Det Kongelige Danske Kunstakademiet.*

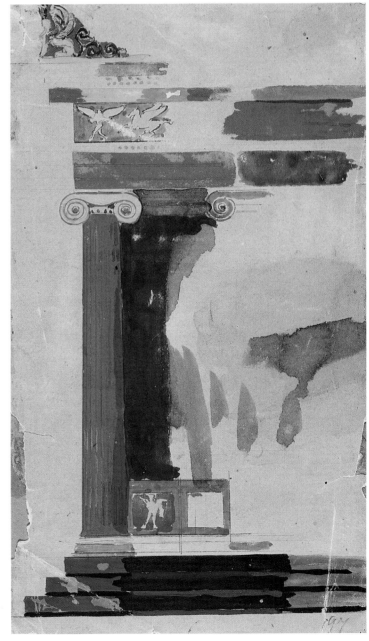

friends were striking at the entrenched Neo-classicism of Quatremère and Raoul-Rochette. They confronted it with the proposition that polychromy was not rule-bound and fixed, but merely the extension of grafitti and the attachment of actual objects. Labrouste's reconstructions of the three monuments at Paestum presented the so-called 'basilica' as just that, not a temple at all, but a meeting hall with irregular inscriptions on its walls and battle souvenirs hung from its rafters. Théodore Labrouste's reconstruction of the Republican temples at Cori showed them not only garishly painted, but the classical shape of one concealed under an awning and with shields and garlands hung or staked around it like a rich foliage (fig. 10, lower left). Delannoy's Tiber Island shows the temples crushed between a jumble of tall apartment houses – making it look like the medieval Ile de la Cité in Paris – wall-paintings, grafitti and shop wares dotted unceremoniously about (fig. 11). Henri Labrouste's personal fantasy watercolour marked "Agrigentum, 1828" shows a temple, a tomb and presumably a palace painted with much Etruscan red, ringed by a double city wall covered with cracking

painted plaster – the inner circuit blue, the outer red – with a broken chariot wheel, shields and a victor's palm strapped over the gateway. When they began designing buildings in Paris during the 1830s they tried to create a more immediate, anecdotal ornamentation. Duban in 1832 made the entrance court of his Ecole des Beaux-Arts a composition of fragments of French national architecture composed as a kind of Pompeiian illusionistic wall-painting in three dimensions. Labrouste in 1843-1850 carved the exterior of his Bibliothéque Sainte-Généviève with the names of authors, picked out in red. Constant-Dufeux made his tomb of the Admiral Dumon d'Urville (1842-1844) a collection or reminiscent objects – an Etruscan chippus painted red; a cylindrical base bearing the explorer's life in flat, painted relief; a ship's prow bearing the subject's portrait bust animated with black painted hair, red lips and blue eyes (fig. 12).

Hittorff had taken a very different attitude to the significance of Greek architectural polychromy when he formulated his ideas in 1830-1851.[22] He saw it not as graffiti-like – immediate and changing – but as a systematic

17. Gottlieb Bindesbøll: the Thorvaldsen Museum, Copenhagen. Photograph by D. van Zanten.

nuancing and enrichment of the fixed vocabulary of the orders it ornamented. The results seemed no less outrageous to the conservatives, especially Raoul-Rochette, who made Hittorff the target of pointed refutation. And Hittorff's mixing of conventional elements could get very complex. He reconstructed the polychromatic treatment of a single example – the tiny prostyle 'Temple of Empedocles' which he had excavated at Selinus in 1823-1824 (figs. 13 and 14) using evidence of all sorts: the cornices from terracottas, the murals from Etruscan tombs, the painting of the exposed ceiling beams from that of the Norman church at Montreale, and a rinceau from the Roman 'Tomb of Jenoshaphat' at Jerusalem. The assumption that made such as jumble of sources possible was that Greek polychromy had been as systematic as the orders themselves so that the same treatment also obtained on each member, even in distant architectural descendants in Jerusalem or Norman Sicily. Hittorff proposed that the function of this polychromy was to express more vividly the particular character of the deities to whom temples were dedicated than Quatremère's vocabulary of the three orders had permitted. This innocent suggestion became a shocking mixing of things – even the sacrosanct orders – in Hittorff's model reconstruction where he shows the philosopher-god Empedocles enshrined behind a part-Doric part-Ionic facade. Hittorff believed that the motifs of architectural history could be mixed and re-arranged to communicate ideas like words in sentences, the individual motifs retaining a fixed meaning through time.[23]

Semper's great hypothesis first tentatively sketched in his *Bemerkungen* of 1834 combined Hittorff's belief in the regularity of the decorative vocabulary with the Labroustians' belief in its origins in actual objects hung about shrines. He extended these aperçus, bit by bit, to embrace the whole of architectural history. Goury's enterprise seems to have been similar. Semper bewailed Goury's death and the loss of his drawings. Jones carried on the work, giving it an ideal, slightly mystical inflection. He believed that underneath later overpainting at the Alhambra he and Goury had discovered the exquisite geometric patterning painted in red, gold and blue in precisely balanced proportions. Citing the optical researches of Michel Chevreul and George Field, Jones hypothesised that the primaries (gold being the equivalent of yellow) were used in juxtaposition to balance each other and to blend into a vibrant white or "bloom" (as Jones called it) like a musical chord. This ultimate, perfect harmony reinforced the regular geometric patterning of the mural decoration.

To Jones, the achievement of this ideal harmony rather than any specific characterisation was the function of architectural colouring. The harmony itself might vary in quality from one civilisation to another. Young societies, he believed, preferred harmonies of primary colours; mature societies those of secondaries; declining societies tertiaries. But this embracing 'bloom' added to architecture was the essence of its beauty. The Greeks had achieved it as well as the Moors at the Alhambra: in 1851 Jones proposed that the Parthenon must have had gilded column shafts below a brilliant red and blue entablature.[24] He believed that iron and glass construction would produce a similar architecture for his own young industrial culture and painted the members of the Crystal Palace in London (1851) in narrow stripes of red, yellow and blue so as to create, down its long brilliantly-lit perspectives, such a vibrant 'bloom' of primary colour.

4. The conception of Greek architectural polychromy evolved greatly from the first hypotheses of 1830 to the painstaking Athenian explorations of 1850. A generation again later, in the 1870s, a last series of imagings appeared, centring around the Parthenon, which was increasingly recognised as the unique, culminating monument of Greek building. In 1879-1880 Benoit Loviot, another French Grand Prix winner studying in Rome and Athens, produced an extraordinary reconstruction (figs 18-22).[25]

Unlike the architects of the late 1840s, Loviot cites no new archaeological evidence. His very summary memoire accompanying the drawings simply cites Hittorff, Paccard and Garnier as well as a scattering of unspecified personal observations. For Loviot this was not a problem of archaeology but one of taste. He ends quoting Paccard that he had not gone far enough in 1846. Loviot's keynote is a sumptuous harmony of Chinese red and Prussian blue, a higher chromatic key than anyone except Semper and Jones had previously dared imagine. He justifies this by noting that archaic buildings would have been covered with brass and gold. He imagines the Parthenon painted in three broad zones: red on the stylobate, yellow across the peristyle shafts (standing before huge mural paintings on blue grounds), red again in the entablature and cornice set off by a blue secondary plane behind the metope and pediment sculptures. Great flat archaic patterns of spidery swirls unify all the architectural surfaces – the frieze, taenia, abaci, cornice fascias and the three faces of the stylobate. Phidias' chryselephantine Athena is repeated in its scale and rhythm by a colossal single register of mural painting reconstructed on the inner and outer walls of the cella.

This was an amazing projection. It was recognised as

18. *Benoit Loviot: reconstruction of the lateral facade of the Parthenon, 1879-1880, ink wash; Paris, Ecole Nationale Supérieure des Beaux-Arts.*

19. *Benoit Loviot: reconstruction of the main facade of the Parthenon, 1879-1880, ink wash; Paris, Ecole Nationale Supérieure des Beaux-Arts.*

20. Benoit Loviot: reconstruction of the Parthenon, 1879-1880, lateral section, ink wash; Paris, Ecole Nationale Supérieure des Beaux-Arts.

21. Benoit Loviot: reconstruction of the Parthenon, 1879-1880, longitudinal section, ink wash; Paris, Ecole Nationale Supérieure des Beaux-Arts.

22. Benoit Loviot: reconstruction of the order of the Parthenon, 1879-1880, ink wash; Paris, Ecole Nationale Supérieure des Beaux-Arts.

essentially an exercise in decorative composition. As such it seemed of a piece with the painted decoration applied to the Ecole des Beaux-Arts glazed courtyard by Loviot's teacher, E.-G. Coquart, in 1874, or the gorgeous red and gold architecture of Gustave Moreau's 'Salome' of 1876. The scholar-architect Charles Chipiez projected something similar in his *Origine des ordres grecs* of 1876 and in the plates of his *Histoire de l'art dans l'antiquité* (with Georges Perrot), 1882-1909, showing rhythmic, decorative projections of ancient architecture. In his texts Chipiez traces the origins of Greek architecture in exotic Eastern sources and in the use of metal and wood construction. He suggests great symbolic power and complexity in the sculptural decorations.[26] The more professional, conservative archaeological studies of polychromy of the late nineteenth century – those of Fenger and Collignon –

seem disappointing and academic by comparison.[27]

The Parthenon had not lost its iconic power in the 1870s. Interpretations of it, however, had shifted away from the light and landscape of Athens itself, as a place (in the 1840s newly accessible to European visitors), and back to the libraries and studios of Northern Europe. The Parthenon came to seem the distant, shimmering quintessence of the vastly complex world of myth being mapped by contemporary philology and the parallel history of decorative style emerging in ethnology and art history.[28] Louis Menard and Gustave Moreau – around 1870 a Parisian hermit-poet and hermit-painter – were formulating extraordinary projections of ancient art from this new thinking. Loviot's sumptuous imaging of a painted Parthenon takes its force from this decade in Paris and remains the most powerful projection of the building as painted.

Notes

1. See the exhibition catalogue *Paris–Rome–Athènes*, Ecole Nationale Supérieure des Beaux-Arts, Paris 1982; Herbert Koch, *Studium zum Theseustempel*, Berlin 1955. Also my *The Architectural Polychromy of the 1830s*, Garland, New York 1977, and Robin Middleton's and my essays in *The Beaux-Arts and Nineteenth Century Architecture*, Thames and Hudson, London 1982, pp. 174-215.

2. See M.-F. Billot, 'Recherches aux XVIIIe et XIXe siècles sur la polychromie de l'architecture grecque', *Paris–Rome–Athènes*, *op. cit.*, pp. 61-128.

3. On the Ecole française d'Athènes: Charles Levêque, 'La Fondation et les débuts de l'Ecole française d'Athènes', *Revue des Deux Mondes*, LXVIII, March 1898, pp. 85-119; Georges Radet, *L'Histoire et l'œuvre de l'École française d'Athènes*, Fontemoing, Paris 1901.

4. *Paris–Rome–Athènes*, *op. cit.*, pp. 162-171; published with a text by Léon de Laborde, *Le Parthénon*, Paris 1848.

5. See for example, Hermann Hermann, 'Bemerkungen über die antiken Dekorations-Malereien an den Tempels zu Athen', *Allgemeine Beuzeitung*, I, 1836, pp. 81-86.

6. Franz Kugler, *Über die Polychromie der griechischen Architektur und Skulptur und ihre Grenzen*, Berlin 1835.

7. Gottfried Semper, *Vorläufige Bemerkungen über bemalte Architektur und Plastik bei den Alten*, Altona 1834; *Die Anwendung die Farben*, Berlin 1834-1836.

8. The basic published study remains Réné Schneider, *Quatremère de Quincy et son intervention dans les arts (1780-1830)*, Paris 1910. In his *Architecture* see the entries Architecture, Ordre, Imitation, Irregulier, Caryatide.

9. In seeking significance in the relation to the landscape, they were preceded by the French scholar and traveller J.-J. Ampère, writing, for example, in the *Revue de Deux Mondes* 'Une course dans l'Asie Mineure' (XXIX, 15 January, 1842) and 'La Poésie grecque en Grèce' (XXXV, 15 June, 1844), or his *Litterature, voyages, poésie* of 1848. German scholars, especially O.M. von Stackelberg, had preceded him in this interest.

10. Emile Burnouf, 'Les Propylées', *Archives des missions scientifiques et littéraires*, I, 1850, pp. 8-38.

11. Ch.-E. Beulé, 'La Polychromie', *Revue générale de l'architecture*, XVII, 1859, columns 193-212.

12. Published by Garnier, *Le Temple de Jupiter panhellénien à Egine*, Paris 1884. See *Revue archéologique*, I, 1854, pp. 193-204; 343-361.

13. Semper has been the subject of considerable study: Heinz Quitzsch, *Die ästhetischen Anschauung Gottfried Sempers*, Berlin 1962; Ernst Stockmeyer, *Gottfried Sempers Kunsttheorie*, Zurich 1939; Hans Prinzhorn, *Gottfried Sempers ästhetische Grundanschauung*, Stuttgart 1909; and especially for our concerns here Leopold Ettlinger, *Gottfried Semper und die Antike*, Halle 1939. Also, Martin Fröhlich, *Gottfried Semper: Zeichnerischer Nachlass an der ETH Zürich*, Birkhäuser, Basel and Zurich 1974.

14. 'On the Study of Polychromy and its Revival', *Museum of Classical Antiquities*, I, 1851, pp. 228-255.

15. These numerous but scattered observations are summarised by Billot in *Paris–Rome–Athènes*, *op. cit.*, pp. 63-76.

16. Karl Hammer, *Jakob Ignaz Hittorff: ein Pariser Baumeister, 1792-1867*, Hiersemann, Stuttgart 1968; Donald Schneider, *The Works and Doctrine of Jacques Ignace Hittorff (1792-1867): Structural Innovation and Formal Expression in French Architecture, 1810-1867*, Garland, New York 1977.

17. The Parisian scholar D.-D. Raoul-Rochette declared that they were, in fact, Greek in origin in the *Journal des Savants*, January-February 1828.

18. Discussed: Neil Levine, 'The Romantic Idea of Architectural Legibility: Henri Labrouste and the Néo-Grec' in Arthur Drexler (editor),

The Architecture of the Ecole des Beaux-Arts, Museum of Modern Art, New York, 1977, pp. 103-179; David Van Zanten, *Designing Paris: The Architecture of Duban, Labrouste, Duc and Vaudoyer*, MIT Press, Cambridge 1987, chapter 1.

19. He devoted two volumes to this, apart from a number of articles in the *Journal des savants: Peintures antiques inédites*, Imprimérie Royale, Paris 1836; *Lettres archéologiques sur les peintures des Grecs*, Paris 1840. Raoul-Rochette's and others' objections are summarised exhaustively in Hittorff's *L'architecture polychrome chez les Grecs*, Paris 1851.

20. H. Bramsen, *Gottlieb Bindesbøll: Liv og Arbeider*, Copenhagen 1959.

21. See Michael Darby's work on Jones, especially *The Islamic Perspective*, World of Islam Festival Trust, London 1983, pp. 61-121.

22. J.-I. Hittorff, *Architecture antique de la Sicile*, Paris 1827-1830; 'De l'architecture polychrome chez les Grecs', *Annales de l'institut de correspondance archéologique*, II, 1830, pp. 263-284; *L'architecture polychrome chez les Grecs, op. cit.*

23. On this aspect of Hittorff, see my essay, 'Architectural Polychromy: the Life in Architecture', *The Beaux-Arts..., op. cit.*, pp. 196-215.

24. In a discussion at the Royal Institute of British Architects reported in the *Civil Engineer's and Architect's Journal*, 1851, p. 49.

25. It was exhibited incomplete with pensionnaires envois in 1879 and (evidently) complete in the Salon of 1880. Published: *Paris–Rome–Athènes, op. cit.*, pp. 230-237. Loviot's memoire: *Revue archéologique*, XXXIX, 1880, pp. 322-329. Reviews: J.-L. Pascal, *Revue générale de l'architecture*, 1879; *La Semaine des constructeurs*, IV, 1880, p. 568. Loviot's was one of the new series of polychrome reconstructions that included Victor Laloux's of Olympia (1883) and Victor Blavette's of Eleusis (1884-1885): see *Paris–Rome–Athènes, op. cit.*

26. Ch. Chipiez, *Origines des ordres grecs*, Morel, Paris 1976, pp. 242-251. See also the study of his friend, Emile Boutmy, *Le Parthénon et le génie grec*, Paris 1870.

27. L. Fenger, *Dorische Polychromie*, Berlin 1886; Maxime Collignon, *Le Parthénon*, Paris 1912.

28. Henri Peyre, *Louis Menard*, Yale, New Haven 1935.

DIMITRIS PHILIPPIDES

The Parthenon as Appreciated by Greek Society

And I, as I watched, was taken
outside time, far from time,
free of forms enclosed
within the ages, of statues and icons[1]

The Parthenon, as a national symbol, occupies a privileged position in modern Greek ideology. We have given this specific social phenomenon the conventional title of 'appreciation', and we propose it as the particular subject of our research.

Among our intentions is an examination of the ways in which the Western European model was received and reproduced in Greece. Without wishing to overlook the relative autonomy of Greek culture, we have chosen to isolate the role given to contemporary Greece as guardian of the patrimony by means of the transmutation of the Parthenon into a universal symbol.

The *desideratum* is a juxtaposition of formal and informal culture, with the specific monument as our field of reference. In other words, we are interested in seeing how a collective myth is transcribed into everyday practice when it is compelled to address itself to the undeniable needs of Greek society as a whole. At the end of the day, this may mean the following: the manner in which the universal symbolism of the Parthenon (that is, its appreciation) is reproduced through a combination of two contradictory definitions, the independent value of the monument regardless of place and time (the Parthenon as global and eternal symbol), and its dependent value within a specific place (Greece) and at a specific time (the 'now' of the given moment).[2] There is a tacit supposition in this that the independent value stems, as a rule, from above, while the dependent value stems from beneath.

In other words, we are proposing a reading of the Parthenon as seen by the 'names' and the nameless of Greek society. We shall allow them all to speak on an equal footing, abolishing the exclusive privileges of those who, as architects, archaeologists or aestheticians are regarded, presumptively, as experts on the study and protection of the monument. We shall refer to the 'experts' only when we judge it essential, so as not to lose sight of the substantive role which they have played in the affair and, in parallel, so as to keep things in historical proportion.

However, over and above the allocation of responsibility for the management of the monument (and thus of the right to talk about it), there is always the problem of the collective nature of such a national symbol. Although the local hagiography of the Parthenon is subject – to a decisive extent, indeed – to specific and identifiable interventions on the part of individuals (e.g., intellectuals as the instructors of public opinion) or groups (e.g., the machinery of state as the voice of power), the ultimate recipient (in the passive sense) and converter (in the active sense) is, allegedly, society as a whole.

However, there are certain basic characteristics of this relationship of which we are ignorant: the manner in which the relevant concepts are diffused, the range over which they are active, the degree of adulteration to which they are subjected in the process of transference, and the way in which they affect behaviour. The collective, then, will emerge as the resultant of evaluation of these factors.

Given that as far as our field of reference is concerned we are examining the way in which 'the Greek people' approaches the Parthenon, we have to conclude that this, in effect, is an anthropological study.[3] In parallel, though, there is also a historical dimension, as can be seen from the breadth of the period of time covered (a century and a half). The historical dimension arises not only so as to allow the identification of any differentiations as evolutionary landmarks, but also – perhaps – so as to convince the reader of the timelessness of our observations, a timelessness which is directly analogous to the eternal quality of the monument itself.

Our first discovery is that we will have to deal with an enormous volume of widely varying material which diffuses outward in a number of directions, both orthodox and unorthodox. Indeed, the importance of the theme is such that the documentation is constantly being enhanced with new data to add to the existing heritage. This sense of an endless amount of material is heightened by the second option taken, that of examining the theme over time and through events of minor importance.

This use of minor events is a consequence of the hypothesis that a great part of the spontaneous and un-conscious approach of the Greeks to the monument has been conveyed via the daily Press, and has thus acquired an informal – and therefore not fully controlled – character. For reasons which will become obvious later on, we are directly interested in this kind of approach. The frequent use of original material from the Greek Press does not preclude occasional references to other sources of information, such as literature or codified history which, as special

1. Philipp von Foltz: Pericles Orating on the Pnyx, 1852; destroyed in the Second World War. Source: Pankosmios Istoria *('World History'), vol. 1, Eleftheroudakis, Athens 1932 (frontispiece).*

categories of writing, are of course connected with each other and with the Press. Furthermore, the interpolation of material from such sources may lead to useful conclusions about the power of suggestion which such ideological intervention may have.

Given that for all practical purposes the documentation is inexhaustible, we arrive at two conclusions: first, that the exposition by juxtaposition of something approaching indexation would be pointless, if not tiresome; and secondly, that exposition of the material *per se* is of secondary importance since we do not expect to be convinced by the volume of the material or by its statistical completeness. It might, perhaps, be marginally possible to have omitted the series of examples altogether, or to have replaced them with others without perceptibly damaging the

2. *Euzones parading in front of the Parthenon. Source: W. Daven-port,* Athens, *Time-Life Books, 1978.*

correctness or objectivity of the theoretical statements.

Consequently, it was seen as absolutely essential that the material should be subjugated to the logic of some form of classification so as to give it internal cohesion and convey a sense that the goals set were being approached in a methodical way. On the other hand, the manner of classification is of the greatest importance, since the manner chosen to organise the material will – directly or indirectly – determine the quality of the final conclusions.

Transformations

After these essential explanations, the time has come to describe the system of classification. The element of symbolism is obviously predominant in any examination of the Parthenon; consequently, it cannot but occupy a central position in the system of classification. On the other hand, there would be relatively little to gain from a strict classification into symbolic 'types': the symbolic property can probably be taken as read in the appreciation of the Parthenon, rather than serving as a *desideratum*, and in practice it is easy to mistake the boundaries between the types. Since such a classification would be inadequate, we need the help of a higher class of correlation, one with adaptive flexibility, the power of abstraction and, over and above that, the ability to function in conjunction with the symbolic categories.

Our search ultimately leads us to the art of literary devices, which seems to fulfil these needs. We have borrowed from it certain terms used in conjunction with *metaplasm* – paragoge, crasis, apocope and aphaeresis – as a convenient means of identifying four distinct categories of phenomena. In this task, metaplasm, "a generic term for any alteration of a word by adjunction, suppression, or inversion of sounds or letters",[4] is obviously being used metaphorically to connote the transformations which pure reason (*logos*) undergoes as it is funnelled through ideology.

The simultaneous use of a number of terms derived from rhetoric redefines the problem as one of the appropriate combination of elements from the two sets of matrices.[5] The basic four-way division can be further sub-divided into groups of similar phenomena wherever needed, so as to facilitate the classification of the examples into positions of affinity. Nonetheless, it should be borne in mind that this approach does not reduce the element of arbitrariness – nor, indeed, was any conscious effort made to do so. As a result, the same examples could (theoretically, at least) have functioned equally effectively in other positions or, when repeated, have been lit from different angles on each occasion.

Paragoge

Paragoge is the addition of "a letter or syllable to the end of the word"[6] so as to satisfy a specified need while retaining the original meaning. In our case, this can be associated with *antithesis* (the "contrasting of two ideas"), *antilogy* ("a contradiction in terms or ideas"), or *antimetathesis* (connecting two words of similar sound but of different meaning).

The fulcrum for this section is the distortion of time as a mechanism for classifying and/or isolating events. This, then, is the place for everything connected with the comparison between past and present, with the Parthenon as the central point of reference. On the one hand, this gives ample opportunity for Greeks to express their discontent: the more brilliant the past appears to be, the more wretched the present seems. In this respect, an element of the category of apologue, which we shall be encountering in the next section, would seem to be inherent in comparison.

On the other hand, a synchronic correlation can also be achieved using approximately the same materials. This approximation – that is, the lack of clarity in which the relationship is enveloped, while in actuality violence is being done to the truth – is, as we have seen, a component part of paragoge. Here we have a game of successive correlations which leads, by logic, to a paradox. Thus, the relationship between the Parthenon (of the Golden Age, fig. 1) and Greece (the modern country, fig. 2) can be shifted first to the relationship between the Parthenon (in its current form) and the city which lies at its feet (modern Athens) and then, by extension, to the relationship between the architecture of the city at that time and the architecture of the present (Greek or foreign).

The synchronic dimension is concealed within the diachronic dimension – as if one were folded into the other. In appreciating the Parthenon (even as a sublime

3. Constantine Parthenis: Around the Acropolis, 1909; Athens, private collection.

4. Nikos Hadjikyriakos-Ghikas: View of Athens; 1940; Athens, private collection.

work of art outside place and time), we are indirectly making comparisons. The comparisons are not so much with other masterpieces in architectural history (for we know that they are not comparable), but with what we perceive directly every day in the built environment around us. In other words, the Parthenon retains its value because nothing has ever been found to surpass it – even more tellingly, because we are dissatisfied with the things we propose ourselves or make in the modern city.

In order for the comparisons to function properly, some degree of simplification is necessary. The Parthenon today is, of course, not Pericles' Parthenon: its content (meaning by that not just its physical being) has been most severely adulterated. And yet there is a magical way in which it is deemed to be the same. In this case, suppression proves the power of the mechanism of antilogy. By severing the bonds with the specific place and time (that is, with the historical environment which surrounded the Parthenon at that time),[7] we create a mesh of completely different relationships which are then deliberately ignored and leave free space for the elaboration of the ideological undertaking.

This confusion of chronological boundaries which we have noted as a characteristic of paragoge could, perhaps, be the most important reason why we are interested in monuments in a more general sense. We are transported into the past, detaching the monument from history, in the service of needs which are predominantly connected with our own search for identity.

Our demand that the Parthenon should provide an answer to the urgent questions of the time, as if it were a kind of Sphinx, is equally paradoxical. Anything which stands outside time, as a sacred object, is supposed to have the power of clairvoyance, of seeing the present as it

truly is and of predicting the future with guaranteed accuracy. In this capacity, the Parthenon is enlisted either to make official revolutionary breaks with the past or as a sacrifice on the altar of progress. We have to admit that this ambivalent relationship is an imported one. The tyrannical presence of the Parthenon in Greece is so overwhelming as to leave no scope for negotiation, while the foreign visionaries who were so bold as to make such sacrilegious use of the symbol of the Parthenon were to have very little impact in Greece.

To sum up, we can distinguish three areas of evidence: that which directly concerns modern Athens as town planning in practice; that which compares the morphological and ontological substance of contemporary and ancient architecture; and that which weighs up the significance of the monument for art today. Wherever we look there are comparisons and, above all, generalisations which lead easily to rhetorical excesses. In each case, the mechanism of antilogy is applied with infuriating accuracy and effectiveness. What is of particular interest is to identify the points of similarity recognised in each case as the basis for comparison in the correlations.

Crowning glory or dunghill? Around the middle of the nineteenth century, the tormenting question was whether the capital city of Athens, as it developed, had managed to escape from its 'Turkish' past and resemble the European cities which it took as its model. Thus, a "general panorama" of Athens in 1853 contained the optimistic view that Athens could lay claim to the description of 'Queen of Cities', with the Acropolis as its crowning glory.[8] Shortly afterwards, another writer contended that Athens would become "the first city of the East" since it possessed "an inexhaustible fund of architecture and art in

5. *The Acropolis and the Anafiotika district. Photographic archive of the Benaki Museum.*

the form of the incomparable relics of the Acropolis", etc.[9] Now that Queen Amalia had embarked on the task of improving the area around the Acropolis, he continued, we could already imagine the access road lined with trees, and could think that we saw "the city of Athens crowned with a brilliant, precious wreath bearing, at its peak, like priceless diamonds, the unique, inimitable antiquities in Pentelic marble which attract the admiration of all the civilised world".[10]

On the one hand, then, we have the vision of a city worthy of its ancient glory, and on the other, we have reality: in the same period, there were complaints that the area around the Acropolis had become "the dunghill of the capital".[11] Thirty years later, the Anafiotika quarter was still provoking odious comparisons: "What Greek, what person feeling mere affection for the much-hymned remnants of the works of ancient Greek genius, could fail to look without grave spiritual pain upon the disgrace wrought on the sacred rock of the Acropolis by dwellings whose wretchedness can hardly be justified even by the destitution of their tenants?" No: Athens could still look like a Turkish village (fig. 5).[12]

Despite this, the visionary discourse was not overcome by the passage of time. Early in the twentieth century, Angelos Tanagras imagined the Athens of the future, and described it, *inter alia*: as "A queen of cities with all the attractions and all the natural beauties, with the Acropolis in her heart and her feet dipped in the waves at Phaleron...".[13] In 1915, things were regrettable again: the building of hovels began along Acropolis Avenue, and it seemed that – thirty years after the decision was taken to demolish Anafiotika – visitors would soon be climbing to

the rock past the washhouses of these humble dwellings: "And the effluvia of chop-houses will drift up to the Parthenon itself, as the incense of the absolute indifference of the administration".[14]

As Athens grew, of course, so more and more buildings were erected and the noose tightened around the Acropolis. Apart from the uproar which broke out over the position of the enormous Palais de Justice by Alexandros Nikoloudis, which Venizelos planned to build on the Makriyannis site,[15] there was also the fuss over the proposal to move the School of Fine Arts to a location next to the Acropolis, which once more outraged foreign commentators.[16] In 1955, history repeated itself: before anyone could intervene, an apartment block began to rise on Dionysiou Areopagitou St. It was proposed that construction be halted, and Kostas Biris went so far as to suggest that the site be turned into an open space so as to reveal the view of the Acropolis.[17] Visual contact with the Acropolis was already endangered. Within a few decades, however, not even that would be of interest to anyone any more, since the Athenian smog would hide the monument even more frequently and effectively from the eyes of the city's residents.

The concept of this outrageous symbiosis between the Parthenon and contemporary town planning practices was well illustrated by a cartoon of an illegal holiday house on the Acropolis (fig. 6), and a similar idea lies behind the sketch of a basketball net in the temple itself which we shall be seeing later on.

The eternal presence. In an age in which the search for

6. *Cartoon by Kyr(iakopoulos) showing an illegal building on the Acropolis. Source: D. Philippides,* Yia tin elliniki poli *('On the Greek City'), Athens 1990.*

an ideal model for the arts was an urgent problem of interest to every Greek creative artist, Lysandros Kaftantzoglou undertook the task of importing into Greece the views of an Italian sculptor and transferring – in its entirety – the ideological backing for them: "... the relics of Pheidias in the Parthenon are capable, by themselves, of shaping the new art of sculpture, and of leading it back to the true and glorious path marked out by our forefathers, free of any tasteless foreign theories".[18]

The way in which these promptings were implemented does not lie within the scope of this text, but let it be said that they acted as expected; for those who wished to see affinities at all costs – for the foreigners, at least – the proof could be found: "This pronaos, the little tower of that megaron, that spacious platform, this splendid staircase, the Caryatids, the fine decorations – everything is testimony to the fact that the soul of ancient Greece still lives".[19] But the situation changed once neo-Classicism – which was ideal for comparisons – had been abandoned. The introduction of Art Nouveau into Athens, for example, caused black thoughts in the minds of a writer who certainly had little enthusiasm for such innovations: "Yet at the foot of the Acropolis and facing the Parthenon, the sight of this new-fangled, uncontrolled Art Nouveau, with its crazy lines and its outrageous curves, is a sad one...".[20]

In the post-War period, the question came up again, though not in relation to some 'style' which was out of place near the Parthenon:[21] this time, it was contemporary architecture in its entirety, and we thus moved from the realm of form to that of content. Spyros Melas imagined himself walking through the neighbourhoods of Athens with an architect; here is part of their dialogue:

"[...] Convenience, only convenience, convenience and nothing more! That is the great modern idea – and the great modern disease. [...] Just look at the Acropolis: how admirably its profile stands out against the blue. [...] That work is a distillation of life, of the struggle against death, of final, magnificent victory. [...] What have those little houses to say to that, what can our office blocks say – even the largest of them – and what can the skyscrapers of New York or Chicago reply?"[22]

The 'Dialogue on the Acropolis' of Panayotis Michelis, written in 1937, takes a similar direction in its imaginary meeting on the Rock between two men of the arts:

"The Amateur: And what about the white houses of the islands?

The Aestheticist: Those are emotional outpourings regulated into a picturesque whole, wedging on the hillside, frightening the sea. But the Parthenon is a work: it is in itself an entire self-contained world, and it has all the intellectual demands, standing in terrible contrast to the narrow, individual joys of a detached house or of picturesque beauty".[23]

Μετά τον Παρθενώνα... τι;

7. A photograph from an interview with Ileana Tounda. Source: Tachydromos, no. 9 (1868), 1 March 1990.

Sacrilege and awe. Given the way in which the sanctity of the Parthenon has been projected on a global scale, it was only natural that it should have provoked a reaction on the part of the iconoclasts of the early twentieth century. At a time when the concept of the 'modern' was assuming revolutionary dimensions, the explosive presence of the Futurist Marinetti stirred up the stagnant waters of Greece. Deliberately provocative, he chose the Parthenon as his target: "My dear Greek students, admit that the Parthenon is to you the decayed, grand stove of Greece. [...]

"Rather than the Parthenon, I prefer the blue and white flag of living Greece which flutters at its foot and on the spine of its granite base. Raise it quickly, as the banner of Futuristic art on the reconstructed metope!"[24]

A few months later, in July 1933, the most important representatives of modern architecture gathered in Athens for the fourth International CIAM Congress. Le Corbusier, who knew how to make the most of every dramatic gesture, delayed his appearance by an hour and a half or so. When he finally arrived, he said in a bewitched whisper, "Oh dear, I forgot all about you. I've been on the Acropolis".[25] Marinetti's committed theatricality failed to convince, but Le Corbusier, just as 'subversive' in his own way, charmed everyone in a single phrase.

A differing kind of questioning was raised in an un-

8. *A view of the Parthenon in 1941. Source: Kostas Paraschos,* I Katochi, photographika documenta 1941-1944 *('The Occupation, Photographic Documents 1941-1944'), Athens 1979.*

published lecture of 1966 by Dimitris Pikionis, who was known for his early reservations about the Modern Movement. Pikionis also had his doubts about the Parthenon as sublime art – in comparison with the Archaic temples. His preferences were based on the concept of the beginning of art: "This was a divine moment, and thanks to them, thanks to this [authenticity], they were more perfect, more sublime than what was to come later, including the Parthenon. In them, there were none of the things destined to happen with the Parthenon."

One more recent trace of the awe which can dishearten us from all activity is connected with the challenge which the Parthenon represents for every creative artist: "It is disgraceful that we still boast of the Acropolis and the Parthenon as the features which characterise us" (fig. 7).[26] Yet in essence even this reaction is operating in accordance with the rules of appreciation: sacred objects are called into question in order to renew our assessment of them. In other words, this area would fit in equally harmoniously with the next literary device, since it deliberately sidesteps the content of the Parthenon.

Crasis

Crasis is "the contraction of two syllables into one", that is, an entire section of a word disappears leaving no perceptible trace. Two additional rhetorical terms could possibly be connected to crasis: *apologue* ("a narrative illustrating some truth", hence the possibility of conveying a certain shade of meaning), and *metaphor* ("transfer from one meaning to another based on an impression or interpretation"). A feature shared by apologue and metaphor which connects them to crasis is a certain change in

the constituent proportions of shades of meaning so as to emphasise a certain part of that meaning. As a result, certain delicate connotations are sacrificed, despite the apparent gain in clarity or directness of meaning.

More specifically, crasis is applied to three major areas of information about the Parthenon. The first consists of the affair of the Elgin Marbles, the second of the commemorative/ceremonial use of the Parthenon, and the third of references in literature, journalism and aesthetics. Taking them in order, in the first case the loss of reality is read as romantic naivety, in the second the transformation of the Parthenon into a national war memorial degrades the monument to the status of a directly utilitarian object, and in the third the concept of *locus* is elevated to the level of an eternal constant.

Is there, one wonders, a correspondence between the three areas of information and the symbolic categories we have described? The answer is, not necessarily: even if there were, it would be difficult to generalise to cover every instance.

The Elgin Marbles. In the earliest Greek reference it has proved possible to find, one of the three illustrations accompanying a text on the British Museum in the periodical *Pandora* (1851), bears the caption "the Elgin Hall".[27] This was reasonable enough, since the Elgin Marbles were certainly the Museum's most famous exhibits. But in 1880 another serial began: the *Illustrated London News* proposed that the Elgin Marbles ought to be returned to Greece.[28] Ten more years passed, bringing us to 1890/91, and a large-scale campaign was launched for the return of the Marbles, once more on the initiative of a non-Greek, the British man of letters Frederic Harrison.[29] Then there was silence, until 1948, when the news came that the Elgin Marbles had been brought out of the stores where they had remained for safety during the War and were back in their Hall.[30] The fact that this was news in Greece does, of course, have something to tell us, but in practice there was no follow-up. One insignificant reference follows[31] before a fresh upsurge of activity in 1961; here the immediate stimulus is unknown to us, but the initiative contained all the essential Greek purple patches and the usual British refusals.[32] Official promises were, at best, politely vague, but this did not downhearten the Greeks, who embarked on the discussion of where to put the sculptures when (not if) they were returned.[33]

If all this sounds familiar,[34] we are not to blame. The exploitation of the Elgin Marbles by both sides can only be played out again and again by the same moves. There are foreign philhellenes whose motives are pure and who wish to rectify an injustice, just as there are Greek philhellenes who make a fuss out of self-interest or naivety. If any other monument were involved, the affair would be a joke, to

286

9. The sixteenth anniversary of the liberation of Athens. Source: Eleftheria, 12.10.1960.

say the least, but things are different where the Parthenon is concerned. The Parthenon, as a national symbol, belongs by right to this country and to the people which still lives in the land of its forefathers. As the legend goes, the exiled Caryatid is mourned by her sisters in Greece,[35] and that means that there is no place here for conventions or international agreements.

All for a flag. Zero hour for the Acropolis coincided with the establishment on the sacred rock, in 1833, of a Bavarian battalion. The first garrison commander, Major Palingen, wrote: "That night, the full moon shed its honeysweet light across Attica and the proud ruins, creating a marvellous image. I pitched my tent under the columns of the Parthenon. [..] At night, with my eyes open, I watched with amazement as all the passions of my youth took on flesh and blood. I saw Pericles on the Acropolis of Athens, Socrates with his pupils, and Demosthenes and Euripides entering the temple of Athena."

But lost in these dreams, the Bavarians forgot to raise the Greek flag. An old sea-captain from Chios, anchored at Piraeus, noticed even at that distance that there was no flag flying over the Acropolis. He went up to the Rock, and asked the Bavarians to have the flag run up over the Parthenon. They agreed, and before long the captain's son and some Athenians clambered to the top of the temple to instal it.[36]

In this scene we can see many of the representative elements which we will also encounter in the later use of the Acropolis. The identification of the Acropolis as the symbolic 'navel' of the nation could not but follow a course parallel to that of the destiny of Greece. Suddenly, in the

midst of the delirium caused by the expansionist triumphs of the Balkan Wars, a certain "K.T." wrote to a newspaper summing up the universal passion: "Dear Sir; Do you not agree that the time has come to raise a vast Greek flag on the pediment of the Parthenon, one as visible as the Acropolis itself, from the surrounding mountains and even as far away as the sea, in memory of these glorious days?"[37] There is no great distance from this point to the disgrace of the swastika flying from the Acropolis.[38] The German occupying forces were perfectly well aware of the significance of such a final gesture, because the Acropolis was the destination to which they headed as soon as they entered Athens. The eloquent photograph in the following day's papers showed the Greek and German flags side by side. The message was unmistakable: everything was over (fig. 8).[39]

The flag made its appearance again in the seemingly endless series of anniversary ceremonies on the Acropolis to mark the end of the German occupation. As early as 1959 we can see the inevitable codification of the symbol: in front is a vast flag, carried horizontally by girls dressed in national costume, with the official guests crowding in behind (fig. 9).[40] The twentieth anniversary happened to coincide with political changes in Greece, whereupon the ceremony assumed other dimensions and there was a plain attempt to exploit the monument as a symbol of renewal in political life.[41] Yet this classic reversal had first taken place two years earlier, when anti-government demonstrations climaxed with the raising, in secret by night on the Acropolis,[42] of a banner bearing the legend "114", a reference to the demand for constitutional legality. What happened in the meantime does not concern us here, but we can move straight to the 1988 photograph of the striking state-sector engineers in front of the Parthenon (fig. 10):[43] a group of agitators disguised as visitors, equipped with a banner bearing their demands.

Our search for the starting-point of such occasions –

10. Striking state-sector engineers in front of the Parthenon. Source: Eleftherotypia, 16.12.1988.

which detach the monument from its historical lethe by violence and connect it (sometimes painfully) with the present – will lead us back to the occasional upsurges of patriotic fervour. At such times, the Acropolis is among the places which carry a great emotional charge and are the venues for similar demonstrations. To mark the anniversary of 25 March (the outbreak of the War of Independence) in 1883, a procession was organised from the Temple of Olympian Zeus (always a meeting-point before ceremonies and other festivities) to the Acropolis, where there was a banquet to the accompaniment of music, etc.[44] Here we can see the convergence of two major strands in the tradition of ceremonies on the sacred rock: the formal tradition of processions, the raising of flags and speeches, and the unofficial tradition of souvenir photographs, which we shall be coming to later.

Self-advertisement and set design. Along general lines, performances on the Acropolis – and in the Parthenon, in particular – have varied in accordance with the intentions that lay behind them. We can discern three uses: as a point of reference to ancient glories, as the place *par excellence* for meetings with persons of recognised fame, and as a pretext for drawing contemporary examples. In accordance with this rationale, an encounter with the Parthenon can be an echo of the impressive humanist tradition, which Greek newspapers are always willing to re-

11. A scene from the film The Roots of Liberty. *The photograph shows the royal couple and the journalist Severine on the Acropolis. Source: El. Vlachou,* Stigmiotypa... ('Incidents...'), *Athens 1987.*

print, either spontaneously (so as to flatter public opinion) or to order (depending on political conditions). The humanist tradition does not cease to be applicable even when all the evidence points to its having vanished; or is that, perhaps, precisely the point at which its invocation becomes a matter of urgency? It is hard to tell.

The feeling of giving a live performance on the Acropolis was conveyed in exemplary fashion – given that he was a man of the theatre – by the actor Mounet-Sully in 1899: "The artist, in a state of ecstasy, stood before each step in the Propylaea in silence or uttering mere monosyllables of admiration. [...]

"'It is a miracle ... it is mad', Mounet-Sully repeated, and then added:

"'If it were possible to perform the Oedipus here, in the open air inside the Parthenon...'".[45]

The recent history of the Acropolis can boast of countless examples of platitudinous references to the monument whose purpose is, indirectly, to consolidate the prestige of the maker of the reference or of the object being connected with the Parthenon. The references have to be platitudinous because the code of communication within the common culture can then function more effectively. This is a broader issue, and so for the time being we shall leave unanswered questions such as whether the message has to be platitudinous in order to get across, and what consequences this has.

One typical example is provided by the impressions of the monument of a certain G. Deschamps, published in a foreign-language review and reprinted in Greek: "I have to admit that the Parthenon is the only monument which did not generate in me a feeling of disappointment. [...] No painting and no imitation in sculpture can convey an exact idea of this architectural miracle."[46]

It was only to be expected that sooner or later the so-called 'Great Idea' of reconstituting the Byzantine Empire would enlist such an apt symbol in its service. The most appropriate way of doing this was by linking antiquity and Byzantium. That was the aim of Lambros Asteris when, in 1892, he cast his mind back to a book which Panayotis Kalevras had published in 1861 under the title *The Most Complete Draft Constitution for the Future Greek Empire of Byzantium*. Article One of the 'constitution' laid down that the national symbol would be "the sun, radiant". This phrase had stuck in Asteris' mind: "And whenever I come to an open place and confront the Parthenon and see the sun shedding its light on it, the phrase 'the sun, radiant' always springs to mind and I cannot take my eyes off it".[47]

The task of transmuting the Great Idea into a literary form was undertaken by D.A. Anastasopoulos in a short story: "Up on the heights of the Acropolis I stood vigilant that night. I had seen the last kisses of the sun brush

12. Iakovos Rizos: Athenian Evening, 1897, oils; Athens, National Gallery.

13. Edward Dodwell: the Acropolis as a castle in Turkish times. Source: E. Dodwell, Views in Greece, London 1821; Athens, Gennadios Library.

across the beautiful carvings of the Parthenon, and the aethereal ancient dream slip through the multicoloured reflections of the sculptures...";[48] and a little further on: "It was the ideal essence of the old Greeks hailing all the ancient renown in the guise of Christian blessedness: the Greek *logos* in the outline of a true God, a Greek God".[49]

The ambitions of Spyridon Paganelis in his short story 'The Good Friday Procession Seen from the Acropolis' are plainer to the eye: "Seated on its topmost step, and resting my back on the base of a truncated column, I looked up at the starry sky and then at the rest of the ruined temple. [...] From the ruins of the Parthenon and the vortex of my thoughts, I turned my gaze to the living, vigilant city, whose voice and existence were transformed into a prayer at that time and on that night." Seeing the candles of the Good Friday procession, Paganelis draws a parallel between the festival of the Panathenaea and the modern religious feast.[50]

In every instance, the Parthenon continues to be a valuable backdrop – indeed, it is sometimes the only *raison d'être* of the entire performance (fig. 12). In the Socratic dialogue conceived by Herriot, once Prime Minister of France, the philosopher is put on the Acropolis a year before his execution by Callicles.[51]

This potential was exploited by German propaganda during the Occupation, when Professor Praschniker of Berlin gave a lecture in Athens on the subject of the Parthenon. By describing the Parthenon as a "superb hymn to the culture and Art of ancient Greece, of which it has to be regarded as the zenith", etc.,[52] the Professor found a roundabout way of stressing the spiritual and intellectual affinity between Greece and Germany.

On other occasions, the reference may be historically accurate, as was the case with the Classicist Pechet, who delivered a lecture in Paris (reprinted in Greek translation) on the subject of: "The Greek Miracle. Pilgrimage to the Acropolis: Chateaubriand and Renan in Athens."[53] Renan, in particular, was regarded as 'one of us'; and simply because he wrote the famous 'Prayer on the Acropolis'. The fact that the content of this singular orison had nothing to do with the monuments on the rock was of no importance whatever: "Oh goddess with the gleaming eyes, I was born to barbarian parents, in the land of the pure, virtuous Cimmerians, who live on the shore of a dark, rocky and forever windswept sea...".[54]

Or, lastly, the reference can be a mere pretext for a critical attitude towards the past, as in the case of the dialogue by Michelis from which we have already quoted. Correspondingly, when Robert Sherwood gave the title *Acropolis* to a play staged in London, he was providing the historical background necessary to set up a period drama.[55]

Perhaps the orotund words of Angelos Sikelianos come

closest, in their Nietzschian grandeur, to the ineffable character of the Parthenon: "As soon as we approach its columns or find ourselves among them, the indefinable or slumbering inner harmony which existed deep within us immediately manifests itself in our nerves and in all our being, [...] and also in this 'living', worldly, universal temple, while at the same time we become detached from the sphere of our narrowly dogmatic and rationalising thought, moving in the direction of a self which is as yet unshaped and is essentially potential".[56]

Apocope

A third category of metaplasm is apocope, the "omission of a letter or syllable at the end of the word", a synonym for which is *ecthlipse*. This could be associated with *metonymy* ("the designation of one thing by the name of some element belonging to the same whole"), since there is an obvious relationship between the two. So as to be as close as possible to the intentions of this section, we could also use the term elision as a metaphor for a shortened meaning which has lost none of its principal contents.

In the case of the Parthenon, we can distinguish three areas which involve the capacity of apocope: the litany of visits to the sacred rock, with the photographs taken there (together with the suicides who jump from the Acropolis, visiting the Underworld through an entrance marked by a given place-name); the figures of speech and cartoons which testify to the centrality of the concept of the Acropolis; and, lastly, the reactions of the anonymous public – the Greek people. In the first case, the use of the Parthenon as an authentic stage set is a guarantee of formality and social publicity. A visit to it pays honour to the national consciousness and offers as much of a taste as possible of eternity to those who enjoy international (or, more rarely, local) fame. In the second case, a representation of the Parthenon as a hieroglyph can stand as a surrogate for the entire city, symbolising it as a whole. This sets up a dialogue with the concept of the city which we encountered in the section on paragoge. Here there is no apparent effort to evaluate, although the presence of the Parthenon acts indirectly as an ironic reminder of the 'glory' that has now submerged beneath the weight of the insignificance all around it. In the third case, the 'people' does not penetrate the depths of the conceptual content of the Parthenon, but, with its instinctive and pedestrian reactions, deprives the monument of its transcendentality and converts it into an easily accessible symbol of antiquity, vulgarising the dictates of the national ideology. Whether this is an act of destruction or purgation we shall be seeing later on.

The point which the three categories of symbolism have in common is the superficiality of their involvement with the monument, an involvement which is unthinking

290

14. *Kallergis gives a banquet on the Acropolis for the British and French. Source:* Illustrated London News; *Athens, collection of Stavros and Stella Stavridis.*

and thus conventional. Since no particular intervention in its content is called for, its meaning declines to a matter of secondary importance and dwindles to something which serves the purposes of a mere transaction. This is the vindication for the use of apocope: the essential content of the Parthenon remains untouched, since nothing can come near it.

The pilgrimage becomes an established custom. In their souvenir photographs on the Acropolis, which we have come to take for granted, famous or quite unknown people gain in significance through being imprinted on paper with the Parthenon in the background, losing their circumstantial and mortal characteristics and stealing some of the monumental nature of the Rock. In other words, they are translated into what we might call monuments in the flesh.

The codification of the photograph as an infallible document was not, of course, present at the start of recent history. Perhaps things were better that way, because the Acropolis which King Othon took over in 1833 was little more than a vast pile of ruins, fortifications and later buildings (fig. 13). Its condition at this time was recorded in drawings, but they are never quite the same thing.[57] As a result, we cannot reconstruct exactly what happened – for instance – during the first ceremony

on the Acropolis, in 1834, attended by von Klenze, as Miliarakis has preserved it for us.[58]

Similarly, we lack any iconographic details of the commemorative meetings of the Archaeological Society, held on the Acropolis each spring.[59] The only exception, for obvious reasons (occupation by the British and French in 1854-57), was the "magnificent banquet" given on the Acropolis by General Kallergis for 160 persons "of the highest standing" (fig. 14)[60], to the strains of a military band.

This lack of information was rectified by the introduction of systematic photography. Although it is not among the first hesitant iconographic documents, the front-page photograph of 60 bishops and archbishops preserved for posterity on the stylobate of the Parthenon (with the banner of the Ayia Lavra Monastery in the centre) is nonetheless impressive.[61] This paradoxical scene brings together two ill-assorted worlds which, at this specific point in time, are emphatically projected as one and the same. This was the time at which the Great Idea was coming close to being given a coat of reality. Similar linkages were also being tried out in the theatre: a few years later, a revue included a scene in which the King was shown "pulling the Parthenon and St Sophia at the end of two little ropes".[62]

Apart from being an undeniable document, a photograph also creates the illusion of direct experience. Under

15. *Somerset Maugham on the Acropolis.* Source: Eleftheria, 8.5.1953.

16. *Eisenhower inspects the Parthenon by helicopter in 1952. Photograph by K. Megalokonomou.*

normal conditions, this is desirable: after the War, for instance, there was significance in the selection of those who were photographed on the Acropolis and then promoted by the newspapers as notable personalities. From writers such as Maxwell Anderson[63] and Somerset Maugham (fig. 15)[64] to the Allied Supremo Eisenhower (fig. 16)[65], Dulles and Stassen[66], we could move gradually on to Oppenheimer[67], the British dance troupe 'The Johnson Girls'[68] or Jackie Kennedy.[69] In general, there was an increase in the extent to which the personalities were glamourous or society figures, as we can see in the caption to a photograph of the Speaker of the Austrian Parliament: "... and he did not omit to visit the Acropolis for what has become the established custom of a pilgrimage to the Parthenon".[70] 'Established' means conventional, and therefore devoid of content. Official or important visitors eventually merged into the anonymous crowd, and the glory which, in vain, they tried to snatch from the monument was reduced to equally stylised poses[71] whose recipients were now only the subjects of the photographs themselves.

In other cases, the photograph had to be promoted as a 'scandal' or an 'event of unusual importance' in order to gain universal value. One early case of this was the ap-

pearance of Mona Paiva, a well-known dancer at the Paris Opera, who succeeded in dancing nude in the Parthenon. She was captured by the famous photographer Nelly, and two of the photographs – one with Mona Paiva clothed and the other nude – were published together (fig. 18).[72] Similar cases included the engagement of Crown Prince Constantine to Princess Anna-Maria, which was sealed with a visit to the sun-drenched Acropolis[73] and the announcement that a fictional wedding between the protagonists of the popular TV serial *The Bold and the Beautiful* was to be filmed on the Acropolis (fig. 19).[74]

Let us return to the ritual among ordinary people of being photographed on the Acropolis. Despite technological advances, memory has preserved the figure of the photographer on his pitch, in his white uniform and with his primitive wooden-cased equipment, taking orders, photographing and printing on the spot. Every family made the pilgrimage to the Acropolis at least once in life, and a photograph with the Parthenon in the background would always be taken. These documents provide a clear expression of individual attitudes and family relationships (fig. 20): the stances are more or less the same strictly defined poses which the same people would adopt in the photographer's studio in front of the fake scenery.

17. Nelly: the dancer Nikolska semi-nude in the Parthenon, 1929. Photographic archive of the Benaki Museum.

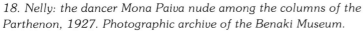

18. Nelly: the dancer Mona Paiva nude among the columns of the Parthenon, 1927. Photographic archive of the Benaki Museum.

The concept of photography would be defective without a mention of its direct exploitation as an element in automatic promotion. Just as the individual or the group acquires proof of his or their presence on the Rock in the photographs they take away with them, so, with the publication of a photograph accentuating the prestige of an event or of certain interests, respect for the monument is translated directly into information which can be exploited. One indicative example is the advertisement for Madame Raymond's school of gymnastics and classical dance, which announced its forthcoming appearance at an Athenian theatre with a photograph of four girl students of the school in typically 'ancient' poses in front of the columns of the Parthenon.[75]

The object of using the Parthenon for advertisements is not necessarily so as to serve the desire of individuals or state functionaries for posthumous renown (fig. 21). At a time at which the aeroplane was establishing itself as beyond question the modern means of travel, the monument most emphatically dominated advertising pictures of this wonderful machine. For those who know of Le Corbusier's controversial linking of the Parthenon and the motor-car in his *Towards a New Architecture* (see p. 47, figs. 26, 27),[76] the examples from Greece

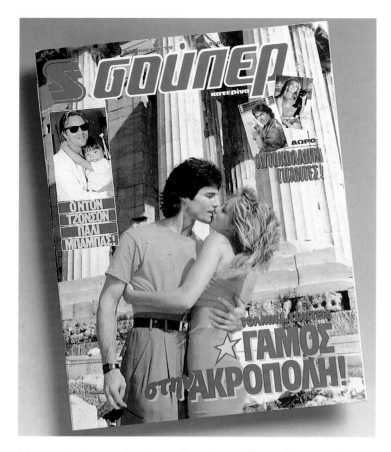

19. A wedding on the Acropolis. Source: Super Katerina, August 1989.

20. A souvenir photograph on the Acropolis; Athens, collection of Dimitris Philippides.

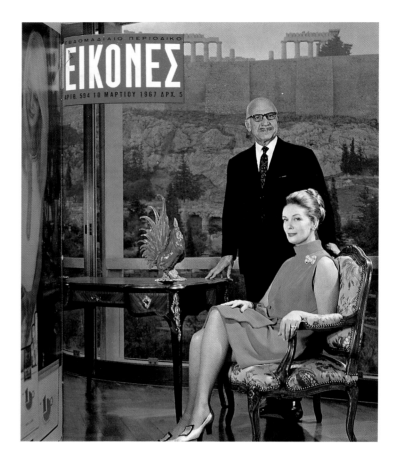

21. 'The Governor of the Bank of Greece and Mrs Xenophon Zolotas in their home in Dionysiou Areopagitou St'. Source: Eikones, 10.3.1967 (cover).

acquire an ironic correspondence.

In 1930, Venizelos himself went up in a German Junkers aeroplane during a demonstration flight above Athens. The plane, microscopic in size by comparison with the monument, is shown flying over a corner of the Parthenon as if completing its broken pediment (fig. 22).[77] A second photograph, taken at a time when general preparations for war were being made, shows the Acropolis reduced to negligible size by a repellent air-raid siren.[78] A third leaps rather unexpectedly out of a historical narrative, to whose story it bears little connection: "German bombers raid the Greek capital...".[79] A fourth and last comes from another period: here the aircraft form the word 'NATO' in the sky to mark the Alliance's anniversary; the photograph shows the Parthenon from the typical angle, and the formation of aircraft are in the background.[80]

This image of an aircraft in conjunction with the Parthenon thus provides an unexpected connection between a respected tradition and modern technology. The full-page advertisement for Lufthansa (fig. 23) is aimed at precisely this: "A country with a historical tradition as long as that of Greece knows how to appreciate the airline with the most modern equipment".[81] Nor is it necessary for the

ΟΥ ΓΙΟΥΓΚΕΡΣ ΕΙΣ ΤΑΣ ΑΘΗΝΑΣ

Τὸ γερμανικὸν ἀεροπλάνον ὑπεράνω τῆς Ἀκροπόλεως κατὰ
τὴν χθεσινὴν ἐπιδεικτικήν του πτῆσιν

22. 'From yesterday's demonstration of the Junkers aeroplane in Athens'. Source: Eleftheron Vima, 23.10.1930.

reference to the wonders of technology to confine itself to the symbolism of the aeroplane. Some advertisements project contemporary interventions in the Parthenon: take, for example, the company which made sealing compounds ("The Parthenon trusted us to seal it: what about you?"[82] fig. 25), or the multinational which sings the praises of the lighting of the monument: "Philips. From the splendour of the Parthenon to the mystery of space" (see p. 24, fig. 7).[83] The Attiko Metro company (fig. 24)

24. The logo of the Attiko Metro S.A.

Μια χώρα με μεγάλη ιστορική παράδοση μπορεί και εκτιμά την πιο σύγχρονα εξοπλισμένη αεροπορική εταιρία.

Μακρόχρονοι, ιστορικοί αλλά και σύγχρονοι – οικονομικοί, πολιτιστικοί, επιστημονικοί – δεσμοί συνδέουν την Ελλάδα και τη Γερμανία.

Αυτούς τους δεσμούς προωθεί και η Lufthansa. Με 30 κατ' ευθείαν πτήσεις κάθε εβδομάδα απο την Αθήνα, τη Θεσσαλονίκη και το Ηράκλειο στη Γερμανία.

Με τα πιο σύγχρονα αεροσκάφη που σας πηγαίνουν σε πάνω απο 160 πόλεις σ'όλο τον κόσμο. Θα χαρούμε να σας καλώς ορίσουμε κοντά μας.

Lufthansa

23. An advertisement for the airline Lufthansa.

25. An advertisement for the Calna insulation company.

ο Παρθενώνας μας εμπιστεύτηκε τη στεγάνωση του εσείς;

Για να τοποθετηθεί ο γερανός μέσα στο ναό του Παρθενώνα για την αναστήλωσή του, έπρεπε επάνω στο μαρμάρινο δάπεδο της εποχής του Περικλή να κατασκευαστεί δάπεδο από μπετόν.
Ταυτόχρονα όμως έπρεπε να προστατευθεί το μαρμάρινο δάπεδο από την υγρασία, που εγκλωβισμένη δημιουργεί μύκητες και διαβρώνει τα μάρμαρα. Η μεμβράνη LESCHUPLAST κλήθηκε να δώσει την λύση, όχι τυχαία, αλλά γιατί είναι δοκιμασμένο και καταξιωμένο υλικό και σε άλλες δύσκολες εφαρμογές.
Η Αρχαιολογική Εταιρεία Αθηνών μας εμπιστεύθηκε ανεπιφύλακτα το πρόβλημα της στεγάνωσης του Παρθενώνα. Περιμένουμε και εσάς για να αντιμετωπίσουμε με την ίδια υπευθυνότητα και αποτελεσματικότητα το δικό σας πρόβλημα στεγάνωσης.

calna ΕΠΕ
• ΟΞΥΜΑΧΑ • ΠΥΡΙΜΑΧΑ • ΜΟΝΩΤΙΚΑ
Αθήνα – Ν. Πλαστήρα 15 – Νεο Ψυχικό
Τηλ. 67.16.877 – 67.26.278
TELEX: 21-8997 ELKE

26. Cartoon by Bost(antzoglou) entitled 'The Wise Vizier', with the Acropolis in the background. Source: Eleftheria, 24.4.1960.

27. Cartoon entitled 'The Acropolis decked out as a ship for the Christmas holidays'. Source: Asty, 210/1.10.1889.

linked the Parthenon with the pioneering technological work being done on the new subway.

These last cases have brought us into another category of use: that of the specialised intervention in the monument which has taken place throughout its modern history. But before dealing with that, we must take a glance at the more abstract areas in which the Parthenon has been used as a metaphor.

True Greeks. Contemporary mass tourism, with all the repellent features of its behaviour towards sacred monuments, is only one aspect of the use of the Parthenon today. With 15,000 visitors a day in peak periods, there is little scope for a qualitative appreciation. Inevitably, one joins the crowds engaged in a superficial contact which leaves no traces. The exceptions, always so touching and so human,[84] will, however, always exist so as to give meaning to something which is threatened with extinction: "They are alone. They look poor; who knows what the trip has cost them in labour and in privation. They sit on the ground, on one of the stones on this most sacred of rocks, and they look: they look, and they look. [...] Then they sink into a contemplation of the monument. In every fibre, in their souls and minds, they are living the greatest of hours, the experience of the Acropolis: the marble, the light, the stiff bush, history, tradition, eternity, the passion of the spirit."[85]

How many of these exceptions – Greeks and foreigners, residents of Athens or visitors to the city – may there be? An early answer is to be found in a guidebook dated 1860: "Our advice is that free admission to the Acropolis should be forbidden and that an entrance fee of half a drachma should be charged. This will motivate those who have never thought of doing so to climb up to the Acropolis at least once a month – and there may be more than a few of such people."[86]

Publication of Milchhoefer's catalogue of the museums of Athens prompted the newspaper *Ora* to write: "Yet how many of the eight hundred thousand Greeks resident around the Acropolis have ever visited, as they ought, this sanctuary of art, and how many of them, having visited it, have understood the relics of human genius located therein and have been inspired by them? [...] Even now, we are not inspired by the life-giving spirit of Greek antiquity and Greek art, and seek teachings about the beautiful not in the ancient sources of which we are the possessors and guardians, [...] but in the researches, and even the misunderstandings, of others."[87] The absence of the Athenians of the time was accepted in a corresponding, though ironic, manner on the occasion of Sarah Bernhardt's visit to the Acropolis in 1893: "... many Athenians know of the Acropolis only from a distance, and are familiar with the Parthenon from photographs. We are not in the habit of ascending the sacred rock, and our souls, worn down by the struggle of everyday life, are unaware that upon its heights they could be revived, could feel emotions, could become the souls of poets."[88]

This description 'from life', dated 1920, is less pessimistic and free of the eternal Greek grumbling: "On Sundays, the Acropolis is a true place of pilgrimage for everyone. Foreigners of every nationality and origin, Greeks from abroad and the enslaved lands, Russian refugees, Athenians of the bourgeoisie and the working classes, little old ladies and society hostesses swamp the Parthenon and the other antiquities. [...] Should the phenomenon be attributed to a belated public love of antiquity, or to some other cause? It is probably the result of the fact that admission on Sundays is free".[89]

In a society which would like to see the Acropolis

monuments as a Greek affair, the proportion of foreign visitors to locals is a matter of importance. The statistical fact that, in 1965, only 7,000 of the 206,000 visitors to the Acropolis in a period of six months were Greek, meant something painful. A tourist guide attempted to interpret the phenomenon:

"Most Athenians feel admiration and pride towards a Greek masterpiece which foreigners come from the ends of the earth to admire. They themselves simply put it aside. The pace of life and the struggle to make a living prevent them from visiting the monument."[90] Six months later, the critical damage which the monuments had been found to have suffered (and which kept alive public interest) provided the stimulus for an opinion poll which restated the matter in the bluntest terms: 80 Athenians out of 100 had never visited the Parthenon, and so Athens was an unknown place to the Athenians![91]

The fact that the Athenians do not visit the sacred rock may not necessarily be proof of negligence; the figures may, once more, be misleading. It may be that the pilgrimage is an essential obligation for those who come from afar 'to climb the Acropolis', but it might equally well not have the same value for the Athenians. Their relationship with the monuments is different right from the outset; they know that the monuments are 'there', and as we have said they are familiar with them from photographs. They see the monuments from a distance as they travel around the city, and they use them as a point of reference (figs. 26, 27) – but that is where all contact with them stops. Climbing the Acropolis as a pilgrimage is seen as something of secondary importance.

That is the way things are: although the Athenians are too busy to find the time to visit the Acropolis, they are perfectly capable of expressing their concern about the fate of their great heritage, and of proposing solutions.[92]

After the War, Petros Haris remembered a different kind of identification with the monument, in a recollection of the first large-scale air raid: "Death flew over Athens, flapping its wings violently like an angry vulture [...], and yet it saluted in respect when it reached the Acropolis, and hastened on, as if taking care not to disturb the serenity and sanctity of the monument. [...] The Athenians still remember [...] how close to the monument they lived on those nights and those days, how close they felt to them, as if they were in a collective embrace. [...] And it was on those days and those nights that their souls went up to make the pilgrimage they had owed for years and years."[93]

Even when conditions are not so critical the bonds of memory can be seen creating a similar relationship. An elderly midwife remembers: "I went out with a boy for the first time beneath the rocks of the Acropolis. [...] I was specially fond of those white marbles. I loved them – be-

28. 'Stones on the Acropolis'. Source: Davenport, op. cit. (rear dust-jacket).

cause they loved me!" Similarly, a student says exactly the same thing in more words: "You see, for the Greeks the Parthenon is not just a symbol of the spirit and of human creativity, it's also bound up with each of us in some separate way. It's the place we first went on a school trip, it's the place where we first heard about 'the land of our forefathers'. And whether we like it or not, [...] we felt our hearts thumping on our first date when we looked at the columns of ancient Greece beneath the fading light...".[94]

The set of scholarly elements in the cult of the Parthenon, in the form of cultural specifications which permeate the social connections of each individual, ultimately blends harmoniously with personal experiences, which stem from a completely different – and much more commonplace – category of images. In the popular consciousness, the two levels cannot be distinguished because there is no point in attempting to make them specific. It is only in the minds of experts that such contradictory dividing-lines exist between 'being' and 'appearing to be', divisions which are capable of confronting them with dilemmas such as those which we shall see today in relation to the reconstruction of the Parthenon.

There is a story about a sea-captain from Cephalonia who had heard so much about the Acropolis that he decided to visit it. When he got home, all he had to say was, "And what was there to see? Stones! Just stones and more stones!" (fig. 28).[95] Even in this anecdote we can see the power which the monument possesses of imposing itself on the popular consciousness: the sea-captain saw none of the wonderful things he had been told about because they are not things you can see with the eye; they belong to another world.

It was that world which Mary Weber, the most celebrated of the Acropolis suicides, invoked before falling to her death from the height of the Parthenon pediment:

29. 'Son et lumière'. A post-card with floodlights in the fore-ground.

"Suddenly, with her red parasol already furled and her arms upstretched, she fell [...] from the dreadful height of some 30 metres [...] on to the stone floor".[96] When, later, people flocked to the Acropolis to see the place from which Mary had fallen,[97] they were doing no more than confirming that what is of value in a monument is that which lies behind the definition of the word itself: "a building erected in remembrance of a person or event", according to Webster. It is no coincidence that one of the examples used to cast light on the word *mnemeio* ('monument') in a Greek encyclopedia concerns the Parthenon: "The Parthenon is the most handsome of the ancient monuments".[98]

The phrase 'cast light on' leads us, by association, to the project of illuminating the Acropolis, better known as 'Son et Lumière' (fig. 29), which began in 1959.[99] There was, of course, nothing new about this; in the past, the Acropolis was always lit up for the visits of important foreign guests to whom the Greeks wished to do particular honour.[100] To put it another way, the night-time uses of the Acropolis have gone through a number of phases; suffice it to recall one of them, the opening of the site on nights when there was a full moon, a custom kept up until only a few decades ago. However, the undisguised attempt to use the 'Son et Lumière' events to boost the Acropolis as a tourist attraction caused a furore, one manifestation of which was the dispute between Spyros Melas (who was responsible for the text heard during the performance, and supported the project) and Marios Ploritis (a sarcastic critic of the project, who called it "the funfair").[101] Ploritis argued for the classic sanctity of the site: "The Rock of inaccessible Beauty has been transformed into a stage set for an opera which some director

with no concept of taste has flooded with spotlights, focusing now here and now there and compelling the Parthenon, the Erechtheum, the Propylaea and the temple of Athena Nike to act as incompetent strolling players". Melas disagreed, on a rather more realistic basis: "For years now, when the mayor of the tiniest village in the backwoods has happened to visit Athens, the Acropolis has been lit up in the most wretched manner. [...] No one called that sacrilege. [...] Nor were the various 'festivities' held in the Parthenon from time to time seen as sacrilegious, [...] not even the pitiful so-called reconstruction of the Panathenaic Festival staged [...] when the University celebrated its centenary."[102]

Figures of speech. Whether in words or pictures, the Parthenon is able to function as a succinct reference to a whole series of concepts bound up with its content. We shall select three of them: the Parthenon as a symbolic landmark of Athens; the Parthenon as a symbol of opposition to violent situations in contemporary history and of a distancing from mortal and worldly things, as an unquestioned masterpiece which challenges all creative artists to interpret it; and the Parthenon as symbol of a value which has suffered incalculable damage.

Let us begin with the primary image which Yeorgios Tertsetis provides in his stage directions for the play *Corinna and Pindar*. In order to depict "the new city of Athens" he records its landmarks: "In it, we can see the Parthenon, Othon's Palace, Sophokleous, Vyronos and Miaouli Sts, the University ...".[103] On the arch erected at the entrance to Athens from the port in honour of Queen Amalia on her return from a journey in 1857, the fourth gate showed "Their Majesties rebuilding Athens, starting with the Parthenon".[104] Such depictions of Athens were characteristic and occurred countless times later, in

30. Cartoon by Ilias Skoulas with the Parthenon made of maize cobs. Source: Apoyevmatini, *19.6.1990.*

ΤΑ ΚΥΒΕΡΝΗΤΙΚΑ ΕΡΓΑ

— Καὶ ἰδοὺ, κύριοι, ποῖα ἔργα συνετελέσθησαν χάρις εἰς τὴν σώφρονα πολιτικήν τῆς κυβερνήσεώς μου!
— Λάθος, κ. πρόεδρε, ἡ ἱστορία λέγει πῶς τὸν Παρθενῶνα τὸν ἔφτιασε οὗ Περικλῆς καὶ τὸ Στάδιου οὗ Ἀβέρωφ!
— Τὸ ἴδιο κάνει! Δικά μας δέν εἶνε; (Τὸ κ. Φωκ. Δημητριάδη.)

31. Cartoon by Fokion Dimitriadis entitled 'The government's achievements'. Source: Eleftheron Vima, 3.6.1934.

paintings,[105] cartoons[106] and the written word.

Next, we move on to the use of the word to set up a sharp contrast. One example is the mocking description of the new Arsakeion building erected in 1902: "A fine building, that one in Stadiou St. Quite a Parthenon – fit only to house pigeons."[107]

During a squabble between Athenian land-grabbers in 1907, a commentator observed: "The other day, quite a number of Greeks were involved in a knife-fight beneath the gaze of the King of the Hellenes and the Parthenon".[108] Another ironic comment came from a foreign journalist in 1922, in reference to the disgraceful state of Athens: "It would be better if you were to employ a few dustmen [...] and then you could be sure you were doing your country a greater service than if you erected a new Parthenon".[109] On the other hand, "new Parthenons" was the fateful phrase Panayotis Kanellopoulos was said to have used on a visit to the Makronisos concentration camp during the civil war of 1946-49.[110] And a distortion of the concept of the Parthenon into a proverb was to be seen in an utterance by A. Athanasopoulos during his trial, when he wished to belittle a foreign witness: "When

32. Cartoon by Kostas Mitropoulos showing a stand selling replicas of the Parthenon next to the monument. Source: Vima, 12.10.1975.

ΜΕΛΙΝΑ ΜΕΡΚΟΥΡΗ
Παρθενώνας

Η Μελίνα Μερκούρη διάλεξε τον Παρθενώνα.
Όταν τη ρωτήσαμε γιατί, μας κοίταξε σαν να τη ρωτούσαμε γιατί η γη είναι στρογγυλή.
«Μα δεν υπάρχει γιατί, απάντησε με σιγουριά. Και είναι προφανές βεβαίως γιατί δεν υπάρχει γιατί!

Η Μελίνα Μερκούρη, Αθηναία, έχει αγαπήσει την Ακρόπολη και τον Παρθενώνα. Έχει βάλει στόχο της ζωής της την επιστροφή των Ελγινείων Μαρμάρων και το Μουσείο της Ακρόπολης. Η Μελίνα σημαίνει Ελλάδα, Ακρόπολη, Παρθενώνας.

33. Melina Mercouri: "This is what I love about Athens". Source: Ena, 25/8.11.1989.

34. A sketch showing the interior of the Parthenon laid out as a basketball pitch and a comment on the turning over of Plato's Academy to be a sports ground. Source: Kathimerini, 29.9.1982.

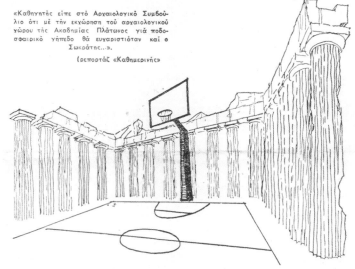

«Καθηγητὴς εἶπε στὸ Ἀρχαιολογικὸ Συμβούλιο ὅτι μὲ τὴν ἐκχώρηση τοῦ ἀρχαιολογικοῦ χώρου τῆς Ἀκαδημίας Πλάτωνος γιὰ ποδοσφαιρικὸ γήπεδο θὰ εὐχαριστιόταν καὶ ὁ Σωκράτης...».

(ρεπορτὰζ «Καθημερινῆς»)

Ὥσπου νὰ ξαναστεγάσει, ὁ Παρθενῶνας τὰ ἐλγίνεια, προτείνουμε μιὰ λύση ποὺ θὰ εὐχαριστήσει καὶ τὸν Ἰκτίνο ...

ΣΚΙΤΣΟ ΕΙΔΙΚΟΥ ΣΥΝΕΡΓΑΤΗ ΜΑΣ

they were still eating acorns, we in Greece were building Parthenons" (fig. 30).[111] Melina Mercouri (fig. 33) betrayed exactly the same mentality in 1990, when Greece was unsuccessful in its bid to host the 1996 Olympic Games: "Coca Cola has beaten the Parthenon!"

The use of the Parthenon as something disconnected from the controversies of the day comes within the same rationale. A cartoon by Fokion Dimitriadis, dating from 1927, shows Prime Minister Kafandaris painting in the Parthenon, without a care in the world. Next to him is the state budget, and the caption is a proverbial expression of self-indulgence which shows precisely this distance from worldly things.[112] Also in this category is the cartoon by Kostas Mitropoulos showing a vendor selling microscopic replicas of the Parthenon beside the monument itself – replicas which are attracting all the attention of the tourists (fig. 32).[113]

The Parthenon can also be used as a symbol of excess; in another cartoon by Dimitriadis, of 1934, the Prime Minister is gesturing towards Athens – that is, the Acropolis from a distance – as his 'achievements', only to receive the reply, "But Prime Minister, history says it was Pericles that built the Parthenon and Averof that built the Stadium!" (fig. 31).[114] In a similar vein is a drawing published on the front page of the newspaper *Kathimerini* in 1982 ith a basketball pitch marked out inside the Parthenon, a

dramatisation of the turning over of the site of Plato's Academy to be a sports ground (fig. 34).[115]

The use of the Parthenon as a symbol of dramatic destruction is rarer. A comment of 1898 compared the destruction of the Parthenon by Morosini to the fate of an Athenian on whom an Italian actress of the day, whom he had previously defamed, took terrible revenge.[116]

G. Tsokopoulos describes a group of late-night revellers walking the streets in 1907 and conveys the prevailing atmosphere of reverence: "At that moment, none of us hated anyone, and none of us remembered what hate meant. Just as the moon glides among the Parthenon marbles and you think that the divine monument is stuck to the sky like a relief, so the serenity of nature passed into our souls."[117] The same atmosphere of supernatural grandeur can be seen in a photograph of an electricity company employee, taken in 1966, with the Acropolis "lit by flashes of lightning during the storm on Sunday night".[118] In the summer of 1965, the Panathenaea of World Sculpture, held on Philopappus hill by the NTOG, organised by Tonis Spiteris and arranged according to a study by Yorgos Candilis, provided another opportunity for the Parthenon to be used as an imposing backdrop.[119]

Aphaeresis

This last category of metaplasm concerns the "drop-

36. *Cartoon showing dealers in illicit antiquities carrying off the Parthenon. Source:* Asty, *126/21.2.1888.*

37. *The logo of the Société Anonyme Athènienne. Source:* Enthymima ton Athinon *('A Souvenir of Athens'), Athens 1985.*

ping of a syllable or a letter from the beginning of a word" – i.e., an action similar to apocope yet differing in the inherent significance of the part dropped: 'beginning' here signifies a principal element of the meaning. *Allegory*, the 'literary image', a visual correspondence to an abstract concept, was found to be the closest term in rhetoric which could represent such an important loss.

Now we will turn to the category of those who are actually the users of the monument, the people whose specific decisions and actions in the implementation of final additions and deletions change its physical condition. These people, by definition, are the experts who serve on committees and councils and who are members of learned associations. When there is a critical outburst of such activity, news of it reaches the general public, which is regularly updated by the Press on what is happening.

Here we can distinguish three thematic units: illegal

trafficking in antiquities, in the general sense; the purist demand for restoration of the Parthenon to its original condition; and restoration itself, with all its emotive implications. We shall discover – without any particular surprise – a number of familiar things: the free use of arbitrary systems of evaluation, the elevation of emotional and subjective impressions to the status of principles, and the extreme difficulty of referring to eternity using the technological and perceptual tools of the immediate present.

Illegal dealers in antiquities. In the early years, illegal dealers in antiquities were to be found side-by-side with the appointed or elected experts (figs. 35, 36). In their own way, they dealt with the increase in interest caused by the excavations of various periods and the emotions they provoked.

Even before Liberation the illegal dealers in antiquities

38. *Nikolaos Gyzis: the medal certificate for the 1896 Olympic Games. Source:* To Pnevma kai to Soma *('The Spirit and the Body'), Athens 1989.*

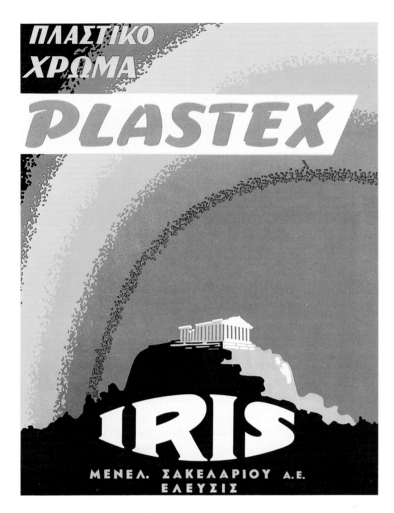

39. Advertisement for the Iris paint company.

40. Front page of a special advertising section devoted to Greece. Source: Time, *date unknown.*

had made their presence felt on the sacred rock, with the familiar affair of the Elgin Marbles as the culmination of their activities. The moving reaction of the Turkish disdar when through the incompetence of Elgin's agent Lusieri a piece of the Parthenon fell and smashed to pieces[120] was indicative of an outdated attitude towards the antiquities, one which was soon to come to an end. As the archaeologists and illicit dealers[121] jostled one another on the Acropolis, vying with one another to appropriate something of its fame, it was often hard to tell one group from the other. One could cite the example of Beulé, who made his not inconsiderable reputation out of a number of insignificant digs around the gate which bears his name today.[122] That systematic looting went on – as was the rule in an age of ignorance and unaccountability – is proved by specific cases reported to the authorities: the French visitor who stole a marble head from the Acropolis and the other gentlemen who departed with two reliefs can be only a tiny proportion of what was actually going on.[123]

This sacrilege, however, was not confined to the actual removal of valuable fragments, but also embraced behaviour towards the Acropolis site. The case of the dancer Mona Paiva, which we have already mentioned, was typi-

cal. There were, of course, others, such as the foreign couple who visited the Acropolis accompanied by their dogs.[124] In this sense, 'illegal dealing' covers inappropriate use of the Parthenon (its picture, or its name) of all kinds, whether in business signs and names or in advertising. We also know of quite a number of other instances (concealed from the public, for obvious reasons) in which the Parthenon was literally sold on the pretext of publicising Greece.

In the last analysis, this has more damaging consequences than putting the facade of the Parthenon on the packaging of a standardised product (figs. 39, 40). In the latter case, the content of the comparison (strength, trust, stability) is entirely in harmony with the content of the monument. Yet official promotion of the monument (figs. 37, 38) means something different: the product on sale is just as counterfeit as the pictures of unspoiled beaches in tourist brochures.

Purism and national consciousness. It is of particular interest that increased public sensitivity towards the Acropolis tends to coincide with the initiatives taken by the state to clear, restore or conserve the monument. The decade of the 1850s, for example, saw a stream of articles and news items describing the excavations on and around the Acropolis, which did much to increase interest in preserving the Greek patrimony.[125] Something similar happened at a later date, after 1880, when the more modern buildings on the Acropolis were finally demolished, together with the castle walls. This was a particularly interesting step, since the demolition altered the appearance of the monuments as known – and thus accepted – down to that time. The statements of support for and opposition to these decisive interventions published in various printed media of the time are still topical even today: they are the direct ancestors of the recent controversy over the restoration of the Parthenon, which has not been restricted to exchanges of fire amongst the experts only. For this reason, we shall dwell at some length on these changing fortunes.

A decisive part in the 'pre-history' of the campaign to

41. A juxtaposition of two different uses of the Parthenon in modern life. Source: Vima, *30.8.1992.*

'tidy up' the Acropolis was played by the construction of the museum on the Rock in 1875. This was an attempt to reconcile two conflicting needs: to provide a home for the scattered finds, yet to do so without affecting the integrity of the monuments. The outcome was of dubious value: "the question is, whether it ought to have defiled the sacred place by its construction. [The works] have been placed in a dungeon."[126]

In the meantime, excavations were being carried out on the south section of the Acropolis,[127] and a year later a major question arose: ought the Venetian tower on the Acropolis to be demolished or not? The views of E. Freeman, published in Vienna, who favoured its retention, sparked off an explosion on the part of Kaftantzoglou: ".. then we saw the Parthenon transformed first into a church of St Sophia to meet the needs of our Eastern Church, later into a Western Catholic church, or lastly into a Turkish mosque, over which – how tragi-comic! – a Turkish minaret was erected".[128]

Here we are dealing with the "disgrace of the successive barbarian conquests",[129] which coincided with a general trend towards 'cultural cleansing' in Greek society. Nonetheless, there were still reactions, such as that of 1888: "The history of many centuries and the vicissitudes of a lengthy period are bound up and identified with the Acropolis of Athens and its ruins. [...] Are the vaults [of the castle], which are being demolished, not testimony to an age? Did the muskets of General Odysseas [Androutsos'] soldiers not thunder out from behind the walls now reduced to dust? [...] Is that, too, not a page in our national history, and a glorious page, at that?

"And what will be the result of throwing down the walls and displaying the rock of the Acropolis naked to the general view? [...] Will the Acropolis of the age of Pericles come back to life in any way? No." (fig. 43)[130]

Kostis Palamas' poem 'The Centuries' captures the same sensation:

"The columns of the golden Parthenons
Were not alone in adorning this land;
The centuries have made the swords which slaughtered it
Into its decorations and its riches".[131]

This dilemma – that is, whether or not we should keep the fortifications where Odysseas Androutsos won his glory during the War of Independence, and, by extension, whether we should retain our hold on the recent history with which we are directly associated – is insoluble. All traces of the War of Independence were removed, because that was the way it had to be. The only exception was the picturesque (that is to say, incongruous) figure of the first custodian of the Acropolis Museum, Zisis Sotiriou. A man of the people and a fighter for freedom who never denied his roots or concealed his passion for the liberation of his own home area, he allowed

42. *The siege of Athens as described by Makriyannis. Source:* Histoire picturale de la Guerre de l'Indépendence Hellénique par le général Makriyiannis, *Paris 1926; Athens, Gennadios Library.*

43. *Karl Krazeisen: Greeks at war among the ancient ruins, 1829, lithograph after Peter von Hess. Source:* Eikonographia tou '21 *('The War of Independence Illustrated'), Aspioti-Elka, Athens 1971.*

himself to be called 'the Greek of Olympus', addressed proclamations to the young people of Greece, and on 25 March each year (anniversary of the outbreak of the War of Independence) held an improvised banquet for his friends on the Acropolis.[132]

By restoring the monuments to their original glory, we deprive them of their immediate historical identity and convert them into objects in the realm of scholars and research. On the one hand, we sever the experiential bonds between society and the site in question, and on the other, in exchange, we gain aesthetic appreciation mixed with confirmation of our national cultural identity. The change can be summed up in the attitude of Makriyannis, who in the heat of the struggle for liberation made a statement of what he was fighting for (fig. 42), but later made a tremendous fuss when the excavations in the theatre of Dionysus deprived him of part of his property.[133]

The conversion of the Parthenon into a symbol *par excellence*, that is, its alienation from any specific functional immediacy, was the process which permitted its ideological exploitation to be freed of any limit or restriction. In the end, it was the absolute and unquestioned sanctity of the Acropolis which came progressively to act as a brake on any attempt to incorporate the monument creatively into the continuous flow of life around it.

Restoration and public opinion. In 1894 a troubled period began for the monument and a natural phenomenon gave cause for anxiety about the Acropolis: "The earthquakes had to happen, the ancient monuments had to be damaged, news of the damage had to be telegraphed to the French newspapers, and those newspapers had to be read in Athens before the committee to repair the damaged parts could be set up".[134] A growing wave of information began after this time, with the intervention in the affair of recognised foreign experts who were consulted for their views.[135]

Perhaps the immediate reaction of the Press is more interesting, combining as it does the past and the present in a superb flight of rhetoric:

"So the Parthenon is unsteady on its feet. It has contracted the chronic arthritis that bedevils everything Greek. The worm that gnaws at all of us, at our foundations and societies, at the columns of Parliament, at the facade of the University, has now spread to the sacred, holy monuments, and is threatening to bring down even these immortal giants of stone and elegance, of beauty and the spirit! [...] The Parthenon is an idea, an entire intellectual cycle. It is all the ancient world summed up in a few lines, in a column or two: it is a true crystallisation of sublime beauty. [...] As such, we must see the Parthenon as the most valuable possession of the Greek land, and the slightest crack in it, even a tiny fissure barely detectable by the eye, must cause horror in the entire nation, must set off a true shudder, must move us from the very depths of our being!"[136]

Between May 1894 and September 1895 the ebb and flow of the controversy retained the attention of the public, which contributed its own recommendations.[137]

In 1905, an international conference of archaeologists[138] was held to debate the crucial question: "In what spirit, and to what extent, should the ancient monuments, and the Parthenon in particular, be renovated?"[139] It codified views which are still to be heard today, for or against restoration which would change the image of the Parthenon familiar down to that time.[140]

The mere fact that the first session of the conference took place inside the Parthenon was enough to raise a protest: "Just think. Inside the ruin there will be a meeting of all those who love and study it only because it is a ruin… It will look like a ceremony in the name of the goddess, but it will be an irony and a lie. The hearts of all those people [...] will lack true faith, love and awe".[141] Here we can see a perceptible difference from earlier practices: it is not sufficient that one should be an expert and take an interest in conserving the monument, one also has to have a metaphysical relationship with it, a prospect which the scholarship of the age did not provide for. This reaction is proof, if of nothing else, that national symbols cannot easily be reduced to mere objects of research. In the intricate windings of ideology, the symbolic charge of the Parthenon does not permit the concept of the rite to be used metaphorically.

When the time came, in 1930, the results of the many years of toil by the architect Nikolaos Balanos were judged with a similar sense of responsibility.[142] The eminent aestheticist Zacharias Papantoniou provided an objective view: "The surprise of those who as of today will see a new Parthenon is certainly understandable. No one likes having his habits disturbed – especially his visual habits. In this respect, people are fanatically conservative. [...]

"Where does the truth lie? [...] The aesthetic theory of empathy has nowhere been expressed more than here. Man has transferred his own ego to the Ego of a glorious ruin such as the Acropolis, suffering its wounds, falling along with the drums of its columns, identifying himself with its destruction and its most beautiful meanings, [...] and discovering incomparable beauty in each aspect of its decay and misfortune".[143]

A new cycle of debate, questioning, fiery denunciations and opportunities for self-criticism began in 1965, once more starting from the diagnosis of the damage suffered by the monuments of the Acropolis. The fact that this time the cause of the damage was different – not an earthquake, but erosion and oxidisation – was not of much im-

portance.[144] The controversy became even more heated in 1988, as soon as the first results of modern intervention (in the Erechtheum) were unveiled. And the debate was widely publicised on the occasion of the international conference held specially on the restoration work proposed for the Parthenon.[145]

This time, the sharpest criticism called into question the social utility of the proposals: "Apart, however, from destroying the authenticity of the monument and distorting its history, the extensive reconstruction of some of the authentic parts of the temple will be catalytic in its consequences. [...] And to think that both the projects claim to be faithful [...] to the grandiloquent but not universally accepted views concerning the 'aesthetic' (and 'artistic') 'enhancing' of the monument and of increasing its 'educational value' or 'readability', for the benefit of the many (and the ignorant)…".[146]

In an emotionally charged atmosphere and striving in vain to establish incontrovertible scholarly foundations, contemporary rhetoric has reproduced, on the one hand, respect for the monument's eternal quality by means of the doctrine (which we have just seen explained) of minimising intervention in it, and, on the other, the concept of identifying the Parthenon with technological progress, which we discussed with reference to aircraft and achievements in space. In this latter instance, if the Parthenon is a superb machine which as a result of historical circumstances has come down to us in fragmentary form, then it is our duty to restore it to completeness on the basis of our level of knowledge today, breaking its enigmatic codes one by one.[147] Between these two traps lies the artistic approach, the most vulnerable and the hardest to define, and for that reason the field for battles without end.[148]

Devices redeemed

Philosophers, aestheticians, writers – all of them have used the monument in one way or another, but always metaphorically. Whatever they have said or written about it has always functioned on the level of meaning, projecting the historical and social problems and the visions of their own age (fig. 41) on to the ruins. Although so much ink has been consumed, these writers did not hit the Parthenon because that was not what they were aiming at. For the same reason, the monument was not affected by the millions of photographs taken on the Acropolis to please the multitudes, or by the post-cards, the plaster models sold in the souvenir shops, or the depictions on the packaging of products of all kinds.

Wherever we look, we can see the corrosive influence of metaplasms, which sometimes subtract and sometimes distort. The Parthenon ultimately exists only to the extent to which it obeys such mutilations of meaning and content. In other words, the existence of the Parthenon results exclusively from its utilitarian value. Without a ritualistic shell, deprived of its nationalistic radiance and without pilgrims, the Parthenon would not exist; it would sink into oblivion. The fact that it has managed to survive and keep its repute high during the century and a half which we have been investigating is the result of its ability to absorb new utilitarian modes. Its adaptability – for example, its shift from the status of proof of ancient glory to tourist tout – is what has ensured it of the power of collectivity in society and thus the ability to reach and move the masses, suffering with them the tribulations of war and breathing with them the poisonous atmosphere of Athens today.[149]

Such an explanation is satisfactory insofar as concerns the collective nature of the response to the Parthenon (what we have been calling appreciation), but it does not explain the monument's relationship with the experts. This can only be done if we accept that the processing of the Parthenon by means of metaplasms is an essential condition for its universal recognition as a sublime masterpiece of art. Its reduction to a pedestrian and everyday level is the essential counterbalance to every high-flown interpretation of its perfection promoted by the priestly caste of experts. Even the successive efforts to 'purify' the monument by means of demolition or restoration are part of this dual approach: the clarification of the historical palimpsest is a response primarily to the need to complete the national vision and make it tangible.

In examining the possible fluctuations in time, we are therefore dealing not with a progressive shift from the earthly (the Serpenje castle during the Turkish occupation) to the heavenly (the modern-day restorations), but rather with a parallel advance in which one element feeds the other. The awe felt by a famous person such as Mounet-Sully, who discovered himself on the Acropolis, coincides with the solitary exercises of Ludwig Ross and Balanos and his successors, whose wish is to perpetuate the material substance of the inconceivable. It also coincides with the obedient crowds of visitors discharging their duty to a unique work of art, just as they would before the Capella Sistina, Notre Dame, and other masterpieces. All this confirms, while at the same time reproducing in its entirety, the symbolic armoury of the Parthenon, which has displaced and reduced to uselessness every objective approach.

In accordance with the above, it will be clear that the purpose of our approach was not simply to understand certain mechanisms, but, through them, to build a bridge across the artificial chasm that separates experts and non-experts. Both sides, in their own ways, have contributed exclusively to alienation from what the Parthenon truly is. If the foregoing text has failed to prove this, it has at least indicated that its existence is no longer axiomatic. Only in this way can we remove – provisionally, at the least – the effect of authority which belongs to the metaplasms and vindicates the chasm.

Notes

1. Angelos Sikelianos, 'The Sacred Way', 1935 (extract).

2. Ultimately, what we are talking about is a competitive relationship between the 'universal' as a compulsory property of every unique masterpiece and the 'local' as the supreme value of a national symbol. Naturally enough, this conflict is directly associated with broader ideological positions in Greek society.

3. 'Folklore' might be a more apt term, but it conceals a number of traps in Greece. On the other hand, it is the only term capable of conveying the concept of the collective nature of the phenomenon under examination.

4. B. Dupriez, *A Dictionary of Literary Devices. Gradus, A-Z*, translated and adapted by A.W. Halsall, University of Toronto Press, Toronto and Buffalo 1991, p. 279.

5. In this translation from a Greek original, an adaptation in the terminology was in order, especially in this particular section of the text. There are, obviously, no literal equivalents in English to word plays such as those used in the Greek text; for example, "passions of vowels" (the term in Greek grammar) used as "passions of reason" (alluding to an ideological substitution).

6. Dupriez, *op. cit.*, p. 316. All subsequent definitions of rhetorical terms, in quotation marks, are from this source.

7. The severeness here takes the form of the inability of the geographical identification *per se* (the Parthenon on the sacred rock for so many centuries) to fulfil the demand for identification with the world of the ancients.

8. 'General Panorama of Athens', *Nea Pandora* 67/1.1.1853, p. 441.

9. *Aion* 1495/31.1.1857.

10. *Athena* 2511/3.1.1857.

11. *Athena* 2590/24.8.1957.

12. N.A. Skias, 'In Favour of the Acropolis', *Asty* 561/21.6.1892.

13. Angelos Tanagras, 'The Athens of the Future', *Acropolis*, 7.7.1902.

14. *Athenai*, 29.11.1915. It is remarkable that in these cases it did not occur to anyone to compare the Athens of the day with the Parthenon as, for example, L. Mumford did (*The City in History*, Pelican, Harmondsworth, 1966, caption to fig. 10), drawing a direct comparison between the houses of Plaka and those of Solon or even Pericles.

15. For only one stage in the various misadventures which befell the Palais de Justice in the pre-War period, see A. Nikoloudis, 'Concerning the Site of the Palais de Justice', *Eleftheron Vima*, 17.10.1930, and E. Hébrard, 'The Site of the Athens Palais de Justice', *ibid.*, 6.11.1930.

16. G. Markantonis, 'While Foreigners are Indignant. A Threat to the Acropolis. A Hard Fight for the School of Fine Art', *Eleftheron*

Vima, 6.1.1936.

17. *Eleftheria* 3433/13.11.1955.

18. L. Kaftantzoglou, 'Speech Delivered at the Memorial to the Late Michail Tositsas on 7 May 1861, Day of the Translation of his Relics', *Avyi* 841/13.5.1861.

19. 'The Greek Capital' (reprinted from the *Times*), *Alitheia* 3174/21.8.1878.

20. Unattributed letter, 'Art Nouveau and Athens', *Athenai*, 17.4.1903.

21. Cf. Pikionis' objections in the pre-War period to the neo-Byzantine architecture of A. Zachos in the (demolished) Pallis house at Dexameni, facing the Acropolis.

22. S. Melas, 'Architecture and Spirit', *Eleftheria* 4474/3.4.1959.

23. P. Michelis, 'Dialogos stin Akropoli' ('Dialogue on the Acropolis', *Aisthitiki Trilogia* ('Aesthetic Trilogy'), Athens 1937, p. 29.

24. 'Raise your Flag. A Manifesto to the Young People of Greece', *Eleftheron Vima*, 10.2.1933.

25. The anecdote was reported by P. Karantinos, 'Proceedings of the Second Panhellenic Conference of Architecture, Thessaloniki', *Technika Chronika* 248/1964.

26. P. Kounenaki, 'After the Parthenon, What?', *Tachydromos* 9/1990, p. 33 (interview with Ileana Tounda).

27. 'The British Museum', *Pandora* 39/1.11.1851.

28. *Aion* 3262/4.7.1880.

29. 'Art-lover', 'The Elgin Marbles', *Asty*, 2.12.1890. Cf. 'Herod Atticus', *ibid.*, 4.12.1890; D., 'Lady Resident Abroad', *ibid.*, 6.12. 1890; an article about the French artist A. Ettecx, who in 1883 wrote a letter to Queen Victoria on the subject (to which he never received a reply), *ibid.*, 11.12.1890; and 'The English 'Banner' on the Elgin Marbles', *ibid.*, 17.12.1890. Seven further articles were published in early 1891.

30. 'Elgin's Marble Sculptures Brought Back and Placed on Display in the British Museum', *Vima*, 28.11.1948.

31. P. Karavias, 'The 'Elgin Marbles'', *Eleftheria* 20.11.1955, and F. Yermanos, 'Are there Marbles from the Parthenon on the Aegean Seabed?', *ibid.*, 29.11.1955.

32. See, for example, A. Kaloyeropoulou, 'The Elgin Marbles. The History of the Famous Sculptures Stolen from the Parthenon', *Eleftheria*, 11.5.1961, and 'The Elgin Marbles will be Returned to Greece only when Nelson Gets his Eye back, Say the British', *ibid.*, 24.5.1961.

33. 'Discussion of Where to Put the Elgin Marbles – when they are Returned', *Eleftheria*, 13.6.1961.

34. See, for example, the recent article by E. Bistika-Katramopoulou, 'The 'Elgin Marbles' on the Road to Justice', *Kathimerini*, 5.2.1989.

35. The tale of the grief of the Caryatids for their lost sister is told by N. Politis in his *Paradoseis* ('Traditions') and was also used by D. Kambouroglou in his book *I Neraida tou Kastrou* ('The Fairy of the Castle').

36. T. Vellianitis, 'The Acropolis Flag', *Athenai*, 13.4.1915. Another version gives a fuller picture: the young garrison commander, Christoforos Nezer, ordered his troops out on parade; as they presented arms, he saluted the old captain with his sword and cried out, with him, "Long live Greece, long live the King!" ('The Acropolis under the Turks. Christoforos Nezer, the First Commander of the Garrison', *Eleftheron Vima*, 14.4.1933).

37. K.T., letter, *Athenai*, 24.2.1913. A week or so later the Archaeological Council hastened to approve the proposal (*Athenai*, 5.3.1913).

38. *Eleftheron Vima*, 28.4.1941. Two weeks later, the same humiliating ceremony, "of a purely military nature", was repeated for the Italian flag (*Eleftheron Vima*, 26.6.1941).

39. Another consequence of the same symbolism was the ultimate act of national resistance, when two youths, Manolis Glezos and Lakis Santos, climbed the Acropolis in secret at night, hauled down the German flag and desecrated it.

40. *Eleftheria*, 13.10.1959. The most imposing photograph was published the following year, having been specially taken from the highest possible point. This was the 16th anniversary (*Eleftheria*, 13.10.1959), and it established a tradition which continued in the years to come.

41. 'George Papandreou on the Acropolis with Representatives of the Allied Forces, Looking Towards the Greek Flag...', *Eleftheria*, 18.10.1964 and 20.10.1964.

42. It was the full moon, and the Acropolis was open until midnight. The banner was spotted by a custodian three hours later.

43. *Eleftherotypia*, 16.12.1988. I owe this detail – and many others – to my friend Panayotis Tournikiotis.

44. *Aion* 4117/21.3.1883.

45. Anon., 'On the Sacred Rock. Mounet-Sully in Athens', *Akropolis*, 30.7.1899. Mounet-Sully gave three performances at the Municipal Theatre and was decorated by King George I.

46. 'Impressions of Greece. A new Article by M. Deschamps', *Asty* 455/6.3.1892.

47. L. Asteris, '29 May. The Great Idea', *Akropolis*, 29.5.1896.

48. D.A. Anastasopoulos of Athens, 'Christ in Paradise', part I, *Acropolis*, 24.12.1900.

49. *Ibid.*, part II, 25.12.1900.

50. S. Paganelis, 'Good Friday Seen from the Acropolis', *Athenai* 3413/22.3.1912 (published in three parts).

51. 'The Greek Spirit. Socrates on the Acropolis. A Page from the Book by M. Herriot', *Eleftheron Vima*, 8.7.1930. We could also put into this category an incident which occurred in 1963, when a film was made, on the Acropolis, about the birth of democracy: a journalist called Severine interviewed the royal couple with the Acropolis as backdrop (*Eleftheria*, 2.4.1963 and 3.4.1963, fig. 11).

52. 'The Greek Spirit. A Hymn to the Parthenon. Yesterday's Lecture', *Eleftheron Vima*, 1.4.-6.5.1944 (in five parts).

53. *Eleftheron Vima*, 28.6.1929.

54. See 'The Writer of the Vie de Jésus. The 'Prayer on the Acropolis'', *Asty* 653/21.9.1892.

55. In the play, for example, Kleon is compared to Hitler ('Pericles' Athens on Stage', *Eleftheron Vima*, 28.11.1933).

56. Angelos Sikelianos, 'Architecture and Music', *Eleftheron Vima*, 10.8.1944.

57. R. Barthes, 'Rhetoric of the Image' (1964), Greek translation in *Eikona – Mousiki – Keimeno* ('Image – Music – Text'), Plethron, Athens 1988, p. 51.

58. A. Miliarakis, 'Ceremony on the Acropolis of Athens', *Estia* 447/22.7.1884, pp. 461-467.

59. 'The Annual Meeting of the Archaeological Society', *Athena* 920/27.5.1842 and 1505/18.6.1848. In the case of the first publication, the comment was a critical one: the Society went through the motions of holding its meeting but was generally inactive.

60. *Athena* 2116/7.6.1854. For the depiction of the event in the *Illustrated London News*, see *1842-1885 Ellada eikonographimeni: mia pliris syllogi istorikon, topographikon kai kallitechnikon documenton* ('1842-1885. Greece Illustrated: A Complete Collection of Historical, Topographical and Artistic Documents'), Athens 1984, p. 38. My thanks to F. Mallouchou for drawing my attention to the source.

61. The representatives of the Church had gathered in Athens for the funeral of King George I (*Athenai* 24.3.1913).

62. At the time, King Constantine was at the Asia Minor front (*Athenai*, 10.6.1921).

63. *Acropolis*, 11.11.1947.

64. *Eleftheria*, 8.5.1953.

65. *Eleftheria*, 7.3.1952.

66. *Eleftheria*, 28.5.1953.

67. "Sitting on a broken column, he gazed at the sky of Attica..." (*Eleftheria*, 28.5.1958), and "yesterday he visited the Acropolis again, and stayed there alone for two hours" (*ibid.*, 29.5.1958).

68. *Eleftheria*, 4.6.1960.

69. *Eleftheria*, 18.6.1961.

70. *Eleftheria*, 7.10.1964.

71. It would be interesting to investigate the typology of the poses struck by famous personalities when being photographed on the Acropolis, covering the entire spectrum from the most frozen frontal views to the completely relaxed and 'individual'.

72. 'Mona Paiva on the Acropolis', *Eleftheron Vima*, 25.10.1925. Cf. the echo in *Journal de Paris* (*ibid.*, 14.11.1925). Mme. Paiva was not the only dancer to perform on the Acropolis: she was followed by Nikolska, whose photographs – also by Nelly – are equally well-known (fig. 17).

73. *Eleftheria*, 31.1.1963.

74. 'A Wedding on the Acropolis!', *Super Katerina*, August 1989.

75. The effect of the teachings of Eva Sikelianou at the Delphi Festival is clear here ('From a Display of Gymnastics and Dancing', *Eleftheron Vima*, 12.5.1931).

76. Of course, the greatest fuss was over the juxtaposition on the same page of the west facade of the Parthenon and the Delage Grand Sport motor-car (p. 107 in the first French edition). The reference to the aircraft of the age is on pp. 111-112 of this edition, with the interior of the cockpit of Caproni's sea-plane next to a detail from the Parthenon entablature.

77. *Eleftheron Vima*, 23.10.1930. This cannot have been the first official linking of the Acropolis with an aeroplane: in 1923, two aeroplanes had flown over the Acropolis and dropped miniature Greek and French flags to mark the centenary of the birth of Renan (*Eleftheron Vima*, 18.3.1923).

78. *Eleftheron Vima*, 8.9.1938.

79. 'The Romance between King Paul and Queen Freideriki. How they Met. A Historical Narrative by Ernst Robert Schuter', *Eleftheria*, 13.9.1952.

80. *Eleftheria*, 5.4.1959.

81. *Kathimerini*, 12.10.1988.

82. *Enimerotiko Deltio TEE* 1542/21.11.1988.

83. *Kathimerini*, 19.11.1989.

84. See the case of the visitor in a wheelchair who was carried up the Acropolis by two workmen (I.M. Panayotopoulos, 'A Visitor. The Passion of the Spirit', *Eleftheria*, 17.6.1956), and of another disabled woman who was carried up on her husband's back (*ibid.*, 1.7.1964).

85. Panayotopoulos, *op. cit.*

86. This was the Greek-French publication whose title could be rendered as: *Modern Athens, or, A Summary Description of the Capital of Greece, with the Departure Times of Steamers, the Value of Greek Coins as against Foreign Currency, the Prices Fixed by the Police for Carriages, etc.* It is cited by Dionysios Romas ('Modern Athens', *Eleftheria*, 1.2.1953).

87. Republished in *Aion* 3610/3.8.1881.

88. Columnist, 'Sarah Bernhardt on the Acropolis', *Asty* 865/24.4.1893.

89. 'The Pilgrimage to the Antiquities', *Athenai*, 2.3.1920.

90. P.V., 'The Athenians Don't Visit the Acropolis very Often', *Eleftheria* 6555/26.1.1966.

91. G.A. Michalopoulos, 'Athens – an Unknown City to the Athenians!', *Eleftheria* 6673/18.6.1966.

92. G. Mich[alopoulos], 'Athenian Concern about the Ancient Monuments. Various Solutions Proposed', *Eleftheria* 6561/2.2.1966.

93. P. Haris, 'A Little Uphill Walk (A Trip to the Acropolis)', *Eleftheria*, 10.7.1952.

94. G. Mich[alopoulos], 'Athenian Concern...', *op. cit.*

95. G. Koutsoukos, 'What Some Greeks See. Stones on the Acropolis', *Eleftheria*, 23.7.1952.

96. 'Young Mary Weber Falls from the Parthenon', *Nea Ephimeris* 56/25.2.1893.

97. Proteus, 'The Cult of the Parthenon', *Akropolis*, 29.10.1894.

98. *Megali Elliniki Enkyklopaidia*, vol. XVII, p. 284.

99. 'Son et Lumière Events Begin on the Acropolis. Speech by André Malraux', *Eleftheria*, 29.5.1959.

100. See the visits by distinguished foreigners and the events to mark national anniversaries in the late nineteenth and early twentieth centuries, such as the visit of the Prince of Wales in 1875 (*Aion* 3174/7.10.1875) and the celebrations for 25 March 1900 (*Akropolis*, 27.3.1900 and 29.3.1905). Cf. on the occasion of the Olympic Games of 1906, *Athenai* 112/9.2.1906. There was a torchlight procession in 1952, as part of the demonstrations over Cyprus (*Eleftheria*, 19.7.1952).

101. Marios Ploritis, 'Son et Lumière, or, the Acropolis as a Funpark', *Eleftheria*, 30.5.1959; S. Melas, 'Passion for Criticism', *ibid.*, 3.6.1959; M. Ploritis, 'Silence and Darkness. "Disclosures" and Scandals', *ibid.*, 5.6.1959; S. Melas, 'Third and Last Passion', *ibid.*, 10.6.1959.

102. We do not need to engage in much of a search for ceremonies on the Acropolis which had verged on the ridiculous, given that patriotic rites there always included mock ancient costume and all the trimmings. Cf. the photograph entitled 'a girl in ancient costume, on the Acropolis, lighting a torch which was then taken to the Monument of the Unknown Soldier', *Eleftheria*, 22.7.1952.

103. G. Tertsetis, 'Corinna and Pindar', *Nea Pandora* 75/1.4.1853, p. 59.

104. *Athena* 2604/12.10.1857.

105. See A. Asteriadis, 'Athens', *Eleftheria*, 22.3.1959.

106. See a series of cartoons by Bost (e.g., *Eleftheria*, 24.4.1960, 19.2.1961).

107. Tim. Stath., 'Architecture', *Akropolis*, 4.10.1902.

108. 'Building Sites', *Asty* 1862/12.1.1907.

109. T. Vellianitis, 'Brandes in Despair', *Athenai*, 6.3.1922.

110. Doubt has subsequently been cast on whether or not Kanellopoulos actually uttered the 'historic' phrase.

111. *Nea*, 16.6.1990, p. 8.

112. *Eleftheron Vima*, 16.1.1927.

113. *Vima*, 12.10.1975.

114. *Eleftheron Vima*, 3.6.1934.

115. 'The Question of Ceding the Use of Plato's Academy to the Re-examined', *Kathimerini*, 29.9.1982.

116. 'The Actress's Tragedy', *Akropolis*, 27.4.1898.

117. G. Tsokopoulos, 'Late Night', *Athenai*, 13.7.1907.

118. *Eleftheria* 6589/8.3.1966.

119. T. Spiteris, 'The Athens Biennale. A Reply to Well-Intentioned Criticism', *Eleftheria* 6745/11.9.1966.

120. Dionysios Romas, 'Scattered Marbles', *Eleftheria* 2528/6.12.1952.

121. Cf. the dispute between Rangavis and Pittakis over the charge that pieces of the monument of Thrasyllus had been used to repair a Byzantine church (*Athena* 1729/1.1.1851 and 1732/17.1.1851). A "learned man of Greek descent" was forcibly turned out by Pittakis for requesting to make a survey of the Herod Atticus theatre (*Athena* 2654/9.4.1858).

122. See the turmoil provoked by his 'discoveries' at the time and the local reaction ('K.', letter in *Athena* 1931/27.11.1852, and 'Acropolis Affairs', *Athena* 1937/20.12.1852).

123. *Athena* 1222/3.6.1845.

124. 'Sacrilege on the Acropolis. The Foreigners and Ourselves', *Akropolis*, 2.11.1894; 'P.S.', a letter about foreign visitors breaking up and sharing out a piece of the Parthenon, *Athenai*, 13.2.1903; German travellers with iron bars detaching "souvenirs of the relief ornamentation" from the Parthenon, *ibid.*, 12.5.1903.

125. See 'Greek Antiquities', *Athena* 2785/11.7.1859 and 2787/15.7.1859; see also the formation of a committee to collect subscriptions to finance excavations (*Elpis* 1280/8.12.1864), and the 'Antiquity-Lovers' Lottery', *ibid.* 1298/13.4.1865.

126. *Aion* 3110/3.3.1875. For later references to the building in the post-War period, see T. Spiteris, 'The Acropolis Museum. The Project of its Renovation', *Eleftheria*, 10.8.1956; the same author, 'The Aesthetic Appearance of the Acropolis Museum', *ibid.*, 10.8.1956; 'The Completed Acropolis Museum Opened', *ibid.*, 9.12.1964.

127. *Aion* 3251/26.7.1876 and 3252/29.7.1876.

128. L. Kaftantzoglou, *Epistolimaia diatrivi pros ton ellogimon E. Friman peri tis katedafiseos tou en ti Akropolei tourkikou pyrgou* ('Representation in the Form of a Letter to the Learned E. Freeman on the Subject of the Demolition of the Turkish Tower on the Acropolis'), 1878, p. 22.

129. *Aion* 4490/2.6.1884.

130. 'Herod Atticus', 'Don't Touch the Acropolis!', *Asty* 141/5.6.1888.

131. *Asty*, 25.12.1896. The date of is particular importance, because at this time the Cretan revolt was in full swing and the disastrous campaign in Thessaly lay only a few months in the future.

132. See A. Kokkou, *I merimna yia tis archaiotites stin Ellada kai ta prota mouseia* ('Care of Antiquities in Greece and the First Museums'), Athens 1977, p. 233, note 1.

133. *Aion* 2027/30.4.1862.

134. 'The Antiquities', *Nea Ephimeris*, 27.4.1894.

135. Apart from the Greek committee, which failed to reach agreement on any point, a number of foreign experts were also consulted.

136. 'Proteus', 'The cult...', *op. cit.*

137. See, for example: N. Solomos, 'The Danger to the Parthenon. Take Care with the Foundations', Akropolis, 9.11.1894; letter from L. Schneider, 'The Reconstruction of the Parthenon', *ibid.*, 23.3.1898; N. Mopoulos, letter on the reconstruction of the Parthenon, *Athenai*, 15 and 16.5.1922.

138. Cf. the poem, in Greek translation, of R.A. Johnson, written on the occasion of the international conference of archaeology the following year, *Akropolis*, 23.3.1905.

139. 'The Glory of the Ruins. Should the Parthenon be Reconstructed? A Fine Reply', *Akropolis*, 23.3.1905.

140. For a series of conservative views, see Routlandos, 'On the Parthenon', *Akropolis*, 25.3.1905.

141. 'G.X.', 'Parthenon', *Athenai*, 6.12.1904.

142. *Eleftheron Vima*, 3.5.1930 (the results were announced on the first day of the Delphi Festival).

143. Z. Papantoniou, 'The Parthenon Changes Form. A Bold Aesthetic Undertaking', *Eleftheron Vima*, 17.5.1930.

144. See, indicatively, 'Acropolis Monuments in Danger of Collapse', *Eleftheria*, 23.5.1965, and a special issue of the periodical *Zygos* (5/June 1965, "If we don't look after them in good time we shall lose the Acropolis monuments").

145. See, indicatively, A. Kaloyeropoulou, 'Unknown Facts about the Parthenon', *Kathimerini*, 12.3.1989; S. Bakoyannopoulou, 'Stone by Stone', *Vima*, 19.3.1989; Anon., 'Facelifting Applied to the Columns of the Temple of Athena', *Kathimerini*, 5.4.1989; C. Kiosse, 'How far should the Parthenon be Restored?' *ibid.*, 9.4.1989; M. Lambraki-Plaka, 'Let's Leave the Parthenon as it is', *Vima*, 16.4.1989; C. Sfaellos, letter to *Kathimerini*, 10.4.1990, and the same author, 'The "Ruin" We're Used To', *Kathimerini*, 15.7.1990.

146. I. Dimakopoulos, 'The Reconstruction of the Parthenon. A Critical Presentation of the Most Recent Proposals for the Pronaos and the Lateral Walls', *Kathimerini*, 21.5.1989.

147. Cf. M. Korres, 'The Parthenon', in *Eikastiki Paideia* ('Education in the Visual Arts'), offprint 1987, publication of a talk delivered on 9.9.1987 to the Union of Art Teachers. Although this is a 'popular' text, it conveys an adequate idea of the vast knowledge which this great scholar of the monument has of his subject.

148. Cf. the views expressed by Y. Miliadis twenty years ago: "Nothing must be implemented [...] if it destroys, damages or changes the artistic form and nature of the works, which we can see in no way other than as works of art" (Ch. Bouras, 'Yannis Miliadis', *Archaiognosia* 4/1988-89, Athens 1990, p. 124).

149. See the photograph accompanying the article 'Athens, City of Slow Death', *Kathimerini*, 26.5.1990, with tourists walking past the Caryatids.

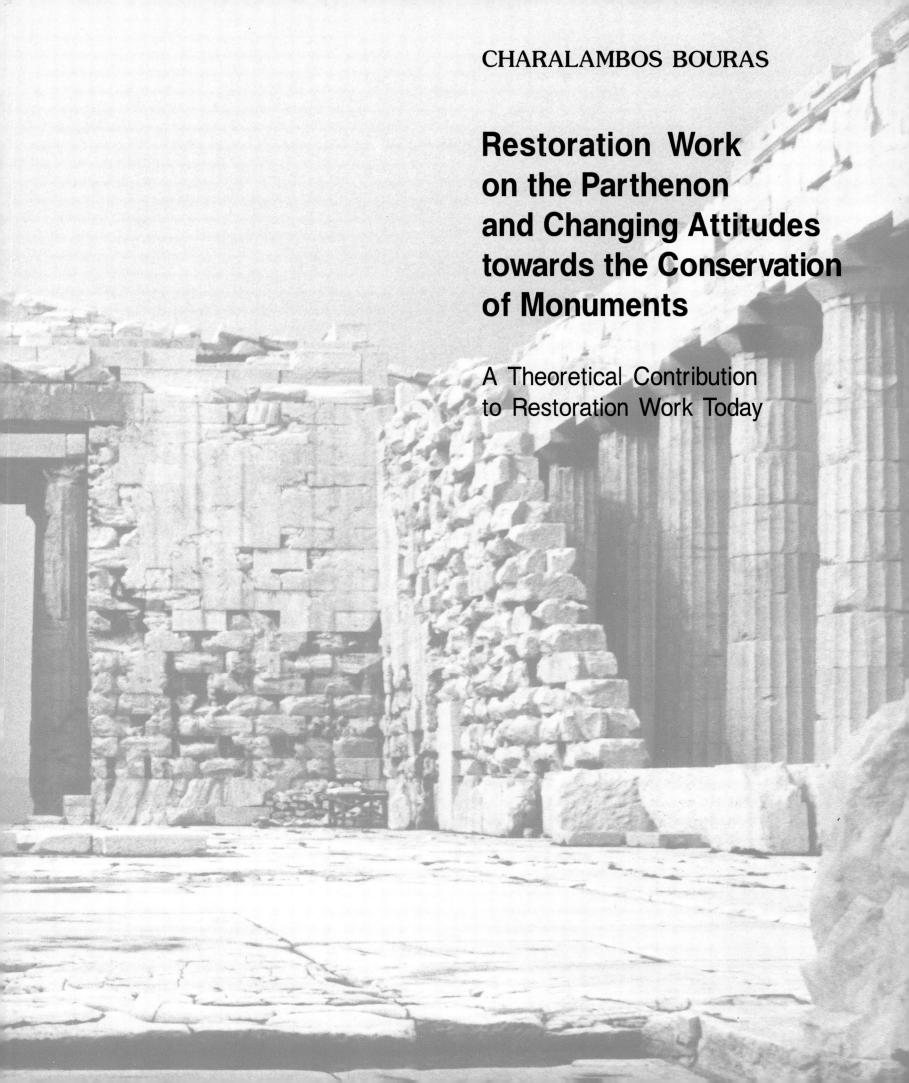

CHARALAMBOS BOURAS

Restoration Work on the Parthenon and Changing Attitudes towards the Conservation of Monuments

A Theoretical Contribution
to Restoration Work Today

The various interventions which have been made in the Parthenon during its long life are connected with the misfortunes, damage and destruction it has suffered from time to time and also to the ways in which it has been used[1] at various periods.

All down the period from antiquity to the present day, the Parthenon has not ceased to change and to distance itself further and further from the state of perfection in which its creators left it. However, these changes – deliberate or unintentional, major or minor – can be seen not to have succeeded in affecting the essence of its presence or of spoiling any of its principal features – those features which make it unique and incomparable. There was never any thought of replacing it. Even when its relationship with mankind was reduced to one of meeting everyday material needs (that is, when only its bare shell was exploited), the spirit won through. In a manner rivalled by few important buildings in the history of architecture, the Great Temple was always there, towering magnificently over human failure and pettiness. More, perhaps, than any other building in the world, it has become an unshakeable proof of the superiority of ancient civilisation, and in recent years it has for many people assumed the character of a symbol. For centuries, the Parthenon made its artistic presence felt to those who had the good fortune – and the eyes – to see it. It became a standard for measuring quality.

As a result, a description and analysis of the various interventions in the Parthenon is highly instructive. All of the work done from time to time illustrates the relationship between society (those who use or manage the monument, or those who simply admire it) and this specific, unique building. Precisely because the temple is a standard for measuring quality, human behaviour towards it is convincing evidence of the level of education and aesthetic cultivation of society in each case. Although there are various imponderables which interpolate themselves into the correspondence, and although we lack some of the information necessary to deal with the question (thus necessitating certain hypotheses), the narrative is one of outstanding interest.

The role of the Parthenon ought, precisely because of its uniqueness and value, to be a central one in the history of monument restoration as it has taken shape in modern times. Similarly, its contribution to crystallising the ethics of managing, conserving and restoring architectural monuments ought to be a decisive one. In reality, however, neither of these things has happened. An analysis of the instances in which interventions have been made in the Parthenon will make plain the reasons for this failure, although we shall also have to accept the imponderable of circumstance, of chance. It will also become clear that the Classical Greek monuments have unique features which distinguish them from those of Western Europe on which the theory and history of the restoring of architectural treasures was moulded over the last two centuries. In the particular case of the Parthenon, however, the entire issue can – to the extent to which we possess the necessary information – be examined starting from a much earlier date, as we have seen, and will produce equally interesting observations.

This allows us to discern eight 'eras' in the life-story of the Great Temple. The constructional interventions of each of these eras have left their marks on the form of the building as we see it today. The text which follows describes and analyses those interventions, drawing parallels with the conditions of each period and the criteria for evaluation applied during them.

1. Thanks to the research work done by various scholars[2] – though especially by I. Travlos[3] and M. Korres[4] – we now know much more about the first major damage to the Parthenon, which took the form of a fire (probably occurring during the invasion of the Heruli in 267 AD) and about the first extensive restoration to the building almost one hundred years later. These repairs may have been constructed with the moral support or even on the initiative and at the expense of the Emperor Julian, with his yearning for antiquity. Travlos has explained the reason for the silence of the written sources about these two important events.[5] Although most of the elements concerning these extensive repairs have disappeared (being destroyed in subsequent disasters to the monument), it is possible to reconstruct what the temple must have looked like after it and also to assess the nature of the project on the basis of some details which have survived.

We know, for example, that the large internal two-level shaped colonnade (which had been completely

1. *The interior of the Parthenon before the beginning of the work of the Committee for the Conservation of the Acropolis Monuments. Photograph by S. Mavrommatis.*

destroyed[6]) was reconstructed with the members of an earlier Doric portico,[7] here re-used (fig. 2). A new wooden roof was installed above the cella, but the peristyle was roofless from now on. The pedestal of the cult statue of Athena was reconstructed, and important interventions were made in both entrances to the cella, which had been severely damaged by the fire (figs. 4, 5), also using pedestals and other members from the Doric portico. Lastly, the parts of the east pediment of the Acropolis which had been affected by the fire were repaired.

These repairs were rough and unskilful; holes and channels for pouring lead were hastily cut into the old stylobates, and the damage to the columns capitals and the entablatures was patched up with mortar stiffened with iron rods (fig. 3). Some of the sculptures seem to have been removed from the pediment – or destroyed – and the entire intervention was makeshift and hurried.

This shows us that as far back as the fourth century the form of the Great Temple had begun to change. The fire was the cause not only of serious direct damage but also of the more obvious appearance of the joints between the architectural members, of the loss of the monolithic impression given by the columns, and of the tacit emergence of a new aesthetic[8] in which the articulation of the members was of prime importance in the visual impression and their construction was accentuated. The effects on the nature of the monument from the re-use of members from another building were much more serious than in other cases: here, the spolia were not inserted in places where they could not be seen. The main feature of the interior of the temple changed, with the introduction of new measures and forms; most importantly of all, the minor defects, patches and 'last resorts' created for the first time an impression of picturesqueness quite alien to the perfection and majesty of the Classical temple. However virtuous the romantic Emperor's intentions may have been, however far their purpose may have been to preserve the ancient cult and the uses connected with it, and however much money may have been spent, the hour of change had struck for the Parthenon. The utilisation of the members from an old portico (possibly the now useless gift of a Hellenistic monarch), coincided with the complete decline of stone-masonry in the Greek world[9] and introduced the aesthetics of what, to recall the words of Levi-Strauss, we might call the 'bricolage culture'. Another reversal of the initial concept was to be seen in the decision to leave the

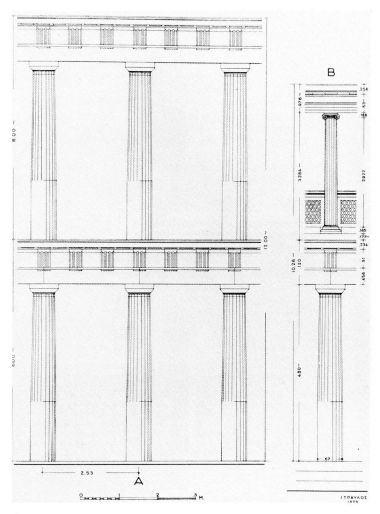

2. Late Roman restoration work: the new internal colonnade in the cella; elevation (drawing by J. Travlos). Source: Archaiologiki Ephimeris, *1973, p. 229.*

peristyle roofless (at least along the greater part of its length), robbed of its coffered ceiling,[10] thus utterly altering the lighting in which the Parthenon frieze was viewed.

The scientific and historical values represented by the temple, which was already more than 800 years old, were of no interest whatever to the restorers of 365. The concept of the 'authentic' was a matter of indifference to them. They tried to give the monument back its old functions, appreciating its ancient values of beauty, use and emotion. For those nostalgic for the past, the temple of Pallas Athena was now the symbol of a better education and a different way of life. As far as beauty – that is, artistic values – was concerned, their efforts failed, whether judged by Classical or contemporaneous criteria. Here we are led smoothly to a first conclusion: in restoring monuments, regardless of intentions, the factor of technical and artistic potential is of the greatest importance – in other words, what can be done at any given time in the framework of new conditions as they emerge.

2. The dedication of the Parthenon to the Christian religion and the work on its conversion into a church took place at an unknown date. Earlier scholars[11] differ in their views, which were based on a heterogeneous collection of written sources. The recent[12] views of Travlos – that the intervention was made towards the end of the sixth century – seems much more convincing. However, this chronological uncertainty makes a theoretical approach to the question more difficult.

Here, too, the destruction of the interior of the cella has, unfortunately, deprived us of much of the evidence we would need to produce a satisfactory reconstruction. The recent researches of Manolis Korres[13] have, on the one hand, done much to enrich our knowledge of the arrangement of the liturgical parts of the church, while on the other hand redating some features[14] to the following (mid-Byzantine) period. However, we can be sure that the Christianisation of the Great Temple did not cause major changes in its general arrangement, particularly in view of the fact that its generally three-aisled layout was easy to adapt to the new use (fig. 6). The west chamber was converted into a spacious narthex[15] and three door openings were constructed in the wall separating it from the main church. To the east, a sanctuary apse was fitted into the large ancient entrance,[16] while an arch was built across the gap left when for liturgical reasons the axial column on the short side of the interior colonnade had to be removed. The external appearance of the Parthenon was, however, considerably altered by the walls erected in the intercolumniation[17] so as to create a kind of precinct[18] used for the various secondary functions associated with large-scale basilicas at this time. Nonetheless, this was a reversible change.

On the other hand, it seems that the most serious damage yet done to the sculptural ornamentation of the Parthenon has to be ascribed to this Early Christian intervention. The east pediment lost its central statues, perhaps so as to make way for a consecration cross. Most of the metopes were so violently defaced that their themes are

3. Late Roman restoration work: mode of restoration of damaged column capitals. Column capitals in the opisthodomos; drawing by J. Durm. Source: N. Balanos, I anastilosis ton mnemeion tis Akropoleos, *Athens 1940.*

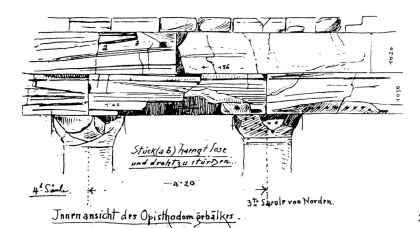

4, 5. Late Roman restoration work: restoration of the west door-
way of the cella, before demolition. Source: Balanos, op. cit.

impossible to distinguish today,[19] and various acts of vandalism were perpetrated on the continuous frieze. This extensive destruction had a tragic effect on the artistic value of the monument (fig. 7).

The alterations of the sixth century, then, did not start out from an act of destruction or a natural disaster, but from a change of use. After various misadventures of which all memory has been lost, the Parthenon – like many other ancient temples – became a church. As we have seen so far, the practical changes to adapt it for Christian worship were relatively unimportant, while by way of contrast the ideological 'uses' proved to be disastrous for the monument.

Far away from Athens, at the decision-making centres or foci of ideological ferment of Constantinople, Asia Minor and Syria, the drama of the condemnation of the ancient world was played out together with that of the rise of a new kind of man and the ruthless destruction of 'graven images' – that is, almost all of the old artistic heritage.[20] In Greece and its ancient sanctuaries[21] archaeological finds show that the silence of the written sources is coincidental and that similar phenomena also occurred there. The era which for many is the "age of spirituality"[22] could

also be described as the age of great confusion and senseless destruction.

In the case of the Parthenon, we unfortunately have no way of knowing what artistic activity took place at this time: whether there were mosaics, for instance, or pieces of metalwork whose quality might have been such as to make up for the loss of the ancient treasures. Nor do we know whether the destruction and acts of vandalism expressed the spirit of the society of the time or were committed on the initiative of a few individuals. The new religion demanded zeal and social stigmatisation, while the new teaching distanced those who received it from the aesthetic cultivation necessary to appreciate ancient works of art. It is typical that only one of the north metopes escaped the hammer: one which in the eyes of the zealots seemed to depict the Annunciation (see p. 119, fig. 41).[23]

However the case may be, during the fifth and sixth centuries the ideals of urban life faded and ultimately disappeared altogether. The uneducated converts, powerful bishops and fanatical monks were incapable of seeing in the Great Temple any values other than purely utilitarian ones (a large and solidly-built meeting-hall), nor could they discern in the sculpture anything beyond the theme (the hated pagan myths). The defaced gods and heroes on the facades of the Parthenon acquired a new use, too: they were a lesson to the society of the age that the great change had come about.

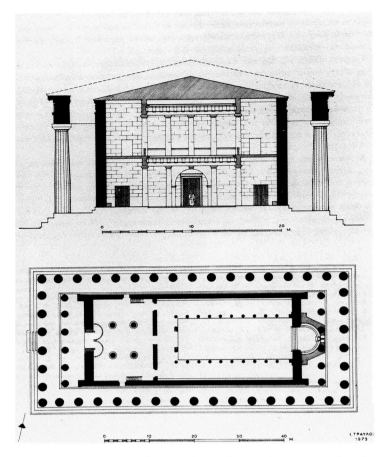

6. The Early Christian change of use: the Parthenon as a church; plan and section (drawings by J. Travlos). Source: Archaiologiki Ephimeris, 1973, p. 234.

7. The Early Christian change of use: a defaced metope. Source: Archive of the Committee for the Conservation of the Acropolis Monuments. Photograph: German Archaeological Institute, Athens.

3. In the twelfth century, Athens was a little town in the Byzantine province of Helladikon. There is very little information to be gleaned about it from the written sources, but we can infer indirectly that the province was in a state of demographic growth, financial prosperity and artistic vigour. Towards the end of the century the phenomena of crisis appeared,[24] and at this time we have more information from written sources.

The fact that the Great Temple – now a church to Our Lady of Athens – retained in the Greek Middle Ages something of its glorious ancient renown and a degree of its fascination can be indirectly deduced from the Imperial pilgrimage to it, a hundred years before, of Basil the Bulgar-Slayer, and directly from the interments in it of the metropolitan bishops: the Parthenon was also used at this time as a mausoleum[25] for eminent Athenian clerics. Today, thanks to the texts of Michail Choniates,[26] Metropolitan Bishop of Athens in 1180-1204 (fig. 8), scholars have quite good access to the society, church and state administration of the time. Choniates was among the learned churchmen from Asia Minor who had connections with circles in Constantinople and whose work in Greece in the twelfth and thirteenth centuries ensured them of a place in history.

At this time, most probably when Nikolaos Ayiotheodoritis was archbishop but also in the days of Michail Choniates, major construction and restoration work was done on the Parthenon.[27] We have direct and indirect evidence of what was done:[28] the older sanctuary apse was replaced with a new structure, semi-hexagonal in shape on the outer side, with a stone bench for the clergy and large double windows on its sides. This has now been demolished. Part of the east wall of the cella and three beams, presumably in a state of near-collapse, were removed. In the opisthonaos, a tall square tower[29] with an internal spiral staircase was erected; access to it was from the narthex, and it rose above the level of the roof. We do not know what its purpose was (figs. 9, 10). Inside the church, the walls were decorated with murals,[30] and all the outer surfaces may have been whitewashed. The fact that considerable numbers of fragments of twelfth-century sculpture have been found on the Acropolis – from screens, door frames, etc. – is an indication that the monument was also enriched with examples of the skills of contemporary marble masons. A long inscription on the bevelled sanctuary (though we do not know in exactly what position)[31] commemorated the works (fig. 11).

These additions to the Parthenon did not make use of

316

8. *Mid-Byzantine use, mid-Byzantine alterations: portrait of Michail Choniates in the church of St Peter, Kalyvia Kouvara. Source:* Deltion Christianikis Archaiologikis Etaireias, *vol. VII (1973-74), plate 27/2.*

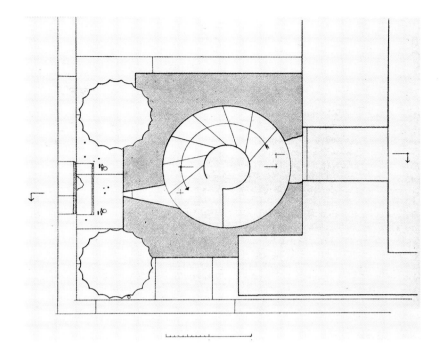

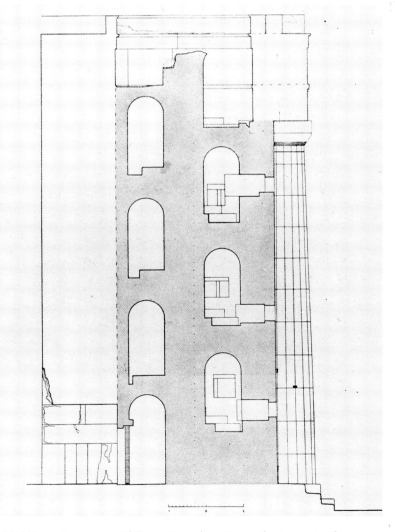

9. *Mid-Byzantine use, mid-Byzantine alterations: the tower in the opisthodomos; plan and section (drawings by Ch. Bouras). Source:* Archaiologiki Ephimeris, *1960, pp. 2, 3.*

the accustomed architectural modes[32] of the time, but were very carefully incorporated into the ancient building. They were constructed exclusively in re-used squared blocks of old marble[33], and their incorporation was rounded off with a general coat of whitewash.

The letters, panegyrics and memoranda of Choniates allow us to comment on this intervention in the Great Temple: one of the very few instances in the entire history of Byzantium in which such correlations can be made over the restoration of a monument.

Choniates, then, was an admirer of the Parthenon. Although – as was only natural for his time – his texts are dominated by rhetoric[34] and a literary approach, his knowledge of antiquity permitted him to glimpse the artistic and historical values of the temple. For this man – who also commissioned a painting showing the Classical city of Athens[35] – what may have been more important was the sentimental value of the monument. Yet respect for its artistic values can be seen in the attempts made by both Choniates and Ayiotheoroditis to incorporate the new elements into the ancient building, although, of course, they did not go so far as to approach the modern belief that new artistic works should not be added to older ones. And by modern standards, their good intentions were let down

10. Mid-Byzantine use, mid-Byzantine alterations: the tower in the opisthodomos. Photograph by M. Korres.

by the limited technical competence of their craftsmen: 'bricolage culture' had left its mark here, too. Lastly, the mere utilitarian value of the vast church would certainly have been reduced by the large number of churches which in the meantime had been built in the lower city.

Choniates' letters confirm for us that Athenian society – the flock of his bishopric – was unable to share his antiquarian interests by reason of its lack of education. For the learned bishop, the criterion to be applied in this instance was that the mid-Byzantine Athenians were ignorant of the ancient tongue. We can thus reasonably suppose that the views only of the bishop himself and those close to him were applied to the mid-Byzantine restoration of the great monument.

4. The chasm between society and those responsible for the fate of the Great Temple widened much further at a later date, under Turkish rule, when the Acropolis became a castle of purely military interest, from which Christians were banned, and the Parthenon was subjected to make-shift conversion into a Muslim mosque. The childish description of Evliya Çelebi (1667)[36] bears witness to the kind of admiration which the temple inspired in the Turks, who appreciated its mythological, magical and sentimen-

tal values over and above the question of utility. However, the people who, pressed by the needs of the Turkish-Venetian war, gave the Parthenon the additional use of a gunpowder magazine were clearly incapable of seeing in the monument anything beyond its value as a building which could withstand artillery fire.

That brought about the disaster of 1687, after which everything changed. The Parthenon ceased to be a mosque and lost its sanctity as an entity, thus opening up the way for looting and further destruction. The little mosque erected inside the ruins of the cella[37] to meet the needs of the Ottoman garrison displayed not the slightest desire to incorporate itself as a building into the environment of the temple.

There was, of course, no question of reconstruction. The Parthenon was a ruin, an open shell ideal for quarrying stone. Absolute ignorance made those who managed it absolutely indifferent to its fate; no one felt any need whatever to protect it.

In the realm of ideas, things gradually began to change in Western Europe, which during the eighteenth century made rapid progress thanks to multifaceted development. The penetration of travellers and artists into Turkish-occupied Greece grew side-by-side with knowledge of antiquity and the spread of science, thus increasing interest in Greece, its ancient monuments and, of course, the Parthenon as the most sublime of those monuments. The European admirers of the monument – whose sensitivity towards matters of art was in sharp contrast to the ignoramuses who managed it – perceived its historical and artistic values and began to study it and copy its forms and sculptures. In the scientific analyses, knowledge of history and pictorial representations which the travellers took away from their trips to Athens, the Great Temple regained some of the prestige it had once enjoyed and a new legend was created. This introduced a new 'use': the

11. Mid-Byzantine use, mid-Byzantine alterations: fragment of the inscription in the sanctuary apse. Photograph by P. Koufopoulos.

12. *The monument after Independence. Purism on the Acropolis: the demolition of the Propylaea ramparts; water-colour by M. Rørbye. Source: Photographic Archive of the Municipality of Athens.*

Parthenon became an exhibit, and more and more foreigners came to visit it.

This proved to be a disaster because of Lord Elgin. Before the managers of the monument had time to realise that a change in attitudes was imminent, Elgin systematically looted the sculptures in the belief that they would be much more useful as exhibits in London than in Athens.[38]

This account is only indirectly connected with the theory and history of the restoration of monuments. The furore over Elgin's shameful rape of the monument reinforced the belief that works of sculpture lose their meaning when removed from the architectural work for which they were created, while the flood of copies, casts and imitations produced at this time strengthened appreciation of the originals, which were unique and incomparable. At this time, too, the ruins served as a supplement to the romantic landscape to create a new aesthetic of monuments which was totally alien to that of the men who had built them. This established the demand that the 'ruinous character' of the monument should be preserved.

A few years later, the Greeks fighting for their freedom took the Parthenon as a symbol of ancient glory, and it became the ideal of the nation. The thoughts about monuments to be found here and there in the works of the illiterate and pious Makriyannis are testimony to the rapidity with which symbols and emotional values can be accepted when historical circumstances are favourable.

5. The founding in Athens, eight years before the War of Independence, of the Society of the Friends of the Muses, an association devoted to the protection of antiquities, shows the extent to which the views of enlightened Europe with regard to the values represented by the monuments had spread to Greek society, still enslaved. Of course, the national awakening did not take place overnight; it would be more correct to see here, too, a process of maturation which was accelerated by reaction to the looting of the first two decades of the century.

It is nonetheless the case that as soon as the war was over and the Acropolis was surrendered by the Turks in 1833, the work of caring for its monuments began. The new managers were Greeks, with Bavarians as their advisers, but interest in the Parthenon was much more widespread and a whole host of philhellenes – academics, antiquarians and politicians from Western Europe – con-

stantly interfered in the affairs of the new state. Fresh intervention began on the Acropolis, in an atmosphere of national rebirth, lively admiration for antiquity and revulsion for the recent past; its nature was clearly that of clearing, collection and research.

The fact that for centuries the rock had been used as a fortress had resulted in the accumulation of a large number of modern utilitarian buildings around and on the temples. Most of these structures had been ruined during the long years of war, while architectural members from the temples themselves were scattered here and there across the rock, under a layer of soil or in full view. It was within the rationale of the age that all these worthless ruins should be demolished and removed; no one saw them as documentation of recent history. As a result, the doctrine of 'purism' established itself on the Acropolis without a word of protest (fig. 12). At a much later date, the historians[39] began to feel rather guilty about having taken such hasty action. Soon, however, the demolition of recent structures was extended to the famous buildings: the little mosque in the Parthenon was knocked down in 1844, and the huge water reservoir on the west side followed it in 1856.

Kyriakos Pittakis began to collect the abundant ancient members of the Great Temple in an attempt to gather together and manage all the materials connected with it, and the symbolic inauguration of the restoration pro-

13, 14. The monument after Independence: C.F. Schinkel's proposal for King Othon's palace on the Acropolis; elevation and floor plan. Source: C.F. Schinkel, Entwurf zu einem Königspalast auf der Akropolis bei Athen, *4th ed., Berlin 1878; Athens, Gennadios Library.*

gramme began as early as August 1834. At a ceremony attended by the young King Othon, the famous architect of Classicism Leo von Klenze[40] restored to its position one of the fallen drums of the temple.

Of much greater importance were the theoretical standards laid out by von Klenze in a report and included in his 'aphoristic comments'.[41] These are the earliest such specifications, and they shed a great deal of light on the concepts of the age: von Klenze recommended the clearing of modern accretions, reconstruction using the ancient materials and a reasonable amount of supplementation, the retention of the ruinous state, and the removal of useless materials from the Acropolis. In other words, his approach involved placing a high estimation on the artistic, environmental[42] and aesthetic values, and a low estimation on the historical and utilitarian values.

In the same year, Karl Schinkel, another leading architect of the time, produced a proposal for building a palace of King Othon on the Acropolis (figs. 13, 14) which is also enlightening as to the beliefs of the period.[43] Here again, the aesthetic and environmental values of the Parthenon

320

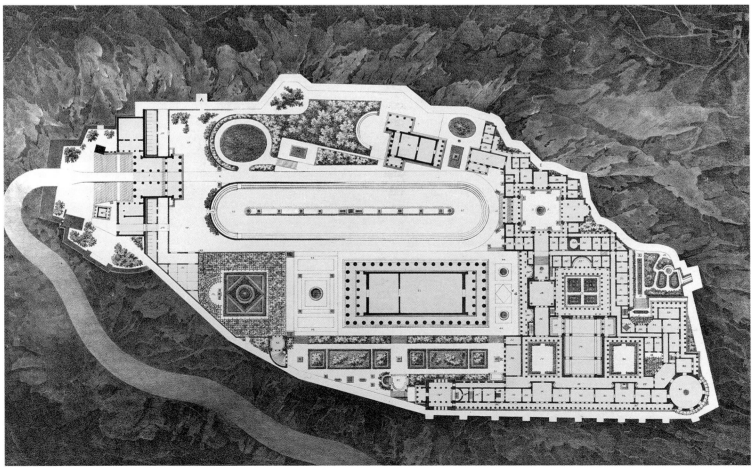

15. *The monument after Independence: Pittakis' reconstruction of the north wall of the cella, using ordinary bricks. Photograph by N. Balanos. Source: Balanos, op. cit.*

were overestimated, while the historical values were completely ignored. Latent in this ambitious plan – which, fortunately, never led anywhere – was the idea (widespread in Europe at the time) that the enlightened monarch should make his mark as a supporter of the arts and sciences and that his palace should occupy a central position in the urban plan.[44]

Kyriakos Pittakis,[45] the Greek archaeologist and a tireless worker in the cause of learning, was certainly not occupied by such theoretical considerations. He accomplished an impressive volume of excavation, collection and arrangement work on the Acropolis, and undoubtedly believed in the principle of purism. The first restoration project planned by him (in 1842-45, with his future opponent Alexandros Rizos-Rangavis) was in effect emergency work, and it consisted of the complete reconstruction with ancient materials of two columns in the north peristyle, the partial reconstruction of two more, and the rebuilding of a large part of the lateral walls of the cella.

We do not know whether Pittakis was aware of von Klenze's specifications, or whether he was influenced by the reconstruction of the little temple of Athena Nike,

which had already taken place.[46] His work was of a markedly improvised character; lacking a theoretical background and with absolutely no previous documentation, Pittakis put architectural members which resembled each other in random positions,[47] used spolia of all kinds,[48] and had no hesitation in making extensive use of unsuitable materials – for instance, the machine-made red bricks which he placed in the walls (fig. 15). However, he did succeed in giving back to the devastated Parthenon a degree of bulk as a building and thus improving it from the aesthetic point of view, while at the same time respecting its character as a ruin. Clearly, it was out of the question at the time that the Parthenon should be left as it was. Equally plainly, the question of practical utility was also of importance to Pittakis, who turned part of the cella into a lapidarium for sculptures and had no hestitation in selling off as ordinary building materials what he judged to be shapeless and useless marbles from the Acropolis.[49]

This is not the place to discuss the studies conducted by archaeologists and architects during the nineteenth century – studies which gave us a new and scientific image of the Parthenon in terms both of its architecture and of its sculpture. This new knowledge made it possible to produce a more correct evaluation of the monument and, consequently, created new needs for its protection, maintenance and aesthetic enhancement.

16. *The period of transition: Kalkos' segmental arch over the west door. Photograph by N. Balanos. Source: Balanos, op. cit.*

The second reconstruction project applied to the Parthenon was conducted in 1872, six years after the death of Pittakis. Recent research by Fani Mallouchou has shown that it was supervised by the architect Panayis Kalkos.[50] It consisted of the repair of the lintel over the west entrance to the cella, using a segmental arch (fig. 16), and the securing of the west frieze and the architrave slabs beneath it. This was the first occasion on which iron bars were incorporated into the temple in modern times. Once again, the project was makeshift and undocumented, was not finally summed up as a published paper, and was aesthetically defective.[51]

For the history of restoration, then, all the interventions in the Parthenon prior to 1894[52] constituted a stage of empiricism, purism and the satisfaction of rudimentary needs. There was undoubted social approval for the projects. There is no point in attempting to draw parallels with the activities being carried out elsewhere in Europe at the same time, since the restoration of monuments there involved dealing with a multiplicity of problems and also had theoretical foundations based on the positions which could be attributed to specific scholars – positions which created the 'schools' of restoration that emerged in the second half of the nineteenth century. Nor is there any point in comparing the work done on the Parthenon with other projects in Greece, since such projects were more or less non-existent at this time.

6. The perceptible changes in the structure and form of the ruined Great Temple continued during the first third of the twentieth century, thanks to two projects which have gone down in history in association with the name of Nikolaos Balanos. This was an instance in which a coincidence of factors enabled the thought and will of a single man to leave their marks on an architectural monument of unique value.

The first project took place in 1899-1902, and the second from 1922 to 1933. During the twenty years which elapsed between the two projects, Balanos restored the Erechtheum and the Propylaea, acquiring experience and a reputation as he experimented with the application of his method to those two fine ancient buildings. Almost down to the time of the Second World War, his was a name to conjure with in relation to the Acropolis and the restoration of monuments in Greece as a whole.[53]

Over those forty years, tremendous progress was made in these matters elsewhere in Europe. In Italy, in particular, where the ancient monuments faced problems similar to those of Greece,[54] activities developed which were based on an in-depth knowledge of each monument, on the transcending of dogma in the theoretical sphere, and

17. Restoration and reconstruction by N. Balanos: Balanos' scaffolding on the SE corner of the temple. Photograph by N. Balanos. Source: Balanos, op. cit.

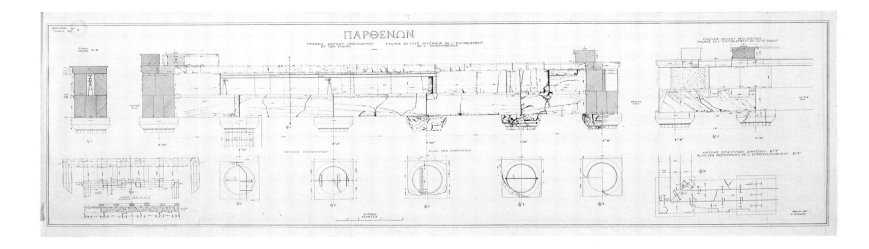

18. *Restoration and reconstruction by N. Balanos: his 'method' applied to the entablature of the opisthodomos. Drawings of the elevation and plan of five column capitals. Source: Balanos, op. cit.*

on the progress being made in specialised technology. But that meant nothing to Balanos; indeed, he deliberately ignored it.[55]

The details of Nikolaos Balanos' projects are quite well known.[56] He himself published a book on the subject,[57] which is valuable for the information it contains but disappointingly inadequate and superficial by comparison with its theme. It is hoped that when his unpublished archive, now lodged with the Archaeological Society, is published[58] we will possess more knowledge about these important projects and about the conditions (financial aspects, relations with the Archaeological Service, the Archaeological Society and public opinion) in which they were carried out.

For late nineteenth century Greek society, with its almost excessive orientation towards the ideals of antiquity, the Parthenon was a sacred symbol of the Nation and tangible proof of its superiority. It was the most honoured, beautiful and valuable thing which Greece possessed. The minor damage caused by the earthquake of 1894 stimulated concern, triggered action on the part of the Archaeological Service, and led to the formation of two committees: a three-man committee of foreign architectural experts[59] and a joint committee to organise and supervise the work to be done.[60] It was from this committee that Balanos, then Prefectural Engineer, set out, taking initiatives which gradually transferred to him the responsibility for the project and making him the unchallenged manager of the Acropolis monuments almost down to the time of his death.

The three theoretical texts produced by the members of the first committee provided a general base[61] which the first project, at least, took more or less as its starting-point and with which it could be inferred that Balanos agreed,[62] though there were instances in which he referred to the principles of Kavvadias and Dörpfeld.[63] He never stated principles of restoration of his own, nor did he appear to be aware of pioneering and very well-known ideas of the time, such as those of C. Boito[64] or L. Beltrami.[65]

Unfortunately, Balanos was never able to overcome the one-sidedness of his training as a civil engineer.[66] On archaeological matters, he was always dependant on the archaeologists, and in the work of restoration he came up with immediate and practical solutions which were testimony of ingenuity (fig. 18) but not of profound thought. In his papers (minutes of the meetings of committees, councils, etc.) we can see him talking round the archaeologists and dealing with the true restorers – though the latter did not make their appearance until 1931, by which time it was too late,[67] and Balanos exceeded in extracting even from them general and vague consent for what he was doing. In his thirty five active years he ignored the ethics of the design project;[68] as a result, he only had to deal with real opposition on one occasion, when Orlandos attacked him in the Press[69] over his plans for the north colonnade. One thus has to arrive at the conclusion that Balanos succeeded in setting his personal seal on the Great Temple and the other monuments of the Acropolis because there was no system for control and criticism of his work on the part either of the state or of public opinion (figs. 19, 20).

The work of Balanos was judged positively while he was still alive,[70] and negatively when its ultimate results[71] – which were truly catastrophic for the monuments – became visible. Today, it is common knowledge that his Achilles heel was one of the details of the method (or rather, the technique) which he applied: the fact that iron expands as it oxidises, causing the ancient architectural members into which it had been inserted to crack. Balanos was exclusively to blame for this terrible disaster: he was directly responsible because he must have known that iron had this property,[72] and indirectly because, apart from anything else, the insertion of metal parts into the ancient marbles involved an irreversible intervention in them.[73]

324

Balanos' ultimate aim was to restore the temple to some of its ancient grandeur, creating a more complete picture of it as if it had suffered less damage.[74] In other words, his purpose was aesthetic and didactic. Thus, while at first his intention was to secure those parts of the temple which were on the point of collapse, he proceeded to drastic reconstruction work in order to enhance the building aesthetically. The aspect of his work which can be looked on most positively was his attempt to incorporate the surviving ancient members into the building and to minimise the addition of new materials, which gained general appreciation for his method and helped to establish the concept of 'anastilosis' internationally.[75] Approval can also be granted for his intentions of: a) respecting the 'ruinous state' of the monument; b) respecting the later stages in the construction of the temple,[76] retaining the tower with its spiral staircase and the door-posts added during the repairs in the time of Julian; c) not removing the sculptures, but in fact adding copies of some of the pedimental sculpture, presumably for didactic purposes; d) respecting the need for it to be possible to distinguish between the ancient material and the modern material with which it was supplemented, and e) not respecting modern elements which disturbed the unity of the structure.[77]

With Balanos' double and drastic intervention, the appearance of the temple changed radically. The historical

19. *Restoration and reconstruction by N. Balanos: the north side of the temple after reconstruction by Pittakis. Source: Balanos, op. cit.*

20. *Restoration and reconstruction by N. Balanos: the north side of the temple after reconstruction by Balanos. Source: Balanos, op. cit.*

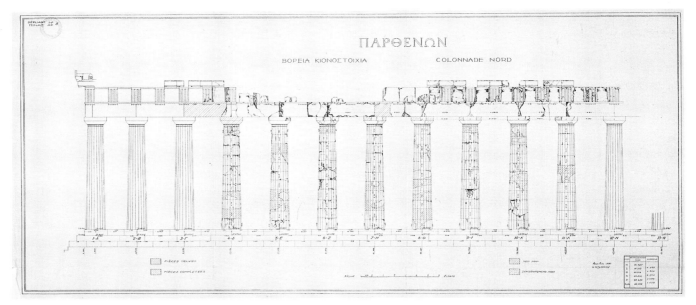

21. Restoration and reconstruction by N. Balanos: a column capital in the west portico supplemented in the Balanos manner. Source: Balanos, op. cit.

and scientific values of the Parthenon obviously interested him little because, on the one hand, he was totally ignorant of the method of interpreting traces on the marbles (as taught since then by Dörpfeld, Dinsmoor, Stevens and Orlandos) and, on the other, he was vigorously opposed to the passive approach of leaving the monuments of antiquity 'as found'.[78]

The negative aspects of the two projects are, unfortunately, numerous. They could be summarised as follows: a) Balanos ignored the special characteristics of each individual architectural member, using those which resembled each other regardless of their original position, and even joined up fragments of different members into new members; b) he ignored the value of the ancient material, cruelly defacing the architectural members so as to create smooth surfaces to which supplementary pieces could be fitted or so as to insert iron rods (figs. 21-25);[79] c) he ignored research and used whatever section iron he could find on the market, without running even rudimentary tests of its properties; d) he ignored the integrity of the materials (sunlight on Pentelic marble) and used cheap cement in vital and obvious positions on the monument; e) he ignored the questions of texture and patina on the new marble sections.

One could round off this reference to the work done on the Parthenon during the first third of the twentieth century by observing that – for all the generally good intentions and favourable conditions – it was of decisive importance that the issue was handled by a single individual. Although Balanos succeeded in aesthetically enhancing the general appearance of the temple, he deprived it of historical documentation, he adulterated its details and

he paved the way for serious damage to occur in the near future.

7. Over the forty years from 1935 to 1975 very few changes came about in the Parthenon despite the fact that the theoretical and practical issues involved were maturing very rapidly. After about 1950, a process of social evolution, modernisation and economic progress began in Greece, based in part on the development of tourism. This created a need for the enhancement of all the country's 'exhibits', and led to the reorganisation of museums, archaeological sites and monuments. Social evolution and a rising level of education also contributed to the need for enhancement, and were the factors which took the monuments out of their role as symbols and, gradually, turned them into social goods. On the Acropolis, this system functioned quite simply, with the successful rearrangement by Yannis Miliadis of the antiquities in the Museum. Plans for major works were confined to the Propylaea, and nothing was done to the Parthenon.

However, over the same period there were a number of events which, while appararently heterogeneous, were of great importance in shaping the situation after 1975. Some of these events were of an organisational and environmental nature, others were connected with the evolution of restoration in Greece (in the theoretical sense, or involving the acquisition of experience), and a third group were of immediate interest for the Parthenon. They could be set out in summary tabular form so as to convey an idea of the dynamics of change, and those which involved the monument itself could be dealt with at greater length.

1943-44: The first cracks are discovered in the marbles of the parts of the Parthenon which Balanos had reconstructed.

1941-44: Systematic study of the monument by Anastasios Orlandos.[80]

1944: The Parthenon[81] is damaged during the December rebellion.

1947-57: Anastasios Orlandos reconstructs the south wing of the Propylaea.[82]

1953: Work begins on the demolition of the tower and staircase in the opisthonaos of the Parthenon; the project is suspended.[83]

1953: The Archaeological Council[84] discusses the work on the Parthenon.

1953-56: The Stoa of Attalus in the Agora is reconstructed.[85]

1953-58: Sections of new marble are prepared to protect the west frieze of the Parthenon.[86]

1956: The Archaeological Council holds a theoretical discussion of the reconstruction of the Stoa of Attalus.[87] When it is opened, Orlandos submits a memorandum.[88]

1956-59: Restoration of the temple of Aphaia[89] on Aegina.

1957: 1st International Conference of Monument Architects and Technicians, in Paris.[90]

1959: Restoration of columns at the Sounion temple.[91]

1959-60: Restoration of the proskenion of the theatre[92] at the Amphiareion, Oropos.

1960: The Archaeological Service is reorganised and brought under the control of the Ministry to the Prime Minister.[93]

1960-64: Work on the Parthenon: on the floor of the cella, the two side entrances to the cella, and the substructure of the crepidoma (figs. 26, 27).[94]

22-25. Restoration and reconstruction by N. Balanos: column capitals on the east side supplemented in the Balanos manner. Source: Balanos, op. cit.

26. The interim period: the side doors of the cella before the intervention of Stikas. Source: Balanos, op. cit.

27. The interim period: the side doors of the cella after the intervention of Stikas. Photograph by S. Mavrommatis.

The question of the demolition of the Byzantine staircase in the opisthonaos brought to the surface, for the first time, the crisis within the group of people responsible for managing the Greek monuments during the Fifties. The crisis took the form of a dispute between the idealistic German-trained archaeologists (Orlandos, Miliadis[101] and Karouzos), who supported a latter-day purism, and the younger archaeologists, who advocated the retention of the historical evidence left by subsequent building phases. Eloquent testimony to this crisis and to the disagreements within the group can be seen in the beams and coffered panels, cut in new marble, which still lie on the ground on the west side of the Great Temple: these were painstakingly made by superb marble-masons (the last descendants of the craftsmen of the time of Classicism) to form a protective roof over the west frieze, but in the end they were never put in place on the monument (fig. 28). The plan was frustrated by the lively opposition to extensive intervention with new materials caused by the recent reconstruction of the Stoa of Attalus, and also by the caution advised by the younger archaeologists and the messages received from abroad.[102] Nonetheless, drastic intervention in ancient monuments continued throughout the Fifties, relying on the prestige and authority of Anastasios Orlandos.[103] However, when his successor in the Service Efstathios Stikas (who signed the Venice Charter on behalf of Greece) carried out some work on the Parthenon, it was painless and on a small scale. Although the disastrous effects on the Great Temple of Balanos' iron rods and of the polluted Athenian atmosphere were now obvious,[104]

28. The interim period: beams and coffered panels on the ground. Photograph by M. Korres.

the civil service department responsible for the monument submerged itself in secondary details.

8. The period since 1975 has been one of lively activity on the Acropolis, thanks to the state's decision to save the monuments there from a number of specific dangers and to enhance their role as social commodities. Much has been written about this endeavour,[105] given that today a multiplicity of information about the management of the cultural heritage is as much of as social necessity as the management itself. Here, then, we shall confine ourselves to that which is strictly essential, referring only to the Parthenon and to questions of the restoration ethics and principles which have been applied during the interventions since 1975.

A number of observations can be made about the new extraneous conditions: a) many issues connected with the country's wealth of monuments have ripened to maturity in Greece, in the sphere of theory and in connection with the methodology and techniques of application. A contribution to this process has been made by the respectable number of architects and technicians who have systematically studied specialised subjects abroad; b) today, monuments such as the Parthenon are regarded as being of international interest. They are no longer national symbols, but priceless documents of Western civilisation with which millions of people are familiar; c) public opinion has become extremely sensitive to the dangers threatening the monuments. Architectural Heritage Year (1975) did much to promote interest in this direction;[106] d) the socialisation of cultural commodities has produced benefits for the monuments (publications, educational programmes, incorporation into the school curriculum) but has also led to

abuses (populism, a tendency towards vandalism, a cheapening of the media). It has also led to the demand that architectural monuments become more didactic; e) the Venice Charter is a useful instrument for understanding and criticism; f) for the Parthenon itself, the publication in 1977 of Orlandos' three-volume work created a base of knowledge of great value for further research.

The Committee for the Conservation of the Acropolis Monuments which was set up by the Ministry of Culture[107] to design and monitor the works was generously endowed with funds and was provided with administrative facilities. The Committee responded by introducing systems of action unprecedented in Greece, such as: a) interdisciplinary composition of the teams which guided and monitored the plans and the work itself; b) a system of successive stages of judgement,[108] whose purpose was to prevent decisions from being taken too hastily or on the basis of personal criteria, and which makes provision for international meetings to share information and spread responsibility; c) the setting up of a technical department with carefully selected staff; d) the promotion of research – that is, of the creation of new knowledge about the monuments or restoration technology; and e) the promotion of a flow of information on all these points and of education by means of exhibitions and educational programmes.

The studies of and intervention in the Parthenon carried out since 1975 can be summed up as follows.

In 1976, the last three statues on the west pediment were taken to the Museum and replaced with copies.

In 1977, the architect Manolis Korres began work on the general study, which was submitted in 1983.[109] It made provision for twelve separate projects. In 1981, a severe earthquake made it necessary to take provisional measures at those points where the Parthenon was on the point of collapse. In September 1983, the first international meeting on the Parthenon was held; it approved the general restoration study and also the first two projects for the east side of the temple.[110] In early 1984 a symposium on the same subject was held in Naples.[111]

The years 1984 and 1985 were taken up with preparation of the mechanical equipment (figs. 30, 31),[112] after which it was possible to begin work at once on the first two projects for the east side of the Parthenon. In parallel – also under the direction of Manolis Korres – the study for the reconstruction of the pronaos was prepared;[113] it was submitted in 1988, the year in which another scientific meeting on the monument was held in Paris (organised by the international body ICOMOS).[114] In April 1989, the second international meeting on the Parthenon was held in Athens, and dealt with the question of the reconstruction of the pronaos. The proceedings of the meeting were published the following year.[115] Research into the surface protection of the marble against atmospheric erosion began in 1975, and a systematic programme of conservation has been continuously in force since 1981.

29. *The works of the Committee for the Conservation of the Acropolis Monuments: the east side fully clad in scaffolding. Photograph by Ch. Bouras.*

The principles on which the intervention in the Great Temple is based and the purposes which it is designed to serve will have become plain from this text so far and are described in detail[116] in the 1983 study. The initial purpose, it will be remembered, was to remove the causes of the continuing damage and wear and to secure the monument. Improved conservation after the completion of the work was another aim. However, it became clear that it would be possible and feasible to go beyond these first targets and extend them to enhancing the values of the Parthenon; this could be done, on the one hand, by eliminating the errors of the past and, on the other, by further reconstruction – that is, by restoring some of the ancient materials scattered around the temple to their original positions on it.

As far as principles are concerned, the designers of the Parthenon restoration projects have stated their views, which have been exhaustively discussed at the international meetings held so far and repeatedly published.[117] They involve certain articles of the Venice Charter, together with five more specific principles which emerge indirectly from the Charter and are particularly suitable

for monuments constructed entirely in articulated stone, such as the temples of Greek antiquity.

The articles of the Venice Charter which the Parthenon studies have taken as inviolable are those numbered 2, 3, 5, 6, 8-12, 15 and 16. Naturally enough, a manifesto whose content is as wide-ranging as that of the Charter is capable of different interpretations at various points – for example, Article 15, of which there has been much discussion.[118]

The five more specific principles which the designers of the Parthenon projects committed themselves to comply with are as follows: a) reversibility: safeguarding of the ability to return the monument to the state it was in prior to the intervention; b) retention of the self-contained nature of the architectural members and their simple static operation; c) restriction of the intervention to those parts of the monument which have already been reconstructed; d) securing of the monument's ability to protect itself in outdoor conditions, and e) minimisation of changes in the appearance of the temple.

Perhaps some clarification of the first two principles[119] – and of reversibility in particular – is required. This principle, which was discussed at length in 1983, can only fully be complied with thanks to the structural nature of the ancient Greek temples. Their structurally (and aesthetically) self-contained architectural members rest in place by their own weight, without any binding material. This means –

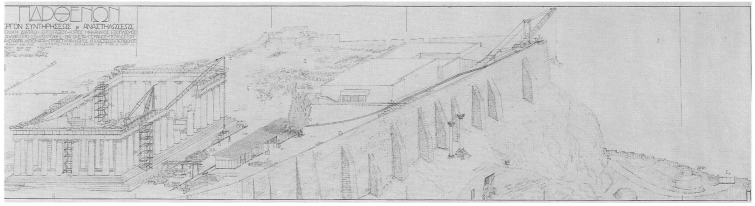

30. The works of the Committee for the Conservation of the
Acropolis Monuments: the mechanical equipment for the project.
Drawing by M. Korres.

31. The works of the Committee for the Conservation of the
Acropolis Monuments: the mechanical equipment for the project.
Photograph by Ch. Bouras.

32. *The works of the Committee for the Conservation of the Acropolis Monuments: the east side at the maximum point of dismantling. Source: Archive of the Committee for the Conservation of the Acropolis Monuments, slide 1188.*

theoretically, at least – that they can be dismantled and reassembled *ad infinitum* as long as they themselves are not damaged. If the ancient technological principle of the autonomy of the architectural members is complied with, any errors that may occur during reassembly can, by definition, be rectified. Mistakes made during the insertion of supplementary material can also be rectified as long as certain technological specifications of reversibility are complied with.

In the Parthenon, then, the architectural members have retained their autonomy and the very simple manner in which they are supported. They are never joined to others, and solutions involving the dynamic weighting of the bearing structure are never used: these were unknown to the architecture of free beams on supports. As D. Mertens has perceptively noted,[120] 'anastilosis' in the strict sense of the term is only possible in buildings constructed entirely in curved stone using the characteristic techniques

of ancient masonry. Korres has stated a supplementary principle,[121] one which has been complied with in the Parthenon: that the interior mass should be taken as an authentic part of the monument – not only of the sections of the monument which have been continuously present, but also of those which have been reconstructed.

This serves as an interpretation of a point made at the start of this article. The Parthenon did not play a decisive role internationally in shaping the ethics of monument restoration because of the particular features of ancient Greek temples by comparison with monuments elsewhere in Europe, because of the fact that views about the monumental heritage only spread recently, and, undoubtedly, because those who managed the monument lacked a clear theoretical background.

Criticism to date of the intervention in the Great Temple which has been taking place since 1976 has focused not so much on the results, which are not yet clear, as on the intentions of the designers and the principles adhered to.[122] The meetings held in 1983 and 1989 did, however, provide opportunities for criticism and the replies to it to be heard; furthermore, publication of the debate in the corresponding *Proceedings* made it accessible to all.

33. The works of the Committee for the Conservation of the Acropolis Monuments: the east side as it is today. Photograph by S. Mavrommatis.

34. The works of the Committee for the Conservation of the Acropolis Monuments: the proposal for restoration of the pronaos as approved by the Committee; model. Photograph by S. Mavrommatis.

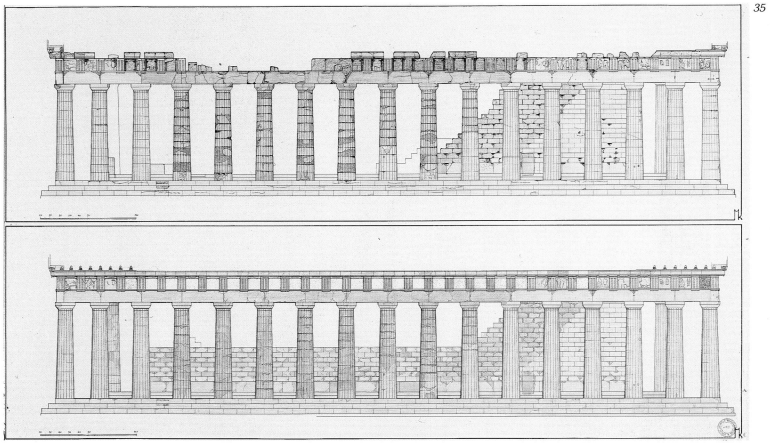

35-37. *The works of the Committee for the Conservation of the Acropolis Monuments: the Korres proposal, 1983. Four pairs of drawings of the facades of the temple, with old and new sections shown in colour. Drawings by M. Korres.*

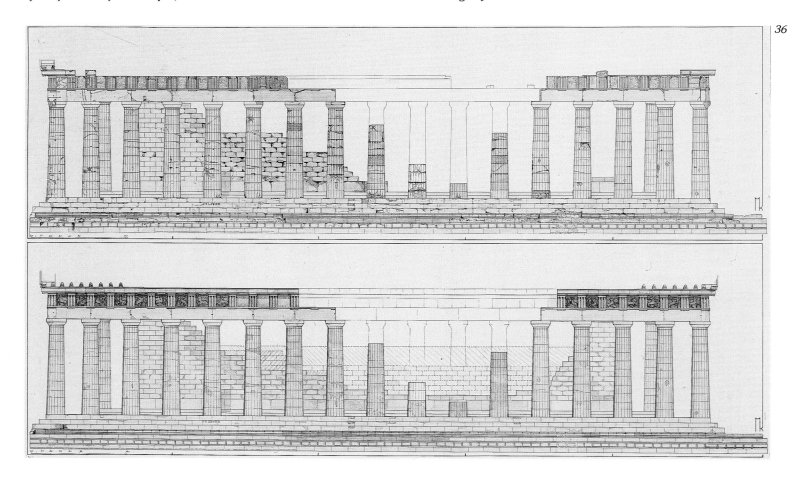

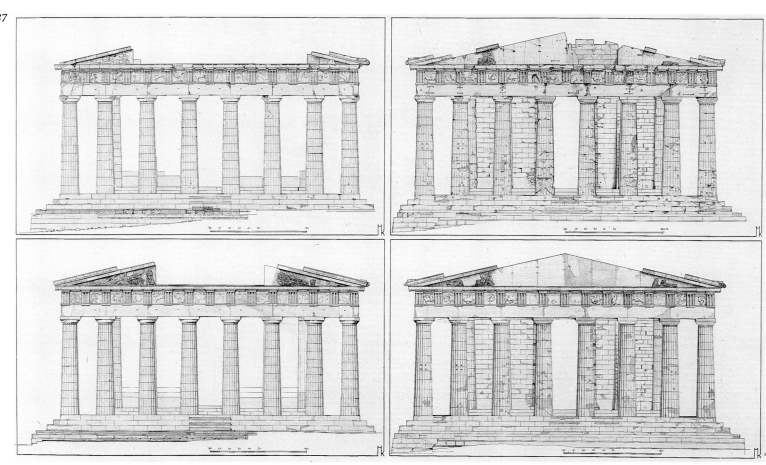

36

37

38-41. *The works of the Committee for the Conservation of the Acropolis Monuments: the Korres proposals for the restoration of the pronaos, 1989; model. Photographs by S. Mavrommatis.*

38

39

40

41

335

42. *The works of the Committee for the Conservation of the Acropolis Monuments: the project in progress with replacement of the SE corner cornice. Source: Archive of the Committee for the Conservation of the Acropolis Monuments, T33576/1191.*

Notes

1. The term 'use' is employed throughout in the broadest sense.

2. W.B. Dinsmoor, 'The Repair of the Athena Parthenos. A Story of Five Dowels', *American Journal of Archaeology* (= *AJA*) 38, 1934, pp. 93-106.

3. J. Travlos, 'I pyrpolisis tou Parthenonos kai i episkevi tou epi Ioulianou' ('The Burning of the Parthenon by the Heruli and its Repair in the Time of Julian'), *Archaiologiki Ephimeris* (= *AE*) 1973, pp. 218-236, and J. Travlos, *Pictorial Dictionary of Ancient Athens*, London 1971, p. 444, fig. 564.

4. M. Korres, Ch. Bouras, *Meleti yia tin Apokatastasi tou Parthenonos* ('Study for the Restoration of the Parthenon'), vol. 1, Athens 1983, pp. 131-149 and especially pp. 136-137, notes 83-113 (= *Meleti* 1).

5. *Ibid.*, pp. 219 and 225.

6. The fragments of columns and coffered panels used as building material in the Agora are so small as to confirm the complete destruction of the interior of the temple. See W.B. Dinsmoor Jr., 'New Parthenon Finds in the Agora', *Archaiologika Analekta ex Athinon'* (= *AAA*) IV, 1971, pp. 264-268. The results of recent research by M. Korres are presented elsewhere in this volume.

7. For the Hellenistic portico (of unknown position), see J. Travlos, *op. cit.*, pp. 227-235, and *Meleti* 1, p. 145, notes 91-96.

8. M. Korres, 'A Consideration of the Tectonic and Plastic Character of the Parthenon as in a Half-Finished State, as Completed, as a Ruin and as Restored', *Proceedings of the 2nd International Meeting for the Restoration of the Acropolis Monuments*, Athens 1985, pp. 116-118.

9. In complete contrast to the state of affairs at this time in, for instance, Syria.

10. The huge coffered panels (weighing 3.6 tons) shattered when the roof above them caught fire, and fell all along the length of the long sides.

11. A. Michaelis, *Der Parthenon*, Leipzig 1870-71; F.W. Deichmann, 'Die Basilica im Parthenon', *Mitteilungen des Deutschen Archäologischen Instituts. Athenische Abteilung* (= *AM*) 63/64, 1938-39, pp. 127-139, plates 21-24; *Meleti* 1, pp. 138-139; A. Frantz, 'From Paganism to Christianity in the Temples of Athens', *Dumbarton Oaks Papers* (= *DOP*) 19, 1965, pp. 187-204 and especially p. 201; Ida Hill, *The Ancient City of Athens*, London 1953, p. 157.

12. See J. Travlos, *op. cit.*, p. 445. Elsewhere, Travlos accepted an earlier date; see J. Travlos, *Poleodomiki exelixis ton Athinon* ('The Town Planning Development of Athens'), Athens 1960, p. 138.

13. *Meleti* 1, pp. 138-139, and especially M. Korres, *Der Parthenon bis 1687, Reparatur-Kirche-Moschee-Pulvermagazin, Die Explosion des Parthenon*, Antiken Museum, Berlin 1990, pp. 17-44 (exhibition catalogue).

14. *Meleti* 1, p. 139.

15. Inside which was the baptistery.

16. This apse, semicircular on the outside, was replaced with another in the twelfth century.

17. For a reconstruction of the walls in the intercolumniation, see M. Korres, *Die Parthenon bis 1687...*, *op. cit.*, figs. 9, 11 and 17.

18. Grooves were cut into the floor of the peristyle to allow rain-water to be collected and led off for use.

19. C. Praschniker, *Parthenonstudien*, Augsburg and Vienna 1928, pp. 48ff; E. Berger, *Der Parthenon in Basel, Dokumentation zu den Metopen*, Mainz 1986, *passim*.

20. Among typical examples of those who instigated such destruction one could cite Maternus Cynegius (P. Athanasiadis, 'Apo tin Romaiki sti Vyzantini Aftokratoria' ['From the Roman to the Byzantine Empire'], *Istoria tou Ellinikou Ethnous* [= *IEE*], vol. VII, Athens 1978, p. 87) and Porphyrius (Marcus Diaconus, *Vios Porphyriou* ['Life of Porphyrius'], ed. H. Gregoire-M.A. Kougener, Paris 1930, pp. 22ff).

21. See J.M. Speiser, 'La christianisation des sanctuaires païens en Grèce', *Neue Forschungen in Griechischen Heiligtümern*, Tübingen 1976, pp. 309-320; F.W. Deichmann, 'Von Tempel zur Kirche', *Mullus, Festschrift Th. Klauser*, Münster 1864, pp. 52-59.

22. B.K. Weitzmann, 'Introduction', *Age of Spirituality: A Symposium*, New York 1980, pp. 1-5.

23. B.G. Rodenwaldt, 'Interpretatio Christiana', *Archäologischer Anzeiger* (= *AA*) 1933, columns 401-405, and E. Berger, *op. cit.*, pp. 48-50, plates 2, 3, 34, 35.

24. Insecurity, strained relations with the central authorities and poverty. See Judith Herrin, 'Realities of Byzantine Provincial Government, Hellas and Peloponnesos 1180-1205', *DOP* 29, 1975, pp. 254ff.

25. A.K. Orlandos, L. Vranousis, *Ta Haragmata tou Parthenonos* ('The Incised Inscriptions of the Parthenon'), Athens 1973. Incised inscriptions nos. 39, 40, 47, 48, 62, 101, 222 and 232, referring to the deaths of bishops, date from the twelfth century.

26. See J. Herrin, *op. cit.*; K.M. Setton, 'Athens in the Later Twelfth Century', *Speculum* XIX, 1944, pp. 179ff; S. Lambros, *Ai Athinai peri ta teli tou 12ou aionos* ('Athens in the Late Twelfth Century'), Athens 1878; G. Stadtmüller, 'Michel Choniates Metropolit von Athen', *Orientalia Christiana* XXXIII, 2, Rome 1934, pp. 268ff. For the texts of the metropolitan himself, see S. Lambros, *Michail Akominatou tou Choniatou ta Sozomena* ('The Remains of Michail Akominatos Choniates'), Athens 1879-80.

27. For a collection of information from written sources, see An. Demetriades-Norré, *Studies in the History of the Parthenon*, Ph.D. dissert., University of California, Los Angeles 1966, pp. 216-217.

28. Principally thanks to the systematic research of M. Korres; see *Meleti* 1, pp. 138-139, and Korres, *Der Parthenon bis 1687...*, *op. cit.*, pp. 20-23.

29. A. Xyngopoulos, 'O mesaionikos pyrgos tou Parthenonos' ('The Medieval Tower of the Parthenon'), *AE* 1960, pp. 1-16. Until the publication of this article, the tower was wrongly thought to be a Turkish minaret.

30. N.H.J. Westlake, 'On some ancient Paintings in Churches of Athens', *Archaeologia* LI, 1888, pp. 174-181, pl. V-VI; A. Xyngopoulos, 'Parthenonos vyzantinai toichographiai' ('Byzantine Wall-Paintings in the Parthenon'), *AE* 1920, pp. 36-51.

31. It has never been published as a whole, but it certainly was not in a *phiale* as was once believed (D. Pallas in *Praktika Christianikis Archaiologikis Etaireias* [= *XAE*] 1932, pp. 19-32).

32. That is, cloisonné masonry, thinner bricks at the window arches, etc.

33. M. Korres is studying the origins of the material from which the tower and staircase were constructed. It is so successfully incorporated into the monument that few visitors to the Parthenon realise it was not constructed in ancient times.

34. See Ch. Bouras in *Deltion Christianikis Archaiologikis Etaireias* (= *DXAE*) vol. 5, 1969, p. 253.

35. P. Speck, 'Eine Byzantinische Darstellung der Antiken Stadt Athen', *Ellinika* 28, 1975, pp. 415-418.

36. K.I. Biris, *Ta Attika tou Evliya Çelebi, Ai Athinai kai ta perichora kata ton 17on aiona* ('Evliya Çelebi on Attica: Athens and its Environs in the 17th Century'), Athens 1959, pp. 7ff.

37. All the information has been brought together by N. Moutsopoulos in *Oi peripeteies tou naou tis Pallados. O Parthenonas tzami* ('The Misfortunes of the Temple of Athena: the Parthenon as a Mosque'), Thessaloniki s.a., pp. 33-40, figs. 15-24.

38. The details of the looting of the temple are common knowledge. See I. Gennadios, *O Lordos Elgin* ('Lord Elgin'), Athens 1930; C.P. Bracken, *Antiquities Acquired, the Spoliation of Greece*, London 1975; W. St. Clair, *Lord Elgin and the Marbles*, Oxford 1967; C. Hitchens, *The Elgin Marbles*, London 1987; D. Hunt, review of the last work in *Journal of Hellenic Studies* (= *JHS*) 109, 1989, pp. 279-280.

39. D. Kambouroglou, *Ai palaiai Athinai* ('Old Athens'), Athens 1922, pp. 351-353, 389-390.

40. See O. Hederer, *Leo von Klenze, Persönlichkeit und Werk*, Munich 1964. See also A. Kaloyeropoulou, M. Prouni-Filip, *AE*, index, Athens 1973, pp. civ-cv, and F.W. Hamdorf, 'Die Restaurierung der Akropolis', *Ein Griechischer Traum, Leo von Klenze, Der Archäologe*, Munich 1986, pp. 182-195.

41. Leo von Klenze, *Aphoristische Bemerkungen, gesammelt, auf seine Reise nach Griechenland*, Berlin 1838, pp. 300-309, 391-395, 422-427, 716-718, 723-724, 772-792. See also A. Kokkou, *I merimna yia tis archaiotites stin Ellada kai ta prota mouseia* ('Care of Antiquities in Greece and the First Museums'), Athens 1977, p. 79, and M. Casanaki, F. Mallouchou, 'Interventions on the Acropolis 1833-1875', *The Acropolis of Athens, Conservation, Restoration and Research*, Athens 1985, p. 13 (exhibition catalogue).

42. It is characteristic that Klenze (*op. cit.*, p. 395) made provision for the founding of a museum on the west side of the Parthenon.

43. K. Schinkel, *Entwurf zu einem Königspalast auf der Akropolis zu Athen*, Berlin 1840.

44. It is no coincidence that Klenze's report proposed the reconstruction of the north colonnade of the Parthenon, which would be visible from the new palace.

45. See Kokkou, *op. cit.*, especially p. 85, note 2.

46. As far back as 1835/36, by L. Ross and the architects Schaubert and Hansen. Their book *Der Tempel der Nike Apteros* was published in Berlin in 1839.

47. That is, without identifying the original position of the members among those which it resembled.

48. Such as the remnants of the sections of the Ionic frieze, which Elgin left after sawing them up: these were used as uprights in the walls.

49. When the Arsakeion was built in 1849, considerable amounts of material from the Acropolis were used, some of which was examined in recent years and returned. Klenze, too, had recommended in his report that the shapeless and useless marbles on the Acropolis be sold off. See also Kokkou, *op. cit.*, p. 236 and notes 1-8.

50. Kalkos also did other archaeological work. See Kokkou, *op. cit.*, pp. 80, 81, 235.

51. The shape of the arch was quite alien to the monument as a whole. Joseph Durm believed the entire project was a failure and that the arch was unsuitable.

52. When a violent earthquake made emergency work to secure the monument necessary.

53. It is not correct to say (J. Dimacopoulos, *Anastylosis and*

Anasteloseis, ICOMOS Information 1, 1985, p. 19) that Balanos did no reconstruction work off the Acropolis. We know that he restored the Philopappus monument, one of the doorways in the theatre at Epidaurus, and other monuments.

54. Among similar cases are the reconstruction of Temple C at Selinous and of the temple of Heracles at Acragas. See, in this connection, C. Ceschi, *Teoria e Storia del Restauro*, Rome 1970, pp. 115-134.

55. Balanos' exclusively French training seems to have prevented him from gaining access to the theoretical texts of two of the great nineteenth century writers, John Ruskin and Alois Riegl. Nor was he acquainted with the Italian restorers.

56. They are described in his book (for which see note 57). A brief account will be found in *Meleti* 1, pp. 154-157, notes 69-116. In even briefer form, they could be summarised as follows: the first project (1899-1902) involved an intervention in the west portico (repair and replacement of column capitals, architrave blocks and revetments of the frieze, additions to the *thranos*), in the spiral staircase, and in the south corner of the east pediment (dismantling and reassembly). It also included an intervention in the west facade of the Parthenon (replacement of sections of the column capitals, securing of the architrave, dismantling and reassembly of the two corners of the pediment and the uprights of its *tympanum*) and the returning to place of cornices and pieces of the *sima*. The second project (1922-1933) involved the "prudent reconstruction" of the north portico – that is, of nine columns with varying degrees of supplementation of their shafts and capitals, cementing and supplementation of the architrave blocks, the installation of eleven ancient triglyphs and an identical number of revetments, and the positioning of sixteen cornices supplemented with concrete. Balanos also intervened in the facade (one column capital, the horizontal cornices – especially those in the corners – and the cornice beneath the pediment, which he supplemented). On the south side, this project involved the complete or partial reconstruction of five columns and corresponding restoration work on the entablature, while in the east portico a complete column, parts of the remaining column and the south anta were restored. Additions were made to the long walls, and Pittakis' bricks removed. Lastly, Balanos removed Kalkos' arch from the west wall of the cella, together with the large lintel and its revetments, which he renewed in concrete.

57. The book was published in two languages: N. Balanos, *Les Monuments de l'Acropole, Relèvement et conservation*, Paris 1938, and N. Balanos, *I anastylosis ton mnemeion tis Akropoleos* ('The Reconstruction of the Acropolis Monuments'), Athens 1940. For this book, see also the judgement of Orlandos in his *I architektoniki tou Parthenonos* ('The Architecture of the Parthenon'), vol. II, Athens 1977, p. xx.

58. The archive is being investigated by Fani Mallouchou-Tufano, to whom my thanks for providing me with certain information from it.

59. Joseph Durm, Lucien Magne and Francis Crammer Penrose.

60. Consisting of X. Vlachopoulos, A. Theophilas, W. Dörpfeld and E. Troump – of whom only the third was an expert in ancient Greek architecture.

61. Joseph Durm, 'I katastasis tou Parthenonos kai ton loipon mnemeion ton Athinon' ('The State of the Parthenon and the Other Monuments of Athens'), *AE* 1895, columns 1-50; F.C. Penrose, 'Peri ton anangaion tou Parthenon episkevon' ('Concerning the Repairs Necessary to the Parthenon'), *Praktika tis en Athinais Archaiologikis Etaireias* (= *PAE*) 1896, pp. 194-200, and *Rapport de Lucien Magne sur les travaux de consolidation du Parthenon*, Paris 1900.

62. Balanos, *op. cit.*, p. 89.

63. In a paper which he presented at the Athens Conference of 1931 (published as recorded by F. Mallouchou).

64. Stated in *Questioni Pratiche di Belli Arti*, Milan 1893.

65. Stated in 1901, in the article 'Il Restauro dei monumenti e la critica', *Il Marzoco* VI, 1901, p. 49).

66. See the entry 'Balanos' in the *Ekpaideftiki Elliniki Enkyklopaideia*, ('Greek Educational Encyclopaedia') vol. 6, Athens 1986, p. 307.

67. At a special meeting on 25 October 1931, in Athens, of the international conference of experts on the study of problems connected with the protection and conservation of monuments of art and history, chaired by C. Karo and with Paquet, Giovannoni, Slothouwer, Pontremoli, Horta, Kieslinger, Anti and Lauer among those present.

68. Although there was no shortage of examples on which he could have drawn; see T. Homolle, 'La reconstruction du Trésor des Athèniens à Delphes', *Comptes Rendus du Congrès Inter. d'Archéologie*, Athens 1905, pp. 167-171.

69. Under the title 'Pro-Parthenone' in the newspaper *Apoyevmatini Protevousa*, 5/18 February 1922. For what ensued, see *Meleti* 1, p. 155, notes 88-92. Certain reservations had been expressed at a much earlier date by writers and artists in Paris; see *Le Musée, Revue de l'art antique*, 1, 1904, pp. 312-313; 2, 1905, pp. 1-3, 5-29.

70. He would seem to have publicised it suitably himself and not to have avoided self-commendation. See, for example, *AE* 1937, p. 807, for the work on the Athena Nike temple. He certainly left his mark on the conference of 1931.

71. The first official denunciation of the destruction was made by Miliadis; see Ch. Bouras, 'O Miliadis kai i syntirisi ton mnemeion tis Akropoleos' ('Miliadis and the Conservation of the Acropolis Monuments'), *Archaiognosia* vol. 4, 1985-86, p. 118, and see also Dimacopoulos, *op. cit.*, pp. 19, 20; *Meleti* 1, pp. 156-158, 296-297, and Casanaki and Mallouchou, *op. cit.*, p. 19.

72. It had been described in detail as far back as the time of Viollet-le-Duc's dictionary. See *Dictionnaire Raisonné de l'Architecture Française*, vol. II, 1867, pp. 400-401. Durm, too, was categorical on the subject in his report (see *AE* 1895, p. 36, and the Greek Government Gazette for 25.8.1898). See, lastly, M. Korres, 'Itan ta technika sphalmata tis Akropolis anapophefkta?' ('Were the Technical Errors in the Acropolis Inevitable?'), *I Nea Oikologia*, 1989, no. 51, p. 16. At the conference of 1931, the delegates Pantremoli, Kieslinger, Slothouwer and Giovannoni spoke out clearly against the use of iron and talked of future damage. See the unpublished proceedings in File X-VIII.5 of the Balanos archive in the Archaeological Society (paper by F. Mallouchou).

73. Strangely enough, the monstrous view that the removal of a mass of marble from the members would have no effect on their form was advocated by a scholar of the prestige of Praschniker (in the *Neue Freie Presse* of 20 March 1926; from the Balanos archive, paper by F. Mallouchou).

74. Balanos, *op. cit.*, *passim*.

75. See Dimacopoulos, *op. cit.*, pp. 16-17.

76. There can have been few serious problems of clearing left, since this had already been dealt with.

77. Such as the segmental arch over the west entrance and the bricks on the side walls, added during the nineteenth century.

78. The English term is also used in Greek. In relation to the temple of Athena Nike, Balanos wrote (*AE* 1937, no. 3, p. 781): "... of the reconstruction of the temple which took place in 1834-38 and which, for an entire century, did not prevent the elegance and beauty of the unique temple from being appreciated. If the temple had not been reconstructed at that time, the Acropolis would have been endowed with yet another pile of marbles, as the famous architect Durm correctly observed...".

79. In this respect, the Propylaea and the Erechtheum are in a far worse state.

80. See Orlandos, *op. cit.*, p. xx.

81. R. Martin, 'Chronique des fouilles', *Bulletin de correspondance hellénique* (= *BCH*) 58-59, 1935, p. 425.

82. E. Stikas, *O anastylotis. Anastasios Orlandos, o anthropos kai to ergon tou* ('The Reconstructor. Anastasios Orlandos, the Man and his Work'), Athens 1978, pp. 417-418, 420-421.

83. *Ibid.*, pp. 413, 419.

84. Acts of 1, 8 and 15 December 1953, unpublished.

85. See Travlos, *op. cit.*, pp. 505-519, with a complete bibliography.

86. Stikas, *op. cit.*, p. 413, and PAE 1953, p. 309.

87. Acts nos. 9, 12, 13 and 15, spring 1955, unpublished.

88. *Nea Estia,* vol. 60, 1956, no. 702, pp. 1314-1315.

89. Stikas, *op. cit.*, pp. 425, 435-439; *PAE* 1959, p. 170; 1960, pp. 221-222.

90. *Congrès International des Architectes et Techniciens des Monuments Historiques*, Paris 1957.

91. Stikas, *op. cit.*, pp. 423, 430, 431.

92. *Ibid.*, pp. 457, 461.

93. *Archaiologikon Deltion* (= *AD*) 16, 1960, part II, pp. 3-6.

94. Stikas, *op. cit.*, 413, 417.

95. I. Papadimitriou in *To Ergon tis en Athinais Archaiologikis Etaireias* ('The Work of the Athens Archaeological Society'), 1961, pp. 20-24, plate 1.

96. Dimacopoulos, *op. cit.*, p. 20.

97. *Zygos*, vol. IX, 1965, pp. 7ff.

98. Ch. Bouras, *I anastylosis tis stoas tis Vravronos* ('The Reconstruction of the Stoa at Brauron'), Athens 1967, pp. 173-174.

99. Principally by Y. Dontas, then Director of the Acropolis; see *AD* 22, 1967, p. 34; 24, 1969, B, p. 19; 25, 1970, B, p. 24; 26, 1971, B, p. 26; 27, 1972, p. 16; 29, 1973-74, p. 27.

100. R.M. Lemaire, R. Sneyers, J. Sonnier, *Rapport sur l'état de conservation des Monuments de l'Acropole*, UNESCO, No 1969 BMS, RD, CTL, Paris 1970.

101. See Bouras, 'Miliadis...', *op. cit.*, p. 120.

102. *Congrès International des Architectes et Techniciens des Monuments Historiques*, Paris 1957, pp. 301ff.

103. See Stikas, *op. cit.*, pp. 393-401, 405ff, and *Charistirion eis Anastasion K. Orlandon* ('Festschrift for Anastasios K. Orlandos'), vol. I, Athens 1965, pp. xxxiii-xliii.

104. Even twenty years later, in 1977, Stikas refused to admit that there were problems with the Acropolis. See 'O peri ta mnemeia tis Akropoleos thoryvos' ('The Fuss about the Monuments of the Acropolis'), *Technika Chronika*, March-April 1977, pp. 33-34.

105. See, indicatively, Y. Mylonas, 'Anastelotikai ergasiai eis tin Akropolin' ('Reconstruction Work on the Acropolis'), *PAA* 55, 1980, pp. 26-58; Ch. Bouras, 'Anastelotika kai alla provlimata stin Athinaiki Akropoli' ('Problems of Reconstruction and other Difficulties on the Acropolis of Athens'), *Idryma N. Goulandri – Mouseio Kykladikis Technis: Dialexeis 1986-1989*, pp. 101-110; Working Group for the Preservation of the Acropolis Monuments, *The Acropolis, Problems, Measurements, Studies, Measures to be Taken*, Athens 1977; Ministry of Culture, *Akropolis '77* (album), Athens 1977; Ch. Bouras, 'A Program for the Preservation of the Monuments of the Athenian Acropolis', *Praktika tou XII Diethnous Synedriou*

Klassikis Archaiologias, vol. I, Athens 1985, pp. 361-365; the same author, 'Introduction', *The Acropolis of Athens, Conservation, Restoration, Research*, 1975-1983, Athens 1983, p. 10, and 'Monuments of Antiquity: The Limits of Restoration', *Actes du Congrès International sur la conservation de la pierre et autres materiaux*, RILEM-UNESCO, Paris 1993, pp. 127-130.

106. See the special issue of *Architektonika Themata*, no. 9, 1975.

107. And later subsumed into its organisational structure.

108. On the part of the committee itself, the Central Archaeological Council and the Ministry of Culture.

109. *Meleti 1*.

110. The proceedings of the meeting were published in English as *Proceedings of the 2nd International Meeting for the Restoration of the Acropolis Monuments, 12-14 September 1983*, Athens 1985.

111. *L'Acropoli di Atene, Conservazione e restauro*, Naples 1985.

112. K. Zambas made a major contribution to his study and to resolving all the civil engineering problems (difficulties of statics and seismic protection). A related research project and study was published independently as P. Theocharis, A. Koronaios, 'Peiramatiki meleti efstatheias tou Parthenonos' ('Experimental Study of the Stability of the Parthenon'), *Pragmateiai tis Akadimias Athinon*, Athens 1979.

113. *Study for the Restoration of the Parthenon*, vol. 2a, Athens 1989, under the direction of M. Korres, with the association of N. Toganidis, K. Zambas and Th. Skoulikidis at the head of a team of restorers; vol. 2b, Athens 1989, under the direction of M. Korres.

114. *Ibid.*, pp. 224-225 (Appendix 2).

115. *3i Diethnis Synantisi yia tin apokatastasi ton mnemeion tis Akropoleos, Praktika* ('Proceedings of the 3rd International Meeting for the Restoration of the Acropolis Monuments'), Athens 1990.

116. *Meleti 1*, pp. 401-405 and 407-412, respectively.

117. Ch. Bouras, 'Athens, The Parthenon', *Monumentum* vol. 27, 1984, pp. 109-120; the same author, 'Principles Observed and that will be Observed during the Operation on the Acropolis Monuments, L'Acropoli di Atene', *Meleti 1*, pp. 11-14, 43-50; the same author, 'The Problems of Conserving the Parthenon and the Possibilities of Improving the Values of the Monument; the Principles which will Guide the Operation', *Proceedings of the 2nd International Meeting*, Athens 1985, pp. 86-94.

118. Dimacopoulos, *op. cit.*, pp. 17, 18.

119. See also the comments of M. Korres in vol. 2a of the *Study, op. cit.*, pp. 80-82, and of Ch. Bouras in 'Anastelotika ....', *op. cit.*, p. 106.

120. See *Planning and Executing Anastylosis of Stone Buildings, Conservation on Archaeological Excavations*, ICCROM, Rome 1984, pp. 121-144, *passim*.

121. See *Study*, vol. 2a, *op. cit.*, p. 82.

122. See the examination of the subject in the periodical *Themata Chorou kai Technon* (vol. 21, 1989, pp. 84-96) with the strong objections of Dimacopoulos and Dontas to the restoration of the Erechteum and, by extension, to Korres' projects on the Parthenon. See also C. de Seta, *Luoghi e architettura perdute*, Laterza 1986, pp. 10-19, and W. Hoepfner, 'Neue Steine für den Parthenon?', *Frankfurter Allgemeine Zeitung*, 22 April 1989.

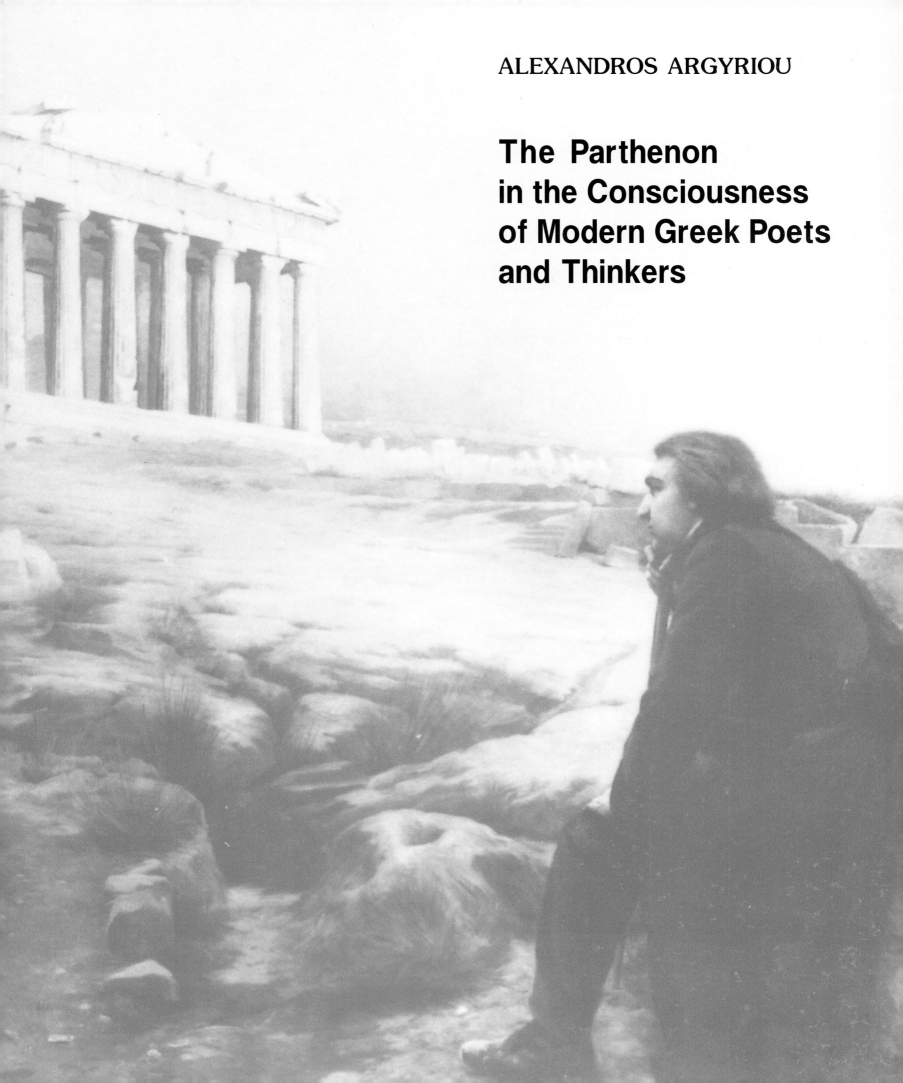

ALEXANDROS ARGYRIOU

The Parthenon
in the Consciousness
of Modern Greek Poets
and Thinkers

It is no surprise to find no reference to the Parthenon in the tomes of Solomos while there is an honourable mention in the *Odes* of Calvos. It is, however, understandable when we bear in mind that Calvos' education was that of a Phanariot Greek, while Solomos' schooling could briefly be described as more vernacular, despite the fact that both authors shared an Italian education from an early age.

In Calvos' poem 'To Glory', we read:

xviii
''On Hymettus
bloomed the bay
a sacred leaf adorning
the ruined relics
of the Parthenon''.

In explaining the absence of the Parthenon from the poems of Solomos (and not only from his work), we could note that the age was still one in which promotion of the Acropolis had not yet assumed a symbolic value in scholarly circles, and the Sacred Rock had not yet been praised by Renan, who visited it in 1865. Yet before his 'Prayer' was published and became known in 1876, there was a fortnightly Greek periodical called the *Parthenon*. It first appeared in March 1871 and, to the best of my knowledge, survived for only a few years despite its ambition of keeping up the tradition of the more successful periodicals of the time. Its name is an indication that in the minds of some Greeks the symbol of the 'Parthenon' had begun to function before the foreigners undertook the task of appreciating it. The periodical had notable contributors, to judge by the fact that some of the best-known young writers of the day appeared in its pages: Dimitris Paparrigopoulos, Spyridon Vasileiadis, N.G. Politis, Angelos Vlachos, Yeorgios Paraschos, Achilleas Paraschos and Timoleon Ambelas.

In *Parthenon* we find a poem by an expatriate Greek, Kleanthis Pappazoglous, entitled 'A Memory of the Parthenon', dedicated – in the most impenetrable archaising language – to the poet Spyridon Vasileiadis.

To finish with this topic, there were three more short-lived periodicals entitled *Parthenon*: one in 1909, in Piraeus, edited by 'Lambros Eftastris' (clearly a pseudonym, though one which cannot be identified from my sources); a second in 1913, edited by P. Xenos, and a third in 1928 under Agisilaos Rallis. The last of these periodicals had high aspirations, terming itself "a monthly illustrated encyclopaedic periodical published under the auspices of Professors of the University of Athens and other scholars". (In this respect, it was a belated copy of the nineteenth-century periodicals which "taught and entertained simultaneously"). Yet the ambitious publication lasted for only a year, running to eight issues from March 1928 to November/December 1928.

In the beginning of the period of which we are speaking (late 1883), the important Greek journalist Vlasis Gavriilidis called his daily newspaper *Akropolis*. Its innovative spirit was to go down in history at a time when obscurantism was triumphant even among students. It is reasonable to assume that Gavriilidis did not hit upon the title of his newspaper by chance; perhaps he wished to link 'tradition' (one of whose sublime achievements he was accentuating) with 'modern life', which had need of lofty and immutable ideals.

Let us return to the poets, however, where the symbols function organically and allusively.

In the sixteen volumes published to date of the *Complete Works* of Palamas, the word 'Acropolis' occurs 88 times, and, in addition: a) in speeches 7-9 of 'The King's Flute', b) in the article 'The Acropolis as a Source of Inspiration' (1927), and c) in 'The Acropolis Moonlit' (newspaper *Akropolis Esperini*, 1.9.1894, signed 'Diagoras', *Complete Works*, pub. Biris-Govostis, vol. 15, pp. 542-544).

In the sixteen volumes, the word 'Parthenon' occurs 91 times, and in addition, in speeches 3 and 7-11 of the 'Flute' (see vol. 5, pp. 521-523, where there is a summary of the 'Flute').

To remain on Palamas, the name of Ernest Renan occurs 18 times for the 'Prayer on the Acropolis' alone in the article 'The Acropolis as a Source of Inspiration' (vol. 13, pp. 347-350).

A brief reference is perhaps in order to this important figure in French literature, whose name has become linked with Greece. Ernest Renan (1823-1892) came to

The covers of the four periodicals published under the title Parthenon.

André Brouillet: Ernest Renan in front of the Parthenon. University of the Sorbonne. Source: Iphigeneia Botouropoulou, O Ernest Renan kai i synchroni Ellada *('Ernest Renan and Modern Greece'), Hadjinikoli, Athens 1993.*

Athens in 1865, as we have seen, and visited the Acropolis, which he spent many days studying. Greatly struck by it, he wrote his 'Prayer to Athena' (first published in the *Revue des Deux Mondes* on 1.12.1876), whose French title is 'Prière sur l'Acropole'. In the text, Renan wrote described this as a "prière que je fis sur l'Acropole quand je fus arrivé à en comprende la parfaite beauté" ('The prayer I made on the Acropolis when I was able to comprehend its perfect beauty'). I do not know whether the prayer on the Acropolis was the main, or indeed the only, reason why Renan became so well known and popular in Greece; many of his works were translated into Greek (such as the *Vie de Jésus, St Paul, The Apostles* and *Antichrist*), and most of them went through numerous editions. Of course, his great renown in Greece may also have been the result of the radical views he advocated, which struck a responsive chord in an age in which a section of public opinion was becoming more intellectually inquisitive. On the other hand, his renown disturbed the established feelings of another section of public opinion, which, naturally, launched severe attacks on him. Nor is it out of the question that another contribution to his prestige was made by his daughter's marriage to Yannis Psycharis, then a professor at the Sorbonne, whose book *To Taxidi Mou* ('My Journey', 1888) stirred up the linguistic controversy at a time when it seemed all hope of doing so had faded. That, at any rate, is the impression we get from the book's reception by Palamas, who praised it but had to admit that its lesson had come too late. To put it in his own words: "... Mr Psycharis introduces system, perfects and embarks on un-

dertakings in prose. We admire and congratulate, but we are very much afraid he is a little too late" (*Complete Works*, vol. 6, p. 310). Fortunately, as Palamas himself might have said, this prediction turned out to be mistaken, but the unpleasant truth is that the 'victory' came after a lengthy delay and was not without casualties.

Yeorgios Drosinis, a 'fellow-traveller' of Palamas, wrote a poem entitled 'A Weed on the Parthenon'. In it, he extols the humble weed which, he said, fulfilled its desire to grow in a "crack" on the Parthenon so as to do honour to its glory and extract honour from it.

We, today, might reasonably compare this poem with Palamas' similar 'A Flower', as a characteristic example of the extent of the poetic range of the two poets.

If we broaden the frontiers of those who partook of Greek education, we will see that the Greeks of communities in other countries sometimes displayed a heightened sensitivity towards the cultural heritage. Perhaps, as the poet says, that is because "distance knows how to convey sublimity"; at any rate, it can be seen in Cavafy's two articles on the 'Elgin Marbles'.

A different approach can be seen as a consequence of unjustified exaggeration. The poem by Asimakis Panselinos preserved in his collection *Taxidi me pollous anemous* ('Journey in Many Winds') is not a paean of praise to the Acropolis. Written around 1930, it bears the misleading title 'Hymn to the Parthenon' and makes ironic capital out of the use of the monument as a symbol of the 'good' and thus, by synecdoche, of 'quality', the role to which it had declined in the language of the market. As an indicative example of this distorted and conventional use, Panselinos mentions the grocer who stuck "it" on a barrel of sardines so as to advertise and pay honour not, of course, to the Parthenon but to the sardines: the signifier and the signified, as a structuralist might say.

Nikitas Rantos (a poet who returned from America after the war as 'Nick Kallas') is another iconoclast whose poem 'Acropolis' involves both Psycharis and Renan, the latter of whom is accused of being the "official verger of the Acropolis" (Nikitas Rantos, *Poiemata* ['Poems'], 1933, pp. 21-22).

The poems of Elytis contain no reference to the Acropolis or the Parthenon, so far as I have been able to discover.

By way of contrast, the equally iconoclastic Nikos Engonopoulos began his poetic career with the poem 'The Tram and the Acropolis', in his collection *Min omileite eis ton odigon* ('Do Not Talk to the Driver'), O Kyklos, Athens 1938, with the motto "beside the driver of the tram". Of course, one has to have the imagination of a Surrealist to connect the Acropolis with the green trams of the pre-War – unless one is among the older members of society, who remember that under the Metaxas dictatorship of 1936 the wise counsel of the dictator could be read on the back of the little paper tram tickets. This was a kind of infallible 'guide' to which there was no answering back, and it was devoted to inanities of the following kind: "Rise up, young people of Greece; only in the traditions of the nation will you find your grandeur once more". Of course, the traditions of the nation included the Parthenon, although Metaxas himself was more attracted to the achievements of Sparta.

Seferis did honour to the Acropolis in another manner; his early prose work 'Six Nights on the Acropolis', published posthumously, is set largely on the Acropolis and the atmosphere of the monument is that which prevails. However, Seferis also measured the significance of the Acropolis with great astuteness (although in few words and as part of a digression) in his 'Dialogue/Monologue on Poetry' (*Dokimes* [Essays], Cairo 1944).

If there are few and infrequent references to the Acropolis and the Parthenon in more recent Greek poetry, I believe we ought to seek for a multiplicity of causes. The most important of them is, perhaps, the fact that such a highly-charged symbol may inspire scholars but it is difficult to convey in 'indirect speech' within a literary context when it has to measure up to the real thing. Perhaps – who knows? – Seferis' friend was right when he said, "I have never seen the Parthenon because I never had a first impression of the Parthenon. I was accustomed to it before I saw it at close quarters" (again from the 'Dialogue/Monologue on Poetry', *Dokimes*, vol. A, 1938, p. 484).

Lastly, we should not be surprised that a thinker of the stature of V.N. Tatakis should write, in his posthumous memoirs, of his first impressions of the Acropolis – impressions which he was able to have because he was not an Athenian (*Apomnemonevmata, Viographiki Mythologia* ['Memoirs, Biographical Mythology'], 1993).

PS. The thesis entitled *O Ernest Renan kai i synchroni Ellada* ('Ernest Renan and Modern Greece'), by Iphigeneia Botouropoulou, published in 1993, has allowed me – belatedly – to form a fuller picture of the Greek translations of Renan's work, in terms both of complete books and of periodicals of various kinds, of which there are far from a few. As for the prayer on the Acropolis, which is of interest to us here, the first translation of it found by Ms Botouropoulou, was by Avra Drakopoulou and was published in 1891 under the title 'Prosevchi epi tis Akropoleos' in the periodical *Evdomas*, pp. 2-3. It was followed, much later, by: b) a translation published in 1953 in the periodical *Eklogi*, p. 66 (unsigned); c) a translation by Kostas Kairophyllas, published in the annual *Philologiki Protochronia* ('Literary New Year'), 1954, pp. 176-184; d) a translation by Kleon Paraschos, published in *Nea Estia*, 1962, pp. 1386-1389, and two more, by A.I. Lazanas (1935) and the poet and actress Tasia Adam (before 1945; if my memory does not fail me, even before 1940), which it has not proved possible to find.

The translation by Professor X.S. Dantis was published as a separate volume in 1960 and a second edition with an introduction, footnotes and a commentary appeared in 1962. We now have the bilingual *Ernest Renan, Prière sur l'Acropole*, containing a translation by Iphigeneia Botouropoulou.

PPS. I was directed by Alexis Politis to the *Nea Poiemata* ('New Poems') of Christos A. Parmenidis (Athens 1858), which contains an 'Ode to the Ruins of the Acropolis'; the first four of its 38 quatrains follow:

"In the ancient days
  When the city of Athens
  Was honoured as the queen
    Of all of Greece,
  And when the voice of Pericles
  Rose on the Pnyx
  And shed its light and shook
    Greece, the people
  Flocked in large numbers from all sides
  With happy faces
  To the city, full of glory
    And famous monuments;
  And from the Propylaea
  They gazed with enthusiasm
  On the handsome Parthenon
    The epitome of Beauty".

General view of the Acropolis. Photograph by Y. Tsangaris.

APPENDIX

CHRONOLOGICAL TABLE OF THE HISTORY OF THE PARTHENON*

566 BC	Celebration of the Panathenaic Festival re-organised – new temple of Athena.
510 BC	Fall of the Tyrants – foundation of democracy.
490 BC	Battle of Marathon – first marble Parthenon (pre-Parthenon).
485 BC	Death of Darius – enthronement of Xerxes – rule of Themistocles – Athens feverishly builds a large fleet and defensive fortifications – possible suspension of temple-building.
480 BC	Second Persian invasion – Athens destroyed – destruction of incomplete pre-Parthenon – Battle of Salamis.
479 BC	Battle of Plataeae, Persians driven out – oath of Plataeae – north wall of the Acropolis, with the prominent incorporation into it of sections of the burned poros temples and drums from the columns of the pre-Parthenon.
477 BC	Foundation of the Delian League.
467 BC	Battle of the Eurymedon – south wall of the Acropolis (wall of Kimon).
461 BC	Rule of Pericles.
454 BC	Treasury of the Delian League moved to Athens.
451 BC	Peace treaty with Sparta – Pericles organises a Panhellenic congress.
449 BC	Peace treaty with Persia.
447 BC	Building of the Parthenon begins, with the use of marbles from the pre-Parthenon.
438 BC	Building of the Parthenon completed – dedication of the colossal chryselephantine statue of Athena Parthenos.
432 BC	Completion of the last sculptures on the pediments of the Parthenon.
431-404 BC	Peloponnesian War.
426 BC	Severe earthquake.
377 BC	Second Delian League.
334 BC	Battle of the Granicus – magnificent Persian shields dedicated to the Parthenon.
307 BC	Demetrius Poliorcetes captures Athens and resides for a while in the Parthenon.
295 BC	The tyrant Lachares removes the gold from the statue and, probably, the Persian shields.
230-c.220 BC	A large Pergamene monument to the Galatian war erected to the south of the Parthenon.
200 BC	Destructive raids by Philip V.
180-c.160 BC	Tall Pergamene monument erected on the east side of the Parthenon.
31 BC	Tall Pergamene monument re-dedicated to Augustus.
27-26 BC	Temple of Rome and Augustus erected facing the Parthenon.

* The chronological table was prepared by Manolis Korres.

61	A votive inscription in honour of Nero installed on the east side of the Parthenon, in the spaces between the new set of fine shields. The inscription is removed directly after the fall of Nero (68).
267	Raid of the Heruli, Parthenon burned, complete destruction of the interior of the temple.
312-313	Edict of Milan.
362-365	Julian, Emperor of Rome – interior of the Parthenon repaired.
395	Raid of the Visigoths (Alaric).
397	Ancient religion suppressed.
402-410	Herculus, proconsul of Illyricum: attempts at reorganisation.
438	Codex Theodosianus (decree of Theodosius II) on the pagan temples and their purification.
529	Suppression of the schools of philosophy.
6th century	The Parthenon converted into a Christian church of Our Lady: 'Our Lady of Athens'.
9th century	The Bishopric of Athens promoted to an Archbishopric (before 841).
10th century	The Archbishop of Athens promoted to the status of a Metropolitan (before 981).
1018	Basil II makes a pilgrimage to the Parthenon.
12th century	The building (as a Christian church) is remodelled under Metropolitan Nicholas Ayiotheodoritis(1166-1175) and decorated with wall-paintings, probably under Metropolitan Michail Choniates (1175-1204).
1204	'Frankish' conquest.
1206	The Parthenon becomes the church of a Latin Archbishop.
1311	Catalan conquest.
1388	Florentine conquest.
1397	Occupation by the Venetians.
1403	Recapture by Florence.
1436, 1444	Visits by Ciriaco de Pizzicolli di Ancona.
1456	Athens falls to the Turks.
1458	The Turks take the Acropolis and convert the Parthenon into a Muslim mosque.
1645-1669	First Turkish-Venetian War.
1685	Start of the Second Turkish-Venetian War.
1687	Venetian siege of the Acropolis – an explosion seriously damages the Parthenon.
1688	The Venetians evacuate the castle, and the Turks return.
1821-1822	The Greeks besiege and capture the Acropolis.
1826-1827	The Turks besiege and recapture the Acropolis.
1833	The Turks surrender the Acropolis to the Greek army.
1834	The Acropolis ceases to function as a military installation – archaeological work begins.
1834, 1842-1844, 1872, 1898-1902, 1911, 1913, 1922-1931, 1960, 1985 *et seq.*	Restoration and conservation work on the monument.

THE ACROPOLIS RECONSTRUCTED

Drawing by M. Korres

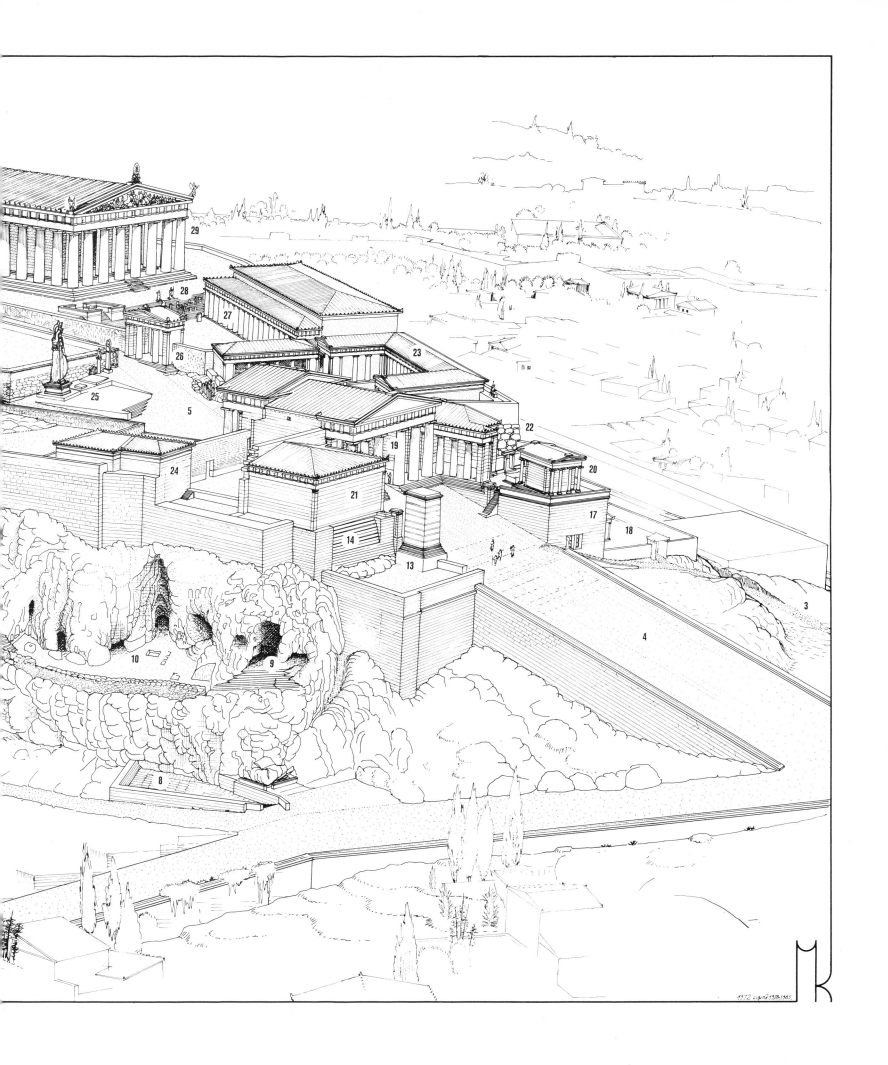

FRIEZE

COFFERS

TYMPANUM

PEDIMENT

CYMATION

CORNICE
MUTULES
TRIGLYPHS
METOPES

GUTTAE

ARCHITRAVE

ABACUS
ECHINUS

STYLOBATE

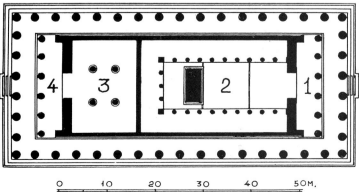

| 0 | 10 | 20 | 30 | 40 | 50M. |

Perspective section of the east side of the Parthenon. Source: A.W. Lawrence, Greek Architecture, *Harmondsworth 1957.*

Plan of the Parthenon: 1. pronaos, 2. cella (Hecatompedos), 3. opisthodomos, 4. opisthonaos. Source: A.K. Orlandos, I architektoniki tou Parthenonos *('The Architecture of the Parthenon'), vol. II, Athens 1977.*

BIBLIOGRAPHY

The bibliography on the Parthenon is vast, in terms both of books and of articles. In some cases, articles have more to contribute than many of the books to study and understanding of the monument. However, the bibliography which follows consists only of books selected from the wide range of works of reference and documentation mentioned by the contributors to this volume. Its purpose is to familiarise readers with the basic bibliography of the Parthenon in all the various aspects of its impact. For a fuller bibliography, see M. Korres and Ch. Bouras, *Meleti Apokatastaseos tou Parthenonos* ('Study for the Restoration of the Parthenon'), Athens 1983, pp. 169ff (ed. Ch. Bouras), and E. Berger (ed.), *Parthenon-Kongress 1982*, Basle 1984, pp 416ff (ed. H. van der Meijden).

Baelen, J., *La chronique du Parthénon*, Paris 1956.

Balanos, N., *Ta ektelesthenta erga pros anastilosin ton mnemeion tis Akropoleos, 1834-1930* ('The Work Performed to Restore the Monuments of the Acropolis, 1834-1930'), Athens 1930.

Balanos, N., *Les Monuments de l'Acropole, Relèvement et conservation*, Paris 1938.

Balanos, N., *I anastilosis ton mnemeion tis Akropoleos* ('The Restoration of the Acropolis Monuments'), Athens 1940.

Berger, E., *Die Geburt der Athena im Ostgiebel des Parthenon*, Basle and Mainz 1974.

Berger, E. (ed.), *Parthenon-Kongress Basel, Referate und Berichte 4. bis 8. April 1982*, Basle and Mainz 1984.

Berger, E. (ed.), *Der Parthenon in Basel, Dokumentation zu den metopen*, Basle and Mainz 1986.

Berger, E. (ed.), *Der Parthenon in Basel, II, Dokumentation des Nord und Ostfrieses*, Mainz 1986.

Boardman, J., Finn, D., *The Parthenon and its Sculptures*, London 1985.

Bodnar, E., *Cyriacus of Ancona and Athens*, Brussels and Bergin 1960.

Bötticher, C., *Bericht über die Untersuchungen auf der Akropolis*, Berlin 1863.

Boutmy, E., *Le Parthénon et le génie Grec*, Paris 1914.

Bowie, T., Thimme, D. (eds.), *The Carrey Drawings of the Parthenon Sculptures*, London 1971.

Brommer, F., *Die Skulpturen der Parthenon-Giebel*, Mainz 1963.

Brommer, F., *Die Metopen des Parthenon*, Mainz 1967.

Brommer, F., *Der Parthenonfries*, Mainz 1977.

Brommer, F., *Die Parthenon-Skulpturen*, Mainz 1979.

Bundgaard, J.A., *The Excavation of the Athenian Acropolis 1882-1910*, Copenhagen 1974.

Carpenter, R., *The Architects of the Parthenon*, Harmondsworth 1970.

Cleghorn, G., *Remarks on the Intended Restoration of the Parthenon of Athens as the National Monument of Scotland*, Edinburgh 1824.

Collignon, M., Boissonas, F., *Le Parthénon. L'Histoire, l'Architecture et la Sculpture*, Paris 1910-1912.

Coulton, J.J., *Greek Architects at Work*, London 1977.

Creighton, W.F., *The Parthenon in Nashville*, Nashville 1968.

Demetriades-Norré, A., *Studies in the History of the Parthenon*, Ph.D. dissertation, University of California, Los Angeles 1966.

Description of the Ancient Marbles in the British Museum, 6, London 1830.

Despinis, G., *Parthenonia* ('On the Parthenon'), Athens 1982.

Fergusson, J., *The Parthenon*, London 1883.

Fougères, G., *L'Acropole. Le Parthénon*, Paris 1910.

Gennadios, I., *O lordos Elgin kai oi pro avtou ana tin Ellada kai tas Athinas idios archaiologisantes epidromeis, 1440-1837* ('Lord Elgin and the Earlier Pseudo-Archaeologists who Raided Greece and Athens in Particular 1440-1837'), Athens 1930.

Gruben, G., *Die Tempel der Griechen*, Munich 1976².

Hambidge, J., *The Parthenon and other Greek Temples. Their Dynamic Symmetry*, New Haven 1924.

Herington, C.J., *Athens and Athena Polias*, Manchester 1955.

Hitchens, C., *The Elgin Marbles*, London 1987.

Jahn, O., Michaelis, A., *Arx Athenarum a Pausania descripta*, Bonn 1901.

Kavvadias, P., Kawerau, G., *I anaskafi tis Akropoleos* ('The Excavation of the Acropolis'), Athens 1907.

Klenze, L. von, *Walhalla in artistischer und technischer Beziehung*, Munich 1842.

Knell, H., *Perikleische Baukunst*, Darmstadt 1979.

Korres, M., Bouras, Ch., *Meleti Apokatastaseos tou Parthenonos* ('Study for the Restoration of the Parthenon'), Athens 1983.

Korres, M., Toganidis, N., Zambas, K., Skoulikidis, Th., et al, *Study for the Restoration of the Parthenon*, vol. 2a, Athens 1989.

Korres, M., *Meleti Apokatastaseos tou Parthenonos* ('Study for the Restoration of the Parthenon'), vol. 2b, Athens 1989.

Korres, M., *Apo tin Penteli ston Parthenona* ('From Penteli to the Parthenon'), Athens 1993.

Korres, M., *Der Parthenon bis 1687, Reparatur – Kirche – Moschee – Pulvermagazin, Die Explosion des Parthenon*, Antiken Museum, Berlin 1990 (exhibition catalogue).

Laborde, L., *Athènes aux XVe, XVIe et XVIIe siècles*, Paris 1854.

Laborde, L., Paccard, A., *Le Parthénon, documents inédits pour servir à la restauration de ce monument*, Paris 1848.

Le Corbusier, *Towards a New Architecture*, London 1946.

Le Corbusier, *Journey to the East*, Cambridge, Mass. 1987.

Le Corbusier, *Keimena yia tin Ellada* ('Texts on Greece'), Athens 1987.

Le Roy, J.D., *Les Ruines des plus beaux Monuments de la Grèce considérées du côté de l'histoire et du côté de l'architecture*, Paris 1758, 2nd ed., Paris 1770.

Lechat, H., *Phidias et la sculpture grecque au Ve siècle*, Paris 1924.

Leipen, N., *Athena Parthenos, A Reconstruction*, Toronto 1971.

Magne, L., *Le Parthénon*, Paris 1895.

Magne, L., *Rapport sur les travaux de consolidation du Parthénon*, Paris 1900.

Magne, L., *La consolidation du Parthénon*, Paris 1905.

Michaelis, A., *Der Parthenon*, Leipzig 1871.

Ministry of Culture, Committee for the Conservation of the Acropolis Monuments, *Proceedings of the 2nd International Meeting for the Restoration of the Acropolis Monuments, Parthenon, 12-14 September 1983*, Athens 1985.

Ministry of Culture, Committee for the Conservation of the Acropolis Monuments, *The Acropolis at Athens, Conservation, Restoration and Research 1975-1983*, Athens 1985.

Ministry of Culture, Committee for the Conservation of the Acropolis Monuments, *Catalogue of the Exhibition 'The Acropolis at Athens, Conservation, etc.'*, Athens 1986.

Ministry of Culture, Committee for the Conservation of the Acropolis Monuments, *Triti Diethnis Synantisi yia tin Apokatastasi ton mnemeion tis Akropoleos, Athina, 31 Martiou - 2 Apriliou 1989, Praktika* ('Proceedings of the 3rd International Meeting on the Restoration of the Acropolis Monuments, Athens, 31 March - 2 April 1989'), Athens 1990.

Omont, H., *Athènes au XVIIe siècle, Dessins de sculptures du Parthénon attribués à J. Carrey et conservés à la Bibliothèque Nationale, accompagnés des vues et plans d'Athènes et de l'Acropole*, Paris 1898.

Orlandos, A., *I architektoniki tou Parthenonos* ('The Architecture of the Parthenon'), vol. A, 1976 (illustrations), vol. B, 1977 (text), vol. C, 1978 (text continued).

Orlandos, A., Vranousis, L., *Ta haragmata tou Parthenonos* ('The Engraved Inscriptions of the Parthenon'), Athens 1973.

Palagia, O., *The Pediments of the Parthenon*, Leiden 1993 (= Monumenta Graeca et Romana VII).

Paris – Rome – Athènes, Le voyage en Grèce des architectes français aux XIXe et XXe siècles, Ecole Nationale Supérieure des Beaux-Arts, Paris 1982.

Pausanias, *Guide to Greece: Attica*.

Pavan, M., *L'avventura del Parthenone, un monumento nella Storia*, Florence 1983.

Pedersen, P., *The Parthenon and the Origin of the Corinthian Capital*, Odense University Press 1989.

Penrose, F., *The Principles of Athenian Architecture*, London 1851.

Picard, C., *L'Acropole d'Athènes*, Paris 1929.

Plutarch, *Pericles*.

Praschniker, C., *Parthenonstudien*, Augsburg and Vienna 1928.

Quatremère de Quincy, A.C., *Restitution des deux frontons du Temple de Minerve à Athènes*, Paris 1825.

Rankin, E.A., *Englishmen on the Acropolis. An Historiography of the Architecture of the Parthenon ca. 1750-1850* (typed doctoral thesis), Johannesburg 1978.

Robertson, A., *The Parthenon Adapted to the Purpose of a National Monument, to Commemorate the Victories of the Late War, Proposed to be Erected in Trafalgar Square or Hyde Park*, London 1838.

Schinkel, C.F., *Entwurf zu einem Königspalast auf der Akropolis bei Athen*, 4th ed., Berlin 1878.

Schwab, K.A., *The Parthenon Metopes and Greek Vase Painting: A Study of Comparison and Influences*, New York University 1988.

Simopoulos, K., *Xenoi Taxidiotes stin Ellada* ('Foreign Travellers in Greece'), vol. A (*333 AD -1700*), Athens 1970; vol. B (*1700-1800*), Athens 1973.

Smith, A.H., *The Sculptures of the Parthenon*, London 1910.

St Clair, W., *Lord Elgin and the Marbles*, London 1967.

Stuart, J., Revett, N., *The Antiquities of Athens Measured and Delineated by ...*, London 1762-1816.

Sutton, R.K., *Americans Interpret the Parthenon: The Progression of Greek Revival Architecture from the East Coast to Oregon 1800-1860*, Niwot, Colorado 1992.

Traeger, J., *Der Weg nach Walhalla*, Regensburg 1987.

Traeger, J. (ed.), *Die Walhalla. Idee, Architektur, Landschaft*, Regensburg 1979.

Van Zanten, D., *The Architectural Polychromy of the 1830s*, New York 1977.

Wiebenson, D., *Sources of Greek Revival Architecture*, London 1969.

INDEX OF PROPER NAMES AND PLACENAMES